# Tradition and Authority in
# the Western Church
## 300-1140

# Tradition and Authority in the Western Church
## 300-1140

KARL F. MORRISON

PRINCETON UNIVERSITY PRESS
PRINCETON, NEW JERSEY
1969

Publication of this book has been aided by grants from
the Louis A. Robb Fund
of Princeton University Press and the
Division of the Social Sciences,
University of Chicago

This book has been composed in Linotype Times Roman

Printed in the United States of America
by Princeton University Press, Princeton, New Jersey

For Anne

. . . e però quella,

Cui non potea mia ovra essere ascosa,

Vôlta vêr me sí lieta come bella:

"Drizza la mente in Dio grata," mi disse,

"Che n'ha congiunti con la prima stella."

—Dante, *Paradiso*, II, 26-30

"Therefore, brethren, stand fast, and hold the traditions which ye have been taught, whether by word or our epistle."

—St. Paul, ii. Thess. 2:15

To confirm the effect of the arrangements [Julian the Apostate] quite courteously admonished the quarrelling bishops of the Christians, who had been introduced into the palace with the divided people. He urged that, since contentions had been laid at rest, each man should boldly serve his own religion, forbidden by no one.

He did this resolutely so that, as freedom increased discord, he need not afterwards fear a united people. For he had learned that the hatred of wild beasts for men is less than the ferocity of most Christians toward one another.

—Ammianus Marcellinus, xxii. 5:3, 4

# Foreword

ONE of the most ancient Christian authors admonished the first-century Corinthians: "Let us leave aside vain and empty hypotheses and come to the well-known and venerable rule of our tradition."[1] And yet, tradition in the Church has never been the sure and manifest rule to which "Clement" resorted. From his day to ours, it has been a supreme authority and an elusive concept.

Prophecies, or the fulfillment of prophecies, the proper understanding of the Scriptures, religious observances, and the faith itself were all considered tradition at some time in the age of the Apostolic Fathers and the apologists. Modern scholars share in this heritage of confusion; there is as yet no common agreement as to what tradition is, or what the apologists themselves thought it to be. Some students of ecclesiastical history have distinguished apostolic tradition, the faith preached by Christ and the Apostles, from post-apostolic or ecclesiastical tradition, the complex of administrative apparatus and legal regulations which grew cumulatively from the apologetic age onward. Others argue that all tradition is ecclesiastical, and that, if distinctions are to be drawn, they should be between tradition as the infallible preaching of the faith by the Church and tradition as the practices and offices which have come about to supplement or to enhance that preaching. And still others maintain that, though there are traditions, or customary practices, there is only one tradition: the content of divine revelation. All these interpretations are indeed present in the writings of the apologists.[2]

Among modern studies of the idea of tradition, only the schematic

[1] I Clement, 7: 2, in ed. K. Lake, *The Apostolic Fathers*, vol. 1 (London, New York, 1912), 18.

[2] Bakhuizen van den Brink distinguishes between the "*traditio Dei*," "*den Inhalt der göttlichen Offenbarung*," and ecclesiastical tradition, or traditions ("Traditio," 77f). Cf. Deneffe, *Traditionsbegriff*, 39: "*Von 180-250 bedeutet Tradition auf die Glaubenslehren angewendet die autoritive kirchliche Glaubensverkündigung, die mit Christus und den Aposteln beginnend ständig von der Kirche ausgeübt wird und die den Glaubensinhalt umfasst, mag derselbe in der Hl. Schrift stehen oder nicht.*" (Reynders, "Paradosis," 174). See Deneffe's distinction (*ibid.*, p. 1) between "*traditio constitutiva*," the original doctrine delivered to the Apostles, "*traditio continuativa*," the elaboration of that doctrine by the Apostles' followers, and "*traditio*" in the form of authentic documents of the faith framed in each generation.

vii

outline of Deneffe has traced its history later than the age of the apologists;[3] and among the studies of mediaeval Church history, none has even drawn attention to the critical role of tradition. Contemporary theologians and historians have, on the whole, examined the concept in discrete ways, according to the methods of their own disciplines, without attempting to establish the historical effects of the theological principle. Thus, the brilliant article by J. N. Bakhuisen van den Brink, *"Traditio* im theologischen Sinne," the antagonistic treatises of Congar,[4] Cullmann,[5] and Holstein,[6] the older essay of Winkler,[7] and even the essay in textual criticism by Flesseman-Van Leer,[8] deal primarily with the theological aspects of tradition. They consider history a necessary subordinate to their exegeses of scriptural and patristic writings. The questions which they pose are indeed historical: whether early Christians considered the Scriptures and tradition opposed, or even mutually exclusive, authorities; what functions or institutions they thought repositories of authentic tradition; whether they judged that the apostolate, the office of transmitting true doctrine by oral instruction (essential to early concepts of tradition), perished with the Apostles, or that it continued in the episcopate, the priesthood, or the body of all the faithful.

The diversity of answers which these issues have evoked reflects the ambivalence and the paucity of available sources. The methods of historical reasoning and textual criticism are insufficient to produce a clear and uniformly accepted resolution. The questions, dealing with theological issues in their historical manifestations, have, in general, been considered and answered theologically; and, with distinguished exceptions, the confessional persuasions of individual authors have all too often supplied the certain resolution which historical methods failed to discover.

Devoted chiefly to the thought of primitive Christianity, theological studies of the idea of tradition render a great service to historians deal-

---

[8] *Traditionsbegriff*. This gap in historical study is shown in the excellent bibliography and essays in Pontificia Academia Mariana Internationalis, *Scriptura*, and in the essay topics in *Ermeneutica e Tradizione* (*Archivio di Filosofia*, 1/2, 1963). The word "tradition" is absent even from the indices of most critical editions and scholarly essays relating to intellectual history in the period under review.

[4] *La Tradition et les traditions; La Tradition et la vie de l'Eglise.*
[5] *La Tradition.*         [6] *La Tradition.*         [7] *Traditionsbegriff.*
[8] *Tradition.* Reference should also be made to B. Gerhardsson's *Memory*, and to his brief *Tradition*. Like Gerhardsson, R.P.C. Hanson, *Church*, is also principally concerned with tradition, not as a category of authority, but as a means of communication.

ing with later epochs. They define doctrinal issues and indicate the complexities awaiting any attempt to measure the historical effects of that idea, or indeed of theological concepts in general. They have still broader implications. Recent studies in the history of ideas in the Middle Ages have shown that theology heavily influenced, when it did not actually inspire, characteristic principles of mediaeval thought, especially that of a political nature. They have shown that the approaches to mediaeval political thought as eminently represented by Gierke and Carlyle, in terms of political institutions and principles inherited from Greek and Roman antiquity, or from Germanic folk practice, are inadequate; for they leave out of account the ecclesiological premises which shaped the principles of some mediaeval thinkers and composed the very substance of thought for others.

Following a suggestion of Maitland, Kantorowicz demonstrated the magnitude of their influence in his last book, *The King's Two Bodies: A Study in Mediaeval Political Theology*.[9] And other works have shown the impact on institutional thought exercised not only by theology in general, but specifically by the concept of tradition and its ancillary aspects. Of those studies, the earliest was D. Van den Eynde's *Les normes de l'enseignement chrétien dans la littérature patristique des trois premiers siècles*, an excellent and incisive study, which set tradition in the context of institutional developments in the early Church. More recently, Ladner has treated the patristic attitude toward that aspect of tradition which required constant renewal of ancient teaching.[10] Among other important contributions, his splendid essay shows the strong interpenetration of law, or constitutionalism, and theology in the Church during the late Roman and early mediaeval period. Dvornik has examined the development of the concept of the apostolate in the patristic and Byzantine Church, and has indicated its critical effects on relations between Byzantium and the West in their political as well as hierarchic aspects.[11] And, concentrating principally on thirteenth and fourteenth century thought, and particularly on that of Innocent III and Wycliff, Wilks has described the vast influence of the juristic concept of the apostolate in Roman ecclesiology.[12] Indeed, the burden of current canonistic studies emphasizes the critical place of tradition's component concepts, such as that of the apostolate, on the development of

[9] See also the review by Kempf, "Untersuchungen," 203-33.
[10] *Reform.*      [11] *Apostolicity.*
[12] "Apostolicus."

theology and constitutionalism in the later Middle Ages.[13] And yet, scholars have on the whole not designated these developments as later stages in the evolution of the ancient concept of tradition;[14] and, except for the exemplary works of Van den Eynde, Ladner, and Dvornik, the impact of that concept on early mediaeval thought has not yet been suggested.

Our task is therefore a modest one. In the following essay, the men and the events discussed, the evidence adduced, and the broad outlines of historical development are all familiar. The work at hand is like restoring a small fragment of a well-known triptych.

+

Three major approaches have guided the study of the problem of ecclesiastical cohesion implicit in the idea of tradition. The first is the position represented by Sohm, who argued that the essence of the Church was the charismatic quality of truth, and that the ecclesiastical order—laws and administrative offices—in the first four centuries of the Church's existence impaired the freedom of the charisma of truth and thus deflected the Church from its proper mission in the world.[15] The second mode of interpretation is represented by Sohm's great antagonist, Harnack, who held that the development of legal order in the Church was necessary to preserve and to transmit intact the doctrine of salvation which Christ delivered to the Apostles.[16] And, finally, there is the interpretation whose major premise was crisply stated by its first exponent, the sixteenth-century Roman Catholic apologist and histo-

---

[13] E.g., on theology, the brilliant work by Obermann, *Harvest*, and the no less profound comment by Tierney, " 'Scriptura.' " On constitutionalism, Tierney, *Foundations*; Wilks, *Problem*. The general absence of the word "tradition" from the sources cited in these works suggests the divorce between the idea and the word that is part of our story.

[14] Chenu, for example, equates tradition with conservatism in his analysis of the struggle between "the Ancients and the Moderns" during the period 1140-1215 (*La Théologie* [ch. 18, Tradition et Progrès], 386ff). Professor L. H. Little kindly drew my attention to this essay, which is now translated as "Tradition and Progress," in M. D. Chenu, Jerome Taylor and Lester K. Little eds. and transl., *Nature, Man, and Society in the Twelfth Century* (Chicago, 1968), 310-30.

[15] *Wesen und Ursprung des Katholizismus* (Leipzig, 1912). *Kirchengeschichte im Grundriss* (11th ed.; Leipzig, 1898), tr. by M. Sinclair, *Outlines of Church History* (Boston, 1958).

[16] Esp., *Entstehung und Entwicklung der Kirchenverfassung und des Kirchenrechts in den zwei ersten Jahrhunderten* (Leipzig, 1910).

rian, Baronius: "There is one spirit among all the Roman pontiffs." Arguing that the forces of historical change have been in suspense since the time of Christ, and that they are so forever, as regards the doctrine of papal government and, consequently, broader questions of Church government, this premise has claimed distinguished advocates from Baronius's day until the present, despite the assertions of others, including Roman Catholic scholars, that it is ahistorical, and that its theological content is at variance with the approved theology of the Church.[17]

Each of these approaches—Sohm's view that change toward legalism destroyed the true character of the Church, Harnack's contrary position, and the argument of immutability—discounts the fundamental character of tradition: the duality of conservatism and change. To appreciate the impact of the concept on the course of intellectual history, one must stand somewhat apart from the legal, theological, and constitutional terms of reference which historians have set in studying the problem of ecclesiastical cohesion, and see that great problem, in all its aspects, as part of a social phenomenon.[18]

From this viewpoint, issues of Church unity must bring us to look for periods that begin and end, the distinctive and precious heritage of every age, ideas that germinate, flourish, and wither, and the factors that make men think in radically different ways about convictions they mutually cherish as much as, or more than life itself. We must look for distinctions, rather than unity, for multiple rather than single meanings.

In the introductory chapter, I have described the basic issues in this essay. A pleasant duty remains: to acknowledge assistance given me in the course of the work. By generous subsidies, the American Council of Learned Societies freed me from the normal distractions of academic life in 1963-1964 and again, jointly with the Institute for Advanced Study, in 1966-1967. The Institute was also a faultless host in the academic year 1966-1967. The librarians at the British Museum, the

---

[17] Ullmann, *Growth*, 2nd ed., X: "It is therefore incomprehensible how some writers nowadays can maintain, amongst other things, that the programme and principles of the medieval papacy underwent radical changes. . . ." Fr. Kempf, "Gewalt," 137, 147ff, 152f (on the first edition of Dr. Ullmann's book). In a response, Dr. Ullmann applied to Fr. Kempf words of Dante: "*Hii sunt impietatis filii, qui, ut flagitia sua exequi possint, matrem prostituunt, fratres expellunt, et denique judicem habere nolunt*" (*HZ*, 191 [1960], 620ff).

[18] For excellent introductions to the sociological and anthropological view of tradition, see Wach, *Sociology*, 21f, 25, 35, 56, and esp. Vansina, *Tradition*, 2, 31, 33f, 36f, 40f, 44, 66, 78, 106.

Warburg Institute, Harvard University, the University of Chicago, Princeton University, the Princeton Theological Seminary, and the Institute for Advanced Study have, without exception, most kindly helped me use their excellent collections. Printing costs have been offset by a generous grant from the Louis A. Robb Fund of Princeton University Press, and by a subsidy from Dean D. Gale Johnson of the University of Chicago.

With great care, Miss Elizabeth I. Horton, Mrs. Helen Keeler, and Mrs. Margaret Sevcenko typed the long and difficult manuscript. Their artistry and kindness more than deserve the thanks of a grateful author. Miss Lalor Cadley of Princeton University Press has been the most exacting and congenial of editors. Mr. Robert J. Berg kindly helped compile the Index.

Professor Robert S. Hoyt encouraged this study from the very beginning. Professors R. C. Dales, Felix Gilbert, Robert M. Grant, Emile Karafiol, Mr. Charles Kletzsch, Mr. Christopher Ligota, and Mr. Christopher Morris have read or discussed with me portions of the essay. Professors Richard Luman and Brian Tierney showed both gallantry and patience in reading the entire manuscript, and they especially have placed me under a heavy obligation by their perceptiveness and knowledge.

Perhaps, given the subject of this essay, it would be appropriate to say in what historical tradition I stand, for teachers and fellow workers always contribute more to one's understanding than can ever be consciously known. Professor J. A. Cabaniss, the late Professor T. E. Mommsen, and Professor Brian Tierney granted me the privilege of studying under their direction, and thus imposed obligations that can never be fully repaid. I may also mention Professor Walter Ullmann, from whose essays I have sometimes differed, but always derived much stimulation and enlightenment.

It would be wrong, however, to suggest that anyone else is responsible for the views stated here. Indeed, these preliminary consultations have revealed most of all that students of Church history and medieval political thought, as well as theologians, labor under the maxim: *Doctrina multiplex, veritas una.*

Finally, Mr. and Mrs. Basil Filonovich and Professor and Mrs. T. G. Stavrou introduced me to the glories of eastern Christendom, and to them as much as to any is due the entire concept of this work.

*Zion, 1967—Chicago, 1969*          KFM

# Contents

CONTENTS

APPENDICES

# Abbreviations

| | |
|---|---|
| Abh. | Abhandlungen |
| AbhMNG | *Abhandlungen zur mittleren und neueren Geschichte* |
| ACO | *Acta Conciliorum Oecumenicorum*, ed. E. Schwartz |
| AHR | *American Historical Review* |
| AUF | *Archiv für Urkundenforschung* |
| Bd | Band |
| Byz | *Byzantion* |
| CH | *Church History* |
| CathHR | *Catholic Historical Review* |
| Corp. Christ., ser. lat. | *Corpus Christianorum*, series Latina |
| CSEL | *Corpus Scriptorum Ecclesiasticorum Latinorum* |
| DA | *Deutsches Archiv für Erforschung des Mittelalters* |
| DOP | *Dumbarton Oaks Papers* |
| DOS | *Dumbarton Oaks Studies* |
| DP | Dictatus Papae (Gregory VII) |
| EHR | *English Historical Review* |
| EO | *Echos d'Orient* |
| ForschDG | *Forschungen zur deutschen Geschichte* |
| GCS | *Die griechischen christlichen Schriftsteller der ersten drei Jahrhunderte* |
| Hft | Heft |
| HistStud | *Historische Studien* |
| HistVjs | *Historische Vierteljahrsschrift* |
| HJb | *Historisches Jahrbuch der Görres-Gesellschaft* |
| HTR | *Harvard Theological Review* |
| HZ | *Historische Zeitschrift* |
| Jaffé, Bib. greg. | P. Jaffé, ed., *Bibliotheca Rerum Germanicarum*, vol. 2, *Monumenta Gregoriana*, Berlin, 1865 |
| JEH | *Journal of Ecclesiastical History* |
| JHI | *Journal of the History of Ideas* |
| JR | *Journal of Religion* |
| JTS | *Journal of Theological Studies* |

| | |
|---|---|
| Mansi | J. D. Mansi, ed., *Sacrorum Conciliorum nova et amplissima Collectio* |
| MGH | Monumenta Germaniae Historica |
| SERIES: | |
| Cap. | Capitularia Regum Francorum |
| Conc. | Concilia Aevi Karolini |
| Conc. Suppl. | Concilia. Supplementum |
| Const. | Constitutiones |
| Epp. | Epistolae |
| Epp. sel. | Epistolae selectae |
| in us. sch. | Scriptores in usum scholarum |
| Ldl. | Libelli de lite |
| Reg. | Gregorii I papae registrum epistolarum |
| SS. | Scriptores |
| MH | *Medievalia et Humanistica* |
| MIÖG | *Mitteilungen des Instituts für Oesterreichische Geschichtsforschung* |
| NA | *Neues Archiv* |
| Pflugk-Harttung | J. v. Pflugk-Harttung, ed., *Acta Pontificum Romanorum Inedita*, vol. I, Tübingen, 1880 |
| PG | J. P. Migne, ed., *Patrologiae cursus completus*, ser. graeca. |
| PL | J. P. Migne, ed., *Patrologiae cursus completus*, ser. latina. |
| QFIAB | *Quellen und Forschungen aus italienischen Archiven und Bibliotheken* |
| RevSR | *Revue des sciences religieuses* |
| RevB | *Revue Bénédictine* |
| RHE | *Revue d'histoire ecclésiastique* |
| RSR | *Recherches de science religieuse* |
| SB | Sitzungsberichte |
| Sudendorf, Registrum | H. Sudendorf, ed., *Registrum merkwürdiger Urkunden*, vol. I, Jena, 1849 |
| TZ | *Theologische Zeitschrift* |
| VigC | *Vigiliae Christianae. A Review of Early Christian Life and Language.* |
| ZKG | *Zeitschrift für Kirchengeschichte* |
| ZkTh | *Zeitschrift für katholische Theologie* |

ZNTW          *Zeitschrift für die neutestamentliche Wissenschaft*
              *und die Kunde der älteren Kirche*
ZfRG          *Zeitschrift der Savigny-Stiftung für Rechtsgeschichte*
  SERIES:
  g. A.       germanistische Abteilung
  k. A.       kanonistische Abteilung
  r. A.       romanistische Abteilung

Tradition and Authority in
the Western Church
300-1140

## CHAPTER 1

# Tradition as a Safeguard of Cohesion

↟↟↟↟↟↟↟↟↟↟↟↟↟↟↟↟↟↟↟↟↟↟↟↟↟↟↟↟↟↟↟↟↟↟↟↟↟↟↟↟↟↟↟↟↟↟↟↟↟↟

### A. INTRODUCTION: CONSTANTS AND VARIABLES

TEACHING and ruling are only two aspects of religion; and religion itself is but one element among several that claim equal priority in the history of any civilization. When a mediaevalist thinks of tradition, he normally has in mind one specific category of religious authority, a small element in Church history, a drop in the great stream of the Middle Ages. Still, it has broader implications. Strictly defined, tradition concerns only the transmission of sacred knowledge; but as such, at least by implication, it stands at the hub of theological enquiry and of other issues to which theology was fundamental, such as Church order and political thought. The doctrine of the Incarnation, directly and by extension, runs like a scarlet thread through the grey fabric of religious and political thought in the early Middle Ages. Tradition was the needle that carried the thread, working out theology's complex and often elusive pattern.

Everyone has some concept of tradition. Art historians speak of various traditions—the Siennese, the Mannerist, the Impressionist, for example. Students of literature recognize, among others, the classical and romantic traditions. The "American way of life," the "honor system" at Princeton University, the changing of the guard at Buckingham Palace, celebrations around the Christmas tree are all traditional. Anthropologists and sociologists use the term more precisely, each in his own way. A distinguished sociologist has described mediaeval society, with its relatively slow change in ethical values and its emphasis on family and tribe, as "tradition-directed."[1] An eminent student of political forms has written about *The American Political Tradition*.[2] Kidnapping and rape, we are told, are still part of "a Sicilian tradition of convincing a girl to marry"; and a violated girl recently made herself an outcast among her own people when she refused to honor the tradition by

---

[1] D. Riesman *et al.*, *The Lonely Crowd: A Study of the Changing American Character* (Yale, 1953).
[2] R. Hofstadter (New York, 1948).

marrying her abductor.[3] Tradition in these senses indicates accepted ways of doing things, conventions sanctioned by old usage.

But for the theologian this is not tradition. Tradition for him is a bond which unifies the Church and separates it from the rest of the world. It is the idea that the true faith exists only within the Church as a community; that the faith and perhaps also the authentic order of the Church was given by Christ to the Apostles; and that it has been handed on unimpaired by subsequent generations of believers. "Tradition" is that "handing on" in its entirety, the preservation and continuance of the faith, the warrant of the Church's existence, the great wall between believers and the outside world.

A fifth-century writer, Vincent of Lérins, composed the classic definition. "The tradition of the catholic Church," he wrote, was one of two necessary canons of orthodoxy, the other canon being Scripture itself. Tradition alone could establish the one true meaning of Holy Writ.[4] It was easy to detect authentic tradition, for it had been believed "everywhere, always, and by everyone. That is truly and properly catholic, as is shown by the very force and meaning of the word, which comprehends everything almost universally. We shall hold to this rule if we follow universality, antiquity, and consensus. We shall follow universality if we acknowledge that one faith to be true which the whole Church throughout the world confesses; antiquity if we in no way depart from those interpretations which our ancestors and fathers manifestly proclaimed; consensus if in antiquity itself we keep following the definitions and opinions of all, or surely almost all, bishops and teachers." Vincent wrote that universality might in itself be an insufficient measure of orthodoxy, since the whole Church could conceivably be infected by heresy. Antiquity too might fail, if no oecumenical councils had considered questions at issue; one might unwittingly mistake an ancient heresy for true belief. Only the consensus of the Fathers was decisive, the judgment of men who had lived in all ages and places, and whose authority was acknowledged. "And whatever [the Christian] finds to have been held, approved, and taught, not only by one or two,

---

[3] *New York Times*, 18 December 1966.

[4] Commonitorium, II (1), ed. A. Jülicher, in Sammlung ausgewählter kirchen- und dogmengeschichtlicher Quellenschriften, Hft 10 (Freiburg i. B. and Leipzig, 1895), 2f. On Vincent's concept of tradition in general see Holstein in Pontificia Acad. Mariana Int., *Scriptura*, 214ff.

but by all equally and with one consensus, openly, frequently, and steadfastly, he may consider tenable without any reservations."[5]

Nothing could be simpler, or more straightforward. What difficulties are there? Does one not exaggerate the problems, in studying this idea, to see change, variety, and inconsistency? Perhaps not. Vincent composed his definition to refute what he considered the dangerous novelties of that Doctor of the Church, St. Augustine of Hippo. And the concept of tradition has always been a focus of debate. During the Reformation of the sixteenth century, men were eager to establish the precise nature of tradition; there is now a renewed interest in the same problem. The Second Vatican Council devoted part of a decree to it, and it periodically rises to vex the World Council of Churches. Beyond a general agreement with Vincent of Lérins about function, enquirers have never reached any common understanding about the degree of correspondence between Scriptures and tradition, about the content of tradition, or about the manner in which tradition is conveyed. Tradition is thus a kind of authority which men understand in clear, but widely different, ways.

This diversity arose in large part through the essential nature of theology. Christian thinkers have to describe a great mystery—the Word made flesh. The Deathless One was born to die. Wisdom became an ignorant child. Power became a feeble child. The Ancient of Days, the Eternal One, was born. This was accomplished so that man might change his inherent nature and be saved by being exalted to reign in and with God, participating in the nature of Divinity. Rationalizing this mystery was yet more complex. Christian doctrine, in contrast with Jewish, depends upon a testament, instead of a covenant. It derives from perceiving truth by unique revelation in Christ's mission, self-sacrifice, and resurrection, rather than from achieving knowledge of divine truth by the cumulative experience and reasoning of an entire people. Both theology and the whole system of moral values which broadly defines Christianity thus rest on a cornerstone of complete, virtually instantaneous, and unrepeatable revelation. Consequently, there is great scope for diversity in interpretation.

Grave differences also arose from another quarter. Vincent of Lérins showed the flaw in his all-too-clear definition when he said that universality could deceive if the whole Church fell into heresy. His ultimate canon was universal consensus; his argument was in fact tautological.

[5] Commonitorium, II (2, 3, 4), ed. Jülicher, 3f.

Interpretations of Scripture vary, he said; consequently tradition must act as a check on the exegesis both of scripture and of patristic texts. The social and political influences—and that most erratic element, personal conviction—which produced different schools of scriptural interpretation likewise affected patristic studies, and conditioned different and sometimes antagonistic standards of conformity among ecclesiological schools. The appeal to tradition was not, as mediaeval thinkers believed, an appeal to a timeless, abstract standard, but to various modes of thought formed by particular circumstances of time and place.[6] That was the fundamental difficulty of our concept, the danger in the sort of certainty that John Knox displayed to Mary, Queen of Scots.

The Queen spoke for many ordinary, perplexed persons in her encounter with Knox. She complained that his doctrine tended one way, and that of the pope and cardinals, another. Whom could she safely follow? Who might judge? Knox represented the self-confidence of most doctrinaire theologians when he answered unhesitatingly that she must follow him. "Ye shall believe God, that plainly speaketh in His Word, and further than the Word teaches you, ye neither shall believe the one or the other. The Word of God is plain in the self; and if there appear any obscurity in one place, the Holy Ghost, which is never contrarious to Himself, explains the same more clearly in other places, so that there can remain no doubt, but unto such as obstinately remain ignorant."[7]

Knox divided the world between himself and his followers, who understood the Holy Ghost, and the others, who were stubbornly ignorant. His attitude was matched in every religious grouping of the period with which we are to deal. Nicene, Arian, Nestorian, Monophysite, and all the rest argued that they held the unchanging truth, the doctrine of salvation. And yet, vast changes did occur in doctrine and in the concepts of the Church, of man's relationship to God, and of how sacred knowledge was properly transmitted.

The very nature of tradition, as early mediaeval thinkers understood it, contained the seeds of diversity, and set the idea apart from the conventional techniques and the clear definitions of historical criticism.

[6] See Ghellink, "Patristique," 403.

[7] John Knox, ed. W. C. Dickenson, *History of the Reformation in Scotland*, vol. 2 (London, 1950), 20. I am heavily indebted to Mr. C. Morris for many kind and helpful suggestions concerning this essay, and, on two specific points, for this reference and for the reference to Hooker's *Polity* on p. 353.

For it maintained that the cohesion of the Church depended both on permanent and on transitory elements, and on conservatism and renewal. Though it exalted antiquity as a prime virtue, it never had the antiquarian character of traditionalism.[8] Vincent of Lérins described this necessary interplay of the eternal and the mutable, when, after discussing the antiquity and universality of tradition, he wrote: "But perhaps someone is saying: 'Will there be, therefore, no development in the Church of Christ?' Obviously, there may be even very great development; for what man is so hateful to men, so odious to God as to strive to deny it? But, to be sure, it must truly be a development, and not a transformation, of the faith. The quality of development is the elaboration of anything, preserving its own character; that of transformation, the change of something from one thing into another. With the passage of the years and the ages of individual men and of everyone, of each man and of the whole Church, understanding, knowledge, and wisdom must grow and develop greatly and powerfully, but [each must grow] only in its own kind, in the same dogma, the same sense, the same meaning."[9] Vincent continued to compare this growth with the development of human bodies, and with plants which, in the "elaboration" of their forms, preserve their original natures.

Vincent's statement was an early acknowledgment that the idea of Christian tradition, a theological concept in origin, also had intrinsically historical and institutional characteristics. The dualism of conservatism and renewal, and the simple passage of time, which removed successive generations of thinkers increasingly far from the Apostolic Age, forced temporal aspects upon a concept whose essence was eternal verity. Conservatism required that tradition be immune from the attrition of time; renewal declared that knowledge of it was subject to mutability, to neglect and corruption, and to correction and recovery. To admit this was to open the door to divergent interpretations and to conflict.

The difficulties in defining the idea of tradition are, therefore, that it meant different things to different people, that these meanings were inconsistent and sometimes contradictory, and, fundamentally, that the ways men understood it were subject to change by circumstances of time and place. Men used the same words, but meant different things. In-

8 Müller, "Bedeutung," 84f.
9 Commonitorium, XXIII (28), ed. Jülicher, 33f.

7

stead of a unitary, immutable, and universal idea, we have to deal with many ideas of tradition.

In discussing the idea of tradition, we shall be concerned to sketch the history of these variations. But the major question we must treat is this: Historically, tradition was a constantly open question for which men framed—as they still do—many different answers. Thinkers who wrestled with this issue saw it, each in his own way, as a concrete matter about which right-minded men could have no doubt. For them, it was a timeless control on the authenticity of rules and official acts in the Church; and it was, at the same time, independent in origin, authority, and ultimate purpose from law and office. We have seen that Vincent of Lérins considered it in effect an abstract principle of right to which, above all, the universal consensus of believers witnessed. In the following essay, we shall try to show the effect of this idea on the way men thought of legitimacy within the Church and of relations between the Church and the world outside it. We shall discuss tradition both as it related to diverse historical contexts, and as men thought it to be.

After a background sketch of how people thought about tradition when the Roman Empire persecuted the Church, the main body of the essay begins with the conversion of Constantine and the slow establishment of the Christian Empire. It traces stages of development through three great crises in the West—the aftermath of Constantine's conversion, the Iconoclastic Dispute, and the Investiture Controversy—before the time of Gratian's *Decretum*, the great systematic book of law that fundamentally changed men's understanding of authority in the Church.

### B. TRADITION IN THE AGE OF THE APOLOGISTS

Any religion that seeks to teach the same doctrine over a long period of time has a concept of tradition. It preaches that, as truth is immutable, each generation has handed on its body of sacred knowledge to the next without essential change; it honors a succession of authentic teachers, men having special gifts as expositors of doctrine, bearers of tradition. Above all, it holds that tradition unifies the faithful and separates them from men outside the religious body. Tradition exists only among the faithful; only they have the doctrine of salvation. But, like a Damoclean sword, there always hangs over believers the danger that even they may lose or corrupt the words of truth and life, and thus suffer the fate of the infidel.

8

These two limitations heavily influenced the attitudes of the apologists toward Roman society, which had no part in Christian tradition, and toward the Synagogue, which, to their minds, had first received tradition, then lost it through corruption and infidelity.[1] From the fourth century onward, Greek and Latin writers tended to think of society as Christian. For them, the standards of personal conduct and just government to which society nominally adhered were those preached by the Church. In fact, this harmony of religion and social order was never complete; before the conversion of Constantine, it was utterly unknown. Society, epitomized in the Roman imperial government, repudiated Christianity and persecuted its followers; Christians rejected the pagan value systems. Christianity and society withstood one another, lacking a basis for consensus, which would have united them, and for close communication, which would have sustained the union.

The dichotomy in the minds of early Christians between believers and non-believers led in extreme instances to total withdrawal from human society (witness the Egyptian hermits). And, despite the efforts of some apologists to prove that the faithful were as other men,[2] those very authors acknowledged the estrangement of Christians from the world in which they lived. Their absence from public functions marked by sacrifices, their condemnations of the love of physical beauty,[3] of wealth and public ostentation,[4] of civil distinctions and public honors,[5] of the pagan gods,[6] and of Rome itself[7] gave rise to the views that Christians were "enemies of the human race"[8] and opponents of the social order, and that they practiced sedition against the Roman Empire.

If, therefore, the charges of social anarchism and sedition against the

---

[1] Cf. Origen, *Against Celsus*, III, 11, 12, 13; *GCS, Origenes Werke* 1, 211f; Molland, "Développement," 14, on Origen's views concerning the apostolic succession. See Congar, *Essai*, 48f, Laurin, *Orientations*, 438, 442ff. For a general survey of the concept of tradition from St. Paul to St. Irenaeus, see Ortiz de Urbina, in Pontificia Acad. Mariana Int., *Scriptura*, 185-203.

[2] E.g., Tertullian, *Apologeticum*, c. 42; *Corp. Christ.*, ser. lat. 1, 156ff.

[3] See *Paedagogue*, III, 1, 2; Origen, *Against Celsus*, VIII, 17-20; *GCS, Origenes Werke* 2, 234ff.

[4] E.g., *Paedagogue*, III, 6-11; Cyprian, ep. I, 1; *CSEL* 3, pt. 3, 465f.

[5] Cyprian, ep. I, 1.

[6] Ellspermann, *Attitude*, 56, 73, 76.

[7] Victorinus, *Commentarium in Apocalypsin*, cc. XIII and XVII; *CSEL* 49, 116ff; Minucius Felix, *Octavius*, XXV, 5-9; ed. A. D. Simpson (New York, 1938), 53f.

[8] Tertullian, *Apologeticum*, c. 37, 8; *Corp. Christ.*, ser. lat. 1, 148f. See Frend, *Martyrdom*, 6ff, 15ff, 104ff.

Christians were misplaced, the very arguments with which the apologists parried them indicate that they actually had some basis in authentic Christian thought. Despite their protestations that they contributed to the welfare of society as a whole, and that they were unfeignedly loyal to the emperors, Christian writers did discourage active participation in public affairs and rejected the values of Roman society. Their absence from temples, theaters, and games indicated both their strong monotheism and their profound alienation from the world in which they lived.

The source of that estrangement lay in the ideological differences between the Christian community and the Roman world; for, on the great questions of life, there was no ultimate agreement between Christian tradition and pagan philosophy. Some thinkers indeed sought a middle ground between the two schools. But Tertullian dismissed them out of hand with his famous questions: "What indeed has Athens to do with Jerusalem? What concord is there between the Academy and the Church? What between heretics and Christians?"[9] In the fourth century, St. Jerome, divinely proclaimed a Ciceronian, asked the same questions: "What has Paul to do with Aristotle, or Peter with Plato? For, as the latter was the prince of the philosophers, so was the former chief of the Apostles. . . ."[10] And again: "What communion has light with darkness? What concord has Christ with Belial? What has Horace to do with the Psalter, Virgil with the Gospels, and Cicero with the Apostle?"[11] Perfidy outside the Church and heresy within it were alike considered the fruits of worldly philosophy.[12] The pagan Libanius touched the crux of this argument when he wrote that literature and the worship of the gods were twin sisters.[13]

Some students of early Christian thought have tended to overemphasize the apologists' rejection of pagan thought. The degree of rejection varied from author to author and sometimes from period to period in the life of a given author. Still, even the most liberal attitude granted pagan learning only relative value. Absolute value belonged to Christian doctrine alone.

St. Augustine drew a very famous parallel between the spoils which the Israelites took from the Egyptians and the things of value which

[9] De praescr. haer., c. 7; Frend, *Martyrdom*, 365ff; Morgenthaler, "Roma," esp. 301ff.
[10] Adv. Pelag. 1, 14, but spoken by the heretic Critobulus, PL 23, 529.
[11] Ep. 22, 29, 6-7; *CSEL* 54, 188f.
[12] E.g., Hilary of Poitiers on Arianism, De Trin., 1, 13, PL 10, 34.
[13] Orat. XVIII, 157.

Christians could derive from pagan learning. Just as the Israelites had taken vessels and ornaments of gold and silver and costly raiment out of Egypt, but had abandoned the idols of their masters, so could the Christian scholar learn from pagan writings some interpretive skills, some moral precepts, and even some truths of divine worship, abandoning what was false and superstitious. Of such spoils, St. Augustine wrote: "Now these are, so to speak, their gold and silver, which they did not create themselves, but dug out of the mines of God's providence which are everywhere scattered abroad, and are perversely and unlawfully prostituting to the worship of devils. These, therefore, the Christian, when he separates himself in spirit from the miserable fellowship of these men, ought to take away from them, and to devote to their proper use in preaching the gospel. Their garments also—that is, human institutions such as are adopted to that intercourse with men which is indispensable in this life—we must take and turn to a Christian use."[14]

Earlier authors, such as Clement of Alexandria, who had accepted pagan learning as of some value, had likewise held that that value was not substantive. Philosophy might bring to the true faith some who could not believe without having been led by reason; skill in rhetorical devices was useful in the exposition of Scripture. But whatever intrinsic worth philosophy and ancient literature had came from imperfect understanding of the knowledge which the Church possessed in full. Some apologists were concerned to show that such understanding as the pagans did have had come from readings of the prophets or of other portions of the Scriptures; and a persistent legend, which the Christians may have derived from the Jewish philosopher Philo, alleged that Plato had been a disciple of Moses in Egypt, and that, through Plato's writings, some elements of the divine truth which Moses had revealed to him were spread abroad in the pagan world.[15] Other apologists, however, maintained that God had utterly deprived Plato, Pythagoras, and all other pagans of knowledge of true doctrine, barring them from any contact with the Jews, who alone, in ancient times, knew the authentic philosophy, the doctrine of salvation.[16] But all apologists, even those who argued that Christians might claim "the spoils of the Egyptians"

[14] De doctrina christiana II, 40 (60); Florilegium patristicum, 24, 46; De doctrina christiana, II, 144f, in *CSEL* 80, 75f. Cf. *ibid.*, II, 42, 163. Florilegium Patristicum, 24, 47f; II, 151, in *CSEL* 80, 78. See Laistner, "Schools."

[15] Ellspermann, *Attitude*, 113, 176; Weltin, "Athenae," 156f.

[16] Cf. Lactantius, Div. Inst. 4, 1, 12; *CSEL* 19, 276.

from pagan learning, agreed that human wisdom was vanity, that the philosophers of Greece and Rome had been blind to eternal truth in its fullness since they had striven towards God, unaided by divine grace, with the insufficient powers of the human intellect, and that the elements of truth to which the pagans did attain brought them unwittingly to bear witness to truth and against their own imperfect, and even depraved, beliefs.

Tertullian's question, "What has Athens to do with Jerusalem?" indicates what he did not say in his defense against the charges that Christians were "enemies of the human race" and subverters of the Roman Empire: namely, that the philosophical systems of classical antiquity, together with the social values they justified, were repugnant to Christian doctrine. Pagans had not shared in Christian tradition; believers likewise had no part in pagan thought, which was for them lifeless, insufficient, and perverse.

This was the judgment of the apologists upon philosophies and societies which had never received tradition. But Tertullian's eagerness to establish the prior antiquity of Christianity over pagan philosophy led him to the significant admission that the philosophers had grasped some elements of truth through their contacts with Jews and through reading some books of the Old Testament. In breaking off from the Synagogue, the Church passed through the three stages of development which Nock distinguished: the periods of prophetic preaching, "wider evangelization," and, finally, institutionalization, when "the experience of what is in time a distant past is mediated to generations yet unborn, as a thing ever fresh, and can harden into a tradition as rigid as the order from which the prophet revolted."[17] The Jews had once been stewards of tradition. At Nock's third stage, how did the apologists judge the Jews?

St. Ambrose's answer is concise: "The Hebrews spoiled the Egyptians and took away their vessels. The Christian people has the spoils of the Jews, and we have all that which they did not know they had."[18] In related terms, St. John Chrysostom viciously attacked the Jews for having the Law and perverting it.[19] Despite the bitterness which they

[17] *Conversion*, 4.

[18] In Ps. 118, 21, 12, 4; *CSEL* 62, 480. On various aspects of this theme, see Welsersheimb, "Kirchenbild," 447; Blumenkranz, "Vie," 466f; Chydenius, *Institutions, passim*; Frend, *Martyrdom*, 18, 31ff, 70ff, 178ff, and Frend's excellent bibliography on 584f.

[19] Seaver, *Persecution*, 39ff; Simon, "Polémique," 406, 408ff.

almost uniformly showed towards the Jews, the apologists acknowledged a close spiritual and even institutional affinity between the Church and the Synagogue. Modern scholars have done much to establish the precise nature of that relationship. From the Synagogue came some Aggadic interpretations of Scripture, liturgical forms, administrative offices, purified texts of the Old Testament, and even the idea of tradition itself.

Many early believers thought that the authority of the Synagogue extended beyond matters of textual exegesis. In the fourth century, judaizing was so prevalent that one author censured Christians for adopting immediately whatever new rites might appear in the Synagogue, even if they had been devised by only a few Jews.[20] Julian the Apostate rightly said, "The Galilaeans [i.e., Christians] say that, though they are different from the Jews, they are still, precisely speaking, Israelites in accordance with their prophets, and that they obey Moses above all and the prophets who in Judaea succeeded him. . . ."[21] The opposition of the apologists to judaizing derived from the thought behind St. Ambrose's statement that Christians had taken the spoils of the Jews. Sensitivity to the charge that their religion was new, or even an heretical deviation from Judaism,[22] had led Christians to the paradoxical position which Julian described, the position that, though they were not Jews, they were the heirs of the covenant which God had made with Abraham, the successors of the Jews as God's chosen people.

They had come into the spiritual heritage of carnal Israel; but the heritage itself carried an admonition, for if the people of God's first election had lost their inheritance, so might that of His second. The author of the apocryphal Gospel of Barnabas, written before 140 A.D., exhorted Christians in this vein,[23] and the admonitory example of the fallen Jews was never far from the thoughts of the later apologists.[24]

The apologists argued that the Jews had blinded themselves to the true understanding of the Law of God by their wickedness, and that they had in fact contravened the Law by establishing contrary tradi-

[20] See Krauss, "Jews" (1892-1893), 126f, 135ff; (1893-1894), 83, 232f, 228; Dix, *Hippolytus*, xlf; Wilde, *Writers*, 92; Oesterly, *Background*, 84ff, 97; Riddle, "Jewish Christians," 32; Blumenkranz, *Judenpredigt*, 62, 80f.

[21] Against the Galilaeans, 253B, ed. W. C. Wright, *The Works of the Emperor Julian*, vol. 3 (London, 1923), 392. On the favor Julian won among the Jews and the Christians' hatred of his judaizing, see Krauss, "Jews" (1893-1894), 90.

[22] Blumenkranz, *Judenpredigt*, 113f.

[23] Wilde, *Writers*, 87, 89. See Frend, *Martyrdom*, 197.

[24] On the Christian's view of moral decay among the Jews, see Krauss, "Jews" (1893-1894), 227.

13

tions of their own contrivance.[25] The teachings of the rabbis had supplanted the love of God in their hearts, and so they had no apprehension of the Word of God. The Jews had early turned from true worship to the worship of idols, of which the Golden Calf was but one; they had not believed the prophets, whom they had in fact put to death. And at length the words of the prophets were fulfilled when the Jews refused to acknowledge Christ and, their perception of the Scriptures entirely distorted by that rejection, slew their Messiah. All the apologists before Augustine attributed the final fall of the Jews to their execution of Christ:[26] the extinction of their nation, the destruction of Jerusalem, and their exile were manifest evidence that God had rejected them as they had rejected His Son. He had cast down the Jews and elected the Gentiles; and since all the elect participated in the nature of Christ, who was by descent of Abraham's seed, all believers became seed of the Patriarch according to the spirit and entered into the inheritance of which his fleshly descendants had long since proven themselves unworthy.[27]

The error of the Jews commenced when they failed to distinguish between eternal and temporal law, and to realize that such holy men as Noah, Melchisedech, and even Abraham had lived righteously and in God's favor without the ritual observances that the Jews required as tokens of orthodoxy.[28] They still mistook the empty rituals for the sacraments they foreshadowed, the image for the reality. And so, unwittingly testifying to the true knowledge of God, they were scattered throughout the world in the invincibility of their ignorance, as witnesses of the prophesies which Christianity had fulfilled.[29]

The Jews were more wretched than the Romans, since they had received the truth and corrupted it; and, to the apologists, their present ignorance, like that of the Romans, illustrated the principle that tradition belonged only to the faithful, and their past fall, that tradition could become corrupted. The blindness of the Jews to the truth of which they were unfaithful stewards, the blindness which led them to mistake tem-

[25] Wilde, *Writers*, 117.

[26] Blumenkranz, *Judenpredigt*, 13f.

[27] Cf. Wilde, *Writers*, 116, 127, 157; Blumenkranz, "Augustin," 233f; *Judenpredigt*, 12, 116f, 131f, 175f.

[28] On the Christian assertion that Jewish prophets, patriarchs, and kings were saints of the Church, see Simon, "Polémique," 412f; "Saints," 98ff; Blumenkranz, *Judenpredigt*, 36ff, 171f; "Auteurs," pt. I, 12, 18, 23, and *passim*.

[29] Wilde, *Writers*, 110f; Blumenkranz, "Augustin et les juifs," 232; "Zeugen," 396-98; "Auteurs," pt. I, 13.

poral observances for eternal law, underscored for early Christians the importance of the manner in which the true tradition could be preserved and the New Israel saved from the fate of the Old.

+

Many of the earliest Christian writers did not mention tradition or the broad problem of preserving the authentic faith. Their treatises, addressed to pagans or to Jews, did not, on the whole, treat of doctrine and discipline within the Christian community; rather, they considered the more general questions of the place Christians could rightly assume in Roman society, and the claim of Christianity that it had replaced Judaism as the religion of God's elect. Indeed, some of them were so far from dealing with theology that they did not even mention the name of Christ.

Other writers of the period revealed two strands of thought about authority: one, inherited from the Synagogue, exalted tradition, as teaching and religious practice based on written works and confirmed by long usage; the other, directly opposite to tradition, gave first place to personal or official authority. Some of the Apostolic Fathers and their successors, the apologists, can be classified as "Jewish Christians," who accepted the Old Testament and some Jewish apocrypha as authentic Scriptures, supplemented them with sayings of Jesus (transmitted orally in the main), and gave the writings that were much later codified in the New Testament importance only as testimonies to these earlier traditions. Papias and Hermas represent this school. Other thinkers, like St. Ignatius of Antioch, held what can be called the Gentile point of view, considering the nuances of tradition secondary, and giving primary authority to the immediate revelations of living men.[30]

Though distinct, these views are often coupled, as they are, for example, even in the Gospels, where Jesus contrasted Pharisaic traditions with "the word of God" at the same time He strove to fulfill the Law. The Jewish and the Gentile views were neither fully reconcilable nor mutually exclusive.

Two disputes in the second and third centuries sharpened each view. The more protracted of those conflicts, the Gnostic controversy, arose early in the second century, and continued in full force for about a cen-

[30] For these early disputes, I draw heavily on the excellent discussion in Grant, *Formation*.

15

tury, leaving a sort of residual legatee in the Manichaean conflict that vexed St. Augustine of Hippo. Gnosticism was strongly opposed to Jewish legalism. It assailed the authority of tradition by arguing that the Apostles had deliberately misrepresented authentic tradition to win converts, and by advancing its own doctrine of secret traditions deriving from revelation and constantly changed and augmented by new revelations. In its elaboration, this doctrine also challenged the nascent doctrine of official authority by emphasizing that the purpose of the secret formulae and practices was to enable each believer to accomplish his own salvation through direct mystical communion with God. The Gnostics renounced the material world; and, in terms of doctrine, this repudiation found expression in contempt for both the Jewish and the Gentile views of authority as external checks on individual belief.

The second conflict, the Montanist dispute, lasted from about 156 until 220. It arose among Phrygian mystics and nature-worshippers. Like the Gnostics, the Montanists emphasized the direct relationship between the believer and God, rather than the believer's adherence to tradition or obedience to religious superiors. Montanus and the two Phrygian priestesses who followed him and continued his doctrine after he died preached direct revelation and the immanent descent of the heavenly Jerusalem. Tradition and formal order were superfluous.

Both Gnosticism and Montanism were extensions of primitive Christianity. The roots of Gnosticism went much further back, beyond the origins of Christianity to oriental mystery religions and to conventicles of philosophers in the classical world. But, as a heresy within the Church, Gnosticism, like Montanism, bespoke the days of the early Church, before the appearance of fixed patterns of congregational government and norms of theology. They were the revivalist cults of their age.

But Christianity's expansion created new social needs, and these were being met by the monarchic episcopate, standards of orthodoxy, and even canons of authentic Scriptures. Gnosticism and Montanism accelerated these developments by convincing their enemies that preservation of the saving doctrine demanded stability, and that stability lay in formalism.

This was the background against which the Apostolic Fathers and, after them, the apologists, viewed problems of authority in faith and order. Then, for the first time, men began to try to set down authentic tradition in writing, and to publish it, in answer to the dangers that

16

Gnosticism and Montanism presented. We know, for example, that St. Ignatius of Antioch, journeying to martyrdom at Rome early in the second century, made such an effort "to attest that tradition [of the Apostles] in writing, and to give it a fixed form for the sake of greater security."[31] But, as Robert Grant observes, "the 'period of oral tradition' did not come to an end when written gospels were produced."[32] Gospels, real and apocryphal, and written compendia of tradition, like those of St. Ignatius and later of St. Hippolytus, did not clear the field of oral teaching. Far from it.

Comments of St. Irenaeus of Lyon, the earliest apologist to express a relatively clear concept of tradition, illustrate the general evolution of thought. Writing in the latter half of the second century, St. Irenaeus asked:[33] "For how should it be if the Apostles themselves had not left us writings? Would it not be necessary to follow the course of the tradition which they handed down to those to whom they did commit the churches? To which course many nations of those barbarians who believe in Christ do assent, having salvation written in their hearts by the Spirit, without paper or ink, and carefully preserving the ancient tradition believing in one God, the creator of heaven and earth, and all things therein, by means of Christ Jesus, the Son of God; who, because of His surpassing love towards His creation, condescended to be born of the Virgin, He Himself uniting man through Himself to God, and having suffered under Pontius Pilate, and rising again, and having been received up in splendor, shall come in glory, the Savior of those who are saved, and the Judge of those who are judged, and sending into eternal fire those who transform the truth and despise His Father and His advent. Those who, in the absence of written documents, have believed this faith, are barbarians so far as regards our language; but as regards doctrine, manner, and tenor of life, they are because of faith very wise indeed, and they please God, ordering their conversation in all righteousness, chastity, and wisdom."[34] Tradition, for Irenaeus, was the confession of faith. Its authority derived from the

---

[31] Eusebius, H. E. III, 36; IV, 8, 2; *GCS, Eusebius Werke* 2, pt. 1, 276, 314; Deneffe, *Traditionsbegriff*, 39f; Flesseman-Van Leer, *Tradition*, 113; Dix, *Hippolytus,* xi, xlviff. On Ignatius's view of tradition, see the varied interpretations of Grant, "Hermeneutics," 181ff; Scripture," 322ff; and Geraets, "Apostolica," *passim.*

[32] *Formation*, 28f.

[33] See Deneffe, *Traditionsbegriff*, 29, 32f; Flesseman-Van Leer, *Tradition*, 103f, 108; Reynders, "Paradosis," 155; Congar, *Essai*, 48.

[34] Adv. Haeres., III, 4, 1, ed. W. W. Harvey, vol. 2 (Cambridge, 1852), 16. See Molland, "Irenaeus," 20ff.

direct action of the Holy Spirit which inscribed the preaching of the Apostles in the hearts of unlettered barbarians.

In Irenaeus's opinion, therefore, authentic documents (even the Scriptures) did not hold final authority. Sts. Ignatius and Hippolytus could well seek to perpetuate apostolic tradition through their writings; but, in the epilogue of his treatise, Hippolytus himself recognized the possibility that he might have omitted something and trusted that God would reveal it "to them that are worthy."[35] St. Irenaeus wrote explicitly that "tradition has not been handed on in writing, but by the living voice,"[36] and that the true meaning of the Scriptures could be learned only with the aid of the direct oral instruction which Christ had given the Apostles, and which they had transmitted to their followers.[37] Fear of deception through writing led the early Fathers to examine with the greatest care those works which claimed apostolic or pre-apostolic origin. The thought that tradition revealed in the written word, even that of the Scriptures, was incomplete and that it had to be verified and supplemented by oral tradition persisted throughout the age of the apologists, from Irenaeus to Augustine.

The attitude derived largely from the fact that the canon of the New Testament had not yet been closed. When the Apostolic Fathers and the apologists wrote of "the Scriptures," they generally meant the Old Testament, though they knew the Gospels and the letters of St. Paul. And, lacking a body of indisputably authentic writings on the new dispensation at the same time that they encountered a considerable number of separate works, some genuine, others spurious, but all claiming apostolic authority, they looked to some channel of inspiration superior to the written word, some charismatic element which would guide them through the confusion and contradictions of Scripture and pseudo-Scripture to true belief. That element was oral tradition.[38]

When Vincent of Lérins composed his classic definition of tradition, he added nothing new except formulaic clarity.[39] Obscure apologists, like Serapion of Antioch and Polycrates of Ephesus, and distinguished ones,

[35] XXXVIII, 4; ed. Dix, cit., 92.

[36] Adv. Haer. III, 2, 1; ed. Harvey, cit., 2, 7: *"Non enim per literas traditam illam [traditionem], sed per vivam vocem."*

[37] Adv. Haer. III, 2, 2; ed. Harvey, cit., 2, 7f. On textual criticism, see ed. Goodspeed, *Die ältesten Apologetiker*, 3, 14; Eusebius, H. E. VI, 7; *GCS, Eusebius Werke* 2, pt. 2, 532f; Origen, Strom. III, 13, 91, PG 8, 1193; Grant, "Criticism."

[38] See Brunhes, "Idée," 118.

[39] Cf. Symonds, "Patristic," 62.

like St. Irenaeus and Tertullian, had anticipated all his canons, as had, indeed, Vincent's elder contemporary, St. Augustine of Hippo.[40] Since the Gnostic controversy in the middle of the second century, when Christian thinkers were forced to define their own concept of tradition in answer to the peculiar Gnostic doctrine that true spiritual knowledge had come down by secret tradition within a closed succession of the elect,[41] authentic tradition had held the attributes of universality, antiquity, and consensus, attributes which it had in good measure inherited from the Jewish concept of tradition. The Scriptures themselves, and the other writings of the apostolic and post-apostolic ages, provided no clear definition of tradition or of how it was to be properly transmitted. Neither they nor oral tradition nor yet the writings of the apologists determined who could judge universal truth from general error, or the ancient faith from early heresy, or distinguish in contrary patristic opinions the reconciling element of consent. Tradition was both oral and written. Who could separate the misplaced rhetorical emphasis from the doctrine of salvation, or sift the defective manuscript reading from the word of God?

With insight born of profound study, Luther distinguished between the Old Testament, as *Schrift*, and the New Testament, as *Predigt*. This is the fundamental problem of Scripture vs. oral teaching that one encounters, for example, in the Gospels, when the commands of Jesus contravene the letter of religious law. But the commands of Jesus and those of St. Paul added a third element to this complex problem when they modified or upset oral teaching itself. In his letter to the Galatians (1: 14), St. Paul remembered his own pre-Christian era, when he "profited in the Jews' religion above many of my equals in mine own nation, being more exceedingly zealous of the traditions of my fathers." Conversion meant departure from traditions as well as from the letter of the law, and St. Paul is careful to say that, for three years after his conversion, he "conferred not with flesh and blood; neither went I up to Jerusalem to them which were apostles before me . . ." After three years, he did confer for fifteen days with St. Peter, but he saw no other Apostle, "save James, the Lord's brother," a man who, like St. Paul himself, entered the apostolic circle after Jesus's death (Galatians 1: 16-19).

[40] But see Reynders, "Paradosis," 164, on the absence of the word "tradition" from some apologetic treatises. Concerning their emphasis on antiquity see Grant, "Appeal," 14ff.

[41] See Symonds, "Patristic," 60.

19

Personal (or official) authority thus implicitly joined Scripture and tradition as a third norm. Early disputes, especially the Gnostic and Montanist conflicts, sharply focused attention on this relation. As Montanism spread into Greece and North Africa, the evolution of the doctrine undercut administrative authority. Only God (i.e., not a bishop) was the sole judge among believers, the Montanists argued. Montanists repudiated bishops for their laxity in ascetic practices, such as fasting, and they advocated utter separation of the faithful from the unbelieving world at the very time when bishops were increasingly concerned with converting Roman society. This sort of thought particularly forced the advocates of formalism to look for a marriage of tradition and office.

The apologists turned their attention to the Apostles, the links between the divine word and mankind, the first human bearers of tradition under the New Dispensation. The personal qualities of the Apostles did not interest the apologists so much as the nature of their office, the apostolate; the different concepts of the Church as an institution which we have mentioned derived precisely from divergent judgments on the powers and nature of the apostolic office. Never a simple matter, tradition became an intricate complex of metaphysical and legalistic thought when the apologists attempted to determine whether the apostolic office was the only means appointed to conserve and transmit oral tradition; if so, whether the apostolate itself could be transmitted, not perishing with the Apostles but passing down from them to each succeeding generation; and, finally, if it were transmissible, in what manner it could be transferred.

The question of the apostolate, like that of tradition itself, first became acute in the second century,[42] and apologists of the earlier period appear to have judged, on the whole, that the apostolate was an office peculiar to the Apostles, and that it died with them. According to this position, the direct action of the Holy Ghost continued tradition among the faithful. Even before the first century had ended, however, another doctrine had appeared: namely, that, while the apostolic teaching had descended to all believers, it had been handed down especially to the clergy—to bishops, priests, and deacons;[43] and early in the second century St. Ignatius of Antioch wrote that priests, and especially bish-

[42] De Wailley, "Notes," 141ff; Labriolle, "Papa," 66f.
[43] Epistola Clementis, 7, 1-12, 3; *GCS, Die Pseudoclementinen*, 1, 10ff.

ops, were stewards of tradition.[44] Later apologists also held this view, without excluding the earlier doctrine of the continual presence of the Holy Ghost in the general body of the faithful. Some, like St. Irenaeus and Tertullian, accepted both views and added yet a third: that each church received its knowledge of the faith from its founder, and that churches founded by Apostles would therefore continue to profess the apostolic faith.[45] It was also generally agreed that laymen of distinguished learning and perception, who remained in the orthodox communion, likewise communicated the authentic tradition and could rightly be acknowledged among the "Fathers" of the Church.

None of these early discussions, however, considered the question of perpetuating the apostolate itself. The concept of succession was surely present: the apologists of the first and second centuries wrote of successions to episcopal sees, of successions in lesser clerical offices, and of successions of spiritual sons to their fathers in the faith. But their concern was with succession to the apostolic faith, and not with succession to the apostolic office;[46] office was no guarantee of orthodoxy, for, as St. Irenaeus pointed out, bishops and priests, for all their special stewardship of orthodoxy, might fall from their succession in the faith by abandoning true doctrine, establishing schismatic bodies, or displaying unworthy conduct,[47] as Judas had lost the apostolate itself through treachery.[48]

By emphasizing the episcopal succession, the early apologists prepared the way for the critical doctrine among western thinkers that both the faith and the office of the Apostles survived them; that the apostolate and the episcopate were identical; that bishops were truly the successors of the Apostles in doctrine and in powers. St. Irenaeus had written that priests and bishops had their succession from the Apostles.[49] But he was the first to state that bishops must be consecrated by bish-

[44] To the Philadelphians, V, 1; to the Ephesians, III, 2, ed. T. Camelot, in *Sources Chrétiennes* (2nd ed.; Paris, 1951), 144, 70.

[45] Caspar, *Geschichte*, 1, 15; Flesseman-Van Leer, *Tradition*, 150ff.

[46] Cf. Caspar, *Geschichte*, 1, 1f, 15.

[47] Adv. Haer. III, 3, 1; IV, 26, 2; ed. Harvey, cit., 2, 8f, 188f. Cf. Grant, "Hermeneutics," 196f. Bakhuizen van den Brink, "Tradition," esp. 20ff, emphasizes a connection in early thought between the episcopate and the transmission of apostolic tradition.

[48] Adv. Haer. II, 36, 1, 3; ed. Harvey, cit., 1, 322, 323f; Reynders, "Paradosis," 188; Molland, "Irenaeus," 26.

[49] Adv. Haer. III, 2, 2; III, 3, 1; ed. Harvey, cit., 2, 7ff; Molland, "Irenaeus," 22.

21

ops. Bishops of Alexandria,[50] and perhaps those of Rome, Antioch, and Lyons as well, were regularly consecrated by priests of their churches until the early third century. The thought had not yet been formulated that the episcopacy was an order distinct from the priesthood, having as its special prerogative the transmission of the Holy Spirit, in priestly ordinations and in episcopal consecrations.[51]

The identity between episcopacy and apostolate never became predominant among eastern thinkers.[52] For them, as for the apologists, tradition remained a rule of faith, prior and external to all formal laws and offices. The coupling of episcopate and apostolate, with all its implications for the idea of tradition, first appears in the writings of St. Cyprian.[53] After pursuing a fruitful career as a lawyer in North Africa, St. Cyprian became a convert to Christianity late in life, and, within a short time after his conversion, he was elected bishop of Carthage. Accustomed by his legal studies to the principles of inheritance and succession, he applied those same principles to the spiritual hierarchy of the works of the Church. Except for his fellow North African, Tertullian, Cyprian seems to have read no apologetic writings, and he either dismissed or did not know the treble canon of universality, antiquity, and consensus as they had laboriously concluded it.[54] Though he did, indeed, emphasize universality, antiquity, and consensus, they were for him not attributes of the apostolic faith only, but much more attributes of the episcopacy through which the faith was transmitted.[55] He glossed Christ's commission to St. Peter to mean that "through the changes of times and successions, the ordering of bishops and the plan of the Church flow onward in such a way that the Church is founded upon the bishops, and every act of the Church is controlled by those same rulers."[56] And, in an equally famous statement: "The bishop is in the Church, and the Church in the bishop; and if any one be not with the bishop, he is not in the Church. . . . The Church, which is cath-

---

[50] Telfer, "Successions," 1ff, 5ff. See the points of difference and agreement in Kemp, "Bishops," 129ff, 142.

[51] Deneffe, *Traditionsbegriff*, 30; Symonds, "Patristic," 59f; Molland, "Irenaeus," 26ff; "Développement," 28.

[52] Dvornik, *Apostolicity*, 44ff.

[53] Simon observes that this process of institutionalization led to the definitive breach between Church and Synagogue ("Polémique," 420f). On St. Cyprian's dispute with Pope Stephen, see Frend, *Martyrdom*, 416, 418ff.

[54] See Flesseman-Van Leer, *Tradition*, 112.

[55] Caspar, *Geschichte*, 1, 76ff.

[56] Ep. 33, 1; *CSEL* 3, pt. 3, 566.

olic and one, is not cut or divided, but it is indeed connected and bound together by the cement of the bishops who adhere one to another."[57] Christ had delivered the faith, the sacrament of His Church's unity, to the Apostles, and through them to their successors, the bishops.[58] The bishops held the office of the Apostles; in them abided the unity of the faith; they were very incarnations of the Church, and rebellion against a bishop was an act of heresy.

For Cyprian, it was imperative that each bishop be consecrated to his office by other bishops; for he could enter into the spiritual powers of his office only if the college of bishops received him as worthy and established him sacramentally as a successor of the Apostles.[59] Men who strove after the episcopal office with violence and schism "succeed no one"; far from entering the apostolic succession, they begin their own wrongful succession.[60] Just as each Apostle had been directly under Christ, so was every bishop directly under God. St. Cyprian did not advocate a hierarchy of episcopal authority.[61] For he concurred in the statement: "It remains that each of us should bring forward what he thinks on this matter [the re-baptism of heretics], judging no man, and rejecting communion with no one if he should think differently from us. For neither does any of us set himself up as a bishop of bishops, nor by tyrannical terror does any compel his colleague to the necessity of obedience; since every bishop, by virtue of the license of his liberty and power, has his own proper right of judgment and can no more be judged by another than he himself can judge another. But let us all wait for the judgment of our Lord Jesus Christ, who is the only one that has the power both of preferring us in the government of His Church, and of judging us in our conduct there."[62]

St. Cyprian, then, differed from earlier apologists and from later eastern thinkers[63] in the high degree of institutionalization he believed to be

[57] Ep. 66, 8; *CSEL* 3, pt. 3, 732f.

[58] Ep. 45, 3; *CSEL* 3, pt. 3, 602f.

[59] Cf. Deneffe, *Traditionsbegriff*, 35; Molland, "Développement," 25, 28.

[60] Ep. 69, 3-5; *CSEL* 3, pt. 3, 752ff.

[61] See Caspar's argument that Cyprian moved from a concept of collegial episcopacy to a concept identifying the pope as heir of St. Peter's powers and the *cathedra Petri* as having primacy over the entire Church, and then further to a refined collegial concept (*Geschichte* 1, 78-83; "Primatus Petri," 68f, 71f). See Harnack's contrary view in "Ecclesia," 139f. Cf. Koch, "Cathedra," 179, "Die Kirche des III. Jhs. kennt kein 'Papsttum.' "

[62] Conc. Carth. (256), sententiae episcoporum; *CSEL* 3, pt. 3, 435f. Cf. Ep. 55, 20-22; *CSEL* 3, pt. 3, 638ff.

[63] Below, pp. 193f, 195ff.

present in the Church. For him, the apostolate was not a vague idea or an office held in the past by the closest followers of Christ, but an office which had continued to be held by a succession of bishops. For him, the apostolic succession was not St. Irenaeus's simple succession in the apostolic faith; it was an explicit official succession. Instead of holding that true doctrine had descended from God to Christ, from Christ to the Apostles, and from the Apostles to the faithful, Cyprian maintained that it had gone from the Apostles to the bishops, their followers in the apostolic ministry, and thence to the people. Oral tradition had come to believers through the apostolate, which, known latterly as the episcopacy, was transmitted through the ceremony of consecration. The same powers devolved upon all bishops, and in the peace of their college, in their harmony and mutual deference, abided the peace and unity of the universal Church. The apostolate lived in the episcopacy.[64]

Thus far, we have followed one school of interpretation by describing Sts. Irenaeus and Cyprian as representatives of the doctrine of collegiate episcopacy. Some scholars, however, have found in the works of each of these authors one passage which they interpret to endorse the contrary doctrine of papal monarchy, and we must digress briefly to refer to those passages. In his treatise, *Against Heresies*,[65] Irenaeus argued that the truth of orthodox doctrine was attested by its antiquity, which clearly showed heretical doctrines to be recent inventions, quite apart from the original teachings of Christ and the Apostles. He referred in his argument to the episcopal succession in Rome. St. Peter was a co-founder of the Roman See, though not the first bishop; he and St. Paul committed the episcopate to Linus. Clement succeeded Linus; as an immediate disciple of the Apostles, he had occasion to state the apostolic teaching in the letters which he sent to settle a dispute in the church at Corinth. Irenaeus then mentioned by name each Roman bishop down to Eleutherius, his contemporary, and concluded with the crucial passage which may be translated as follows: "In this order, and by this succession, the ecclesiastical tradition from the Apostles, and the preaching of the truth, have come down to us. And this is the most abundant proof that there is one and the same vivifying

[64] See Bakhuizen van den Brink, "Traditio," 85f.
[65] III, 3, 1ff; ed. Harvey, 2, 8ff.

faith which has been preserved in the Church from the Apostles until now, and handed down in truth."[66]

Scholars who have thought this section the earliest assertion of papal supremacy have so argued because in their view St. Irenaeus seems to say that the faith of the whole Church has been preserved in the Roman succession, and thus, by implication, that the faith of the Roman Church, or even more the faith of the Roman bishops, is the canon of orthodoxy. This interpretation, however, leaves out of account two factors: the technical question of manuscript tradition and the context of Irenaeus's remarks. Irenaeus wrote *Against Heresies* in Greek, but soon afterwards a Latin translation of it appeared which, as far as we can tell, was not consistently faithful to the original text. The Greek text survives only in fragments; the translation alone preserves large sections of the treatise. One such section is the passage in question. Any translation of this passage must do violence to the text as it stands. The confused syntax in the critical statement indicates that the translator did not accurately understand Irenaeus's text, or that the translation itself has become garbled. In either case, the Latin version as it stands does not represent exactly Irenaeus's thought. Furthermore, the context of the section argues strongly against the strict Romanist interpretations; for Irenaeus continued in the section immediately following the one in question to eulogize Polycarp of Smyrna as a bishop who had learned his doctrine from the Apostles themselves and ardently transmitted it, and whose testimony was handed down by the churches of Asia and by the men who succeeded him, and to recall that "the church in Ephesus, founded by Paul, and having John remaining among them permanently until the times of Trajan, is a true witness of the tradition of the Apostles."[67] Whatever his meaning in citing the Roman episcopal succession, Irenaeus clearly did not intend to designate the Roman See as the exclusive repository of true doctrine, or as anything other than a see which cherished the heritage of faith which it shared with other apostolic churches such as Smyrna and Ephesus.

The disputed passage by St. Cyprian likewise presents textual difficulties. Indeed, these remarks in Cyprian's *On the Unity of the Cath-*

---

[66] III, 3, 3; ed. Harvey, 2, 11f. See also the edition by F. Sagnard in *Sources chrétiennes* (Paris, 1952), 108.

[67] III, 3, 4; ed. Harvey, 2, 12.

*olic Church* (c. 4) occur in three independent readings,[68] one of which exalts the Roman pre-eminence with the classic doctrine of Petrine primacy, the second, emphasizing the equality of the Apostles, and the third, much the shortest, indicating without elaboration the unity of the Church prefigured in the unity of the Apostles. This diversity of texts, all of which occur in authentic manuscript traditions, has been the source of much partisan contention. It seems unlikely that, as some extreme Protestant scholars have maintained, the affirmation of Petrine primacy was a willful falsification by "Romish editors." The reliability of the manuscript traditions supporting each of the versions indicates that the three recensions occurred very early, and that they may indeed have been executed by Cyprian himself. But if the problem of authenticity can be clarified by assuming that the different readings represent three quite sharp and important changes in Cyprian's thought, the problem remains of establishing their sequence. If Cyprian were the author of all three versions, which one states his mature judgment?

The crux of the dispute is whether Cyprian thought the unity of the Church abided first in St. Peter as the Prince of the Apostles, and later in his see, or first in the whole college of the Apostles and afterwards in the episcopacy as a whole. Scholars who favor the most fully developed statement of Petrine primacy cite in support of their view another passage in a letter of the Father. There, discussing the appeal of some heretics to Rome, he wrote: "After such things as these, moreover, they still dare—a false bishop having been appointed for them by heretics—to set sail and to bear letters from schismatic and profane persons to the throne of Peter, and to the chief church whence priestly unity takes its source, and not to consider that these were the Romans whose faith was praised in the teaching of the Apostle, to whom faithlessness could have no access."[69] But, in this letter to Pope Cor-

---

[68] *CSEL* 3, 212; Caspar, *Geschichte* 1, 76 does not discuss these difficulties, but see *ibid.*, p. 82. See the review of opinions concerning this passage in Bévenot, " 'Primatus,' " 19ff. Frend's admonition is very apt: "It is well to remember that the De unitate ecclesiae with its disputed chapters 4 and 5 was written mainly as a pamphlet against the Novatianists, not as a formal theological treatise" (*Martyrdom*, 415).

[69] Ep. 59, 14; *CSEL* 3, pt. 3, 683: *"Post ista adhuc insuper pseudoepiscopo sibi ab haereticis constituto navigare audent et ad Petri cathedram adque ad ecclesiam principalem unde unitas sacerdotalis exorta est ab schismaticis et profanis litteras ferre nec cogitare eos esse Romanos quorum fides apostolo praedicante laudata*

nelius, Cyprian continued to deny that the Bishop of Rome could rightly judge the case appealed to him on the principle that every bishop must judge definitively the cases which arose in his see, and that once his judgment had been given there could be no appeal. The appropriate bishops had already decided the case, and Cyprian admonished Cornelius to have nothing to do with the appellants. In describing Rome as "the chief church whence priestly unity takes its source," Cyprian consequently seems to have meant no more than the man he called his "master" meant in a similar passage. Tertullian once wrote of Rome as the see whence apostolic authority had come to the hands of North Africans,[70] but, in that passage, he also referred to Corinth, Philippi, Thessaloniki, and Ephesus, all "apostolic churches, where the very thrones of the Apostles preside and their own authentic writings are read, uttering the voice and representing the face of each of them severally." Tertullian assigned no administrative headship to these apostolic sees, and in denying Rome adjudication of North African matters, Cyprian indicates that he was of the same mind. Indeed, the meaning of the controverted passage in *On the Unity of the Catholic Church* may be indicated by the chapter which immediately follows it, in which Cyprian explicitly stated his doctrine that the unity of the Church stood in the unity of the college of bishops.

The passages by Sts. Irenaeus and Cyprian which are sometimes adduced as testimonies to Roman primacy are, therefore, textually unclear, and their elucidation is consequently uncertain. The context of these two chapters, the burden of other works by the same authors not clouded with textual difficulties, and the policies which the two bishops followed in their official actions all indicate that in their different ways they subscribed not to the Petrine theories read into these passages, but to the doctrine of episcopal collegiality. But the precise interpretation of these passages must await resolution of the textual problems.

Shortly before St. Cyprian formulated his doctrines, Roman thinkers had advanced toward similar, but significantly different, conclusions. In the year 217, a disputed election to the Roman See occurred between Calixtus I and Hippolytus, the author of the "Apostolic Tradition." The divisive issue was whether persons guilty of mortal sins could, on re-

---

*est, ad quos perfidia habere non possit accessum, quae autem causa veniendi et pseudoepiscopum contra episcopos factum nuntiandi?"*

[70] De praescr. haer., 36; *Corp. Christ.*, ser. lat., 1, 216f.

pentance, reenter the Church, as Calixtus's party maintained. The exact circumstances of the election and the arguments of the two claimants are imperfectly known. It is clear, however, that the doctrine that bishops were the successors of the Apostles and the heirs of their powers did appear, together with another doctrine which came to be characteristic of Roman ecclesiology: namely, that Christ had conferred powers on St. Peter beyond those which he had bestowed on the other Apostles, and that the bishop of Rome, as the successor of St. Peter, exercised those same powers.[71]

With the emergence of the first principles of Petrine primacy and the development of St. Cyprian's ecclesiology, three views of the apostolate were current in the Church of the apologists: first, that the apostolate had died with the Apostles, but that the tradition which it had preserved was kept alive by the succession of faithful people, especially clergy, by learned and orthodox teachers, and most of all by the continual action of the Holy Ghost; secondly, that the apostolate survived in the episcopacy; and finally, that it survived in the episcopacy, and principally in the See of Rome. Two ecclesiastical disputes, one in the second century and the other in the third, are, in a sense, historical paradigms of the divergent ecclesiological theories in the age of the apologists, and we may turn to them by way of summarizing the doctrines we have discussed.

The earlier of the two controversies centered upon a specific liturgical point,[72] the date on which Easter should be observed. During the visit of Bishop Polycarp of Smyrna to Rome about 150 AD, the issue first arose whether the churches of Asia Minor were to be followed in observing Easter at the Jewish Passover, or whether Easter should be celebrated, as it was in the other Christian communities, on the Sunday immediately following the first full moon after the vernal equinox. Polycarp and the bishop of Rome, Anicetus, discussed the question; but, even though he disapproved the judaizing tendency of the Asian practice, Anicetus took no measures against it. The matter had, however, assumed general interest for all churches, and, after four decades of intermittent controversy, it arose again when Victor was bishop of Rome.

We do not know what brought the crisis to a head about 190 AD; the historian, Eusebius of Caesarea, simply writes that assemblies of bishops were held—in Palestine, in Rome, in Pontus, in Gaul, and in many

---

[71] Caspar, *Geschichte* 1, 24-28, 36-39.
[72] Caspar, *Geschichte* 1, 19ff.

other places—to determine the correct time of Easter, and that they were unanimous in rejecting the Jewish Passover as unsuitable.[73] The bishops of Asia Minor, however, led by Polycrates of Ephesus, defended their observance on the grounds that their predecessors had since apostolic times "observed the day when the people put away the leaven." Their defense had been put forth in response to "terrifying words" from the bishop of Rome, and in the spirit of those who had said, "We ought to obey God rather than man." And on receiving this response Victor sought to cut off the churches of Asia Minor from the orthodox communion, declaring all the bishops who had concurred in Polycrates's statement excommunicated.

His action aroused vigorous protests from other bishops, who "besought him to consider the things of peace and of neighborly unity and love. Words of theirs are extant, sharply rebuking Victor." St. Irenaeus was one of those who thought Victor's action extravagant, and he wrote pointing out that the Asian observance was but a custom, an ancient custom, deriving from the simplicity of early Christians, and that it did not jeopardize the faith. He reminded Victor of the interview between Polycarp and Anicetus, admonishing him to follow their example: "For neither could Anicetus persuade Polycarp not to observe the practices he knew John the disciple of our Lord had observed, and the other Apostles with whom he had always been, nor did Polycarp persuade Anicetus to abandon what he said that he ought to preserve in the fashion of his elders. But though they regarded each other in this way, they communed together, and Anicetus conceded the administration of the eucharist in the Church to Polycarp, manifestly as a mark of respect. And they parted from each other in peace,

---

[73] Grumel, "Problème," 161, argues cogently that this dispute began because of a change in the method of computing the date of the Jewish Passover, at the end of the second or the beginning of the third century. Tertullian may have been referring to this incident when he wrote that the heretic Praxeas had so misled a bishop of Rome "by importunately urging false accusations against the prophets themselves and their churches, and insisting on the authority of the bishop's predecessors in the see" that the bishop withdrew his favor from the churches of Asia and Phrygia. Adversus Praxean, I, 5; *Corp. Christ.*, ser. lat., 2, 1159: "*Nam idem tunc episcopum Romanum, agnoscentem iam prophetias Montani, Priscae, Maximillae, et ex ea agnitione pacem ecclesiis Asiae et Phrygiae inferentem, falsa de ipsis prophetis et ecclesiis eorum adservando et pracessorum eius auctoritates defendendo coegit et litteras pacis revocare iam emissas et a proposito recipiendorum charismatum concessare.*" The treatise belongs to Tertullian's Montanist period.

both those who observed, and those who did not, maintaining the peace of the whole Church."[74]

Eusebius leaves us there; we do not know how the affair was settled. Since Rome and Asia Minor were soon again in communion, Victor seems to have lifted his excommunications. The particular matter at issue was far from settled; it arose again to trouble the Council of Nicaea (325). Objectively, the controversy was inconclusive: Victor's judgment had been rescinded, in practice if not by an explicit act, and the diversity which had caused the dispute had not been resolved.

When the second controversy began, about sixty years later, the doctrines which were only nascent in Victor's day had gained distinct form. The question at issue in this later dispute was whether persons baptized by heretics should be re-baptized on their conversion to the orthodox faith. The principal antagonists were Bishop Stephen I of Rome, and the bishops of Asia and North Africa, for whom St. Cyprian was a major spokesman.[75] The issue was very profound, especially as it involved the indelible character of the priesthood by asking whether a man, ordained to the priesthood in the orthodox church, lost his sacramental powers on lapsing into heresy. St. Cyprian represented the predominant judgment of Christendom by arguing that priestly powers could be exercised only within the true Church, and that when a priest lapsed from the faith he simultaneously departed from the Church and lost his powers. Persons who had been baptized by heretics must, therefore, be re-baptized on converting to the authentic faith; rather, they must be baptized, for the ceremony to which they had as heretics submitted was of no effect.[76] Stephen denounced the practice with the stinging sentence that "it is unnecessary to add any innovation contrary to the tradition which has been held from the beginning."[77] In his mind, baptism was effective even if it were performed by heretics, and he gave an edge to his judgment by refusing communion with bishops in Asia Minor who re-baptized heretics,[78] on the ground that they had departed from the tradition of the apostles.[79]

---

[74] Eusebius, H. E., V, 23, 24; *GCS, Eusebius Werke* 2, pt. 1, 488ff.

[75] Caspar, *Geschichte* 1, 75ff.

[76] Cf. above, pp. 14, 21; below, p. 122.

[77] Caspar, *Geschichte* 1, 80; Deneffe, *Traditionsbegriff*, 527; Bakhuizen van den Brink, "Traditio," 69; Dölger, "Nihil," 80. For references to this sentence by St. Cyprian and Vincent of Lérins, see Symonds, "Patristic," 62.

[78] Eusebius, H. E., VII, 3-5; *GCS, Eusebius Werke*, 2, pt. 2, 638ff.

[79] Firmilian, Cyprian, Ep. 75, 6; *CSEL* 3, pt. 3, 813f.

Stephen's appeal to "most ancient custom and ecclesiastical tradition" and his strong measures against the eastern bishops provoked a widespread and vigorous response. Other great prelates, such as Dionysius of Alexandria, wrote to Stephen and to his successor, Sixtus, protesting that the Roman judgment was contrary to "the sure and immovable teaching and tradition begun by our Lord after His resurrection from the dead . . . preserved and fulfilled by his successors, the blessed Apostles, and by all the bishops prior to ourselves who have died in the holy Church and shared in its life."[80] Utterances of the sort Stephen had made were dangerous, for, in contravening this tradition, they prejudiced the harmony of church and church, bishop and bishop, elder and elder.[81] But the strongest protests came from St. Cyprian and Firmilian of Caesarea in Cappadocia.

Stephen had condemned Cyprian as "false Christ, false apostle, and practicer of deceit," because he advocated re-baptism;[82] and the Bishop of Carthage reciprocated in kind.[83] Since the headship which Stephen claimed was unwarranted, by the example of St. Peter, he could not force his brethren to accept his views. Even worse, his judgment opposed the authentic tradition of the Church. The bishop of Rome, wrote Cyprian, had confounded human tradition and divine precepts; he insisted on a practice which was mere custom, and "custom without truth is the antiquity of error."[84] Whence came the "tradition" on which Stephen insisted? Cyprian answered that it came from human presumption.[85] Subverting the Church from within, Stephen wished the Church to follow the practices of heretics by accepting their baptisms, and to hold that those who were not born in the Church could be the sons of God.[86] And, finally, Cyprian urged that bishops (Stephen was meant) lay aside the love of presumption and obstinacy which had led them to prefer custom to tradition and, abandoning their evil and false arguments, return to the divine precepts, to evangelical and apostolic tradition, whence arose their order and their very origin.[87]

In a letter to Cyprian, Firmilian endorsed everything the bishop of Carthage had said and added a few strokes of his own.[88] One of those

[80] Conybere, "Letters," 113.　　　[81] *Loc.cit.*

[82] Firmilian, Cyprian Ep. 75, 25; *CSEL* 3, pt. 3, 827.

[83] See Caspar, "Primatus," 298, 312ff.

[84] Ep. 74, cc. 3, 9; *CSEL* 3, pt. 3, 801f, 806f: "*Nam consuetudo sine veritate vetustas erroris est.*"

[85] Ep. 74, c. 2ff; *CSEL* 3, pt. 3, 799ff.　　　[86] Ep. 74, c. 7; *CSEL* 3, pt. 3, 804f.

[87] Ep. 74, c. 10; *CSEL* 3, pt. 3, 808.　　　[88] Caspar, *Geschichte* 1, 82f.

with whom Stephen had refused communion, Firmilian felt most keenly the Roman rebuke that re-baptism was unwarranted by apostolic tradition, and that he himself, in practising re-baptism, had fallen from orthodoxy. Recalling the earlier dispute about the date of Easter, he upheld the practice of Asia Minor by commenting that, in the celebration of Easter and in many other matters, the Romans did not observe the practices established in the age of the Apostles, though they vainly claimed apostolic authority for their aberrant forms. The decree of Stephen was the most recent instance of such audacity, an instance so grave that Firmilian ranked Stephen among heretics and blasphemers and compared his doctrines and discipline with the perfidy of Judas.

The Apostles did not command as Stephen commanded, Firmilian wrote, nor did Christ establish the primacy which he claimed. "But how great is the error and how deep the blindness of him who says that remission of sins can be granted in synagogues of heretics, and does not abide on the foundation of the one Church which was once based by Christ upon the rock. . . . And in this respect I am justly indignant at this very open and manifest folly of Stephen. He who boasts exceedingly of the place of his episcopate, and contends that he holds the succession from Peter, on whom the foundations of the Church were laid, introduces many other rocks and establishes new buildings of many churches maintaining that there is baptism in them by his authority. . . . He does not understand that he darkens the truth of the Christian Rock and in a measure breaks it away when he thus betrays and deserts unity."[89]

To the Roman custom, Firmilian, like Cyprian, opposed the custom of truth, "holding from the beginning that which was delivered by Christ and the Apostles."[90] And, Firmilian argued, by his violence and obstinacy, Stephen had apostatized from the communion of ecclesiastical unity; far from cutting heretics off from his communion, he had cut himself off from the orthodox and made himself "a stranger in all respects from his brethren, rebelling against the sacrament and the faith with the madness of contumacious discord. With such a man can there be one Spirit and one Body, in whom perhaps there is not even one mind, slippery, shifting, and uncertain as it is?"[91]

[89] Cyprian Ep. 75, 16f; *CSEL* 3, pt. 3, 820f.
[90] *Ibid.*, c. 19; *CSEL* 3, pt. 3, 822.
[91] *Ibid.*, c. 25; *CSEL* 3, pt. 3, 826.

Estranged from Roman society, the apologists saw the integrative functions of tradition as operating only within the community of the faithful. But, in fortuitous and improvised ways, disputes in the early Church led men to propose two new kinds of authority beside oral tradition: Scripture, as a partial, written testimony to ancient teachings, and the episcopal office, as the ground in which not fixed doctrine, but understanding, which was at the same time true and variable, flourished anew in each generation. The seeds of yet a fourth authority, Church law, had begun to grow, but the implications of this development and its place in the general structure of doctrine and order remained to be worked out.

These four elements were part of the overriding conflict between the "Jewish" and the "Gentile" views of authority, a conflict basic to the whole history we are to trace. As we shall see, a thousand years of conflict in the West failed to resolve the tension between them.

The vague, divisive concept of tradition was the "law" to which Victor, Stephen, Polycrates, Cyprian, and Firmilian all appealed. In defending the Eastern practice against the exclusive claims of Rome, Polycrates had invoked the antiquity of his church and the sanctity of his predecessors, writing to Victor, "For in Asia also great lights have fallen asleep, which shall rise again on the day of the Lord's coming, when He shall come with glory from heaven, and shall seek out all the saints."[92] But, for all their glory, those great lights, and the others which had fallen asleep in the West, spoke in voices indistinct and elusive to living men, to whom they were as the heavenly bodies were to Lorenzo:

> Sit, Jessica. Look how the floor of heaven
> Is thick inlaid with patines of bright gold:
> There's not the smallest orb which thou
>       behold'st
> But in his motion like an angel sings,
> Still quiring to the young-eyed cherubins.
> Such harmony is in immortal souls;
> But whilst this muddy vesture of decay
> Doth grossly close it in, we cannot hear it.[93]

[92] Eusebius, H. E., V, 24; *GCS, Eusebius Werke*, 2, pt. 1, 490.
[93] *Merchant of Venice*, Act V, 50.1.

33

## BOOK I

Tradition as Warrant of Schism:
The Church in the Later Roman Empire

# PART I

# Multiple Centers of Cohesion

CHRISTIANITY'S path to dominance in the Roman Empire was neither smooth nor certain. Constantine merely set it on its way. For the next century, pagan reactions in the imperial government, popular devotion to the ancient gods, and the caprice of fortune challenged its ascendancy. And yet its power continued to grow; despite adversities, it became by stages the official cult of the Empire and the private religion of the Empire's subjects.

In practical terms, the conversion of Constantine drew a far more pronounced caesura across Church history than did Theodosius I's approval of the Nicene doctrine or the closing of pagan temples by Arcadius and Honorius. Before Constantine's conversion, Christianity was a persecuted sect whose members, scattered throughout the Empire, followed widely diverse practices. Suddenly, Constantine's favor catapulted Christianity into the *de facto*, though not yet *de jure*, role of a State Church.

To do this was to force Christianity into a role for which it was utterly unprepared. In organizational terms, there was no unitary Church. There were many churches, which shared in a loose way the same confession of faith. It beclouds the facts to say that Constantine struck an alliance with "the Church." The Emperor himself thought in those terms, and that was the chimerical fantasy that always led him on and eluded him in the Donatist, Meletian, and Arian conflicts.

Nothing in Christianity's earlier history had suited it for the task Constantine and his successors set: namely, to weld all bishops, clergy, and people into one corporative body, and to establish norms of universal conformity. The emperors thrust upon Christianity not merely the role of a universal religion, but more exactly that of a universal administrative order. Christians welcomed the change; they grasped avariciously the privileges and wealth which the Empire offered. But they were unready to deal with the broader critical issues which the Empire posed. The proper relations of Church and civil government had to be resolved.

The whole range of authority in the Church—magisterial, legislative, and hierarchic—had still to be defined.

Only the most carefully reasoned answers, derived from the trial-and-error of long experience, would have satisfied these demands. But Christians, living at a level of political existence to which they were quite unfamiliar, lacked the experience required. They could meet the new demands only by improvisation, and their improvisations were colored by highly diverse forces of social conventions and personal ambition. Believers in the patristic age, then, had to deal with the most essential, and the most difficult, issues that have ever arisen in the history of Christianity. What were the issues as they saw them, and what answers did they give?

The paramount question was that of authority, and we have taken the specific concept of tradition as a window on the way men understood that wider issue. The newest and, in some ways, the most urgent issue concerned the authority of the Empire in the Church.

CHAPTER 2

# Paradoxes of Unity

## A. THE CHURCH AND CIVIL POWER:
### ASSIMILATION THROUGH EQUIPOISE

THE fact that Constantine had ended persecution and restored to Christians their liberty of conscience was itself of the highest importance to the Church; that he had gone still further and bestowed privileges and emoluments upon the clergy and their churches was revolutionary; and that he himself had adopted the religion his colleagues persecuted reversed an imperial policy which had begun with Nero. The Church and the Roman world alike were unprepared for this change. The whole heritage of the Church impelled it to mistrust and curse the Empire which had persecuted it intermittently for three hundred years and in whose social and political values it saw nothing but the vanity, the corruption, and the burning malice of Antichrist. Rome was Babylon, the scarlet whore of the Apocalypse, the kingdom of Satan, the serpent between whom and man God had put eternal enmity.

The doctrine of tradition, as formulated in disputes of the second and third centuries, held that the right understanding of the Scriptures was transmitted from one generation of the faithful to the next. Different theories appeared concerning the precise instrument which preserved apostolic doctrine; but all schools agreed that tradition existed only within the Church, and that the world and worldly government had no power to receive or transmit tradition. Pre-Constantinian ecclesiology, therefore, was deeply stamped with the alienation believers generally felt from the persecuting Empire; and ecclesiology after Constantine preserved as a first principle the premise that the Empire was external to the Church, and wholly alien to ecclesiastical tradition. The Empire had no part in the definition or the teaching of doctrine.[1] The maintenance of this position, however, became difficult when the imperial powers nurtured instead of persecuting and when the Emperor

[1] From this point of view, see the fuller exposition in Morrison, *Rome*, 20ff.

considered himself in some sense a "bishop,"[2] or the "equal of the Apostles," and wished his body to be buried amid relics of the Apostles so that, after death, he could share the devotions offered to them.[3]

But an attitude of hostile separateness continued even beyond the time of Constantine.[4] Realizing that Constantine, the *pontifex maximus,* had not cast out the ancient gods, the Fathers did not acclaim the conversion of Constantine as the beginning of a Christian Empire. They knew that Constantine had turned to their benefit the same powers that the persecutors had used against them, and that rulers after him might revive the earlier policy. Indeed, pagan emperors and imperial usurpers still arose. The Fathers saw yet another threat equally as great if not greater than that of a pagan revival: the intrusion of civil power into the constitution of the Church, and especially into the teaching and interpretation of doctrine.

A formidable task confronted the Fathers: to preserve the integrity of tradition, and thus the integrity of the Church, from the violence it would surely suffer if the conventions of Roman law prevailed in imperial dealings with the Church, and, at the same time, to preserve the benefits of imperial patronage. A solution was found, slowly and falteringly, in the long, intricate series of controversies that spanned the mid-fourth century. The Fathers discovered that, if they could neither resist the encroachment of a benevolent Empire upon ecclesiastical liberties by force, nor yield to that advance, they had to fight legal claims with legal counter-claims. If the emperor asserted his authority to direct Church affairs on the basis of precedent and legal convention, the Fathers had to assert their independence of that authority on equally strong legal grounds.

The Fathers generally granted that, in ecclesiastical matters, the em-

---

[2] Vita Const. IV, 24; *GCS, Eusebius Werke* 1, 126. On this term, see Seston, "Constantine," *passim*; Straub, "Kaiser," 695; Frend, *Martyrdom*, 546; Dörries, *Selbstzeugnis*, 256f, 295f. On Constantine, see especially Morris, *Thought*, vol. I, 189ff.

[3] Vita Const. IV, 60; *GCS, Eusebius Werke* 1, 141f. For another viewpoint, see Dörries, *Selbstzeugnis*, 424: "*Das ist der Sinne seiner Grabanlage: 'heilsamer Nutzen für seine Seele.' Schutz, nicht kultische Verehrung!*" In general, see the excellent account in Setton, *Attitude*, 40ff; Aland, "Haltung," 600; and Dörries, *Selbstzeugnis*, 400f. Still, on the continuity of pagan practices under Constantine, Alföldi, *Conversion, passim*; Jones, *Constantine, passim*; Telfer, "Purpose," 166; Dörries, *Selbstzeugnis*, 286ff, 329ff; Jones, *Empire*, 2, 938ff.

[4] Cf. Hilary of Poitiers, Tractatus in psalmum I, 10; *CSEL* 22, 25. On the general state of affairs, see the excellent discussion in Jones, *Empire*, 1, 83ff; 2, 933ff.

peror might legitimately exercise the powers normally his according to the conventions of Roman law, and add to judgments of synods the corroboration and enforcement of temporal power. They understood that, in some degree, an emperor could rightfully deal with them in the context of the *ius sacrum*. He could construct, confiscate, and grant church buildings. He had punitive powers over clergy in their civil actions, in their administration of Church property, and in all their other functions, official or personal, which were not directly part of their sacramental duties. These were also the lines of the entente which Rome and the Synagogue had worked out in the years after the fall of Jerusalem, and, in view of the Church's Jewish heritage, it was natural that the New Israel should enter into legal privileges comparable with those of the Old.[5]

To the Donatist question, "What has the Emperor to do with the Church?" the orthodox writer Optatus of Milevis responded with St. Paul's admonition to pray for "kings and powers" so that the faithful might lead a quiet and peaceable life. He observed that the Church was in the Empire, not the Empire in the Church, and that Christ even called the Empire "Lebanon" in the Song of Songs when He said, " 'Come, my spouse, out of Lebanon, . . .' that is, out of the Roman Empire, where priesthoods, morality, and virginity are sacred, as they are not among the barbarian peoples, and if they were, they could not be safe."[6] In his own argument against the Donatists, Augustine provided a yet fuller exposition. The Donatists had protested that the Empire had no right to take their churches from them. Augustine answered: "Possessions are owned through the laws [*iura*] of kings. You have said, 'What has the king to do with me?' Say not your possessions, for you have renounced them according to the very human laws by which they are possessed."[7] The complex history of Bishop Athanasius of Alexandria's struggle displayed the whole range of imperial intervention against a bishop by confiscation of church buildings, by banishment, and by at least the threat of capital punishment. But neither Athanasius nor his supporters protested the illegality of any of these temporal intrusions.

Likewise, there were prerogatives and conventions of ecclesiastical government which the Empire did not dispute; for, if emperors did intervene in Church affairs in a strong and partisan fashion, they still

[5] See Morrison, *Rome*, 9ff, 19, for further bibliographical citations.
[6] De schismate Donat. III, 3; *CSEL* 26, 74.
[7] Tract. VI in John Ev., c. 26; *Corp. Christ.*, ser. lat. 36, 66f.

acknowledged at least in form that only bishops, collectively, had the power to define articles of faith, to judge disputes in which the faith was a crucial factor, to transmit the episcopal office, and to depose clergy —in short, to define the authentic faith and to oversee its teaching. Constantius II at Rimini-Seleucia, and Theodosius I at the series of synods in Constantinople beginning in 381, and perhaps even Constantine at Nicaea I, had prejudged the decisions of their councils. Technically, they acted merely as protectors of the assemblies, as guarantors of synodal integrity. They summoned the councils, not on their own initiatives, but on the petition of clergy. Though they made their wishes clear to the assembled bishops, they did not preside over them. Bishops presided even in Constantine's presence at Nicaea; Constantius appeared neither at Seleucia nor at Rimini; and, when the Council of Constantinople met (381), Theodosius was absent from the capital on a military maneuver. The councils issued their definitions in their own right, as their free and deliberate judgments. As such, the rulings had intrinsically all the canonical force of synodal decrees, and the imperial confirmation they later received, on petition of the issuing council, merely extended their validity to dimension of civil law. The brutal methods which Constantius used to extort condemnation of Athanasius and approval of Arian symbols from his several synods shows how firmly convinced he and his bishops were that judgments of the sort they wished could come only from synodal assemblies.

When Theodosius set out to purge Constantinople of the creed Constantius had established there, and which Valens had confirmed, he too approached his work with a fixed purpose. But he also required the approval of ecclesiastical authority before he could impose the policy he had already determined. At the Council of 381 and the Synod of 382, he acted merely as the summoner and protector of the assemblies. He corroborated their judgments, confirming their creeds by rescript as orthodox and binding throughout his lands, and ratifying their sentences of deposition with the temporal sentence of exile. These efforts failed to achieve the unanimity which the Emperor wished. Before the Synod of Constantinople (383), the Emperor again "discussed with Bishop Nectarius how to bring Christendom into harmony and to unite the Church." Theodosius proposed a great council to debate the issues which still, despite his best efforts, divided the orthodox, the Arians, and the Macedonians. Nectarius, however, feared that yet another open dispute would hurl the Church into catastrophe, and he consulted his *lector* Sisinnius, a wise and learned man, schooled both in theology and in philosophy. He too was convinced that disputation would but confirm the partisanship of the heretics instead of healing schisms, and "advised him to avoid dialectical encounters, to appeal to the sentences of the ancients, and to put the question to the heresiarchs from the Emperor, whether they accepted the teachers who belonged to the Church before the schism or repudiated them as aliens to Christianity. For if they rejected their authority, they could venture to anathematize them; but if they attempted that, the people would drive them out."[8] Theodosius adopted this evasion of debate, exiling those who rejected the ante-Nicene writers, as he had exiled others in 381 and 382; but he preserved the technical argument that he was merely executing the sentences of the earlier synods against those who rejected the faith of the Fathers.

An equipoise of jurisdiction between the Church and the civil power —a division of juridical competence between ecclesiastical and imperial courts—was, therefore, generally acknowledged, even when emperors unswervingly pressed their predetermined religious policies. The principal conflicts between the Fathers and the temporal power did not arise when the clergy judged that an emperor had upset the balance of this order, by unrighteous use of his powers in the *ius sacrum*; for the use of those powers fell outside moral limits. They arose rather through the unrightful extension of civil powers into matters beyond the competence of civil government, or, more often, through the perversion of ecclesiastical order to allow such an extension. Imperial intervention in two kinds of legal action especially concerned the Fathers: the promulgation of creeds, and the trial of clergy on religious grounds. They judged that in these actions lay the greatest danger that the Empire would destroy the Church's freedom to teach true doctrine.

The Fathers particularly condemned the Arian Constantius II for his intervention in the composition of creeds. "He writes," Athanasius observed, "and while he writes, he repents; and while he repents, he is exasperated. And then he grieves again, and, not knowing how to act, he shows how bereft his soul is of understanding."[9] "You are like unskillful workmen," St. Hilary of Poitiers wrote to him, "to whom their own works are always displeasing. You are always destroying what

[8] Mansi 3, 643f.
[9] Historia Arianorum, 70, 1; *GCS, Athanasius Werke* 2, 221.

you are always building."[10] On the Emperor's insistence, "We define yearly and monthly creeds about God. We repent of our definitions; we defend those who repent, and anathematize them whom we have defended; we condemn our own doings in those of others, or others in us, and, gnawing each other, we nearly devour one another."[11]

The Fathers argued that the faith was immutable,[12] and that the constant reformulation of creeds which Constantius required was evidence both of heresy and of the Empire's presumptuous arrogation of power in spiritual matters outside its rightful competence.

Creeds were definitions of the faith. Bishops framed the creeds; they were the supreme teachers and interpreters of the faith. Jurisdiction over them was very complex, chiefly because ecclesiastical thinkers acknowledged temporal jurisdiction over clergy in some matters.[13] Constantine the Great severely censured the Donatists for appealing to his court from synodal judgment,[14] and, at Nicaea, he utterly declined to judge charges against bishops, saying, "God has established you bishops and has given you power of judging us; thus are we rightly judged by you. But you cannot be judged by men. Wherefore, look for the judgment of God among yourselves, and let your disputes, whatever they are, be reserved to that divine review."[15] Constantine's conduct in other cases, however, gave rise to objections that he had given religious cases over to secular judges and to unbelievers. Still, he always sought synodal approval of his high-handed acts. The Synod of Tyre's verdict on St. Athanasius is perhaps the pre-eminent example of how the Emperor held to the form, but contorted the sense, of the canons.

Under Constantine, this sort of meddling with the doctrine and the teachers of the Church was a tendency; under his son, Constantius II, it became a decided program. Constantius commanded the Synod of Milan (355) to condemn Athanasius with the words, "Whatever I will, be that considered a canon";[16] and this sentence seems to epitomize his view.

[10] Contra Constantium, c. 23; PL 10, 598.

[11] Liber II ad Constantium, 5; *CSEL* 65, 201.

[12] See below, pp. 57ff.

[13] On the following section, see the fuller discussion in Morrison, *Rome,* 23ff, 25ff.

[14] PL 8, 488.

[15] Rufinus, Hist. eccles. X, 2; *GCS, Eusebius Werke* 2, pt. 2, 961. See Marot, "Conciles," esp. 219ff.

[16] Athanasius, Historia Arianorum, cc, 33, 34; *GCS, Athanasius Werke* 2, pt. 1, 201f.

By his "mingling Roman sovereignty with the constitution of the Church,"[17] Constantius had attempted to make the Church a "civil senate," and had led the Arians to consider "the Holy Place a house of merchandise and a house of juridical business for themselves."[18] The teachers of the Church were constrained to accept the Emperor's doctrines or to go into exile; the teaching of the Church was imperiled; the doctrine of salvation, the character of the Church as the body of Christ, the sacred mysteries themselves had become the prey of the civil power. Constantius observed the letter of the canons; he acknowledged that only bishops could define and teach doctrine, and judge those who erred from the authentic faith; but he used the conventions of Roman law to impair their freedom of definition and instruction. In destroying the liberty of the Church, in denying the incarnation of God, in casting the Church into confusion, Constantius had, St. Hilary wrote, "set his hands against Christ Himself."[19] Hilary bitterly reproached the Emperor for enslaving the Church with honors and wealth, and yearned for the days of the ancient persecutors, Nero and Decius, when torture and death led to freedom.[20]

Among the Fathers, only St. Ambrose seems to have understood that the tension between the legal claims of the Empire in the *ius sacrum* and the Church's demand for freedom could be resolved only by curtailing the imperial prerogatives. "We, by the law of our Lord Jesus Christ, are dead to this [temporal] law. . . . The law did not gather the Church together, but the faith of Christ."[21]

Even Ambrose's somewhat inconsistent restriction of imperial powers exceeded the thought of his contemporaries. The tension between the demands of civil law and the requirements of theology remained. For the Fathers of the fourth and early fifth centuries, it sufficed to argue that the essence of the Church and the truth of its tradition abided in its sacramental functions, and to admit temporal intervention into all other aspects of religious observance and ecclesiastical administration. It is difficult to establish consistent schools of thought and to distinguish, as

[17] *Ibid.*, 202.

[18] *Ibid.*, c. 78, 226f. Cf. PG 26, 1189. On the changes that occurred in Athanasius's attitude toward Constantius, see Setton, *Attitude*, 73-81; Frend, *Martyrdom*, 599f; Hagel, *Kirche*, 47ff.

[19] Contra Const., c. 11; PL 10, 589. See Setton, *Attitude*, 100f.

[20] Contra Const., c. 4; PL 10, 580f.

[21] Serm. contra Aux., 24; PL 16, 1057. See Setton, *Attitude*, 109ff. For a fuller discussion of Ambrose's thought, see Morrison, *Rome*, 40ff.

some scholars have done,[22] the Arian doctrine of kingship from the Nicene, and the Alexandrine from the Antiochene. The only fixed premise for any thinkers in considering temporal power was that if the emperor intervened in support of the position they themselves approved, he had acted righteously and according to the will of God and the tradition of the Fathers. If he did not, he had violated the canon of orthodoxy. Still, one further point was clear. The actions of the emperors showed plainly enough that only the Church could convey tradition, the surety of its cohesion. The coupling of politics and religion under Constantius II taught a plain lesson. The Church could never enter an institutional union with the Empire and at the same time preserve its freedom to define and teach true doctrine. The Church held a timeless, immutable doctrine; the Empire required varying creeds, to suit the emperor's whims or to endorse his political actions. The coupling of politics and religion juxtaposed expedience and eternity. The relationship must remain an alliance, or, at the most, a symbiotic union.

Within the century after Constantine's conversion, a union of this sort had occurred. The problems encountered in establishing it had led to many permanent and decisive changes in the administrative pattern of the Church and in the concept of the Church itself. But the concept of the Empire too was changing in a way which reflected the ambivalence of its symbiosis with the Church. The iconographic representations of Christ in the fourth century show a remarkable transformation of the qualities conventionally attributed to Him. At the beginning of the century, He appeared as the Good Shepherd, a simple pastor with His sheep; but, gradually, this representation gave way to Christ the King, girt about with imperial splendor, radiant with the awesome majesty of Universal Empire. Christ, the Pambasileus, supplanted Christ, the Good Shepherd. The concept of God, and of Christ as a King, the Ruler of all men, is of course scriptural. It recurred in early Christian thought, as, for example, in the writings of Clement of Alexandria, who equated the relationship of the king to his realm with that of God to the world. A recent study[23] has shown most clearly, however, that the implications of this parallelism began to be fully realized only when the rulers of the Roman world had adopted Christianity.

Champions of ecclesiastical liberty, such as Ambrose, seized upon the concept of Christ as King. For them, it affirmed a government whose

22 Cf. Williams, "Christology," pt. 1, 11ff. Cf. Beskow, *Rex*, 316ff.
23 Beskow, *ibid.*, 313ff.

qualities and powers transcended those of any worldly government, and a King mightier and more terrible than Caesar. But another interpretation arose simultaneously. Pagan thought had, since the Hellenistic period, drawn similar parallels; the translation of the pagan Theomimesis to the Christian Christomimesis was easy. For the emperors and their courtiers, the new parallel identified the divine ruler with the earthly and ascribed to Caesar powers of the Eternal King. On the ambiguity of these two interpretations, reenforced by conventions of Roman law, hinged much of the tension between the Church and the Empire in the century after Constantine; on it turned much of mediaeval political thought. The liberties of the Church were secure as long as the Empire followed only the admonition its greatest poet had put in the mouth of Anchises: "Remember, O Roman, that you are to govern peoples by empire. These will be your arts: to impose habitual peace, to spare the downcast, and to overwhelm the proud."[24]

But, in her last century of imperial splendor, Rome had transformed her own character, cast off the ancient gods whom Virgil celebrated, and assumed a "foreign" religion. A new concept of imperial goals likewise emerged, which made the defense of a particular creed the chief duty of the emperor, and which earned him the adoration due "the vicar of God on earth."[25]

+

By the beginning of the fifth century, the religious revolution which Constantine the Great rather tentatively began was complete; and the great doctrinal conflicts which ran throughout the century posed incessantly and elementally the Empire's place in teaching and interpreting doctrine. There persisted and became increasingly extreme the quasi-hieratic concept of the imperial office, which Rome had received from the East and which, in a Christianized form, had justified temporal direction of the highest ecclesiastical affairs. The acclamation of Theodo-

---

[24] Aeneid, VI, 851-53: "*Tu regere imperio populos, Romane memento;/ Hae tibi erunt artes, pacisque imponere morem,/ Parcere subjectis et debellare superbos.*"

[25] Ambrosiaster (or Pseudo-Augustinus), Quaetiones Veteris et Novi Testamenti, CXXVII, c. 91, 8; *CSEL* 50, 157: "*Rex enim adoratur in terris quasi vicarius dei, Christus autem post vicarium impleta dispensatione adoratur in caelis et in terra.*" See also Eusebius of Caesarea's oration for Constantine's Tricennalia (Baynes, "Eusebius," 13; Frend, *Martyrdom*, 545).

sius II as "High Priest" by the *synodus endemousa* which condemned Eutyches, and later of Marcian by the Council of Chalcedon,[26] and the consecration of the deposed emperors Avitus and Glycerius as bishops indicated this tendency to identify the imperial office with the episcopal. At the same time, an important interpenetration of temporal and spiritual terminology and forms sharpened and imperialized the conventional thought of churchmen.

And yet, even as the Empire and the Church approximated each other in modes of expression, in ceremonial practices, and in the claims to real power which such usages expressed, each institution remained jealous of its own integrity. As the acclamation of Marcian at Chalcedon shows, the Church countenanced and even encouraged the quasi-priestly pretensions of contemporary emperors. Even Leo I, an unswerving defender of the Church's liberty, wrote of one eastern emperor that "royal power and priestly diligence" flourished in him "to the salvation of the whole world,"[27] and, of others, that they showed, "not only a Christian, but even a priestly disposition."[28] By such acquiescence in prevalent civil ideology, ecclesiastics may have meant no more than that an emperor, by some special act of piety or of benefit to the Church, had revealed particularly the sacerdotal character which he shared with all the faithful, who became in baptism both kings and priests. On his part, Leo I ascribed no strictly hieratic powers in Church affairs to emperors, however "priestly" their disposition.

Clergy sought the force of imperial law for their decrees in religious matters. Synods and councils from Nicaea I onwards based their mode of procedure on that of civil assemblies, and petitioned emperors for civil ratification of their sentences; in the fifth century, synods and great prelates framed some of their decrees on precedents in Roman law. Still, just as they regarded the quasi-hieratic attributes of the emperors with reserve, the Fathers also failed to accept imperial law, and the authority which issued it, as normal parts of Church administration. They came to consider the special rights the Church enjoyed under Roman law only just, and to condemn as sacrilege any attempt to impair them. In their minds, the imperial edicts they quoted were auxiliary to the canons of synods and the orthodox prescriptions of individual

[26] Mansi 6, 733 A; 7, 177, and ACO II, 1, ii: [353] 157 (20). On Church-State relations in the eastern and western empires, see Morris, *Thought*, vol. I, 201.

[27] Ep. 115, c. 1; *ACO* II, 4: 67.

[28] Ep. 85, c. 3; *ACO* II, 4: 45.

bishops. The edicts were valid in Church matters because they accorded with canonical regulations and because they had been requested and approved by authorities in the Church.[29] The Empire remained an "external power"; and, though they might invoke its laws, the Fathers still were careful, at least in form, to exclude "human presumption" from the consideration of sacred matters.

The Empire also took precautions to guard its own integrity in its symbiotic union with the Church. Its measures in this regard tended increasingly to restrict episcopal jurisdiction to purely ecclesiastical matters, and to redefine the *privilegium fori* in such a way as to increase temporal jurisdiction over clergy. In the years of persecution, cases of every description were pleaded before episcopal courts by persons, clerics or laymen, who could not in good conscience or with safety appear before secular judges. Consequently, a juridical system of general competence developed outside the imperial system. On present evidence, Constantine did not eliminate the duplication of competences when, after his conversion, the imperial courts were open without prejudice to Christians. Civil order and the great elaboration of ecclesiastical institutions and power in the fifth century required the Empire, in its own interest, to limit the scope of ecclesiastical jurisdiction according to the personal qualifications of pleaders, the nature of cases, or both. A ruling which Arcadius first imposed on the East (398) and which Honorius, in the next year, applied to the West was designed to assure the integrity of the imperial courts by curtailing the comprehensive scope of ecclesiastical jurisdiction.[30] Though their powers of judgment in religious cases remained unimpaired, bishops ceased in civil cases to have any powers beyond those of arbitration between parties to whom episcopal council was mutually acceptable.

A decree of Valentinian III[31] took these restrictions still further, by providing that a lay accuser might invoke the force of the civil government to bring a cleric before a temporal court. In practice, clerics in Italy, Africa, and Gaul so far disregarded the *privilegium fori* by appearing before secular judges that synods in those regions, as well as contemporary popes, repeatedly imposed the severest penalties for such deliction. The practice, however, favored imperial interests; in recognizing an existing situation, Valentinian's decree regularized a prac-

---

[29] Jonkers, "Gelasius," 334.
[30] Cf. the excellent comments in Gaudemet, *L'Eglise*, 235f, 241f.
[31] Novella 25.

tice which curtailed what remained of the effective influence of Church courts in civil matters, and correspondingly enhanced the juridical power of the waning Empire.[32]

Beyond these measures, the western rulers abstained even from the kinds of temporal intervention in Church affairs which had grown usual in the East, and which tended to subject tenure of clerical offices and matters of faith to review by secular judges. The western Empire, for example, did not even claim the right to mediate in disputed episcopal elections.[33] So thorough was the reserve of the western emperors in religious matters that Valentinian III was the first to acknowledge even the ancient doctrine of Roman primacy.[34]

This reticence can only be explained politically by the assumption that it was not profitable in the West for the imperial government to control religious affairs. Profit in such a context can be equated with public order. Doctrine, the precedence of sees, and political reliability of bishops did not normally play an important role in the West. There the population was more widely dispersed and perhaps also less numerous than in the East. Barbarian invasions had both scattered the indigenous population and reduced the proportion of orthodox inhabitants by interjecting large numbers of Arians and heathens. Episcopal sees in any given province numbered in the tens instead of in the hundreds. The fluidity of population and the progressive constriction of lands effectively ruled by the Empire excluded both the possibility and the necessity of masking national aspirations with the subterfuge of religion. And, finally, the presence of only one autocephalous Church, Rome, obviated for the West the divisive questions of primatial order.

For western emperors the ill-defined relationship of interdependence, despite its instability, remained viable. The peculiar social and political structure of the East, however, made it impossible for the Byzantine Empire to maintain a similar distance from Church affairs; but even there the clergy vigorously upheld the integrity of the Church and countered the institutional amalgamation towards which the quasi-hieratic concept of emperorship inclined. The Oecumenical Councils of Ephesus (431) and Chalcedon (451) and the so-called Robber Synod

[32] Gaudemet, *L'Eglise*, 236, 244f.

[33] *Ibid.*, 410.

[34] *Ibid.*, 423ff; Caspar, *Geschichte*, 1, 440-46; Fuhrmann, "Patriarchate" (1953), 158. Cf. Klinkenberg, "Papsttum," 47.

of Ephesus (449) show that their work was neither hopeless nor without success.

In the form which had grown usual during the fourth century, the emperor, on the advice of clergy, convoked each council, specifying the day and place of convention. He summoned bishops—in some cases individually and in others by general orders to metropolitans. He provided commissioners to see that the debates were conducted with due order, and a military force to defend the councils from external intrusions and mob demonstrations. He confirmed by imperial decree the Fathers' decisions; and, finally, he prorogued the assembly. In view of the civil implications religious issues held, the disposition of eastern cities to lapse into terrifying riots, and the chronic ebullience of the Fathers themselves, such disciplinary measures were necessary both to ensure orderly debate of issues and to give the conciliar judgments some chance of general acceptance among the faithful. The eastern emperors did not venture formally to enlarge this protective role.

When he named Count Candidian "protector" of the Council of Ephesus, Theodosius II explicitly instructed him to take no part in the doctrinal discussions, as such matters could rightly be considered only by bishops.[35] He also commanded Candidian to bar monks and curiosity seekers from the sessions, to preserve order in the debates, at the same time allowing each Father unlimited freedom to elaborate his views. Nightmarish confusion ensued when Cyril of Alexandria prematurely convened a synod of his adherents, contrary to the protests of Candidian and some bishops, and proclaimed it the true Council of Ephesus. When Cyril's opponents, on arriving late in Ephesus, heard of his irregular procedure they immediately convened their own synod, likewise claiming that it was the authentic Council. In the melée, Candidian found it impossible to discharge his commission, which Cyril had arbitrarily declared null, and he submitted an immediate and urgent report to Theodosius. The Emperor confirmed the decrees of both splinter synods, including the later group's condemnation of Cyril, and dissolved the Council. Cyril again flaunted imperial authority by escaping from captivity and returning triumphantly to his see.

It would be ludicrous to pose the question of imperial control of the Council of Ephesus; Cyril's contempt for imperial authority had in effect voided even Candidian's lenient commission, and it was precisely the absence of tight control by the Commissioner which allowed the

[35] Janin, "Rôle," 98. Grillmeier, *Christ*, 329ff, 374ff, 413ff.

chaos in Ephesus and the schism and civil disorders which followed throughout the East. That Theodosius's intervention was warranted for political reasons is clear, and no objection to it occurred on canonical grounds. Indeed, from the West, Pope Celestine I wrote of his efforts that temporal government was most beneficial in sacred matters, "since worldly power belongs to God who faithfully holds the hearts of governors."[36] In one letter, Celestine commended Theodosius for his interest in religious affairs, and, admonishing him to give greater care to matters of faith than to those of government, he urged him to follow the examples of Abraham, Moses, and David in devoting his primary concern to the cult of God.[37] In another letter, written after the Council, Celestine's hyperbolic praise mounted to claim glory equal to that of Elias for Theodosius, who, like the Prophet, had cast down and punished the false teachers.[38]

The Robber Synod of Ephesus saw a considerable display of imperial force.[39] Theodosius II repeated the actions he had taken on behalf of the Council of 431, setting the time and place of convention, summoning members of the projected synod, and delegating imperial commissioners to assure orderly debates. There is no evidence whether he had nominated a president for the earlier assembly, or whether he had given the Council specific instructions for its debates. He took these steps in 449. He designated Dioscorus of Alexandria as president and commanded the Fathers neither to add to nor subtract from the canons and the Faith of Nicaea. These measures did not of themselves constrict the liberty of the synod. His orders and the eminence of his see qualified Dioscorus for the presidency, which he shared at least in form—on the first day of the Council—with Roman legates, and the Nicene decrees were universally accepted as an authentic rule of faith and discipline. On the command of the imperial commissioners, imperial troops indeed contributed to the cruelty and gross injustice of the Synod; the Fathers drafted their judgments under the sharp swords of Theodosius's soldiers. But such acts of coercion as the secular arm committed were done at Dioscorus's behest. Theodosius placed his commissioners and his troops under Dioscorus's command, and the military violence which did occur expressed the Patriarch's tyrannical will more than imperial manipulation of the Synod. Theodosius confirmed the acts of the Synod and refused to subject them to synodal review,

[36] Ep. 16; PL 50, 501.
[37] Ep. 19, c. 2; PL 50, 511f.
[38] Ep. 23, 2; PL 50, 545.
[39] Janin, "Rôle," 100f.

even when petitioned to that end by Leo I and his imperial cousins of the West. In this attitude, he did not uphold principles of imperial supremacy over the Church, but rather the position that the Robber Synod had been canonically constituted, and that its decisions, framed under the presidency of the successor of St. Mark, were just and binding.

The Council of Ephesus served only to sharpen the Nestorian dispute by precipitating a schism between John of Antioch, Nestorius's principal supporter, and Cyril of Alexandria, his bitterest enemy. As a basis of compromise, John subsequently issued a letter defining the doctrine of the Incarnation as he had "received it both from the divine Scriptures and from the tradition of the holy Fathers," adding nothing to the Nicene Creed.[40] Cyril accepted this profession, and the two bishops were reconciled by the Formulary of Reunion (433). The Formulary scandalized both Cyril's followers, who suspected that he had joined the Nestorians, and the Nestorians, who considered the settlement a betrayal of the faith.[41] The dispute, therefore, continued and led to another council under imperial auspices.

Theodosius's successors, the joint rulers Pulcheria and Marcian, acquiesced in the demands for a revisionary synod and convoked the Council of Chalcedon[42] with the reluctant consent of Pope Leo I.[43] Likewise, their commissioners brought to decision matters which Leo expressly feared and against which his legates strenuously protested. As the records of the debates show, not only the imperial pair, but also the majority of the assembled Fathers demanded these actions. The commissioners indeed moderated the debates strictly, but not arbitrarily, and, though the decrees of the Council never ran overtly counter to the will of Pulcheria and Marcian, the Fathers exercised considerable freedom and even took issue directly with some imperial intrusions into ecclesiastical matters.

In a debate on hierarchic rank (Canon 12), they declared the broad principle that no imperial intervention in episcopal elections or in matters of precedence which transgressed the canonical limits was valid. Marcian acceded to this sentence, responding through his commissioners that, in matters concerning bishops, actions by the imperial govern-

---

[40] Sellers, *Chalcedon*, 17.

[41] *Ibid.*, 22.

[42] Janin, "Rôle," 101ff; Grillmeier, *Christ*, 480.

[43] See Klinkenberg, "Papsttum," 83, 61: "*Das Konzil soll unter Rom gebeugt werden.*"

ment should be considered of no effect if they contravened conciliar canons.

The repudiations of imperial direction at the Council of Ephesus, the ancillary role of the troops at the Robber Synod, and Chalcedon's exclusion of uncanonical influence by the Court in episcopal accessions and matters of hierarchic precedent are not sufficient to prove the consistent development of a doctrine, or the programmatic activity of an ecclesiastical party in the eastern Empire which required total freedom of the Church from the civil government. They rather show that the eastern Church, like the western, continued to maintain conventions of institutional integrity which had been transmitted from the time of persecution. Byzantine clergy did this despite the dangers, sometimes insidious and sometimes overt, that the Empire presented through the peculiarly close interdependence of ecclesiastical and imperial interests that had arisen in the East. More than Ravenna, Constantinople was forced to seek to identify its interest with those of the churches in its lands. But the methods the Empire used left the clergy considerable freedom to create its own laws (the canons) and to live according to them, to assemble for discussions of important doctrinal and disciplinary matters, to judge such disputes with canonical liberty, and even to resist imperial authority. Indeed, the clergy retained such a large degree of freedom that the first great period of Byzantium's search for identity of interests with the Church ended vainly in the Monophysite Schism, when most Coptic and Syriac churches withdrew from communion with the patriarch of Constantinople.

Christian thinkers thus rationalized the Church's new role in society, as regards the imperial government, in two chief ways. Some powerful churchmen accepted the emperor as truly the vicar of God in the Church, and thus as an arbiter in religious matters as well as in temporal government. Eusebius of Caesarea was an early and very distinguished representative of such men. In his hyperbolic praise of Constantine's conduct of ecclesiastical affairs, Eusebius left a clear model of the basis on which the doctrine of Caesaropapism later arose. The Syriac bishops, who, Constantius II boasted, accepted that Emperor's word as canon, also held this position as did all those other prelates who obediently followed imperial changes of creed throughout the Byzantine period.

Still, even advocates of the quasi-hieratic doctrine of imperial supremacy were forced to accept some limits: for example, emperors could not perform the eucharistic liturgy, consecrate deacons, priests, or

54

bishops, or discharge any other of the sacerdotal functions on which the survival of the Church depended. These limits led the second body of thinkers to very different conclusions. In explaining the relation of the Church to the world, they held that the emperor had to be considered as a layman, and thus as part of the world, not of the Church. Athanasius and his sympathizers sought imperial support in what they judged the cause of truth. But, to their minds, the Empire was an auxiliary; it intervened on sufferance as an external power in the Church, where it had no organic connection.

This second view continued the apologists' suspicion toward the Empire; the first view cast it aside. But both positions shared one fundamental thought: if the emperor could not convey the Church's common experience in sacraments, he could not convey it in doctrine or in order. Constantius II's brutal subjection of synods to his fickle will, Theodosius I's pose as executor of the Fathers' doctrine, and the role of emperors in the oecumenical councils of the fifth century showed the flaw in the fabric of Caesaropapism. Standards of religious conformity could be set only by synodal or conciliar decrees, sanctioned by patristic authority. Conformity could be imposed by temporal coercion; but, in this, the emperor acted as executor rather than as framer of the norms. Clergy, especially bishops, were the sole authentic bearers and interpreters of the Church's common experience in sacrament, doctrine, and order. This functional monopoly set formal limits in theory beyond which the Empire could not go, however much ambition, bribery, and power might circumvent them. When they rationalized the relation of Church and Empire, thinkers of each school were therefore forced to contemplate in their different ways the paradox of assimilation through equipoise.

## B. HIERARCHY: UNIVERSALITY IN PARTICULARISM

### (1) Arianism: Legalization of Tradition

The issue of imperial authority within the Church was a new and enormous problem in itself; but it also sharpened yet more complex questions of authority with which the apologists grappled.

The churches prospered. Their adherents and lands multiplied; their administrative orders developed; their ceremonies grew increasingly elaborate and opulent; they framed ample and ever more precise laws and doctrines. Through its laws, the Empire was both the fosterer and pattern of their growth in wealth and organization; and it is fair to speculate that, without imperial favor, ancient differences would have driven believers farther and farther apart, and reduced doctrine to an anarchic muddle. Still, even the briefest survey of Church history in the patristic age shows that the growth of administrative order in particular sees went hand in hand with universal schism. There were many antagonistic centers of unity in the Church. This elaboration of order merely sharpened the issues of cohesion that had plagued the apologists: Who bears authentic doctrine? How can doctrinal conflicts be judged? What authority can settle them definitely?

The apologists had considered tradition the ultimate rule of faith. But even they found that solution inadequately vague, and adduced Scripture and the episcopal office as cognate authorities. Conflicts in the age after Constantine's conversion demanded increasing elaboration of the apologists' leads into legalism.

There was no canon of scriptural exegesis, no rule of faith, free of the distortions and inexactitude of human language; and thus there was no unerring test for heresy. St. Augustine suggested the confusion which had ensued on this point when he wrote of two compendia of heresies, the works of Epiphanius of Cyprus[1] and Philastrius of Brixen, showing that some doctrines that one author had thought heretical had been considered orthodox by the other, even though the men were contemporaries reviewing much the same evidence.[2]

The first great doctrinal conflict was, of course, the Arian dispute, the forerunner of many controversies between two schools of scriptural interpretation: the Alexandrine, which emphasized Christ's divine nature, and argued that man's salvation lay in union with God, and the Antiochene, which held that Christ showed His perfection as a man especially in his submission to God and that men were saved, not by changing human nature through union with the divine, but by fulfilling their human natures through obedience to God.[3]

Behind the contested exegeses, the repeated formulation of creeds, the fierce debates over the words "*homoousios*" and "*homoiousios*," and the shifting political conformations which the Arian dispute cast

[1] On Epiphanius's view of tradition as a source of instruction supplemental to Scripture, see Adv. haer. panarium 61, 6; PG 41, 1048; and the comment of Deneffe, *Traditionsbegriff*, 42.

[2] Ep. 222; *CSEL* 57, iv: 446ff; Grabowski, *Church*, 242f.

[3] See especially Manoir, "L'Argumentation," 445ff; Ghellink, "Patristique," 403. On the distinctions between Antiochene and Alexandrine, see the brilliant discussion in Ladner, *Reform*; Sellers, *Chalcedon*, xv, 158.

over the ecclesiastical landscape, lay the critical issue of tradition. That was the issue which went unresolved at Nicaea, which plagued Athanasius and his enemy Eusebius of Nicomedia alike, and through which the Arian controversy exerted its most lasting influence. How could authentic doctrine be determined, if the Scriptures provided no clear answers to theological issues? What were the norms of Church unity?

The greatest norm was Scripture. Even in the days of the apologists, the charge had been common that the chief characteristic of heretics was their twisting Scripture to suit their own ends.[4] The charge revived in the Arian conflict. After comparing Arianism with several other heresies and collating the scriptural passages from which they claimed legitimacy, Hilary of Poitiers summed up the case: "They all speak of the Scriptures without the sense of Scripture, and without faith, they pretend faith. For the Scriptures exist, not in reading, but in understanding, nor do they stand in prevarication, but in love."[5] Even more exactly, St. Ambrose made right faith a condition for the correct understanding of Scripture. He did not mean the literal interpretation of the Scripture. When he glossed St. Paul's statement, "the letter killeth but the spirit giveth life" (II Cor. 3: 6), he observed that the Jews had fallen away from God by rejecting the inner meaning of Holy Writ and following only its literal sense.[6] The true Church alone possessed the authentic faith, all the commands of the Old and the New Testaments.[7] Sects and heresies claimed scriptural warrant for their doctrines, but the difference between their teachings and that of the Church was not due to contradictions in the Scriptures. The interpretation of the Arians, not Scripture itself, contained the error.[8] The Gospels were eye-witness accounts of Jesus's life and immediate testimonies of His doctrine. "[John] has told me what he heard, and what he heard from Christ I cannot deny as truly of Christ. Therefore, what he heard, I have heard, and what he saw, I have seen."[9] But in the Gospels and in other portions of the Scriptures occurred many passages which were so obscure as to be incomprehensible. To these passages especially, St. Ambrose applied the critical techniques he had mastered: the collation of manuscripts, particularly of Greek transcriptions, the investigation of contexts, and

---

[4] See above, pp. 15ff, *passim*.

[5] Liber II ad Constantium, c. 9; *CSEL* 65, 204.

[6] Exposit. in Luc. 2, 42; *CSEL* 32, 65; Huhn, "Bewertung," 394.

[7] *Ibid.*, 388.

[8] *Ibid.*, 394f.

[9] De inc. dom. sac. 22; PL 16, 859; Huhn, "Bewertung," 387.

the allegorical method of exegesis he had learned from Alexandria. But, above all, he trusted that faith would enlighten what was obscure and open his ears to the word of God.[10]

From Nicaea onwards, Athanasius was the chief spokesman of the orthodox and the historian of the controversy; he has left us the most complete statement of his party's position. All the emphasis of the Arians upon Scripture was vanity, he wrote, since they had begun the controversy with terms they themselves framed anew or distorted from scriptural allusions. Likewise, their complaints against the *homoousion* were groundless, he sophistically argued, since it was etymologically grounded in Scripture, and, moreover, since the word itself had long been used by bishops, especially at Nicaea.[11] The Scriptures themselves were sufficient to teach the doctrine of salvation without the human inventions to which they had resorted. *Homoousios*, unlike *homoiousios*, was totally harmonious with the sense of Scriptures. On this point, his argument resembles that of Hilary of Poitiers, who wrote that, from the Scriptures, he knew the two concepts, the true and its opposite, before he knew the words.[12]

Athanasius maintained that the Scriptures must be read in the light of the frequency and variety with which critical terms and images occurred, with close regard for the context of important passages, and most of all, in view of their total message. The *"skopos"* or the sense of Scripture, referred entirely to the doctrine of the Incarnation, God's eternal design for the redemption of the world made plain in the Old and the New Testaments. Through all the Scriptures ran the message that in Christ the works of the Devil would be destroyed, and that all men would be "deified," made the sons of God by participation in the humanity, and thus also in the divinity, of the Incarnate Word.[13]

Tradition was the message of Scripture in another form: the teaching and the preaching by the Church of "the sound and orthodox faith which Christ bestowed upon us, the Apostles preached, and the Fathers from all our world who met at Nicaea have handed down."[14] Tradition

[10] *Ibid.*, 389, 391ff, 395.
[11] Ad Afros, c. 6; PG 26, 1040.
[12] De Synodis, c. 91; PL 10, 545.
[13] De decretis Nicaenae synodi, c. 8ff; *GCS, Athanasius Werke,* 2, pt. 1, 7ff. In this section I draw heavily from the brilliant essay of Pollard, "Exegesis."
[14] Ad Afros, c. 1; PG 26, 1029.

was, therefore, oral confirmation of what was written fully and sufficiently in the Scriptures, and, as such, a guide to correct exegesis.[15]

In these canons of scriptural interpretation, Athanasius followed closely the thought of the apologists. The peculiar demands of the Arian controversy forced him to go further, and to place particular emphasis on the means by which tradition was preserved. The Arians too argued from Scripture; they knew the criteria of scriptural exegesis; they appealed to tradition, the teaching they had received from the beginning. Athanasius countered with an argument which proved a landmark in the history of the concept of tradition; he took up the thought of the apologists that bishops were the chief conveyors of true doctrine, and he worked it into a great and powerful principle of Church unity. He was within the polemical conventions of an earlier age when he protested that the Arian doctrine was not the teaching which the Church had received or transmitted, and that it must consequently be condemned. But the elaboration of his argument was new and important; it turned on the article that tradition was transmitted by the Fathers.

Who were the Fathers? To Athanasius's mind, as to St. Cyprian's earlier, they were the bishops. The tunic of Christ is one and undivided, Athanasius wrote, and the unanimity of bishops in confessing to articles of faith proves their authenticity. "It is, as our Fathers have handed it down, certain doctrine, and the sign of true teachers if they confess the same thing among themselves and vary neither from one another nor from their own Fathers. For those who lack this character are to be called not true teachers, but corrupt. Thus, the Greeks do not have the true doctrine, for they do not confess to the same things, but quarrel among themselves. But the saints and the heralds of the Being of truth are in harmony with one another, and do not differ among themselves. For, though they lived in different times, yet they all follow the same path, being prophets of one God and preaching harmoniously the same Word."[16]

The Fathers at Nicaea had reached such unanimity; but the Arians had departed from it, and, in this, they had falsified the tradition of the Fathers. Each generation of bishops must guard the faith and pass it intact "from Fathers to Fathers" in the episcopal ordination. "But

[15] See Smulders, "Le Mot," 57f.
[16] De decretis Nicaenae synodi, c. 4; *GCS, Athanasius Werke*, 2, pt. 1, 4.

59

you," Athanasius asked the Arians, "O modern Jews and disciples of Caiaphas, whom do you have to show as Fathers to your phrases? Say not one of the understanding and wise, for all abhor you, but the devil alone. Only he is your father in this apostasy, who both in the beginning scattered on you the seed of this impiety, and now persuades you to slander the Oecumenical Council. . . ."[17] Having no Fathers, the Arians were illegitimate sons; they had neither the faith nor the episcopate. True belief was preserved only by the fidelity of each successive generation of bishops to the establishments of its predecessors. The Arians had abandoned the faith of the Fathers, overturning the establishments of earlier bishops, discrediting themselves.[18] For "how are they themselves to be trusted by those whom they teach to disobey their teachers?" Their secession from the teaching of bishops who had gone before implicitly condemned those Fathers as heretics and thus overturned the episcopal ordinations they had performed, including those of the Arian innovators.[19] They were, therefore, by their own argument proven to be false bishops. Athanasius acknowledged that, in disciplinary matters, the Fathers might differ.[20] But differences in faith and contradictions in the interpretation of Scripture did not occur among the Fathers, the true bishops, and the Nicene Creed was both a sign and a guarantee of their universal concord.

Athanasius thought the numerous creeds of the Arians a token of their error. When, toward the end of Constantius's reign, they sensed the decline in their influence, the semi-Arians too came to a position close to Athanasius's, a conclusion which foretold the reunion with the orthodox which many semi-Arians later undertook. At the Synod of Seleucia they were urged to subscribe the Anomoian creed, but declined. "If," said the leader of the Anomoians, "the Nicene faith has been altered many times since, nothing forbids us to dictate another creed now." The response of the semi-Arians was worthy of Athanasius: "This Synod is held not to learn what it has already learned, nor to receive a creed, as though it lacked one before, but, adhering to

[17] Athanasius, De decretis Nicaenae synodi, c. 27; *GCS, Athanasius Werke,* 2, pt. 1, 24. On the Christologies involved, see esp. Wolfson, *Philosophy, passim;* Schneemelcher, "Athanasius," *passim,* esp. 255f; Grillmeier, *Christ,* 183ff, 190ff, 194ff, 217ff.

[18] See Deneffe, *Traditionsbegriff,* 42.

[19] De Synodis, c. 13; *GCS, Athanasius Werke,* 2, pt. 1, 240f.

[20] De Synodis, c. 43; *GCS, ibid.,* 268.

the creed of the Fathers, to stand by it in life and in death."[21] The creed meant was not the Creed of Nicaea, but the Arian Dedication Creed (341). Still, the semi-Arians had come to think along lines which Athanasius had made familiar. On the defensive, both the Alexandrine and the semi-Arians appealed to the authority of synods which had declared their doctrines authentic. They had not invoked the Scriptures, but the teaching of the Church, the tradition of the Fathers, as canonized in synodal decrees.

From this time onward, the appeal to patristic authority became a regular and important technique of doctrinal argumentation, and the character of legalism which marks mediaeval theological treatises began to develop. Tradition was no longer a vague "rule of faith," or even the oral teaching of the Church, a means of instruction collateral with the Scriptures. It was assuming concrete form, independent of the Scriptures and supplemental to them. Athanasius accepted the *homoousion* although it was unscriptural and although it had been anathematized by the synod that condemned Paul of Samosata. He clearly judged the term authentic, because the "Fathers" had used it for more than a century, and, more important, because it had been approved by the Council of Nicaea.

Eusebius of Caesarea recorded that at least one author towards the middle of the third century had collated patristic authorities to counter the heresy that Christ was a mere man, invoking works of second-century authors such as Irenaeus of Lyon and Justin Martyr, and "psalms and hymns written by the brethren from the beginning."[22] Athanasius, his fellow orthodox writers, and later the semi-Arians added a critical element to this eclectic method of argumentation. The third-century author directed his work towards establishing a consensus of authors whose authority was generally acknowledged. That done, his case rested. The disputants in the Arian controversy accepted the canon of consensus, but they added to it the principle that the authority of a synod was far above that of a single author, and indeed that some synodal decrees defined the message of salvation more precisely than the Scriptures themselves. Each believer heard that message, but, as Athanasius argued, its perpetuation was the special office of the bishop, who transmitted it intact through episcopal consecration. St. Cyprian had thought similarly. But Athanasius went beyond his concept that com-

---

[21] Socrates, Hist. eccles., II, 40; PG 67, 341.
[22] Hist. eccles., V, 28; *GCS, Eusebius Werke*, 2, pt. 1, 500.

mon charity united bishops and produced consensus among them. For Athanasius, synods of bishops were the winnowing-floors of doctrine, and, by their conference, the "stewards of the divine mysteries" distinguished mere opinion from faith, and cast out the chaff of error. Their judgments were the authentic interpretation of Scripture, the voice of tradition, the very sentence of God. On the other hand, heretics who pretended the title "bishop" had separated themselves from the episcopal succession which imparted true doctrine and renounced their own ordinations; having repudiated the Fathers, they spoke singly or in synod with the voice of their real father, the Devil.

To the criterion of consensus, therefore, was added the sub-category of concordance with the decrees of authentic synods; these were the first elements of the science of canon law. But the argument from authority did not yet have the quality of antiquarianism it later acquired. To be sure, the disputants argued that the creeds which they invoked stated the original, the ancient, faith of the Church, the faith handed down from the beginning. But they were polemicists as well as theologians. In Athanasius's argument, for example, the value of the Nicene Creed was surely not its antiquity—Athanasius himself had a part in framing it—but its substantiation of the doctrines for which he was fighting. It served an immediate, vital purpose. In invoking it, Athanasius had no thought for ossified traditionalism; his whole concern was to defend the living and vivifying tradition which, under his own eyes, the Nicene Fathers had received from their Fathers and framed in writing to instruct those to whom they would hand it on. Neither Athanasius nor the semi-Arians appealed to ancient creeds, though there were many such professions of faith of widely diverse length and complexity, especially in the form of private statements and the baptismal creeds used in churches. When Eusebius of Caesarea produced one symbol of this sort, the baptismal creed of his own church, at the Council of Nicaea, it became the basis of the debate which ended in the formulation of the Council's creed. Though older than the symbols to which Athanasius and the semi-Arians appealed, these creeds lacked both the sanction of synodal authority and the immediacy and doctrinal relevance of the Nicene and Dedication Creeds. The disputants did not contest the claims of the older creeds to represent the tradition of the Church, but, to them, the apostolic teaching was clearer and more useful in debate as set forth in the creeds of recent synods.

By the end of the fourth century, the impact of the Arian dispute on concepts of Church unity was clear. The twilight hour of paganism was waning towards the night of things past. The symbiotic union of Church and Empire had made the Roman world a vast tribunal for religious disputes. Theology was no longer a matter for private thought and conviction. It involved civil rights, property, freedom, and life itself. The Empire had made doctrinal conflicts political affairs; it had made the Church hierarchy a foster child of civil government, having much political influence. Theological disputes thus became legal matters involving the political interests of the Empire, of the hierarchy, and of social or ethnic groupings. The Arian conflict was the first great clash of those interests. The conjunction of religion and politics in the Church brought men to think of Church unity in terms of legal exegesis and official action.

The Arian dispute centered upon two unscriptural terms, *homoousios* and *homoiousios*; it was not a dispute over what the Scriptures literally said, but over what they meant. Exegesis was therefore more important than the actual text. Theology and concepts of Church cohesion had shifted from repetition of scriptural passages to their interpretation, from the text to the gloss. True believers were no longer simply those who upheld the Scriptures as true, but those who shared a particular understanding of the Scriptures' inner meaning or implications.

If the cohesion of the Church depended upon a specific exegesis of Scripture, it also required an authority to define that exegesis and, perhaps, to impose it upon dissenters. These were the tasks of councils and of imperial troops. As to the specific work of defining authentic articles of faith, men of Athanasius's generation took the lead of the apologists and framed a doctrine of tradition and Church unity which made study of patristic writings a legal exercise, and which exalted the magisterial actions of synods as legal definitions and sentences. But Athanasius and his contemporaries never framed an abstract rule by which some written sources could be accepted and others discounted, or some synods obeyed and others condemned, or the coercive power of the Empire defied. Legalism always leads men in different paths; fourth-century thinkers had no sure means, other than their own convictions, to show them one true path. As a rule of faith, tradition was uniquely independent of laws and offices; in its very nature, it was not amenable to legalization. The alliance of Church and Empire thus brought men to rationalize concepts of Church unity in important new ways, but they left their successors incomplete formulations, paradoxes without solutions.

### (2). Monophysitism: Hierarchic Cohesion and Universal Schism

Thinkers in the Arian dispute showed clearly that each religious grouping—heresy, sect, or hierarchic order—would frame a concept of Church unity in its own idiom, according to its own circumstances. In the new, but highly developed, administrative framework of the Church, this was more than the simple sectarianism that earlier led the Gnostics, Montanists, and other schismatics to claim each in his own right to represent the whole Church. That ground of separatism survived, but it had become encased in civil and ecclesiastical orders of government, and crystallized by identification with ethnic and social groupings. The path lay open to the incessant conflicts of the fifth century, when the concept of cohesion within the Church became increasingly constricted by the degree of authority that autocephalous sees claimed, and by political struggles throughout the East.

When Pope Gregory VII considered Christian history, he saw a sharp distinction between the earliest days and the age of the Fathers. He wrote that, "although the primitive Church had disregarded many things, these were afterwards corrected by the Fathers with careful scrutiny when Christianity had been established and religion was advancing."[23] Men living in the age Gregory praised realized that they witnessed a change in the fabric of Christianity. St. Augustine saw, for example, that the concept of ecclesiastical cohesion in his day was not that advanced by earlier thinkers. In an enlightening passage, he said that no universal synod had been held before Nicaea, "because the whole world was held together by the powerful bond of custom; and this was deemed sufficient in itself to oppose those who wished to introduce what was new, because they could not comprehend the truth."[24] But "the bond of custom" had utterly dissolved. To be sure, the Scriptures were absolutely true and right. Still, St. Augustine observed, a body of canonistic writings had grown up for Church government, and they were all liable to change. Letters of bishops could be nullified by the discourses of wiser men and by the weightier authority of councils. Regional and provincial councils yielded in authority to "plenary councils,

[23] Reg. VII, 11; MGH Epp. Sel. 2, 474. On this statement, see Miccoli, "Ecclesiae," 479f.
[24] De Baptismo, II, ix, 14; CSEL 51, 189.

64

which are formed for the whole Christian world." And even plenary councils were liable to correction by later ones when "things are brought to light which were before concealed."[25]

Other thinkers in the patristic age deplored this incessant change. Protesting against an archbishop of Alexandria who luxuriously decorated his church at the same time he oppressed his people, an Egyptian hermit admonished the prelate to consider that, although the Church in the time of the Apostles had had no buildings, it had been rich in the gifts of the Holy Ghost. In their own day, he said, church buildings shone with costly marbles, while the Church itself had lost its spiritual gifts.[26] St. John Chrysostom likewise wrote that from the apostolic Church, the Church of his day had inherited only the symbols without the substance, which was Heaven itself.[27] The Egyptian and the Antiochene, like Gregory VII and Augustine, saw that the patristic age had departed from the ways of the primitive Church. For them, that departure was not the correction of earlier negligence, but the loss of the Holy Ghost. Everywhere they saw disunity instead of the concord that Athanasius and the apologists before him looked for as a sign of true doctrine. There was no consensus among Christians on the most essential elements of belief.

In view of St. Athanasius's reliance on councils as oracles of tradition, it is ironic to think that this disintegration came about largely through a sequence of synods and councils. Far from acting as channels of authentic tradition, corporative teachers and interpreters of the true faith and heralds of unity, those assemblies exasperated differences. The principal theological issues that they had to consider had developed out of doctrines framed in the Arian dispute: Nestorianism and Monophysitism, the last, titanic antagonists in the struggle between Antiochene and Alexandrine theologies.

Even in the fourth century, men had questioned the practical advantage of conciliar discussion. They realized that, far from reconciling differences, it brought them into full elaboration and ended with juridical decisions which many disputants could only accept insincerely, if at all.[28]

---

[25] *Ibid.*, II, iii, 4; II, iv, 5; *CSEL* 51, 178ff.

[26] Isidore of Pelusinum, Epp. II, 246; PG 78, 685.

[27] In ep. I ad Cor. homil. XXXVI, 4f; PG 61, 312f.

[28] Fear of aggravating already serious divisions persuaded Sisinnius, in 381, to argue against Theodosius I's projected council on Arianism and Macedonianism (see above, p. 43).

The council, as a supreme court, foundered on this point, for the validity of its decrees on the faith, and of its judgment in disputes among patriarchs depended either upon the voluntary acceptance of its canons by the parties involved or upon the military power which the Council could invoke from the Empire to enforce its decisions. The lack of acceptance in the West which the Council of Constantinople (381) encountered indicated the flaw in the concept of oecumenity; the schism between Alexandria and Antioch following the Council of Ephesus and Rome's flat rejection of the decrees of the Robber Synod, which were accepted in the East, showed the flaw in the clearest light. The Council of Chalcedon led to its complete development.[29]

For very different reasons, Leo I, Pulcheria, and Marcian combined their efforts in convening Chalcedon. That Rome and the court of Constantinople had allied was itself an unusual fact, in view of the antagonism which had grown up between the two imperial sees in the fourth century, and which had received sharp expression when Rome broke communion with Constantinople in protest against the deposition of John Chrysostom and again when she joined the New Rome's archenemy, Alexandria, in bringing down Nestorius. Indeed, the formation of their joint effort was almost coincidental. When they insisted that a general council be held, against Leo's objections, Pulcheria and Marcian suggested that they had more definite goals in mind than the mere reversal of the Robber Synod, which Leo was content to see progressing without any extraordinary measures. Leo wished orthodox diophysitism to prevail; it was already returning to dominance. The imperial court sought more: first, the clear definition of orthodox doctrine, to clarify the confusion of faith into which the East had fallen; and second, the exaltation of the see of Constantinople above the dignity of Alexandria, thus to place its bishops beyond the reach of the successors of St. Mark who had, in the lifetime of Pulcheria, humiliated and deposed three bishops of the imperial city. These grand purposes required a general council. For the court, the restoration of amiable relations between Constantinople and Rome was not an end in itself, but a means to achieve ecclesiastical changes of direct benefit to the see of Constantinople.

To win the sanction of oecumenicity for their council, Pulcheria and Marcian required that the Roman see be represented; for the dignity of his see, Leo, finding a general council summoned despite his pro-

---

[29] Sellers, *Chalcedon*, 301, 254f.

tests, was forced to send legates. Such were the tenuous lines of the alliance.

In his instructions to his legates and in his order that they withdrew from the Council if they found it impossible to discharge their commission, Leo had attempted to avert precisely the two discussions which Pulcheria and Marcian most wished. Flattery of every sort was heaped upon Leo and his legates; masterly rhetorical structures, sonorous acclamations, sumptuous ceremonies, all celebrated the unfailing orthodoxy and ecclesiastical pre-eminence of Rome. The Council could receive Leo's *Tome* with artful rapture: "That is the faith of the Fathers! That is the faith of the Apostles! We all believe thus! The orthodox believe thus! Anathema to him who does not believe thus! Peter has declared these things through Leo!"[30] The presidency of the Council could easily be given to the Roman legates jointly with Anatolius of Constantinople, under the supervision of the nineteen imperial commissioners. The Council's decrees could even be sent to Leo for approval, accompanied by an insinuatingly adulatory letter.[31] But, as Leo's legates understood during the Council, and as the Pope himself furiously declared on receiving the Council's decrees, all this was subterfuge.

Every point of Leo's instructions was discarded. Contrary to his express demands, Dioscorus was admitted to the first session of the Council, the faith was discussed, and the order of primatial sees was changed to include Constantinople in the second place, after Rome.[32] The Roman text of the Nicene Canon which, Leo argued, forbade this last measure, began, "The Roman church has always had the primacy." When Leo's legates read it, the imperial commissioners could not find that reading among the transcripts of Nicaea and barred it as inauthentic, recalling at the same time the pronouncement of the "oecumenical" council of 381 in favor of Constantinople. Indeed, Jerusalem too was recognized as an autocephalous see, to the detriment of Antioch; and all these indignities were compounded when many of the eastern Fathers denounced Leo's *Tome* as Nestorian.

Still, Leo's one victory in the Council was securing the approval of the *Tome* as an authentic document of the faith. This approval, however, and the incorporation of Leo's phrasings in the Council's defini-

---

[30] *ACO*, II, 1, ii: [272] 81 (23).

[31] See the Latin translation, *ACO*, II, 3, ii: [352] 93f.

[32] Sellers, *Chalcedon*, 109. Cf. the argument of Klinkenberg that Chalcedon merely ratified what Leo had already decided ("Papsttum," 93ff).

tion of the faith, was a victory whose disastrous results Leo himself had attempted to avert when he protested against the summoning of the Council. He had written, in the *Tome*, a masterly exposition of the faith from the viewpoint of western theologians, and he had submitted it for the instruction of the eastern clergy, whether of the Alexandrine or of the Antiochene school. The Council received it with the acclamation that Leo and Cyril taught the same thing—which was true except in the three sections suspected of Nestorianism, particularly in the affirmation that Jesus was not "*of* two natures," but "*in* two natures," a statement which was totally unacceptable to the Monophysites and even to the orthodox but extreme followers of Cyril. Adoption of this phrase into the Council's definition and approval of Leo's *Tome* brought on the full violence of the Monophysite Schism.

When Leo first received the canons of Chalcedon, he declared that he would repudiate Chalcedon as he had repudiated the Robber Synod. But, after a delay of more than one year, he agreed to approve only those canons relating to the faith. At the same time, he inveighed in the strongest terms against the twenty-eighth canon.

The East renounced the decrees as a whole. Historians have called the Chalcedonian definition the triumph of Antiochene theology. To the clergy and people of Egypt, Palestine, and Syria, it was the triumph of heresy. They saw that, though the Council affirmed that Leo and Cyril taught the same doctrine, the Fathers had not adopted Cyril's Twelve Anathemas among the documents they named canonical. Furthermore, leaving unmentioned Cyril's critical phrase, "the one nature of the incarnate Word," they had affirmed the two natures. The Council, in their judgment, had betrayed the Fathers and Cyril, and espoused Nestorianism. Leo, the West, and all who subscribed to Leo's *Tome* were Nestorians, "dividers" of Christ.[33] Extreme violence broke out in Jerusalem, Alexandria, and later in Antioch.

Monophysitism, however, had not wholly carried the day. Chalcedonianism remained predominant in Byzantium, and it held some highly articulate followers even in Syria, Palestine, and Egypt. When he reentered Constantinople after overthrowing a Monophysite usurper, the

[33] Sellers, *Chalcedon*, 169. For examples of Monophysites' recourse to the Fathers, see Timothy Aelurus's confession (Le Bon, "Christologie," 700) and, from the sixth century, Severus of Antioch's *Liber Contra Impium Grammaticum*, esp. Oratio I, c. 12, trans. by J. Le Bon in Corpus Scriptorum Orientalium, SS. Syri, ser. IV, t. iv (Louvain, 1938), 42.

Emperor Zeno saw the Empire torn asunder by religious dispute and their civil effects. Relying on the advice of Bishop Acacius of Constantinople and Peter Mongos, the Monophysite patriarch of Alexandria, Zeno tried to calm the dispute and ease political factionalism by issuing the Henotikon, a decree which forbade the use of the theological terms which had been the catch words of disunity since Cyril's day. Perhaps unwittingly, he followed the example of Constantius II, who had prohibited the use of the words *homoousion* and *homoiousion*. His success was even less than Constantius's; indeed, the Henotikon opened a second stage in the protracted controversy.[34]

Zeno proclaimed that the creeds framed at Nicaea and Constantinople, and confirmed at Ephesus, were full and sufficient definitions of the faith. Anathematizing both Nestorius and Eutyches, he approved Cyril's Twelve Anathemas; and, maintaining that Jesus was "one, not two," he also censured those who "confused" the natures. All men who taught any new doctrine, at Chalcedon or at any other place, were anathematized; and, finally, Zeno exhorted all believers to return to the one communion of the true Church. This decree was a complete reversal of the religious policy which the imperial court had followed since the Council of Chalcedon, and as such it found opponents among the Chalcedonian clergy. It was likewise resented by the extreme Monophysites, who wished an explicit and complete repudiation of Chalcedon. But on the whole the Henotikon found general acceptance in Constantinople and Alexandria, under the joint authors of the decree, and, after sharp resistance, in Antioch. This reception was superficial and illusory. But to Zeno, Acacius, and Peter Mongos, the Henotikon seemed, at least for the moment, to have set at rest the disputes which had divided the East for half a century.[35]

Their concern for the East, however, had led them to infringe deliberately upon the dignity of the Roman See. Probably they understood that they risked a schism with Rome; but they could hardly have perceived fully the disintegrative consequences that the schism would evoke.

The Empire's situation was desperate enough to blot out schism with Rome as a pressing danger in Acacius's mind. He took enormous risks in pinning his hopes for ecclesiastical unity on the Henotikon, only to be utterly frustrated. Peter Mongos departed ever more widely from

[34] Sellers, *Chalcedon*, 278f; Caspar, *Geschichte* 2, 22ff.
[35] Caspar, *Geschichte*, 2, 29, 36.

69

the terms of the settlement, and when he died (489), he was preparing to condemn Chalcedon overtly and to break off relations with Constantinople. His successor did withdraw from communion with the imperial see. Rancor between Monophysite majorities and ardent Chalcedonian minorities, and antipathy between each of those parties and the moderates, who upheld the Henotikon, tore every province of the East apart. The Empire fell into internecine strife.

The oecumenical council had become an instrument of division instead of an institution with powers of supreme mediation and judgment. The autocephalous character of the patriarchates, combined with reassertions of national feelings in the eastern Empire, opposed and finally negated the Council's potential for ultimate jurisdiction within the Church and gave free reign to the forces of schism.

On another level, Rome had broken communion with eastern sees before the Acacian Schism, but the separation to which the Henotikon led was the first to divide Rome simultaneously and for a long time from all the great churches of the East, from Byzantium, Egypt, and Syria-Palestine. In 452, the orthodox bishop of Alexandria, Proterius, held a synod which accepted Chalcedon and declared Timothy Aelurus and other Monophysites deposed; but this was an ineffectual action repudiated or ignored by Timothy and by Egypt as a whole. The majority judgment was shown by the mob which tore Proterius limb from limb.

The East was divided against itself. From the end of the fifth century onwards, Syria, Palestine, and Egypt went their own ways, firmly Monophysite, and ceased to exert any direct influence on the West; only Chalcedonian Byzantium retained meaningful relations with the See of Peter. But for nearly forty years even this connection with the East was severed.

In this sequence of disputes, fact ran counter to theory. The fact was that every bishop was in effect autocephalous. He could repudiate even the decrees of episcopal synods and councils if he judged them heretical or unjust. The theory was the ancient idea of the faith's essential unity. The fact led to schism in every ecclesiastical province; the theory led the concept of tradition to new degrees of legalization.

From the second century onward, men sought to commit the apostolic tradition to writing; but, readily acknowledging the possible incompleteness of their work, they never attributed any compelling authority to what they had written, beyond its alleged apostolic origin. The urgent requirements of the fourth and fifth centuries gave an abstract, external authority to the writings of the Fathers which these early expositors never claimed. What was required was an authentic interpretation of Scripture which could, as it were, stand up in court. Oral tradition, or even the testimony of many living men in a synod or council, could not prove what the true faith had always held. That could be done only by examining critically the works of authors living and dead whose orthodoxy was unquestioned, and by collating them with the records of orthodox synods to establish a consensus of interpretation. By the end of the fourth century, the textual proof of consensus in patristic writings had taken its place as a touchstone of orthodoxy together with the testimony of apostolic churches and the charismatic quality of the apostolic succession.

But, in the patristic disputes, there was never uniform understanding about which writers were worthy to be thought Fathers, or whether the dissenting opinion of a few Fathers might be valued more highly than the concurrence of many, by virtue of personal sanctity or extraordinary learning. Even when opponents consulted the works of the same author, their interpretations of his remarks often differed radically. In disputes among themselves and against the Empire, Egypt, Armenia, and Syria all produced elaborate doctrinal compendia proving that the consensus of the Fathers showed their faith to be orthodox. Especially in the later years of the fifth century, Rome too adopted this method of argumentation in asserting her orthodoxy and juridical supremacy against the counter-claims of the East. In this way, tradition indeed sharpened its integrative functions among groups predisposed to unity by ethnic, political, or linguistic factors; but, on the supraterritorial level, its effect was completely disintegrative.

Whom could polemicists suitably choose as their "Fathers"? When challenged on this point by Donatists, St. Augustine and his companions answered evasively that only God was their Father, the source of their doctrine.[36] Few authors proved a more consistent answer. Vincent of Lérins required that the Fathers must be approved and distinguished teachers who persevered in the faith and communion of the orthodox Church, and that the enquirer should seek what was "held, approved, and taught, not merely by one or two, but by all equally and with one assent, openly, often, and incessantly."[37] In one letter, Cyril of Alexandria recommends, as a corrective for heresy, careful reading of "the

[36] Collat. cum Donat., III, vii, 8; *CSEL* 53, 3: 58.
[37] Above, pp. 4f.

71

ancient Fathers, whose orthodoxy is universally acknowledged,"[38] apparently alleging that preference should be given to writers whose careers were spent in the orthodox communion before his own day; that is, to authors of authentic faith whose views could not be affected by current disputes. The patristic compendium compiled by the Council of Ephesus, under Cyril's supervision, conforms to this rule: the authors cited had all flourished in the fourth century. But, as Dioscorus's invocation of Cyril's authority, together with that of Athanasius and Gregory Nazianzus, shows, antiquity was not an inevitable criterion. In his compilation on behalf of Diophysitism, Leo I likewise included excerpts from Cyril's books, though the other writers he consulted were contemporaries of Athanasius.[39] The prevalent view held that, though the great theologians of the fourth century invited universal confidence, men recently dead, or even yet alive, might also deserve the title "Father." The Robber Synod acclaimed Dioscorus by crying, "These are the words of the Holy Spirit! Guardian of the rules! Through you live the Fathers! Guardian of the faith!"[40] and Chalcedon declared that the Fathers, and even St. Peter, had spoken through the mouth of Leo. The frequent acclamation of bishops assisting synods and councils as "Fathers," together with the equivalence in contemporary sources of the words "papa" ("Father") and "episcopus" ("Bishop") further show that even living men could be acknowledged as having patristic authority if they held episcopal orders and if the ancient Fathers lived in them by faith.[41] Thought had thus regressed almost to the third-century stage. Perhaps because of the uncertain credit that councils could command during the Monophysite dispute, St. Athanasius's sharp focus on conciliar decrees as touchstones of authenticity was lost.

Though it was a critical development in the technique of doctrinal

[38] Apologia, ACO, I, 1, 7: 48 (64); Manoir, "L'Argumentation," 460f, 482ff, 552, 536.

[39] Ep. 165; PL 54, 1173ff; ACO, II, 4: 113ff.

[40] ACO, II, 3, 1: 65: "Haec voces sancti spiritus. Custos regularum. Per te vivent patres. Custos fidei." See also Dioscorus's address to the Council, ACO, III, 3, 1: 62: "Piissimus et Christianissimus noster imperator pro aliquibus quae emerserunt, iussit hanc congregari synodum, non ut fidem nostram exponamus, quam exposuerunt iam patres nostri, sed ut inquiramus quae emerserunt, si conveniant sanctorum patrum nostrorum statutis. Oportet ergo ea quae contigerunt primitus inquirere et nos probare si consonantia sint statutis a sanctis patribus. Aut vultis fidem sanctorum patrum innovare? Sancta synodus dixit: 'Si quis innovat, anathema sit. Si quis discutit, anathema sit. Sanctorum patrum fidem servemus.' "

[41] Labriolle, "Papa," 71ff; Manoir, "L'Argumentation," 442, 444, 460f; Congar, Essai, 60f.

argumentation and in the concept of canonistic authority, the search for patristic consensus did not appreciably clarify the question of what authority transmitted the authentic faith. Like the idea of the apostolate, to which it was distantly related, it provided no specific canon of orthodoxy, and no closed company of unimpeachable doctors. Though explicit, its criteria were not sufficiently exclusive to prevent vagueness, misunderstanding, and conflict. A few authors such as Athanasius and the Cappadocian Fathers were generally accepted as authoritative. But the production of forged letters and treatises masquerading under venerable names, the very different approaches of acknowledged writers to the same questions, and the great number of authors of divergent views who had claim to the title "Father" made the quest for consensus little more than an ornament of pedantry for any disputant who wished to have it. Authority was, so to speak, in the eye of the anthologist.

In a broader context, the identification of imperial interests with ecclesiastical, which obtained in the East from the late fourth century onwards, served to create permanent divisions among believers. Political necessity demanded the settlement of religious disputes by law, when, to the contrary, reconciliation of the disputants required avoidance of juridical debate and positive judgment. There was no hope of general acceptance for a decision issued by any authority other than an oecumenical synod; and yet the sentences of the fifth-century councils proved even that hope vain. Indeed, the great schisms of the fifth century were largely due to the alliance between Empire and Church which Constantine instituted, and which both brought form out of the anarchic pre-Constantinian Church, and, in doing so, ruinously changed ancient differences in ecclesiology, doctrine, and social values into causes of estrangement and intransigent discord by insisting that orthodoxy and right order could and must be determined juridically. Neither in the West nor in the East, however, was the clergy subserviently bound to the imperial will; and, even in the East, where imperial intervention in Church affairs was normal and sometimes coercive, the clergy still asserted and exercised its ancient liberties. Bishops individually decided whether to accept the decrees of imperial councils.

As a channel of political aspirations, this abiding freedom ran counter to Byzantium's attempts to achieve uniformity and harmony in religious matters, inflamed the religious disorders of the fifth century, disrupted civil government in the East, and confounded the hallowed illusion that all the faithful were one spiritual brotherhood in this world and that,

73

despite differences in language, ceremonial practice, and hierarchic order, Christian unity in the faith was a real, present, and living force in the affairs of men.

Dionysius Exiguus exhibited a measure of this fragmentation when he addressed his third rescension to Pope Hormisdas, so as to teach the Pope "by what [rule] the eastern churches are governed."[42] Earlier generations had assumed Christian unity to be fact, and had considered evidence that their faith was both universal and true. Without reservation, St. Cyprian and other writers in his age and later considered this unity and the charismatic charity which, they believed, sustained it real, present, and effective within the Church. But, in the face of the theological disputes, hierarchic contentions, and great schisms of the fifth century, unity and charity became real only in apocalyptic promises, and present and effective only in hope. The episcopal throne, rather than the council, was the ultimate seat of judgment. The patristic age lost the immediacy of the ideal of cohesion without conformity, and gradually defined cohesion in terms of conformity to articles of theology and law.

[42] Peitz, *Studien*, 273f.

# PART II

# The "Janus Complex"
# in Roman Thought

## CHAPTER 3

# The Conflict of Tradition and Discretion

ALL the developments considered so far tended to undermine the idea of tradition as an effective category of authority prior and external to any structure of laws and offices. Tradition demanded unbroken continuity. Though it might make room for progressive elaboration, it still required a complete chain of teachers, a steady transmission of authentic doctrine from one generation to the next. This sort of authority suited a primitive, loose-knit, and persecuted sect; but it could not meet the pressures which Christianity bore as the imperial state cult. In our rapid survey of fourth-century thought, we have seen new patterns of authority arise which in time corroded tradition's place as a genuine check on authentic teaching. Imperial favor from Constantine's day on brought into conjunction highly disparate kinds of authority: particularly, for our purposes, temporal government, hierarchic order, and tradition. There was no thorough rationalization of how these three elements should function in Church affairs.

Such solutions as did appear were improvised and paradoxical. Two "paradoxes of unity" have especially concerned us. The first—assimilation through equipoise—held that the interests of Church and Empire could be harmonized and even fused, while each body retained its institutional integrity. The history of the Arian conflict, and especially the whole series of creeds framed under Constantius II, showed that this identity of interest could produce great changes in scriptural interpretation. It revealed the partly realized potential of "renewal," "reform," or "correction" of doctrine. As yet only by implication, it admitted the possibility that true teaching might be impaired, and that the succession of authentic teachers might lapse; and thus it undercut tradition's *continuum*. "Universality in particularism" was the second paradox that challenged tradition's confirmative function. It held, in effect, that each bishop was the final judge of true faith and practice in his see. He could decide whether, for his church, decrees of specific councils were "oecumenical" (i.e., orthodox) or heretical. On this level, discretion as a spontaneous official power ran counter to tradition; not the general confession of "everyone, everywhere," but the immediate rule of particular bishops determined authentic faith.

The corrosive effects of imperial and hierarchic authority on the idea of tradition as an abstract rule of faith appear nowhere more clearly than in the letters of Roman bishops during the fifth, sixth, and seventh centuries. "Reform" imposed by imperial interests did not figure significantly in papal thought until the Byzantine reconquest of Italy. We shall take up this aspect of the story later. Episcopal discretion, however, appeared early in the fifth century. It was part of that general, slow, and momentous shift toward legalism that we have described. For the apologists, tradition had been above all a bond within the Church; it united true believers and set them apart from the rest of the world. From the fourth century on, many thinkers transferred these functions to the bearers of tradition. They saw Church unity in the light both of concurrence in doctrinal interpretation and of obedience within an administrative order. Increasingly, men thought of the power to teach as one aspect of the power to govern, and of submission within a hierarchic grouping as an outward sign of orthodox belief.

There was no sharp break; as in most slow transitions, the old merged unobtrusively with the new. For the popes, the shift combined the concept of a *continuum* of authentic knowledge, with the idea of spontaneous, administrative authority. Roman thought became a "Janus complex" of tradition and discretion.

$$+$$

## A. COHESION THROUGH JURIDICAL ORDER (TO CA. 426)

From the fourth century, a most critical century in the history of the Church, only thirty-three papal documents survive. They come from different times; they have different forms; and some of them are fragmentary. Documentation is satisfactory only from the pontificate of Innocent I (402-417) onward.

The first hint of the direction Roman thought was taking occurs in a letter of Pope Julius I repudiating the sentence of the Synod of Tyre against Athanasius and other imperial acts of force in the Church. Julius stressed the injustice of these intrusions by an external power into the inner concerns of the Church. The canons, the apostolic tradition, the peculiar law of the Church, must remain vigorous; they are the "traditions of the Fathers," which have been handed down from the Apostles. To violate them is to tear apart the limbs of Christ.[1]

Very early, the Greek historians Socrates and Sozomen found the spirit, but not the letter, of the tendency toward legalism in Julius's judgment. They interpreted his letter to mean that "contrary to the canons, they [the Arians] had not called him [Julius] to the Synod, although it was forbidden by ecclesiastical regulation that anything be decided by the churches without the sentence of the Roman pontiff," and that "the priestly law is that whatever things are done without the sentence of the Roman bishop should be considered void."[2] Julius had actually said that it was customary for matters at issue to be referred in writing to the bishop of Rome, and that "what is just be decided."[3] But he also proposed that yet another synod be called to hear Athanasius's case. The thoughts which the historians attributed to him may not have been far from his mind.

At any rate, they became explicit in papal correspondence in 371, when the Roman Synod under Damasus repudiated the creed of Rimini, first because it deviated from the "faith which was established at Nicaea by the authority of the Apostles," and secondly, because the "Roman bishop whose sentence must be sought before all others," had not been represented or consulted.[4] Paucity of evidence clearly keeps us from appreciating Damasus's hierarchic thought fully, but it does indicate that his pontificate marked a turning point in the development of the idea of papal supremacy. In his day, Roman thinkers began to use the term "the Apostolic See" as a synonym for Rome. Damasus glorified his see with many buildings and commemorative inscriptions. He commissioned St. Jerome to translate the Scriptures into Latin, and he secured from the Emperor Gratian a promise that the Empire would enforce papal judgments at least in Italy and perhaps in the entire West.[5]

---

[1] Athanasius, Apologia II, 30; GCS, Athanasius Werke, 2, pt. 1, 109; Caspar, Geschichte 1, 142ff, 152ff. For a brief survey of papal thought about tradition from Innocent I to Gelasius I, see Holstein, in Pontificia Acad. Mariana Int., Scriptura, 218-21.

[2] Socrates, H. E., II, 17; PG 67, 217f; Sozomen, H. E., III, 10; GCS, Sozomenus Kirchengeschichte, 112f.

[3] Athanasius, Apologia, cc. 30, 31; GCS, Athanasius Werke, 2, pt. 1, 109f; Caspar, Geschichte 1, 152: "In der Tat stand Julius I. in der Verteidigung."

[4] PL 13, 348f.

[5] Caspar, Geschichte 1, 211ff, 250f, 253.

At the end of the fourth century, Pope Siricius clearly indicated the drift Roman thought had taken.[6] In the age of the apologists, Popes Victor I and Stephen I had argued that only Roman tradition was authentic. The evidence is too fragmentary, however, for us to know whether they forecast Siricius's further point. In his letters appears for the first time a curious pairing. The idea of tradition, with all the intellectual hardware of the apologetic age, is joined with a curious new idea running directly counter to it. Siricius argued that apostolic doctrine survived in Rome because St. Peter himself ruled in the Roman bishops.[7] He never lost sight of the older idea, or of its emphasis on a long succession of authentic teachers, or bearers, of tradition. At the same time, his new concept of an imperishable and immediate, rather than an inherited, apostolicity rendered the idea of tradition logically irrelevant. If the spirit of St. Peter, dwelling in his successors, intended to correct an ancient error commonly accepted as truth, judgments of the Fathers must give way.

Designedly or not, Siricius was in fact using conventional terms to veil a new doctrine of spontaneous administrative power. He set discretion up as an authority beside tradition. He was using the word tradition to cover a concept of order directly counter to the rules of universality and consensus. Siricius's successors worked out the implications of this development. His own letters to the bishops of Spain, Gaul, and North Africa give strong indications of where he was leading. He wrote to the Church of North Africa that no episcopal ordinations were to be performed without the knowledge of the Roman bishop.[8] And he set out to emend diversities of practice that had sprung, he said, from arrogant departures from the tradition of the Fathers, and to recall bishops to the unitary faith, discipline, and tradition preached by the Apostolic See. Apostolate and episcopate began in Christ through St. Peter, and, by this inheritance, Siricius governed, wishing not to command any new precepts, but to restore what the Apostles and the Fathers had once established.[9]

The bold inconsistency in Siricius's thought had to wait until the pontificate of Leo I for full elaboration. It did, however, mark the thought and actions of intervening popes, who themselves contributed important refinements. Innocent I, for example, a brilliant student of legal sources, added a new, more highly legalized element.

---

[6] *Ibid.* 1, 261ff.  [7] PL 13, 1133.  [8] PL 13, 1157.
[9] PL 13, 1187f, 1155f, 1164, 1182.

As far as he thought of tradition—as distinct from the nascent idea of administrative flexibility—Innocent concurred entirely with Siricius. He quoted almost verbatim a passage in which Siricius asserted that both apostolate and episcopate originated in Christ through St. Peter, that he wished, not to establish new precepts, but to restore the old, and that the Roman Church was the very form of authentic discipline.[10] He went further and wrote that since the authentic tradition was one, there must be no diversities, no variations in the liturgical services, especially those of ordination and consecration. Such deviations crept in through human presumption, and were a stumbling-block to the faithful, who understood from them either that the churches had fallen into discord or that the Apostles or "apostolic men" had taught contrary things. Authentic tradition had been given to the Roman Church by St. Peter, and there it still survived, without addition or diminution, the type to which all churches must conform. Novelties must be uprooted and the true custom, the custom of Rome, be universally established. "This is especially so, since clearly, in all Italy, the Gauls, the Spains, Africa and Sicily, and the islands between, no one has instituted churches except those whom the venerable Apostle Peter or his successors constituted bishops. Let them read whether any other of the Apostles is found in these provinces, or is read to have taught there. And if they do not read this—since they will never find it—they ought to follow what the Roman church preserves, from which they manifestly took their beginning. . . ."[11] "Especially as often as the order of the faith is at issue," he wrote to an African synod, "I think all our brethren and fellow bishops are obliged to refer nowhere but to Peter, that is, to the author of their name and honor."[12]

This view of Rome as the font of authentic, unitary tradition and of judgment in matters of faith echoes Siricius's thought. But, as regards administrative authority, Innocent framed in clear, legal terms what Siricius had only suggested. For both of them keeping tradition meant not "transgressing the limits set by the Fathers." But, for Innocent, this meant explicitly observing a definable body of law which he called "the tradition of the elders" (*traditio maiorum*). The "elders" were the

[10] PL 20, 470. On the general importance of Innocent's work, see Caspar, *Geschichte* 1, 296f.

[11] PL 20, 551f. Repeated, in different words, by John II, Mansi 9, 760.

[12] PL 20, 590. See also cols. 515, 517, 527f, 555; Caspar, *Geschichte* 1, 309ff; Fuhrmann, "Patriarchate" (1953), 173ff. See also the special relationship which Innocent attempted to establish with Antioch (Dvornik, *Apostolicity*, 13).

"Fathers," the "apostolic men," whom Innocent mentioned with the Apostles as transmitters of tradition.[13] Who were they? His predecessors were *apostolici*,[14] the "elders" whose judgments be studied.[15] To others, he himself spoke "with an apostolic tongue."[16] The canons, however, were the principal store of the "tradition of the elders." "No priest," Innocent wrote, "should be ignorant of the norm of ecclesiastical canons."[17] But the canons themselves were subject to review by the Roman Church. Among them were the so-called Apostolic Canons, those "ancient rules, transmitted by the Apostles, or apostolic men, which the Roman Church preserves,"[18] and also, most important, the canons of Nicaea, "for the Roman Church admits no other canon."[19] The authority of the Nicene Synod alone set forth the thinking of all priests throughout the world.[20] And, as Innocent read its canons, it established that judgments of ecclesiastical cases in any province must be issued "without prejudice to the Roman Church," and that such decisions could always be appealed to the Apostolic See.[21]

Siricius's concept of the Roman bishop as in some sense the incarnation of St. Peter had a counterpart in Innocent's belief that he spoke "with an apostolic mouth." And Innocent gave administrative meaning to Siricius's doctrine of immediate apostolicity in the care with which he asserted Rome's general supervision over trials of bishops, and in his efforts to have an oecumenical council summoned to hear the case of John Chrysostom and thereby sustain, perhaps even supplement the canons of Nicaea.[22] Innocent revered antiquity, but he honored it less than what he considered apostolic sanction of administrative flexibility; the freedom to dispense with ancient norms, such as those governing consecrations in Gaul, and established hierarchic order, such as that in Macedonia.

Innocent's successors, Zosimus and Boniface I, framed yet more sharply Siricius's pairing of tradition and immediate apostolate. A choleric and irresponsible man, Zosimus pressed his claims to general primacy so far as to incite disobedience among the clergy of Gaul and

---

[13] PL 20, 532.          [14] PL 20, 516.          [15] PL 20, 535.
[16] PL 20, 536, ore apostolico.
[17] PL 20, 605.          [18] PL 20, 531f.          [19] PL 20, 495.
[20] PL 20, 547; Caspar, *Geschichte* 1, 317.
[21] PL 20, 472f.
[22] PL 20, 505. On Innocent's exalted concept of Roman primacy, as expressed in his dealings with the East, see Demougeot, "Interventions," 23ff.

North Africa.[23] He denounced the uproar he met on every hand by claiming, first, that antiquity, to which the Fathers commanded reverence, lived unimpaired in Rome,[24] and, second, that "the tradition of the Fathers granted to the Apostolic See such great authority that no one may take exception to its judgment."[25] The antiquity he had in mind was an ancient carte blanche for unlimited judgment, or so it seemed to the offended bishops. When he invoked as warrant for his measures in North Africa two of the appeal canons of Sardica, which he alleged to be Nicene, the issue was fairly joined.

Of the Sardican records, only the letter of the Arians had reached Africa; the canons of the orthodox bishops were unknown. When the papal legates added to their abusive tone the assertion that Nicaea warranted their procedure, the Synod of Carthage called for investigation. They looked up the copies of the Nicene canons that they had, including a transcript made by a participant in the Great Synod, and found no trace of the canons in question. They decided to send to the Greek churches for authentic transcripts, particularly to Antioch, Alexandria, and Constantinople, and meanwhile to admit the papal claims pending confirmation. They sent this decision to Boniface I, Zosimus's successor.[26] On receiving the transcripts they requested, the Africans reopened the proceedings and discovered that the disputed canons did not occur in the Nicene canon. In a letter to Celestine I, who had just succeeded Boniface, they repudiated in the strongest terms both Zosimus's claims to normal judgment over North African cases and the specious Nicene basis for his assertions.[27]

This refutation led neither to modification of Roman claims nor to correction of papal transcripts of Nicaea. Celestine I and his successor, Leo I, repeated the claims that Innocent I and Zosimus had made, with the same confounding of Nicaea and Sardica.

Boniface I expressed the Roman position concisely in a letter to the papal vicar, Rufus of Thessaloniki, and other eastern bishops. The thought of Siricius and the words of Zosimus reappear in Boniface's assertion that, by ancient right, indeed by Christ's commission to St.

---

[23] Caspar, *Geschichte* 1, 344-59.

[24] PL 20, 666. Zosimus's letters contain many references to Rome as the preserver of tradition and the ancient norms. See also PL 20, 642f, 653f, 661, 666f, 669, 670, 672. See Demougeot, "Interventions," 37f.

[25] PL 20, 676; Deneffe, *Traditionsbegriff*, 53.

[26] PL 20, 755.

[27] See Caspar, *Geschichte* 1, 369f.

Peter, the Roman See had free judgment over bishops, that no one could review its judgment, and that any men who infringed Rome's privilege fell into "new usurpation" against the "decrees of the elders," and became servants of the Devil, the master of pride.[28]

These comments indicate how far Roman thought had progressed since the time when Julius I undertook to defend Athanasius.[29] The old claim to pre-eminence recurred, but it was buttressed, not only by the Petrine commission, but by the force of convention, by antiquity, by the decrees of the elders, and by "ecclesiastical law," to use Boniface's term. No longer did Boniface suggest, as Julius had, that his judgment might be reviewed by yet another synod. No one, he said, repeating Zosimus, may review the judgments of the Roman See. Alexandria and Antioch must defer to the chair of Peter. Resistance to Rome is contumacy, rebellion, a crime which bars its perpetrator from heaven.

Roman thought had become strongly legalistic, hedged about with patterns of administrative relationship, privilege, and juridical competence. Discretion had the upper hand over tradition.

### B. ROMAN THOUGHT IN THE NESTORIAN AND MONOPHYSITE CRISES

For the apologists, tradition had been a device for teaching authentic doctrine. But they had also set up other categories of authority beside, and antithetic to, tradition. At least from Siricius on, Roman bishops honored tradition and used the vocabulary of the apologists to describe it. But the burden of their thought completely undercut the conventional idea. The apologists had argued that the three principal signs of authentic tradition were antiquity, universality, and consensus. The Roman bishops picked up another strand in the apologists' thought— the resort to personal or official authority—shaped it to suit their see, and ultimately rendered antiquity irrelevant by arguing that St. Peter still lived in the Roman bishop. What need of tradition, and a long succession of authentic teachers, if the Apostle himself spoke directly to each generation? Universality had no validity because only Roman tradition was authentic; variation from it in practice or belief was error by definition. Argument from consensus carried no weight, since resistance to correction by Rome was rebellion against divine order. In form, Siri-

[28] PL 20, 781. See Boniface's other statements on Petrine primacy. PL 20, 760, 762, 774f, 777, 779.
[29] Cf. Caspar, *Geschichte* 1, 379ff.

cius and his successors accepted the apologists' views of tradition. But in fact they invalidated the older position by their new, though incompletely formulated, doctrines of administrative order. To see the full development of their curiously ambivalent thought, we must turn to the works of popes from Celestine I onward, and especially to those of Leo I.

During the fifth century, Roman thinkers occupied themselves increasingly with one aspect of the argument from consensus: that is, with the study and collection of synodal canons. The exegetical method of textual collation, in this context, assumed an explicitly legal character. Universality, antiquity, and the ancillary qualities of tradition became the tests of proper juridical and administrative order.[1] The citations of Nicaea and, under Nicaea's name, Sardica by Innocent I and Zosimus, and of the African Canons by Celestine I were early hints of the great movement that culminated in the so-called Gelasian Renaissance at the end of the fifth and the beginning of the sixth century. Then, the legal tendency of Roman thought took form in a number of canonical collections which remained classic sources of Church law[2] throughout the Middle Ages.

Consensus was sought, however, to prove a predetermined point: Rome's unchecked juridical powers in the Church. Innocent I gave the tone of the movement when he said that authentic canons were the ones the Roman Church accepted; and the contents of the new collections bore this out circumstantially. There were in the same period canonistic collections in the East. These tended increasingly to lack one class of canonistic source that western collections included: papal letters. In the East, the circulation of decretals was complex. It required translation from Latin into Greek, Syriac, or Coptic, and, more important, the approval of the emperor, patriarch, or bishop to whom the letters were sent. As a result, few decretals were preserved in the oriental churches, except in special collections of correspondence such as were made at the time of the Council of Chalcedon, and none entered the normal compendia of Church law. The western, and especially the Roman, attitude was quite different. Latin was universally understood, at least by higher civil and Church officers, and papal judgments were esteemed as legal sources. Valentinian III acknowledged them as having the force

[1] See below, pp. 91, 104, and *passim*.

[2] On these collections, see A. Van Hove, *Prolegomena* (Mechlin-Rome, 1945), 145ff.

of law to some degree. Bishops of Rome themselves demanded this respect at least as early as the time of Siricius, who wrote that "no priest of the Lord is free to be ignorant of the establishments of the Apostolic See or the venerable judgments of the canons."[3] His successors, particularly those in the fifth century, repeated the same thought.

Order for them was itself part of the substance of tradition, the requisite corollary of the doctrine of salvation. In their judgments the bishops of Rome taught authentic doctrine and imposed the religious practices that tradition demanded. In their decretals, collectively with the approved canons of synods and councils, lived the ancient and universal rule of faith and the consensus of the Fathers, the "tradition of the elders," a Roman Law term applied to Church order.

This progress in legal study potentially limited the more extreme current in Roman thought. For example, Celestine I's strongly legal position marked a refinement of the unadorned, authoritarian stand that Zosimus had taken. Celestine's legate at the Council of Ephesus, to be sure, revived Siricius's metaphor when he said that St. Peter always lived and judged in his successors. But the Pope's own majestic and often profoundly moving letters are replete with allusions to the legal content of tradition, and to the limits it imposed on right government in the Church.

Episcopate and apostolate were the same. Judas, he wrote, had lost his "episcopate" to another;[4] and, in a letter to the Fathers at Ephesus, he described them, and all bishops, as successors of the twelve Apostles, obliged to preserve, by their common labor, the doctrine of Christ. He wrote of Pope Damasus as "the man of apostolic memory,"[5] and of Cyril as "an apostolic man" discharging "the office of the Apostle."[6] Faith and order alike depended on fidelity to what the Apostles had handed down. Just as he wrote to Nestorius urging that he adhere to "the symbol transmitted by the Apostles,"[7] he also admonished bishops of Gaul to honor the ancient practices of the Church, "for," he wrote, "if we begin to be eager for novelty, we will trample under foot the order handed down to us by the Fathers to make room for empty superstitions."[8] To the bishops of Apulia and Calabria, he wrote, "No priest may be ignorant of his canons, nor can he do anything contrary to the rules of the Fathers. For what will we preserve as worthy if the norm

[3] PL 13, 1146.
[5] Frag. serm., PL 50, 458.
[7] Ep. 13, c. 4; PL 50, 475.
[4] Ep. 25; PL 50, 550.
[6] Ep. 25; PL 50, 552.
[8] Ep. 4, c. 1; PL 50, 431.

of established decretals be broken according to the taste of some men.
. . ."[9] The duty of bishops, the successors of the Apostles, was to govern canonically. "The people must be taught, not followed."[10] And this
was particularly the duty of the men in whom St. Peter lived and judged.
"Let the rules be our masters; not us, the masters of the rules. Let us be
subject to the canons, since we observe the precepts of the canons."[11]

Still, legal limits on papal authority remained only potential in Celestine's own thought, and his acknowledgement of tradition's force
left no residual check on papal discretion in the thought of his successor.

## (1) Leo I

In this age of great crises and of the ever widening division between
East and West, Rome was fortunate in being governed for twenty-one
years (440-461) by Leo, one of the most learned and judicious of its
bishops, whose ardor for the dignity of his see was accompanied by
a rare conciliatory spirit. He was a man of spacious and receptive intellect, and of great courage; and it fell to him to give the doctrine of
Petrine primacy the most refined expression it had until then received.

By Leo's day, that doctrine was a Janus complex. Part of it looked
backward to the primitive authority of tradition, and part anticipated a
newer doctrine of administrative authority. It stressed apostolic foundation as a requirement for primacy; yet it did not admit all apostolic
churches (for example, Smyrna and Corinth) as primatial sees. Equating apostolate and episcopate, it did not admit episcopal equality. It
held that, since St. Peter was the head of the Apostolic College, his
episcopal successors should have directive powers over all other bishops.
Yet it denied to Antioch, St. Peter's first see, the supreme jurisdictional
and executive powers it claimed for Rome. Its premises were paradoxical; but the dogmatic quality of the Petrine doctrine transcended paradox and inconsistency, limited criteria of patristic consensus and universality, and certified elaborations in law and theology according to
their consonance with the discretionary force of papal judgment. This
was the raw material with which Leo had to work. It was small wonder
that, when he declared his own position, his enemies taxed him with
having transgressed the commands of Christ and the teaching of the
Apostles and the Fathers.[12]

---

[9] Ep. 5; PL 50, 436.    [10] *Ibid.*, col. 437.    [11] Ep. 3; PL 50, 428.

[12] Lauras, "Léon," 166f. On Leo's general position, see Caspar, *Geschichte* 1,
456ff. Cf. Ullmann, *Principles*, 39: "Allegorically speaking, the pope might be said

Leo's doctrine of tradition was of a piece with his interpretation of the Christian past. In his mind, Church history combined the unchangeable divine plan for man's salvation with the abrupt break with the past effected by Christ's advent. The nativity of Christ, he wrote, was the beginning of the Christian people; for the birth of the head was the birth of the body.[13] It was, likewise, not a new plan of God's for mankind, but the fruit of His ancient compassion, the same cause of salvation for all men which He had established from the beginning of the world,[14] the day of "new redemption, ancient preparation, and eternal joy."[15] The novelty of Christianity touched Rome particularly, where, after imbuing the East with the laws of evangelical teaching, St. Peter carried the ensign of Christ's cross. Divine providence had prepared the Roman Empire as a device for spreading its grace throughout the world, uniting many kingdoms into one realm and many peoples under the rule of one city. Through Christ, Rome was delivered from the errors of all nations and miraculously freed from the tight bonds of the Devil. Through the See of St. Peter, Rome truly became the holy nation, an elect people, a priestly and royal city, the head of the world, whose government extended more widely by religion than by earthly dominance, and whose gains by military victories fell far short of what Christian peace had won.[16]

In religion, too, the Advent was a continuation and a severance. He who spoke to Moses also spoke to the Apostles;[17] Christians were "true Israelites" and the "seed of Abraham."[18] But the New Testament revealed in light what the Old had veiled in symbols; and the "Jew according to the flesh" could never share in that joyful transformation

to stand with one leg in heaven and with the other on earth. In the late fifth century this function of the pope as the *Schnittpunkt* between heaven and earth prompted the appellation of him as *sanctus*." In Dr. Ullmann's article, "Leo I," the *Schnittpunkt* metaphor is applied explicitly to Leo I (p. 45). On this metaphor, see C. H. Haskins, *The Renaissance of the Twelfth Century* (New York, Meridian Books, 1962), 9. I cannot follow Dr. Ullmann in his further comments on Leo's "peremptory commands" and his "unbending and unyielding attitude" ("Leo I," 25). The evidence reviewed below, pp. 90ff., suggests to me an inclination to honorable compromise, always saving the dignity of the Roman See. Cf. Schmidt, "Papa," *passim*, sharing Dr. Ullmann's view.

[13] Serm. 26 (25) in nativ. Domini, 6, c. 2; PL 54, 213.
[14] Serm. 23 (22) in nativ. Domini, 3, c. 4; PL 54, 202.
[15] Serm. 22 (21) in nativ. Domini, 2, c. 1; PL 54, 193.
[16] Serm. 82 (80) in natal. app. Pet. et Paul., cc. 1, 5; PL 54, 422f, 425.
[17] Serm. 95, de grad., c. 1; PL 54, 461.
[18] Serm. 30 (31) in nativ. Domini, 10, c. 7; PL 54, 234.

of darkness into light. His blindness and malice still hid evangelical truths under the pall of the Law,[19] in the prefigurative observances of ritual; and he was still bound by guilt in the death of Jesus. "On you, on you, false Jews and princes of the people of sacrilege, weighs the whole weight of this crime. . . . Whatever sin Pilate's judgment or the duty of the soldiers committed in the punishment of Christ makes you the more worthy of the hatred of the human race."[20] Through their rage against Christ, the Jews had lost their inheritance. The promises of God passed from the sons of the flesh to the sons of the spirit, and Christ was sacrificed, "offering Himself to the Father as a new and true sacrifice of reconciliation, not in the Temple, whose reverence was now at an end, nor within the walls of the city, for the merit of snatching away its shame. But He was crucified outside, beyond the camps, so that, as the mystery of the ancient victims fell away, a new victim might be laid upon the altar, and the cross of Christ might be the altar, not of the Temple, but of the world."[21]

Through this new sacrifice, the old was transformed into the new, and the desires of the soul superseded, in newness of life, the concupiscence of the flesh.[22] "Let the people of God know," Leo said in a sermon on the Resurrection, "that, in Christ, they are a new creature, and let them vigilantly see by whom they have been acknowledged and whom they will acknowledge. Let those things which have been made anew not return to the infirmity of their old existence, and let not him who has set his hand to the plow leave his work."[23]

In his thought concerning tradition, Leo made room for corresponding change, an ideological development or elaboration comparable in tone, though not in magnitude, with the revelation by the light of truth of what the pall of the Law had hidden. He held the conventional view that authentic doctrine and practice descended from the Apostles through the succession of the Fathers to his own day, and, in the letters he wrote in the dispute over Chalcedon, he reiterated that he had learned and taught only what "the preaching of the holy Fathers and

[19] Serm. 60 (58) de pass. Domini, 9, cc. 1, 2; Serm. 66 (62) de pass. Domini, 15, c. 2; PL 54, 343, 365f.

[20] Serm. 59 (57) de pass. Domini, 8, c. 3; PL 54, 339.

[21] Serm. 59 (57) de pass. Domini, 8, c. 5; PL 54, 340. On Leo's comments concerning the mnemonic value of nearness to the Holy Places, see Honigman, "Juvenal," 260.

[22] Serm. 63 (60) de pass. Domini, 12, cc. 6, 7; PL 54, 357.

[23] Serm. 71 (69) de resurr. Domini, 1, c. 6; PL 54, 389.

the authority of the unchangeable symbol" imparted.[24] This transmission of authentic doctrine from generation to generation assured that the immutable faith was the same in all places and at all times, neither added to nor subtracted from.[25]

The faith was one and indivisible, true and universal; it was also given once for all in Christ's own teaching. But man's understanding of the faith could grow,[26] as disciplinary regulations developed according to necessity. Tradition (in the form of religious practices or disciplinary rules) was augmented by ecclesiastical customs which the changing needs of the Church required.[27] Never in conflict with the faith, rules of observance and definitions of faith alike were framed by the Fathers, the teachers of true doctrine in each generation, under the direct inspiration of the Holy Ghost.[28] In its administrative and magisterial characters, tradition received elaboration.

The authority of the Fathers was consequently exercised, not merely in transmitting the faith they had learned from their predecessors, but also in devising regulations for the proper government of the Church, consonant with the commands of Christ. The Advent had suddenly and radically revealed the substance of the faith; Leo admitted the possibility that the slower process of synodal review could effect a more gradual change in the body of tradition.[29]

Leo himself never explicitly formulated his thought on this point, but he was in fact very close to Vincent of Lérins, who wrote: "The Church of Christ is a zealous and careful guardian of the dogmas deposited with her. She never changes, subtracts, or adds anything; she does not cut off what is necessary, nor apply what is superfluous; she does not lose what is her own, nor seize what is another's. But with all industry she works to the end that, by faithfully and wisely considering the old, she may care for and refine the things which were formed and begun in former days, confirm and strengthen what are now expressed and laid

[24] Lauras, "Léon," 167, 172. An inventory of Leo's references to tradition and dogma is in Deneffe, "Tradition." Epp. 89, 90, c. 2; 102, c. 2; PL 54, 930, 933, 985f; *ACO*, II, 4: 47f, 53.

[25] For passages to this effect, see ep. 10, c. 1; ep. 119, cc. 2, 3; ep. 129, c. 3; PL 54, 628f, 1041f, 1077; ep. 119, *ACO*, II, 4: 73.

[26] Lauras, "Léon," 175.

[27] Serm. 9, 3; PL 54, 162; Serm. 79, 1; PL 54, 419.

[28] Serm. 16, 2; PL 54, 177; Serm. 50, 2; PL 54, 307.

[29] Lauras, "Léon," 170f, 183f. Cf. Deneffe, "Tradition," 554, arguing that the views of Leo I and Tertullian were fundamentally the same.

open, and guard what are now confirmed and defined. Furthermore, for what else has she striven with the decrees of councils except that what was earlier believed in simplicity subsequently be believed more accurately, that what was preached before somewhat remissly should afterwards be preached more diligently, that what was before observed quite carelessly, should later be anxiously perfected? This, I say, the catholic Church has always accomplished by the decrees of her councils, when she has been aroused by the innovations of heretics; and [she has accomplished] nothing else except that what she had before received from the elders by tradition alone, she might then also certify to later men with the surety of writing. . . ."[30]

Leo's Monophysite opponents vehemently charged that he had destroyed ecclesiastical tradition in his assertion of the Petrine doctrine. It is true that his thought was revolutionary, but its novelty existed principally in his acute understanding of the paradox in the ancient concept of tradition: that Christ gave the authentic tradition in its fullness to the Apostles and that, even though each generation transmitted it intact to the next, men's understanding of it developed. Exegetical methods, such as the argument from consensus, were in a sense accommodations to this uneasy pairing of immutability and change. Leo resolved this paradox with another, forecast in Siricius's thought, a brilliant reassertion of the Petrine doctrine which was, on one hand, firmly conservative in matters of doctrine and, on the other, subtly revisionist in the degree of emphasis on hierarchic powers. Such changes as occurred in human comprehension of divine teaching were not doctrinal; they amounted rather to the elaboration of the administrative lines of authority established by Christ and the Apostles.

The central aspect of Leo's ecclesiology was his concept of hierarchic order. The office, not the personal attributes of its incumbent, determined a bishop's authority. "No pontiff is so perfect, no prelate so unsullied, as not to offer sacrifices of reconciliation for his own sins when he offers them for the sins of the people."[31] Dioscorus's impiety did not diminish the prerogatives of Alexandria,[32] nor was the dignity of Rome lacking in an unworthy heir of St. Peter.[33] The episcopate was a comely

---

[30] Commonitorium, XXIII (32); ed. A. Jülicher, *Sammlung ausgewählter kirchen- und dogmengeschichtlicher Quellenschriften*, Hft 10 (Freiburg i. B. and Leipzig, 1895), 36.

[31] Serm. 5 (4), c. 1, anniv. access; PL 54, 153.

[32] Ep. 106, c. 5; PL 54, 1007; ACO, II, 4: 61.

[33] Serm. 3 (2), c. 4, in anniv. access; PL 54, 147.

body, held together by unanimity and concord; and yet this harmony was assured by a hierarchy of precedence and obedience. Following the distinction of power among the Apostles, headed by the See of St. Peter, bishops shared the same dignity, but not the same order. "Let him, therefore, who knows that he is set above some not take umbrage that someone is set above himself; let him rather give the obedience he requires."[34]

Leo's concept of ecclesiastical government was dominated by this hierarchic order of bishops, metropolitans, and prelates "in greater cities," culminating in the successor of St. Peter. In his view, this order was both prefigured among the Apostles and, equally important, prescribed canonically. When Hilary of Arles attempted to raise his see to primatial standing, Leo condemned severely his affront to the dignity of the Apostolic See as a violation of the order "which has been transmitted to us by our Fathers."[35] He likewise denounced "new and unheard-of" irregularities in Antioch,[36] and attempted to cut short the ambitions of Dioscorus of Alexandria on his accession by reminding him that "the most blessed Peter received the apostolic principate from the Lord," and that, since "the Roman church abides in his establishments it is wicked to believe that his holy disciple Mark, who first governed the Alexandrine church, framed the decrees of his traditions by other rules; for, without doubt, disciple and master had one spirit from the same font of grace, nor could the ordained transmit any thing other than what he received from his ordainer."[37]

But this quasi-monarchic view was not the only great element in Leo's concept of the Church. His conventional insistence that universality was a proper test of authentic practices as well as of the true faith led him to equate decrees of orthodox synods with the judgment of the universal Church.[38] Such was his attitude toward the canons of Nicaea, "the canons of the holy Fathers established by the Spirit of God and consecrated by the reverence of all the world."[39] Like the rule of faith, they were "inviolable" by any person or synod.[40] Although Innocent I

[34] Ep. 14, c. 11; PL 54, 676. On Leo's hierarchic views, cf. Ullmann, *Growth*, 7ff.

[35] Ep. 10, c. 2; PL 54, 629.    [36] Ep. 119, cc. 2, 3; PL 54, 1041f.

[37] Ep. 9; PL 54, 624f. See Stockmeier, *Beurteilung*, 205ff, 210.

[38] Ep. 94; PL 54, 941; *ACO*, II, 4: 49f. See Deneffe, "Tradition," 554.

[39] Ep. 14, c. 2; PL 54, 672.

[40] Ep. 119, c. 4; PL 54, 1043f; *ACO*, II, 4: 75. See also ep. 105, c. 2; PL 54, 999; *ACO*, II, 4, 57f. Cf. ep. 19; PL 54, 709.

had declared that the Roman See accepted only the Nicene judgments as authentic, historical circumstances realized for Leo what Innocent had only acknowledged as a possibility: an oecumenical council to be venerated equally with Nicaea. He honored the decrees of the Council of Ephesus. But, after overcoming his bitter antipathy to Chalcedon, Leo set that council uniquely beside Nicaea in his scale of precedence.[41]

The great size of the Chalcedonian assembly, the dignity it won by sitting in the imperial presence, and its critical place in the eastern controversies would have in themselves commanded respect. Chalcedon had overturned the "contemptible judgment" of Ephesus.[42] For Leo, there was one further telling point: the Council had received his *Tome* as a canonical document of faith. More than simple pride of authorship, the knowledge that this acceptance firmly committed Byzantium to a Diophysite creed brought Leo to exalt the Chalcedonian decrees in the faith to the level of sacred doctrine. Chalcedon, he wrote, and the *Tome* expressed the will of "the universal Church."[43] Knowing that it was being circularized in the East and that the Gallican bishops had accepted it "as the symbol of faith,"[44] he might at one time have believed that there was indeed some equivalence between the approval of the Great Council and that of the whole Church.[45] The Monophysite reaction soon showed how specious was that identity. As the eastern controversy grew increasingly grave during the last decade of his life, Leo resorted with great emphasis to the oecumenicity and the orthodoxy of Chalcedon. "We dare not undertake consideration of matters judged, as pleased God, at Nicaea and at Chalcedon, as though those things were doubtful or without strength, which such great authority has established through the Holy Ghost."[46] Chalcedon was celebrated "by all the provinces of the Roman world with the consent of the whole earth, and at one with the decrees of the most sacred Council of Nicea."[47] Its sentences were those of the universal Church, sufficient definitions of the teaching of the Fathers;[48] repositories of apostolic tradition, they had "truly proceeded from heavenly judgments."

[41] See ep. 156, c. 2; PL 54, 1129; *ACO*, II, 4: 101ff.
[42] Ep. 139, c. 1; PL 54, 1103; *ACO*, II, 4: 92.
[43] Ep. 130, c. 3; PL 54, 1080; *ACO*, II, 4: 83f.
[44] Ep. 99; PL 54, 966ff.          [45] Lauras, "Léon," 183.
[46] Ep. 162, c. 3; PL 54, 1145; *ACO*, II, 4: 105f.
[47] Ep. 164, c. 3; PL 54, 1150; *ACO*, II, 4: 111.
[48] Ep. 157, c. 3; PL 54, 1133; *ACO*, II, 4, 109f. Ep. 149, c. 2; PL 54, 1120; *ACO*, II, 4, 98. Ep. 161, c. 2; PL 54, 1142; *ACO*, II, 4, 108.

This was, however, no digression from Leo's hierarchic views. Although Leo accepted progressive development in the understanding of the faith and in disciplinary regulations through conciliar decrees, his acceptance was subject to some severe qualifications. For all its oecumenicity, the Council of Chalcedon enacted its twenty-eighth canon elevating Constantinople to the second rank among primatial sees, a regulation which Leo utterly denounced, and which nearly persuaded him to repudiate the Council itself. General councils, he wrote, were convened "by the precept of Christian princes with the consent of the Apostolic See."[49] Of their decrees, the bishops of Rome were the chief executors, the principal watchmen against "wrongful innovation."[50] And beside the canons of oecumenical councils there was another supplementary and possibly restrictive body of canonical authority: papal decretals. For, as Leo wrote, all the decretals established by Innocent I or any of his predecessors concerning ecclesiastical order and canonical discipline must be observed together with the canons themselves.[51]

For Leo, then, the administrative side of Rome's ecclesiological Janus dominated tradition's side. He was not prepared to accept synodal or conciliar decrees which, in his judgment, abruptly deviated from the established rule of faith or order. He repudiated the Robber Synod because "to infringe the catholic faith and confirm an execrable heresy, they stripped some of the privilege of honor, and tainted others with impiety by association.[52] In a letter to the Empress Pulcheria, Leo's legate to the Robber Synod and, later, his successor as pope confirmed this position when he wrote that Leo and his synod had utterly forbidden that the West receive what the assembly under Dioscorus had done "contrary to the canons."[53]

His strongest protests, however, were entered against the order established by the twenty-eighth canon of Chalcedon "against the reverence of the canons of the Fathers, against the statutes of the Holy Ghost, against the examples of antiquity."[54] The holy and venerable Fathers who condemned Arius at Nicaea "established laws of ecclesiastical canons to last until the end of the world and in their constitutions they

[49] Ep. 114, c. 1; PL 54, 1029; *ACO*, II, 4: 71. See Stockmeier, *Beurteilung*, 158ff, 167.

[50] Ep. 19; PL 54, 709.

[51] Ep. 4, cc. 1, 5; PL 54, 610, 614.

[52] Ep. 95, c. 2; PL 54, 943; *ACO*, II, 4: 51.

[53] Ep. 46, c. 2; PL 54, 838f.

[54] Ep. 104, c. 2; PL 54, 993; *ACO*, II, 4: 56.

live with us and throughout the whole world."[55] And yet, the framers of the canon had even dared to contravene those "spiritual decrees."[56] Certain that political considerations as well as clerical ambition had inspired the canon, Leo wrote to Marcian about the Patriarch Anatolius: "Let, as we hope, the city of Constantinople have its glory, and, with the protection of God's right hand, may it enjoy the lasting rule [*imperium*] of Your Clemency. But the ordering of temporal matters is one thing; that of divine matters, another. Nor can any edifice be sure apart from that rock which the Lord set as a foundation stone. The man who covets what is not owed him looses what is his own. It is enough that, by the aforementioned aid of Your Piety and the assent of my favor, [Anatolius] obtained the episcopacy of so great a city. Let him not disdain a royal city, which he can not make an apostolic see; nor let him hope that it can be increased through the misfortunes of others. For the privileges of churches, established by the canons of the holy Fathers and fixed by the decrees of the venerable Nicene Synod, can be overturned by no wickedness, changed by no innovation."[57]

This opposition to a canon of the very Council which he set on a level with Nicaea indicates the crux of Leo's thought on tradition, the dimensions of his conservatism and his revisionism. The decree to which he objected conformed entirely with his views on appropriate change in the administrative order of the Church. Since it was framed by an oecumenical council that had been summoned by imperial edict and papal assent, it expressed the consensus of the Fathers, the ratification of the universal Church, as much as did the approval of Leo's *Tome*. The criteria of episcopal agreement, conciliar approval, and universality urged its legitimacy. Against it, Leo advanced only the sixth canon of Nicaea in a sense which the East had steadfastly repudiated for at least a century, and the warning that nothing could be firm apart from the rock of St. Peter.

Leo's synthesis of Roman legal and ecclesiological thought thus contained a bold inconsistency roughly analogous to the much later canonistic theory that when doctors of the Church differed from judgments stated in papal decretals they were not to be considered "masters" on the disputed points. Affirming that councils held after Nicaea, like Chalcedon, could elaborate articles of faith, and that the canons of the Fa-

[55] Ep. 106, c. 4; PL 54, 1005; *ACO*, II, 4: 61.
[56] Ep. 105, c. 2; PL 54, 999; *ACO*, II, 4: 58.
[57] Ep. 104, c. 3; PL 54, 994f; *ACO*, II, 4: 56. See Lacy, *Appellatio*, 41.

thers could also add to ecclesiastical "traditions," Leo sharply confined this growth to those matters which did not threaten the Roman concept of hierarchic order. The immediate apostolate of St. Peter in every pope carried greater authority than a long sequence of acknowledged teachers. Papal discretion, rather than tradition, was the ultimate rule.

Some scholars have suggested that Leo's "monarchistic" interpretation of Church order was directly patterned on Roman imperial usage, and that he wished to create in the Church an administrative pattern parallel with that of the Empire, the bishop of Rome being the counterpart of Caesar. There are in his works many terms and concepts supporting this view. His description of St. Peter's "principate" over the other Apostles and of the Heavenly Keybearer as their "prince"; his use of the terms "*auctoritas*" and "*potestas*"; his assertion of the "universal care" of the Roman Church; his reference to papal letters as "decretals," and his allegation of the "common utility" of the faithful were all clearly derived from imperial terminology. The decree of Valentinian III giving judgments of Roman bishops the force of law likewise indicates Leo's imperializing tendency.

But behind all this was the theological concept of St. Peter's preeminence among the Apostles by virtue of his pure confession of faith, strengthened by the doctrine, perhaps suggested by Roman law, that the Roman bishops, in whom he still lived and judged, had inherited his special powers. "From the whole world, one Peter is elected to preside over the vocation of all peoples, and over all Apostles, and over all the Fathers of the Church in such fashion that, although there be many priests and many pastors in the people of God, Peter rules as his own all whom Christ also principally rules."[58]

So strong was Leo's effect on the course of ecclesiastical development that even four centuries later one of his successors applied to him the words of the Apocalypse (5: 5): "Behold, the Lion of the Tribe of Judah [*Leo de tribu Juda*] hath prevailed to open the book, and to loose the seven seals thereof."[59] The men who followed him immediately to the throne of St. Peter likewise honored his achievement and

---

[58] Serm. 4 (3) in anniv. access., c. 2; PL 54, 149f. On Leo's concept of Church-Empire relations, see especially Stockmeier, *Beurteilung*, 217: "*Keineswegs wird das Imperium von der ecclesia aufgesogen, so wenig wie letztere vom Reiche. Beide bewahren ihren Selbstand; doch existieren sie nicht in kalter Gleichgültigkeit nebeneinander, sondern in Zuordnung aufeinander.*" See also 94, 108, 170.

[59] Caspar, *Geschichte* 1, 514, a reference of Nicholas I.

developed the uneasy but splendid synthesis of tradition and discretion which he had shaped.

## (2) The Late Fifth Century

The major disputes which Leo's successors met were later stages of the same issues with which he had come to grips: the Monophysite dispute, the Henotikon controversy, and the Acacian Schism. In dealing with these issues, they brought Leo's conservative and revisionist thought to its ultimate subjection of tradition to papal discretion. They reiterated the conventional claim that they merely preserved the ancient faith handed down by the Holy Fathers: ". . . we are neither more judicious than our elders were, nor is it lawful for us to speak anew other than as the elders once learned and taught. We are not, as students and expositors of the Nicene Council, more learned than those many and great prelates, venerable men, either in wise understanding or in faithful preaching. Thus, if we all hold this doctrine in common, with a sincere mind and a true heart, peace abides; and, if we keep intact the rules which the Church received from those same Fathers, peace abides."[60] But for them, as for Leo, hierarchic order was the central element in Church government. They declared their personal unworthiness of the Roman See,[61] and Felix III implied that Rome was governed by a college rather than by one man only, when he wrote that Peter the Fuller had been deposed "by me and by those who rule the apostolic throne with me."[62] Still, neither the sense of personal inadequacy nor the yet primitive concept of collegial government mitigated Rome's claims to primacy. The bishops of Tarragona sensed the drift of Roman thought when they wrote that they sought the faith from Pope Hilary I's "apostolic mouth, seeking answers from the place whence nothing is commanded by error, nothing by presumption, but all things by pontifical deliberation."[63]

Felix III and his successors received the Council of Constantinople (381) as an authentic synod to be ranked with Nicaea and Chalcedon;[64] Chalcedon itself remained a talisman of orthodoxy, a council held "as much by the authority of the Apostolic See as by the consent of the universal Church."[65] But the bishops of Rome undeviatingly repudiated the canon which the Fathers at Constantinople and at Chalcedon

---

[60] Felix III, Tract; PL 58, 954.
[61] E.g., PL 58, 40, 971.
[62] Ep. 4; PL 58, 912.
[63] PL 58, 14f.
[64] Epp. 3, 5; PL 58, 907, 919.
[65] Felix III, ep. 15; PL 58, 975.

had approved, raising Constantinople to second place among the great sees, and asserted that throughout the entire Church only the Roman concept of hierarchic order was legitimate. In effect, they judged that councils which went against that concept lost their oecumenical character in canons on the hierarchy. As the Church was one, so must its universal order be one with Roman discipline; it was impious to violate "the divine constitutions or the decrees of the Apostolic See."[66] Councils might issue their decrees; but the touchstone of their legitimacy was consonance with Roman ecclesiology.

Three events prepared the way for a full exposition of this theory in the pontificate of Gelasius I (492-496): Acacius's consecration of a bishop of Antioch under circumstances which plainly violated the canons of Nicaea (479); the accession of Peter Mongos to the see of Alexandria; and the promulgation of the Henotikon, with the attendant result of Acacius's entering communion with Peter (482). As the secretary of Felix III (483-492), Gelasius framed the strong declarations with which Felix immediately met these events; and, on his accession, he had cause to reiterate under his own name the position which Felix had taken.[67]

He firmly declared that the whole body of the Church should follow the discipline observed "where the Lord placed the principate of the entire Church,"[68] and that "all things, as has been said, are placed within the power of the Apostolic See. And so, that in a synod which the Apostolic See has confirmed has gained force; what it has rejected, cannot have validity. It alone annuls what a synodal assembly had thought to seize upon beyond the right limits of order."[69] Charged by eastern bishops with "pride" and "arrogance," with diminishing the privileges of his see by obstinacy,[70] and, most important, with transgressing the canons,[71] he answered that his opponents could invoke canon law against him only because they were ignorant of what the canons said.[72] Not he, but his detractors, had departed "from the ancient tradition of the Church."[73] They objected that the bishop of Rome had no authority to declare Acacius excommunicate and deposed without the concurrence of a synod, or at least of the bishops of the other great sees. Indeed, they argued, the standing among the primatial sees which the Fathers

---

[66] Hilary I, epp. 1, 6; PL 58, 12f, 23.   [67] Caspar, *Geschichte* 2, 34.
[68] Ep. 9, c. 9; PL 59, 51.   [69] Tomus de anath; PL, 59, 107.
[70] PL 59, 30, 46, and (Felix III) PL 58, 961, 965.
[71] Ep. 4; PL 59, 27f.   [72] Ep. 4; PL 59, 28.
[73] Ep. 13; PL 59, 61.

at Chalcedon had acknowledged as due the bishop of Constantinople, "the pontiff of the royal city,"[74] forbade that procedure.

Gelasius rejected this argument out of hand. "The voice of Christ," he wrote, "the tradition of the elders, and the authority of the canons confirms that [Rome] may always judge the whole Church."[75] And, repeating Zosimus and Boniface I, he stated the focus of his position: "Furthermore, we do not keep silent what the whole Church throughout the world knows: that the See of St. Peter, the Apostle, has the right to loose what the sentences of any pontiffs have bound, since, though it has the right to judge of every church, no one may judge of its judgment, even as the canons allow appeals to it from any part of the world, though no one is allowed to appeal from it."[76] As for the conciliar authority adduced by his opponents, Gelasius recounted, without scrupulous historical precision, instances from the case of Athanasius onward in which Rome had overturned synodal judgments.[77] The Robber Synod showed that councils sometimes went contrary to the Scriptures, the doctrine of the Fathers, and ecclesiastical rules. Such a council could not be received by the Church, nor, especially, could the Apostolic See approve it; an unrighteous synod must be canceled out by a righteous one, as Chalcedon had countered the Robber Synod. A synod properly celebrated must not be superseded in that fashion. Rome held the authority to judge whether a synod was just or whether it required, through its innovations and pestilential error, a corrective assembly. His adversaries had quite misconstrued the order of judgment established by the canons. The ancient establishments were entirely sufficient;[78] Gelasius's action was warranted by "the series of patristic canons and manifold tradition."[79] "By what tradition of the elders do they call the Apostolic See into judgment?"[80]

Wholly repudiating the defense of Constantinople's pre-eminence on the basis of the Chalcedonian decrees, Gelasius went on to deny altogether its hierarchic primacy.[81] He was more careful than any of his predecessors to apply the adjective "apostolic" only to the Roman See. Other popes had referred to Alexandria as the see of St. Mark and to Antioch as the first see of St. Peter; Gelasius called them only the "second" and the "third" sees, entirely disregarding their apostolic founda-

---

[74] Ep. 13; PL 59, 61.
[75] Ep. 4; PL 59, 30. Cf. Caspar, *Geschichte* 2, 47.
[76] Ep. 13; PL 59, 66.    [77] *Loc.cit.*    [78] Ep. 4; PL 59, 28.
[79] Ep. 8; PL 59, 45.    [80] Ep. 4; PL 59, 28.    [81] Caspar, *Geschichte* 2, 57ff.

tion.[82] His attitude toward Constantinople was more severe. When the dispute over the twenty-eighth canon of Chalcedon began, Leo I objected that Constantinople could not be numbered among the great churches because it was not an "apostolic see." Having in effect discounted the claims even of Alexandria and Antioch to apostolicity, Gelasius carried his predecessor's argument to an extreme point. Not only, he wrote, could Constantinople not be ranked with Rome, or with the "second" and "third" sees; "according to the canons," it could not even be counted among the metropolitan churches. Indeed, so far was it from primacy that it was canonically subject to the metropolitan church of Heraclea, a small town near Constantinople mentioned in the Nicene canons.

Gelasius thus dismissed the claims advanced that, on ecclesiastical grounds, Acacius was immune from Rome's unilateral sentence of deposition. The easterners had objected that the hierarchic standing of Acacius's see prohibited his deposition by one of his primatial colleagues. Gelasius responded by repudiating the canonical basis of the objection, paradoxically, a canon of Chalcedon, and by denying Constantinople any standing other than that of a simple bishop. The eastern bishops had protested that, if Acacius were guilty of a heresy, a synod must be called to define the heresy and prescribe the proper sentence. Gelasius brushed this position aside with the crisp observation that by entering communion with Peter Mongos, Acacius had fallen into Monophysitism and consequently incurred the existing sentence of the Council of Chalcedon. One further objection remained: that Acacius, as bishop of a royal city, had primatial dignity. In refuting this argument, the same thought expressed in the twenty-eighth canon of Chalcedon, Gelasius showed more clearly than any of his predecessors the implications of the Roman concept of tradition in ecclesiastical relations with the civil power.

"We laughed," he wrote, "because they wish Acacius to gain precedence as bishop of a royal city. Did not the emperor reside many times at Ravenna, Milan, Sirmium and Trier? Did the bishops of those cities usurp to their dignities anything beyond the measure anciently ascribed to them? . . . The power of worldly rule is one thing, the allotment of ecclesiastical dignities, another; for, just as a small city does not diminish any prerogative of the government in it, neither does the im-

[82] Dvornik, *Apostolicity*, 111.

perial presence change the religious dispensation."[83] Felix III had encountered a similar argument when Acacius consecrated a bishop of Antioch, and soon after, when he disregarded Rome's excommunication of Peter Mongos, acknowledged him as true bishop, and received him into communion. Then, Acacius's defenders argued, he had acted on imperial orders. Felix and his secretary, Gelasius, protested that this evasion was admitting that the civil power might intrude into ecclesiastical affairs, and that it satisfied the will of man, but defied the will of God. He admonished Acacius to recognize the limits of his powers, to give his support to the sanctions of the Fathers and the judgments of Nicaea and Chalcedon,[84] and he urged the Emperor Zeno, most of all to submit to the priests of God in matters concerning God, learning from them rather than presuming to teach.[85] On the day of judgment, Felix wrote, God would require of bishops the Church as they received it from the Fathers;[86] and, knowing this, Acacius ought to have resisted the imperial will even to suffering martyrdom rather than acquiescing in the perversion of right.

In attempting to exclude imperial direction of Church affairs, Pope Simplicius tried a few years earlier to win his point by accepting in a conciliatory way the very hieratic concept of the imperial office which sanctioned secular intrusion. He wrote to Zeno exulting that he had "the spirit of the most faithful priest and prince."[87] But neither Felix nor Gelasius was prepared even to pay lip-service to the imperial doctrine. Gelasius epitomized their thought in two statements which became *loci classici* in mediaeval political writings. Before Christ's advent, he wrote in one treatise,[88] some men, such as Melchisedech, rightly acted as kings and priests. Among his own, Satan imitated this practice; thus, the pagan emperors were also called "*pontifices maximi*." After Christianity prevailed, kings and priests, acknowledging themselves as discrete members of Christ, the true King and Priest, accepted the division of their offices. Mindful of human frailty, Christ tempered this functional division in such a way that kingship and priesthood remained interdependent: Christian emperors required pontiffs to achieve eternal life, and pontiffs needed imperial support in temporal matters so that they might remain free of worldly care. The second passage occurs in a letter to the Emperor Anastasius. Gelasius admonished the Emperor to remem-

---

[83] Ep. 13; PL 59, 71f.
[85] Ep. 9; PL 58, 935.
[87] Ep. 14; PL 58, 51f.

[84] Ep. 1; PL 58, 895f.
[86] Ep. 1; PL 58, 898.
[88] De anath. vinc., c. 11; PL 59, 109.

ber that there were two which ruled the world, the hallowed authority of pontiffs and the royal power. In this order, the burden of the priests was the heavier since they must give account even for the kings in the Last Judgment. Although in his office he presides over the human race, the Emperor must in sacred matters submit to the bishops and await their counsel in regard to ecclesiastical affairs and to his personal salvation. He must know that he ought to submit to religious order rather than preside over it, especially inasmuch as he received his Empire by divine dispensation and as bishops obey his laws in civil matters.[89]

One interpretation of these statements holds that they assert positive and unconditional dominance of the temporal power by the ecclesiastical.[90] Corroborative evidence is gleaned from Gelasius's catalogue of the kings who were withstood by priests and prophets, from Nathan's rebuke of David to the measures of Popes Simplicius and Felix against Zeno, and from his strong assertion "that Christian princes are not used to set their own power above the decrees of the Church, and that the prince is accustomed to bow his head to bishops, not to submit them to capital judgment."[91] But it is difficult to see in Gelasius's letters and treatises any sentiment more extreme than the most definite and vigorous defense of the Church's freedom from civil control in its internal matters. His emphasis was on the correlation of two separate, but interdependent, powers; and his goal was the integrity of the Church from temporal intervention, not the positive subjection of the Roman Empire to the Church.[92]

Some elements of later hierocratic thought are surely present in Gelasius's insistence that the Emperor submit to religious counsel in matters concerning his own salvation and the welfare of the Church. But his exclusive application to ecclesiastical matters of his claims to supremacy over the temporal ruler and his acknowledgment that clergy were rightly subordinate to the Empire in civil matters show the essential duality of his thought. He asserted no constitutive power over the Emperor or the imperial office. His ultimate appeal was not to the punishment he could inflict upon a delinquent ruler, but to the spiritual welfare of the emperor himself. Most probably, Gelasius's own thoughts were expressed in a letter in which Felix III admonished Zeno to receive "the confes-

[89] Ep. 8; PL 59, 42.    [90] Ullmann, *Growth*, 20ff.    [91] Ep. 15; PL 59, 95.
[92] Caspar, *Geschichte* 2, 67-72. Cf. Ullmann, *Growth*, 23: "We need not dwell on the ingenuity with which Gelasius turned the imperial argument of the divine derivation of imperial powers into an argument with which to establish control over the emperor." See also *ibid.*, 28.

102

sion of the prince of the Apostles to whom the keys of the Kingdom were granted by the Saviour, and who also will prepare for your most Christian empire a place in Heaven with the holy angels." He described the Church personified, saying, "O, Emperor, beloved of Christ, do not allow the bond of my sanctity to be dissolved, in which multitudes of the faithful are united. Do not allow the worship of Christ, even the Only Begotten Son of God, to be transgressed, which has saved your city when it was endangered. Preserve rather the incorrupt tradition of the angels."[93] But, if the Emperor did not heed this counsel, Gelasius neither held nor claimed any coercive power over him. The choice to heed or disregard was the Emperor's; Gelasius's was to yield or suffer. As he wrote, using the words of St. Paul, " 'For I believe, I hope, I trust in Christ that neither tribulation nor distress nor the sword, nor persecution, nor life, nor death, can ever separate me from His love [Romans 8: 35].' Let persecution press on; let the laws rage. To the soldier of Christ it is more glorious to die than to conquer, and better to forfeit the rewards of the present than to loose those of the time yet to come."[94]

By emphasizing the division and the interdependence of the Church and the civil power, Gelasius's thought pointed up a critical, though conventional element in patristic ecclesiology: the exclusion of the civil power from the ecclesiastical tradition. Implicit in Leo's writings, and especially in his comments on the twenty-eighth canon of Chalcedon, this position came to classic formulation in the letters of Felix and Gelasius when imperial judgment was openly and strongly urged as a warrant for changes of the first magnitude in Church order. In the Henotikon dispute and the Acacian Schism, these two popes, and Gelasius in particular, were obliged to refute this insidious doctrine and to reaffirm that secular rule was one thing and ecclesiastical order another; that the Scriptures, the ancient tradition of the Church, and the canons, not imperial decrees, were the authentic law of the priesthood; and that God would at the last hour require them to render up His Church as they had received it from the Fathers, scarred by persecution, but with its freedom untrammeled by compromise with worldly powers, and its doctrine still the incorrupt tradition of the angels.

Though their attitude toward temporal power was largely negative

[93] Ep. 5; PL 58, 917f. I agree entirely with the interpretation in Cavallera, "Doctrina," passim.
[94] Ep. 14; PL 59, 90.

and, indeed, defensive, their ecclesiological position was vigorously assertive. (Gelasius, however, made extensive use of Roman law in his administration.)[95] Leo had synthesized the thought of his predecessors—conservative in demanding that faith and order must accord with ancient tradition, and revisionist in affirming that the body of tradition could be elaborated by acceptable customs, papal decretals, and synodal enactments according to the need of the times. The intrusion of civil power in securing Constantinople's elevation to the second place among patriarchates provoked the most precise formulation of the doctrine. He said that the preservation of ecclesiastical integrity required not only the exclusion of secular control as entirely external to the Church's fabric, but, more important, the maintenance of the hierarchic order which, according to the customary Roman interpretation, the Council of Nicaea had established and which, indeed, Christ had instituted among the Apostles. This was more than a matter of honorific precedence.

It was, to Leo's mind, a system of inferior and superior courts, corresponding with the ranks among bishops, who in their episcopal, metropolitan, or primatial synods exercised appropriate degrees of jurisdictional competence. Councils were an extraordinary, but legitimate, element in this juridical structure. But above them all was the See of St. Peter, to which appeals could go from any priest in any part of the world, to which, through Christ's commission to St. Peter, the general government of churches inalienably belonged. On the preservation of this order depended the proper judgment of cases of discipline and doctrine, and the preservation of the Church from heresy. The curtailment of any privileges in the scale weakened the entire system, destroyed the apostolic disposition, and endangered the liberty of the Church. The key to Leo's synthesis was, therefore, formalism, the understanding of tradition in juridical and administrative aspects.

The thought of Leo's successors, especially of Felix III and Gelasius, conformed to his pattern and refined some major points. Even more than Leo, they were concerned to present themselves explicitly as defenders of the canons. The strongly legalistic character of their arguments, the redundant affirmation that the canons of the Fathers authorized their actions against the greatest eastern sees, and the consistent representation of Petrine primacy in its jurisdictional quality crystallized the juridical and administrative concept of tradition and left as enduring tokens of their intensity the codifications of the Gelasian Renaissance.

[95] Jonkers, "Gelasius," 335f, 339.

It fell their lot to declare, even more vehemently than Leo, that none but the Church could teach and interpret her tradition and the laws which safeguarded it, and that, within the Church, the sign of orthodoxy in doctrine and practice, the guarantee of what was truly the ancient and universal consensus of the Fathers, was consonance with Roman ecclesiology.

$$+$$

At the end of the fifth century, a case arose which showed graphically the tension in Roman thought between the authorities of tradition and papal discretion.[96] At issue was a decree of Anastasius II regulating the ecclesiastical jurisdiction of Arles and Vienne to the detriment of Arles's claim to hold an apostolic vicariate.[97] With a penchant for unfortunate judgments, Anastasius had taken preliminary steps toward reconciling Rome with Constantinople and thus ending the Acacian Schism. For this, according to his biographer, divine providence struck him dead. Though his decision in the case of ecclesiastical jurisdiction had less dramatic consequences, it was equally ill-advised. Jealous of the primacy which, they argued, popes since Zosimus had conferred upon their see, the bishops of Arles opposed any diminution of their power. This was part of the broader contest between Arians and orthodox in Gaul and Burgundy, and Pope Symmachus found himself in the awkward diplomatic position of assuring the bishops of Arles that the ancient privileges of their church would not be infringed upon, and, at the same time, promising the bishop of Vienne that Anastasius's decree would not be rescinded.

His correspondence with the bishops of Arles is full of emphasis on the antiquity of their rights. "It is reasonable," he wrote to Caesarius, "that the holy Church of Arles enjoy her proper privileges; new presumption ought not to violate what antiquity has provided and the authority of the Fathers has confirmed."[98] To Aeonius, Caesarius's predecessor, he had declared himself moved by the argument that, under Anastasius, a wrongful decree had gone out from the Apostolic See in favor of the bishop of Vienne, contrary to the rules of church constitution

[96] Caspar, *Geschichte*, 2, 124ff.

[97] The basis of this claim was in Zosimus's dealings with Patroclus of Arles. After his conflict with Hilary of Arles, Leo I carefully avoided establishing a vicariate in Gaul. See Caspar, *Geschichte* 1, 451, and 2, 10f; Fuhrmann, "Patriarchate" (1953), 149ff.

[98] PL 62, 66.

105

and the considered judgment of the canons. He assured Aeonius that he would ordain nothing new, nothing but what the decrees of the Fathers and his predecessors prescribed for the case.[99] In a fuller exposition of his thought, he wrote to Aeonius that Anastasius had issued the objectionable decree on the ordination of bishops in consideration of the profound civil confusion prevalent in Gaul, and that under cogent necessity, Anastasius had commanded some things to be observed contrary to custom, thus transgressing the ordination of his predecessors. Symmachus commented that this action, necessity aside, was unseemly. For, following the pattern of diversity in unity set by the Trinity, all bishops shared in one priesthood, and they must honor the commands of their predecessors. Every power relating to the sacrosanct catholic religion would be infringed if all establishments of bishops, once issued, were not considered eternal; there could be no stability if bishops gave no vigor and confirmation to the acts of their predecessors. In the matter of ordinations, he therefore admonished Aeonius to preserve the ancient order, for only through reverence for antiquity could new ambitions be held in check[100] (Oct. 499; Sept. 500).

To Avitus of Vienne, however, Symmachus wrote less evasively (Oct. 501). He urged Avitus not to take umbrage at the letters he had sent Aeonius, since there were ways to set things right. Though the decree of Anastasius was issued outside the limits of the Church's custom and the ancient statutes of his predecessors, and thus could not be tolerated, it was nonetheless not to be reconsidered. Indeed, Symmachus rejoiced that Anastasius had not attempted an uncanonical act, since what is done outside the limit of the rule for a just cause does not break the rule. Only obstinacy and contempt for antiquity infringed the rule. For, although the decrees of the Fathers must be diligently observed, the rigor of the law could be relaxed for a good purpose, which would have been provided for in the law itself, if it had been foreseen. Often it would be cruel to insist on the letter of the law when its strict observance was prejudicial to the Church; laws were after all established to benefit and not to harm. On consideration of Anastasius's measure, Symmachus therefore rejoiced in the Lord that "Anastasius of blessed memory had done nothing which must be reviewed."[101]

The ambivalence—one might even say "double-dealing"—of Symmachus's policy in this case indicates the perils that tradition held for

---

[99] PL 62, 49.  [100] PL 62, 50f.  [101] PL 62, 51f.

the doctrine of papal discretion when pressed to the extreme. On one hand, the Pope claimed to preserve the decrees of the Fathers, and, in that vein, he wrote to the bishops of Arles, taking exception to Anastasius's action as contrary to the custom of the Church and the establishments of his predecessors. On the other hand, he acknowledged that the severity of the law might be relieved in a good cause, and, thus, he wrote to Avitus of Vienne that Anastasius had done nothing censurable. In either case, Symmachus brought into question the continuity of papal administrative policy, and even the steadfastness of the throne of Peter, disparaging in his letter to Arles the action of Anastasius, who had in turn abandoned the conventional policies of his predecessors; and, in his letter to Avitus, framing the more latitudinarian policy that the establishments of the Fathers could be modified according to necessity.

Symmachus's ambivalent attitude in the dispute between Arles and Vienne was an early symptom that the simple assertions that the bishop of Rome had the universal care of churches and that there was no appeal from his judgment were in themselves inadequate to indicate a clear and systematic program for papal policies. The disputes of the age had outstripped contemporary ecclesiologies in complexity and sophistication, and such dangers to the Petrine doctrine as arose among Roman thinkers derived from the primitive stage of their thought concerning all but the first elements of Petrine primacy. A doctrine adequate to meet contemporary demands would have required a firm concept of patterns of hierarchic relationships and of powers of legislation, legislative review, original and appellate jurisdiction; and it would have required above all flexibility within its clear definitions which would allow it to sacrifice the point without violating the principle.

But the formulation of such a doctrine lay six centuries and more beyond the time of Symmachus. The actions of synods and councils, emperors, eastern prelates, and even Roman bishops and clergy placed on Roman ecclesiology the demands of conservatism and of radical change; and the ecclesiology had not yet attained sufficient maturity to resolve the ensuing tensions on juridical and administrative points.

Other views prevailed in other places. The oriental bishops at Sardica excommunicated Julius I for his intervention in eastern affairs; the Illyrian bishops, encouraged by Theodosius II, repudiated the Roman vicariate in Thessaloniki; and, before Chalcedon, Dioscorus of Alexandria excommunicated Leo I, the very man who framed the Roman doctrine of tradition and discretion in its classical formulation. The Antiochenes considered their patriarch "oecumenical," "the holy pope and the patriarch of all the earth," and "the general Father of the whole Church."[102] The Armenians had their *Catholicus*; the Syriacs had theirs; the Alexandrines saw in their bishop "the holy pope and patriarch of the whole earth." Such views were not likely to bend before the thundering of the bishop of Rome, remote as he was and rendered politically impotent by the barbarian tribes which had engulfed his see. Indeed, for many easterners, the bishop of Rome had proven himself obdurately heretical. Like all other Diophysites, he had no place in the true Church.

Even among Diophysite believers, many contested the Roman stand. Boniface I's emphatic letter was addressed to bishops who were continuing a long series of efforts to throw off the papal vicariate in Thessaloniki.[103] And the thought of Athanasius and the other eastern bishops, and that of the early North African thinkers, had become highly refined. In a primitive form, the conflict between the collegiate and the monarchic concepts of Church government occurred in the dispute between Pope Stephen I and St. Cyprian. In its new array of law and privilege, it recurred in the conflict between Zosimus and Celestine I and Cyprian's successor, Aurelian of Carthage.[104] St. Augustine, a participant in the latter dispute, may well have spoken for many of his North African colleagues when he acknowledged an inconsistent development in his thought about the authority of St. Peter in the Church. He wrote that he had sometimes glossed the Petrine commission to mean that St. Peter was the rock on which the Church stood, and, at other times, applied the rock metaphor to Christ Himself. Augustine gave no solution. "Let the reader choose which of these two interpretations is the more likely to be correct."[105] Did Christ give supreme powers of

[102] Vries, *Kirchenbegriff*, 7ff, 20ff, 91ff. See Domnus of Antioch's protest against the anathema that Dioscorus of Alexandria issued against him at the Robber Synod of Ephesus. The successor of St. Mark, he said, had no right to take such a measure against him, the successor of St. Peter, who was St. Mark's teacher and the teacher and head of all the Apostles (Flemming, *Akten*, 121f).

[103] Cf. Völkers, *Studien*, 375f.

[104] See Deneffe, *Traditionsbegriff*, 50f.

[105] Retractationes, I, xx, 2; *CSEL* 36, 97f. Cf. the famous statement by St. Optatus in De Schismate Donat., 2, 3. *CSEL* 26, 36f. St. Augustine's views on tradition as an authority in the Church command a separate study. For purposes of the present general survey, I despaired both of digesting the enormous volume of scholarly literature on the subject and of reconciling the different views that St. Augustine himself presents especially in his anti-Donatist and anti-Manichaean

binding and loosing to St. Peter to hold in his own right, or did He give them to him as to the representative, though not the head, of the whole Church, and especially of all the apostles and of their successors, the bishops? After the affair of Apiarius, only a few years before his own death, Augustine could only write, "Let the reader choose."

Scattered in his writings are the broad outlines of a position apparently much like that of the early apologists. He placed little emphasis on the doctrine of apostolic succession[106] and much on the authority of councils in defining matters of faith and practice.[107] And yet his view of authority went beyond the powers of councils to the "tradition of the universal Church."[108] He held that tradition was what all churches held, not only what councils established, or what authoritative writings prescribed.[109] The authenticity of tradition was proven by the universal consensus of the Fathers, and by the practice, not of one church, but of all churches.[110] This was the meaning of his famous sentence, "I should not believe the Gospel unless the authority of the catholic Church impelled me."[111] Whatever Augustine's personal ambivalence may have been, the papal claims had weighted the choice and removed all doubt for the Synods of Carthage in 418 and 426, in which he participated.[112]

Thinkers in Rome itself could not follow the extreme claims entered on behalf of papal discretion. Popes Zosimus and Boniface I held as the basic premise of their ecclesiology that no one might appeal from or review the judgments of the Roman See. And yet, the process against Pope Symmachus at the end of the century raised the question whether the bishop of Rome, the supreme judge, might himself be

---

writings. The above remarks seem to present the gist of the Father's views on our particular theme, but a full investigation is needed. On St. Augustine's political thought, see the judicious comments in Morris, *Thought*, vol. I, 208ff. For the broad outlines of St. Augustine's concept of tradition, see the summary by Holstein in Pontificia Acad. Mariana Int., *Scriptura*, 206ff.

[106] See Molland, "Développement," 28f.

[107] De bapt. II, iii, 4-ix, 14; *CSEL* 51, 178-90.

[108] Ep. 54, 2, 3; PL 33, 201; De Baptismo, II, vii, 12; *CSEL* 51, 187.

[109] De baptismo IV, xxiv, 31; V, xxiii, 31; *CSEL* 51, 259, 289; ep. 54, 1; *CSEL* 34, 152; Contra Julianum II, 34; PL 44, 698; Holstein, *Tradition*, 19; Deneffe, *Traditionsbegriff*, 46.

[110] Contra Julianum I, 14; VI, 11; PL 44, 649, 829. See also Augustine's emphasis on universality of practice in *ibid.*, I, 13-16; PL 44, 648-51.

[111] Contra ep. fundamenti, 5; *CSEL* 25, 197.

[112] Caspar, *Geschichte* 1, 338ff.

109

judged, and, consequently, whether his sentence might be subject to revision.[113] Later, Pope Agapetus gave an affirmative answer when he reversed Boniface II's anathematization of the Anti-Pope Dioscorus as "contrary to the canons."[114]

Indeed, as Symmachus's intervention in the dispute between Arles and Vienne showed, even the Janus character of papal thought carried within itself severe tensions. One part, the emphasis on discretionary powers, looked forward to a universal hierarchic order motivated by variable judgments of the Apostolic See. The other part, reverence for tradition, looked backward to tradition as the apologists had understood it. The tensions between these two positions were all the more severe because popes used the terms proper to tradition to describe discretion. Therein lay the chance that, even for the popes themselves, the language of tradition might undermine the concept of discretion.

Factionalism within the papal court greatly influenced later thinkers through the five Symmachian forgeries, rebuttals to the synodal process that the Antipope Laurentius' partisans brought against Symmachus. Earlier popes wrote that no one could review Rome's judgments. These apocrypha extended the immunity to the pope's person. They argued that a pope, personifying the Apostolic See, could be tried only with his own assent. But, as historical proof, they gave specious case histories of Pope Marcellinus, who under persecution sacrificed to pagan gods, of Pope Liberius, who lapsed into Arianism, and of other popes, impeached but exonerated. On these "precedents," the forger insisted that only popes could deal with charges against them, either voluntarily submitting to a synod or clearing themselves by purgation; but this merely perpetuated in writing current doubts that the voice of a heretical or grossly immoral pope was the voice of Christ.

The quasi-hieratic doctrine of Byzantine rulership and the counter-ecclesiologies of North Africa and the East severely challenged the Roman concept of Church order. But, at least from Symmachus's pontificate on, it was clear that, in internal crises and in relations with western churches, members of the Roman Church itself were divided on the juridical and administrative principles of the Petrine doctrine. These challenges from within and without the Apostolic See carried vast impact in the sixth and seventh centuries.

[113] See the brilliant discussion, with a bibliographical summary, in Zimmermann, "Papstabsetzungen," I, 2ff.
[114] Liber pontificalis, Vita Agapiti, ed. Duchesne, vol. I, 287.

## CHAPTER 4

# The Byzantine Papacy: Tradition Reaffirmed

AMONG fifth-century popes, tradition gradually became the handmaid of discretion. What we have called the paradox of "universality in particularism" ran its course unchecked, and the spontaneous authority of office superseded tradition's *continuum*. With the Byzantine reconquest of Italy, the picture changed radically. Because Byzantium honored tradition, tradition resumed its pre-eminence as a category of authority in papal thought. But, as in the fifth century, the language of tradition was used to mask an utterly different reality. Unchallenged by discretion, tradition encountered fresh dangers from the civil power. The threat of temporal dominance to tradition, and indeed to all categories of authority in the Church, which Leo I and his successors had anticipated and fought against came to maturity. In the fourth and fifth centuries, the East had seen the Empire repeatedly use the language of tradition to sanction "reforms" and "corrections" of dogma; it had undermined the theory of anciently transmitted teaching with the fact of new, politically expedient formulations. In the sixth and seventh centuries, the Empire reached the height of this dogmatic virtuosity. The paradox of "assimilation through equipoise" became a matter of life and death for Byzantium; and the bishops of Rome felt fully the ebb and flow of its great struggles.

The letters of six-century popes reveal patently the effects of challenges from the Empire upon conventional Roman ecclesiology. The premises of Innocent I, Leo I, and Gelasius I recur—majestic assertions that Rome had the supreme headship of all churches. But the political force exerted upon Rome by the eastern rulers considerably sharpened the effects of eastern counter-theories; economically weak and subject to military and civil pressure from the Ostrogoths and later both from the Lombards and from the Empire, the popes could not assert the conventional doctrines in practice or even in theory. Inheriting the residual animosity of the Acacian Schism, they were precipitated into the dispute of the Three Chapters and the ensuing western schism before the middle of the century, often forced, between the conservatism

111

of the West and the revisionism of the East, to modify the conventional doctrine of Roman primacy when they did not frankly compromise it.[1] Of the two strands in papal thought, the rule of discretion lost its brilliance, and was supplanted by the older rule of tradition. But, as a commonly understood, definable authority, tradition itself was subverted by the Empire's "reforms."

## A. BEFORE THE RECONQUEST OF THE WEST

The Henotikon had left the East in the midst of religious warfare. Confusion deepened in the reign of Anastasius I, who tried from 502 onward to secure his border against Persian assault by favoring Monophysite majorities in the eastern provinces. He gradually abandoned the settlement outlined in the ineffectual Henotikon. He expelled Chalcedonian bishops and replaced them with Monophysites, and soon his policy became general for the whole Empire, not merely a *modus vivendi* with Syria. From 512 until his death six years later, Chalcedonians in Constantinople and in the western provinces rose repeatedly in armed rebellion. Anastasius's Monophysitizing failed, as thoroughly as the Henotikon, to establish religious conformity and unify the Empire. His successors, Justin and Justinian, tried new devices which included both the eastern churches and Rome.[2]

The pontificate of Hormisdas was a tranquil prelude to the ferocious storms visited on his successors as a result of these experiments. He reasserted the discretionary claims of fifth-century popes. And yet, some aspects of even his greatest triumph—when he presided with the Emperor Justin over the healing of the Acacian Schism—undermined the brilliant "Janusism" of his see. The eastern Empire had often changed its doctrines. Basiliscus had, in succession, condemned and embraced Chalcedon, and creedal changes under Zeno and Anastasius carried dogmatic virtuosity to unsuspected heights. Justin's return to Chalcedonianism was simply one more link in the long, tangled chain of variations, for all of which tradition was claimed as sanction. Moreover, Byzantine clergy put their own interpretation on the reconciliation with

[1] In his rapid survey of pre-Carolingian thought, Dr. Ullmann describes none of these modifications (Ullmann, *Growth*, esp. 31ff). On the Byzantine impact on western culture generally, see the excellent analysis in Geanakoplos, *Byzantine East*, 11ff.

[2] PL 63, 373f. On Rome's negotiations with Byzantium in the reign of Anastasius I, and on the whole course of the Henotikon dispute, see esp., Charanis, *Church*, 15ff, 56ff.

Rome, an interpretation of authority far different from Hormisdas's. The Empire's power to impose doctrinal reform and Byzantine views of authority in the Church had a critical impact on Roman thought after Byzantium conquered Italy; they cast deep shadows even over Hormisdas's assertions of the Roman doctrine. But Hormisdas did not live to see their potential fulfilled.

Unlike his successors, whom circumstances put in a defensive position, Hormisdas enjoyed considerable advantages in his negotiations both with western churches and with Byzantium. The bishops of Thrace and Illyria, abandoning the Monophysitism of the Empire, restored communion with Rome; even though the four eastern patriarchates were Monophysite, the Chalcedonians in Syria, Palestine, and especially in Constantinople itself looked to Rome for spiritual leadership against the imperial policies.

Upon Justin's accession, the position of the Roman bishop became still more favorable. The pope was potentially a powerful representative of imperial interests in Ostrogothic Italy. On another level, Justin, as an Illyrian, held to the orthodox creed himself, and, at the insistence of the people of Constantinople, he restored the faith of Chalcedon to imperial favor. Even earlier, the Monophysite emperor, Anastasius, had proposed reconciliation with Rome in the hope of quelling religious disaffection among the eastern Chalcedonians, inviting Hormisdas to participate in a new council to settle the Monophysite dispute, holding out the hope of rehabilitating Chalcedon and Leo the Great,[3] and even paying oblique lip service to the primacy of St. Peter among the Apostles.[4]

Under these circumstances, Hormisdas was able to repeat without qualification the strong statements of primacy which his predecessors, most notably Gelasius I, had made. His emphasis, however, was on the magisterial aspects of the claim. The principal ecclesiological advance for which Hormisdas was responsible is very close to the critical statement in the Decretum Gelasianum that the Roman Church was "without spot or wrinkle."[5] In reestablishing communion with separated clergy, Hormisdas required their subscription to a profession of faith which began with this article: "The first condition of salvation is to hold the rule of right faith and never to deviate from the establishments of the Fathers. The sentence can not be passed over of our Lord Jesus

---

[3] PL 63, 382.      [4] PL 63, 370.      [5] PL 59, 159.

Christ, who said, 'Thou art Peter and upon this rock I shall build my Church . . . ' and this statement is proven true by the outcome of affairs, for the catholic religion has always been preserved unspotted in the Apostolic See. Wishing in no way to be separated from this hope and faith, and following the decrees of the Fathers, we anathematize all heresies, and especially Nestorius, the heretic, who was once bishop of Constantinople. . . ."[6] This statement was Hormisdas's test for reunion, with its lofty premise of the unerring purity of the faith in the See of St. Peter, and its deliberate contrast of Rome with Constantinople by numbering among the condemned heretics Nestorius and Acacius, each specifically designated as a former bishop of the eastern capital.

The underlying elements of Hormisdas's ecclesiology seem to have been the ones his predecessors had made conventional. Hieratic doctrines of rulership did not initimidate Hormisdas; neither did he yield before counter-ecclesiologies. Ecclesiastical government belonged to bishops; for, denouncing the precipitate ordination of laymen as bishops, Hormisdas wrote that the orders of laity and episcopacy were discrete. Though laymen might please God by their lives, a long probationary period, a time of learning rather than of teaching, must necessarily precede assuming government in the Church.[7] He showed his view of other concepts of Church order when he wrote to the people of Constantinople urging them to abandon the councils and the communion of the "heretics" who acted as their ecclesiastical superiors.[8] Furthermore, Hormisdas preserved the ambivalence of tradition and discretion as developed by his predecessors. Throughout his correspondence runs the very strong thought that bishops must follow the ancient rules. The regulations of the Fathers must be on the lips and in the hearts of bishops and handed on, like the ancient law; "for, as it is written, let us tell them to our sons that they may consider them in their hearts sitting at home, walking by the way, sleeping, and rising."[9] The venerable wisdom of the Fathers, Hormisdas wrote, had designated certain ancient books as authoritative to keep each man from inclining more to his own will than to the edification of the Church. And in those canonical books, synodal precepts, and rules established by the Fathers stood the unchanging and inviolable limits of the Christian faith.[10] Still, he

[6] PL 63, 460; JL 788 (498); Caspar, *Geschichte* 2, 133ff.
[7] PL 63, 423f; JL 787 (497).
[8] PL 63, 404; JL 794 (504).
[9] PL 63, 425; JL 787 (497); Deut. 6, 7.
[10] PL 63, 492; JL 850 (554).

114

preserved the full vigor of discretionary thought; "the communion of the catholic Church" and concord with the Apostolic See were identical.[11] His predecessors, Hormisdas wrote, were uniquely ministers of the tradition of the Fathers and guardians of right faith.[12] The schism of eastern churches from Rome was due to their "obstinacy," which had cut them off from the "apostolic communion"—that is, from "the communion of St. Peter, prince of the Apostles"—and the schism could end only when the errant believers undertook obedience "to the rules of the Apostolic See."[13]

The reconciliation which Hormisdas and Justin effected did not, however, lead to a general conversion of eastern clergy to Roman ecclesiology.[14] Even the letters of John of Constantinople showed how far acceptance of Roman ecclesiology was from being an integral part of the reunion. John professed to hold the doctrine of the most holy Apostles according to the tradition of the holy Fathers, and, in token of that, to restore the name of Leo to the diptychs and add Hormisdas's name.[15] But in the very letter in which he subscribed to the anathematization of Nestorius and Acacius, each referred to as "once bishop of the city of Constantinople," and affirmed that he followed in all things the Apostolic See and preached what was decreed by it, he placed a severe qualification on his oath by one sentence: "I accept," he wrote, "the most holy churches of God—that is your elder and this new Rome —and I judge the see of the Apostle Peter and of this august city to be one."[16]

John might well rejoice at the reunion, "understanding that both churches, that of the elder and that of the new Rome, are one, and judging that there is rightly one see between them both."[17] A synod of Constantinople under Epiphanius, John's successor, could likewise without scruple take satisfaction in the peace restored between the two Romes. For no point had been sacrificed of the ecclesiology which Acacius gave practical meaning, the doctrine which asserted that Constantinople was the peer of Rome. Epiphanius could write to Hormisdas in good conscience that he wished to be united with the pope, since

[11] PL 63, 393f; JL 782 (492).
[12] PL 63, 370; JL 771 (482).
[13] PL 63, 431f; JL 777 (487), *apostolicae sedis regulis*. Cf. PL 63, 446.
[14] Cf. PL 63, 410ff.
[15] PL 63, 429.
[16] PL 63, 444. Caspar, *Geschichte* 2, 157f, 159-60.
[17] PL 63, 450.

nothing was more precious than the divine teachings which had been handed down from the disciples and Apostles of God, especially to the See of St. Peter, the chief of the Apostles;[18] for to his mind the reconciliation had not changed the proper hierarchic order of the Church. Neither John nor Epiphanius were of one mind with Hormisdas in understanding Christ's commission to St. Peter. They understood the critical verse of St. Matthew in the general fashion implicit in a letter of Syriac and Palestinian clergy to Justinian, the fashion long before grown conventional among eastern exegetes.[19]

For them, St. Peter was the representative and the first spokesman of the Church's true confession, not the first bishop of one particular see, and, in claiming that Constantinople and Rome were one see, John of Constantinople gave an important hierarchic cast to this thought. He undercut Hormisdas's ecclesiology with the premise that his see and Rome were, not equal, but identical.

Hormisdas made acceptance of conventional Roman ecclesiology a condition of reunion. John, in accepting the condition, turned it to the advantage of his see. Constantinople and Rome had been reconciled. And yet, their reconciliation was but a preliminary to a bitter dispute in which Roman ecclesiology, challenged by imperial political doctrines and Byzantine ecclesiology, could not be defended merely by repeating formulaic claims to supremacy, and in which the credit of the Roman church was shaken in the West as well as in the East.

### B. VIGILIUS AND PELAGIUS I

That dispute was the controversy about the Three Chapters, part of the aftermath of the Council of Chalcedon. The feeling among Monophysites that Chalcedon had betrayed the doctrine of St. Cyril and overturned the decrees of the Council of Ephesus (431) led to the alignment of the four eastern patriarchs against the bishop of Rome at the end of the fifth century. This period of Monophysite dominance, which began with the antecedents of the Acacian Schism, achieved its zenith under Emperor Anastasius (498-518), and ended in 518 with the Chalcedonian reaction of which Emperor Justin was patron.

Many Monophysites, however, remained unshakeably steadfast in their faith. The persistent dispute between them and the orthodox continued to be chronic and ruinously divisive throughout the first thirty years of Justinian's reign. In the sixth century religious dissent was as

[18] PL 63, 494f.          [19] PL 63, 503.

much a political concern as it was in the age of Theodosius II and Marcian; heresy and schism were still vehicles of civil disaffection, ideological warrants of revolt. In weighing matters of government, the Empire had always to consider its religious divisions, the prevalence of Diophysitism in Greece and the territories ecclesiastically subject to the see of Constantinople, the predominance of Monophysitism in Syria, Palestine, and Egypt, and the presence of both parties in every region.

Impelled by the desire to restore the universal government of the Roman Empire, Justinian had to come to terms with the Monophysites in Syria, Palestine, and Egypt before he could consider reestablishing imperial power there. On the other hand, his efforts to recover the West, and the Diophysite predominance in Byzantium itself, forced him to make common cause with the Chalcedonians. Politically unable to condemn either doctrine, Justinian was likewise unable to satisfy the adherents of either. His strongest effort to placate the Monophysites, the condemnation of the Three Chapters, estranged the Diophysites, who held that the condemnation had overturned Chalcedon, despite the contrary protestations of Justinian and the Council of Constantinople (553). The controversy abated only when the Persian Empire overran great portions of Syria and Palestine, effectively separating predominantly Monophysite lands from chiefly Diophysite.

In the West, the way for radical changes in Roman ecclesiology was prepared by Byzantium's defeat of the Ostrogothic kingdom and the subjection of the papacy to its civil and military dominance. Ostrogothic power over the papacy definitely brought Felix IV and Hormisdas's son, Silverius, to the throne of St. Peter; it almost certainly influenced intervening papal elections and the conduct of papal affairs. The deposition of Silverius and the enthronement of Vigilius by the victorious Byzantine general, Belisarius, were part of Justinian's reassertion of civil headship over Rome.[1]

There is little in the writings of Pope Vigilius issued before the year 550 to distinguish his thought on the nature of the Church from that of his predecessors.

This confidence soon failed before Justinian's bipartite design for religious accommodation of the Monophysites in the East and for the reconquest of the West. There can be little doubt that he was motivated by considerations of political necessity in his dealings with Vigilius

[1] Caspar, *Geschichte* 2, 193f, 230f; Zimmermann, "Papstabsetzungen," I, 8.

117

from 546 onward, rather than by any desire to degrade the Roman See for the advantage of Constantinople, or by explicitly Caesaropapistic doctrines.[2] Indeed, he extended many signs of unusual honor to the bishops of Rome. When Pope John I visited Constantinople in the reign of Justin, Justinian apparently inspired his uncle to ask to be crowned by the Pope, though he had already received the crown by Byzantine rite.[3] And even when relations with Vigilius were most thinly frayed, Justinian took care to preserve communion between Byzantium and the Roman See, to establish Rome's precedence over Constantinople, and to command all eastern churches to subject themselves to Roman headship.[4] Scholars are not in agreement as to whether Justinian moved under the pressures of circumstance from honoring Roman precedence to regarding the authority of oecumenical synods as supreme,[5] and finally to Cesaropapism,[6] or whether he honored Rome's pre-eminence sometimes merely by outward signs.[7]

But Justinian's political goals led him to extreme measures, which finally gained Vigilius's subscription to the decrees of the Fifth Oecumenical Council. When he first arrived in Constantinople (547), the Pope stood firmly by his refusal to condemn the Three Chapters; to Justinian's representatives, he defiantly said, "Although you hold me captive, you cannot make St. Peter the Apostle captive."[8] But Vigilius's severe illness and the acts of intrigue and violence against him and his supporters led to numerous changes in his attitude.[9]

Within one year, he had approved the imperial policy. The reaction against his Iudicatum, condemning the Chapters, and the ensuing rise of Neo-Chalcedonianism[10] showed how gravely Vigilius had jeopardized

---

[2] Cf. Caspar, *Geschichte* 2, 214ff. Dr. Ullmann gives an excellent interpretation of Justinian as Caesaropapist (*Growth*, 31ff). On the whole question of Caesaropapism, see the incisive "reconsideration" in Geanakoplos, *Byzantine East*, 55ff.

[3] Batiffol, "L'Empereur," 210.

[4] Ensslin, "Justinian I," 114ff.

[5] His decree on the *privilegium fori* curtailed that ancient clerical immunity by recognizing as legitimate the trial of clergy by imperial courts, although he forbade the execution of civil punishment until the condemned clerics had been degraded by their bishops (Beck, *Pastoral Care*, 63). And it is safe to assume that, in matters concerning Roman precedence, he likewise inclined to modify the rule without breaking it.

[6] Batiffol, "L'Empereur," 203ff, 221, 261.

[7] Ensslin, "Justinian I," 127. Dr. Ullmann argues cogently for an inflexible Caesaropapism (*Growth*, 33f).

[8] PL 69, 115.

[9] Caspar, *Geschichte* 2, 234ff.      [10] Galtier, "L'Occident," 56f.

the credit of Hormisdas's axiom that "the catholic religion has always been preserved unspotted in the Apostolic See." From the year 550 onward, he went to great pains to prove that his alternating rejections and approvals of condemnation did not violate the decrees of Chalcedon or the judgments of his predecessors, especially Leo I. "We have done nothing," he wrote in 550, "contrary to the faith and the preaching of the four venerable synods." Indeed, he had on all counts resisted the adversaries of the four synods and Pope Leo. His repudiation of the "blasphemies" of Theodore of Mopsuestia, and of his person, of the letter to Maris ascribed to Ibas, and of those writings of Theodoret opposed to the right faith and to the Twelve Chapters of St. Cyril was in harmony with the definition of Chalcedon, which was, in turn, a confirmation of the faith of the three earlier councils. In his repudiation, he claimed to have preserved inviolate, in similar continuity, the establishments of his predecessors and of the four great councils.[11] In his Encyclical (552), Vigilius described his retraction of the condemnation, and his admonition to Justinian that the policy which had scandalized "bishops of the Latin tongue" be submitted to a synod of Latins and easterners, or at least that the sense of the western clergy be taken by correspondence. He threatened that, if this were not done, clergy in favor of the imperial policy would be suspended from communion with the See of St. Peter. He affirmed that he wished only to hold and to defend the faith which had been handed down by the Apostles and guarded inviolably by their successors, and that Christ had conferred upon St. Peter the office of preserving the Church from the ferocity of error. After a full profession of faith, he concluded with the assertion that disapproval of condemnation accorded with the faith handed down by the Apostles and affirmed by the four great councils.[12] The Constitutum with which he actually retracted the condemnation of the Chapters states the same assertions that Vigilius was upholding the apostolic tradition and opposing innovation.

Throughout all his apologetic letters runs the theme that Vigilius had stood by the faith handed down by the Apostles and inviolably preserved the decrees of the oecumenical councils, by the judgments of his predecessors, and by the writings "of the other Fathers whom the pontiffs of the Apostolic See received and followed," and that he had

[11] PL 69, 51f; JL 924 (604).

[12] PL 69, 53f, 56ff; JL 931 (610). On Origenistic Christology at the Council of 553, see Grillmeier, *Christ*, 292.

119

condemned by apostolic authority those who worked against the true faith.[13]

Finally, in 553, he was brought to acknowledge the inconsistency of his declarations. He had first rejected, then accepted, and latterly rejected the condemnation. Now, he had confirmed the decrees of the Council of Constantinople, and moreover declared null all writings published by him or by other men in defense of the Three Chapters. In this last statement, he vindicated his condemnation of men whom Chalcedon had received as orthodox with a telling reference to St. Augustine: "The reason of wisdom demands in every affair," he wrote, "that something under investigation be reconsidered unashamedly when elements which were omitted from the beginning are lately found through zeal for truth and brought forth in public. How much more suitable is it to observe the same order in ecclesiastical disputes? Especially since it is clear that our Fathers, and most of all the most blessed Augustine, who was illustrious in [the interpretation of] divine scriptures, a master of Roman eloquence, reconsidered his own writings, corrected his statements, and added what he had omitted and then found." Vigilius wrote that, inspired by these examples, he had advanced his investigations in the controversy of the Three Chapters, and concluded that the writings of Theodore were contrary to the right faith and to the doctrines of the holy Fathers, and that the Fathers themselves had written against him, leaving the judgment of his treatises to the learning of the general Church. With similar discoveries about Theodoret and the letter to Maris, Vigilius reconsidered his earlier defense of the Three Chapters, withdrew it, and declared that it was most clear that the holy Fathers, and most of all the Council of Chalcedon, required absolute repudiation of the "blasphemies" listed in the Three Chapters.[14]

Vigilius thus introduced not only grave suspicion of Roman constancy, but the first explicit statement of a doctrine which allowed indefinite review of disputed points, the overthrow as heretical of what had been earlier considered orthodox, and the total confusion of any doctrine of undeviating continuity in the apostolic tradition. Pelagius I, who was his companion in Constantinople, and whom Justinian selected as Vigilius's successor, inherited both the suspicion of Rome's orthodoxy which Vigilius had engendered and the apologetic doctrine of indefinite review and correction.[15]

[13] PL 69, 41f; JL 925 (605).       [14] PL 69, 124; JL 936 (615).
[15] Caspar, *Geschichte* 2, 291ff.

In Vigilius's pontificate, Pelagius had defended the Three Chapters, and in view of his later acceptance of their condemnation, he was subject to the same charge of inconstancy with which the Neo-Chalcedonians had taxed Vigilius. The burden of his apology was the same as that of his predecessor. He recalled that St. Paul had reproved St. Peter to his face, and that St. Cyprian had considered that apostolic reprimand an example of the harmony and patience which should bind the episcopal college together. To err was but natural to human infirmity; correction was effected by divine grace. Not only he, but the bishops of the whole Orient, of all Illyria, and of all Africa had cast aside the shadows of their former ignorance to enter the gleaming light of truth. Those who reproved him for having corrected his error proved themselves ignorant of the rules of the Fathers, ecclesiastical custom, and the canonical Scriptures, all of which command that those in error correct themselves; and indeed punishment was intended for those who refused correction, rather than for those who undertook it. Like Vigilius, he invoked the example of Augustine, "that evangelical man who, enlightened by divine grace, corrected himself, not in one meaning, or in one work, but in nearly all of his books."[16]

As evidence of his personal orthodoxy, Pelagius issued letters, including an encyclical "to the whole people of God," in which he paid exaggerated tributes to Leo I,[17] and anathematized those who deviated from the Chalcedonian decrees "in one syllable, or in one word, or in understanding."[18] This was the burden of his personal vindication.

In defending his official integrity, Pelagius followed similar lines, shifting his emphasis, however, from the rightness of correcting previous error to the universal correction expressed in the condemnation of the Three Chapters. He directed this argument particularly against the dissidents in Gaul;[19] the emphasis of his remarks was not that Rome preserved supremely the essence of the Church's universality, but rather that Rome's condemnation of the Three Chapters represented the consensus of the apostolic churches. Again, in his admonition to schismatics in Tuscany, he asserted that, by repudiating the Council of Constantinople and thus by showing contempt for the Apostolic See, they had divided themselves from the universal Church. In an abstraction of a statement by St. Augustine, Pelagius argued that the foundation

---

[16] Gasso-Batlle, no. 19, 55ff. Cf. no. 80, 196f.
[17] *Ibid.*, no. 7, 21f; *ibid.*, no. 11, 36-40.
[18] *Ibid.*, no. 3, 6f.          [19] *Ibid.*, no. 19, 60.

of the Church abided in the apostolic sees (which he did not name), and that whoever separated himself from the authority and communion of the bishops of those sees was in schism. Pelagius maintained that, by refusing to name him in the sacred mysteries, the Tuscan bishops had separated themselves from the communion of the whole world, since in him, unworthy as he was, abided the strength of the Apostolic See, exercised with no deviation from the holy Fathers.[20] He returned repeatedly to the vindication of his position by reference to the fabricated sentence of St. Augustine, which appears in several forms, taking advantage of the rare intercommunion of the five great patriarchates in his day to reenforce the position of his own see. Schism from one of the apostolic sees was schism from them all, separation from the universal body of the faithful.[21]

Indeed, he reproduced a "conciliarist" citation from Cyprian when he wrote to a schismatic bishop: "Has the truth of the catholic mother [the Church] failed you, who are set in the highest rank of the priesthood to such a degree that you do not at once see that you are schismatic, since you have withdrawn from the apostolic sees? Established to preach to the peoples, have you not read that the Church was established by Christ, our God, upon the prince of the Apostles, and so its foundation, so that the gates of Hell cannot prevail against it? But if you have read it, where did you believe the Church to be apart from him in whom, one man, are all the apostolic sees, on which equally with him who had received the keys, the powers of binding and loosing was bestowed? Therefore, what He was to give first to one, He also gave to all, so that, according to the exposition of that sentence by the martyr St. Cyprian, the Church might be shown to be one."[22]

Tacitly reversing the judgment Pope Stephen I had issued against St. Cyprian three centuries earlier, Pelagius argued that priests who divided themselves from the members of Christ lost their sacramental powers. "But the man who is divided from the inmost parts of the Church and separated from the apostolic sees desecrates, rather than consecrates," he wrote. "Inasmuch as they are not one in unity, inasmuch as they wish to be apart, inasmuch as they have not the Spirit, they cannot have the Body, the Sacrifice of Christ."[23] The efforts of the "schismatics" in the provincial synods of northern Italy to overturn the Council of Constantinople was grossly irregular, for "a particular synod has not

[20] *Ibid.*, no. 10, 31-34.  [21] *Ibid.*, no. 35, 95ff.  [22] *Ibid.*, no. 39, 111f.
[23] *Ibid.*, no. 24, 73, 75f; no. 35, 96-99.

been allowed and will never be allowed to gather for the purpose of judging a general synod." Their repudiation of the Great Council merely confirmed their schism from the universal Church and from the apostolic sees.[24]

Too little of Pelagius's intellectual predilections is known for modern scholars to understand fully the principles of his thought. In view of his extraordinary departure from conventional Roman ecclesiology, it may, however, be an important clue that his letters contain six explicit citations of St. Cyprian, and that his view on the indelibility of priestly orders and on the concordance of apostolic sees correspond with the judgments of that bishop of Carthage, rather than with those of the bishop of Rome who condemned Cyprian as Antichrist. The enormous dangers of multiple schism in the West, added to the always complex difficulties of relations with the eastern churches, placed on Pelagius the heavy burden of advancing ecclesiological doctrines which would both preserve the dignity of his see and accommodate the objections of the schismatics, doctrines which would provide a basis for the reestablishment of communion between them and the See of St. Peter. Pelagius's solution was the collegiate doctrine of the African apologists, a doctrine which, given the momentary concord of the five patriarchates, set a difficult task for the schismatics: to prove that their position, contrary to the judgment of a great council and of all the major sees of Christendom, represented the true faith.

His church in poverty,[25] his personal orthodoxy doubted, his official actions repudiated, Pelagius turned to the civil power for support. With brutal incitements to repression, he declared that the canonical Scriptures and the rules of the Fathers taught that the civil powers must put down the evil of schism,[26] and crush those obstinate and insolent men who could not be won back to communion with the apostolic sees.[27] The ferocity of these appeals reflects no credit upon the spirit with which Pelagius waged his difficult struggle for ecclesiastical unity; but it does indicate the intransigence of the clergy whom he considered schismatics, and who, in turn, considered him heretical.

In Pelagius's thought, the proud assertions of Hormisdas and of Vigilius in the early years of his pontificate retreated before the challenge of healing a graver schism than the West had ever known. The axiom that the true faith had always abided unsullied in the Roman

---

[24] *Ibid.*, no. 59, 155f.     [25] *Ibid.*, no. 94, 223f.     [26] *Ibid.*, no. 52, 136f.
[27] *Ibid.*, no. 59, 158. Cf. 159f, 172f.

See, and the Roman claims of juridical primacy alike had come under determined attack along with their very basis, the Roman concept of Petrine primacy. Pelagius discarded the exclusive application of the term "apostolic see" to Rome, which appeared most notably in the correspondence of Gelasius I, and appealed to a consensus of apostolic sees in whose harmony abided the very foundation of the Church. His efforts toward religious comprehension enjoyed indifferent success; the schism in northern Italy continued into the seventh century. But the new cast of Roman ecclesiology which he advanced, together with the doctrine of indefinite review and correction which he shared with Vigilius, set men thinking about the nature of Church government in unfamiliar ways long after the churches of Milan, Ravenna, and Aquileia had reestablished communion with the See of St. Peter.

## C. GREGORY THE GREAT

The profound effects of these new elements in Roman thought became apparent in the writings of Gregory the Great. Among the severest difficulties Gregory met, was the task which Vigilius and Pelagius I had undertaken but left incomplete: the reconciliation of Rome and the Neo-Chalcedonians of the West. Schism persisted in Gaul and in northern Italy, and many of Gregory's letters, like those of Pelagius I, contain earnest apologies for Roman orthodoxy. But, since the schism had hardened over half a century and since Italy's Lombard conquerors had joined the schismatics, Gregory could have entertained only a slight, if earnest, hope of reunion.

The lines of his defense were on balance the same which Pelagius had used. In a letter to the eastern patriarchs, he wrote that he venerated the five oecumenical councils, including the Council of Constantinople (553), repudiating those whom they repudiated, embracing those whom they revered, "since as they were established by universal consent, whoever presumes to release those whom they bound, or to bind those whom they loosed destroys, not the councils, but himself."[1] In the letters composed for negotiation with the schismatics, Gregory diplomatically neglected to rank Justinian's Council with the first four oecumenical councils. Still, he steadfastly defended the condemnation of the Three Chapters on the grounds that the universal Church and especially all the patriarchs had approved their condemnation. Repeatedly, he affirmed that nothing contrary to Chalcedon

[1] Reg. I, 24; MGH I, 36.

had been done in the time of "Justinian of pious memory," and that he received "the four synods of the holy universal Church as the four books of Holy Gospel."[2]

To the Frankish queen, Brunhilda, he wrote in this tenor, attesting his veneration for Chalcedon. His detractors, he said, were deluded by their own ignorance, shunning by malice, not by reason, the whole Church and the four eastern patriarchs, and thus separating themselves from the universal Church.[3] He was disturbed to find that Greek codices of Chalcedon and Ephesus had been falsified, and that the Roman transcriptions of Chalcedon were "much more accurate" than the Greek.[4] For the Ephesene records, he suggested a collation of texts with codices in Alexandria and Antioch.[5] But there was no question of Christendom's division on a matter of faith. Condemning the Three Chapters, the eastern churches followed the faith and doctrine of Leo I; with Rome, they guarded and revered the holy synod of Chalcedon and considered no one a true bishop who did not accept it. Indeed, whenever men were ordained in the four principal sees of the East, they sent letters to their colleagues professing their fidelity to Chalcedon and the other general synods, and it was clear that any synod later acknowledged to be general would hold its title by virtue of adherence to Chalcedon's honor and authority.[6] When the Lombard queen, Theodelinda, was won to the side of the schismatics, Gregory wrote that she had suspended herself from the communion of catholic unity, giving ear to ignorant and irresponsible men. Professing his reverence for the four first councils, "most of all, however, for Chalcedon," he admonished her to have no further doubt concerning the Church of St. Peter, prince of the Apostles.[7] Theodelinda's doubts lingered; and, in the next nine years, Gregory had to repeat twice his assurance that the faith of Chalcedon had not been vexed in Justinian's day, and that the Apostolic See remained faithful to the *Tome* of Leo and to the "four holy synods."[8] His letters to Bishop Constantius of Milan, whose see had remained in internal schism since the early days of the controversy over the Three Chapters, and to the clergy and people of Ravenna, who were similarly afflicted, repeated the points that the honor of Chalcedon had not been impaired by Justinian's council, that, indeed, the universal

---

[2] Reg. III, 10; MGH I, 170.  [3] Reg. VIII, 4; MGH II, 7.
[4] Reg. VI, 14; MGH I, 395.  [5] Reg. IX, 135; MGH II, 134.
[6] Reg. IX, 147; MGH II, 144f.  [7] Reg. IV, 33; MGH I, 268f.
[8] Reg. IV, 4; XIV, 12; MGH I, 236; II, 431.

Church, in condemning the Three Chapters, had remained true to Chalcedon, and that to repudiate Rome's condemnation of the Chapters was to reject the sentence of the universal Church, and thus to withdraw from the orthodox communion.[9]

Though he appealed to the concurrence of the patriarchs, Gregory did not describe that agreement in Pelagius's terms, as the consensus of apostolic sees. To a Greek bishop, he once wrote of "the holy synods which the apostolic Church venerates,"[10] "apostolic" being apparently interchangeable with "universal." He acknowledged Alexandria and Antioch as "apostolic sees," together with his own Church. But the emphasis of his thought was not so predominantly on the apostolate as upon the universality of belief.

+

Behind Gregory's defense of Rome's condemnation of the Three Chapters lay the broader premises of his ecclesiology, and particularly his evident conviction that true faith and order were proven by universal consensus, as manifested in the agreement of the patriarchates. The nature of the western schism prevented him, as it had prevented Vigilius and Pelagius, from expecting that the work of conciliation would be effectively served by repeating the thought or the words of Hormisdas's axiom. Invoking the collective testimony of apostolic sees, Pelagius I had taken up one alternate test of orthodoxy proposed by the apologists. Advancing the doctrine of universality, Gregory adopted another.

Tradition was the central element of his thought, though strangely enough he never used the word in its ecclesiological sense. He strongly maintained that living bishops were under an absolute obligation to leave to posterity the special institution of synodal assembly which they had received from the Fathers,[11] and he found it of great significance that, despite linguistic differences, the doctrine of Alexandria was like in spirit to that of the Latin Fathers. This latitudinarianism is suggested by his attitude toward ritual practices.[12] Unlike Innocent I and John II, Gregory did not include ritual practices of local ceremonials in the body of what the Apostles handed down to the whole Church. In a famous letter to St. Augustine of Canterbury, the authenticity of which

9 Reg. IV, 3, 37; VI, 2; MGH I, 235, 272f, 381f.
10 Reg. XI, 55; MGH II, 330.  11 Reg. IX, 218; MGH II, 209.
12 Reg. X, 21; MGH II, 257.

126

has been disputed and defended,[13] Gregory (or pseudo-Gregory) came to grips with the problem of liturgical diversity. Augustine asked how differences had come about in customary observances, and especially in the order of masses as celebrated in Rome and in Gaul. Gregory answered that the Roman Church kept the observance in which it had been nourished, but he added that Augustine might find things pleasing to God in the Gallic services or in the observances of other churches, and he urged him to adopt for the service of the newly established English church whatever he could collect from many churches. For, he wrote, the observances were not respected for the place from which they came; but the places were honored for their good observance. "Choose, therefore, from the several churches the things that are pious, religious, and right, and set them as custom, collected as though in a packet, before the minds of the Angles."[14]

Much the same thought appears in an indisputably genuine letter. Gregory answered in the same tenor when taxed with the allegation that the liturgy of Rome followed that of Constantinople. Responsible for changes in the Roman service, Gregory affirmed that he had in some respects "cut off the custom which had been transmitted here by the Greeks," and that on the most obvious point which the two liturgies had in common, the singing of the Kyrie, Roman practice differed from Greek. As the prayer of consecration, the Greeks used the composition of a scholar; the Romans, "the same tradition which Our Redeemer composed over His Body and Blood." The charge of imitation was misplaced, since Gregory had "repaired" former Roman practices or introduced new and useful ones which imitated no others, and especially since Constantinople was subordinate to the Apostolic See. Gregory did not condemn the liturgical variations of Constantinople from Roman practice; he himself introduced innovations into the Roman liturgy which departed both from the earlier Roman order and from the orders of other churches; and, finally, he concluded his remarks with a comment much like that supposedly addressed to St. Augustine: "I am prepared to imitate even my subordinates to whom I forbid what

[13] It was accepted as genuine at least from the early eighth century onwards. For a review of current scholarly opinion, see G. Constable, "The Treatise 'Hortatur nos' and Accompanying Canonical Texts on the Performance of Pastoral Work by Monks," *Speculum Historiale* (ed. Clemens Bauer, *et al.*, Munich, 1964/5), 570, n. 25. See also Wallace-Hadrill, "Rome," 523ff, where the "greater part" of the letter is accepted as "authentic."

[14] Reg. XI, 56 a; MGH II, 334.

is wrong. For the man is stupid who thinks himself too exalted to learn things he sees to be good."[15]

The essence of Christian belief—what other authors called "tradition"—was, for Gregory, the faith itself, and his concept of the faith, as well as his latitudinarian attitude towards ritual, was influenced by his keen sensitivity to historical development within the Church. His tripartite division of history into the ages before the Law, after the Law, and under Grace, to be terminated by the end of all things,[16] was an integral part of the exegetical method by which he won a distinguished place among mediaeval thinkers. "For first," he wrote, "we place the foundations of history, and then by allegorical meaning we raise the fabric of the mind to the arch of the faith. Finally, through the grace of morality, we cover the building as though with the finishing color." He held that an interpreter who neglected "the words of history" in their literal meaning hid the light of truth which had been given him;[17] and he applied this principle with good effect in his own consideration of the election of the Jews as God's chosen people, their fall through blind adherence to empty forms, and their supplanting by the Gentiles.[18]

The elaboration of religious knowledge itself followed a tripartite historical development. Gregory expressed his thought on the spiritual development of the human race in a sermon on the book of Ezekiel, with a sense of progression much like that which Vincent of Lérins stated in his famous description of legitimate growth in the tradition of the Church. The holy Fathers, Gregory wrote, who lived before the Law knew God, obeyed His commands, lived pure lives and often, in seeing angels, won the palm of contemplation. After the Law had been given, however, the Hebrews were also schooled in the Ten Commandments, but they still lacked knowledge of the Trinity. "When Grace came on through the New Testament, the whole faithful people knew that the Trinity was one God and completed the virtue of the Decalogue in knowledge of Him."

As time passed, therefore, the spiritual Fathers' knowledge increased. "Moses was more learned in knowledge of Omnipotent God than Abraham; the prophets, more than Moses; the Apostles, more than the prophets. . . . The man, therefore, who remembers to mediate in the

[15] Reg. IX, 26; MGH II, 59f.

[16] Reg. V, 44; MGH I, 341, and below, n. 19.

[17] Reg. V, 53 a, cc. 3, 4; MGH I, 356.

[18] Cf. Moralia II, xxiv, 55, 56, 57; XXVII, xliii, 75, Homil. in Ev. I, iii, 1; PL 75, 583; PL 76, 441, 1086.

law is proven to understand more than all who teach him and more than the elders, for he shows that he has received more divine knowledge than Moses. But how are we to show that the holy Apostles were more learned than the prophets? Truth says with certainty, 'Many kings and prophets have wished to see what you see, and to hear what you hear, but they have not.' They knew more of divine knowledge than the prophets, therefore, since they saw physically what they [the prophets] had only heard in the spirit. . . . For the more closely the world is led to its end, the more widely is the approach to eternal knowledge opened to us. . . ."[19]

Gregory knew that, simultaneously with the growth of doctrinal knowledge, powerful developments had occurred in the institutions of the Church. His admission of the liturgical orders of other churches as legitimate indicates an apparent conviction that, though the spiritual development of authentic belief might have advanced uniformly, the historical elaboration of observances and offices in the visible Church had progressed unevenly in different places. But what were the checks on legitimate growth, the signs of authentic development, the safeguards of unity?

Jealous of the prerogatives of his see, Gregory once wrote that he was readier to die than to allow the Church of St. Peter to be dishonored in his day;[20] he was mindful of any injury to himself or to his predecessor.[21] As governor of the Apostolic See in St. Peter's stead, he was forced to lead the Church in general warfare against the Devil.[22] He held the Roman convention that the higher God had raised the Apostolic See above other churches, the more carefully Rome was obliged to oversee the consecration of their bishops,[23] and, despite his own liturgical reforms, he did not modify the statement of African bishops that Rome preserved the practices, particularly the form of ordination to the priesthood, which St. Peter had established.[24] What the Apostolic See confirmed never lacked force.[25] And Gregory was careful to assert the privileges of Rome in his legatine commission and in the "incardination" of clergy,[26] the translation of priests or bishops from the churches in which they were ordained to a vacancy in another church, the institutional origin of "cardinal" clergy.[27] Over synods too, Rome

---

[19] Homil. in Ezech. II, iv, 10-12; PL 76, 979ff.

[20] Reg. V, 6; MGH I, 286.     [21] Reg. II, 50; MGH I, 154.

[22] Reg. II, 46; MGH I, 146.     [23] Reg. III, 30; MGH I, 188.

[24] Reg. I, 75; MGH I, 95.     [25] Reg. IX, 216; MGH II, 204.

[26] E.g., Reg. I, 1; MGH I, 1f.     [27] Kuttner, "Cardinalis," 132ff, 142f.

held precedence; Gregory maintained that their acts had no force without the authority and consent of the Apostolic See.[28]

In the thought of fourth- and fifth-century popes, these powers had represented Roman supremacy as the cohesive element in Church order. Innocent I, Leo the Great, and Gelasius I, most notably, conceived the universal Church as an official hierarchy, bound together by the exercise of Rome's ultimate, general, and discretionary authority. Gregory preserved the claims of precedence, but, in his thought, they lost their quality of administrative, or juridical, cohesiveness. With Roman precedence accepted only in ceremonial terms in the East and flatly denied by the Neo-Chalcedonians in the West, Gregory saw the cohesive element of the Church not in administrative hierarchy, but in the virtue of humility.

Humility, he wrote, was the "mother and guardian of virtues," through which the unity of the universal Church was preserved.[29] His thought about the position of St. Peter in the Church, and thus of papal precedence, was profoundly influenced by this emphasis. In commenting on the dispute between Sts. Peter and Paul over the circumcision of Gentile converts, Gregory swept away as false the mitigating thought that when he wrote that he withstood Peter to his face, St. Paul referred to a namesake of the Apostle. Paul had indeed, Gregory wrote, described Peter as "reprehensible" and since, in his letters, Peter said that Paul was to be admired, Gregory inferred that St. Peter himself approved the censure. The man who was first in the apostolate was also first in humility. In punishing the wicked, as, for example, in striking Ananias and Sapphira dead with a word, Peter showed what great power he had over others. In reversing his opposition to the reception of the Gentiles, and particularly, in receiving the centurion Cornelius, Peter showed the moderation with which the faithful must be dealt. For, although "Peter had received the power of the kingdom of Heaven, so that whatever he bound or loosed on earth were bound or loosed in Heaven, he had walked on the sea, he cured the sick by his shadow, killed sinners with a word, and raised the dead by a prayer," he reasoned with the faithful, and even accepted reproof from them. In this attitude, Peter set a pattern for all bishops: "If the shepherd of the Church, the prince of the Apostles, who exceedingly performed signs and miracles, did not disdain humbly to defend himself in the case

[28] Reg. IX, 156; MGH II, 158.
[29] Reg. II, 52; MGH I, 156.

of his rebuke, how much more ought we sinners, when we are censured for some reason, to pacify our accusers with an humble defense?"[30]

Gregory's treatise on *Pastoral Rule* is in a sense an essay on humility as the unifying element of the Church. Not once did Gregory discuss, in that treatise on episcopal government, hierarchic relationships, canonical obligations, or any legal aspect of Church administration. "Our ancient Fathers," he wrote, "are recorded to have been shepherds of flocks, not kings of men."[31] In the *Pastoral Rule*, as in other works, Gregory held that St. Peter was supreme in the Church in the struggle with sin, and in the exercise of his spiritual authority, but that among the righteous he honored the rule of common equality. Bishops must not vaunt themselves on their office: they are, by nature, like other men, though they must preserve the honor of the episcopacy by not yielding to fleshly lust and by avoiding every other pursuit that would degrade their office in the eyes of their people.[32] Gregory numbered doctrinal learning among the qualifications for the episcopacy. For, after the prophets, the Apostles came to instruct the Church, and after them the Fathers, including contemporary expositors of the Scriptures,[33] with whose erudition the Church strengthened its unity.[34] But learning was insufficient. The bishops must teach; by preaching, they must take the Church to the untutored[35] and, above all, reprove the sinful.[36] They must exemplify in their conduct the doctrine they preach,[37] consoling the widowed and the desolate, and comforting those impaired in earthly estate.[38]

When Gregory wrote of the Fathers in the *Pastoral Rule*, he referred not to the growing body of canons and regulations, but to the pattern of life recommended by the example of earlier saints. The bishop was to contemplate incessantly the lives of the elders, for he could keep within the proper limits of order by following in their footsteps and checking wrongful thoughts.[39] In Church administration, the bishop must unite with his spiritual sons in the concord of love so as to prove himself their

[30] Reg. I, 24; XI, 27; MGH I, 34; II, 293f. Reg. Past. I, 6; PL 77, 19f; Homil. in Ezech. II, vi, 9f; PL 76, 1002f.
[31] II, 6; PL 77, 34.      [32] II, 6; PL 77, 35.
[33] Moralia XXVII, viii, 13f; PL 76, 405f.
[34] Reg. VIII, 2; MGH II, 3.      [35] Reg. Past. II, 11; PL 77, 49.
[36] Reg. I, 24, 24a; MGH I, 32, 37. Reg. Past. I, 5; PL 77, 18f.
[37] Reg. Past. I, 2; PL 77, 15f.      [38] Reg. I, 13; MGH I, 13.
[39] Reg. Past. II, 2; PL 77, 27f; Reg. I, 24; MGH I, 29f.

131

father in deed as well as in name;[40] all bishops of the universal Church were like the stars of Heaven, shining by life and word among the sins and errors of men as though in the shades of night.[41]

Bound together by humility, their offices defined in terms of moral conduct, bishops were still "princes," the rulers of the Church, who were called "kings" and "consuls."[42] But even in their hierarchical relations, they were ranked by virtue. As Gregory wrote of North African bishops, "Command the council of catholic bishops to be admonished not to make a man primate by virtue of official precedence, disregarding the merits of [his] life, since, with God, the action of the better life is tested, not the choicer rank."[43]

Gregory was much concerned with matters of hierarchic order, and with the canons. His letters reveal fastidious attention to canonical rule, and, in negotiations with the Franks, he repeatedly insisted that synods be held to uproot clerical abuses. "The man who does not know to obey the holy canons," he wrote, "is unworthy either to minister or to take communion at the holy altars."[44] And in his dispute with John the Faster, he wrote to that Bishop, "If you do not keep the canons, and if you wish to overturn the statutes of the elders, I do not know who you are."[45]

But the canons held their authority from a source other than the administrative authority of the bodies which had framed them, indeed, from the very source of unity in the faith: from Christ, whose will was testified by the consent of the universal Church. In his defense against the Neo-Chalcedonians, Gregory, therefore, invoked the fundamental principle of his ecclesiology. Though Gregory cherished the precedence of his see, he did not judge its pre-eminence, absolute in administrative and juridical offices, as the unifying element of the entire Church. His emphasis on the Petrine commission in the conventional Roman sense was qualified by the eastern understanding that the rock upon which the Church was built was not St. Peter, but Christ Himself.[46] In his mind, the oecumenical councils held a similar position —"for on them as on a four-square stone, the structure of the holy faith rises"—"because they have been established by universal consent."[47]

[40] Reg. II, 47; MGH I, 148.     [41] Reg. V, 44; MGH I, 340.
[42] Moralia IV, xxxi, 61f; PL 75, 670f.     [43] Reg. I, 72; MGH I, 92.
[44] Reg. III, 7; MGH I, 168.     [45] Reg. III, 52; MGH I, 209.
[46] Reg. IX, 135; MGH II, 133.
[47] Reg. I, 24; MGH I, 36. See above, pp. 59f, 93ff.

Like articles of doctrine, some matters of discipline—as, for example, prohibition of the "most damnable depravity" of simony[48]—were binding on all believers because they had been defined by the "holy universal Church." Indeed, this universality of common belief and special points of discipline distinguished the Church from heretics, who, not sharing in the Church's unity, were divided against one another by their depraved doctrines.[49]

The great popes of the fifth century had argued vehemently that the canons of the Council of Nicaea and of other eminent synods confirmed Rome's administrative headship of all churches, and they had entered this assertion particularly against the claims of the eastern patriarchates to autonomy. Gregory, however, advanced no such doctrines, and towards the great eastern sees, he maintained a "collegiate" rather than a "monarchic" policy.

He stated his thought on hierarchic questions concisely when he wrote, "far be it from me that I should infringe what the elders have established for my fellow bishops in any church, for I do myself injury if I confound the rights of my brethren."[50] The rights of the other patriarchates were very great; Gregory eschewed any effort to curtail them to enhance the glory of his own see. In striking contrast with Leo I's magisterial letter to Dioscorus of Alexandria, Gregory encouraged Anastasius of Antioch with the thought that, since he ruled an apostolic see, he was everything to all men; neglecting assertions of Roman supremacy, he wrote that he and Anastasius shared the glory of St. Ignatius of Antioch, since they had in common Ignatius's master, the Prince of the Apostles.[51] Gregory's letters to Eulogius of Alexandria show a similar congeniality unmarked by thoughts of hierarchic precedence. As in the letter to Anastasius, he made much of the relationship between disciple and master, in the case of Alexandria, between Sts. Mark and Peter. The benediction of St. Mark was more truly that of St. Peter, he wrote,[52] and the relationship of unity between disciple and master had remained so unimpaired between Alexandria and Rome "that I should seem to preside in the see of the Disciple, because of the Master, and you in the see of the Master because of the Disciple."[53] In response to a letter in which Eulogius glorified Rome and Gregory by saying that St. Peter still occupied his episcopal throne, sitting in the

[48] Reg. V, 62; MGH I, 377.
[49] Reg. VIII, 2; MGH II, 3.
[50] Reg. II, 50; MGH I, 154.
[51] Reg. V, 42; MGH I, 336.
[52] Reg. VIII, 28; MGH II, 29.
[53] Reg. VI, 58; MGH I, 432.

133

persons of his successors, Gregory received the compliment on behalf of his see, but disclaimed the magnification of his own position. Repeating the words of the Petrine commission, he returned Eulogius's courtesy, by applying the commission itself to the three sees with which St. Peter was immediately united. "Although the special honor in no way delights me, I rejoice greatly that you, Most Holy, have given yourself what you apportioned to me. For who does not know that the holy Church has been confirmed in the steadfastness of the Prince of the Apostles, whose firmness of mind is expressed in his name, since Peter is derived from "petra" [rock]? To him was said by the voice of Truth: 'To you I shall give the keys of the kingdom of Heaven.' To him it was again said: 'And, when you are converted, confirm your brethren,' and once more: 'Simon, son of John, lovest thou me? Feed my sheep.' Wherefore although there are many Apostles, only the see of the Prince of the Apostles suffices in authority for this principate, the see which, in three places, belongs to one man."[54]

Much the same collegial concept was in Gregory's mind when he denounced John the Faster for assuming the title "oecumenical patriarch."[55] His protests that to countenance the title was to lose the faith, that the title was contrary to the civil laws,[56] to the decrees of the Fathers, to the canons, to the establishments of the Gospels, and to the commands of Christ,[57] were ancillary to his principal contention. More critical were his comments on Christ's commission to St. Peter, who received the "care and principate of the whole Church" without being called "universal Apostle,"[58] and his frequent assertion that, though the Council of Chalcedon wished to honor St. Peter by conferring the disputed title upon his see, all of the Roman bishops declined its use as an infringement of the rights of other bishops.[59]

His point was wider, however, than the defense and increase of Roman primacy; he concurred in the judgment of his predecessors and objected when the bishop of Alexandria addressed him as "universal

---

[54] Reg. VII, 37; MGH I, 485.

[55] Caspar, *Geschichte* 2, 366f, 452-56. See the diametrically opposed view in Ullmann, *Growth*, 36ff. According to Dr. Ullmann's interpretation, Gregory acted in this conflict specifically to uphold the *principatus* of Rome over all Christian society.

[56] Reg. V, 45; VII, 24; MGH I, 344, 469.

[57] Reg. V, 37, 41; MGH I, 321ff, 332.    [58] Reg. V, 37; MGH I, 321f.

[59] Reg. V, 37, 41, 44; VIII, 29; MGH I, 322f, 332, 341; II, 31.

pope."[60] The law, the canons, and Roman prerogatives had not suffered alone. The full force of Gregory's argument struck in the protest that there could be no "universal patriarch," no "universal pope," no "general Father" of the universal Church.[61] Rome declined the offensive title in Gregory's mind for the same reason John should have shunned it: it deprived the other patriarchs of their titles and rights;[62] it denied the glory of the episcopate to all other bishops.[63] For, he argued, if there were one universal bishop, there could be no other bishops,[64] and the "absurd" or "demented" position must be maintained that the universal Church stood or fell in the person of one man.[65]

The title was "proud," "arrogant," and "wicked." As for John, Gregory could only invoke the fate of Lucifer, admonishing John to forswear his wrongful and disruptive course, and to return to the true unity of the Church, not the unity of administrative power, but that of virtue. "Love humility, therefore, most beloved brother, with all your heart; through it the harmony of all brethren and the unity of the holy universal Church can be guarded."[66] Disappointed in his hope of John's repentance, Gregory addressed the new bishop of Constantinople on the same matter, urging him to cast the scandal of the proud title out of the Church quickly. For the faithful could not live in faith unless in thought and deed they honored humility and trod underfoot profane self-exaltation; the unity of the Church lay in the one spirit, one mind, one love, one bond of harmony in Christ which stayed in the dwelling-place of the Holy Spirit.[67]

Without frequently using the word "tradition," Gregory therefore said much that was important about the transmission of faith and observances. He did write explicitly that articles of belief, special disciplinary regulations, and the hierarchic structure of the Church had been "handed down" by the elders, or the Fathers, and that they must be kept inviolate.

The strained ecclesiastical relations of his day, however, led him, as they had led Pelagius I earlier, to modify the conventional Roman concept of tradition in its magisterial sense. He supplanted the predominately administrative and juridical cast of his predecessors' thought

[60] Reg. VIII, 29; MGH II, 31, *universalis papa*.
[61] Reg. V, 44; MGH I, 340ff.  [62] Reg. V, 41; MGH I, 332.
[63] Reg. V, 44; MGH I, 341.
[64] Reg. VIII, 29; IX, 156; MGH II, 31, 157.
[65] Reg. V, 37; VII, 24; MGH I, 322, 469.
[66] Reg. V, 44; MGH I, 340.  [67] Reg. XIII, 43; MGH II, 406.

with theological premises much like those advanced by the early apologists. The controversy of the Three Chapters and the schisms to which
it led brought the principle of earlier Roman ecclesiology under the severest pressure; the familiar tension between conservatism and change
in the intellectual appreciation of tradition achieved bitter reality in the
conviction that Rome had abandoned Chalcedon and the true faith.

While they professed undeviating loyalty to Chalcedon, Vigilius and
Pelagius I resorted in their apologies to the principle of indefinite review, an insecure support for any argument that the Church's confession
of faith was immutable. To it, Pelagius added the further argument, inspired perhaps by St. Cyprian, that the true faith was witnessed by the
consensus of apostolic sees, in which abided the unity of the Church.
These two premises represented a considerable departure from the
thought of fifth-century popes, and Gregory's adaptations of them prolonged the divergence and replaced the rather provisional formulation
it seems to have had in Pelagius's mind with an intellectually refined
structure.

He framed the doctrine of indefinite review in terms of historical development, pointing out the serial quality of the first five oecumenical
councils, and applying to the whole body of theology the rule that sacred knowledge increased steadily the nearer the end of the world approached. He broadened the argument from agreement of the apostolic
sees to a doctrine that the consent of the universal Church, and especially of the patriarchal sees, testified authentic belief, and, presumably, kept the elaboration of doctrine within the bounds of orthodoxy.
This testimony was not necessarily expressed through councils, for universal consent confirmed the orthodoxy of councils rather than the reverse. Nor was it declared by one eminent patriarch; indeed, the common assent of all the patriarchs, vigorous witness to universality as it
was, claimed validity as evidence of the quite uninstitutionalized, indeed, mystical or charismatic, consensus of all believers, and especially
of all bishops. None of his predecessors exceeded Gregory in devotion
to the dignity of the Roman See; but, in replacing administrative and
juridical supremacy with the virtue of humility as the cohesive element
in the Church, and in supplanting definition by decretal with justification by universal assent, Gregory departed fundamentally from the
Roman ecclesiology of the fifth century.

In his day, Roman ecclesiology was defensive rather than aggressive
as it had been in the time of Leo the Great and Gelasius I. It had to

136

meet singularly grave challenges. Divisions among the Roman clergy, suspicion in Gaul, and schism in north Italy, all accompanied by doctrinal assaults, forced perhaps more than other elements an enlargement of theological aspects in Roman thought and an extreme modification of its administrative and juridical aspects. They raised more fundamental issues than Rome's competence in appellate jurisdiction; they disputed the very orthodoxy of the See of St. Peter and contested the whole structure of thought supporting Hormisdas's axiom that the Christian religion had always remained unsullied in the Roman Church.

Under such pressure, Roman ecclesiology approximated the eastern doctrines of the Church which, in its earlier form, it had fiercely disputed. But the challenge to Roman thought presented by the Byzantine concept of rulership persisted; it received no strong response from the sixth-century popes. Indeed, the power which had stirred up the conflict over the Three Chapters, consistently demanded and won submission of the bishops of Rome. Hormisdas dealt in great dignity with Byzantium, and there is evidence that Justin and his successors did not wish to impair Rome's ecclesiastical pre-eminence.[68] And yet, they stopped short only at capital punishment to gain papal concurrence when political ends required it. The deposition of Silverius, the abuse and banishment of Vigilius, the dependence of Pelagius I on imperial force to sustain his position all testify to the constraint of judgment which the Empire imposed on the papacy.

Gregory gave a spirited defense when the exarch of Ravenna accused him of treason for entering negotiations with the Lombards; he bitterly reproached the Empire for its negligent and ineffectual defense of its own subjects in Italy; he carefully developed the material resources of the papacy.[69] But generally his attitude towards Byzantium was submissive. Instructed by the demands of humility, Gregory gave extraordinary evidence of deference to imperial authority even in such purely ecclesiastical matters as episcopal elections and the admission of men into monasteries. To be sure, he showed, in some comments, a contrary attitude. He wrote to a usurper bishop that he and all men knew "that the most pious lords [i.e., the emperors] love discipline, preserve the orders, venerate the canons, and do not mix in the legal cases of bishops."[70] But, in a letter to the Emperor Maurice, he showed that he had

[68] Above, pp. 112ff.  [69] Caspar, *Geschichte* 2, 409ff.
[70] Reg. VI, 25; MGH I, 403.

not described the actual practice. Gregory admonished Maurice to forswear his untoward intervention in ecclesiastical affairs, to remember that the Scriptures, in the words of God Himself, call priests "gods" and "angels" and command that they be rendered all reverence. He reproved Maurice with the example of Constantine the Great who, at Nicaea, refused to judge complaints against bishops, saying "You are gods established by God. Go and decide your cases among yourselves, since it is not worthy for us to judge gods." And, Gregory wrote, even before Constantine, the pagan emperors showed the greatest honor to priests who served gods of wood and stone.[71] But these indications that Gregory strongly opposed imperial intervention in Church affairs on principle are rare.

The predominant tendency of his thought was suggested by his use of the term *"sancta res publica,"*[72] and it received full expression in his comments on the attitude of David to Saul. The sanctity of authority precluded any rightful resistance to rulers; David's refusal to harm Saul, when the advantage was his, was an historical example of the principle that subjects must be obedient, even towards evil rulers, since disobedience was an affront to God, who granted temporal power.[73] On several occasions, Gregory had the opportunity to apply this lesson. His remarkably extensive use of Roman law as a canonistic source was,[74] in a sense, evidence of the obligation of Church officials to obey imperial commands; and, when taking issue with Maurice, he wrote that God had made the Emperor guardian of ecclesiastical peace.[75] He considered the "will of the Prince" admissible in episcopal elections.[76] When his decision on a case involving the episcopal affairs in Corfu conflicted with Maurice's, he refrained from publishing his own judgment to avoid seeming to act in contempt of the Emperor's order. He urged reconsideration of the imperial command with a view to rescinding it, but he took no public action against it.[77] He bitterly contested Maurice's decree prohibiting the admission into monasteries of men obliged to service in civil or military offices, and held before the Emperor the anger which the edict would arouse in the Eternal Judge when he came amidst burning skies and burning earth and dissolving elements, accompanied by angels and archangels, thrones, dominions,

---

[71] Reg. V, 36; MGH I, 318.
[72] Reg. II, 34; MGH I, 130. Cf. Reg. I, 16a; MGH I, 18.
[73] Reg. Past. III, 4; PL 77, 54ff.       [74] Cf. Reg. XIII, 50; MGH II, 414ff.
[75] Reg. VII, 6; MGH I, 449.       [76] Reg. V, 16; MGH I, 296f.
[77] Reg. XIV, 8; MGH II, 427.

princedoms, and powers. And yet, he concluded this extensive denunciation with one anticlimactic sentence in which he said that he had published the offensive decree "through the various regions" even though it opposed God Himself.[78] As in the case of episcopal administration in Corfu, Gregory took issue with the imperial judgment privately, but submitted to it in his public actions.[79] The disedifyingly servile letter of congratulations which Gregory sent the Emperor Phocas, after Phocas had slain Maurice and his sons in an appalling general slaughter, shows to what extreme Gregory pressed the moral he drew from the relationship of David and Saul.[80]

In the last analysis, Gregory's thought on the relations of Empire and Church was not far from that of his opponents, the schismatic bishops of Istria, who wrote to Maurice urging him to convene a synod to judge the lingering issue of the Three Chapters. The good order of the Councils of Constantinople (381), Ephesus, and Chalcedon was due, they wrote, to direct imperial intervention in them. The scandal to the Church which the Robber Synod generated came about "through the absence of the most Christian princes" which gave occasion of Dioscorus's irresponsible behavior. Only the presence of Marcian at Chalcedon had ended the grievous effects of the Robber Synod and restored catholic peace to the universal Church.[81]

Gregory extended notable deference to the Germanic rulers as well as to Byzantine emperors. He urged them to summon synods, to oversee reforms of Church order, and to intervene in Church affairs, even with great force, so as to secure the good repute of the clergy. He wrote with special reverence to the Frankish kings, applying to his relations with them the concept of sacral kingship which framed his thought in dealings with Byzantium. The Frankish rulers were beacons of faith and defenders of the Church; Gregory extravagantly praised whatever passed for virtues in them, just as he glorified Phocas. "By as much," he wrote to King Childebert, "as the royal dignity surpasses other men, by that much clearly the loftiness of your kingdom excels the kingdoms of other peoples. To be a king is no wonder, since there are others; but to be a catholic is enough, since others are not worthy of it. For as the splendor of a great beacon shines with the clarity of its light

---

[78] Reg. III, 61; MGH I, 221f.    [79] Cf. Reg. VIII, 10; MGH II, 12f.
[80] Caspar, *Geschichte* 2, 465-70, 479ff, 487ff.
[81] Reg. I, 16a; MGH I, 19.

in the shadows of earthly night, so the clarity of your faith glows and flashes among the dark perfidy of other peoples."[82]

In his ecclesiology, Gregory accommodated principles to bear the tensions of doctrinal conflict. But, like his immediate predecessors, he failed to respond to the challenge with which the Byzantine concept of emperorship endangered his concept of the Church. For the sixth-century popes from Vigilius onward, obedience to the civil power was a way of survival, and perhaps for some even a way of life. Imperial direction of Church affairs was normal; it should not be openly resisted. Extended also to Germanic rulers, the concept of sacral kingship prepared the way for conflict in a later age, when the Frankish kings, supplanting Byzantium as defenders of the Roman Church, adopted a pattern of temporal headship, and the papacy, having overcome the other challenges to its ecclesiology, repudiated subservience to earthly princes.

### D. PAPAL THOUGHT IN THE SEVENTH CENTURY

The defensive ecclesiological premises advanced by Pelagius I and Gregory the Great depended on the fundamental harmony of the patriarchates. In the seventh century, such specious concord as Justinian had been able to establish among them dissolved; the western schisms which gravely impaired Roman ecclesiastical hegemony were healed, and the precedence of the See of Peter among the churches of the West was again generally acknowledged. The basis of the defensive ecclesiology and the schisms primarily responsible for it were thus removed almost simultaneously.

The interlude of patriarchal consensus had ended; the defensive arguments of Pelagius I and Gregory I thus lost their historical warrant; and, with the pre-eminence of their see restored in the West, the popes of the seventh century returned to the apologetic claim of their fifth-century predecessors: that by special grace Rome preserved the true doctrine of salvation.

This assertion was not the exclusive axiom of some thinkers that Rome was the only font of authentic dogma for the entire Church; nor did the disturbed political conditions of Europe, practical impediments to juridical process, give occasion for a restatement of the claims to supreme appellate jurisdiction which popes from the late fourth century onward had made.

The juridical claims were never, to be sure, lost sight of. The thought

[82] Reg. VI, 6; MGH I, 384.

of seventh-century popes, however, was closer to that of their immediate predecessors than to the position of those in the fifth century. The burden of the apologetic ecclesiology of Pelagius I and Gregory I had fallen on magisterial, rather than on the administrative and juridical aspects of the Church. Sixth-century popes were not concerned, since they had no occasion, to assert that the cohesion of the Church depended upon the maintenance of a hierarchic order, and of a corresponding juridical structure, organized as a papal monarchy. Leo the Great and his immediate successors wrote in such terms; in the ninth century, administrative and juridical problems resumed a predominant place in Roman ecclesiology. But Roman thought in the seventh century still bore circumscriptions imposed by the crises which began in the time of Vigilius. Magisterial, not hierarchic, authority was the major question in the great disputes of that age; isolated from the other patriarchates, Rome met the requirements of controversy by neglecting the doctrine of consensus among the apostolic or patriarchal churches and restating the axiom of Hormisdas that "the catholic religion has always been preserved unspotted in the Apostolic See."

The old challenges to Roman ecclesiology remained alive. Counter-doctrines continued to claim the adherence of some western clergy.[1] To be sure, from the East hyperbolic affirmations came invoking the assistance of Martin I against Monothelitism, and two monks from Asia Minor addressed the pope as "supreme and apostolic pope, head of all the priestly order beneath the sun, supreme pope truly oecumenical, apostolic pope and coryphaeus."[2] In 681, the Byzantine bishops wrote to the Emperor Constantine IV on concluding peace with the Roman See, "The supreme prince of the Apostles worked in concert with us; for we have had as patron his imitator and successor in his see, to explain in writing the mystery of the divine sacrament. . . . Peter spoke through Agatho."[3] But these exalted phrases, recalling the acclamation of the Council of Chalcedon that Peter had spoken through Leo, were little more than diplomatic instruments. The power of the Byzantine Empire and the quasi-hieratic doctrine of rulership to which it adhered continued to endanger the concept of Roman primacy in the erection of two autocephalous sees, Ravenna (666) and Nea Justiniana (*ca.* 686), and in acts of force, of which the abduction, trial, and hu-

---

[1] See above, pp. 121ff.    [2] Pargoire, *L'Eglise*, 199.
[3] Mansi 11, 665; Pargoire, *L'Eglise*, 193.

miliation of Martin I was but the most flagrant. The ambitions of eastern prelates and their ecclesiological doctrines likewise remained an active counterpoise to Roman thought, particularly in Constantinople, where the myth of that see's apostolic foundation achieved full formulation in the late seventh century, the last requisite for hierarchic parity with Rome.[4]

Despite these points of opposition, Rome assumed the role of defender of apostolic tradition from the beginning of the Monothelite dispute, maintained the part vigorously, and at length, when the political goals of Monothelite doctrine were permanently lost, achieved a measure of recognition of her precedence from the Byzantine churches.

From the pontificate of Honorius I onward, Roman bishops, restored the word tradition to the frequent usage it had lost in Gregory's correspondence; in view of the doctrinal estrangement between them and the eastern sees, they emphasized the antiquity, the apostolic character, of their own creed and thus, implicitly, the novelty of Monothelitism. Though he was later condemned as a fomenter of Monothelitism, Honorius I vigorously objected to the doctrine of Cyrus of Alexandria as "a new invention," departing from the received faith of the Church,[5] and, with the orthodoxy of Rome again in question, he attributed the apostolic character to his predecessors: Gregory the Great was, he wrote, "of apostolic memory."[6] His successor, John IV, writing to condemn the Ekthesis and, at the same time, to vindicate Honorius's doctrine, likewise repudiated Monothelitism as a "novelty" contrary to the *Tome* of Leo, the Chalcedonian definition, and the doctrine of universally acknowledged Fathers.[7]

But the letters of Honorius and John are few and much too concisely written to represent the development of Roman ecclesiology. Most of the relatively few documents extant from the seventh century which suffice for that purpose derive from the period of thirty-three years between the synodal condemnation of Monothelitism by Martin I and Leo II's acceptance of the Sixth Oecumenical Council as orthodox: they are principally the letters and synodal decrees relevant to the Lateran Synod of 649, the letters of Agatho, especially his Dogmatic

---

[4] Dvornik, *Apostolicity*, 160ff.
[5] Ep. 5; PL 80, 474f; JL 2018 (1564), *scandalum novellae adinventionis*.
[6] Ep. 6; PL 80, 476; JL 2019 (1565), *apostolicae memoriae*.
[7] Ep. 2; PL 80, 606f; JL 2042 (1583).

Tome, composed in anticipation of the Council of Constantinople (680/81), and Leo II's letters approving the Council.

With the greatest emphasis, the authors of these documents reiterate the apostolic character of the Roman faith in its origin and at every stage in its transmission. Vindicating specific opponents of Monothelitism, Agatho referred to Popes Theodore, Martin I, and Donus, as "of apostolic memory,"[8] and honored Leo I, the foe of earlier eastern heresy, as "holy Leo of apostolic memory," and "apostolic Father."[9] Leo II likewise honored Agatho "of apostolic memory."[10] To earlier popes, they referred generally as "holy and apostolic predecessors,"[11] and "apostolic pontiffs,"[12] who, with the Apostles, prophets, and doctors, had guarded and transmitted the authentic faith, "the apostolic and patristic doctrine," "the pious tradition of the saints."[13] The faithful composed the "apostolic, catholic Church,"[14] the "one, holy catholic and apostolic Church of Christ."[15] Christ, coming in glorious, terrible power to judge the earth, would by a sign of His hand prove the true belief of apostolic tradition.[16]

This general emphasis on the apostolate was subordinate to the prevalent object of the papal writers: to reaffirm that bishops of Rome were, by the unfailing charisma of their office, vicars of the Prince of the Apostles,[17] and that consequently, the faith of the Roman Church was indeed the firm and blameless faith of the Apostles, "the apostolic tradition of apostolic pontiffs and of the five general councils."[18] They asserted that the "apostolic tradition" was the "tradition of this Apostolic See," and that the Roman confession was a canon of orthodoxy.[19] In their work appears the concept of Rome as a microcosm of the universal Church: the "one, holy, catholic, and apostolic Church of

[8] Epp. 1, 2; PL 87, 1161, 1205, 1224; JL 2109 (1624), 2110 (1625).

[9] Ep. 1; PL 87, 1177; JL 2109 (1624).

[10] Ep. 3; PL 96, 401; JL 2118 (1630); ep. 4; PL 96, 414. JL 2119 (1631); ep. 7; PL 96, 419; JL 2120 (1632).

[11] Agatho, ep. 1; PL 87, 1164; JL 2109 (1624).

[12] *Ibid.*, col. 1165; ep. 2; PL 87, 1217; JL 2110 (1625).

[13] Martin I, ep. 13; PL 87, 193f; JL 2072 (1606).

[14] *Ibid.*, col. 196, *apostolica catholica ecclesia.*

[15] Agatho, ep. 1; PL 87, 1209; JL 2109 (1624), *intra unam sanctam catholicam atque apostolicam Christi ecclesiam.*

[16] Leo II, ep. 4; PL 96, 415; JL 2119 (1631).

[17] *Loc. cit.*

[18] Agatho, ep. 1; PL 87, 1165; JL 2109 (1624).

[19] *Loc. cit.*

143

Christ" had its eponym and chief representative in Rome, "this apostolic Church of Christ,"[20] this holy, apostolic see, the mother of all churches."[21] Despite the error of other sees, notably Constantinople,[22] and considerable adversities, the bishops of Rome themselves had never fallen into error. In condemning the Ekthesis and the Typos, Martin I invoked the examples of his predecessors who had destroyed heresy and torn the catholic Church from the error of perverse teachers;[23] and he recalled that the "damnable novelty" of Monothelitism had been repudiated "by almost all the God-beloved bishops of other provinces and by the apostolic pontiffs established in this Elder Rome."[24] Remembering Martin's arrest, humiliation, and death, Agatho and Leo II made similar claims to Roman steadfastness in the true faith despite all dangers.

To the East, Agatho wrote that the light of the catholic, apostolic, and true faith, never shaded by the darkness of heretical error, had shown forth through Sts. Peter and Paul, the princes of the Apostles, and through their disciples and their apostolic successors in series to Agatho himself. Undaunted by adversities, the "apostolic pontiffs" had honored—and still honored—the limits of the catholic and apostolic faith, publishing it in their admonitory decretals and synodal definitions.[25] He reiterated that position more crisply in another letter to Constantine IV. Christ, he wrote, had granted care of his spiritual sheep to St. Peter, whose apostolic church had never deviated from the path of truth.[26] Though he confirmed the condemnation of Honorius I by the Sixth Oecumenical Council, Leo II found no logical difficulty in making the same assertions. Like Cyrus, Sergius, and the other Monothelites, Honorius had striven against the purity of the apostolic tradition; by negligence, he had fanned the flame of the heretical doctrine, instead of extinguishing it at the beginning;[27] he consented to the defilement of the immaculate rule of the apostolic tradition which he received from his predecessors;[28] rather than illuminating the Aposto-

---

[20] *Ibid.*, PL 87, 1164; JL 2109 (1624).
[21] Leo II, ep. 4; PL 96, 413; JL 2119 (1631).
[22] Agatho, ep. 1; PL 87, 1172; JL 2109 (1624).
[23] Ep. 1; PL 87, 125f; JL 2058 (1594).
[24] Ep. 3; PL 87, 142; JL 2062 (1596).
[25] Ep. 3; PL 87, 1217-20; JL 2110 (1625).
[26] Ep. 1; PL 87, 1169; JL 2109 (1624).
[27] Ep. 4; PL 96, 414; JL 2119 (1631).     [28] Ep. 7; PL 96, 419; JL 2120 (1632).

lic See with the doctrine of apostolic tradition, he strove by perverse betrayal to subvert the unsullied faith.[29] And yet, Leo II was able to write that the Roman Church until his own day preached the true doctrine, which descended from apostolic tradition to the Fathers and the doctors of the Church and which the "apostolic successors" of St. Peter had with great labor transmitted intact to Leo himself.[30] The condemnation of Monothelitism by the Sixth Oecumenical Council was, for him, an acknowledgment that "this holy Church, sustained by divine assistance, preaches and preserves the rule of apostolic tradition."[31]

In his own mind, Leo II clearly distinguished between the see and the particular bishop, much as Augustine had when he wrote that the orthodoxy of the apostolic succession in the Roman See would not be impaired even if some "traitor" to true doctrine insinuated himself as bishop. The implications of Roman orthodoxy in the minds of Leo, Martin, and Agatho, were, however, far wider than those in Augustine's thought; for they exalted Roman doctrine as a canon of authentic faith against which patristic writings and synodal decrees must be judged. The principles of the Decretum Gelasianum on the magisterial aspects of ecclesiology received new expression in the repeated assertions that Fathers and synods had accepted the faith of Rome, and that the acceptance of their writings and decrees as authoritative depended upon close correspondence between their doctrine and the tradition of the Apostolic See. Martin and Agatho numbered the first five oecumenical councils with the Apostles, the Fathers, and the doctors as oracles of the faith; Leo II added the sixth. But, for none of the three popes did conciliar decrees or the patristic writings to which those decrees appealed for justification have magisterial authority entirely independent of Roman acceptance. Martin I "confirmed" the "holy Fathers."[32] Leo's reference to the decrees of the Council of Constantinople (680-681) as vindication of the customary teaching of the Apostolic See was designed to emphasize the statement that the apostolic tradition had been preserved in Rome despite severe adversity. Leo once wrote of heretics "whom the holy, catholic, and apostolic Church rejects from the catalogue of faithful Fathers."[33] Though it is not clear whether he then referred explicitly to the Roman See, his thought was not far from that

---

[29] Ep. 2; PL 96, 408; JL 2118 (1630); Deneffe, *Traditionsbegriff*, 53; Caspar, "Lateransynode," 133f.

[30] Ep. 6; PL 96, 416; JL 2121 (1633).　　[31] *Ibid.*, col. 417.

[32] Ep. 1; PL 87, 128; JL 2058 (1594).　　[33] Ep. 3; PL 96, 408; JL 2118 (1630).

of Agatho, who recommended for doctrinal instruction "the testimonies of other holy Fathers whom this apostolic church of Christ has accepted,"[34] appealed to the "magistracy of the holy Fathers whom the holy, apostolic, and catholic Church and the venerable synods receive,"[35] and declared to Constantine IV: "This, His [Christ's] apostolic Church has never deviated from the way of truth in any degree of error. Every catholic church of Christ and universal synods always faithfully embracing its authority, or rather the authority of the Prince of all the Apostles, have followed it in all matters; and all venerable Fathers have embraced its apostolic doctrine, through which also have shone the most excellent lights of the Church of Christ. Holy, orthodox doctors have venerated and followed it; but heretics have reproached it with false accusations and malignant dishonor. This is the living tradition of the Apostles of Christ which His Church holds everywhere. . . . This is the rule of true faith which this apostolic Church of Christ, the spiritual mother of your most tranquil Empire, has vigorously held and defended in prosperity and in adversity; she is shown, through the grace of Omnipotent God, never to have erred from the path of apostolic tradition or to have succumbed, seduced by heretical innovations."[36]

The popes rendered high honor to oecumenical councils. Agatho wrote that the first five had confirmed and strengthened the foundations of the catholic Church of Christ, the apostolic tradition.[37] But their place in seventh-century papal ecclesiology is perhaps clearest in Leo II's statement confirming the decrees of the Sixth Council of Constantinople (680-681). He judged that it had acted in accord "with the rules of the elders," the canons of the first five Councils,[38] and that its judgments were consonant with the statements of apostolic men.[39] The critical factor, however, was that its confession agreed with that of Rome.[40] "The holy, universal, and great sixth synod," he wrote, had followed "in all matters the apostolic doctrine of the established Fathers. And since, as has been said, it preached most fully the definition of right faith which the Apostolic See of St. Peter the Apostle (in whose ministry we serve, although inferior to him) reverently accepts, we, and through our office

[34] Ep. 1; PL 87, 1164; JL 2109 (1624).    [35] Ep. 2; PL 87, 1221; JL 2110 (1625).
[36] Ep. 1; PL 87, 1169; JL 2109 (1624).    [37] *Ibid.*, col. 1165.
[38] Ep. 3; PL 96, 404f; JL 2118 (1630).
[39] *Ibid.*, and ep. 4; PL 96, 413f; JL 2119 (1631).
[40] Ep. 2; PL 96, 404; JL 2118 (1630).

this venerable apostolic see, therefore, assent harmoniously and with one spirit, to what it has defined, and confirm it by the authority of St. Peter. . . ." Leo then ranked the Council with the "holy five universal councils," and declared that "the bishops of Christ's Church who faithfully convened in it must be counted among the holy Fathers and doctors of the Church."[41]

Stating anew the axiomatically expressed thought of Hormisdas and of the Decretum Gelasianum, the popes of the seventh century tacitly laid aside the doctrine of the consensus of apostolic sees, or of the patriarchates, which had been critical in the apologies of Pelagius I and Gregory the Great. Actual ecclesiastical relations deprived that argument of any immediate value; it did not correspond with present facts. When the Monothelite dispute broke, Rome stood alone against the great eastern sees, as it had in the Monophysite controversy. Later, as Alexandria, Antioch, and Jerusalem fell into Islamic control, the dispute actively involved only Rome and Constantinople, and, Islamic advances having dashed forever any possibility of reconciliation between Monophysite and orthodox through Monothelitism, Byzantium came to terms with Rome. The condition of agreement was acceptance of papal concepts of apostolate, tradition, and the authenticity of Roman doctrine. No occasion had arisen for a fresh assertion of Roman pre-eminence in administrative and juridical matters, but acknowledgment of magisterial primacy laid the doctrinal basis for such claims in the next century.

The papal emphasis on magistracy also prepared the way for important elaborations in political thought by reviving, if only in a tentative way, the position that the temporal ruler must learn, not teach, matters of religion. The reconciliation effected at the Council of Constantinople (680-681) was not an unqualified victory for Roman ecclesiology. It was in fact principally an achievement of the Emperor Constantine IV, and, in confirming the decrees of the Council, Leo II sanctioned the imperial power which had summoned the assembly, presided over it, and guided it to its predetermined conclusions. It was the same power which constrained Vigilius to condemn the Three Chapters, which established the Ekthesis and the Typos as standards of orthodoxy, and which abducted and cruelly abused Martin I. Both Agatho, who spoke for Rome in the preliminary negotiations, and Leo II, who saw recon-

[41] Ep. 2; PL 96, 405; JL 2118 (1630).

ciliation achieved, knew that, though the Empire accepted Rome's magisterial assertions, it could later repudiate them to serve changed political requirements or to accommodate new intellectual currents in the East.

Their praise for Constantine was lofty; instructed by caution, they based their praise on the Emperor's cultivation of the apostolic tradition, his adherence to the doctrine confessed by their see. Gregory the Great had written of the "holy commonwealth" (*sancta respublica*); Agatho wrote more specifically of the "Christian commonwealth,"[42] and of the "most Christian Empire."[43] Though he referred to Rome as a "servile city" of the Empire,[44] Agatho repeatedly identified the prosperity of imperial interests with the welfare of the Roman See, "Christ's apostolic Church of the Empire which God has preserved,"[45] "the spiritual mother of your most happy Empire, the apostolic Church of Christ."[46] The faith of Rome, never corrupted by heresy was "the living tradition of Christ's Apostles . . . which preserves the Christian Empire of Your Clemency, which brings great victories from the Lord of Heaven to Your most pious Fortitude, which accompanies you in battles and defeats enemies, which protects on every side as an invincible wall your Empire, which God has preserved, which smites enemy nations with terror and casts them down by divine wrath, which, in wars, grants the palms of triumph from Heaven through the dejection and conquest of enemies, and, in peace, always guards secure and joyful your most faithful principate."[47]

Agatho admonished Constantine to provide for the welfare of tradition; Leo commended him for his orthodox zeal. "O Lord," he rhetorically exclaimed, "keep safe our most Christian king and hear him in the day when he shall cry unto Thee. Through his zeal, inspired of God, the piety of apostolic and true tradition flames throughout the whole earth, while the foul darkness of heretical perversion has vanished."[48] In collaboration with the Sixth Oecumenical Council, Constantine had overcome the heretics and become truly the "son of St. Peter

[42] Ep. 1; PL 87, 1161, 1165; JL 2109 (1624).
[43] Ep. 2; PL 87, 1224; JL 2110 (1625).
[44] *Loc. cit.*; ep. 1; PL 87, 1164; JL 2109 (1624).
[45] Ep. 1; *ibid.*, 1165, *a Deo propagati imperii apostolica Christi ecclesia.*
[46] *Ibid.*, 1163. Cf. *ibid.*, 1172.
[47] Ep. 1; *ibid.*, 1169.
[48] Ep. 2; PL 96, 404; JL 2118 (1630).

the Apostle,"[49] "our most pious and most Christian son, or rather, the son of the Church of God."[50]

In referring to Constantine as his "son," Leo used terms much like those in Ambrose's claim that Christian emperors must be spiritually subject to clerical direction, and in the assertion of Felix III that emperors must take no initiative in religious matters, but learn the proper course from bishops. The careful phrasing of the addresses to the Emperor both from Agatho and from Leo indicates that such a concept of the temporal ruler's dependence upon episcopal counsel in spiritual matters was present in their minds, and that they were determined that the Emperor's ecclesiastical advisers must hold firm to "the tradition of the Apostolic See."

In the eighth century, these reservations were critically important in papal thought about relations between the Church and the civil power. But in the immediate historical context of the late seventh century, they constituted a strong, if qualified, approval of the imperial direction of Church affairs which had become a normal part of Byzantine life. Leo praised Constantine, not only for his pious work, but for the dominant part he assumed in achieving the reconciliation: summoning the Council of Constantinople, laying aside the cares of state to assist in the Council, causing a careful examination of patristic testimonies and papal assertions to be made, and giving papal legates leave to expound the true faith.[51] To say even this much was to approve the concept of rulership which had inspired the ecclesiastical conflicts from the time of Leo the Great onward, and to admit the challenge to Roman ecclesiology which that concept by its very nature presented.

Though development in the magisterial aspects of Roman ecclesiology was most fully stated in documents concerning disputes in the East, it also figured briefly but decisively in relations between Rome and the Germanic peoples of the West. It appeared, for example, in the few surviving documents concerning Roman negotiations with Gaul. Its clearest manifestation occurred in dealings with the Anglo-Saxons. The differences in practice and observance which distinguished the Celtic from the Roman missionaries among his people led King Oswy of Northumbria to convene the conference of Whitby (664). In a preliminary address, Oswy said that it behooved those who served one God to serve

---

[49] Ep. 4; PL 96, 413; JL 2119 (1631).    [50] Ep. 7; PL 96, 419; JL 2120 (1632).
[51] *Loc. cit.*

one rule of life, and that they must enquire which tradition—Celtic or Roman—was the truer and then follow it in common. Colman, a great missionary from Iona, defended the Celtic observance, especially in the manner of computing the date of Easter, by affirming that it had been held by his "elders," by all his Fathers, and St. John the Evangelist, the disciple especially beloved of God. The testimony of St. John, who was worthy to recline on the Lord's bosom, was very great; great, too, was the authority of St. Columba and the other Celtic Fathers, who gave by signs and miracles evidence of their sanctity.

Wilfrid of York spoke for the Roman position; his comments, as rendered by the Venerable Bede, are an outline of Roman ecclesiology. He argued that the observance in Rome, where Sts. Peter and Paul lived, taught, suffered, and were buried, was universal. In Italy, Gaul, Africa, Asia, Egypt, Greece, and the whole earth, among divers nations and tongues, it prevailed; only the Picts and the Britons on two remote islands—and not even all of them—fought against the entire world. St. John observed the letter of the Mosaic law, since the early Church judaized in many things. But in Rome, St. Peter established the authentic observance, the "evangelic and apostolic tradition" which fulfilled the Law, and to which St. John's successors in Asia, and indeed the whole Church, had converted. Wilfrid objected that the Celts in fact followed neither the example of St. John, nor that of St. Peter, neither the Law nor the Gospel. To the prophecies and miracles of the Celtic Fathers, Wilfrid cruelly applied the verses, "Many will say to me in that day, Lord, Lord, have we not prophesied in thy name? and in thy name have cast out devils, and in thy name done many wonderful works? And then will I profess unto them, I never knew you: depart from me, ye that work iniquity" (Matt. 7:22f). Colman and his companions must heed the decrees of the Apostolic See, or rather of the universal Church; they must honor first, not their Fathers, who, though they may have been saints, were few in number, but the universal Church of Christ. However holy and mighty in wonders Columba was, if he were of Christ he could not be preferred "to the most blessed Prince of the Apostles to whom the Lord says: "Thou art Peter, and upon this rock I shall build my Church, and the gates of hell shall not prevail against it, and I shall give you the keys of the kingdom of Heaven.' "

At this point, Oswy asked Colman whether Christ had actually spoken thus to St. Peter, and whether any such power had been given

150

to Columba. When Colman confirmed the authenticity of the Petrine commission and entered no claim of corresponding power for St. Columba, Oswy declared for the Roman observance. He did not wish, he said, to stand against the heavenly door-keeper, but rather to obey his establishments so that, when he came to the gates of the kingdom of Heaven, the key-bearer would not bar his entrance.[52]

Pope Vitalian subsequently wrote to Oswy commending him for acting as befitted a member of Christ, "eternally following in all matters the pious rule of the Prince of the Apostles, in the celebration of Easter, or in all matters which the holy Apostles Peter and Paul transmitted, since, as the two lamps of heaven illumine the world, so their doctrine daily enlightens the hearts of believing men."[53] Though centers of Celtic observance continued to exist for another century, the doctrines of magisterial supremacy which the Council of Constantinople later accepted won the allegiance of Northumbria at the conference of Whitby.

The seventh-century popes thus reasserted in the magisterial aspects of ecclesiology those premises which their predecessors had held until the time of Hormisdas, and upon which historical circumstances, particularly the western schism of the sixth century, had forced severe modifications. Wilfrid's remarks at Whitby show as clearly as papal correspondence the tendency of Roman thought: the identification of Roman practice as the right practice of the universal Church, the assertion of Rome's magisterial pre-eminence by virtue of the Petrine commission. Pelagius I and Gregory I saw the general consensus of the apostolic sees or of the patriarchates as a test of authenticity. Universal assent proved orthodoxy of doctrine; the creed of Roman bishops was shown to be authentic by its concordance with the confessions of other principal churches. Patriarchal consensus broken and the dangerous western schism healed, the popes at least from Martin I onward reversed that position: since, they argued, Rome had never erred in doctrine, the Roman creed was a canon of true faith. Their thought suggested corresponding developments in ecclesiology toward a reformulation of the monarchic thought of fifth-century popes, and in political thought toward the subjection of the civil rulers to direction by clergy in religious matters. But for these elaborations Roman thinkers of

[52] Bede, Hist. eccl. gent. Ang. III, 25; ed. C. Plummer, vol. I (Oxford, 1896), 183ff.
[53] Ep. 5; PL 87, 1004f; JL 2089 (1613).

151

the seventh century restored only the essential doctrinal basis, the identification of Roman creed and apostolic tradition; their first, tentative fulfillment waited until the age of Charlemagne.

Discretion was resuming its place in Roman thought; though the language of tradition continued to be used, tradition itself lost ground as an authority beside the spontaneous powers of the papal office.

On a still broader plain, the disputes of the sixth and seventh centuries showed that, even when it was invoked as a primary authority, tradition gave ambiguous testimony. Like any history of compromise, the story of Byzantium's efforts to reach common ground with the Monophysites is full of projects begun, but not achieved, policies formulated, but not enacted, positions taken and subsequently abandoned. Changing political requirements sometimes altered radically the terms of potential compromise and led to corresponding changes in doctrine and governmental policy. Only the goal of reconciliation remained constant; consistency in doctrine and in administrative methods, and adherence to fixed and changeless doctrine were sacrificed to it. The Empire launched Monothelitism as a compromise doctrine, but, with the East lost to Islam, Byzantium was freed of the necessity, and even the chance, to compromise with the Monophysites. The old problems no longer mattered. In all this complex history, it was clear that politics gave the answers which the language of tradition masked. Supporters of imperial policy in the sixth and seventh centuries frankly raised the double breach of "reform" or "correction"—first, when men fall into error and second, when men renounced error—to a level with tradition. The disruption of reform undercut the *continuum* of tradition. In practice tradition had become a catchword; in theory, it remained a supreme authority, the cryptic oracle whose meaning political expediency made plain.

152

PART III

# Beginning a New Era

CHAPTER 5

# The Eighth-Century Crisis:
# Papal Reassertion and Frankish Dissent

THE Council of Constantinople (680-681) marked the end of the age of Christological disputes which had begun with Arianism. It rejected both Monophysitism and Monothelitism, and it espoused Chalcedonianism; doctrine no longer divided Constantinople from the Roman Church. But politics removed Rome as well as the Monophysite East from Constantinople's religious schemes. Rome no longer fell into Byzantium's political orbit, and, as far as the Roman bishops were concerned, there were far brighter lights in the political firmament than the Byzantine emperor. For the West, the critical issues of Church unity were beginning to be fought in Rome, Rheims, or Lyon, rather than in the city on the Golden Horn.

The Byzantine loss of Italy determined, above all other events, the course of the papacy's intellectual and political history in the eighth century. From the end of the seventh century on, Byzantium's effective control of Italy, and particularly of Rome, declined. At the expense of the Empire, the Lombards extended their territories. Its lands threatened by their advances, and imperial support failing, the papacy concluded a complex and inconsistent series of defensive treaties with the dukes of Spoleto and Benevento, with the Franks, and with the Lombards themselves. Finally, the Lombards extinguished the exarchate of Ravenna, the papacy emerged as temporal ruler of the regions of central Italy, and, at length, the Franks took the role of defense for the Roman city and church. Except for some territories in the extreme south of Italy, the Empire had lost control of the peninsula. An autonomous papacy appeared.[1]

The Donation of Constantine reveals the lofty aspirations that exhilarated Roman thinkers at this moment. Forged in the late eighth or possibly the early ninth century, the Donation declares that Constantine,

[1] Caspar, *Geschichte* 2, 643ff, 730ff. Cf. Ullmann, *Growth*, 45. On the supposed "emancipation plan" to free the papacy from Byzantium, the clearest possible statement is in Ullmann, *Growth*, 51f.

in gratitude for his miraculous recovery from leprosy, resolved to exalt the See of St. Peter, his healer. After quoting Christ's commission to St. Peter, pseudo-Constantine granted the highest honors to St. Peter's See, decreeing, in ecclesiastical matters, that it should have a "principate" (*principatus*) over Antioch, Alexandria, Constantinople, Jerusalem, and all other churches, and that it should have general review of all matters of cult or doctrine. In other matters, he ceded the Lateran Palace to the Roman bishops, together with ample revenues from the Mediterranean basin. He bestowed upon Pope Sylvester, "supreme pontiff and universal pope of the City of Rome and upon all of his successor bishops who are to sit in the See of St. Peter the Apostle until the end of the world," imperial insignia, including the diadem, a retinue parallel with that of the emperor, and control of the entire West. Out of reverence for the "Heavenly Emperor" whose representative sat in Rome, pseudo-Constantine resolved to move his own capital to Byzantium.[2]

A radical intellectual change indeed is indicated by the appearance of the title "universal pope" in this forgery; for Gregory the Great had rejected that title in the strongest terms, and condemned it as contrary to the very faith. It first appears with approbation in the records of the Lateran Synod (649), and then in two entries in the *Liber Diurnus,* a book of official formulae added to at various times between the sixth century and the beginning of the eighth. The entries in question date not long after the sixth oecumenical council.[3] Thereafter the term appears rarely, except in official documents of the Roman See;[4] and a similar term was coined for the Roman Church: "the holy, universal Roman church of God," as Pope Paul I put it, or, in Hadrian I's words, "our holy, catholic, and apostolic, universal Roman Church.[5]

It was natural that Gregory I's reservations concerning the title "uni-

[2] In *Decretales Pseudoisidorianae*, ed. Hinschius, 252ff. On the dating, see Gerike, "Schenkung," esp. 72ff; Fuhrmann, "Schenkung" (1959), 523-40; and now, Gerike's rebuttal to Fuhrmann "Schenkung" (1961), 293ff, and his developed argument on one aspect of the question in "Glaubensbekenntnis."

[3] *Liber Diurnus*, ed. Foerster, V85-C66-A61, 162f. See the inventory of usages in Gelzer, "Streit," 552ff, and Vaihé, "Titre," 65f, 68. Similar titles had been used by bishops of Constantinople from the late fifth century onward (Caspar, *Geschichte* 2, 747; Ullmann, *Growth*, 15).

[4] PL 89, 1169; MGH Epp. 4, k. a. 2, no. 3, 20. Cf. the Frankish Laudes in Kantorowicz, *Laudes*, 15.

[5] Codex Carolinus, ep. 36; MGH Epp. 3, k. a. 1, 545; MGH Epp. 5, k. a. 2, no. 2, 41.

versal" should be set aside precisely when oriental influence was at its height in Rome. In the seventh and eighth centuries, Islam and adverse imperial policies drove many Greeks and Syriacs and some Egyptians to seek safety in Sicily and Rome. From among them came, not only members of the Schola Graecorum and Greek and Syriac monasteries in Rome, but also a large number of popes. A distinct series of oriental bishops began with the Greek Boniface II, and, in the hundred and fifty years after his death, nearly half the bishops of Rome were of Greek or Syriac origin. Altogether, they ruled more than seventy years. The Greek and Syriac popes who consented to be called "universal" and applied that adjective to their see had in mind the same, quite conventional, meanings as prevailed in the minds of their Monophysite compatriots when they used the terms "catholicus" and "universal patriarch." For both, the term carried connotations of ecclesiastical precedence within a communion, of supervision over an inhabited area, and, above all, of orthodoxy.

But it meant rather more in the framework of conventional Roman thought. The acceptance of the title was an advance of the greatest importance. It utterly resolved the inconsistency which we have observed in the thought of Leo I between the demands of the Petrine doctrine and the authority of synods and councils as spokesmen of authentic tradition; it cut the Gordian knot that Siricius first tied between the apologists' idea of tradition and the papal idea of administrative flexibility. It inferred explicitly what Siricius, Leo, and their successors had only implied: namely, that the bishop of Rome was by virtue of being universal pope the supreme interpreter, and even the source, of tradition. It was the last major touch required to complete the structure of Roman thought on the relationship between the pope and tradition; it corresponded with the familiar Roman claims to exceptional jurisdiction within the Church. It also supplemented positions long before formulated in regard to two of the three qualities of tradition, when Pope Zosimus wrote that antiquity lived unshaken in the Roman See, and when, in the dispute over the twenty-eighth canon of Chalcedon, the Roman bishops firmly maintained that no consensus of the Fathers was valid if it ran counter to papal decrees. When universality too became a quality of the papacy, the conceptual structure was complete.

The accommodation of Roman thought to eastern ecclesiologies which had occurred in the sixth century was totally discarded. The eighth-century popes showed the greatest reverence for the works of

157

Gregory the Great, but their ecclesiological concepts differed radically from his. They could well accept his doctrine of the historical development of sacred knowledge;[6] but, abandoning his fear of the titles "oecumenical patriarch" and "universal bishop," they likewise departed from his broad and tolerant attitude toward matters of practice and hierarchic structure. They insisted that magisterial headship conferred administrative and juridical precedence. Exclusivism supplanted the latitudinarian principles of Gregory the Great. Discretion resumed its predominance over tradition in papal thought.

In this development, tradition was subsumed under hierarchic structure, as is shown particularly well in papal dealings with St. Boniface.[7] Commanding Boniface to observe the "tradition of the Fathers,"[8] Gregory II made it clear that tradition was subject to "the unshaken authority of St. Peter,"[9] and that Gregory taught by the grace of Him who opened the mouth of the mute and made the mouths of children learned.[10] The tone of Gregory III's correspondence is even stronger. Declaring that he presided over the "catholic and apostolic Church of God," and that he had commissioned Boniface "by apostolic authority,"[11] he specifically obliged the missionary and his people alike to adhere to "the rule and norm of the apostolic and catholic faith of the Roman church,"[12] "the holy, catholic, and apostolic tradition of the Roman see."[13] Obedience to "the tradition of the Roman Church" must be the guiding principle of Boniface's establishment of canonical order among the German clergy, and the warrant for his inclusion "in the company of the holy, established Fathers."[14]

Pope Zacharias, successor to the two Gregories, added to their thought a special emphasis on the canons and on the undeviating consonance of Roman decrees with the canons. The sentences of Celestine I and Martin I had counterparts in Zacharias's statements that "what may be found to be contrary to the establishments of the Fathers or of the canons are not issued from the Apostolic See." "It does not behoove us," he wrote, "to preach anything other than what we have learned from the holy Fathers."[15] And, again, "This we admonish Your Sanctity to hold most firmly: that you must follow in all respects the

---

[6] E.g., MGH Epp. 5, k. a. 3, 51f.
[7] Caspar, *Geschichte* 2, 695ff.
[8] Ep. 26; MGH Epp. 3, k. a. 1, 275.
[9] Ep. 12; MGH Epp. 3, k. a. 1, 258.
[10] Ep. 26; MGH Epp. 3, k. a. 1, 275.
[11] Ep. 44; MGH Epp. 3, k. a. 1, 292.
[12] Ep. 43; MGH Epp. 3, k. a. 1, 291.
[13] Ep. 45; MGH Epp. 3, k. a. 1, 293.
[14] *Ibid.*, 294.
[15] Ep. 51; MGH Epp. 3, k. a. 1, 304f.

establishments of the holy Fathers and the counsel of the holy canons, for we preach and act in no other way."[16] In a letter to Pippin and to the higher clergy and nobility of the Franks, Zacharias gave impressive evidence of his canonistic knowledge, with rich citations of conciliar and papal decrees, and of the Apostolic Canons, to illustrate "what we have, handed down by the holy Fathers, what the authority of the canons has sanctioned, and also what, with God's inspiration, we have been able to decide, by apostolic authority."[17] His admonition in that letter to obey "the apostolic mandates,"[18] and the other statements emphasizing consonance between Roman judgments and the canons, far from implying subordination of papal adjudication to a superior law, tended to identify what was done contrary to the canons with what was done against "the catholic and apostolic church."[19] Like his predecessors, Zacharias held that orthodoxy was proven by consonance with the tradition of the Apostolic See, and that St. Boniface's preaching and canonical reforms had validity because they were ratified "by the authority of St. Peter the Apostle."[20]

His rejection of the Gallican rite illustrates the burden of his thought. Zacharias wrote to St. Boniface: "As for the benedictions which the men of Gaul perform, they vary, as you know, Brother, with many corruptions. For they do not do this according to apostolic tradition; but they work through vainglory, bringing upon themselves damnation, since it has been written: 'If any man preach any other gospel to you than what has been preached, let him be anathema.' (Gal. 1:8) You have received the rule of Catholic tradition, most beloved Brother. Preach to all men and teach them all as you have learned from the holy Roman church, which, by God's action, we serve." The assertions of Innocent I and John II in liturgical matters were thus revived, and, together with corresponding developments in thought concerning hierarchy and faith, they composed a broad doctrine of ecclesiastical monarchy.[21] The defensive character of Roman ecclesiology under Pelagius I and Gregory I had given way to an aggressive and unaccommodating doctrine. For the moment, papal thinkers could overlook the dangerous fault that tradition introduced into their monarchic doctrine, the

---

[16] Ep. 60; MGH Epp. 3, k. a. 1, 324.
[17] Codex Carolinus, ep. 3; MGH Epp. 3, k. a. 1, 480.
[18] *Ibid.*, 486.
[19] Ep. 60; MGH Epp. 3, k. a. 1, 323.
[20] Ep. 51; MGH Epp. 3, k. a. 1, 302f; ep. 52; MGH Epp. 3, k. a. 1, 306.
[21] Ep. 87; MGH Epp. 3, k. a. 1, 371.

flaw that had split open in the sixth century. Other thinkers could see little but that flaw. A strong and highly articulate counter-doctrine had emerged among the Franks.

✝

Charlemagne, the scholars at his court, and his clergy all acknowledged Roman headship in the Church. From Rome, they sought and received an authentic book of ecclesiastical law, the Dionysio-Hadriana, a sacramentary of Gregory the Great, a copy of the Benedictine Rule, the manner of religious chant, in short, the very pattern of Church government and liturgical observance.[22] And yet, there were elements in Frankish ecclesiology which led Charlemagne to challenge papal administrative claims even in Church affairs, which inspired Hadrian I with fear that Charles meant to depose him,[23] and which won Charlemagne's approval for the proposed trial of Leo III. In the Iconoclastic Dispute, this divergence allowed the Frankish clergy to condemn as heretical the position which Rome had previously confirmed as orthodox.

Unlike eastern ecclesiologies which ran directly counter to the Roman concept of the Church, the ecclesiological principles expressed in Alcuin's works and in the writings of Frankish authors modify rather than contradict the papal doctrine. Roman thinkers asserted that the "tradition of the Apostolic See" was the talisman of true doctrine, that only the writings which the Roman Church accepted as orthodox would be taken as authentic statements of faith, and that those writings must be understood in the sense which Rome placed upon them. Deeply influenced by the revival of patristic studies which Charlemagne fostered, Alcuin and the Frankish authors advanced a less exclusive doctrine of tradition. They professed that Rome held the unsullied faith of the Apostles, and they considered Fathers those whom Rome had approved. But with the Fathers whose works they studied, they held that the apostolic tradition was not the peculiar property of the See of St. Peter; the body of patristic teaching was supplemental, though not contrary, to Roman decrees; and the interpretation of the writings of

[22] Codex Carolinus, praef; MGH Epp. 3, k. a. 1, 476. See Ullmann, *Growth*, 73 and *passim*. I agree entirely with Dr. Ullmann's excellent comments on p. 119. Cf. Delaruelle, "L'Eglise," 143ff. See the brilliant résumé by Ganshof, "L'Eglise," 95ff.

[23] MGH Epp. 3, k. a. 1, no. 92, 629. On Hadrian I and Leo III, see Zimmermann, "Papstabsetzungen" I, 26, 30, 76.

the Fathers was subject to the judgment of the entire Church, not to the approval of one see. Roman thinkers claimed the character of universality for their own see; following the early North African and Greek Fathers, the Franks ascribed it to the whole company of orthodox churches in every place and age, of which Rome was the pre-eminent representative.

Alcuin expressed profound veneration for the See of St. Peter and for Roman bishops. He acclaimed Hadrian I as the "vicar of the most holy see," and the "heir of St. Peter's wondrous power,"[24] and Leo III as "most holy Father, pontiff elect of God, vicar of the Apostles, heir of the Fathers, prince of the Church, fosterer of the one unsullied dove."[25] And he anticipated the Day of Judgment, when he would see Leo III sitting in the judgment seat among the apostolic men, apportioning with the Apostles the rewards of the faithful people.[26]

When a faction in the Roman Church charged Leo III with perjury and adultery, Alcuin denounced the proposal that Leo be brought to trial. "I remember reading once, if I rightly recall, in the canons of St. Sylvester that a pontiff must be accused and presented for judgment by no fewer than seventy-two witnesses, and that their life [i.e., the life of the accusers] should be such that they could stand against such an authority. Moreover, I read in other canons that the Apostolic See is to judge, not to be judged. . . . What pastor in the Church of Christ can be safe if he who is the head of the churches of Christ is cast down by evil doers?"[27]

He wrote, in terms reminiscent of comments by Gregory the Great, of St. Peter's frailty in denying Christ.[28] After His resurrection, Christ "recalled him to the principate of the former dignity and commended to him the sheep which he redeemed with His own blood, to the end that the good shepherd might understand that the errant should not always be censured with harsh reproach but often corrected with the admonition of pious consolation."[29] This reference to St. Peter's denial and to the restoration of his principate has great interest in view of

[24] MGH Epp. 4, k. a. 2, no. 27, 68. See Dr. Ullmann's brief remarks in *Growth*, 117f.

[25] MGH Epp. 4, k. a. 2, no. 94, 138.

[26] MGH Epp. 4, k. a. 2, no. 234, 379.

[27] MGH Epp. 4, k. a. 2, no. 179, 297. See Ullmann, *Growth*, 117f; Zimmermann, "Papstabsetzungen," I, 30, 76.

[28] Dr. Ullmann does not mention this aspect of Alcuin's thought.

[29] MGH Epp. 4, k. a. 2, no. 113, 165.

Alcuin's reference to Paulinus of Aquileia as "guardian of the gates in the City of God,"[30] and his statement that all true bishops held the power to bind and to loose, the gift which "Christ gave to the Apostles, and, through them, to their successors."[31]

The compromise between the Roman doctrine and collegial ecclesiology which these remarks suggest appears in Alcuin's letter admonishing Bishop Felix of Urgel to abandon his adoptionist teachings. The burden of his argument is that Felix's doctrine did not accord with teachings of the universal Church. He asked, "Where is the power given to Peter, the prince of the Apostles: 'Thou art Peter and upon this rock I shall build my Church' etc.? Has this power been taken from him and transmitted to you, to the end that upon you, at the end of time and in a corner of the world, a new Church might be built disagreeing with the apostolic traditions?" He urged Felix to return to the fold which Christ commended to St. Peter. His purpose in these remarks, however, was neither to exalt the dignity of the Roman See above that of other churches, nor to define the Roman creed as the exclusive canon of faith. The tendency of his argument is much like that of St. Augustine's remarks in which Peter was said to have received the power of the keys, not in his own right, but as the representative of the entire Church. Without contesting Rome's primacy of honor, St. Augustine held that all the Apostles, and all their successors, the bishops, shared equally in the powers which Christ granted St. Peter.[32] Alcuin wrote similarly that Christ gave the power of binding and loosing "to His holy Church," and he went on to mention four canons of orthodoxy: they were, in order, the whole authority of the Gospels, the sayings of the Apostles, the creed of the breadth of the world, and the preaching of the Roman Church. He thus upheld the dignity of Rome but appealed to proofs of orthodoxy other than the Roman confession. The context of his remarks reveals his intent still more clearly. In terms like those of St. Augustine and of still earlier African apologists, he wrote that concord and charity preserved the unity of the Church. Those bonds secured the "one holy Church of God," the "one holy, catholic, and apostolic Church" confessed in the orthodox creed. Her doctrine attested by the interpretation of the holy Fathers, that Church, "the universal Church," held the power to bind and to loose and preserved

[30] MGH Epp. 4, k. a. 2, no. 139, 221.
[31] MGH Epp. 4, k. a. 2, no. 111, 161.
[32] Above, pp. 108f.

the "Apostolic and Gospel doctrine." It was she of whom Christ said, "One is my dove, my perfect one, my spotless one."[33]

As a principal figure in the Carolingian revival of patristic studies, Alcuin naturally referred often to the works of the Fathers and the doctors as defenses of "the apostolic tradition,"[34] to the "patristic traditions" as safeguards against novelty.[35] To his mind, the test of the authority of a given author or work was consonance with the "most certain testimonies of the holy Fathers," among whom he mentioned Jerome, Augustine, Gregory the Great, Hilary of Poitiers, Leo I, Fulgentius, Ambrose, Cyril of Alexandria, Peter of Ravenna, the Venerable Bede, Gregory Nazianzus, Isidore of Seville, and Juvencus. In his work against Felix of Urgel, he included citations of Origen and John Cassian, "although they seem in some places of their writings to wander from the faith." He felt secure in making these references since they were in harmony with St. Jerome and the other doctors. St. Jerome, he wrote, had himself followed that method, as had St. Paul in his references to pagan writings, and almost all the holy doctors in their references to heathen philosophers and poets.[36] The final test of orthodoxy for Alcuin was, therefore, the consensus of orthodox writings, a collation of "many testimonies from the Gospels or the Apostles or also from the traditions of the holy Fathers."[37]

In the magisterial aspects of papal ecclesiology, assertions of the unfailing "tradition of the Apostolic See" and of the transcendent authority of Rome to define the faith predominated. By contrast, the emphasis of Alcuin's thought fell on the broader concepts of "apostolic tradition" and the "traditions of the Fathers," and his method of argumentation was consequently comparative and exegetical rather than authoritarian. The Scriptures and the confession of the universal Church were proofs of orthodoxy together with, but not necessarily subordinate to, the preaching of the Roman Church.

This general position on Church order seems to have been very similar to Charlemagne's own view. In praising Offa of Mercia for being "not only the strongest protector of the earthly realm, but also the most devoted defender of the holy faith,"[38] Charlemagne had in mind the parallel role to which God had called him as king of the Franks

---

[33] MGH Epp. 4, k. a. 2, no. 23, 61f.   [34] MGH Epp. 4, k. a. 2, no. 213, 356.
[35] MGH Epp. 4, k. a. 2, no. 166, 269. Cf. *ibid.*, no. 291, 449.
[36] MGH Epp. 4, k. a. 2, no. 203, 337.   [37] MGH Epp. 4, k. a. 2, no. 205, 340.
[38] MGH Epp. 4, k. a. 2, no. 100, 145.

and Lombards and patrician of the Romans. He also had in mind some ecclesiological premises which he perhaps grasped imperfectly, but which in any case were not those of the Roman Church.

One of these premises may well have corresponded with Alcuin's emphasis on patristic consensus and especially with its legal manifestation in the canons. Alcuin had made "the most holy unanimity of the universal Church" a coordinate proof of orthodoxy with "Roman authority,"[39] and his correspondence shows that he considered the canons a special test of that unanimity. Only two generations earlier, St. Boniface found that the canons had been neglected for eighty years;[40] the importance which canonistic learning assumed between the time of Boniface and that of Alcuin was due largely to the encouragement of Charlemagne himself, on whose initiative Hadrian I had sent a transcript of the Dionysio-Hadriana to the Frankish court.

In an important statement on the growth of religious knowledge among the faithful, Charlemagne wrote that there were always, as in the days of the patriarchs and Apostles, many men endowed with one or more of the gifts of the Holy Spirit, which, according to the promise of Christ, would not fail even at the end of the world. "We believe," he wrote, "that this Holy Spirit of seven-fold grace existed among the Fathers and the Apostles, and that He is now inspired by the divine gift into the sons of Holy Mother Church, who are daily reborn in Christ to the increase of His people."[41] But this constant action of the Holy Ghost among the faithful did not modify the requisite conservatism in doctrine, of which, Charlemagne judged, the canons were the supreme safeguard. Once admonished by a patriarch of Aquileia to keep the canons safe from transgression,[42] he took the extraordinary measure of instructing Leo III to honor the canons. Sending an envoy to the recently elected Pope, Charlemagne directed him "to admonish him diligently concerning the respectability of his life and especially concerning the observation of the holy canons concerning the pious government of God's holy Church."[43] In a letter to Leo, he repeated the charge more gracefully: "May the prudence of your Authority adhere in every way to the canonical sanctions and always follow the statutes of the holy

[39] MGH Epp. 4, k. a. 2, no. 137, 211.
[40] MGH Epp. Sel. I, no. 50, 82. See the brilliant comments by Ladner, *Reform*, 301.
[41] MGH Epp. 4, k. a. 2, no. 21, 530f.    [42] MGH Epp. 4, k. a. 2, no. 8, 505.
[43] MGH Epp. 4, k. a. 2, no. 92, 135f.

Fathers, to the end that examples of all sanctity may shine forth for all men in your conversation and that the exhortation of holy admonition may be heard from your mouth, to the end also, that your light may shine before men that they may see your good works and glorify your Father who is in Heaven."[44]

The mandatory tone of this letter is even clearer in Charlemagne's description of the relationship he wished to establish between himself and Leo. He wrote that he wished to establish with Leo as he had with Hadrian I "an inviolable alliance of faith and charity." His duty, he wrote, was to defend the Church of Christ by force of arms from the external attacks of pagans and the ruin of infidels, and to fortify it internally with knowledge of the catholic faith. The Pope's responsibility was to assist Charlemagne's army with prayers so that the Christian people might conquer its enemies and the glory of Christ's name might spread throughout the earth.[45]

Charlemagne's admonition to Leo concerning the observance of the canons and his description of the pope as a prayerful auxiliary of his army show how far Charlemagne was from accepting conventional Roman ecclesiology.[46] He ignored the argument of Felix III and Gregory II that laymen must learn, not teach, in ecclesiastical matters. Hadrian I's fears that Charlemagne meant to depose him and the favor the King initially gave the proposal that Leo III be subject to formal trial are measures of the degree of difference between the concepts of right order in the Church and of the proper relations between Rome and the Frankish kings which Charlemagne and his contemporary popes held. On this evidence, the two concepts seem diametrically opposed: a doctrine of temporal supremacy against one of universal papal headship.

Still, the few letters purporting to state Charlemagne's own ecclesiological and political views provide no consistent or detailed exposition;[47] and it is likely that his thought in those matters differed less radically from the Roman position than his letters seem to indicate. Like

---

[44] MGH Epp. 4, k. a. 2, no. 93, 137f. Leo himself, however, was assured by monks from the Mount of Olives that the entire world had been committed to him by virtue of Christ's commission to St. Peter (MGH Epp. 5, k. a. 3, no. 7, 65f).

[45] MGH Epp. 4, k. a. 2, no. 93, 137f.

[46] See also Charlemagne's frequent enactments concerning religious instruction and the preservation of canonical order (MGH Cap. I, nos. 19, 20, 22, 33, 35, 36, 38, 90, 92, 121, 124; 44f, 47, 53f, 57, 61, 93, 103, 107, 110, 190, 194, 239, 295; MGH Epp. 5, k. a. 3, no. 1, 242.

[47] See the very systematic exposition in Ullmann, *Growth*, 102ff.

Alcuin's thought, it may well have been a modified version of Roman ecclesiology, rather than a blatant counter-doctrine.

Eighth-century popes were elaborating doctrines drawn from the age before Justinian reconquered the West. Frankish thinkers looked back to the same period. At about the time when the Decretum Gelasianum was composed, Cassiodorus wrote a divergent comment on authority and change in the Church. In compiling his catalogue of orthodox texts, Cassiodorus encountered much diversity of opinion among the Fathers on certain points. Well aware of historical progression in the series of oecumenical councils and of development in theological schools, he resolved the tension between antiquity and change by appealing to a pervading, supra-historical unity of intent. Beyond any doubt, his zeal for the judgments of the Fathers was great. The ancient masters, he said, had been able to complete works beyond the powers of the new.[48] He wrote disparagingly of men who thought it laudable if they held an opinion contrary to that of the ancients and discovered some new approach that would make themselves seem skillful. Against such men, the universal councils of Nicaea, Constantinople, Ephesus, and Chalcedon had issued their decrees. They struck down arrogant inventors of new heresies and decreed that no one should launch novel enquiries, but that, without craft or perfidy, men should be content with the authority of those whose credit was established of old.[49]

Still, Cassiodorus acknowledged that there were new "masters" in the Church,[50] and that the decrees of councils, framed at different times to meet different circumstances, were sometimes at odds. He was not disturbed by divergences between old and new authorities. Rather, he accepted them as natural. In his own mind, he seems to have reconciled them with the thought that he applied explicitly to the early Fathers and to the decrees of Nicaea and Chalcedon. The many Fathers, he wrote, and the two councils, "spoke, not contrary things, but diverse, but they all, through their divisions, reconciled the divine books with meet sureties, just as it is proven to be the effect in the harmony of the Evangelists, where the matter of faith is one and the order of words, diverse."[51]

Cassiodorus sought concord between new and old in the realm of metaphysical unity. He found a basis for reconciliation in textual criti-

[48] I, praef., 4; ed. Mynors, 5.    [49] I, xi, 1; ed. Mynors, 35.
[50] I, xvii, 3; I, xxiii, 2; ed. Mynors, 57, 62f.
[51] I, xiv, 3; ed. Mynors, 40.

cism, especially in the collation of texts by different authors and, above all, in an historically transcendental unity shared by all testimonies to the true faith.

This seems by and large to have been the concept of authority prevalent among eighth-century Franks. Among them, tradition took precedence as an authority over papal discretion. Charlemagne acted upon this general position at the Synod of Frankfurt (794), which he summoned principally to consider the Adoptionist heresy.[52] To define the "orthodox faith handed down by apostolic teachers,"[53] he directed the assembly to the writings of the Fathers and to the separate statements submitted by the Pope, "together with the holy Roman Church and the bishops and catholic teachers abiding anywhere in those parts," by the "ecclesiastical teachers and bishops of Christ's churches" in north Italy, and by "the holy Fathers, the bishops, and venerable men" in Germany, Gaul, Aquitaine, and Brittany. Charlemagne added his assent to the decrees of these "Fathers," aspiring to refute the Adoptionists' "new assertion," and to sustain the "Apostolic See and the ancient and catholic traditions from the beginning of the nascent Church."[54] The Roman See was pre-eminent; but the bishops were "rectors, in different sees, of Christ's city." Final authority in doctrinal matters belonged, not to one see, but to the "pious unanimity and the tranquil study" of the Fathers.[55] Together with many other thinkers in their day and earlier, Cassiodorus and the author of Decretum Gelasianum drew the lines of dispute; the first great confrontation of their views occurred in another matter before the Synod of Frankfurt, the Iconoclastic Controversy, in the arguments of Frankish and Roman thinkers.

[52] MGH Conc. I, no. 19 F, 159.

[53] MGH Conc. I, no. 19 F, 158. Cf. *ibid.*, no. 19 E, 143. Dr. Ullmann argues (JTS, 17 [1966], 193) that it is "mirth-provoking to read" that the Synod of Frankfurt was called to combat the Adoptionist heresy, rather than to consider the decrees of Nicaea II. The Synod did indeed consider the issue of Iconoclasm; the second Council of Nicaea was condemned in c. 2. of its decrees. But many other matters, including the case of Tassilo of Bavaria, coinage, episcopal jurisdiction within dioceses, and various general and specific problems of clerical discipline were also considered. Chapter 1 of the decree, however, declares that Adoptionism was the primary issue (MGH Conc. 2, 165), and Charlemagne himself wrote that he convened the Synod chiefly to counter Adoptionism (MGH Conc. 2, 159).

[54] MGH Conc. I, no. 19 E, 160.

[55] *Loc.cit.*

## CHAPTER 6

# Confrontation and Disengagement:
# Tradition and Political Groupings
# in the Iconoclastic Dispute

THUS FAR, we have mentioned the Byzantines, Romans, and Franks as the three major political components in eighth-century Europe, and sketched their different concepts of right order in the Church. We have now to consider a great dispute in which their ideas conflicted. Religion's main social function is to explain the relation of believers to society. Controversies from Constantine's day onward proved that in each society this function was discharged in an idiomatic way. The Church's common religious experience was expressed in different theological and philosophical terms, in different artistic conventions, and in different liturgical orders. The Iconoclastic Dispute, at the end of the eighth century, centered upon one issue, the veneration of sacred images. But it brought into debate a wider and more fundamental problem: idiosyncratic concepts of tradition as an authority in the Church.

As early as the fourth century, antagonism developed between those who considered religious images useful means of instructing the illiterate, and those who considered them heretical and idolatrous.[1] In letters often cited in the eighth-century controversy, Gregory the Great undertook the defense of sacred images against iconoclasm in Gaul,[2] and the contention between iconodules and iconophobes continued unabated until the great conflict under Leo III and Constantine V. Critical as the religious issues were in the Iconoclastic dispute, they were very old, and they achieved general importance principally because they inspired an imperial policy which Byzantium prosecuted by force of arms for half a century.

The Iconoclastic Controversy was primarily a struggle within the Empire, in which Rome joined a large party of easterners in opposing

[1] For still earlier evidence on the veneration of images, see Alexander, *Nicephorus*, 25ff.

[2] Reg. IX, 147, 208; XI, 10; MGH II, 147ff, 195, 271.

imperial religious policy, rather than a conflict between eastern and western canons of orthodoxy. Instead of articles of faith, the dispute concerned one religious practice: the adoration, or veneration, of sacred images. But to the iconodules of Byzantium and to those of Rome, the imperial prohibitions against pictorial representations of sacred themes and the destruction of religious art touched the faith itself. John Damascene expressed the view of iconodules both in the West and in the East when he wrote, "we do not change the eternal limits which our Fathers established. We maintain the traditions as we received them; for if we begin to destroy the fabric of the Church even in a small thing, gradually the whole of it will be cast into ruin."[3]

The parties to the dispute had some important points in common. Dogma, for example, did not divide them. To be sure, the Byzantine iconoclasts argued that pictorial representations of Christ violated orthodox Christology; but articles of Christology itself were not debated. On the value of art, there was likewise no division. The iconodule Council of Nicaea could have been speaking for its adversaries as well as for itself when it declared that all manual arts were of value in man's life, and that the beneficent or malign effect of a painting depended upon the subject represented.[4] Furthermore, all disputants used the same tests and methods of argumentation to establish the content of authentic tradition, which they all considered normative. All parties invoked textual criticism, the establishment of patristic consensus, and the deliberation of episcopal synods.

Still, there was no agreement on the issue which Leo III raised in 726: namely, the function of icons as expressions of the Church's common religious experience. Four principal attitudes emerged: (1) that icons were simply ornaments; (2) that they were mnemonic or didactic devices through which the experience of the holy was communicated; (3) that they were means of experiencing the holy directly, through divine presence immediate in the icons, or indirectly, through the icons as intermediaries; and (4) that they were idolatrous images the very creation of which was contrary to orthodox doctrine.

Variations on this immediate issue expressed the social values of na-

[3] De Imagin., II; PG 94, 1297f. Cf. Orat. I; III, 41; PG 94, 1284, 1355. See also Ladner, "Image Concept," 5. On the cult of imperial images in the fourth century, see Setton, *Attitude*, 196; and the splendid essay by Kitzinger, "Cult," 87, 90ff, 103, 123ff; Grabar, *L'Iconoclasme*, 77.

[4] Actio VI, Mansi 13, 241, 344.

tional groups. The iconoclasts were inspired by the artistic modes of the eastern provinces, where Islamic conventions against representations of the human form profoundly influenced Christian thought, and whence came the Isaurian emperors and many of their troops.[5] It is certainly important to know, as Father Dvornik has pointed out, that Constantinople was largely resettled by Syriacs and Armenians after its depopulation by plague in 747.[6] The iconodules in Byzantium and Rome held to the established artistic conventions of their societies. And, in condemning the Council of Nicaea II, the Franks upheld their own conventions, which Anastasius Bibliothecarius described when he wrote that throughout the Church only the Franks had not seen the "utility" of "the venerable images." "For they say that no work of human hands is to be adored—as though the codex of the Gospel, a work of human hands which they daily adore by kissing, were not more venerable than a dog, which they freely admit is not a work of human hands."[7]

To appreciate the hermeneutic concepts of tradition held by these schools and their social implications, we must now describe separately the general tenor of their arguments.

### A. THE ICONOCLAST POSITION

The destruction of iconoclasts' writings, including the official records of their synods, was so thorough that, except for a handful of fragments and short treatises, the historian must reconstruct their argument from the works of their enemies.[8] Fortunately, the iconodule Council of Nicaea (787) chose to refute the decrees of the iconoclast Synod of Hiereia (754) point by point, and, by quoting verbatim the debated passages, preserved a large portion, perhaps all, of the decisions it condemned. In their variety and comprehensiveness, these excerpts can be considered representative of the iconoclast position toward the middle of Constantine V's reign. There is no comparable monument from any other period of iconoclastic dominance; and the following remarks primarily concern the 754 decree.

The Synod of Hiereia confirmed the critical part which the emperors played in establishing iconoclasm. It wrote that Jesus had inspired the emperors with the same Holy Spirit given to his disciples and that He had raised them in wisdom and strength to be the counterparts (ἐφαμίλλους) of the Apostles for the perfection of doctrine and the de-

---

[5] See Bréhier, *La querelle*, 13.

[6] Dvornik, "Quomodo," 167f.

[7] Mansi 12, 983.

[8] Martin, *Controversy*, 111.

struction of demonic battlements being raised against the knowledge of God.[9] The laudes of the Synod also described the emperors as leaders in the struggle against error: they were acclaimed as the "peace of the world"; through them, the universal Church was pacified; they had exterminated idolatry.[10] And yet, the very convocation of the Synod of Hiereia showed that Constantine V had become convinced that his religious policies required the highest ecclesiastical confirmation. Constantine had at length summoned a synod which called itself oecumenical, and even in the laudes, the emperor and the Synod alike acknowledged the insufficiency of the imperial office to set ecclesiastical policies. "Let the holy and universal Synod say," the emperors asked, "whether the definition which has now been read may be promulgated through the consent of all the most holy bishops." To this the Synod responded that they all believed what had been read and that it was the faith of the Apostles, the Fathers, and the orthodox. The emperors had confirmed orthodoxy, the Synod exclaimed, for, having destroyed idolatry by discerning the unconfused and inseparable natures of Christ, they had confirmed the dogmas of the six holy and universal councils.[11]

Throughout the Iconoclast argument in 754 ran the thought that the imperial policies merely enforced the decrees of earlier oecumenical councils, which the assembly at Hiereia ratified, and that the oecumenical councils themselves were obedient to a primordial rule of faith fully stated in the Scriptures and in the writings of the Fathers.

The Synod was concerned, on one hand, to defend iconoclasts from the charge of perverting Christian doctrine with Jewish prohibitions and, on the other, to establish that iconodules had departed from the faith. It consequently alleged that Christianity was between Judaism and paganism, sharing the ceremonies of neither, and barring alike the blood sacrifices of Judaism and the pagan veneration of idols.[12] After Christ's advent, the Church became paganized by the introduction of idols,[13] and, though the councils and the Fathers always opposed idolatry, the private devotions of many believers and even the public services of churches continued the forbidden practice. The extinction of idolatry remained for the emperors to accomplish, but the work of the Synod of Hiereia was to sanction the imperial policy by drawing a line of identity between iconoclasm and orthodox Christology, between its own de-

---

[9] Nicaea II, Actio VI; Mansi 13, 225.  [10] *Ibid.*, 352f.
[11] *Ibid.*, 352f.  [12] *Ibid.*, 273.
[13] Cf. Alexander, *Nicephorus*, 11.

crees and the doctrine of salvation to which the oecumenical councils had witnessed. The Synod called itself the "holy, great, and universal seventh Synod";[14] it decreed that anyone who rejected "this holy and universal seventh synod," and did not embrace what the Synod had defined according to the doctrine of divinely inspired Scripture, was anathema to the Father, the Son, and the Holy Spirit, and to the seven oecumenical councils.[15] It professed in elaborate detail its acceptance of the oecumenical councils of Nicaea I, Constantinople (381), Ephesus, Chalcedon, Constantinople (553), and Constantinople (681),[16] and affirmed that the members of those councils were their spiritual fathers and masters, who had preserved intact the faith of which Christ had left His disciples and Apostles the teachers.[17] The makers of religious images, they argued, erred with Arius, Dioscorus, Eutyches, and the other heresiarchs condemned by the Great Councils,[18] for to paint an image of Christ was, theologically, either to confuse Christ's divine, unrepresentable nature, the efficient agent of salvation, with His human nature, or to divide the two natures. No portrait of the Word of God could be painted, nor could the special sanctity of the Blessed Virgin or the virtues of the saints, which alone set them apart from other men, be painted. Consequently, pictorial representations of Christ fell under the ancient condemnations of oecumenical councils, because their very existence expressed theological error; and paintings of the Blessed Virgin and of the saints, likewise not representing the effective qualities of the persons, were sheer vanity, anathematized according to the Fathers.[19]

In extending its argument beyond Christological questions, to touch upon representations of the Blessed Virgin and the saints, the Synod showed that it wished to establish conformity, not merely to the decrees of earlier councils, but even more to the pervading doctrine of salvation of which Christological issues were but a part. Indeed, earlier councils supplied only a small proportion of the total documentation which the Synod adduced; the bulk of its evidence derived from the Scriptures, from hagiographical works, and from doctrinal treatises. Concerned as they were to identify their judgments with the decrees of

---

[14] Mansi 13, 208. Cf. Grabar, *L'Iconoclasme*, 110.

[15] Mansi 13, 349, the six earlier councils, now accepted as oecumenical, plus itself.

[16] *Ibid.*, 233ff.       [17] *Ibid.*, 217.

[18] *Ibid.*, 252.         [19] *Ibid.*, 333, 336, 341, 344f, 340f.

oecumenical councils, the bishops at Hiereia summed up their argument without reference to the councils, referring only to "scriptural and patristic testimonies."[20] The breadth of their remarks and their citation of "an infinite multitude" of authorities[21] show an appeal beyond the specific judgments of oecumenical councils to the broader truth of which the councils were partial witnesses; by the methods of textual analysis and the establishment of a patristic consensus, they sought their ultimate justification in what they vaguely described as "the tradition of Christ, and the Apostles, and the Fathers."[22]

The "extirpation of idolatry" was, for them, the abolition of a devotional practice contrary to the essence of true doctrine, and the recovery of the long-obscured preaching which Christ had delivered to the Apostles, the renewal of that tradition which united all believers.

### B. THE ICONODULE ARGUMENT

Long before these arguments were framed, iconodules advanced, by similar methods, an entirely different view. The earliest important spokesmen for the iconodules were Germanus of Constantinople and John of Damascus. The latter, though not within the Empire, so strongly influenced iconodulic thought that he was one of those men explicitly anathematized by the Synod of Hiereia. Indeed, the Synod indicated his relative importance by entering four curses against him, and only one each against Germanus and George of Cyprus.

Entered before either party had fully explored the doctrinal implications of its position, Germanus's defense was loose and improvised. Iconoclasm, he wrote, was a novelty, a departure from the ancient custom of the Church. The Jews, who charged Christians with idolatry, lacked all shame, for their own fathers had not only fallen into the service of idols, but even acted contrary to the Law which they boasted of keeping.[1] Venerating images of the prophets, Apostles, and saints was merely honoring examples of fortitude and virtue. Venerating images of Christ and the Blessed Virgin was honoring the persons depicted. Such images had been received from the earliest bishops, and, after the time of persecution was over, universal councils down to his own day had established rules concerning images. These regulations and ancient usages, he wrote, were cogent evidence in favor of iconodulism, but still more convincing was the testimony of universal practice. All

---

[20] *Ibid.*, 324.     [21] *Loc.cit.*     [22] *Ibid.*, 268.

[1] PG 98, 168.

Christians throughout the entire world were under the single yoke of the Gospel, serving God with their distinctive confession. This unity was secure, for Christ had promised that He would be with the Apostles until the end of time, and that He would be present whenever two or three gathered in His name. Surely, on these assurances, that practice should be followed to which adhered, not a few insignificant cities, but almost all regions and great and pre-eminent churches.[2]

In the thought of John of Damascus, these suggestive but broadly defined principles achieved systematic formulation. It was not a recent device, but the early tradition of the Church that images be made and venerated. All things transmitted by the Law, the prophets, the Apostles, and the Evangelists must be accepted without qualification;[3] and to those authorities John added the Fathers and the councils.[4] With very fine distinctions, John pointed out that icons were but one form of imagery used in the Church. There were images according to nature, as Christ was the image of God; according to imitation, as man was the image of God; according to prefiguration, analogy, or plan, as the Scriptures revealed God's plan for salvation; and, finally, according to recollection.[5] Liturgical symbols too were images: the cross, the sacred vessels, and even the Eucharist had the same representative functions as icons.[6] To forbid one form of symbolism was to threaten them all.

Against the iconoclasts' argument that they were restoring obedience to the Second Commandment, John argued that if they wished to honor the Law by abolishing sacred images, they ought also to observe the Sabbath and the circumcision and keep the Passover nowhere but in Jerusalem. Still, if they observed the Law, Christ would profit them nothing. For God said of the Old Testament sanctions, "I have not given them good precepts," because of their hardness of heart.[7] Indeed, neither the Old Testament nor the Gospel referred by name to the Trinity, or to consubstantiality, to the one nature of Divinity, to the three Hypostases, or to the one person and the two natures of Christ. The holy Fathers, finding the same meaning in the words which they read in Scripture, defined all those terms, and the faithful received them.[8] Study of the Scriptures was laudable. It must, however, be done with

[2] *Ibid.*, 172f, 176.    [3] De Fide I, 1; PG 94, 789, 792.
[4] Orat. III, 3; PG 94, 1320f.
[5] E.g., Orat. I, 15, 22, 23; PG 94, 1244f, 1256. Orat. III, 18-23, 26; PG 94, 1337ff, 1345.
[6] Orat. I, 16; PG 94, 1245. Orat. II, 14, 15; PG 94, 1300f.
[7] Orat. II, 15; PG 94, 1302.    [8] Orat. III, 11; PG 94, 1333.

great caution; for, though there was one God of both the Old and the New Testament, He spoke in many different ways through the Fathers (John meant the Jewish patriarchs), the prophets, and, most recently, through His only-begotten Son, differently to diverse regions, differently to the sick and to the well, to the child and to the man. He spoke things suitable to the changing seasons and needs.[9] The Second Commandment addressed the Israelites' peculiar historical circumstances, but its relevance to Christians could be seen only in the light of the rule of grace which had superseded the Law.

The guide to proper understanding of the Scriptures lay in the ecclesiastical discipline which the eyewitnesses and ministers of the Word had established, not only by writing, but also by certain traditions never committed to writing.[10] The unity of the Church abided in tradition, for, as Gregory the Theologian said, one swallow does not make a spring, nor does the judgment of one man have such force that it can overturn the tradition of the universal Church, which is spread from one end of the earth to the other.[11] As sons, believers received much from their spiritual Fathers by unwritten tradition, including the institution of sacraments and liturgical practices; and, as St. Basil writes, the teachings transmitted by apostolic tradition were of equal force with those conveyed in writing.[12]

The making and veneration of religious images was one of the practices which John attributed to unwritten tradition. His rich citations of Scripture and patristic writings,[13] and his references to miraculous images, like the achiropoeta of Edessa,[14] were designed to prove his case by patristic consensus and by historical evidence that Christ Himself and His immediate followers had approved and encouraged the devotional use of images.

Leo III's iconoclastic decree consequently represented both a misunderstanding of the true meaning of scriptural injunctions and a danger to one of the two channels of true doctrine. The Manichees, John said, had written the Gospel according to Thomas; the iconoclasts were now perhaps to write that according to Leo. Not imperial edicts, but the establishments of the Fathers—written and unwritten—gov-

---

[9] Orat. III, 4; PG 94, 1321, 1324.     [10] Orat. I, 22, 23; PG 94, 1256.
[11] Orat. I, 23; Orat. II, 16; De Fide IV, 16; PG 94, 1256, 1301, 1304, 1172f, 1176.
[12] Orat. I, 23; Orat. II, 16; PG 94, 1255, 1301, 1304.
[13] PG 94, 1260ff, 1311ff, 1360ff.     [14] De Fide IV, 16; PG 94, 1173.

175

erned the Church. For just as the Gospel was spread throughout the world without literary monuments, so was it established and transmitted throughout the world that Christ, God incarnate, and the saints might be represented by images.[15] Emperors had no power to sanction the laws of the Church, for the Apostle did not include them among the Apostles, prophets, pastors, and teachers whom God set in the Church for its perfection. Emperors had charge of civil government; the pastors and teachers, of ecclesiastical. And temporal rulers might well be warned by the deaths of Saul, Jezebel, and Herod what severe punishment might await those who usurped powers not rightly theirs in afflicting Germanus and many other bishops who remained faithful to the ancient limits, the traditions which they received from their Fathers.[16] The Emperors had not received the power of binding and loosing; their religious decrees contrary to ecclesiastical order could not be obeyed.[17] For, in dismembering the anciently received and confirmed tradition, Leo threatened to divide the seamless tunic of Christ and to tear His Body asunder.[18]

For Germanus and John the cohesive element in the Church was ecclesiastical tradition, sustained by the continual presence of Christ among His people. They argued that the consonance of iconolatry with true religion was proven by the antiquity and the universality of the practice, and, in exegetical terms, by the testimony of Scripture and by patristic consensus. John extended his argument to mark some logical inconsistencies in the iconoclasts' doctrine of symbolism and to draw the ultimate conclusions that only clergy, and especially those who held the apostolic powers of binding and loosing, could judge of tradition, and that Leo's usurpation of their office mutilated tradition and, with it, the Body of Christ.

These arguments profoundly influenced later iconodulic thought. But the introduction of Christological associations by the iconoclasts under Constantine V, and the convention of the professedly Oecumenical Council of Hiereia forced the followers of Germanus and John to amplify the theological and ecclesiological aspects of their defense. The principal refutation of iconoclasm from the late eighth century occurs in the records of the Second Council of Nicaea. Summoned specifically to discredit the Synod of Hiereia, the Nicene assembly discussed the Horos of 754 premise by premise, patristic citation by citation, and with

[15] Orat. II, 16; PG 94, 1302, 1304.    [16] Orat. II, 12; PG 94, 1296f.
[17] Orat. I; PG 94, 1280f.    [18] Orat. I, 1, 2; PG 94, 1232f.

the minutest care rebutted the doctrinal justification of iconoclasm. Between the two arguments, however, there was a close correspondence in ideology and method. For, just as Hiereia looked for ultimate authority beyond oecumenical councils, to tradition, Nicaea, following Germanus and John, saw tradition as the cohesive bond of Christians and the paramount rule of faith.

The Synod of Hiereia referred to three principal authorities by which the veneration of images had been put down: the emperor, oecumenical councils, and tradition. Accordingly, the Council of Nicaea's refutation was concerned to show how the iconoclasts' understanding of these authorities erred. The Nicene comments on the imperial office are the least categorical of all, perhaps because the three iconoclast emperors from Leo III onward were both the predecessors and the progenitors of the reigning emperor, and perhaps also because the convention of the Council of Nicaea and the enforcement of its decrees depended upon imperial sanction. Its comments on the iconoclast emperors, though critical, are moderate. Indeed, its principal objection was not that Leo III, his son, and his grandson had destroyed the sacred images, but that the Synod of Hiereia had acclaimed Constantine and his son as the subverters of idols. In his address to the people of Constantinople, made at his nomination to the see, Tarasius asserted that Leo III had overturned the images and that the Synod of Hiereia, following his initiative, had presumed to uproot the ancient practice handed down in the Church.[19]

The Council of Nicaea, however, did not go even that far in censuring the iconoclast emperors. Certainly, the Council made a reference in its canons to Constantine V's irregular manipulation of ecclesiastical affairs; for it affirmed that the only true laws of the Church were those published by the Apostles through the Holy Spirit (the Apostolic Canons), those promulgated by "the Six Holy and Universal Synods and those councils which have been locally assembled," and, finally, those issued by the Holy Fathers (i.e., in their letters and treatises), for all these authorities were illuminated by the same Spirit. Imperial decrees were omitted from this list, and the tacit criticism of Constantine's Church policies became obvious in the second and third canons, which required a bishop-elect to promise as a condition of consecration that he would obey the canons, and which forbade the election of bishops by emperors.[20]

[19] Mansi 12, 990.    [20] Mansi 13, 417, 420.

Against Hiereia's description of the emperors as "counterparts of the Apostles," Nicaea entered no objection.[21] Indeed, at no point did Nicaea come firmly to grips with the imperial intervention which precipitated the iconoclastic dispute, or even enter censures against the policies of the iconoclast emperors. Nicaea's quarrel was with Hiereia; its objection was not to imperial policy but to Hiereia's allegation that the emperors had destroyed idolatry. Nicaea acclaimed Constantine VI and Irene as "overthrowers of novelty," for their hostility to iconoclasm,[22] but it judged the corresponding claim entered for the iconoclast emperors theologically untenable. Christ alone freed mankind from the error and deception of idols. The emperors might justly be acclaimed for their military victories and for subduing the barbarians.[23] But to acclaim them for destroying idolatry was either to assert that, in the eight hundred years since Christ, true doctrine had been obscured, or that a change had early occurred in the Church, laws and ordinations being introduced other than those which Christ instituted. Nicaea paraphrased Hiereia's acclamation to mean that, since the doctrine of the Apostles had become antiquated, they must enact a new doctrine, as did Moses and Aaron. Claiming a grace superior to that of the Apostles, they assembled at Hiereia allegedly to perfect themselves and their teaching; but, in fact, they renounced the doctrine of the magistracy and the tradition of the Apostles and the Fathers.[24]

Nicaea's comments on oecumenical councils are fuller and more to the point. In their letters of summons convening Nicaea, Constantine VI and Irene described the function of such a council. It was, they said, to confirm what had been handed down by the Apostles and all other orthodox teachers. Especially, they wished the ancient tradition concerning images to be established,[25] and the whole legislation ($\theta\epsilon\sigma\mu o\theta\epsilon\sigma i\alpha\nu$) of the Fathers to be followed.[26] The Church was presently torn asunder, East from West. But God had assembled the Council from all parts of the world, with vicars from the bishop of Rome and from the great bishops of the East, to expel all novelty and to restore wholeness to the body of the Church, strengthening it with the tradition of the Fathers.[27]

Nicaea argued that Hiereia had failed precisely on those points. Hiereia had called itself "the holy, great, and universal seventh synod."

---

[21] Actio VI. Mansi 13, 225, 228.  [22] Actio V. Mansi 13, 201.
[23] Actio VI. Mansi 13, 356.  [24] Actio VI. Mansi 13, 228.
[25] Mansi 12, 985f.  [26] Actio I. Mansi 12, 1003.
[27] *Ibid.*, 1006f.

178

But, Nicaea asked, how could it be "great and universal" when the prelates of other churches repudiated and anathematized it, when the bishop of Rome was present neither in his vicars nor in an encyclical letter, as the law of councils required, and when the patriarchs of the East were also unrepresented? Their sound had not gone forth into all the earth, after the fashion of the Apostles, nor had their words, after the fashion of the six holy and universal synods.[28]

Moreover, Hiereia's attempt to establish a line of identity between its own decrees and those of the six Great Synods was vain.[29] Though the iconoclasts professed to honor the decrees of the earlier councils, they in fact contravened the tradition which had been held by all the saints. They could not pretend that the veneration of images was a new practice, introduced in the seventy-odd years between the Sixth Oecumenical Council and themselves. It was introduced by the preaching of the Apostles and witnessed by the Holy Fathers, and indeed the Council in Trullo, supplementing the canons of the Sixth Council, approved the representations of the Lamb of God. To be sure, heresies had arisen against the Church, and the Six Councils had put them down, confirming all things which had been transmitted in the Church from ancient times, whether by writing or without writing. But the veneration of images was among those ancient practices; it was a means of teaching the Gospel visually, just as the readings of the Word taught orally.[30] Hiereia's profession that it held the articles of faith set forth by the Six Councils was meaningless. Nestorius accepted Nicaea I and Constantinople (381); Eutyches and Dioscorus accepted Ephesus; Monothelite heresiarchs, including "Honorius of Rome," accepted Chalcedon, Constantinople (552), and the preceding councils. Though they acknowledged the Holy Synods, the orthodox Church still expelled them for their heresy. Hiereia's repudiation of religious icons was evidence that, in the same way, it departed from the authentic tradition.[31] Hiereia's assertion that makers of images erred with Arius, Dioscorus, Eutyches, and all others who confused or separated the natures of Christ invited the response that the making of images was not an invention of painters, but the approved legislation and tradition of the orthodox Church (τῆς καθολικῆς ἐκκλησίας ἔγκριτος θεσμοθεσία καὶ παράδοσις).[32]

[28] Actio VI. Mansi 13, 208f.
[29] Actio VI. Mansi 13, 349, 353.
[30] Actio VI. Mansi 13, 216, 220.
[31] Actio VI. Mansi 13, 233, 236f.
[32] Actio VI. Mansi 13, 252.

Those who made and venerated images did not fall under the condemnations which the Six Councils entered against the heresiarchs; they were true to the unwritten tradition spread by the preaching of the Apostles.[33] But the iconoclasts were at one with the Manichees, the Marcionites,[34] and those who confused the natures of Christ.

Like their adversaries, the iconodules at Nicaea found ultimate authority, the infallible rule of faith, in tradition, of which emperors were but executors and oecumenical councils, partial witnesses. Early in Nicaea's debates, Tarasius acknowledged the supremacy of tradition by quoting the words of St. Paul: "Therefore, brethren, stand fast, and hold the traditions which ye have been taught, whether by word or our epistle,"[35] and his admonition to Timothy and Titus to "avoid profane novelties of speech."[36] Hiereia's corresponding claims on scriptural and patristic testimony that iconoclasm accorded with authentic tradition commanded no respect. For, Nicaea argued, like all heresiarchs, the iconoclasts used the words of Scripture, adulterating what the Holy Spirit correctly dictated with their own malign interpretations.[37] By textual criticism, Nicaea discovered that Hiereia's patristic citations were sometimes distorted out of context or misquoted, and that one author quoted as an authority was tainted with heresy.[38] Indeed, the iconoclasts are unwilling to submit to the tradition of the Church, infatuated as they are with their novelty, which is contrary to wholesome definitions and laws. They simulate words of piety, but they speak with their own distorted sense, not receiving God's true judgment, and trampling under foot ecclesiastical traditions. They ought to speak one harmonious voice, and confirm the ancient tradition, which the universal company of the faithful has held and confessed by the tradition of the Apostles and Fathers. For the things which have been handed down in the orthodox Church admit no addition or subtraction.[39] Of them, one cannot say, "it is and it is not"; they exist in truth and abide uncorrupted and unaltered forever.[40]

Hiereia gave evidence of its deficient understanding when it declared

[33] Actio VI. Mansi 13, 268.
[34] Actio I. Mansi 12, 1031; Actio VI. Mansi 13, 296.
[35] II Thess. 2, 15.
[36] Actio I. Mansi 12, 1054. Cf. II; Tim. 2, 16; Tit. 3, 9.
[37] Actio VI. Mansi 13, 281. Cf. Actio VI. Mansi 13, 348f.
[38] Eusebius of Caesarea, Actio VI. Mansi 13, 313, 316. Cf. Actio V, Actio VI, Mansi 13, 192, 292f, 296.
[39] Actio VI. Mansi 13, 324f, 328.       [40] Actio I. Mansi 12, 1002.

that Christianity stood midway btween Judaism and paganism, sharing the ritual of neither; for the things of the Old Testament, which the Israelites held, were the tradition of God, while the observances of pagans belonged to demons.[41] In the seventh century, Leontius of Cyprus had been concerned to defend the Church against Jewish allegations of idolatry. Leontius affirmed that reverence for images was entirely consonant with the Old Testament, and that it was indeed "a tradition of the Law, and not of our making" (νομικὴ γὰρ αυτη ἡ παράδοσις καὶ οὐχ ἡ μετέρα).[42] With Leontius's treatise ready in their dossier, the bishops at Nicaea adopted his argument that veneration of religious images, not iconoclasm, was the true tradition of God, revealed to the people of the Old Dispensation and transmitted to the New Israel. The "Judaic council"[43] at Hiereia wrongly interpreted the injunctions of the Old Testament; for not only had the Church received the veneration of images as law from ancient times, from the first teachers of Christian doctrine and their successors, but, according to Scriptures, the practice was also observed by the Old Israel.[44]

Iconoclasm, not the veneration of images, was the novelty wrongly introduced into the Church's ancient order, the corruption of the rule of faith which God first revealed to the Israelites. Nicaea asserted that it truly held "the ancient legislation of the orthodox church" (τῇ ἀρχαίᾳ θεσμοθεσίᾳ), the laws (τοὺς θεσμούς)[45] of the Fathers, in anathematizing the "novelty." Hiereia spurned the teachings of the holy Fathers and the tradition of the orthodox church; they assumed the voices of Arius, Nestorius, Eutyches, and Dioscorus; their doctrines were not transmitted by the Old or the New Testament, the doctrines of the Fathers, the holy synods, or authentic tradition. The Church had never, as they taught, fallen into idolatry;[46] rather, in venerating images, it had preserved the ancient tradition of the Fathers, who established the practice "in all God's churches, and in every place of His dominion."[47]

The Synod of Hiereia, therefore, erred not because it departed from the decrees of oecumenical councils, but because it violated the Church's written and unwritten tradition.[48] In contrast, Tarasius entered Nicaea's own claims to oecumenicity when he declared: "Thus our sound will go forth into all the earth, and the power of our words to

[41] Actio VI. Mansi 13, 273, 276.
[43] Actio IV. Mansi 13, 132.
[45] Actio V. Mansi 13, 201.
[47] Actio IV. Mansi 13, 132.

[42] PG 94, 1381. Baynes, "Icons," 98.
[44] Mansi 13, 404.
[46] Actio I. Mansi 12, 1010f.
[48] Mansi 13, 400.

181

the ends of the earth; for we do not remove the limits which our Fathers set, but, instructed apostolically, we hold to the traditions which we have received."[49] The iconoclasts had striven to add to the teachings of the Scriptures, the canons, and the Fathers, and thus to extinguish the truth;[50] men who were the princes of bishops had become the princes of heretics, and scattered contention among the people.[51] Withdrawing from the tradition of the orthodox Church, they lost the understanding of truth, and failed to distinguish between the holy and the profane. But Christ, who promised to be with His Church until the end of time, provided that the common decree of Nicaea would confirm the divinely inspired teaching of the Fathers and the tradition of the entire Church throughout the earth—the tradition proper to the Holy Spirit, which lives in the Church.[52] Contrary to truth, the iconoclasts had changed the apostolic and patristic tradition of the Church to suit their purposes; but, inspired by the grace of one Spirit, Nicaea preserved unchanged all that belonged to the Church,[53] raised up what had been tyrannically destroyed, and reshaped it into the ancient and apostolic tradition.[54] "Contention subsides," Tarasius said at Nicaea, "and the dividing wall of enmity is cast down. East, west, north, and south—we have been brought under one yoke and in one agreement." The Holy Synod said: " 'Glory be to you, o Lord, who hast united us.' Tarasius, the most holy patriarch said: 'Thanks be to Christ, the bearer of peace, our true God, with the Father and the All-Holy Spirit forever. Amen.' "[55]

For the bishops at Nicaea as well as for those at Hiereia, the ultimate bond of union in the Church was tradition, and the means for determining authentic tradition were exegetical devices. Techniques of textual criticism and the establishment of patristic consensus were the tests of orthodoxy, rather than any official declaration or synodal decree. To be sure, each party emphasized its own oecumenicity and professed identity between its own decrees and those of the first six oecumenical councils. But even the oecumenical councils were important only in their magisterial function, not in any juridical or administrative action. Their pronouncements, limited to specific cases, did not present a full rule of faith; they were rather testimonies to parts of a greater body of

[49] Actio IV. Mansi 13, 4. Cf. canon 7; Mansi 13, 427.
[50] PG 98, 1480.
[51] Mansi 13, 401ff.
[52] Mansi 13, 376f.
[53] Mansi 13, 408f.
[54] Actio III. Mansi 12, 1134f.
[55] Actio III. Mansi 12, 1154.

written and unwritten discipline transmitted by Christ to the Apostles, and by them to the Fathers in every age, and thence to the faithful, always sustained in every place by the continual presence of the spirit of Christ. Nicaea objected that Hiereia could not be considered "great and oecumenical" because no representatives from Rome and the great eastern sees assisted in it,[56] and because they had repudiated its decrees. But Nicaea's further arguments that Hiereia was not "universal," although it accepted the decrees of the first six oecumenical councils, the claims it entered of its own oecumenicity, and, finally, its acceptance even of the decrees of local councils as laws of the universal Church show that the matter of representation was relatively superficial. According to Nicaea, Hiereia lacked what it claimed to have, and what Nicaea affirmed to be its own: consonance with the tradition of the Apostles and the Fathers, and harmony with that Spirit which alone unified the Church.

We must now turn to the radically different thought of the Franks and the Romans.

## C. FRANKISH THOUGHT

A Byzantine legation in 767 and Frankish bishops at the Roman synod of 769 informed Gaul of the dispute, but the earliest extant Frankish statement on iconoclasm was composed about 791.[1] There is no general agreement as to the authorship of the *Libri Carolini*. Charlemagne himself,[2] Alcuin,[3] and Theodulf of Orleans[4] have all been proposed as authors. Uncertainty on this important and highly technical question, however, does not cloud the fact that the *Libri* were promulgated by Charlemagne as a declaration of official policy, and consequently that he and his advisors accepted the ecclesiological doctrine it expresses.

A monument of the Carolingian patristic revival, the *Libri* were composed as a refutation of the decrees of the Second Council of Nicaea, which it knew from an inaccurate Latin translation of the Council's acts prepared in Rome. In complete disagreement with what he knew of the Council and with the commendation with which Hadrian I had sent its decrees to Gaul, the author or authors contested the pro-

---

[56] Cf. Dvornik, *Apostolicity*, 171.

[1] Haendler, *Epochen*, 19.
[2] Winston, *Hammer*, 274f. Cf. Haendler, *Epochen*, 31.
[3] Wallach, "Author," 469-515.　　　　[4] Freeman, "Further Studies," 203-89.

priety of the veneration of images. Without going so far as iconoclasm, he argued that the use of religious representations as sanctioned by the Council, and thus by Pope Hadrian's legates at Nicaea, was contrary to orthodox practice.

With the magisterial aspects of ecclesiology foremost in his mind, he framed a doctrine which, like Alcuin's, combined universal consensus with "Roman authority." Before undertaking the refutation of the Nicene decrees, the author, in Charlemagne's name, set forth as a basic premise that "the holy, Roman, Catholic, and apostolic Church, exalted above all other churches, must be explicitly consulted when a question arises concerning matters of faith." He wrote that no Scriptures could be considered authentic except those which the Roman Church received as canonical, and that only the teachings of those doctors whom Gelasius I (i.e., the *Decretum Gelasianum*) or other Roman pontiffs approved could be embraced. He attributed to St. Augustine an argument that approval by the apostolic sees was a necessary warrant of canonical authority, and applied this statement particularly to Rome, which, he said, was exalted above all other apostolic sees, as those sees themselves were over all other churches. This pre-eminence derived not from synodal establishments, but from the authority of Christ Himself, in His commission to St. Peter. All catholic churches should seek assistance in fortifying the faith from Rome, after Christ; for, having neither spot nor wrinkle, she trod upon the heads of heretics and confirmed the minds of believers in the faith. Though many had withdrawn from Rome's communion, the Frankish church had always sought apostolic instruction from her. This was true particularly concerning the liturgical reform instituted by Pippin and continued by Charlemagne, who, "wishing to elevate the condition of the holy Roman church and striving to obey the salutary exhortations of the most reverend Pope Hadrian," had spread "the tradition of the Apostolic See in singing" throughout Gaul, Italy, Saxony, and the lands of the north.[5]

These ascriptions of primacy were narrowly circumscribed. They introduced a treatise which repudiated doctrines and decrees which Rome had at least implicitly approved. Portions of the treatise were concerned with defending the Frankish profession of the Filioque, which, as the author acknowledged, was not part of the Nicene or Chalcedonian professions, and which the Roman Church refused to accept.[6] The pro-

[5] I, 6; MGH Conc. II, Suppl., 21f.
[6] III, 1, 3; *ibid.*, 106f, 112; MGH Epp. 5, k. a. 3, no. 7, 65.

fession of Charlemagne's obedience to Hadrian I ignored the numerous occasions on which the King had acted directly contrary to Hadrian's commands.

Differences between the magisterial aspects of Roman ecclesiology and the corresponding thought expressed in the *Libri* were equally distinct. The whole passage acknowledging the supremacy of the Roman Church appears to have been little more than a diplomatic courtesy to the see whose judgment the treatise was designed to refute. For the references to the *Decretum Gelasianum*—including both the statement that the Roman Church was without spot or wrinkle and the assertion that only the Scriptures which Rome received as canonical and the dogmas of the Fathers whom Rome accepted could be considered authentic—conceal profound differences from the position of the *Decretum* itself and from the general premises of eighth-century papal thought.

These divergences concerned two principal elements: the designation of specific writings or thinkers as authoritative, and the establishment of a standard interpretation of patristic doctrine. Roman thinkers wrote of "the Fathers whom the Apostolic See has accepted," and required that their works be understood according to Roman exegesis. In the passage cited from the *Libri Carolini*, the author significantly modified this position. He referred principally to doctrine, rather than to authors, writing that only the "dogmas" of the teachers whom Gelasius and other Roman bishops approved could be embraced. He therefore implied that writers other than those whom Rome specifically approved might be considered authoritative if their teachings corresponded with those of the approved writers. To establish that correspondence, it was critical to fix a standard interpretation; the author left that vexed question unanswered in his self-conscious and qualified ascription of primacy to Rome.

The *Decretum* was cited several times more as a catalogue of authentic writings. In those citations, the author betrayed the tendency of his thought by invoking the judgment of "other catholic and orthodox men,"[7] or of "the doctrines of other Fathers,"[8] as criteria together with the *Decretum*. He rejected writings deficient in learning or in style, or errant in doctrine, works lacking "the learning of heavenly magistracy," not because of any authoritative decree, but because they departed "from the norm of the ancient Fathers." He accepted those which

[7] IV, 10; MGH Conc. II., Suppl., 189.
[8] IV, 11; *ibid.*, 190.

185

the "holy and universal Church" approved as "blameless," "according to the institution of the holy Fathers."[9]

The author of the *Libri* thus found the standard interpretation of authentic teaching in what he considered the consensus of patristic judgments and the universal confession of all orthodox believers. This aspect of his thought is particularly clear in his specific refutation of the Second Nicene Council. He argued that the Council had striven to anathematize the "catholic church" and "the churches of the whole world," had departed from ancient institutions, and had sought to withdraw from the universality of the Church's body.[10] The Council had called itself "universal," but the author of the *Libri* contended that the title was unwarranted. "The holy and universal Church" rejected the practices the Council approved,[11] and, most important, the Council had not been assembled "from the universal Church." Neither did it have the unshaken purity of the universal faith, nor did its acts stand confirmed by the authority of all churches. He observed that the "universal Church" was called, in Greek, the "catholic church";[12] whatever did not depart from the unity of the Church was, therefore, "catholic," and every Christian doctrine, constitution, or tradition must suit the "universal Church." Heretics in different parts of the world betrayed their errors by lacking ecclesiastical unity. Citing St. Augustine, the author observed that whenever the bishops of two or three provinces gathered, their judgments would be catholic if their establishments did not depart from the teachings of the ancient Fathers. Indeed, their decisions might be called universal, since, even though not framed by the bishops of the whole world, they conformed to the faith and traditions of all believers. "Everything that is ecclesiastical is catholic; everything that is catholic is universal; and everything that is universal lacks profane verbal novelties." Assemblies of bishops from two or three provinces, like the Nicene assembly, which established "new things," could not be called universal, since their establishments diverged from the understanding of the whole Church, and since their work, consequently, was not catholic. Therefore, the Nicene Council could not be called universal. Discontented with the teachings of the ancient Fathers, it violated the doctrines of the universal Church,[13] and willfully distorted scriptural verses to suit its own interpretations.[14]

[9] I, 11; IV, 11; *ibid.*, 30, 192.    [10] III, 11; *ibid.*, 123.    [11] IV, 2; *ibid.*, 175.
[12] Cf. Alcuin, MGH Epp. 4, k. a. 2, no. 19, 53ff.
[13] Cf. IV, 28; MGH Conc. II, Suppl., 227.
[14] Praef., I, 9; *ibid.*, 4, 27f. Cf. I, 5, 18f.

The author acknowledged that antiquity was not inviolable and that changes might occur in the Church; but, to be legitimate, they must accord with "the ancient tradition of the Fathers and of the Church,"[15] with "the apostolic tradition."[16] His reference to the sacrament of the Eucharist as "a new antiquity, and an ancient novelty,"[17] expressed the combination of conservatism and change which he required of every authentic development. The Church itself had once been "new," growing among the Jewish people, and later expanding to include the Gentiles;[18] the Apostles succeeded to the partiarchs and prophets;[19] the New Testament revealed the truth which the Old had declared in the Law and the prophets.[20]

This mutability admitted corruption of the authentic tradition through the perverse intent of schismatics,[21] the introduction of novelty without the corroboration of antiquity. The author of the *Libri* argued that the Nicene Council had fallen into that error, abandoning the tradition of the early Fathers and schismatically introducing new establishments into the Church. The "most impudent tradition" of the Council ran contrary to the prophetic, Gospel, and apostolic Scriptures, to the teachings of the holy orthodox Fathers, and to the six oecumenical councils.[22] And, by their insolent disparagement of the tradition of their spiritual Fathers, the schismatics had lost their powers to consecrate the eucharistic elements, to bless by the imposition of hands, and to bind and loose.[23]

Knowing that the Nicene decrees had been framed through the influence of Irene and Constantine VI, the author of the *Libri* took exception to their concept of rulership. They had, he wrote, introduced new and unsuitable constitutions into the Church, and yet they allowed themselves to be called "divine." Roman ambition, the ambition of pagan emperors, admitted the title *Divus*,[24] a barbarism and a solecism; apostolic tradition opposed it. The author understood that Constantine and Irene had claimed that God ruled jointly with them.[25] The assertion, he wrote, was absurd. For, though God might reign in men, by their faith in Him, His Kingdom was as different from human government as His existence was from human life. Men could not "co-rule" with God

---

[15] II, 31; *ibid.*, 102.  [16] I, 17; *ibid.*, 42.  [17] II, 27; *ibid.*, 88f.
[18] Cf. I, 20; II, 13; *ibid.*, 48, 73.  [19] I, 21; *ibid.*, 49.
[20] I, 20; II, 4; *ibid.*, 45ff, 66.  [21] I, 18; *ibid.*, 43.  [22] Praef.; *ibid.*, 4f.
[23] II, 31; *ibid.*, 100.  [24] Cf. IV, 5; *ibid.*, 180.
[25] I, 1; *ibid.*, 8f, . . . *Deum sibi conregnare etiam dicunt.*

as long as they were "robed with the tunic of this mortality."[26] It was absurd to argue that men far inferior to the Apostles in personal merits and in spiritual powers, men who did not even follow the Apostles, should be called their "counterparts."[27] Just as the followers of truth spurned the false gods of paganism, so should they spurn pagan titles, for the Apostle said: "What has light to do with darkness, or Christ with Belial?"[28] In similar terms, he denounced the ceremonial adoration of imperial images in Byzantium as an inheritance of the Roman Empire from the Babylonian, deserving to be uprooted by followers of the true religion.[29] And yet (with Charlemagne in mind no doubt) the author of the *Libri* did not disparage the royal office. On the contrary, he represented Heaven as a kingdom whose Lord was its light;[30] and of earthly rulers, he wrote, describing the honor which David showed Saul, a wicked king: "As long therefore as he is in this office, he is to be honored, if not for his own qualities, then for his order. Whence the Apostle says: 'Be ye subject to all the higher powers. For there is no power but of God.' And, in another place, 'Fear God, Honor the King.' "[31]

Like Alcuin in his signed works, the author of the *Libri Carolini* attributed the sanction of divinity, without the attributes of divinity itself, to the royal office. In repudiating the Council at which Hadrian I had been represented and whose decrees the Pope had instructed Charlemagne to approve, he also showed the degree of difference between Roman and Frankish ecclesiology. His very treatise is a refutation, of the Nicene decisions as well as of the papal assertion that Roman approval was sufficient to establish the writings of individual men or the decrees of synods as authentic statements of faith. Without rejecting papal authority, as represented by the *Decretum Gelasianum*, he appealed to another coordinate canon of orthodoxy: tradition, as attested by the consensus of the universal Church.

It would be sheer hypothesis to suggest that Charlemagne himself framed the sophisticated ecclesiological position stated in the *Libri*. He did give it his official approval, however; and, in issuing the *Libri* as a public document, Charlemagne declared that he, his religious advisors, and the Frankish clergy as a whole held a concept of the Church rad-

[26] I, 1; *ibid.*, 12.
[27] IV, 20; *ibid.*, 211f.  [28] I, 3; *ibid.*, 16.  [29] III, 15; *ibid.*, 135.
[30] II, 3; *ibid.*, 65.  [31] III, 29; *ibid.*, 166.

ically different from that advanced by their contemporary popes. For the Franks, as for the African apologists, distinguishing heresy from schism was a work of exegesis and collation rather than an authoritarian act.

The thought of the eighth-century popes followed from the premises that Christ's commission to St. Peter gave the Roman Church "principate" over all the earth, that both apostolate and episcopate began through Christ in St. Peter, and that the "tradition of the Apostolic See" was the measure of orthodox faith and practice. Alcuin and his Frankish colleagues advanced a doctrine in which the approval of the universal Church and the sanction of Roman authority were coordinate tests of orthodoxy. For Roman thinkers, they were identical, since St. Peter's See was the holy, universal, and apostolic Church.

### D. THE ROMAN POSITION

When the iconoclastic dispute opened, Gregory II expressed the Roman position in two vehement letters to the Emperor Leo. Gregory said that Leo had commanded Roman obedience, writing, "I am Emperor and Bishop [*sacerdos*]." Surely, earlier emperors had shown themselves true pontiffs and emperors by seeking the welfare of the Church jointly with bishops. Constantine the Great, Theodosius the Great, Valentinian the Great, and Constantine IV were rulers of that sort, governing religiously, gathering synods at one with the counsel and purpose of bishops, enquiring into the truth of doctrines, establishing and adorning churches. They were indeed priests and emperors; though Leo held the Empire, he had not guarded the judgments of the Fathers, for he had stripped the churches of their ornaments and laid them waste. Gregory admonished Leo to cease his wrongful intrusion into religious matters and to "follow the Church." "Dogmas do not belong to emperors, but to pontiffs; for we have the sense of Christ. The institution of ecclesiastical establishments is one thing; the sense of secular establishments is another." Just as the pontiff has no power to intrude into the palace and confer royal offices, so the emperor has no power to intrude into the churches, to direct clerical elections, to consecrate, to administer the symbols of the holy sacraments, or to participate in the work of the bishops. Leo must honor and glorify the holy Fathers who, according to God, dispelled the blindness from men's hearts and eyes; he must restore the veneration of images, which had been handed

189

down from the very beginning of human life; and thus, by obedience, he might truly be pontiff and emperor.[1]

Leo had proposed a general council to judge the dispute. Gregory rejected the proposal as useless, since true doctrine concerning religious images was already manifest. Leo had proposed to destroy the image of St. Peter in Rome, "which all the realms of the West consider a god on earth"; Gregory promised armed retribution. The Emperor proposed to seize Gregory and send him in bondage to Constantinople, as Constantine had captured Martin I; Gregory defied him. The Pope could withdraw twenty-four *stadia* to safety in the Campania; the Emperor would chase the winds. "The whole West offers the fruits of faith to the holy Prince of the Apostles. But if you send men to destroy the image of St. Peter, lo, we declare to you, we are innocent of the blood which they will shed; but may these things fall . . . on your head."[2]

The Emperor, Gregory wrote, was "the head of Christians," but he had violated the commands of the Scriptures, of the Fathers and doctors, and of "the six synods in Christ," the six oecumenical councils, which had transmitted the true faith.[3] Rome was free of his error and contemptuous of his assertion of ecclesiastical authority. Later, when the controversy had ended its first period, Hadrian I wrote in the same vein to Charlemagne, providing a very full statement of the Roman case in the Iconoclastic Dispute.

When Hadrian I took up the debate, it was clear that political matters weighed more heavily on his mind than doctrinal issues. The Roman concept of the functions of images seems, in fact, to have been very close to the Nicene position. At least one miraculous image was revered at Rome; and, in an early defense, Pope Gregory II needlessly confirmed the worst fears of the iconoclasts by affirming that all the kingdoms of the West considered a particular image of St. Peter to be a god on earth (*deum terrestrem*).[4] Acceding to the desire of Irene and Constantine VI, Hadrian sent legates to Nicaea. They participated in the debates and subscribed the Council's definition. Four years later, Hadrian wrote that he had made no response to Constantine concerning the Council,[5] and, in 794, his legates joined the Frankish clergy at the Synod of Frankfurt in repudiating Nicaea. This apparent *volte-face*

[1] Ep. 13; PL 89, 521-24; JL 2182 (1674).
[2] Ep. 12; PL 89, 517-20; JL 2180 (1672).
[3] *Ibid.*, 513.                                    [4] PL 89, 520.
[5] MGH Epp. 5, k. a. 3, no. 2, 57. See below n. 16.

was not prompted by aversion to the doctrines affirmed at Nicaea, but, as Hadrian himself wrote, by Byzantium's failure to acknowledge Roman primacy in some eastern dioceses. But Hadrian never approved or rejected the Council in his own right; his ambivalence was part of a cautious diplomatic enterprise.

Apart from political matters, ecclesiology was, for the Pope, the chief matter of debate; conventionally, the doctrine of papal monarchy was the starting point. He acknowledged that "the ancient tradition" was "the orthodox faith."[6] But the concept of the bishop of Rome as "universal pope" and of the Roman Church as "universal" had ancillary principles corresponding precisely with those which Gregory the Great saw and feared in the title "oecumenical patriarch." Hadrian contrasted "the Church of Constantinople," which had converted from error, with the "holy, catholic and apostolic Roman church, which has always held to justice, as it has been written, 'the see of justice, the house of faith, the hall of uprightness [*pudoris*].' "[7] "The holy catholic and apostolic Roman church," he wrote, was the "head of the whole world," and, since the gates of Hell would not prevail against it, the sanctions issued from "the most blessed and apostolic See of St. Peter" must be reverently observed forever by all the faithful. The tradition of the Fathers showed that Rome held that principate over all the earth which Christ granted personally to St. Peter and which that Apostle's Church after him had held and would always retain. The churches of Constantinople, Alexandria, and Antioch were subject to the "holy, catholic, and apostolic Roman Church." With utter disregard for the furious protests of Leo I and Gelasius I, Hadrian wrote that that subjection was especially clear in the fact that Constantinople had assumed second rank among the patriarchates "by the consent of the holy Roman church," and that Alexandria and Antioch, though opposed to the new ranking, had not dared to resist the Roman definition. Borrowing a turn of phrase from Innocent I, Hadrian went on to say that the West was particularly subject to Roman supremacy, "for, as the decrees of the holy pontiffs have established in all Italy, the Gauls, the Spains, Africa, and Sicily, and the islands in between, no one instituted churches but those whom the venerable Apostle Peter or his successors established as bishops." The clergy in those regions must follow what Rome, the origin of their faith, ordained. Paraphrasing a sentence of Zosimus,

[6] Hadrian I. Ep. 2; MGH Epp. 5, k. a. 3, 29.
[7] *Loc.cit.*

Hadrian concluded that all the Church knew that the See of St. Peter had the right to reverse the judgments of anyone, that it had the privilege of judging every church, that no one might judge of its judgment, and that, if anyone presumed to dispute the ruling of the Apostolic See, he was anathema.[8]

Concerning the immediate issue of iconoclasm, he professed—in the very words of his predecessor—to follow the ancient traditions of the Fathers and to depart in no way from their doctrine; for thus he hoped to attain their full grace.[9] If heretics had not assailed the holy, catholic, and apostolic Church, the six oecumenical councils would have been unnecessary; but ancient heresies had arisen, and, in iconoclasm, a new heresy, "novelties," appeared against which Hadrian and his immediate predecessors had defended the true faith handed down by their elders, and the dignity due St. Peter.[10] The authority of the Fathers established that sacred images be adored and venerated;[11] that was the ancient tradition of the holy, catholic, and apostolic Roman Church, the ancient doctrine of Hadrian's predecessors, the holy pontiffs, and the tradition of right faith.[12] Such was the command of the oecumenical councils; such was the tradition of "the holy, catholic, and apostolic, universal Roman Church."[13] Hadrian's condition for reconciliation with Constantinople had been the invalidation of the inconoclast Synod of Hiereia, whose decree "was framed irregularly and irrationally, without the Apostolic See and against the tradition of the venerable Fathers."[14] The Synod of Hiereia represented both the religious doctrine and the concept of rulership against which Roman bishops had contended for fifty years, the chief victory of powers and ideologies opposed to Roman ecclesiology, the papacy's greatest defeat in the conflict which Pope Paul I described when he wrote: "These most wicked Greeks persecute us for no reason other than for the holy and orthodox faith and the venerable and pious tradition of the Fathers, which they wish to destroy and to crush."[15]

The Second Council of Nicaea rendered the atonement which Hadrian demanded. The decrees of Hiereia were overturned; at least in form, the demands of Roman ecclesiology were accommodated in

---

[8] Ep. 1; *ibid.*, 3-5.    [9] Ep. 2; *ibid.*, 27f.    [10] *Ibid.*, 51.
[11] *Ibid.*, 15f.    [12] *Ibid.*, 7.    [13] *Ibid.*, 11.
[14] Ep. 57; PL 96, 1237, 1240. JL 2449 (1883); Deneffe, *Traditionsbegriff*, 53f. See Wallach, "Versions."
[15] Codex Carolinus, ep. 30; MGH Epp. 3, k. a. 1, 536.

Byzantine ecclesiology and political thought. These terms of reconciliation were superficial; iconoclastic revivals and continuing animosity toward Rome allowed them little more than transitory, ceremonial
importance.[16]

+

The dispute over the social functions of icons brought into question
modes of communicating the Church's common religious experience.
That, in turn, led to new thought concerning cult and organizational expressions of the common experience; the basic doctrinal expressions
remained unchanged. As we have seen, the principal arguments of
the dispute advanced from the particular cult expression of the common
experience to the stage of arguing the meaning of tradition itself: that
is, to the general means by which the common experience was initially
communicated anterior to social expression in cult, doctrine, or organization. The iconodules and iconoclasts in Byzantium differed radically
in their over attitude toward cult expression though they lived within the
same society. All the same, they worked intellectually within the
same organizational terms; they expressed their differences secondarily
in secession and regrouping. On the other hand, the differences among
Byzantine, Frankish, and Roman thinkers toward the social function of
icons only suggested the extreme variations in organizational expression
which divided them. Conflict merely sharpened these indigenous
groupings.

Resorting to the norm of universality and thus implicitly to the canons
of antiquity and consensus by no means clarified the content of tradition. It rather exasperated different understandings of what the cohesive
element of the universal Church was. Byzantine thinkers considered
universality demonstrable by general consensus: first, the consensus of
the Fathers and orthodox councils, as attested by a critical study of their
works, and secondly, the consensus of all the faithful in matters not
defined in Scripture or in patristic writings. The Franks similarly held
that the test of universality was an exegetical collation of scriptural and
canonistic sources, the establishment of a patristic consensus. Upholding the standard of textual criticism and collation of texts, Roman think-

---

[16] On Hadrian's acceptance of Nicaea II as a "local council"—i.e., not an oecumenical council—see Alexander, *Nicephorus*, 105. Cf. Codex Carolinus, ep. 32;
MGH Epp. 3, k. a. 1, 539.

193

ers affirmed moreover that in any case the "tradition of the Apostolic See" and "the tradition of the universal Church" were identical, for the See of St. Peter was not only "holy," and "apostolic" but also "universal." The disputes of the patristic age and the ever more refined doctrinal definitions made the ancient concept of ecclesiastical cohesion without conformity obsolete. Cohesion followed precisely from conformity in cult, doctrine, and order, and standards of conformity were set by political expedience.

## CHAPTER 7

# Summary: The Progress of Transvaluation

FROM the Church's earliest days, the force of tradition had been qualified by other forms of authority. The power of prophets to cast down ancient laws and practices survived in the power of bishops to reinterpret earlier precepts anywhere along the spectrum between rigid literalism and wildest allegory, or even to ignore them. The literal meaning of writings—such as the Scriptures themselves, canons, and the letters and treatises of acknowledged Fathers—stood as a third force beside episcopal discretion and tradition. Thinkers dealt with these different strains in improvised and fortuitous ways; traces of "constitutionalism" appear only in retrospect.

Into this variegated and amorphous body of authorities, the conversion of Constantine and its aftermath intruded yet another element: the extraneous authority of civil government. This cataclysmic series of events revised issues of authority in the Church and brought them to an unprecedented level of sophistication, and it also cast into high relief one general problem, which had touched even the apologists: the effect of society on religion.

In the West, these forces, particularly episcopal discretion and interests of civil government, slowly emptied the word "tradition" of the meaning it had had for the apologists, term and concept grew separate.

The disputes in the era of the Byzantine papacy greatly heightened the tension between conservatism and reform implicit in the concept of tradition. At the beginning of the fifth century, Vincent of Lérins wrote of that tension in theological terms as a harmonious duality of conservatism and change, in which understanding, wisdom, and knowledge increased while the sense of doctrine remained unaltered. Many synods between the sixth and the eighth century showed the same concern in institutional terms, when they affirmed that they had restored to vigor the ancient canonical decrees which had long fallen into disuse, and further, as one Synod declared, that they had "believed that new statutes had to be added according to the state of the cases and the

195

times."[1] Vincent's contemporary, St. Augustine, had suggested the disorder to which the process of renewal and addition might lead when he wrote that lesser councils must yield in precedence to greater, and that plenary councils "of the whole Christian world" could and did "correct" the judgments of earlier plenary councils when "things are brought to light which were before concealed, and that is known which previously lay hid."[2] But the full implications of synodal renewal of ancient statutes and addition of new ones, of the process of review and correction which St. Augustine observed, the full degree of antagonism between conservatism and reform both in the doctrinal and the institutional aspects of tradition, became apparent only in the disputes following the Council of Chalcedon.

In the patristic age, this tension was resolved in the minds of some thinkers, like Leo I, by the doctrine that tradition might be elaborated and developed by the thought of each generation, always holding unchanged the principal teachings of the faith. In the period between the accession of Justin and the imperial coronation of Charlemagne, an equally distinct and important change occurred in the concept of tradition. The age of the Fathers was largely an era of exposition; the period which followed was one of reformation under the name of recovery. Repeatedly, the decrees of the Fathers were called into question and even repudiated, not merely to elaborate or to supplement them but overtly to correct them. The position that the Fathers might have erred in doctrine, practice, or discipline was totally foreign to the concept of tradition as it was held by the Apologists and by the Fathers after them. Indeed, the substance of their thought was that each generation had transmitted the full, pure, and necessary doctrine of salvation to the next, and that the chief duty of the believer was to preserve and pass on unchanged the teachings of his predecessors in the faith. From the time of Justinian onward, however, the judgments, the practices, and even the confessions of faith framed by earlier bishops and councils were reviewed, modified, or condemned on the grounds that tradition had in some way been suspended at particular times or on specific issues, and that by reviewing past actions the truth was only being recovered and revealed. In the time of Justinian, the dispute over the Three Chapters opened reconsideration of the decrees of Chalcedon concerning Theodore of Mopsuestia, Theodoret, and Ibas; and many great

[1] Orléans III (538); MGH Conc. I, 73; Ladner, *Reform*, 302ff.
[2] See above, pp. 64f.

contemporaries judged that the condemnations issued by the Council of Constantinople (553) against the persons and works of Theodore and Theodoret and against one treatise ascribed to Ibas reversed the Chalcedonian decrees. For Chalcedon had passed over in silence the charges of heresy against Theodore, who had died shortly before in communion with the orthodox Church, and it had received Theodoret and Ibas as true believers on their anathematizing Nestorius and Eutyches. The opponents of this revision resisted it first as the repudiation of decrees of an oecumenical synod, and next, as the posthumous condemnation of persons whom their contemporaries had formally declared orthodox.

And yet, the "correction" of decrees and practices of predecessors continued.[3] The Council of Constantinople (553) condemned the Three Chapters; the Synods of Milan, Ravenna, and Aquileia repudiated the Council. The Synods of Constantinople and Alexandria (638-639) approved Monothelitism; the Lateran Synod (649) condemned it. Finally, in the eighth century, the Iconoclast Synod of Hiereia (754) repudiated the practices and establishments of earlier generations in favor of religious images and declared that, in overthrowing the judgments of their predecessors and in condemning men and practices which had been considered orthodox in earlier days, they were in fact regaining the authentic tradition of the Church. The decrees of Hiereia were overthrown by the Second Council of Nicaea (787), which was in turn rejected by the Synod of Frankfurt (794).

In themselves, these theological crosscurrents are strong evidence of the Empire's widening social and political fragmentation. The "correction" of earlier decrees, and the condemnation of men who in their times were thought to teach the true faith corroded the very substance of tradition as the Fathers understood it. For who was surely a "Father," who beyond doubt transmitted the faith of the Apostles, if men who died in the odor of sanctity among their contemporaries could be post-

---

[3] In defense of the condemnations of the Three Chapters, Justinian and his Council referred to a controversial incident in the Roman See: the condemnation by Pope Boniface II of the dead Pope (or anti-Pope) Dioscorus, whose orthodoxy was unquestioned. Rome knew other such incidents. This condemnation of Dioscorus was itself overturned by Boniface's successor, Agapetus, who condemned the decree as "contrary to the canons" and publicly burned it (Harnack, "Papst," *passim*). Similarly, Pope Leo II later condemned the establishments of his predecessor, Honorius I, as deviations from the tradition of the Fathers, and accepted synodal decrees which numbered Honorius among the heresiarchs (see above, p. 144).

humously condemned as heretics? The early Fathers argued that tradition must continue unbroken from generation to generation, always in its full truth, though its expression might be gradually elaborated. Cyrus of Alexandria, a formulator of Monothelitism, crisply stated the predominant theme of religious politics in Byzantium: conciliation at any cost. His new doctrine, he said, was a ground of compromise with the Monophysites; it healed a schism nearly two centuries old. In teaching it, he followed the example of the ancient Fathers who, to save souls, had modified doctrinal expressions without sacrificing orthodoxy. He argued that it was wrong for him to engage in semantic disputes when the salvation of tens of thousands of men was at stake.[4]

The old concept of transmitted authority survived. But the question of the recovery, or even of the discovery, of tradition disputed the conventional argument that special writings and offices had unerringly preserved the teaching of the Apostles. From the sixth until the late ninth century, the great disputes gradually impelled thinkers to consider insufficient the patristic doctrine of transmission and elaboration, and to seek a more practicable canon of orthodoxy for resolving the tension between conservatism and change, a norm which sanctioned necessary and even radical innovation. They found it in a concept of universality, as molded by civil and social groupings, an elaboration of what we have called for the patristic age, the paradox of universality in particularism. Contemporaries understood that politics influenced hierarchic relationships, but they seem not to have appreciated the profound divisions which that influence produced, or their ultimate social causes.[5]

Roman thought illustrates this impact of political orientations on ideas of authority in the Church. Caught between their Byzantine masters and the Neo-Chalcedonian schismatics, Pelagius I and Gregory the Great departed from the claims of their predecessors to juridical and magisterial pre-eminence. Their ecclesiology was strongly apologetic, rather than polemical, and the basis of their defense was the consonance of Roman doctrine with that of the other apostolic or patriarchal sees. In the seventh century, Roman bishops, increasingly free of Byzantine control, resumed claims to magisterial supremacy, which had been in abeyance since the day of Honorius I; and their successors in the eighth extended these claims to administrative questions as well as magisterial.

[4] See K. J. Hefele—H. Le Clercq, *Histoire des Conciles*, vol. 3, pt. 1 (Paris, 1909), 339ff.
[5] Cf. Charlemagne to Michael I, MGH Epp. 4, k. a. 2, no. 37, 556.

For them, "the tradition of the Apostolic See" and "the tradition of the universal Church" were identical; for the See of St. Peter was "holy," "apostolic," and "universal."

The historical variations in Roman thought as its emphasis alternated between apology and polemics all preserved intact the basis of the Petrine doctrine: that Christ had given special authority to St. Peter and, through him, to his successors. Under the influence of political circumstances, the authority was sometimes described as properly exercised in concert with other prelates, sometimes as valid without their corroboration and, indeed, in defiance of their judgment. It was at times conceived in primarily juridical terms; at others, in magisterial; at still others, in administrative. In any construction, Roman thought remained an assertion of official precedence, not merely in honor, but in some degree of authority.

This continuity was possible because Roman thought itself was inconsistent. The "Janus complex," the two antithetical strands of tradition and discretion, gave the flexibility that allowed Leo I and Gregory I, in their very different ways, to stand true to the conventions of their see. The history of Roman ecclesiology in this period is like an exercise in counterpoint, in which sometimes the air predominates, and sometimes, the descant. Leo emphasized the strand of discretion; Gregory, that of tradition. We have seen that social conditions, and especially political circumstances, forced the shift in thought from Vigilius on, and that they likewise prompted another great change in the eighth century. Even in Hadrian I's day, when discretion had won the palm, and when history had amply demonstrated the dangers of the concept of tradition for any doctrine of administrative flexibility, the popes continued to give lip service to tradition. To be sure, it was little more than a theatrical prop for their true doctrine. But the conservatism of religion would not let it go, especially as clergy in the East and in Gaul still considered it a real and effective authority. It was, in a sense, part of the *lingua franca* of the Church, and, though for them it held no practical meaning, the popes had no alternative to preserving its empty form. At least in appearance, Janusism survived.

Throughout its Byzantine period, the papacy lived at the normal level of the eastern clergy. It worked within a politico-religious structure in which the civil power, however uncanonically, designated bishops, established new dioceses, summoned oecumenical councils, and directed all other great ecclesiastical matters. Resistance to this order was

199

common. But while the order prevailed, no one could imagine, much less establish, a fixed juridical or administrative order as the permanent and unwavering expression of Church unity. The structure of Byzantine society required flexibility, indeed opportunism, of its clergy in hierarchic matters. Patriarch Anastasius of Constantinople gave but one example of this in the eighth century when he altered his views on the adoration of images three times to suit political circumstances. This order was in some degree comparable with the relation between throne and mitre among the Franks. It was natural, therefore, that Byzantine thinkers, rather like the Frankish, predominately considered doctrine and cult the chief expressions of the Church's common religious experience, and sought unchanging rules of faith and observance outside the order of Church government: that is, in the Scriptures, in the writings of the Fathers, and in ancient usages.

Because of their place in feudal, or proto-feudal, government, western clergy carried this emphasis beyond the strictly theological level achieved in Byzantium. Government, rather than doctrine, was the chief issue. Assimilation of churches into political groupings thus led to a certain obsolescence of the idea of tradition in the West. That idea was from the beginning a concept of abstract control prior to and independent of laws and offices. In its earliest days, it was a check on scriptural exegesis; but, as the structure of Church offices grew more elaborate, it became the sanction of limits in the magisterial, juridical, and administrative functions of the Church. From the eighth century onward, western thinkers were increasingly preoccupied with patterns of authority within the hierarchy. In seeking lines of responsibility within the hierarchy, they raised the primary questions of political, or constitutional, thought: the basis of official authority, its extent, and the restrictions upon its use. What earlier thinkers had considered partial witnesses to tradition assumed exclusive importance for them. They sought ultimate definitions of hierarchic relationships in the writings of the Fathers, official acts of bishops, and the decrees of synods and councils.

The concept of tradition as such lost its normative role in questions of doctrine, cult, and order, to canonistic argumentation, which detached itself from theology as a discrete, though related, form of reasoning. From the age of the apologists until the late eighth century, thinkers had appealed to tradition, the unwritten rule of faith, as the measure of orthodoxy. But social and intellectual pressures in the West modified this view in Justinian's day and later until, by the end of the ninth century, the complex of legal qualifications put upon it assumed to a large extent the normative role of tradition itself. This conceptual change was a slow, progressive, and fortuitous, transvaluation in fact, rather than an abrupt rejection in theory.

The eighth century saw the first fruits of this process. It also saw the birth of political conformations in the West that subsequently impelled the transvaluation through centuries of conflict. In entering a defensive covenant with the Frankish kings, the papacy adopted a diplomatic expedient which had great consequences both in political and in ecclesiological questions. For the eighth-century popes, the Franks became a military adjunct of the patrimony of St. Peter, defenders of the Roman Church and of its tradition. The kings owed their royal function and the patriciate to papal favor; they were the "adoptive sons" of St. Peter, subject to the direction of his vicar. Later, when the Frankish covenant was sealed by the imperial coronation of Charlemagne, papal thinkers argued that the imperial office itself was the creature of the Roman bishops, who had "translated" it from Byzantium to the West, and thus that emperors, like Frankish kings before them, were subordinate to the papal will.[6]

But for this new manifestation of Roman ecclesiology, as for its purely ecclesiastical aspects, Frankish thought framed an antagonistic counterpart. Charlemagne, whom even Hadrian I called a "new Constantine,"[7] conceived his duties of defense as extending not merely to the Roman See but to all churches, and as including not merely military defense but also doctrinal instruction. His courtiers called him the vicar of God;[8] the Synod of Frankfurt acclaimed him as "king and priest."[9] Far from seeing himself as subordinate to the papcy, he acted aggressively toward both Hadrian I, whose judgment on the Council of Nicaea he ignored and whose political instructions he brushed aside, and Leo III, for whom he planned a synodal trial.

The Frankish ecclesiology, with its emphasis on assent, and the

---

[6] See Ullmann, *Growth*, 97: "The historic significance of the act [the imperial coronation of Charlemagne] is only heightened when this twofold objective is appraised: the coronation was aimed against the empire as well as against the Frankish king. The seat of the empire was where the pope wished it to be—the seat of the *Roman* empire was *Rome*, not Constantinople, not Aix-la-Chapelle."

[7] MGH Epp. 3, k. a. 1, no. 60, 587: "*Ecce novus christianissimus Dei Constantinus imperator his temporibus surrexit, per quem omnia Deus sanctae suae ecclesiae beati apostolorum principis Petri largiri dignatus est.*"

[8] Cathvulf. MGH Epp. 4, k. a. 2, no. 7, 503.

[9] MGH Conc. I, no. 19 D, 141f.

201

Frankish concept of kingship were complementary: subsequent conflicts between the papacy and northern peoples were both hierarchic and civil. For, though they repudiated the hieratic aspects of Byzantine rulership, the Franks still considered the king a "higher power" ordained by God, to whom subjection was a religious obligation. His kingdom was an earthly type of that City "in which is eternal felicity, supreme blessedness, perpetual joy, in whose palaces reigns the King of whose kingdom there shall be no end, whose tribunals glitter with the Senate of patriarchs, whose court glows with banks of prophets, whose walls are arrayed with the vast army of martyrs, whose gates are adorned with apostolic hosts, whose streets overflow with virgin throngs, whose habitations are full of legions of confessors, which needs not the sun, since the Lord is its light, and through whose every place is sung, Alleluia."[10]

[10] Libri Carolini, II, 3; MGH Conc. II, Suppl., 65. For a schematic outline of the Frankish Church structure, see Santifaller, *Geschichte*, 15ff.

BOOK II

Tradition Transvaluated: Tradition, Discretion,
and Political Groupings in the West from the
Ninth to the Twelfth Century

## CHAPTER 8

# The New Political Order

FOR THE concept of authority in the West, the role of the clergy as a political class, unheralded in the late Roman and Byzantine Empire, led to changes as distinct as those which Constantine's conversion had produced. Byzantium normally excluded the clergy, individually and as a class, from affairs of government. It retained the administrative forms of the Roman Empire, and thus felt no need to admit the clergy into governing the themes, dispensing civil justice, commanding field armies, or participating in the higher counsels of state. Civil or military officers regularly discharged these duties. Disqualified by their orders, the clergy nevertheless remained an extremely wealthy and influential social class, having great political influence without formal political powers. The Byzantine princess Anna Comnena, alludes to this essential difference between Byzantium and the West in her description of a Latin priest in a sea battle: "For the rules concerning priests are not the same among the Latins as they are with us. For we are given the command by the canonical laws of the Gospel, 'Touch not, taste not, handle not. For thou art consecrated.' Whereas the Latin barbarian will simultaneously handle divine things and wear his shield on his left arm and hold his spear in his right hand, and at one and the same time he communicates the Body and Blood of God, and looks murderously and becomes 'a man of blood,' as it says in the psalm of David. For this barbarian race is no less devoted to sacred things than it is to war."[1]

By the late eighth century the papacy in the West had freed itself from the civil disfranchisement of the Byzantine clergy and had assumed the full powers of temporal government. At the same time, the higher clergy in the emergent Germanic realms became members of the military landed aristocracy of feudal, or proto-feudal, government. They were governors, judges, generals, and counsellors of state.

A clear break occurred in the fourth century between the concept of authority held by the Church under persecution and that held by the Church in power. A second revolutionary break occurred in the

---

[1] *Alexiad*, X, 8, trans. E.A.S. Dawes (London, 1928), 256.

West in the ninth century between the concept of authority held by the Church as a social class under Byzantine rule, and that advanced by churchmen who commanded immense political power, as members by birth and by office of a military, landed aristocracy. Eastern clergy lived in a world increasingly remote from their counterparts in Italy and Gaul; they did not share this change.

As in Byzantium, the interplay of politics and religion produced "national" churches. But their political power set an unprecedented context in which western clergy had to interpret Christian Antiquity, and the whole question of authority in the Church. The concept of tradition, as framed and reframed and modified in disputes from the fourth century onward, did not suit their needs. They forged a new link in the history of the idea of tradition by ascribing tradition's functions to other authorities. Elaborating the thought of eighth-century thinkers, they completed the rough work of transvaluation, which their successors refined; they reinterpreted the question of authority in the Church according to the social order which was to rule Europe for nearly seven centuries; and thus they prepared the way for the great conflicts of Church and State which set a hallmark on the Middle Ages, and of which the Investiture Conflict in the eleventh century was the first.

Before the Islamic conquests of the seventh century, the pattern of relations between civil and ecclesiastical authorities centered upon the presence of several autocephalous sees within one autonomous Empire. This pattern continued in theory until the Byzantine recession from Italy. Then the pattern for the western Church consisted of one autocephalous see and several autonomous realms. The questions of autocephality, apostolic foundation, and the pentarchy, which confounded ecclesiastical affairs from the fourth century on, scarcely appeared in western thought between the eighth century and the Crusades.

The freedom of Western thinkers from Byzantine influence permitted them to work out the relevance of this new cast for the problem of ecclesiastical cohesion. As we saw, the positions taken in the first stages of the Iconoclastic Dispute proved that the Church unity which Byzantium's civil and military structure produced in Justinian's age had in great measure dissolved.

In the ninth century, the independent development of Byzantine, Frankish, and Roman ecclesiologies continued. Some major points of debate, broad ecclesiological issues, and basic lines of argument remained those formulated in the eighth century. But, unmodified by common intellectual engagement, the inherent differences of the three schools drew them increasingly far apart. The later stage of the Iconoclastic Controversy illustrates this separation well, particularly the loss of grounds for normal, frequent, and originative interaction between the Byzantine and Roman schools; it began about 815.

The iconoclastic revival seems to have had no comment from western authors until 824, when the Emperor Michael II wrote to Louis the Pious. In terms derogatory to Louis's imperial dignity, Michael asked his western counterpart to intercede with the pope, urging him to deny refuge to those who had fled to Rome to escape iconoclastic persecution. With papal permission, Louis convened the Synod of Paris (825) to review the issue of iconoclasm.[2] The Synod differed from the author of the *Libri Carolini* in accepting Nicaea II as having ecclesiastical authority and in adducing a very great volume of patristic citations.[3] But it followed him in impugning the position of Nicaea, and it added an explicit rejection of Hadrian I's argument in favor of Nicaea. Nicaea was extreme, it said, and deliberately misinterpreted the sense and the intent of patristic writers. Hadrian's patristic authorities were irrelevant; he had erred in ignorance rather than in malice. With the *Libri Carolini,* the Synod affirmed that the destruction and the veneration of icons were equally wrong; images were useful mnemonic and didactic devices. Though it professed utmost respect for the successors of St. Peter, the Synod took exception to the "superstitious reverence" popes rendered images,[4] drafted a letter in Louis's name admonishing the pope to accept the Frankish definition and to send envoys with Louis's own representatives to Byzantium, and finally, framed a second letter, in the Pope's name, to Michael commending the Synod's judgment as authentic. The Frankish envoys to the Pope urged that the tone of these documents might drive him into "irremedial obstinacy," and that the desired goal required a more diplomatic approach.[5] The results of the legation are not known; Louis's representatives went from Rome

---

[2] Cf. Ladner, "Bilderstreit," 13; Martin, *Controversy*, 110, 150ff; Alexander, *Nicephorus*, 189, 244f; "Iconoclastic Council," 46; Grabar, *L'Iconoclasme*, 137, 148; Dvornik, "Photios," 69ff; *Schisme*, 116. On Leo the Armenian's sudden change from iconodulism to iconoclasm, see Bréhier, *La querelle*, 32f.

[3] Haendler, *Epochen*, 104, 109, 130, 170.

[4] MGH Cap. 2, 484. Ullmann, *Growth*, 126f emphasizes the Synod's professed respect for Rome, but does not mention its criticism of Roman practices.

[5] MGH Cap. 2, 533. Cf. Haendler, *Epochen*, 49f.

to Byzantium, but it seems likely that they failed to win papal collaboration.[6]

Subsequently, Agobard of Lyons composed a treatise against the veneration of images, and still later other Frankish writers—Aeneas of Paris, Hincmar of Rheims, and Ratramnus of Corbie—composed, at the request of Nicholas I, refutations of the Byzantine policy. These authors and the Frankish clergy generally had no direct experience of iconoclasm as a normal aspect of ecclesiastical discipline or as a policy of state. But in their extant treatises—those of Agobard, Aeneas, and Ratramnus—the independent attitude of the Parisian Synod persisted. Ultimate authority resided in scriptural and in patristic writings, not in the consensus of all patriarchs nor yet in the Roman See. When reproved in the name of Paschal I, the iconoclast Claudius of Turin, a Spaniard by origin, expressed the prevalent thought of Frankish bishops when he wrote, "Certainly a man is not to be called 'apostolic' because he sits in the seat of an Apostle, but because he fulfills the apostolic office. Of them who hold the place and do not fulfill the office, the Lord has said, 'The scribes and the Pharisees sit in Moses's seat. Observe, therefore, and do all things which they shall bid you; do not according to their works, for they say, and they do not.' "[7]

After the time of Hadrian I, Rome became involved in the Iconoclast Controversy only as in a matter tangentially related to greater issues.[8] Until 880, the Roman Church withheld acceptance of Nicaea II as an oecumenical council; even then, that recognition was part of a broader settlement.[9] The principal issue which invited Roman intervention in the Dispute was the Photian Controversy, which fell into three periods, corresponding with the first and second patriarchates of Photius (858-867, 878-886) and the second patriarchate of Ignatius (867-877). In papal letters, statements upholding the veneration of images are perfunctory; we shall return to them in another context. The degree to which ninth-century popes were excluded, in part voluntarily, from the issue of iconoclasm is indicated by the absence of any direct attack by a Roman bishop upon iconoclasm, by Rome's neglect to send a joint legation with the Frankish envoys in 825-826, and by the absence of Roman legates at the Synod of Constantinople which restored the ven-

---

[6] Haendler, *Epochen*, 48f; Martin, *Controversy*, 253.

[7] MGH Epp. 4, k. a. 2, no. 12, 613. On Claudius, see Russell, *Dissent*, 14ff.

[8] Cf. Nicholas I (866), MGH Epp. 6, k. a. 4, no. 91, c. 6, 522f.

[9] Dvornik, "Patriarch Photios," 96.

eration of images (843). Whenever Rome and Constantinople reached accords in the Photian dispute, as, for example, in 869 and 880, the two sees joined in an affirmation that the veneration of images was an orthodox practice. But the major issues for Rome were the authority to judge Photius's disputed election, and administrative jurisdiction over some eastern provinces, especially over those held by the Bulgars. The age had ended in which relations between Rome and Constantinople as genuinely autocephalous sees were close enough to engage in conflict and schism.

Roman ecclesiology and the papacy's role as an independent principality partially explain this breach. But Byzantine hostility or indifference toward western ecclesiastical affairs also contributed to it. The particularism which eastern clergy had shown towards Rome from the fourth century on survived as a settled attitude in Byzantine thought; it was modified only in consideration of cogent diplomatic or political reasons, and even then it retained characteristic qualifications.[10]

From the eighth century onward, Byzantium formulated its religious policies independently of Rome. Claiming apostolic foundation for their see,[11] and asserting on occasion that primacy belonged to the bishop of the imperial city, Byzantine thinkers lost all common ground with their Roman counterparts.[12] In the eleventh century, Cardinal Humbert did not exaggerate when he wrote that the Byzantines affirmed that "excepting the church of the Greeks, the Church of Christ, the true sacrifice, and baptism had utterly perished from the earth."[13]

The lack of common intellectual engagement among the Byzantine, Frankish, and Roman ecclesiological schools, the recession of Byzantine power from Italy, and the close civil relations between the Franks and the Roman bishops meant that Byzantium had ceased to influence Western thought fundamentally and that Western ecclesiology would in future turn on the axis of Gaul and Rome. Further, the profound legal studies at the poles of that axis meant that the antagonism shown in

[10] Cf. Alexander, *Nicephorus*, 94.

[11] Dvornik, *Apostolicity*, 156ff.

[12] Cf. Ladner, "Origines," 149. On the distinctly insular attitude of Byzantine thinkers, see Hoffmann, "Schwerter," 100; Bach, "Imperium Romanum," 143f; Alexander, "Strength," esp. 348ff.

[13] PL 143, 1063: ". . . *sicut Donatistae affirmant, excepta Graecorum ecclesia, ecclesiam Christi et verum sacrificium atque baptismum ex toto mundo periisse.*" A century earlier, Liutprand encountered the same attitude (Legatio, cc. 21, 11; MGH in us. schol., 2d ed., 145).

794 and in 825 would assume, not merely theological, but, even more important, institutional expression. The paradoxes of universality in particularism and assimilation through equipoise survived in this changed social context.

# PART I

# The Ninth and Tenth Centuries:
# Tradition and Official Spontaneity

CHAPTER 9

# The Popes and the Franks

### A. PAPAL DOCTRINE: UNIVERSALITY AND IRRESPONSIBILITY

A PRECIOUS HERITAGE belonged to the popes of the ninth century. The judgments of their predecessors stretched back for half a millennium in an ample, if broken, sequence. Administrative procedures had precedents in the remote past, beyond the rise of the Germanic kingdoms, and even beyond the crumbling of the western Empire. The writings of the Fathers from the age of the apologists, the whole series of conciliar decrees from the patristic era on lay at Rome's disposal.

For the Carolingians, as for ninth-century popes, the accumulated body of patristic authorities was the cornerstone of thought about the Church, and about its place in the world. Men with hard Germanic names, like Agobard and Hincmar, ruled bishoprics in the north by the same laws that men with mellifluous Greek and Latin names applied to the See of Rome. They all consulted the records of synods and councils held in the patristic era; they all honored the decretals of such popes as Innocent I, Leo the Great, and Gelasius I; they invoked the same maxims of Roman Law, and used the same historical events as precedents.

As we have seen, the antithetical authorities of tradition and administrative discretion, drawn from this body of law, flourished side by side in papal thought. Hadrian I and his successors gave discretion full weight and tacked across the flood of tradition. Some Frankish thinkers accepted their monarchic principles. Others accepted only its magisterial aspects, and put a significantly different interpretation on the authorities they all shared.

In a new guise, this was the old issue of control, or "tradition." The issues now under debate concerned Church order rather than the faith. But the categories of authority were ancient. Even in the sixth century, Cassiodorus and the author of the *Decretum Gelasianum* were using terms venerable with age when they represented the conflict between the authoritarian and the exegetical concepts of authority. Franks and popes, on balance, advanced the two concepts along separate paths in the Iconoclastic Controversy. In the ninth century, their successors brought the divergent views to mature expression.

$$+$$

There are few papal documents from the period between the death of Hadrian I (795) and the accession of Nicholas I (858). Surviving letters of Gregory IV and Leo IV provide no full exposition of Rome ecclesiology, but they do indicate that those popes continued, and perhaps even sharpened, the thought of their eighth-century predecessors. They both found the essence of the Church's cohesion in the hierarchic privileges of St. Peter's throne, and, secondarily, in the canonistic sources that confirmed and witnessed to them.

The letters of Nicholas I contain the first general outline of papal thought about ecclesiastical cohesion in the ninth century. Elevated to the papacy largely through the influence of Louis II, Nicholas proved to be one of the most brilliant and effective popes in the early Middle Ages, an ardent exponent of papal supremacy within the hierarchy, and, ironically, a steadfast opponent of temporal intervention in ecclesiastical affairs. In his major disputes with Byzantium, opposing Photius's accession, with Lothair II, repudiating that King's effort to secure a divorce, and with Hincmar of Rheims, supporting Rothad of Soissons' appeal from a provincial synod to the papal court, Nicholas formulated a broad and coherent concept of conservatism and change within the Church.

Because his knowledge of patristic sources was profound, Nicholas often invoked the ancient concept of tradition. He used the word "tradition" in various terms, of which he seems to have considered the singular and plural forms interchangeable.[1] In some senses, "traditions which

[1] *Traditio* about fasting (MGH Epp. VI, k. a. 4, no. 99, c. 60, 589); *traditiones quas antiquitus a patribus nostris suscepimus* concerning general administrative order (*ibid.*, no. 100, 604); *apostolica traditio* concerning the proper method of computing the date of Easter (*ibid.*, no. 90, 502) and general matters of faith and order (*ibid.*, no. 82, 434); *traditio ab apostolis instituta* about hierarchic jurisdiction over Sicily (*ibid.*, no. 82, 439); *paterna traditio* about the obedience of monks to bishops (*ibid.*, no. 110, 626), scriptural exegesis (*ibid.*, no. 87, 454), and general Church order (*ibid.*, no. 86, 450), and in the plural, reverence for episcopal order (*ibid.*, no. 100, 604), the manner of episcopal accession (*ibid.*, nos. 86, 90, 91: 450, 508, 535), and general Church order (*ibid.*, no. 88, 484); *canonica paterna traditio* concerning the appeal from provincial synods to Roman judgment (*ibid.*, no. 69, 385); *sanctorum patrum traditio* concerning the venera-

we received from our Fathers of old," "apostolic tradition," "patristic tradition," "ecclesiastical tradition," and "tradition of the Apostolic See" were interchangeable, as were, in a second class, "canonical patristic tradition" and "ecclesiastical tradition," and, in yet a third class, "patristic traditions," "tradition of the approved Fathers," "tradition of the Church," and "tradition of the Apostolic See." The imprecision of this usage is also shown by an affinity between "tradition" and "custom" (*consuetudo*) in Nicholas's thought. The Pope once mentioned as incentives to action "zeal for the house of God, zeal for patristic traditions, ecclesiastical order, ancient custom, the care of all churches of God which we bear and the privileges of our own see, divinely received by St. Peter and transferred to the Roman church." Clearly, he distinguished each of these six terms.[2] Their interrelation, however, was so close and the connotation of long usage so fundamental both to "tradition" and to "custom" that occasional semantic elision was natural. Nicholas wrote, for example, of a liturgical "custom anciently observed in the Roman church,"[3] and he commanded that "canonical custom" (*consuetudo canonica*) prevail in ecclesiastical jurisdiction.[4] But this elision was not extreme or uniform. Nicholas placed a severe restriction upon the validity of custom when he forbade that any custom supersede sanctions of the Roman pontiffs,[5] and when he wrote that the diverse customs held by different churches must all be judged by "canonical authority" (*canonica auctoritas*) and rejected if they ran counter to

tion of sacred images (*ibid.*, no. 82, 437); *traditio patrum* concerning diocesan administration (*ibid.*, no. 59 a, 368); *probabilium patrum traditio* concerning the manner of episcopal accession (*ibid.*, no. 92, 535); *ecclesiae traditio* about the manner of episcopal accession (*ibid.*, no. 100, 607); and generally to fasting, creed and hierarchic order (*ibid.*, no. 100, 605); *ecclesiastica traditio* concerning the status of metropolitans (*ibid.*, no. 127, 648) and, in the plural, concerning the appeal from provincial synods to Roman judgment (*ibid.*, no. 57, 357) and general Church administration (*ibid.*, no. 88, 482f); and *traditiones apostolicae sedis* concerning the manner of episcopal accession and deposition (*ibid.*, no. 100, 608) and general matters of faith and order (*ibid.*, no. 100, 605).

[2] *Ibid.*, no. 88, 484: ". . . *zelus domus Dei, zelus paternarum traditionum, ordo ecclesiasticus, antiqua consuetudo, atque sollicitudo quam circumferimus cunctarum ecclesiarum Dei necnon et privilegia propriae sedis, quae in beato Petro suscepta divinitus et in ecclesiam Romanam dirivata universalis celebrat et veneratur ecclesia. . . .*"

[3] *Ibid.*, no. 26, c. 7, 292, *consuetudo in Romana ecclesia antiquitus observata.*

[4] *Ibid.*, no. 85, 446. Cf. Nicholas's confirmation of a decree of Benedict III, *ibid.*, no. 59, 366.

[5] *Ibid.*, no. 86, 448.

what the Fathers had promulgated.[6] In contrast, tradition and the canons were complementary authorities, and it was an "abominable shame" to allow "those traditions which we have received of old from our Fathers" to be infringed.[7]

The ascription of canonical authority to tradition and the application of the term "tradition of the Apostolic See" to matters of general order and to the mode of episcopal accession suggest the primary tendency of Nicholas's thought. Rome was the font of tradition for the whole Church, and this function was expressed first of all in hierarchy.

Nicholas held that the universal Church received all those in communion with the Roman Church, either when they were alive or when, after their deaths, their positions were vindicated. He adduced the example of St. Peter, whose enemy, Simon Magus, inflamed the princes to seek his death; of Victor, whose judgment in computing the date of Easter drove other bishops from his communion; of Felix III, despite whose decree Acacius remained patriarch of Constantinople, protected by the temporal power and in communion with nearly all Eastern bishops; and of Silverius and Vigilius who suffered for refusing to recognize Anthimus as a true bishop. Many other Roman bishops had endured much after the fashion of "Victor, pope and martyr, who thus is truly 'victor,' since as a martyr for the apostolic tradition, he was reproved for obstinacy by the prelates of almost the whole Church, whereas the whole Church is now of his mind and preaches that what he did was worthy of praise."[8] The identification between Rome and tradition is even clearer in Nicholas's extensive quotation of Innocent I's decretal to Decentius condemning diversity of practice as the result of human presumption, affirming that the Roman Church retained intact what had been transmitted to St. Peter and commanding general adherence to Roman norms.[9]

In his own remarks to the Emperor Michael, Nicholas wrote that his

[6] *Ibid.,* no. 86, 450f.

[7] *Ibid.,* no. 100, 604: "*Ridiculum est enim et satis abominabile dedecus, ut temporibus nostris vel falso insimulare sanctam Dei ecclesiam permittamus vel eas traditiones, quas antiquitus a patribus nostris suscepimus, pro libitu semper errantium infringere patiamur.*"

[8] *Ibid.,* no. 90, 502f: "*Quid autem mirum, si nobis pro ecclesiastica correctione laborantibus manum non datis, sed et duritiae redarguitis, cum videamus Victorem papam et martyrem, qui ideo vero victor est, quia martyr pro apostolica traditione, pene a totius ecclesiae praesulibus pertinaciae redargutum; quandoquidem ecclesia tota nunc cum illo sapit et quod fecit laude praedicat dignum.*"

[9] *Ibid.,* no. 118, 637.

predecessors, "most blessed, orthodox pontiffs," had preserved the pristine tradition of the holy Fathers and that the Roman See, "this holy catholic and apostolic Church," still held and defended it unchanged.[10] Understanding of the apostolic tradition remained with the Roman see and pontiff, without whose consent no ecclesiastical decision was final.[11] The whole Church throughout the world, he wrote to Photius, bowed in reverence to the judgment of Celestine I and Leo I;[12] the "traditions" of the Roman Church and the "traditions of the Church" were synonymous in Sabbath fasting, in the procession of the Holy Ghost (both of which Byzantium challenged), and in the hierarchic order which Photius violated by boasting that, when the emperors moved from Rome to Constantinople, the primacy of the Roman See had likewise moved to the eastern capital, and by presumptuously assuming the title "archbishop and universal patriarch." The Roman Church held what it had received from St. Peter when Christianity began to spread through the world; in every region it taught this same tradition to churches it established. Even by comparison with these daughter churches, the See of Constantinople was of recent foundation.[13]

Nicholas himself referred to the legend of Pope Marcellinus who lapsed from the faith in the persecution under Diocletian; his conclusion was that of the Symmachian forgeries, that "the first see shall not be judged by anyone."[14] The personal defection of a Marcellinus did not counterbalance Victor's loyalty to the apostolic tradition or impair his see's transmission of authentic teaching. "Blessed Peter lives and presides in his see, and gives the truth of faith to them that seek it. For the holy Roman Church has always been without spot or wrinkle, exactly because he founded it whose confession of faith was divinely approved."[15] In this peculiar relation with the Roman See, Peter had never ceased to fortify the structure of the universal Church with his prayers.[16] His authority worked through the individual popes,[17] and a line of identity stretched through the sequence of papal decrees.[18]

---

[10] *Ibid.*, no. 82, 437. This discussion is entirely consonant with Dr. Ullmann's statement concerning the ninth century: "Perhaps the most characteristic feature of the papal-hierocratic theme had always been its conservatism and reliance on tradition" (*Growth*, 177). On Nicholas I, see *Growth*, 191ff.

[11] *Ibid.*, no. 82, 433f.  [12] *Ibid.*, no. 92, 535.

[13] *Ibid.*, no. 100, 605.  [14] *Ibid.*, no. 88, 466.

[15] *Ibid.*, no. 99, c. 106, 599f.  [16] *Ibid.*, no. 82, 433.

[17] *Ibid.*, no. 18, c. 2, 285.

[18] *Ibid.*, no. 91, 516. Nicholas frequently referred to himself with the conventional term "our apostolate" (*apostolatus noster*)—ibid., nos. 12, 15, 26, 29, 33:

Two Frankish bishops whom Nicholas deposed may indeed have caught Nicholas's identification of Peter, see, and pope when they wrote that "Nicholas, who is called pope, numbered himself an apostle among the Apostles."[19]

This point was critical; for, beyond magisterial functions, Nicholas ascribed great administrative and juridical prerogatives to his see on the ground of its steadfast fidelity to apostolic tradition. He insisted that consecration of the archbishop of Syracuse must continue a privilege of the Roman See lest "the tradition instituted by the Apostles" be violated.[20] And freedom of appeal from provincial synods to the Roman See was established by "canonical, patristic tradition,"[21] and by "ecclesiastical traditions";[22] it could be violated only "in contempt of the blessed prince of the Apostles, Peter, through whom, in Christ, the apostolate and the episcopate took their beginning."[23]

"Having neither spot nor wrinkle nor anything of that kind,"[24] the Roman See stood in contrast with other churches, especially with Constantinople whose dissensions, conspiracies, and hatreds were, Nicholas wrote, portents of the end of the world.[25] The "principate of divine power" (*principatus divinae potestatis*), though given to all the Apostles, abided chiefly in the immovable faith of Peter, and in the See of Peter.[26] The special privileges which the Roman Church consequently held were Christ's.[27] They were the surety of privileges for the whole Church, the arms of Peter against every depraved attack;[28] from them derived the privileges of other churches, and upon their integrity depended the integrity of their derivatives.[29] These great privileges were to be judge over all priests, to establish laws in all Christ's Church, to issue decrees and to promulgate judgments.[30] "If any one disregard the teachings, mandates, prohibitions, sanctions, or decrees beneficially promulgated by the head of the Apostolic See for the catholic faith, for ecclesiastical discipline, for the correction of the faithful, for the improvement of wrongdoers or for the prohibition of imminent or future

---

278, 282, 290, 296, 302f, and *passim*—but his reference to his own "apostolic mind" (*noster apostolicus animus*) was less usual—*ibid.*, no. 3, 269.

[19] PL 121, 379.
[20] MGH Epp. VI, k. a. 4, no. 82, 439.
[21] *Ibid.*, no. 69, 385.
[22] *Ibid.*, no. 57, 357.
[23] *Ibid.*, no. 69, 385.
[24] *Ibid.*, no. 88, 475, a frequent usage.
[25] *Ibid.*, no. 93, 540.
[26] *Ibid.*, no. 82, 433.
[27] *Ibid.*, no. 60, 371.
[28] *Ibid.*, nos. 57, 60: 360, 371.
[29] *Ibid.*, no. 58, 363f.
[30] *Ibid.*, no. 29, 296.

evils, let him be anathema."[31] All these powers, including particularly the power to judge bishops, were established by Christ Himself; no synod had ever dared judge of the Roman Church since all things were granted Rome by the Lord's own words. Synods and universal councils had merely acknowledged and venerated Rome's privileges.[32] The power to legislate and generally to supervise legal authorities within the Church was equally important. Nicholas mentioned "decretals established by the Apostolic See" as definitions together with the holy canons, of the limits which the Fathers had set.[33]

In an important letter to the Frankish bishops, he affirmed that the legislative power was a continuing attribute of the Roman See. The Franks had argued that only those papal decrees contained in the "*codex canonum*" (probably the Dionysiana or the Dionysio-Hadriana) could be considered canonical. Nicholas denounced this position as tending to diminish the power of the Apostolic See. The letters of Gregory the Great and other popes before and after him were not in the *codex canonum*, though their teaching and judgments were universally revered. Neither the Old nor the New Testament was in the codex of ecclesiastical canons; they could obviously not be discarded on that ground nor could the omitted papal decretals be erased from their books. Decretal letters of Roman pontiffs must be received whether in the codex or not, according to the commands of Innocent I and Leo I. They were too numerous to be comprehended within the limits of one collection; but no distinction existed "between those decrees of pontiffs of the Apostolic See which are contained in the *codex canonum* and those which, because of their great number, are scarcely found in single volumes; since we have shown that the excellent bishops, namely Leo and Gelasius, commanded that all things—both the decretals established by all their predecessors and decretal letters which most blessed popes issued at various times from the City of Rome—must be reverently received and observed."[34]

[31] *Ibid.*, no. 18, c. 5, 286.     [32] *Ibid.*, nos. 71, 88: 398f, 474f.
[33] *Ibid.*, nos. 90, 91: 496, 515.
[34] *Ibid.*, no. 71, 394f. "*His ita divina favente gratia praelibatis ostendimus nullam differentiam esse inter ea decreta, quae in codice canonum habentur sedis apostolicae praesulum, et ea, quae prae multitudine vix per singula voluminum corpora reperiuntur, cum omnia et omnium decessorum suorum decretalia constituta atque decretales epistolas, quas beatissimi papae diversis temporibus ab urbe Roma dederunt, venerabiliter fore suscipiendas et custodiendas eximios praesules, Leonem scilicet et Gelasium, mandasse probavimus.*"

219

Photius presented another challenge to Nicholas's concept of Roman legal powers. Nicholas came to consider falsification of canonical sources a normal Byzantine practice,[35] but he was outraged when Photius asserted that the Sardican canons and the papal decrees which the Pope invoked were unknown at Constantinople. In Nicholas's eyes, this was tantamount to deleting a large and critical segment from the body of ecclesiastical law. Knowledge of the Sardican canons among Byzantine clergy had been proven by appeals to the Roman See, by Greek transcriptions of the canons, by the fact that Greek and Latin speakers had joined in promulgating the canons at Sardica, and by their presence in the canonical collection of Johannes Scholasticus, patriarch of Constantinople under Justinian.[36] The whole Church had received Sardica: How, Nicholas asked, could the holy Church at Constantinople reject it? As for papal decretals, Nicholas concluded that Photius disclaimed knowledge of them because they forbade the process by which Photius had come to the patriarchate.[37] The decrees of which Photius professed ignorance contained only what the law of nature, the Mosaic law, and the law of grace commanded, and what Sardica defined.[38] Abiding without spot, without reproach, without transgression, Rome must uphold the "patristic traditions" which Photius had violated, and vindicate the establishment of all the holy Fathers.[39]

Roman judgment in legal matters was irreversible and unreviewable. It was always, Nicholas wrote, undertaken with such great moderation of counsel, prosecuted with such great maturity of patience, and issued with such great gravity of deliberation that it never required reconsideration or adjustment unless it contained specific provision for review.[40] Otherwise, no one could judge the Apostolic See's judgment or review its sentence, since no inferior could judge his superiors,[41] and the universal Church had its head in the See of Peter.[42]

Rome's unparalleled eminence was not qualified by the apostolic succession of other bishops either in synods or individually. Indeed, Nicholas wrote that no assembly could be called a synod unless it received the pope's approval;[43] otherwise it was fraudulent, a "Robber-Synod."[44]

---

[35] *Ibid.*, no. 88, 457. See Wallach, "Versions," 110f.
[36] *Ibid.*, no. 92, 537f.      [37] *Ibid.*, no. 86, 450.
[38] *Ibid.*, no. 92, 537.      [39] *Ibid.*, no. 86, 450f.
[40] *Ibid.*, no. 53, 348. Cf. no. 8, 274.
[41] *Ibid.*, nos. 45, 46, 88, 100: 321, 323, 480f, 606.
[42] *Ibid.*, no. 71, 393.      [43] *Ibid.*, no. 29, 296.
[44] *Ibid.*, nos. 18, 70, 91: 285, 389, 518.

The episcopate itself derived from the Apostolic See,[45] which retained the power to judge all bishops, even metropolitans and patriarchs.[46] The glory of St. Peter honored Antioch and, through St. Mark, Alexandria as well as Rome; and the government of Sts. Peter and Paul still remained principally in those three churches.[47] Among the patriarchates, they were the apostolic sees; subsequently, Constantinople and Jerusalem were called patriarchates, though they lacked the full authority of the three great sees. Constantinople was neither established by an Apostle nor mentioned by Nicaea; its bishop was called patriarch by the favor of princes rather than by due cause (*ratio*). Honored by ancient custom and by Nicaea, Jerusalem in fact claimed only the dignity of a metropolitan, despite the honorary title of patriarch. Among them all, Rome was the premier see,[48] and Alexandria held second rank. Though he boastfully claimed the title "oecumenical patriarch," the bishop of Constantinople was in fact subject to the Bishop of Rome, as was proven historically by the fact that popes had deposed many bishops of the imperial city.[49]

When Nicholas referred to Leo I as "universal pope,"[50] he had in mind both the premise that Leo dealt with the "faith, which is universal, which is common to all, which pertains not only to clerics but also to laymen and generally to all Christians,"[51] and the structure of legal privileges which lay behind his statement that those who withdrew from Roman communion fell from communion with the universal Church.[52] He conceived universality as a quality of the faith, the cohesive element of the Church. But he also thought of it in a geographical sense, when he identified the Church and the earth,[53] and in an administrative sense when he wrote that the Roman Church had received and contained within itself what God commanded the universal Church to re-

---

[45] *Ibid.*, no. 18, c. 3, 285.
[46] *Ibid.*, nos. 29, 71: 296, 396f; cf. no. 31, 300.
[47] *Ibid.*, no. 88, 475. Cf. no. 84, 442.
[48] *Ibid.*, no. 99, cc. 92, 93: 596f.
[49] *Ibid.*, nos. 88, 100: 469, 604f. Cf. his instructions to the Bulgars on establishing a patriarchate, demanding: "*Vos tamen, sive patriarcham sive archiepiscopum sive episcopum vobis ordinari postuletis, a nemine nunc velle congruentius quam a pontifice sedis beati Petri, a quo et episcopatus et apostolatus sumpsit initium, hunc ordinari valetis.*" He was not to be consecrated, "*priusquam pallium a sede Romana percipiat, sicuti Galliarum omnes et Germaniae et aliarum regionum archiepiscopi agere comprobantur*" (*ibid.*, no. 99, cc. 72, 73: 592f).
[50] *Ibid.*, no. 87, 452.
[51] *Ibid.*, no. 88, 470. Cf. no. 82, 433.
[52] *Ibid.*, no. 47, 327.
[53] *Ibid.*, no. 88, 475.

ceive and contain, that the supervision of the universal Church conse-quently descended to the bishops of Rome,[54] and, finally, that "the whole, universal Church of Christ" honored the privileges of the Apos-tolic See.[55]

In a term from Roman law, used by Gregory IV, Nicholas conceived the Church as abiding chiefly among the priests;[56] that is, as a clerical community, functionally and legally discrete from political divisions and civil laws. The cohesive element in the Church was apostolic teach-ing and practice, integrally preserved in the Roman Church. The ex-ternal, but fundamental signs of orthodoxy were communion with the Roman See and, correspondingly, acknowledgment of Rome's supreme magisterial, administrative, and juridical privileges. Preserved from error by St. Peter's continual presence and prayers, Rome was the para-mount guardian of authentic doctrine, cult, and order; the traditions of the Apostolic See were the orthodox traditions of the Church. This structure unified the Church, and likewise set it apart from civil orders which did not functionally teach or administer tradition. The temporal power did not bear tradition; it had no proper supervision over doctrine, cult, or order; consequently it was neither below nor above ecclesiastical administration.[57] Christian kings were subject personally to ecclesiastical censure, even to the ultimate censure of excommunication; but no judgment of the Church conferred their office or withdrew it. Es-pecially in the "national" churches of Byzantium and Gaul, temporal power itself remained external to the Church, but an unchecked threat to the integrity of tradition—a threat epitomized in the imperial support which Photius received when, despite Nicholas's sentence of excommu-nication and deposition, he continued in full possession of his patri-archate and decreed Nicholas himself excommunicate (863).

In his work, Nicholas encountered two principal barriers: in theory, ecclesiologies which ran counter to his position, and, in practice, the in-tervention of temporal rulers in matters of doctrine, cult, and order. These were persistent obstacles to any centralized doctrine of Church order, and neither Nicholas's elaboration of papal ecclesiology nor his vigorous entreaties to worldly rulers permanently overcame them.

The assertive formulation of Roman ecclesiology which Nicholas framed and which his successor, Hadrian II, seems to have adopted closely corresponded with the thought of popes in the late fifth cen-

---

[54] *Ibid.*, no. 88, 478.
[55] *Ibid.*, no. 55, 354. Cf. no. 105, 614.
[56] Morrison, *Kingdoms*, 38f.
[57] See Appendix A.

tury. Like the Monophysite Schism, Byzantine disregard for Roman judgments in Photius's case and Frankish threats to depose Gregory IV and Hadrian II showed that other ecclesiologies, responding to particularistic ethnic or social influences, rejected on principle the Roman concept that ecclesiastical cohesion derived from a monarchic structure of the Church. The assertive expressions of Roman doctrine issued in the fifth century by various popes and now by Nicholas and Hadrian were prompted, in the first instance, by the personalities of the men in St. Peter's chair, and, more generally, by the coincidental freedom of their see from external political direction. Just as the papal concept of ecclesiastical cohesion changed in the time of the Byzantine papacy, preserving conventional terms by changing its conceptual emphasis, it experienced modification after the death of Hadrian II when constant military pressures both outside and within Rome greatly weakened the papacy's own resources and prepared for the day when, in the late ninth century, the See of St. Peter became subject to the Roman nobility.

The grave disorders of his pontificate led John VIII to compromise ecclesiological points for the sake of a military alliance with secular rulers.[58] John's complaint that none of his predecessors had suffered evils comparable with those he endured[59] was not mere hyperbole, for the disorders with which he had to contend led, without remission, to the utter debasement of the papacy in the last decade of the ninth century. Amidst these political pressures, John continued to affirm the general principles of Roman ecclesiology. His rare uses of the word "tradition" all point toward Roman authority as the safeguard of ecclesiastical cohesion.[60] For him, tradition was little more than a catchword which enhanced papal dignity.

---

[58] On John VIII, see Ullmann, *Growth*, 219ff. See Appendix A.

[59] MGH Epp. VII, k. a. 5, no. 82, 77.

[60] John professed eagerness to preserve "inviolable traditions of the Fathers" (*paternae traditiones inviolabiles*) (*ibid.*, no. 29, 290). "The tradition of the Apostolic See" (*traditio sedis apostolicae*) once referred to orthodox doctrine (*ibid.*, no. 200, 160), the equivalent of what John elsewhere calls "the doctrine of the holy Roman church" which must be followed "according to the approved tradition of the holy Fathers" (*ibid.*, no. 276, 244, *sanctae Romanae ecclesiae doctrinam iuxta sanctorum patrum probabilem traditionem sequi debere monuimus*). He wrote that "the tradition of divine law" had regulatory force, together with "the censure of canonical authority" and "examples of the ancient Fathers" (*ibid.*, no. 5, 4, *divinae legis traditio*). "Canonical tradition" denotes the norms of archiepiscopal administration (*ibid.*, no. 255, 223, *canonica traditio*).

Many of John's claims to sweeping power were conventional; so too was his attitude that every priest must know the canons and that no action could rightly be taken contrary to them.[61] But John's attitude toward ecclesiastical law reveals the major ecclesiological difference between his position and the views of Nicholas and Hadrian: namely, his emphasis upon the pope's discretionary powers by virtue of the imperishable apostolate of St. Peter. As represented by Anastasius Bibliothecarius, John reversed a judgment of "Pope Stephen" (Sergius I is meant) that only fifty of the Apostolic Canons could be accepted as genuine. John declared that all the 85 Apostolic Canons should be accepted, together with all rules and establishments of approved Fathers and holy councils, on the condition that they were not contrary to right faith or good morals, and that they in no way ran counter to decrees of the Roman See. Thus, Anastasius observed, some decrees of the Council of Constantinople (680-681) which opposed earlier canons "of the holy pontiffs of the see" or good morals could never be accepted.[62]

By his rule of discretion, Anastasius records, John admitted without individual examination virtually all ecclesiastical documents concerning faith and order as legal authorities; he acknowledged that a kind of "common law" was developing within the Church, and he imposed upon it no control other than general consonance with orthodoxy, morality, and Roman decrees. To establish this point, however, John had rescinded a decree of his predecessor, "Stephen," and severely modified its implicit principle that canonistic sources must be individually approved. His own decree refuted the concept that all papal decrees were identical in sense, and it opened the way for further modifications of the Roman concept of ecclesiastical law, according to the discretion of individual popes.

The importance of discretionary powers in John's thought appeared in his administrative and juridical actions, particularly in his translation

---

[61] *Ibid.*, no. 35, 34. On what follows: John knew from the Council of 680/81 and Nicaea II that Dionysius Exiguus' translation of only 50 Apostolic Canons misled earlier popes.

[62] Mansi 12, 982. Anastasius seems to refer to the canons of the Quinisext which condemn specific Roman practices. John exercised similar powers of discretion at the Synod of Troyes (878) when he commanded that a Frankish decree on fines for the crime of sacrilege be added to the Gothic code, "at the end of the codex of temporal law" (Mansi 17 A, 351). He may indeed have acted on the premise that his predecessor, John II, and Justinian had jointly "made Roman law" (MGH Epp. VII, k. a. 5, no. 111, 103).

of Bishop Frotherius from Bordeaux to Bourges, in his rulings on the use of languages other than Latin in the liturgy, and in his negotiations, concerning the case of Photius. Commanding Frotherius's translation, John acknowledged that the canons forbade moving a bishop from one see to another. Under normal circumstances, the canons must be observed. The special necessity of Bourges, which had been devastated by the Vikings, required that they be kept "with discretion and dispensation." Compassion for the brethren warranted the translation, "according to the example of the elders."[63] In dealing with St. Methodius, John reversed Hadrian II's privilege for a Slavonic translation of the liturgy, and one year later, restored the privilege. In 879, he professed outrage at learning that Methodius had had masses sung in the "barbaric, Slavonic tongue," instead of Greek or Latin, the two languages in which the whole Church throughout the world sang."[64] But in 880 he wrote again that there was no objection to singing the mass or other offices, or to reading the Gospel or the divine lections of Old or New Testament, well translated into Slavonic, since God had not only created Hebrew, Greek, and Latin, but all other tongues as well to His praise and glory. He commanded however that in all churches the Gospel be read first in Latin, and then in Slavonic.[65]

In Photius's case, John executed a similar double reversal. Ignatius's actions in the last years of his second patriarchate gave John cause to compare Photius favorably with him, especially since Ignatius had made a considerable effort to supplant Roman ecclesiastical hegemony in Bulgaria with his own. John wrote furiously to Ignatius that he had cast the decrees of the Fathers underfoot and utterly forgotten the beneficence of the Apostolic See toward him.[66] John wrote that even Photius had never attempted usurpation of Roman privileges in Bulgaria, and that his predecessors had absolved Ignatius of the sentence against him on condition that he attempt nothing contrary to "apostolic rights" (*iura apostolica*). If he made no such attempts in Bulgaria, he was truly absolved; if he did, he was still bound by the former sentence. To emphasize his point, John excommunicated and deposed

[63] MGH Epp. VII, k. a. 5, nos. 14, 38: 12f, 37.

[64] *Ibid.*, no. 201, 161.

[65] *Ibid.*, no. 225, 224. Five years later, Pope Stephen V again reversed this privilege, condemning Methodius's translations as presumptuous, tending "to superstition rather than to edification" (*ibid.*, no. 1, 357).

[66] *Ibid.*, no. 68, 63.

the Greek clergy whom Ignatius had sent into Bulgaria,[67] and later threatened Ignatius himself with excommunication and deposition.[68]

Two years after Photius returned to the patriarchate, Basil I invited John to participate in the synod which he had summoned to clear Photius's title (879-880). Having at least gravely questioned the title of Ignatius, whom Nicholas I and Hadrian II had acknowledged as true patriarch, John then accepted the claims of Photius, which his predecessors had vehemently rejected. As in Frotherius's translation, John invoked the special necessities of the case. Without consultation with the Roman See, Photius had indeed usurped the office explicitly forbidden him; but as Nicaea I, Gelasius I, Leo I, and Felix IV testified, necessity allowed the canons to be disregarded without prejudice to the apostolic establishments or impairment of the rules of the Fathers. The patriarchs of Alexandria, Antioch, and Jerusalem, and all archbishops, metropolitans, bishops, and clergy subject to Constantinople had consented to Photius's restoration; and John also received him as a "fellow minister in the pontifical office," absolving him of the earlier sentences against him by virtue of the supreme powers of binding and loosing which Christ granted St. Peter. Disregarding Hadrian's declarations against Photius, John commented only that, at the Council of 869, Hadrian's legates had subscribed the judgment against Photius, deferring final review to their bishop. John professed to act on that referral, recalling that Rome had absolved other patriarchs of synodal condemnation, but also providing that no bishop of Constantinople should in future be chosen, as Photius had been, from among the laity.[69] John explicitly declared to Photius that this acknowledgment was conditional upon withdrawal of Byzantine clergy from Bulgaria.[70]

The exercise of papal discretion in these three cases was largely dictated by Rome's difficult political circumstances; they served John's great effort to establish Roman hegemony in disputed ecclesiastical provinces and to secure military support for his see. Frotherius's transfer served the efforts of Charles the Bald to establish political order in the valleys of the Loire and the Cher, efforts which in 866 had prompted the elevation of Wulfhad of Bourges in view of the pagan invasions and general instability of the region.[71] Indeed, it answered an explicit request of Charles, and thus it reinforced the interest of John who, at the time of

---

[67] *Ibid.*, nos. 71, 37: 66, 294f.  [68] *Ibid.*, no. 68, 63.
[69] *Ibid.*, no. 207, 168-71.  [70] *Ibid.*, no. 209, 185f.
[71] Ep. 5, PL 124, 874; Morrison, *Kingdoms*, 156f.

the translation, had crowned Charles emperor and demanded military defense in return.[72] The decrees concerning Slavonic translations were part of Rome's effort to exclude Byzantine influence from Moravia, and John's conduct toward Photius was clearly directed with a view toward Byzantine military assistance and cession of the Bulgarian dioceses to Rome.

In a letter written after the Synod of 879-880, John stated the practical reasons for his action. Basil I had placed men in John's service to defend the lands of St. Peter; he had restored the monastery of St. Sergius, in Constantinople, to Roman jurisdiction; and, finally, he had allowed Rome to have the Bulgarian diocese. Thanking Basil for these concessions, John asked for continued assistance in defense; and, in a curious sentence, he suggested that his acceptance of Photius's claims depended upon the future course of Byzantine-Roman relations. He professed to rejoice at Photius's restoration; but, in words recalling his evasive comments on the Council of 869, he ended the letter with a curt statement that if his legates had acted "contrary to apostolic command" he would not receive the judgment of the Synod of 879-880 or attribute any validity to it.[78] Shortly afterwards, when, despite Basil's assurances, Byzantine clergy continued to work in Bulgaria, John took up the implicit option by excommunicating Photius.

At least by implication, John VIII's diplomacy had an important effect on the broad issue of ecclesiastical cohesion. His emphasis on discretionary powers in ecclesiastical cases enabled him to provide grounds for diplomatic negotiation, especially with Byzantium and the Franks. Nicholas I had held that papal judgments were irreversible and unreviewable; but the reversals and modifications of earlier papal judgments to which John's diplomacy led jeopardized the principle of continuity throughout the whole series of papal judgments. For John, precedents gave way to spontaneity. Like his predecessors, John wrote that St. Peter lived and ruled in the Roman See, which consequently retained Peter's imperishable apostolate.

And yet, the "Janus complex" in papal thought survived. Discretion pure and simple was the basis of John VIII's action, and it was the core of Nicholas I's elegantly reasoned concept of papal power. But tradition survived in their thought, as much a flaw in their monarchic doctrines as it had been in the thought of Leo I and his successors. In

---

[72] MGH Epp. VII, k. a. 5, no. 9, 9.
[73] *Ibid.*, no. 259, 229f. See Engreen, "John," 319ff.

the sixth century, political events had hammered that flaw until the whole system of thought based on discretion collapsed, a shattering blow which forces at work in the ninth century threatened to repeat.

The justified instability which John's concept of papal discretion implied reopened the question of whether the heir of Peter could lose the constancy of Peter. Nicholas's recollection of the lapsed Pope Marcellinus and Hadrian II's acknowledgment of Honorius I's condemnation as a follower of heresiarchs showed that papal thinkers admitted the possibility in matters of faith as well as of discipline.[74] In Rome itself, distinctions between the See of St. Peter and his individual heirs, which strongly undercut the doctrine of Petrine primacy, found vicious expression in the posthumous trial and deposition of Pope Formosus (897), and in the reconsiderations of the charges against Formosus, first under John IX and later under Sergius III.[75] Among Frankish thinkers, it inspired important developments in ecclesiology and in political thought, not only in the days of John VIII, when the papacy slipped gradually into the hands of the Roman nobility, but also in the days of its strength, under Nicholas I and Hadrian II.

### B. THE FRANKISH DOCTRINE: CONDITIONAL AUTHORITY

For Frankish thinkers, the pre-eminence of the Roman bishop and his see were indisputable. In the ninth century, Franks normally accorded popes the title "universal pope,"[1] often combined with "supreme pontiff."[2]

---

[74] Dr. Ullmann does not discuss this aspect of Roman thought in *Growth*. Cf. esp. pp. 190ff.

[75] On the trial of Formosus, see the brilliant and detailed discussion in Zimmermann, "Papstabsetzungen" I, 48ff, esp. pp. 61, 72. Zimmermann's comment on the much earlier deposition of Pope Constantine is a very prudent caution against taking at face value extreme statements of papal headship in the eighth century. *Ibid.*, I, 19: "*Seine Deposition war somit nicht bloss eine Angelegenheit der römischen Kirche, sondern der gesamten Christenheit und müsste überall Anerkennung finden, zumal die Rechtmässigkeit eines in so unruhigen Zeiten gefällten Urteils leicht in Zweifel gezogen werden konnte.*" The evidence we have just reviewed puts a similar caution upon interpreting ninth-century statements.

[1] Synod of Paris (825), MGH Conc. 2, 535, no. 440. Cf. PL 124, 867; PL 119, 747; Cap. ab Odone prop., MGH Conc. 2, no. 36, c. 3, 351.

[2] DC II, 413, no. 418; MGH Epp. 6, k. a. 4, no. 1, 209; Annal. Bert. (a. 869), MGH in us. sch., 99. Cf. the addresses to Nicholas I by Adventius of Metz (MGH Epp. 6, k. a. 4, no. 8, 219f): "*gloriosissimo Dominici gregis pastori, domino et beatissimo Nicolao, summo et universali papae,*" and Ratbod of Sens (PL 119, 751): "*coangelice papa cum apostolorum meritis cooperante ac suffragante.*"

An appeal of Nicholas I in 867 evoked several treatises defending Roman precedence and practices against Byzantine attack. In his *Contra Graecorum Opposita*, Ratramnus provided the fullest argument for Rome against Constantinople's pretensions.[3] The authority of Constantinople could never be greater than that of Rome, which the Greek and Latin Fathers alike acknowledged as "the head of all Christ's churches." Nor could an assembly of 150 bishops, like that recently gathered in Constantinople, prescribe for all bishops of the whole world, forbidding to the Roman pontiff and to all churches what it claimed for itself.[4] Indeed, Roman pontiffs had presided over councils —in person or in their legates—from Nicaea onward. Whatever councils the Roman bishop approved stood; those he condemned could never have any authority.[5] The Roman pontiff had the "principate of bishops" (*principatum obtineat episcoporum*); by his judgment synods were assembled and their agenda set.[6] Neither antiquity nor any decree of the elders, nor any ecclesiastical or human right exalted the patriarch of Constantinople over all other churches, unless the contemporary emperors assumed powers which their predecessors had not claimed, powers to dispose of the Roman Church at will and to change the authority which Christ and the whole Church had granted to St. Peter. The entire West, Africa, and the East, with a few exceptions, had fallen from the emperor's control.[7] By contrast, their predecessors in the fourth, fifth, and sixth centuries had ruled the whole world. They had acknowledged Rome's precedence in their edicts. Far from establishing the pre-eminence of Constantinople, they exalted Rome over the "second Rome."[8] The bishop of Constantinople had no primacy, except over his own diocese. But the Roman bishops had from antiquity borne solicitude for all churches and the power to dispose all ecclesiastical affairs; their decrees were observed as laws by all churches in the East and in the West.[9]

Even so, many Frankish thinkers placed severe qualifications on the doctrine of Roman primacy. St. Cyprian and the Donatists had argued that a priest might lose his sacramental powers through personal unworthiness, and after the patristic age this argument remained for many thinkers an elementary principle of ecclesiology. Among the Franks, Jonas of Orléans expressed it when he wrote that unjust priests

---

[3] Cf. Aeneas of Paris, Liber adversus Graecos, praef.; PL 121, 689.
[4] II, 2; PL 121, 245.    [5] IV, 8; PL 121, 337.    [6] IV, 8; PL 121, 338.
[7] IV, 8; PL 121, 343f.    [8] IV, 8; PL 121, 337ff, 344.    [9] IV, 8; PL 121, 343.

lacked the power granted to holy pastors.[10] Haimo of Auxerre wrote that a bishop who was defective in doctrine lacked the effective powers of his office, though he might retain its title,[11] and Hincmar of Rheims affirmed that, if he rejected the canons or *decreta*, he would cast himself from the episcopacy and from the Church.[12]

The qualifying effects of this general thought upon the specific doctrine of Roman primacy appeared in the records of the Synod of Paris (825). The Synod declared that God had deigned to establish an apostolic vicariate in the Roman See and that the resulting pre-eminence of Roman bishops was acknowledged by the title "universal pope." But since charity, the unifying bond of the Church, required mutual assistance in all circumstances, the pope could not rightly be called "universal" if he failed to struggle with all his powers for the universal welfare of the Church.[13] This collegial concept had already appeared in practice when the Frankish bishops threatened to depose Gregory IV for violating the authority of ancient canons.[14]

Contrary to papal doctrine, some Franks therefore held to the premises that the personal unworthiness of a pope might impair the "universal" character of his office and that a national synod, not a universal council, could depose a bishop of Rome without his voluntary submission to its judgment. This thought sprang from a concept of legal authority within the Church fundamentally different from that of Nicholas I and his successors. We have already alluded to a dispute which suggested the lines of divergence: namely, the conflict over legal authorities in the case of Rothad, in which Frankish clergy argued that only papal decretals included in the *codex canonum* were legally binding and Nicholas I responded that the privileges of the Roman See, not a particular act of codification, conferred authority upon decretals and that consequently all of them held equal authority, whether recent or ancient, whether in the *codex canonum* or not.[15] At issue in this dispute was the authority of the Pseudo-Isidorian Decretals, which Rothad

[10] De cultu imag. III; PL 106, 379f.

[11] Exposit. in Eph. 4, 12; PL 117, 720.

[12] LV Cap., c. 4; PL 126, 300.

[13] MGH Conc. 2, 522, no. 44. Ullmann, *Growth*, 127, overlooks this qualification, but cf. *ibid.*, 132f.

[14] *Vita Walae* II, 16, MGH SS. 2, p. 562; *Vita Hludowici Imperatoris*, c. 48, MGH SS. 2, p. 635. Cf. Hincmar of Rheims to Hadrian II, ep. 27, PL 126, p. 180. On Frankish "episcopalism," see Ullmann, *Growth*, 132ff.

[15] MGH Epp. VI, k. a. 4, no. 71, 394f; above, p. 219.

invoked as warranting his appeal from Hincmar of Rheims's provincial synod to papal judgment. In opposing Rothad's appeal, Hincmar (who himself invoked the Pseudo-Isidorian letters on other occasions) condemned the critical decrees as "contrary to the holy rules" (*sacris regulis obvias*) "and not sent out by apostolic authority, but compiled by some men's cunning. For the Apostolic See cannot be contrary to or inconsistent with itself."[16]

Aroused by what he considered contradictions between the Pseudo-Isidorian decrees and papal decrees in the *codex canonum* which he accepted as genuine, Hincmar argued that the former had not come from the Roman See. The principle behind this conclusion—that the Apostolic See could not issue contradictory or inconsistent decrees—implied that even if they had been authentic decretals they would have been invalid as they opposed "the holy rules" and acknowledged canons. This thought ran directly counter to that of Nicholas I and, especially, of John VIII, who claimed broad discretionary powers for the Roman See, and who argued that papal decrees were primary norms for the validity of canons, rather than the reverse.

Hincmar's comments on the Pseudo-Isidorian decrees reveal the thought that there was in generally accepted canons an abstract standard of authenticity which limited the legal authority of papal decrees. Frankish thought imposed limits of another sort by claiming legislative powers for "national" and even provincial synods. Without claiming universal validity for their decrees, the numerous Frankish synods of the ninth century consciously exercised powers of originative legislation and thus tacitly enacted a doctrine counter to the monopolistic concepts of Roman thinkers.

Early in the ninth century, Agobard of Lyons wrote protesting against the argument that Gallic canons were "superfluous and useless" (*superflui et inutiles*) because no Romans had commended them. The ancients, he wrote, had revered them because they were framed by venerable and holy men. In any case, the Lord, having promised to be

---

[16] Ep. 47, Opp. ed. Paris, 1645, 2, 778: "*nec auctoritate apostolica fuisse missas, sed compilatas quorumcunque vafricia credimus. Non enim sibi ipsi sedes apostolica potest esse contraria vel diversa.*" See also MGH Epp. 8, k. a. 6, no. 160, c. 21, 131: "*. . . quoniam aliter erga fratres non agimus, quam apostolicae sedis papae fieri placet quamque quod ipsa prima in toto orbe terrarum sedes fiendum esse decrevit. Quae non inter se adversa neque diversa tenemus.* Cf. Cap. Presbyteris data, PL 125, 792: "*Et sicut evangelicae sententiae inter se non discordant, ita nec apostolica sedes est sibi ipsa diversa, sive adversa, quae secundum canones . . . permittit.*"

present where two or three gathered in His name, was surely present when twenty, thirty, or many more gathered in His name, learned in the faith, distinguished for wisdom, revered for sanctity, and terrible in their signs and prodigies. All decrees which episcopal assemblies issued to meet ever-changing necessities must be received with equal authority; for this was the consensus of Nicaea, Chalcedon, and the other general councils.[17] Neither the absence of a Roman legate nor the silence of imperial decrees deprived them of validity.[18]

Almost a century later, Regino of Prüm described this thought in similar terms. Defending inclusion of many canons from Gallican and German councils in his *De Synodalibus Causis*, he wrote that he had taken particular care to include what he knew to be helpful in his own perilous times. Many kinds of difficulties had occurred which were unknown in earlier days; for them only "recent rules of the Fathers" (*modernis patrum regulis*), which had no ancient counterparts, were applicable. Just as divers nations differ among themselves in descent, habits, language, and laws, so also does the holy universal Church dispersed throughout the earth differ in ecclesiastical customs, although it is unified by a common faith. Different customs prevailed in the ecclesiastical offices in the kingdoms of the Gauls and Germany, in the eastern kingdoms, and in regions beyond the seas. The "recent rules" thus belonged among the laws and decrees which the Fathers established and which could be transgressed only with arrogant presumption.[19]

[17] MGH Epp. V, k. a. 3, no. 3, c. 12, 163. Cf. *ibid.*, no. 5, c. 4, 167.
[18] *Ibid.*, no. 5, c. 20, 174f.
[19] Praef., ed. F.G.A. Wasserschleben (Leipzig, 1840), 2: "*Si quem autem movet cur frequentioribus nostrorum, i.e., Galliarum ac Germaniae conciliorum usus sim exemplis, accipiat responsum et sciat, quia ea maxime inserere curavi, quae his periculosis temporibus nostris necessariora esse cognovi et quae ad susceptum propositae causae negotium pertinere videbantur. Illud etiam adiiciendum, quod multa flagitiorum genera hoc pessimo tempore in ecclesia et perpetrata sunt et perpetrantur, quae priscis temporibus inaudita, quae non facta, et ideo non scripta et fixis sententiis damnata, quae modernis patrum regulis et damnata sunt et quotidie damnantur. Nec non et illud sciendum, quod sicut diversae nationes populorum inter se discrepant genere, moribus, lingua, legibus, ita sancta universalis ecclesia toto orbe terrarum diffusa, quamvis in unitate fidei coniungatur, tamen consuetudinibus ecclesiasticis ab invicem differt. Aliae siquidem consuetudines in Galliarum, Germaniaeque regnis in ecclesiasticis officiis reperiuntur, aliae in orientalium regnis, transmarinis regionibus. Monet praeterea scriptura, terminos, id est, leges et decreta, quae patres nostri posuerunt, omnimodis observandos, nec ullatenus temeraria praesumptione transgrediendos, quapropter antecessorum nostrorum vestigia sequens, diversorum patrum diversa statuta in ordine digessi, lectoris iudicio derelinquens, quid potissimum eligere ac approbare malit.*"

Thus, the Church had strongly particularistic qualities for Frankish thinkers. Asserting the position of the clergy as a political, as well as a social, class, which had autonomous powers of legislation, adjudication, and administration in religious matters, they expressed two views on the order of government in the priestly "commonwealth." One position accepted the doctrine of Roman primacy. The other held that all bishops alike were successors of the Apostles. It contested the doctrine that St. Peter still ruled his see, and argued that the personal qualifications of popes affected the validity of their actions; it gauged the legal authority of papal decrees by the higher authority of the canons; it subjected the pope himself to judgment and possibly to deposition by "national" synods. Both views were in the mainstream of Frankish thought. To ninth-century thinkers, they were not of necessity mutually exclusive; indeed, some authors affirmed one at one crisis and the other at another. The fundamental difference between them concerned the problem of change, or rather the offices which held power spontaneously to change and to modify. The Romanists, of course, held that the Roman See exercised supreme discretionary power. But advocates of the second position argued either that they were shared by the pope and his fellow bishops or that they were principally held by synods and councils.

## C. BENEDICTUS LEVITA AND PSEUDO-ISIDORE

By contrast with Romanists, advocates of Frankish collegiality stressed patterns of institutional relationship which qualified the pope's discretionary powers, even when they accepted his supreme appellate jurisdiction. The compilations of Benedictus Levita and Pseudo-Isidore and the works of Hincmar of Rheims preserve three variant statements of the Frankish position, and we must now assess the new cast they gave to the concept of tradition in the broad context of ecclesiastical cohesion.

Neither Benedictus nor Pseudo-Isidore frequently used the word "tradition." Benedictus's few references are incidental.[1] By contrast, Pseudo-

---

[1] Benedict wrote that the "tradition of the holy Fathers" (*sanctorum patrum traditio*) set the goods of the Church apart as the offerings of the faithful and the patrimony of the poor (I, 208, PL 97, 726) and that the "traditions of the holy Fathers" (*sanctorum patrum traditiones*) submitted every order of clergy to episcopal direction (III, 2, PL 97, 803). He also described the observance of four great fasts in the year "as it has been handed down in the Roman Church" (I, 151, PL 97, 721) and, in the words of the Synod of Paris (829), he wrote that

233

Isidore's allusions, though only slightly more numerous, refer almost exclusively to the Faith, and specifically to Rome's unerring preservation of authentic doctrine.[2] Like the popes contemporary with him, Pseudo-Isidore considered Rome as the repository of apostolic doctrine and practice,[3] by virtue of St. Peter's imperishable apostolate in the Roman See.[4] The imperishable apostolate survived in St. Peter's election and consecration of Clement, described in a letter of Pseudo-Clement,[5] and in Clement's preservation of the doctrine he had learned directly from St. Peter, repeated in the specious letters of his successors.[6] Pseudo-Sixtus II was made to affirm (in the words of Siricius) that St. Peter survived in the person of the Roman bishop to bear the burdens of all the heavy-laden.[7] Even this slight notice of the concept of tradition was probably given not by conscious decision of Benedictus and Pseudo-Isidore so much as by the incidental presence of the word "tradition" in texts which they excerpted for their forgeries. The paucity of references, indeed, indicates that the two authors found the element of ecclesiastical cohesion not in the concept of tradition, but in the structure of offices within the Church to which they devoted their primary attention.

In the last analysis, it is difficult to judge precisely what degree of precedence Benedictus ascribed to the Roman See. Clearly, he thought

the body of the Church was divided chiefly between the priestly and the royal persons "as we have received what the holy Fathers handed down" (I, 319, PL 97, 742: "*sicut a sanctis patribus traditum accepimus*").

[2] Pseudo-Lucius and Pseudo-Felix I both affirmed that, through divine grace, the Roman Church had never erred from the path of apostolic tradition or succumbed to heretical novelties (ed. Hinschius, 179f, 205f, cc. 8, 18: *a tramite apostolicae traditionis nunquam errasse*). Pseudo-Pius distinguishes between the "tradition of men" (*traditio hominum*), which concerned astrology, philosophy, and elements of the world, and "right tradition" (*traditio recta*), which concerned Christ (Ep. I, c. 1, ed. Hinschius, 116f). Pseudo-Clement and Pseudo-Marcellus refer to doctrines handed down from the apostles, or the Fathers, to the writers' generations (Ps.-Clem., ep. 3, c. 70; ep. 5, c. 83; Ps.-Marc. ep. 2, c. 7, ed. Hinschius, 57f, 65f, 227).

[3] Ps.-Anacletus, ep. I, c. 11; Ps.-Eusebius, ep. I, c. 2; ep. III, c. 19; Ps.-Calixtus, ep. I, c. 2; Ps.-Felix, ep. I, cc. 6, 7; Ps.-Gaius, c. 7; Ps.-Fabianus, ep. II, c. 8; ed. Hinschius, *ibid.*, 70, 230, 239f, 136, 119f, 218, 160.

[4] Pseudo-Isidore provided specious evidence of this unbroken continuity of apostolic teaching and practice in the address of St. Peter in Pseudo-Clement's letters and in the sequence of forged decretals from Clement and his successors down to Melchiades.

[5] Ep. I, cc. 1-4, *ibid.*, 30ff.

[6] Cf. Ps.-Clement, ep. II, cc. 45, 54, 55; *ibid.*, 46f, 52.

[7] Ep. II, c. 8, *ibid.*, 193.

that the bishop of Rome stood at the head of the episcopal order, and could be judged by no one.[8] According to the Lord's command and St. Peter's merits, Rome, the origin and head of all churches, held the singular authority to assemble synods; and by the decrees of the canons, the Fathers likewise transmitted to it the unique power to summon synods for trying bishops.[9] The great liturgy,[10] the mode of chant, lections,[11] and fasts[12] must all conform to Roman usage. On the other hand, Benedictus's ascription of pre-eminence to the Roman See seems to have been somewhat limited by his emphasis upon the common functions of all bishops as successors of the Apostles, vicars of St. Peter, and vicars of Christ.[13] Furthermore, two of his chapters mention confirmation by a Frankish synod of Roman establishments, certainly a modification of the doctrine that judgments of the Apostolic See could not be reviewed.[14]

Benedictus clearly thought that the cohesion of the Church consisted in this hierarchy of juridical competence, and this lay at the basis of the most fundamental and redundant theme in his work: his insistence that temporal courts must not decide clerical cases. He commanded laymen to obey priests of every hierarchic rank and thus to show obedience to God, whose vicars the priests were.[15] But he also considered the hierarchy itself bound together by degrees of obedience, particularly in appellate recourse. The mode in which Benedictus chose to express his thought, a very long sequence of disjointed chapters, prevented any systematic exposition, and apparent contradictions and the lack of definitions make it difficult to understand precisely the lines of Benedictus's structure of authority. For example, the competence of synods and coun-

---

[8] I, 302, PL 97, 739f.

[9] Addit. IV, 24, PL 97, 892; II, 381, PL 97, 793.

[10] II, 74, PL 97, 759.    [11] II, 256, PL 97, 776.    [12] I, 151, PL 97, 721.

[13] All bishops, he wrote, were vicars of Christ (II, 99, PL 97, 761f; cf. III, 390, PL 97, 847) and vicars of St. Peter, sharing his powers to bind and loose (I, 315, PL 97, 741; cf. I, 116, PL 97, 715). They were the columns of the Church, the doors of the eternal city, the doorkeepers of Heaven (loc.cit.). Only they had the power to transmit the Holy Spirit by the imposition of hands (I, 320, PL 97, 742f; cf. III, 260, PL 97, 530f).

[14] I, 392, 393, PL 97, 752f. Perhaps mindful of the title "supreme pontiff and universal pope," he included an African canon which commanded: *Ut primae sedis episcopus non appelletur princeps sacerdotum aut summus sacerdos aut aliquid huiuscemodi, sed tantum primae sedis episcopus* (III, 29, PL 97, 805). See above, p. 23. Of course, he may have preserved the original intent of the canon, referring to primates or metropolitans.

[15] III, 390, PL 97, 847.

235

cils, from diocesan assemblies to oecumenical councils, is never even schematically described, and the relative powers of bishops, metropolitans, primates, and popes in administrative matters, other than jurisdiction over clergy, likewise went undefined. These matters may well have been extraneous to Benedictus's primary purpose, which was obviously to provide a series of *capitula* purportedly of his own kings excluding royal authority from administration of Church property and adjudication over clergy.

The purpose of Pseudo-Isidore, by contrast, was to compose a book of discipline for the clergy; his hierarchic definitions are correspondingly more ample, though not always more precise, than those of Benedictus. In the words of the ancient Letter of Clement, he expressed his concept of Church order metaphorically, with the image of a ship sailing through the tempest of this world. Christ stood as captain (*gubernator*); the bishops were pilots (*prorete*); priests were sailors (*nautae*); deacons were quartermasters (*dispensatores*); catechizers were mechanics (*nautologae*), and "the multitude of the whole fraternity," the laymen, were naval fighters (*epibatae*), sitting each one in his place so as not to impede the progress of the ship.[16]

Like Benedictus, Pseudo-Isidore thought of the Church chiefly as the priesthood, hierarchically ordered according to degrees of juridical competence.[17] True belief was the general cohesive element of the Church, but within the hierarchy cohesion resulted from conformity manifested in obedience of lesser officers to greater. Pseudo-Isidore's forgeries were designed to provide ancient and apostolic proof that the hierarchy he described was the authentic form of Church order. They show as well that Pseudo-Isidore himself thought that the order he described required the corroboration of canonical sources. In the history of the idea of tradition, his collection was of the greatest importance, both as an indication of tendencies in ninth-century thought and as a body of sources which profoundly influenced subsequent thinkers; for in concentrating upon order, Pseudo-Isidore transferred to order and to the documents which prescribed it the qualities which earlier authors ascribed to tradition. Benedictus's compilation also shows this transfer-

---

[16] Ps.-Clement, ep. I, cc. 13-14; *ibid.*, 34f. The Greek text of the letter is printed in GCS, *Pseudoclementinen* 1, 16f (Epistola Clementis 13, 5). I cannot subscribe to Klinkenberg's position that Pseudo-Isidore completed the grand design of Leo I ("Primat," 10).

[17] Ps.-Pius, ep. II, cc. 7, 8, ed. Hinschius, 118f.

ence, but the lines of Pseudo-Isidore's thought reveal it completely. Antiquity, universality, and consensus were the marks of authentic canonistic sources, and the warrants of the order which those sources prescribed. The false decretals repeatedly command obedience to the rules and establishments of the Fathers and portray Rome as the foremost guardian, and thus the first subject, of the canons.[18]

Reverence for antiquity is shown by Pseudo-Isidore's very frequent repetition of the scriptural command against transgressing the limits which the Fathers set,[19] by the argument implicit in the very plan of the collection that the doctrines stated in the letters descended from St. Peter and the other Apostles,[20] and by his insistence that the hierarchic order he described came not only from the first days of Christianity but even from anterior pagan practice.[21] Universality and consensus appear in the importance assigned to the Fathers as confirmers of legitimate order. Legitimate change became a function of juridical review within the hierarchy, according to the appearance of new problems.[22]

In his preface, Pseudo-Isidore dealt with canonistic problems of his work, indicated his standards of authenticity, and suggested their effects upon his concept of order, particularly upon the unresolved tension in his own mind between the concept that the Church was ruled collegially by bishops and the position that it was governed monarchically by the bishop of Rome. He began the preface alleging that bishops and other servants of God had prevailed upon him to collect in one volume canonical statements (*canonum sententias*); for diverse interpretations had led to variant statements, some longer, some shorter, but all with the same sense. Truth, he said, was to be sought in plurality. He wrote that he had chosen to begin the volume with a statement on how a synod should canonically be celebrated. Next came the Apostolic Canons which, Pseudo-Isidore wrote, were included even though some

---

[18] Cf. Ps.-Dionysius, ep. II, c. 4; Ps.-Marcellinus, ep. 1, c. 1; Ps.-Cornelius, ep. II, c. 3; *ibid.*, pp. 196, 220, 172.

[19] Ps.-Alexander, c. 1; Ps.-Victor, ep. I, c. 6; Ps.-Calixtus, ep. II, c. 13; Ps.-Fabianus, ep. II, c. 15; Ps.-Eusebius, ep. II, c. 13; *ibid.*, pp. 95, 128, 139, 163, 238; Deut. 27:17; Prov. 22:28.

[20] Cf. Ps.-Anacletus, ep. III, c. 28; *ibid.*, 82.

[21] This emphasis upon antiquity is excellently described in an as yet unpublished dissertation by Dr. Shafer Williams, "Pseudo-Isidori Visio Aetatis Aureae Ecclesiae," University of California (Berkeley), 1951. Dr. Williams very kindly lent me his own copy.

[22] Ps.-Gaius, c. 4; cf. Ps.-Fabianus, ep. I, c. 3; *ibid.*, 215, 157.

considered them apocryphal, because they were applicable to all synods, because many accepted them, and because the holy Fathers confirmed their sentences by synodal authority and placed them among the canonical establishments.[23] There followed the (forged) decretals from popes up to Sylvester, the decrees of Nicaea I, divers Greek and Latin synods, and finally decretal letters of Roman popes up to and including Gregory I, "in which, because of the loftiness of the Apostolic See, there is authority not unequal to that of councils."[24] After invoking some relevant parallel sanctions in secular law,[25] Pseudo-Isidore turned to the fundamental problem of the precedence of papal over synodal judgments.

The Apostolic See, he wrote, held sole power (*privata potestas*) to assemble synods; no synod was valid without having been assembled or sustained by Rome's authority, as was witnessed by canonical authority, substantiated by ecclesiastical history, and confirmed by the holy Fathers. On the other hand, the four principal councils held the complete doctrine of the Church: Nicaea, whose acts the oriental brethren affirmed to be as long as the four Gospels; Constantinople (381), which framed the creed recited in Greek and Latin churches alike; Ephesus, which condemned Nestorius; Chalcedon, which renewed the sentence against Nestorius, condemned Eutyches and Dioscorus, and defined the two natures of Christ. These were the chief and venerable synods which perfected catholic faith. But Pseudo-Isidore admitted the complete validity of any other synods which, like Constantinople (553), the holy Fathers sanctioned at the inspiration of the Holy Ghost. For the guidance of future synods, he appended directly to his preface an order for the celebration of a council.[26]

In these remarks, Pseudo-Isidore acknowledged two supreme authorities which he clearly believed to be coordinate: the synod and the Roman See. His statement concerning Roman authority over the assembly and approval of synods is disharmonious with the equivocal statement that decrees of Roman bishops held "authority not unequal" with that of councils, with the thought that the four great councils had "perfected" the faith, and with the admission of any other councils which the holy Fathers—not explicitly the Roman Church—had sanctioned.

[23] Praef., cc., 1-4, *ibid.*, 17. Above, p. 224.
[24] Praef., c. 4, *ibid.*, p. 18: *in quibus pro culmine sedis apostolicae non impar conciliorum exstat auctoritas.*
[25] Praef., c. 7, *ibid.*, p. 19.
[26] Praef., cc. 9-11, *ibid.*, 19f.

Pseudo-Isidore's position seems to have been very close to that of the later thinkers who judged papal decretals normative among canonistic sources, and argued that the validity of other sources was proven, not necessarily by their individual approval in decretals, but more usually by simple consonance between their content and that of papal decrees.

Yet it would be inexact to attribute this position to Pseudo-Isidore. He nowhere distinguished the relative competence of oecumenical councils and the Roman See, even in the juridical structure of the Church which he defined with special care. Since his forgeries were all ascribed to the period before the Council of Nicaea, such a definition fell outside the limits of his creative activity; he may well have judged that the genuine documents which he appended represented the position he thought proper. It is difficult for the modern reader to gauge exactly what that position was. Certainly, his approval of the eighty-five Apostolic Canons, thirty-five of which Rome had repudiated as forgeries,[27] suggests a norm of ecclesiastical law besides that of papal decrees. In the same fashion, Pseudo-Isidore's distinction of juridical competence within the hierarchy, and his general subordination of diocesan affairs, including discipline of lower clergy, to individual bishops, left great areas of ecclesiastical administration in which no allowance was made for papal authority. Pseudo-Isidore's scheme of appellate recourse within the hierarchy is more amply developed than Benedictus's; but the two authors alike expressed an ecclesiological doctrine which might faithfully be called a form of "mixed monarchy."

That Pseudo-Isidore did not consider the papal monarchy absolute is shown by his ambivalent attitude toward relative authority of synods and popes, by his ascription of broad powers of administrative competence to each bishop, and by his inclusion of synodal processes against Popes Sixtus, Vigilius, and Symmachus.[28] Rome's appellate powers did not curtail the mastery that Pseudo-Isidore ascribed to bishops in diocesan affairs or the broad powers he attributed to them in metropolitan synods. In juridical process within the hierarchy, Rome was supreme. But in the normal government of the Church, all bishops shared the powers of the Petrine commission. Episcopal sees were thrones of judgment, repositories of the power to bind and loose; the sentence of a bishop was to be feared, even if it were unjust.[29] Christ committed the

---

[27] See above, p. 224. John VIII's approval was yet to come.
[28] *Ibid.*, 603f, 562f, 628f, 675ff.
[29] Ps.-Urbanus, ep. I, cc. 7, 8; *ibid.*, 145.

universal Church to bishops,[30] all of whom, in keeping with the precepts of the Church, declared the same doctrine.[31] They were the keys of the Church, the columns of the Church,[32] whose fall meant the fall of the Church itself.[33] They were the rulers of the Church,[34] holding the place of the Apostles,[35] and the vicariate of Christ.[36]

### D. HINCMAR OF RHEIMS

The writings of Hincmar of Rheims reveal a similar emphasis on hierarchic order as the safeguard of ecclesiastical unity, but they also present a more comprehensive understanding of relevance among legal sources than that evidenced by Benedictus or Pseudo-Isidore, and an ecclesiology more consistent than theirs. Like Nicholas I, Hincmar was led by an extraordinary knowledge of canonistic sources to an unusually keen appreciation of the concept of tradition, as earlier writers understood it, and to a sophisticated adaptation of the concept to suit his own circumstances and preconceptions. The degree to which Hincmar, like his contemporaries, departed from the ancient concept of tradition as oral teaching is shown by his reference to "writings of ecclesiastical tradition."[1] "Holy and apostolic men, namely the successors of the Apostles, established laws on the basis of their tradition."[2] Whenever some new matter concerning catholic faith or sacred religion appeared, Hincmar required that bishops must deal with it, not according to unwritten tradition, but according to written sources, "the authority of sacred Scriptures, the doctrine of orthodox masters, canonical authority, and decrees of the Roman pontiffs."[3] The "presumption of novelties" (*novitatum praesumptio*) was feared, not as a breach of faith, but as a violation of the "regular establishments of our Fathers" (*regulares con-*

[30] Ps.-Eleutherus, c. 6; *ibid.*, 127.
[31] Ps.-Evaristus, ep. I, c. 2; *ibid.*, 88.
[32] Ps.-Clement, ep. I, c. 37, 41.
[33] Ps.-Sixtus II, ep. II, c. 4; Ps.-Eusebius, ep. III, c. 18; *ibid.*, 191, 239.
[34] *Loc.cit.*, and Ps.-Stephanus, ep. II, c. 13, 188.
[35] Ps.-Urbanus, ep. I, c. 2; *ibid.*, 144.
[36] Ps.-Eusebius, ep. III, c. 17; Ps.-Evaristus, ep. II, c. 4; Ps.-Lucius, c. 7; Ps.-Alexander, ep. II, c. 12; Ps.-Clement, ep. III, c. 59; Ps.-Zepherinus, ep. II, c. 13; *ibid.*, 239, 90, 178, 102, 53, 134.

[1] Ep. 11, PL 126, 81: "*scripta ecclesiasticae traditionis.*"
[2] De Div., PL 125, 652: "*sancti et apostolici viri successores videlicet apostolorum ex eorum traditione leges statuerunt.*"
[3] MGH Epp. VIII, k. a. 6, fasc. 1, no. 131 b, 71: "*scripturarum sanctarum auctoritate et orthodoxorum magistrorum doctrina atque secundum canonicam et decreta pontificum Romanorum.*"

*stitutiones patrum nostrorum*).[4] Accusations that men fell into error by following their own senses rather than the understanding of the Fathers continued. Athanasius and Hilary of Poitiers had brought the same charge against the Arians. But, for Hincmar, the charge likewise concerned the interpretation of legal sources, rather than doctrine.[5]

In this transference, no blurring of distinctions occurred between tradition and custom (*consuetudo*). Hincmar considered custom a valid warrant for administrative actions within the Church,[6] but he did not attribute to it more than a quasi-legal relevance. Using an expression of Roman law, he wrote that custom which did not impede the public welfare was to be considered as law.[7] By contrast, tradition, in its canonistic form, retained a genuinely normative role in Church affairs. In some contexts, the "tradition of the elders"[8] and "ecclesiastical tradition"[9] denote, in the sense of the apologists, a source of information. The same meaning, with a reference to the Old Testament, seems to have been meant when Hincmar (?) wrote that Charles the Bald had been anointed "according to divine tradition"[10] and "according to ecclesiastical tradition."[11] Generally, Hincmar invoked tradition as the authority for Church order in the performance of sacramental functions,[12] as, for example, in ecclesiastical discipline over clergy and laity, in the trial of clergy, and especially in the pattern of official relationships within the hierarchy.[13] Hincmar often cited it with other authorities, such

[4] *De ecclesiis*, ed. Gundlach (ZfKG, 10 [1889]), 108.

[5] LV Cap., c. 32. PL 126, 414: ". . . *Non ut sicut Iudaei legem eosdem canones pro suo libitu ad suum sensum inflectant, sed ut sensum eorum praecepta sequendo. . . .*" MGH, Epp. VIII, k. a. 6, fasc. 1, no. 123, 59; cf. LV Cap., c. 43; PL 126, 441, 448; Flodoard, *Hist. Rem. eccl.*, III, 23; MGH SS 13, 519.

[6] Ep. 2, PL 126, 39ff; MGH Epp. VIII, k. a. 6, no. 160 a, c. 1, 122. Cf. De Div., PL 125, 658.

[7] De Div., PL 125, 679: "*ita ut scriptum legimus, consuetudo quae publicis utilitatibus non impedit pro lege est retinenda.*" Cf. Cod. Th. V, 20, 1 int., Br. V, 12, 1 int.

[8] *De Ord. Pal.*, c. 1; MGH Cap. 2, 518; Ep. 15, PL 126, 96: *traditio maiorum.* On the treatise, De Ordine Palatii, see Brühl, "Hinkmariana," 54ff.

[9] LV Cap., c. 16; PL 126, 339: *traditio ecclesiastica.*

[10] MGH, Cap. 2, no. 297, 439: *divina traditio.*

[11] *Ibid.*, no. 300, c. 3, 451: *traditio ecclesiastica.*

[12] Ep. 6, PL 126, 514: *traditio Domini*; De offic. episc. PL 125, 1087: *traditio ecclesiastica.*

[13] *Traditio* applies to the Christian faith (LV Cap., cc. 20, PL 126, 360) or to approved conduct (LV, cap., c. 24, PL 126, 376), *Traditio Domini*, to the sacramental system (ep. 6, PL 126, 514). *Traditio apostolica* to hierarchic order (Ep. 31, c. 3, PL 126, 210; LV Cap., c. 13, 17-25, Libellus, c. 28, PL 126, 326, 344,

as "Gospel truth, apostolic and canonical authority, and the way of the Holy Scriptures."[14]

Given the considerable bulk and the extraordinary variety of Hincmar's works, the term "tradition" in any of its forms occurs rarely in his writings. But Hincmar's erudite use of the term in its historically correct senses, his attribution of normative force to it, his invocation of it particularly concerning matters of order, and the predominance of the legalistic term "tradition of the elders" suggest the major outlines of his highly juristic and collegial ecclesiology.[15]

No less than Benedictus and Pseudo-Isidore, Hincmar considered the Church principally a priestly corporation, united by sacramental functions and by the general law of the canons. Among the kinds of Church law,[16] the canons were normative: they were the distinctive

---

387, 614), and to the role of the king as God's avenger (*Conc. Duz., Acta,* c. 7, Mansi 16, 670); *Traditio divina* to the anointing of Charles the Bald (MGH Cap. 2, no. 297, 439); *Traditio antiqua* to the transmission of knowledge (LV Cap., c. 16, PL 126, 338), the hierarchic ranking of Jerusalem (LV Cap., c. 17, PL 126, 343); *Traditiones sanctae,* consistently in a quotation from Pope Hilary I, to ecclesiastical order (*Conc. Duz., Responsio episcoporum,* Mansi 16, 657; Libellus, c. 35, PL 126, 630; LV Cap., cc. 19, 36 [two citations]; PL 126, 352f, 430; epp. 32 [c. 24], 33, PL 126, 242, 247. Letter in the name of Charles the Bald to Hadrian II, ep. 8, PL 124, p. 893); *Traditio doctorum* to a matrimonial case (ep. 22, PL 126, 142); *Traditio(nes) maiorum* to measures of authenticity in canonistic sources (LV Cap., c. 20, PL 126, 360); source of information (*De Ord. Pal.,* c. 1, MGH Cap. 2, p. 518; ep. 15, PL 126, p. 96); the manner of episcopal administration (*De Ord. Pal.,* c. 3, MGH Cap. 2, 518; LV Cap., 24, PL 126, 376; LV Cap., c. 4, PL 126, 301; letter in the name of Charles the Bald to Hadrian II, ep. 7, PL 124, 879; epp. 6, 10, PL 126, 514, 533; *Conc. Duz.,* Acta, c. 9, Mansi 16, 671, 675); to hierarchic order (LV Cap., c. 16, PL 126, 539); to clerical discipline (*Conc. Duz., Respona episc.,* Mansi 16, 655, 657); to order of synodal trial (*Conc. Duz.,* c. 1, Mansi 16, 643). *Traditio ecclesiastica* to sacramental order (*De offic. episc.,* PL 125, 1087; ep. 53, PL 126, 275); to source of information (ep. 11, PL 126, 81; LV Cap., c. 16, PL 126, 339); mode of synodal trial (ep. 4, PL 126, 50; Conc. Suess. II [853], Actio I, Mansi 14, 983); to the manner of royal coronation (MGH Cap. 2, no. 300, c. 3, 451). *Leges ex traditione* to synodal canons (*De Div Responsio* V, PL 125, 652). One reference to the *traditio apostolicae sedis,* which is not clearly Hincmar's, may also be included. It concerns the effects of deposition upon a bishop's official acts (Conc. Suess. II (853), Actio V, Mansi 14, 986.

[14] E.g., letter in the name of Charles the Bald to Hadrian II, ep. 7, PL 124, 879: "*evangelica veritate et apostolica atque canonica auctoritate secundum tramitem sanctarum Scripturarum traditionemque maiorem.*" On the term "tradition of the Apostolic See," see above, n. 13.

[15] Morrison, *Kingdoms,* 37f.

[16] De Div., PL 125, 746: "*Unum regnum, una Christi columba, videlicet sancta*

law of the priesthood,[17] just as the law of Moses was the law of the Jews; and they were eternal,[18] for, like Moses, the priests who established them received their laws from the divine oracle.[19] Persons who were not priests, had nothing to do with the canons. A bishop who cast aside the holy canons and decrees of the Catholic Church deposed himself from the episcopate and fell into schism;[20] for the canons received their legal force from the "assent of the universal Church,"[21] the approval of "all bishops throughout the whole world."[22]

The other forms of law must conform with the canons, and their legal relevance declined as the conditions they were designed to meet disappeared. To be sure, additions were made even to the body of the "eternal" canons as circumstances required by "modern and Gaulish bishops" as well as by the ancient Fathers.[23] And Hincmar included the canons with papal decretals and the Scriptures themselves when he wrote that contrarieties appeared in Church law because its components were framed "according to the quality of times, circumstances, and causes." With time, some laws came to be understood in a spiritual sense, some were changed, some were entirely lost, and others remained as they had been established.[24] But in general he argued that conciliar decrees, especially those of oecumenical councils, were "fixed and immobile,"[25] and that they were the "decrees of the saints" to which new constitutions and even papal decretals must conform.[26]

Explicitly, Hincmar argued that to promulgate laws was, first, to judge the laws, and, second, to judge according to them and to declare their

---

ecclesia, unius Christianitatis lege, regni unius et unius ecclesiae, quamquam per plures regni principes et ecclesiarum praesules gubernacula moderentur." On Hincmar's categories of law, see Morrison, *Kingdoms*, 85ff.

[17] *De Ord. Pal.*, c. 7, MGH Cap. 2, 520.

[18] LV Cap., c. 32, PL 126, 414: "*quoniam canones et patrum regulae canones et regulae sunt sacerdotum eo modo sicut lex Moysi dicitur et lex Iudaeorum. . . .*" Cf. *Pro. Lib.*, PL 125, 1055.

[19] Ep. 8, PL 124, 892f; LV Cap., c. 32, PL 126, 414; cf. *De Div.*, PL 125, 643f. See Hincmar's description of the ancient Jews as "*ecclesia veteris populi*," in LV Cap., c. 13, PL 126, 326.

[20] LV Cap., c. 4, PL 126, 300.

[21] LV Cap., c. 47, PL 126, 465; cf. *ibid.*, c. 43, col. 448: *assensus universalis ecclesiae*.

[22] LV Cap., c. 43, PL 126, 444.

[23] Ep. 21, PL 126, 126; cf. Ep. 22, PL 126, 142.

[24] LV Cap., c. 20, PL 126, 353f: *pro temporum et rerum ac qualitate causarum*.

[25] E.g., LV Cap., c. 36, PL 126, 428.

[26] LV Cap., c. 34, PL 126, 419.

observance and judgments to all men. Ecclesiastical laws established holy orders. That was beyond the power of the Roman bishops, who could only prescribe discipline within the orders which the laws established.[27] Once the immediate circumstances to which a decretal was addressed had past, the edict lost its intrinsic applicability and preserved a measure of legal relevance only if it were included or excerpted in conciliar decrees.[28]

The body of canons held its position as the supreme law of the Church because it had been defined by the approval of "all bishops throughout the whole world," by "all the catholic Church."[29] Oecumenical councils were special channels of that universal assent. There were many "catholic" synods, Hincmar wrote, but only six specifically called "general," "since they were called on a matter general to all Christians. They could not, nor can they be regularly assembled without the special command of the Apostolic See."[30] Hincmar rejected the claims of Nicaea II to oecumenicity on the grounds that its decrees lacked sound understanding and that it had met "without the authority of the Apostolic See." On the other hand, he described the Synod of Frankfurt (794) as a "general synod" (generalis synodus),[31] meeting under the command of the Apostolic See and Charlemagne's imperial (sic) convocation, and overturning Nicaea II "according to the way of the Scriptures and the tradition of the elders." To elucidate his point, Hincmar quoted a passage from the Libri Carolini which rejected Nicaea II's claims to universality.

If any synod avoided novelty and held the teachings of the ancient Fathers, it could be called universal, the Libri said; but, since Nicaea II had run counter to the teachings of the universal Church, it could not claim the title "universal."[32] It is not clear how far Hincmar accepted this definition, which recurred, differently cast, in a quotation from St.

[27] LV Cap., c. 10, PL 126, 318ff.

[28] LV Cap., argumenta, PL 126, 283.

[29] LV Cap., c. 43, PL 126, 444: "omnes episcopi per universum orbem . . . omnis catholica ecclesia."

[30] LV Cap., c. 20, PL 126, 359: "Unde cum plura catholica habeantur concilia sex synodi tantum generales specialiter appellantur, quia pro generali ad omnes Christianos causa pertinente sunt convocatae, quae sine speciali jussione sedis apostolicae regulariter congregari non poterant, neque possunt."

[31] Cf. Chron. Moissiac. (a. 794), MGH SS. 1, 330f, where the Synod of Frankfort is called "universalis synodus," "sancta et universalis synodus," and "universale concilium."

[32] See above, pp. 178f.

Augustine;[33] for he pointed out that the Synod of Sardica and the North African Synods of the patristic age were not reckoned universal councils, although they were orthodox and although the Apostolic See and the universal Church had accepted them.[34] He likewise left unclarified the question of conciliar autonomy. Though Chalcedon met under papal command and imperial summons, Hincmar pointed out that the Apostolic See did not receive its disciplinary decrees, especially canon 28, which the Council had approved with imperial concurrence, but in prejudice to Rome's privileges.[35] In a treatise against Hincmar of Laon, Hincmar obviously considered the legal relevance of these canons to have been impaired; but he neither explicitly denied them any relevance nor resolved the institutional conflict between papal and conciliar powers which broke out at Chalcedon. Indeed, in the same treatise, he observed that, according to a decree of Chalcedon, the rules which the Fathers had earlier established at their several synods had independent validity. In another context, he himself invoked as valid canon 9 of Chalcedon, which he was at pains to disallow in the dispute with Hincmar of Laon.[36]

Oecumenical councils were thus special instruments for expressing the universal assent, marked by two principal characteristics: that the Roman See command that the council be held; and that the empire summon it. Taken with his reservations about Sardica and the North African synods, Hincmar's quotation from the *Libri Carolini* suggests the argument that synods, which lacked the chief characteristics of oecumenical councils, could still issue decrees that were "universal," if they accorded with the decrees of the Fathers and if the Apostolic See and the universal Church accepted them.

Hincmar left open the question of whether papal discretion or universal assent as expressed in synodal decrees took precedence. He appears to have accepted papal precedence, and the corresponding discretionary powers, in disallowing the disciplinary canons of Chalcedon. But on other occasions he rejected papal discretionary powers. For example, he argued that the Roman See could not issue contra-

[33] LV Cap., c. 25, PL 126, 388.
[34] LV Cap., c. 20, PL 126, 361.
[35] LV Cap., c. 23, PL 126, 368f.
[36] LV Cap., c. 10, PL 126, 322: "*Inspice canonum libros et videbis omnia illa concilia quae a maioribus servanda suscepimus, celebrata ante Chalcedonensem synodum, quae decrevit regulas sanctorum patrum per singula eatenus concilia constitutas proprium robur obtinere. . . .*" *De ecclesiis*, ed. Gundlach (ZfKG, 10 [1889]), 99.

dictory decrees; he advocated limited conciliar superiority by maintaining that papal decrees could not rightly depart from the Nicene canons,[37] and that the judgments of the Roman bishop were valid and the pope himself immune from synodal deposition only so long as his decrees accorded with the "laws established by the assent of the whole Church."[38] The bishop of Rome retained the power to bind and loose only when he exercised that privilege of Peter with Peter's equity.[39]

Hincmar's view of hierarchic order, the vessel of universal assent, complemented his concept of authority in canonistic sources. Many passages in Hincmar's works attest his profound reverence for the See of St. Peter. He accepted the Donation of Constantine as evidence that Constantine the Great had translated his capital to Byzantium out of love and honor for Sts. Peter and Paul.[40] Rome held the exclusive power to establish general observance for all priests.[41] Gaul had received its religion from Rome,[42] and thus it was particularly subject to St. Peter's principate as expressed in the power to review judgments of metropolitan and episcopal sees.[43] The canons of Sardica and Nicaea I confirmed this power to review and overturn or confirm provincial and general synods;[44] and it was an indisputable premise that the Roman Church must be consulted whenever doubtful or obscure matters arose concerning right faith and dogma.[45]

Yet, there were checks upon even this general pre-eminence. The "principate of judiciary power" (*principatum iudiciariae potestatis*) which Christ granted St. Peter was shared by all bishops,[46] and the privileges which they consequently held severely limited Rome's powers of immediate and appellate jurisdiction.

Hincmar's concept of hierarchic relations differed from Pseudo-Isidore's chiefly in the degree to which he identified metropolitans

[37] See above, p. 231.
[38] Ep. 8, PL 124, 883, 894ff.
[39] Ep. 8, PL 124, 894; cf. *ibid.*, col. 883. Leo I, PL 54, 151.
[40] De Ord. Pal., c. 13, MGH Cap. 2, 522.
[41] MGH Epp. VIII, k. a. 6, fasc. 1, no. 108 b, 54: "*scribere procuravi non quasi ex meo singulari iure generalem omnibus Domini sacerdotibus, quod solius est apostolicae sedis, imponens observantiam. . . .*"
[42] Ep. 52, PL 126, 271.
[43] LV Cap., c. 5, PL 126, 306.
[44] *Loc.cit.*; De Div., PL 125, 748.
[45] De Div., PL 125, 623.
[46] MGH Epp. VIII, k. a. 6, fasc. 1, no. 160 a, cc. 23-25, 132f.

with primates.[47] Hincmar was perfectly prepared to quote, as proceeding from apostolic tradition, Leo I's statement that different ranks of bishops held varying degrees of power, though they all shared the same dignity.[48] But, whereas Leo intended to enhance papal supremacy by that observation, Hincmar invoked it to buttress his broad claims of metropolitical autonomy. Hincmar quoted passages from Pseudo-Clement and Pseudo-Anacletus rendering the historical descent of hierarchic rank and distinguishing between metropolitans and primates.[49] But he once pointed out that the canons often referred to some archbishops or metropolitans as primates if, without consulting another primate, they could be ordained by bishops of any province, if their predecessors had normally received the pallium from the Apostolic See, and if they could oversee the election of bishops in their own provinces and ordain them without the permission of another primate.[50] In another comment, he omitted the second of these qualifications and added another characteristic function: the power to convoke synods and to provide for necessities in their provinces.[51] These special powers could not rightly be superseded by the claims of another see. Hincmar discussed in this regard the honorary primacy which Nicaea granted Jerusalem, a simple bishopric, preserving the rights of the metropolitan see to which Jerusalem was subject, and the similar case of Constantinople, which was numbered among the patriarchates and primatial sees by imperial sanction and consent of the Apostolic See and of a "general synod," but which remained a suffragan see of the metropolitan of Heraclea. Neither imperial edict, nor the bestowal of a pallium by the Apostolic See, nor synodal decree could rightly detract from the powers of a metropolitan see. For, as Hincmar pointed out, the bishop of Constantinople was excommunicated by bishops of Rome for presuming to use primatial powers "contrary to the rules."[52]

Hincmar's view concerning metropolitan powers was naturally one aspect of his effort to establish the pre-eminence of Rheims in Gaul and to identify Rheims, at least in its provincial administration, as the parallel of Rome. St. Remigius, the founder of the see, was an

[47] Ep. 30, c. 5, PL 126, 191: "*Illis metropolitanis qui et primates multoties in sacris canonibus appellantur. . . .*"

[48] E.g., *loc.cit.*; LV Cap., c. 13, PL 126, 326f. See above, pp. 91f.

[49] LV Cap., cc. 15, 17, PL 126, 329ff, 34.

[50] LV Cap., cc. 6, 17, PL 126, 311f, 341; Ep. 30, cc. 4, 5, PL 126, 190f.

[51] LV Cap., c. 17, PL 126, 344.

[52] *Ibid.*, 347ff.

"apostolic man,"[53] the "apostle of the Franks."[54] Hincmar quoted, and may have composed, the forged appointment of Remigius by Pope Hormisdas to be papal vicar "throughout all the realm of our beloved and spiritual son, Clovis . . . , reserving the privileges which antiquity has granted to metropolitans." He alleged that this position had been confirmed by Pope Hadrian I's grant to Archbishop Tilpin, and by Leo IV's cession to Hincmar himself.[55] Just as Roman bishops argued that St. Peter lived in them, Hincmar maintained that St. Remigius lived in his successors. Just as Alexandria and Antioch were subject to Rome, Laon, the see of his rebellious nephew, was rightly subject to Rheims.[56] At Chalcedon, Dioscorus had been condemned "not because he sinned against the faith, but on account of ecclesiastical order alone, and because, contravening the sacred canons, he had rebelled against his archbishop."[57] Laon's defiance of Rheims' authority was "civil war" against "the privilege of the metropolis"[58] and resistance to a power ordained of God.[59]

Hincmar of Laon asserted that the powers his uncle claimed, especially in judiciary authority, derogated from the privileges of Rome.[60] The Archbishop's conduct in the case of Rothad had led Nicholas to the same conclusion, and Hincmar was forced to write protesting that he had not acted "in contempt of the Apostolic See" by judging Rothad in provincial synod after the accused had appealed to Rome.[61] Rothad was charged with alienating treasures and lands of his church arbitrarily, without the consent of his metropolitan and of his fellow bishops, and without the consent of the oeconomus, priests, and deacons of his own church. The charges were proven true.[62] This was the sort of case, Hincmar argued, that the canons of Nicaea and other councils and the decrees of Roman bishops prescribed must be terminated by

[53] *Vita S. Remigii*, c. 31, MGH SS. RR. Mer. 3, 330: *viri apostolici.*

[54] Ep. 15, PL 126, 97: *Francorum apostoli.*

[55] LV Cap., c. 16, PL 126, 338f. He also invoked the precedent of the vicariate of Arles, as supposedly established by Pope Zosimus (MGH Epp. 8, k. a. 6, no. 160 a, c. 6, 124f).

[56] LV Cap., c. 16, PL 126, 334, 337f.

[57] LV Cap., c. 27, PL 126, 397: *"non quia in fidem peccaverit, sed propter solum ecclesiasticum ordinem et quia contra suum archiepiscopum sacris canonibus obvians rebellaverat est damnatus."*

[58] LV Cap., c. 44, PL 126, 454.

[59] LV Cap., c. 5, PL 126, 303; Romans 13:1ff.

[60] LV Cap., c. 45, PL 126, 456.

[61] Ep. 2, PL 126, 28; see Fuhrmann, "Patriarchate" (1954), 37f.

[62] *Ibid.*, 32f.

metropolitans in provincial synods. To have burdened Nicholas's supreme authority with it would have shown scant regard for the privilege of the Roman Church. Hincmar argued that referral to Rome of cases concerning bishops could canonically occur only if clear judgments were not apparent in the sacred rules, and if, for that reason, the provincial synod could reach no settlement. A bishop deposed in a provincial synod could appeal to the Roman bishop, who could then, according to the Sardican canons, re-open the case. But a metropolitan, ordained duly and by ancient custom bearing the pallium granted by the Apostolic See, had the canonical privilege of issuing his sentence in such a case before judgment was imposed. After judgment, the case could go to Rome.

Indeed, the Sardican canons prescribed, not that the Roman bishop could of his own right restore a deposed bishop, but rather that for rehearing he must return the condemned man to the province where the case arose. The Carthaginian canons and Roman Law confirmed this procedure.[63]

Rothad defied Hincmar's admonitions, alleging that he held full competence over the affairs of his diocese. The Archbishop judged him "incorrigible and useless in the sacred ministry" (*incorrigibilem et ministerio sacro inutilem*), and summoned him to answer before an episcopal synod. Charles the Bald issued a complementary summons. Rothad, however, denied the competence of the synod to judge him, demanded sentence against Hincmar, and appealed to Rome. He was consequently deposed as one "always disobedient to the sacred rules, to the royal dignity, and to the metropolitan privilege."[64]

Hincmar of Laon and Rothad invoked two principles of Pseudo-Isidore: that bishops had full powers over the administration of their dioceses, and that they could evade judgment before provincial synods by accusing their metropolitan of partiality and appealing directly to Rome. Hincmar of Rheims, however, argued that supervision over all his province belonged to the metropolitan,[65] and that cases concerning more than one diocese within the province must be adjusted by the provincial synod which could be summoned only by the metropolitan,[66] by judges whom the metropolitan should name, or by arbitrators com-

---

[63] *Ibid.*, col. 36.

[64] *Ibid.*, cols. 28ff: "*semper inobediens et sacris regulis, et regiae dignitati, et metropolitano privilegio.*"

[65] Ep. 52, PL 126, 275.     [66] LV Cap., c. 28, PL 126, 397.

monly chosen by the disputing parties acting under the general super-intendence of the metropolitan. In matters of general concern, neither could the archbishop act without his suffragans, nor could the suffragans act without the consent or order of their archbishop.[67] Matters concerning the general observance of all priests could not be decided without approval of the metropolitan.[68]

The metropolitan himself could receive appeals from the courts of any of his suffragans.[69] But Hincmar was equivocal about what course disputing or accused bishops might follow if they suspected the partiality of their archbishop. In one text, he wrote that they must petition him to designate judges or to approve the judges they themselves had selected, and to designate a place where synodal hearings would be held.[70] In another treatise, he adduced canon 9 of Chalcedon, which allows bishops to appeal from their metropolitan to " 'the primate of the diocese or the see of the royal city,' which, for us, is Rome." But Hincmar argued, it would be harsh to submit the metropolitan or primate of a province to this process. Far better procedure would be to follow a canon which Hincmar attributed to a synod of Orleans (now unidentifiable). That canon prescribes that bishops might present their grievances against metropolitans in their provincial synods, if the metropolitans failed to give prior satisfaction. Hincmar added that the common decision should be binding upon the metropolitan and upon other bishops.[71] In any case, an appeal to Rome would, according to Sardica, return a case to the province whence it came, and thus if not to the metropolitan's judgment, then at least to his sphere of influence.

In Hincmar's mind, metropolitan privilege was a distinct limit upon the juridical competence of the Roman See. It virtually excluded Rome's immediate jurisdiction over matters outside its own province and erected a barrier of privilege between bishops and the successor of St. Peter. To be sure, in some texts Hincmar attributed complete directive powers only to metropolitans, who enjoyed special distinctions such as the use of the pallium. But in his general comments, these unusual qualifications were lost sight of, and Hincmar completed the identification of metropolitan and primate against which ninth-century popes,

---

[67] MGH Cap. 2, no. 297, c. 1, 428.
[68] E.g., LV Cap., cc. 27, 45, PL 126, 396, 456.
[69] De ecclesiis, ed. Gundlach (ZfKG, 10 [1889]), 98.
[70] LV Cap., c. 6, PL 126, 311.
[71] De Ecclesiis, ed. Gundlach (ZfKG, 10 [1889]), 98f.

Benedictus Levita, and Pseudo-Isidore had all protested. In advocating this hierarchic structure, Hincmar argued that he preserved ecclesiastical tradition and that he was "not the author of a new constitution, but the executor of what was anciently established."[72]

✝

Ninth-century thinkers wrestled with enormous problems of ecclesiology and political thought. Their victories and their defeats alike command respect. They were the first to think comprehensively about the role of churchmen as princes, as temporal rulers and military commanders in political realms. What obligations did such men owe to the civil power that gave them their state, and to the Church that gave them their office? These problems were the warp and woof of the clergy's life. Social developments from the time of the Germanic migrations prepared them; Alcuin and his circle had encountered them; they did not suddenly confront men in the age of Hincmar and Nicholas I. Consequently, thinkers approached them as matters that could be dealt with out of the mixed bag of experience. There were no systematic analyses of the problems, and it is more than likely that ninth-century thinkers had no idea of the revolutionary importance of their work.

They were in fact reinterpreting the teachings of Christian antiquity to suit the needs of mediaeval society. Their answers set forth principles in a cast, and often of a kind, that no previous age would have grasped, but that their successors in Western Europe shared for at least seven centuries. Their success in re-examining the problem of authority in the Church was perhaps greater than that in dealing with the relations of Church and State.

Hincmar and Nicholas I were singular in the degree to which they explicitly referred to the concept of tradition. Moreover, it is important to know that nearly all of Nicholas's references to tradition occur, not in letters to western princes and clergy, but in letters to the East. There —to take one distinguished example—the records of the Synod of Constantinople (869) show that the concept of tradition luxuriantly

---

[72] LV Cap., c. 6, PL 126, 313: "*quia, ut beatus monstrat Gelasius, in his non novae constitutionis auctor, sed veteris constituti exsecutor existam.*" The other viewpoint is represented most crisply by John Scottus's bitter epitaph for Hincmar: "*Hic iacet Hincmarus cleptes vehementer avarus / Hoc solum gessit nobile, quod periit,*" MGH Poet. Lat. 3, 553).

flourished in all its ancient trappings. Nicholas was using the polemical language of his opponents. The rarity with which Hincmar and Nicholas used it, and its neglect by other writers suggest that other concepts had assumed the ecclesiological functions which it once discharged, and that it had become an archaism useful only to experts in Church law. Even Hincmar and Nicholas described tradition not as the principal safeguard of ecclesiastical cohesion, but as a secondary expression of that safeguard. Their understandings of universality epitomized this emphasis and the different casts it had in their broad concepts of Church order.

Nicholas argued that true bishops, "bishops of the universal Church," were members of the Church, and that the Apostolic See was its head. Care of the universal Church, and especially the power to judge any bishop, rested in the See of St. Peter.[73] For Nicholas, juridical primacy naturally implied magisterial primacy. Apostolic teaching was direct in each generation, by virtue of the imperishable apostolate of St. Peter in the Roman See. Tradition, in his mind, was not so much the conveyance of a body of ancient doctrine and practice as it was immediate and spontaneous instruction expressed through Rome's supreme juridical powers.

Hincmar, however, did not identify juridical and magisterial primacy, and, concerning each, he denied Rome the degree of precedence which Nicholas claimed. As for powers of adjudication, his argument that all bishops shared the "principate of juridical power" which Christ granted to St. Peter, and his views on the metropolitanate left Rome only the most eminent member of the episcopal college. In magisterial matters, the supreme ecclesiastical sanction he invoked—the consensus of all bishops, the approval of the universal Church—was more metaphysical than institutional; it could not be expressed by one see or even by one council. Like Nicholas, Hincmar held that each generation must witness primordial truth in its own right; ecclesiastical law, even the canons, changed according to necessity. Like Nicholas, he judged

---

[73] E.g., MGH Epp. VI, k. a. 4, no. 71, 393: "*Quomodo, rogo per vos, quorum vel in singulis provinciis habetur prima sententia vel qui in maioribus urbibus constituti sollicitudinem suscipitis ampliorem ad unam Petri sedem universalis ecclesiae cura confluit, ut de minoribus sileam, qui de deponendis episcopis nil ad notitiam nostram deferre curatis? An episcopi de universali ecclesia non sunt, ut de illis dampnandis per vos aliquid ad unam sedem Petri non deferri curetur? Vel quomodo nil usquam a suo capite dissident, cum de adiudicandis praecipuis membris ecclesiae, id est episcopis, a capite, id est a sede apostolica, dissentitis? An sedes apostolica caput non est?*"

that official functions, not tradition, certified authentic changes and preserved the unity of the Church. But these essential functions belonged to all bishops, rather than to one see.

For Hincmar, Nicholas, and their contemporaries who did not invoke tradition, official powers had assumed the functions which earlier writers ascribed to tradition: they united the Church and divided it, as a religious grouping, from external institutions. Aside from orthodox faith, which all authors took for granted, the cohesive element in the Church was obedience within the hierarchy. Obedience was construed not as a pattern of normal administrative accountability so much as one of juridical competence, and especially of appellate recourse. The classic tension between conservatism and change became a matter of preserving the legitimate powers both of individual officers and of whole ranks within the hierarchy at the same time as procedures and regulations were adapted to meet particular circumstances. Accordingly, normative authorities were those which regulated due juridical process, setting the limits within which conventional powers could be modified, suspended, or excluded, and giving new administrative and juridical regulations legal validity. The Church's cohesion depended upon conformity to the establishments of these authorities, whose very existence expressed apostolic tradition. But was cohesion to operate in the pattern advocated by the popes, in that of the Frankish "episcopalists," or in yet another scheme?

Beyond this lay one, great question: How was the tension in papal thought between the language of tradition and the fact of discretion to be resolved? Nicholas was within the conventions of his great predecessors when he tried to make tradition into a pillar of discretion. For him, only the Roman See and pontiff correctly understood tradition; thus the traditions of Rome had to be those of the entire orthodox Church, and the Roman pontiff, the universal judge of authentic faith and order. But to exalt the authority of tradition, even with these qualifications, was to undermine the force of papal discretion at least by setting up a joint, corroborative authority. More than that, it gave a strong handhold to thinkers in Rome and in the "national" churches north of the Alps who would have reversed Nicholas's priority by making papal discretion a pillar of tradition. Disputes in the ninth century failed to resolve this tension; in the drama of ecclesiastical thought, the papacy still had the role of Janus.

253

# CHAPTER 10

# The Tenth Century: Hardening the Lines

WITH the possible exception of Gerbert, intellectual achievements in the tenth century can hardly be compared with those of the ninth. There are no thinkers of Hincmar's stature, or Nicholas I's, and no compilers either as ambitious or as accomplished as Benedictus Levita or Pseudo-Isidore. Yet it would be harsh to call the century, as Baronius did, an age of iron, an age of lead, and an age of darkness;[1] for it witnessed the dawn of new societies which reached their brightest magnificence in the next two centuries.[2] Intellectual life was scarred by shattering disasters. The first half of the century saw Europe repeatedly ravaged by Scandinavians and Magyars; there was no stable and effective political order. The great achievement of Otto I was the establishment, by about the middle of the century, of a strong government in Germany, without peer in western Europe. But Otto's own reign was uneasy; for his son and grandson, the struggle to maintain political order was terrifyingly unequal. At the end of the century, Bruno of Querfurt, representing the lament of the Church, beleaguered by unrelenting enemies, recalled the "golden times" of the first Otto, when her world was truly happy.[3]

In political thought, the tenth century was an age when ideas were in steady flux, when exceptions were the rule, and when only the most general norms remained constant. The extant sources concerning ecclesiology are meagre by comparison with sources surviving from the ninth and the eleventh century. But such evidence as there is indicates that, in contrast with political thought, ecclesiology experienced no abrupt or far-reaching changes, but rather certain shifts in emphasis, elaborations of conventional premises, and sharpening of old differences.

However diverse their general positions, ninth-century thinkers agreed that the cohesive element in the Church was hierarchic obedience, based on legal authorities and enforced through established patterns of juridical process.[4] The means of salvation were conveyed

[1] *Annales Ecclesiastici*, in ed. A. Theiner, 15, 467.
[2] Lopez, "Renaissance," *passim.*
[3] *Vita Adalberti*, 9, MGH SS. 4, 598; see Mommsen, *Studien*, 30.
[4] See above, p. 253.

through Church order. This was the fruit of work done in other profoundly troubled times, when men like St. Wilfrid of York laid special emphasis on prayers, fasts, and vigils, read the scriptures, and studied the canons.[5] The simple studies of Anglo-Saxon missionaries and their Frankish disciples gradually led to the profound learning of ninth-century scholars in Gaul. While disturbed social and political conditions engendered corruption of clerical discipline throughout the West in the tenth century,[6] the study of the canons continued. In the so-called age of papal pornocracy no less than in the ninth century, western thinkers defined the Church primarily in terms of legal order.

Despite their vulnerability to political coercion and moral rebuke, the popes reaffirmed and in some ways elaborated the answers which their predecessors had given these questions. It has been argued that the texts of tenth-century papal letters are misleading in that they repeat claims to supremacy made in the patristic age, but with radically different meanings.[7] That is certainly true in some instances, as, for example, when Leo VII intervened in a case of Gerard of Passau, quoting and paraphrasing the famous letter of Innocent I concerning diversity of practice among churches.[8] But even in Leo's decretal, and in most other tenth-century papal documents, the influence of patristic quotations is not so confusing as to hide the greater influence of ninth-century papal thought.

The popes did not appeal to convention or to tradition, as had their predecessors in the fourth and fifth centuries; Leo VII's letter deliberately omits Innocent's references to tradition. They appealed rather to the spontaneous powers of their office, sanctioned, to be sure, by ancient practice and by Christ Himself, but not directed or bound by old or common usage. This very unpatristic concept of authority appears throughout papal correspondence in the tenth century, despite the variations in fortune experienced by individual popes. The old themes do, of course, recur—in the emphasis on maintenance of "the decrees of

[5] Eddius Stephanus, *Vita Wilfridi*, c. 11, in ed. B. Colgrave (Cambridge, 1927), 24: "*Prae caeteris ei speciale officium erat, ut ieiuniis et orationibus et vigiliis incumberet, scripturas legens—memoriam autem miram in libris habuit—percurrens canones, exempla sanctorum imitatus, cum fratribus pacem implens. . . .*"

[6] See the invective of Ratherius of Verona against the contempt of Italian clergy for the canons in their hunting, whoring, and warring (*De contemptu canonum*, I, 17; II, 1; PL 136, 504, 515f).

[7] Klinkenberg, "Primat," 12ff. For critiques of Klinkenberg's method and conclusions, see H. Fuhrmann (review), D. A. 13 (1957), 280f, and Keller, "Kaisertum," 354, n. 134.

[8] PL 132, 1085f. Above, p. 81.

the ancient Fathers,"[9] in frequent references to the Petrine commission,[10] in the establishment of papal vicariates in Gaul,[11] in the subordination of other patriarchal sees, such as Aquileia,[12] and in sweeping claims to the "universal ministry throughout the earth" which inhered in the See of St. Peter.[13]

And yet the actions of tenth-century popes, and the sanctions which they invoked, were more closely related to the work of Nicholas I and John VIII than to that of Innocent I and Leo the Great. Among the earliest letters in the century is one of Sergius III to Adalgar of Bremen annulling actions done "by the wicked agreement of Pope Formosus and King Arnulf," in which the archbishops of Cologne and Mainz and other bishops had concurred, and confirming what Nicholas I and other popes had established.[14] John XII came to grips with the *nova Christianitas* in eastern Europe by granting the petition of Otto I: he transformed the monastery at Magdeburg into an archbishopric, raised the monastery of Merseburg to a bishopric subordinate to Magdeburg, regulated the establishment of other new sees in the East, and required that the bishops of these establishments be consecrated by the Archbishop of Mainz, the premier bishop of Germany and, at that time, papal vicar.[15] John's successors, John XIII, Benedict VI, and Benedict VII, attempted to gain tighter control of the whole structure of the German church, including the vast, newly Christianized areas, by establishing apostolic vicariates in Mainz and Trier.[16]

In Sergius's flat repudiation of Formosus's action, in John XII's strong assertion of papal power to establish new sees and thus to regu-

[9] E.g., Marinus II to Sicus of Capua, PL 133, 873f: "*contra statuta canonum atque antiquorum patrum decreta*," with reference specifically to Celestine I and the Council of Chalcedon.

[10] E.g., John XII to William of Mainz, PL 133, 1014f.

[11] E.g., Agapetus II to William of Mainz, PL 133, 915.

[12] Leo VIII to Rodoaldus of Aquileia, PL 134, 991.

[13] John XIII, encyclical; PL 135, 975: "*universaleque in toto orbe terrarum ministerium suscepimus.*" This arenga is repeated by Benedict VI, PL 135, 1083. Both letters confirm privileges of the archbishops of Trier.

[14] PL 131, 975: "*iniquo consensu Formosi papae et Arnolphi regis et machinatione Hermanni archiepiscopi.*" A similar *volte-face* occurred later, when Pope John XIX at first denied Grado patriarchal rights and then confirmed them on the ground that Poppo of Aquileia had originally deceived him (PL 141, 1138, 1140f).

[15] PL 133, 1028; Fuhrmann, "Patriarchate" (1955), 175.

[16] PL 137, 318, 321; Fuhrmann, "Patriarchate" (1955), 105ff, and preceding note. Cf. the specious grants to Salzburg, PL 135, 1081f and Passau, PL 137, 315ff.

late the development of the mission field, and finally in the purposeful establishment of vicariates, principles of administrative power were stronger than principles of tradition. The popes were perfectly aware that the challenges of their age differed greatly from those of earlier times.[17] Their effective powers were limited; but they went beyond their predecessors in the degree of competence they claimed. Earlier popes had struggled to establish the principle that any bishop might appeal to Rome for trial. On the precedent of Julius I, "who judged liable to deposition even oriental bishops who disdained to come to a synod," Gregory V restated this principle, suspending from office the bishops of Gaul who had not answered his summons in Arnulf of Rheims' case.[18] Benedict VII had already broadened the implicit principle beyond adjudication over bishops to allow the pope to ordain as priests and deacons men whose proper metropolitans would not ordain them without simony.[19] The authority even of an ecclesiastical office could not be defined principally in terms of anciently transmitted charisma of office or of long usage. It existed in the degree of competence which the incumbent could spontaneously exercise; and the actions of tenth-century popes suggested the great centralization to which that principle might lead in the hands of strong pontiffs.

Churchmen in northern Europe likewise continued and strengthened the ecclesiological thought of their predecessors. For them, conveying the means of salvation was not a papal monopoly. Through most of the tenth century, the principle of papal accountability, as framed by Hincmar of Rheims and his colleagues, remained latent in the confession of six oecumenical councils[20] (instead of the seven confessed by Rome),[21] in emphasis on the paramount authority of the canons,[22] in such assertions as that the archbishop of Mainz was *pontifex*

[17] Cf. Leo VII to Guy of Lyon, PL 132, 1080, and John XII's use of the term *nova Christianitas.*

[18] PL 137, 913, c. 1: "*Auctoritate Julii papae sancitum est, qui etiam orientales episcopos ad synodum venire spernentes, depositionis reos judicavit. . . .*"

[19] *Concilium Romanum* (981), PL 137, 338.

[20] See, in general, Klinkenberg, "Primat," 51.

[21] Gerbert, *Professio fidei*, in ed. Havet, no. 180, 162: "*Sanctas sinodos VI, quas universalis mater aecclesia confirmat, confirmo.*" Cf. Marinus II to Sicus of Capua, PL 133, 874: "*Quapropter Dei omnipotentis et beatorum apostolorum principum Petri et Pauli et omnium sanctorum et septem universalium canonum* [sic] *auctoritate te excommunicando, mittimus. . . .*"

[22] See below, pp. 260ff.

257

*maximus*,[23] in emphasis on the apostolate of St. Remigius,[24] and in the importance ascribed to universal consensus, especially as expressed in general councils.[25]

The position was potentially the same as that expressed by an anonymous Gallic author much later, after the Synod of Sutri (1046). He maintained that the deposition of Gregory VI was invalid, and that, consequently, Clement II was not a true pope. The people confessed to the priest, he wrote, the priest to the bishop, the bishop, to the "supreme and universal pontiff," whom God reserved solely to His own judgment. Though emperors were subject to excommunication by bishops, as the submissions of Constantine the Great and other pious rulers proved,[26] some rulers had attempted to pervert right order, as did Constantius II in exiling Liberius for refusing to sanction Arianism, and, recently, Henry III at Sutri. The deposition of Gregory VI was therefore wrongful, but the anonymous author went further: bishops functioned in the place of Christ,[27] and their ordinations depended upon the judgment of the episcopal order, in each province for a bishop, in the whole world for the supreme pontiff. Since they had not consented to Clement's consecration, the French bishops owed him no obedience.[28] Not the sentence of a Roman synod, but the universal consensus of bishops was decisive.

For his generation, Fulbert of Chartres restated the latitudinarian view that had often opposed the monarchic principles of Roman ecclesiology. Diversity in observances, he wrote, gives no offense, since it does

---

[23] Widukind, *Res gestae Saxonicae*, II, 1; MGH SS. in us. schol., 5th ed., 64.

[24] Gerbert, ep. 70 in ed. Havet, 67. Gerbert, as pope, Appendix IV in ed. Havet, 239.

[25] On Ratherius of Verona, see Klinkenberg, "Primat," 16f, 21. Cf. Ratherius to Pope John XII, ep. 5. PL 136, 656f: "*domine reverendissime, archipraesulum archiepiscope, et si de ullo mortalium jure dici possit, universalis papa nominande.*" Annales Hildesheimenses (a. 997), MGH SS. 3, 91: "*Johannes [XVI] . . . ab universis episcopis Italiae, Germaniae, Franciae, et Galliae excommunicatur.*" Zimmermann, "Papstabsetzungen" II, 275, n. 45. Gerbert, ep. 193 in ed. Havet, 183: "*. . . et nunc ad votum meorum hostium, quia ex toto orbe fieri non potest, saltem ex toto principum nostrorum regimine, ut universale cogatur concilium, modis quibus valeo elaboro.*" Thietmar, Chron. IV, 46. MGH SS. n. s. 9, 184: "*Qui [Giseler of Magdeburg] sapienti consilio usus generale sibi postulat dari concilium sicque indiscussa dilata sunt haec omnia usque dum haec Deus finire dignatus est nostris propiciis temporibus.*"

[26] *De ordinando pontif.*, MGH Ldl. I, 12ff. On this treatise, see Zimmermann, "Papstabsetzungen" III, 80ff.

[27] *Ibid.*, 9.  [28] *Ibid.*, 11.

not destroy the unity of the faith. Greece differs from Spain, and the Roman and Gallic church differs from them; indeed, the Church stands as a queen at the right hand of her King, arrayed in a golden robe of varying hues. There are many churches throughout the earth, and yet, because of the unity of faith, there is only one holy, catholic Church, composed of believers who keep to the narrow way of the Fathers, contemplating their examples, upholding what they had understandably done, and not destroying what they had done according to spiritual counsel, but beyond the full comprehension of later men.[29]

This was the appeal beyond hierarchic order, the subjection of all priests, even the most exalted, to the rules of the Fathers, which Hincmar of Rheims advanced in his conflicts with Rome. In the tenth century, it likewise led to important disputes,[30] but to none better documented or, thus, more instructive than that over Gerbert's accession to Hincmar's see. Indeed, by quoting excerpts from Hincmar's works frequently and at length, Gerbert showed himself in conviction as well as in office the successor of the great Archbishop.

Adalbero of Rheims apparently designated Gerbert as his successor, but when Adalbero died (989), Hugh Capet had Arnulf, an illegitimate son of King Lothair, elected to the see. Arnulf persuaded Gerbert to remain in Rheims. Late in 989, Arnulf perjured himself of his oath of fealty to Hugh Capet by giving Rheims up to Charles of Lorraine. Gerbert sided with the Capetians, and when Rheims fell to Hugh (991), the King convened the synod of St. Basle, where Arnulf was deposed and Gerbert elected his successor. The case against Arnulf had already been submitted to Rome for review, but after the synod of St. Basle, Arnulf's supporters formally appealed his conviction to the papal court. Hugh strongly supported Gerbert. In 992-993, the papal legate found it impossible to hold his investigations in France; in 994 he withdrew to Germany, where, at the synod of Ingelheim, he asked the German bishops to overturn the sentences against Arnulf. The threat of John XV to enforce this sentence by excommunicating Gerbert and all other participants in the Synod of St. Basle aroused Gerbert to bitter defiance. But after the death of Hugh Capet (996), Gerbert was unable to retain his see. He took refuge at the court of Otto III, and succeeded

[29] Ep. III (II); PL 141, 192ff. Cf. Liutprand's comments on divergencies among the Romans, Byzantines, and Saxons (Legatio, cc. 21, 22, MGH in us. schol. 2nd ed., 145).

[30] E.g., the rebuke of John IX: "*summo pontifici et universali papae, non unius urbis, sed totius orbis,*" by German bishops (PL 131, 34ff).

in 998 to the see of Ravenna and, the next year, to the See of St. Peter.

The fullest statements of ecclesiological principles occur in the debates of St. Basle and in Gerbert's letters. At the Synod, debate centered principally on one article of Arnulf's defense: that the case should be referred to Rome.[31] The plaintiffs swept this objection aside: the court of the Roman bishop was notoriously venal, they said, and the African bishops in their dispute with Popes Zosimus, Boniface I, and Celestine I had left as a model "what they wished to be thought concerning the power of the Roman bishop."[32]

Arnulf of Orleans led the attack. The Roman Church, he said, must always be honored because of St. Peter's memory, and, saving the authority of the Nicene Council which the Roman Church had always revered, the decrees of Roman pontiffs should not be withstood. Yet the canons must be kept by all men, since they were eternally valid, established as they were in diverse places and at diverse times, but by the same spirit of God. Two things must be guarded against: the silence or the "new establishment" (*nova constitutio*) of a Roman pontiff which might "prejudice the promulgated laws of the canons or the decrees of earlier men." Silence could be resisted with silence. As for a new establishment, "what profit are established laws, when all things are directed according to the judgment of one man?"[33]

Arnulf of Orleans declared that he did not wish to derogate from the privilege of the Roman pontiff. Not at all. When the bishop of Rome was a wise and virtuous man, neither silence nor new establishment was to be feared. Ignorance, fear, and cupidity had come in, but "when tyranny prevails at Rome, then much less are the same silence and new establishment to be feared. For he who is in any way against the laws cannot prejudice the laws."[34] There was much to lament in Rome. The clear light of the Fathers—the Leos, the Gregories, Gelasius, and Innocent—had been clouded by monstrous shadows. License and wickedness of every sort prevailed. What sat on the supreme throne, radiant in vestment of purple and gold, was Antichrist sitting in the tem-

---

[31] Cf. Synod of St. Basle, c. 23, PL 139, 308f.

[32] C. 27, PL 139, 311f: "*quid de Romani episcopi potestate sentiri vellent.*"

[33] C. 28, PL 139, 312: "*Si autem nova constitutio, quid prosunt leges conditae, cum ad unius arbitrium omnia dirigantur?*"

[34] C. 28, PL 139, 312f: "*Romae tirannide praevalente tunc multo minus idem silentium et nova constitutio formidanda sunt. Non enim is qui quolibet modo contra leges est, legibus praejudicare potest.*"

ple of God as though he were God. "But perhaps someone should say that according to Gelasius the Roman Church judges of the whole Church, without coming under the judgment of anyone or having her judgment judged by anyone. I say let him who might say this establish a man for us in the Roman Church whose judgment can not be judged, although the African bishops judged this very thing impossible, 'unless perhaps,' they say, 'there is someone who believes that our Lord can inspire any one man with justice of inquiry and deny it to innumerable bishops gathered in council.' "[35]

Sardica favored the privileges of Rome, but it sanctioned the procedure followed against Arnulf of Rheims: judgment by a provincial synod.[36] Hincmar of Rheims and the African canons confirmed the same process. Pope Damasus had written, to the contrary, that without the authority of the Roman See, no synod could be catholic. But, Arnulf of Orleans asked, what if the encircling swords of barbarians prevented passage to Rome? Or what if Rome itself were subjugated to a barbarian and incorporated at his pleasure into some kingdom? "Will there be no councils in the meanwhile, or, at the cost of harm to their kings and of desolation by enemies, will the bishops of the whole earth wait for counsel and councils concerning matters that have to be decided?"[37]

Nicaea had commanded that synods be held twice each year. The African canons had perhaps stressed that regulation too much, to the detriment of Roman privileges; Arnulf of Orleans alleged that whenever the *status regnorum* allowed, the bishops of Gaul consulted Rome on important matters, as indeed they had in the present case. And yet, this could not be inevitable practice. The Church had experienced profound divisions since the "fall of the Empire" (*imperii occasum*). Rome had lost control of Alexandria, Antioch, Africa, Asia,

[35] C. 28, PL 139, 314: "*Quod si quispiam dixerit, secundum Gelasium Romanam ecclesiam de tota ecclesia judicare, ipsam ad nullius commeare judicium, nec de ejus unquam judicio judicari, is, inquam, qui hoc dixerit, eum nobis in ecclesia Romana constituat, de cuius iudicio iudicari non possit, quamquam hoc ipsum Africani episcopi impossibile iudicant: Nisi forte, inquiunt, quisquam est qui credat, unicuilibet posse Dominum nostrum examinis inspirare iustitiam et innumerabilibus congregatis in concilium sacerdotibus denegare.*" See above, p. 83.

[36] C. 28, PL 139, 315.

[37] C. 28, PL 139, 319: "*Quid ergo si barbarorum gladiis circumsaevientibus licentia commeandi Romam intercludatur? Vel si Roma barbaro cuilibet serviens, motu libidinis eius in aliquod regnum efferatur? Num interim aut nulla concilia erunt, aut orbis terrarum episcopi ad suorum regum dampna vel interitus ab hostibus disponendarum rerum consilia et concilia expectabunt?*"

261

and Europe. Constantinople had withdrawn from her, and her judgments were unknown in the interior of Spain. Churches and nations were divided.[38] Religion had fallen into such confusion "that even supreme pontiffs despise the cult of divine religion itself."[39] In the midst of this fragmentation, Rome had withdrawn to herself, taking counsel with no others and pronouncing judgments without due consultation and without regard for the canons.[40]

Arnulf of Orleans' point was that Roman judgment could not be hastily accepted because of the moral turpitude of contemporary popes, because canons took precedence of papal decrees both as norms of judgment and as procedural regulations, and, finally, because political circumstances made it impossible for Rome to issue an informed judgment. The bishops in "Belgica" and "Germania" were morally better qualified to judge than the venal bishops of Rome,[41] and indeed canonical norms and the expedience to which political divisions gave rise alike granted them the precedence in judgment which the Roman claims threatened to corrode.

Gerbert's own comments upon the case similarly emphasized the natural and legal limits of papal competence. Arnulf's partisans argued that final judgment belonged to the bishop of Rome. "Could they say," Gerbert asked, "that the judgment of the Roman bishop is greater than the judgment of God?"[42] The Romans' first bishop, St. Peter, had declared that one should obey God rather than man. When Pope Marcellus (*sic*) burned incense to Jove, all other bishops did not have to follow his example. In fact, if a Roman bishop should persevere in wrong doing despite admonition, he must be considered a heathen and a publican. Even if he considered men unworthy of his communion because they refused to follow his unscriptural doctrines, he could not separate them from the communion of Christ. Any formal sentence of his contrary to established laws was invalid, for Leo I had written, "the privilege of Peter is not had wherever judgment is not derived from his equity."[43]

[38] C. 28, PL 139, 320: "*Fit ergo discessio, secundum Apostolum, non solummodo gentium, sed etiam ecclesiarum.*"

[39] C. 28, PL 139, 320: "*ipsius divinae religionis cultus, etiam a summis sacerdotibus contemnatur.*"

[40] C. 28, PL 139, 320.

[41] C. 28, PL 139, 314.

[42] Ep. 192 in ed. Havet, 180: "*Poteruntne dicere, Romani episcopi iudicium Dei iudicio maius est?*"

[43] Ep. 192 in ed. Havet, 181. Above, p. 246 n. 39.

In a long apology to the Archbishop of Strassburg, Gerbert described fully the concept of law which strengthened his defiant attitude. The law of nature, he wrote, had been succeeded by the written law (the Old Testament), which the law of grace had later transcended. The law of grace was expressed by the Apostles, by the "pontiffs of the first see" in their decrees, and by the counsel "of innumerable bishops." The relative authority of individual expressions was determined by "whether God speaks, or man, and, if man, whether an Apostle, or simply a bishop." Further, the authority of statements by bishops varied according to the number of them responsible for a given decree, the knowledge displayed in it, and the place where it was drawn up. Sheer plurality yielded as a criterion to the weight of reason and truth; that was shown at the Synod of Rimini, where the orthodox were greatly outnumbered.

There were, then, three forms of law: that declared by Christ, the Apostles, and the prophets; that confirmed by the consensus of all catholics; and that brought forth into the light of understanding by individual men of great knowledge and eloquence. In establishing these categories, Gerbert professed to show no contempt for papal decrees. He adduced the *Decretum Gelasianum* to show in his defense that (Pseudo-)Gelasius had mentioned as legal sources conciliar decrees and the works of orthodox Fathers before decretal letters of Roman bishops. He quoted extensively from Hincmar's *Opusculum LV Capitulorum* to elaborate his point that papal decrees were neither the source nor the supreme expression of law.[44]

Gerbert then applied these general principles to the dispute with Arnulf. The bishops of the Gauls, he said, had not established new laws against Arnulf; rather, they had assiduously executed established laws.[45] In contrast, the Pope had prejudiced the laws by his "new establishment" (*nova constitutio*), and Gerbert was forced to say, with St. Jerome: "If authority is sought, the world is larger than the City." He repeated the statement of Leo I which he understood to mean that inequitable judgments masked by the privilege of St. Peter were invalid, and he asked how the laws established at Nicaea could last forever, if they could be changed or circumvented at the pleasure of one man. Gerbert's enemies said that Arnulf ought to be judged only by the bishop of Rome. Gerbert himself recalled the dispute between the North Africans and Pope Zosimus in the case of Apiarius, and concluded:

[44] Ep. 217, in ed. Havet, 206ff. On Hincmar, see above, pp. 243f.
[45] Ep. 217, in ed. Havet, 220.

"The bishops of the Gauls were therefore warranted in having said 'anathema' to Arnulf—alive, confessed, and convicted—as a heathen and a publican. It was warranted, I say, to follow the Gospels, Apostles, prophets, sacred councils, and the decrees of apostolic men not conflicting with these four [categories], always kept, and always to be kept, in use."[46]

The dispute had an unexpected denouement when Gerbert, as Pope Sylvester II, restored Arnulf to full pontifical honor.[47] But in the very unconciliatory arguments which we have described, Gerbert and Arnulf of Orleans showed the degree to which some bishops north of the Alps rejected the most fundamental elements of papal ecclesiology. They denied that Rome was the unfailing conveyer of the means of salvation. Followed to its extreme conclusions, Arnulf's argument certainly suggests that Christians could lead devout lives and enforce canonical government without the support, the guidance, or even the communion of the Roman Church. Gerbert's views on law lead to the same conclusions on a more abstract level. In magisterial functions, as well as in administration and adjudication, the bishop of Rome was not free to change laws and constrain all other believers to follow him in new ways. Arnulf of Orleans pointed out with great emphasis that worldly matters might deflect papal judgments from the eternal verities. Both he and Gerbert argued that the rest of the world must be free not to follow Rome into error. Consensus had legislative effect; papal authority did not. They were saying in effect that the obedience rendered a pope depended upon the consensus which his decrees found. That consensus was due not to the papacy as an office, but to the righteousness which might find one expression in papal decrees, and which had an ageless testimony in the canons of the Great Council of Nicaea.

[46] Ep. 217, in ed. Havet, 222: "*Licuit ergo episcopis Galliarum viventi Arnulfo, confesso, et convicto, tanquam hetnico et publicano dixisse anathema. Licuit, inquam, sequi evvangelia, apostolos, prophetas, sacra concilia, virorum apostolicorum decreta ab his IIIIor non discordantia, semper in usu habita, semper habenda.*" Cf. Klinkenberg, "Primat," 34.

[47] Appendix IV, in ed. Havet, 239.

# PART II

# The Investiture Controversy:
# A Test of Accountability

A KIND of doctrinal counterpoint played among men who thought deeply about Church unity. If the air held that Rome conveyed the doctrine of salvation through papal discretion, a strong descant ran that papal actions must be gauged by higher authorities, and that, while the pope might testify to the true faith in a uniquely authoritative way, his witness was not the substance of truth. This counterpoint played most distinctly between popes and thinkers north of the Alps, as we have seen especially in reviewing positions in the ninth century generally, and, for the tenth century, in the case of Arnulf of Rheims. But it recurred also even in Rome itself. Time and again the "Janus complex" of papal thought appeared, by implication as in the thought of Nicholas I, or directly as in the case of Pope Formosus.

The Investiture Conflict again brought these tensions to the fore. The split between Rome and "national" churches and divisions within the Roman See itself became acute. In the sharp and prolonged conflict, there was no chance for dissidents to tack calmly across the flood; they had to state their positions frankly and give them life through action. All the questions of ecclesiastical cohesion that we have considered came to a head in this great conflict. The familiar antithesis between discretion expressed in reform, which postulated a double breach with the past—first, when corruption entered, and second, when it was repulsed—and tradition, which required an unbroken *continuum* of knowledge and practice, carried these issues to new levels of sophistication.

The whole character of the dispute was set by the fact that men knew no distinction between constitution and administrative order. Concerning ecclesiastical as well as temporal government, constitutional thought was still in its pre-rational, even intuitive, stage. Thinkers understood the cohesion of the Church in terms of law and order, but none of them conceived a broad system of government based on principles of justice. Advocates of every persuasion actually expressed relatively primitive conceptions of administrative procedure, instead of fully rationalized theories of government. To be sure, they spoke of justice—though many of them understood *justitia* in a moral sense, as righteousness— and behind their statements were often simple, and sometimes crudely defined, abstract principles of equity. Later thinkers did systematize such principles into constitutions and constitutional theories. We are perhaps most familiar with the succession of legists and canonists beginning in the twelfth century whose work reached a peak of refinement in the sixteenth and seventeenth centuries. But, in the age of the Investiture Controversy, clear constitutional patterns did not exist, either in Church or in kingdom. What did exist was an amorphous body of written authorities, accumulated since the apologetic age, and diverse, often contradictory ways of doing things. Into them, thinkers read right order according to their personal convictions.

The prime issue in the conflict was old: it was the question of what unified the Church, of what communicated the authentic means of salvation. But the growth of the higher clergy as a third party beside pope and king, which had begun in the Frankish period and achieved full development in the Ottonian, made any straightforward answer unfeasible. Metaphysics and politics were inseparable. The Ottonian period set the lines of interest in Germany; Christian antiquity as interpreted from the ninth century onward provided the conceptual battle lines.

The Investiture Controversy has general importance as the first great conflict between Church and State. In some aspects it was indeed a struggle between pope and king for supremacy over the clergy. Many scholars would add that, at least in some crises, it was also a struggle between them for supremacy over the whole order of government, temporal and ecclesiastical. And yet, the contest of Empire and Papacy came relatively late in the Gregorian reform. It was not an issue from the start. Rather, it emerged from other questions and, from the ecclesiological point of view, it always remained subordinate to more fundamental matters. For disputants on each side, the basic question was not whether Church or Empire should be supreme. It was, instead, whether evil practices, having crept into the Church, had corrupted communication of authentic doctrine. We have to deal, not literally with a conflict between "Church" and "State," but with one among churches.

The controversy has been described as a struggle for "right order in the world." That phrase is a bit deceptive, as well as attractive, in its clarity. To struggle for right order implies a preconception of what right order should be, a fairly detailed systematic understanding of administrative patterns. Sophisticated constitutional thought was evident in no party during the Controversy. Despite obvious administrative issues, the combatants understood it rather as a struggle for "righteousness," a war to sweep away the wickedness that hindered transmitting the means of salvation through preaching and sacraments.

CHAPTER 11

# Tradition Discarded: the Gregorians

FROM the ecclesiological point of view, the issue of relations between Church and Empire was less critical than questions concerning papal responsibility. The conflict between the papacy and temporal rulers could be settled by a straightforward, political engagement; the Concordat of Worms was a pragmatic agreement of that sort. Issues of authority within the Church, however, could be settled only by delicate rationalization, by theoretical explanations that former practice had been erroneous in some degree, though it was commonly judged right, and that it had been corrected by new establishments.

The intellectual terms at issue were legal; the subject of dispute was authority. Perhaps exaggerated by the excitement of conflict, distorted by enthusiasm for personal or partisan interests, or modified in hope of compromise, the views expressed are often without logical order. Many fundamental questions of Church order were not even asked, especially concerning the nature and purpose of law and office, and the proper pattern of institutional relationships. But one issue was plainly drawn: the legal relevance of canons and the degrees of responsibility that they imposed upon each hierarchic rank.

Some thinkers held the view, familiar as early as in the papacy's Byzantine period, that the canons comprised an immutable rule of order binding upon all bishops.[1] Writers thoroughly disciplined in canonistic thought, however, had long understood that canons were not immutable. Despite his insistence that the canons were "eternal," Hincmar of Rheims once acknowledged that they were framed to answer particular requirements, and that they lapsed into desuetude with the passage of time.[2] That seems also to have been the view of Agobard of Lyons and Regino of Prüm,[3] and in the late tenth century Abbo of Fleury expressed it once more. Canons sometimes contradicted each other, Abbo observed, and one synod commanded what another for-

---

[1] E.g., Othloh of St. Emmeram, *Vita S. Bonifatii*, praef. MGH SS in us. sch., 113f.
[2] See above, p. 243.    [3] See above, p. 232.

269

bade, because the rules of various provinces normally changed according to the influence of geography, historical circumstances, and other necessities.[4]

Pope Victor II stated the Gregorian position when he wrote that the Lord had established the Roman Church over nations and kingdoms, "to root out and destroy and plant and build in His name. Indeed, [He commanded this] so that, as long as His holy Church, spread throughout the whole earth, shall be subject to temporal mutability, and shall alternate in the various and constant changes of waning and waxing, like the moon in its monthly course, it may unceasingly be discerned in the Church what the assiduous husbandman ought to root out or plant and what the wise architect should destroy or build."[5]

Advocates of papal ecclesiology neither resolved nor even seriously raised the critical issue of official responsibility. In their eyes, that question was moot because of the special relationship between Christ and St. Peter and the inherently apostolic character of the papacy, through succession to St. Peter;[6] because of identification of dissent from the Roman Church with heresy and even idolatry;[7] and because of Rome's juridical supremacy.[8]

All reformers understood that popes had great latitude in legal matters. But was the papal authority unlimited? There was no general agreement. The lines of debate were never clearly drawn, but all issues derived from one basic question: How far was the pope bound to observe old laws and to honor old practices? Did the popes have power merely to restore, to lead the Church in some details back to the good,

---

[4] *Collectio Canonum,* PL 139, 481f, cc. 8, 9.

[5] PL 143, 835: *"Sanctae Romanae et apostolicae sedis apicem ideo super gentes et super regna in principe apostolorum suorum, Petro, constituit universitatis Dominus, ut evellat, et destruat, et plantet et aedificet in nomine ipsius. Siquidem donec sancta ejus ecclesia in toto terrarum orbe diffusa, temporalitatis mutabilitati subjacebit, variis et continuis defectuum et profectuum suorum vicissitudinibus, velut luna suis menstruis, alternabitur, ut sine intermissione deprehendatur in ea quod industrius hortulanus debeat evellere, vel plantare et quod sapiens architectus destruere vel aefidicare"* (Jer. 1, 10; I Cor. 3:10).

[6] E.g., Paschal II, PL 163, 50, 57: *"apostolicae memoriae Gregorii VII et Urbani II."* PL 163, 420: *"quae a b. Gregorio Anglicae gentis apostolo."* PL 163, 32, 48, 74, 201, 297. Innocent II, PL 179, 353 (a frequent arenga. Cf. cols. 431, 433, 444, 464); 172, 180, 222, 318 (on the *cathedra Petri*); 178f, 327, 333, 342 (on the apostolate of the papacy); 291, 393 (referring to papal letters as *apostolica scripta*).

[7] Paschal II, PL 163, 55.

[8] E.g., Innocent II, PL 179, 334, 342, 345, 364, 369, 436.

old order, or did they have the greater power to destroy the old root and branch and set up new orders?

What was the Gregorian position? In terms of law, the Gregorians based their reform on the freedom to modify or even to exclude ancient rulings and to create and execute new ones. They declared that the correction of abuses they had undertaken was merely reform, the recovery of an ancient order. Peter Damian knew that the Gospel was in constant danger, and that the base desires even of one schismatic man could overturn the labor of the Apostles and darken the splendor of the universal Church.[9] When a reformer, Gregory VI, acceded to the papacy, after a long series of flagrant simoniacs, Peter wrote to the new Pope rejoicing that the golden age of the Apostles would return through the reflowering of discipline.[10] He found in the lives and precepts of the Fathers since that age a continuation of apostolic teaching which the corruption of his own "iron age" had interrupted.[11] After the Synod of Sutri, he wrote to Henry III in similar terms: "Let the heavens rejoice, therefore, let the earth exult, since truly Christ is known to rule in His King, and now at the very end of time, the golden age of David is renewed."[12] Gregory VII also wrote that he labored to restore the Church to the state of ancient religion,[13] and, in a striking metaphor, he commended the Empress Agnes and Beatrice and Mathilda of Tuscany for their support. "And so, because of you a new example of ancient joy, because of you, I say, these women who once sought the Lord in the tomb often return to our memory. For just as, with love's wondrous ardor, they went to the Lord's sepulchre before all the disciples, so with

[9] Epp. VII, 3, PL 144, 437.

[10] Epp. I, 1, PL 144, 205.

[11] Opusc. 12, c. 3; Opusc. 16, 3, PL 145, 253, 369.

[12] Epp. VII, 2, PL 144, 436: "*Laetentur ergo caeli exsultet terra, quia in rege suo vere Christus regnare cognoscitur, et sub ipso iam saeculi fine aureum David saeculum renovatur.*" Cf. Serm. in S. Matt., PL 144, 779. Peter Damian was keenly aware of the force of change in ecclesiastical affairs; he wrote of the birth of the Church at Christ's crucifixion (Serm. 63, PL 144, 861), of the historical relations between Church and Synagogue (Opusc. 60, c. 30, PL 145, 858: "*nam de Synagoga fit ecclesia*"; Opusc. 22, c. 4, PL 145, 471. Cf. ep. II, 13, PL 144, 284f), of the mode of communal life in the "infancy" of the Church which had largely been lost (Serm. 53, PL 144, 806), of the historical development which led the Greeks and the Latins to different doctrines about the procession of the Holy Ghost (Opusc. 38, c. 2, PL 145, 635f), and, most clearly, of the corruption in the church, even in the Roman See, which he hoped would be blotted out by the reappearance of the golden age of the Apostles (epp. I, 1, PL 144, 205).

[13] Epp. Coll., no. 2, ed. Jaffé, *Bibl. Greg.*, 522f.

pious love do you visit the Church, as one set in the sepulchre of afflictions, before many—indeed before all the princes of the earth. And, as though instructed by angelic replies, striving with all your powers to the end that she may rise again to the state of her liberty, you call forth others to succor the endangered Church."[14]

The movement, however, was more than an effort to recover a lost order, to revive the tormented, but fully formed, body of Christ. In their work, the Gregorians advanced a curiously ambivalent view of the past, and particularly of the concept of tradition. Gregory, as well as the reformers who preceded him and those who followed, identified their work with the ancient truth of the Church. Leo IX consciously imitated the customs (*mores*) of Leo I;[15] the popes from the time of Clement II to the conflict between Innocent II and Anacletus II chose their pontifical names from the lists of Roman bishops in the apostolic and patristic ages;[16] and all the reformers, including Gregory VII, steadfastly maintained that they were not introducing new doctrines and observances, but only restoring the doctrine of the Fathers.[17]

Yet none of the canonistic anthologies of the period contains a specific entry or cluster of entries concerning tradition, and, despite its importance for twelfth-century polemicists, the word "tradition" itself rarely occurs in the Gregorians' letters.[18]

[14] Reg. I, 85, MGH Epp. Sel. 2, 122: "*Per vos itaque novum exemplum antique letitiae, per vos inquam ille mulieres olim querentes Dominum in monumento sepe nobis ad memoriam redeunt. Nam sicut ille pre cunctis discipulis ad sepulchrum Domini miro caritatis ardore venerunt, ita vos ecclesiam Christi quasi in sepulchro afflictionis positam pre multis, immo pene pre omnibus terrarum principibus pio amore visitatis et, ut ad statum libertatis suae resurgat, totis viribus annitentes quasi angelicis instructae responsis ceteros ad suffragium laborantis ecclesiae provocatis.*"

[15] Vita Leonis IX, c. 3, PL 143, 489; Ullmann, "Pontifex," 239.

[16] Cf. Schmale, *Studien*, 74, 197f.

[17] Cf. Ladner, "Letters," 236; Ullmann, "Humbert," 111.

[18] Leo IX once invoked "canonical tradition of the holy Fathers" (PL 143, 676f: "*sanctorum patrum canonica traditio.*" Gregory VII declared that recent neglect "of the tradition of the Fathers" had led to the decay of right order (Reg. II, 61, MGH Epp. Sel. 2, 216: "*patrum traditio*"), and he referred to "canonical traditions and the decrees of the holy Fathers" as establishing hierarchic privileges (Reg. I, 60, *ibid.*, 88: "*canonicas traditiones et decreta sanctorum patrum*"). "By tradition of writings" he learned of past misfortunes in the Church (Reg. II, 45, *ibid.*, 183f). Humbert, Boniface *et al.* to the Empress Agnes, in Peter Damian, epp. VII, 4, PL 144, 442: "*Ipsi siquidem pontifices ex antiquae traditionis usu ad apostolorum debent limina properare et hoc sine quo metropolitani esse non possunt signum consummendae suae dignitatis* [the pallium] *accipere.*" Urban II

In dealing with other churches, the reform leaders militantly opposed ancient forms and usages. They refused to acknowledge as legitimate the extraordinary diversities which separated believers. For them, the unity of faith and universality of the Church were largely synonymous, and the factors which had divided Christendom must be dismissed as conducive to schism and replaced by Roman norms. By the end of the period under review, Rome had first allowed, and then forbidden, the use of vernacular languages in the Divine Office, commanded Milanese, Armenian, and Spanish prelates to replace their own rites with the Roman, and declared that those who did not adhere to Roman disciplinary practices (such as the enforcement of clerical celibacy) were outside the Church.[19] Rome was seeking by spontaneous administrative action to establish the Church as an institution, and to supply the uniformity of language, discipline, and creed necessary to that plan.

Other comments of the reformers concerning Rome itself reveal a settled contempt for antiquity unrecommended by other qualifications. A fragmentary letter attributed to Gregory VII quotes with approval the comment of St. Cyprian that the Lord did not say, "I am custom," but "I am truth," and that any custom, however old or widespread, must be subordinated to truth and discarded if it ran contrary to truth.[20] Together with the Gregorians' assertions of papal supremacy, the Cyprianic passage epitomized the thought of an early reformer, perhaps Humbert of Silva Candida, who wrote that the Roman See commanded such respect that all men sought the discipline of the holy canons and the ancient institution of the Christian religion from the mouth of its governor (*presessoris*) rather than from holy writings and the traditions of the Fathers.[21] Gregory once wrote that the Fathers had corrected the neg-

---

adduced the "traditions of the holy Fathers, namely Pelagius, Gregory, Cyprian, Augustine, and Jerome," as evidence that sacraments performed by heretics were invalid (PL 151, 532). And Cardinal Deusdedit identified "apostolic tradition" and the "custom handed down from the Apostles" concerning the manner of episcopal election (*Lib. contra invas. et symon.* I, 2, MGH Ldl. 2, 302ff: "*apostolica traditio . . . consuetudinem ab apostolis traditam.*" See *ibid.*, I, 17, 317: "*Non mutent traditionem ecclesiae a Deo institutam. . . .*")

[19] See Schramm, "Zeitalter," 104.

[20] See Tellenbach, *Church*, 164; Ladner, "Letters," 225ff; Krause, *Papstwahldekret*, 39. For similar uses of the verse (John 14:6) in the patristic age, see Ladner, *Idea*, 138. Even if Gregory himself did not write this passage, St. Cyprian's sentence was current among his followers (Urban II, PL 151, 356; Godfrey of Vendôme, MGH Ldl. 2, 691. Cf. Becker, *Studien*, 237, n. 126).

[21] Schramm, *Kaiser*, 2, 128. Cf. Miccoli, "Ecclesiae," 477.

ligence of the primitive Church;[22] in his own reforms, he undertook what he clearly considered a similar breach with received conventions, a selective rejection of the teachings and practices of the immediate past.

It was paradoxical that the Gregorians adopted as their own the sentence which St. Cyprian wrote against a bishop of Rome, that they rejected immediately received conventions and, at the same time, claimed sanctions of antiquity for their work. This ambivalence was resolved according to the Gregorians' thought by a doctrine of unlimited papal discretion in legal matters. Only Rome could distinguish between ancient error and truth, suspend the force of just canons in need, or promulgate new laws to meet unprecedented necessity. The antiquity of Roman discretionary powers was, in the last analysis, the only rule of antiquity which the reformers unreservedly accepted.

The first reformer pope owed his pontifical accession to uncanonical procedure; his successors defended him by arguing that the normal force of the canons had been voided by necessity.[23] Throughout the period under review, there were thinkers who argued more generally that the canons were not in any case binding upon Roman bishops. As Bernald wrote, "For no pope deprives his successor of the privilege of the Apostolic See to mitigate, according to the necessity of his time, not only the canons but also the sanctions of his predecessor. In this he does not repudiate his predecessor, since he knows that his own establishments may sometime be mitigated."[24]

Gregorians considered temporal law external to the law of the Church. An imperialist writer, Petrus Crassus, wrote that God established two kinds of law: assigning one to clergy, through the apostles and their successors, and the other to laymen, through emperors and kings. Each law benefited the other, however; and the Church used both bodies of law.[25] The reformers, however, were concerned to draw the

[22] Above, p. 64.

[23] Bonizo, *Lib. ad amic.* V, MGH Ldl. 1, 584f, 586.

[24] *De incont. sacer.*, MGH Ldl. 2, 23: "*Nullus enim apostolicus suum successorem privilegio sedis apostolicae privat, quin pro sui temporis necessitate non solum canones sed et sui antecessoris sanctiones valeat mitigare; nec tamen in hoc suo predecessori repugnat, quem et propria statuta aliquando mitigasse non ignorat.*" See also Bernald's comment on Cassiodorus (*ibid.*: 10): "*Se huius viri persona, quantumvis veneranda, non poterit annullare canonicas sanctorum patrum institutiones. . . .*" Cf. Leo IX's prefatory letter to the *Liber Gomorrhianus* of Peter Damian (PL 145, 160), and Leo's effort to avert modification of one of his own privileges (PL 143, 721f).

[25] *Defens. Hen.*, c. 4, MGH Ldl. 1, 438f. Cf. Manegold, *Ad Geb.*, c. 12, MGH Ldl. 1, 334.

line of legal relevance sharply. Though they may have lacked full knowledge of Roman law,[26] their familiarity with it was sufficiently detailed to persuade them that no regulation of Roman law could be invoked in ecclesiastical cases unless it accorded with the canons.[27] A very similar position led Hildebrand to argue, in 1059, that a decree of Louis the Pious on canons regular was invalid. Louis, he said, had no right to change the "apostolic rule . . . without the authority and consent of the Holy Roman and Apostolic See; for although an emperor and a devout man, he was a layman. But neither could any bishop do that, for it is not their part to introduce a new rule into the churches by their office or judgment alone, especially a rule contrary to [the Roman See]. . . ."[28] Deusdedit argued on broader grounds, but to the same end, that the foundation of the faith stood in the patriarchal sees, particularly in Rome, Alexandria, and Antioch. If one of the three fell, two would stand; if two fell, the faith of the Roman patriarch would never fail. Secular powers had no share in this structure. "For God is read to have spoken to pontiffs, not to emperors, 'Who hears you, hears me, and whoever spurns you, spurns me,' etc. And again, 'Whatever you shall bind on earth will be bound also in heaven,' etc." Therefore temporal rulers had no power to change "the Church's tradition, established by God," for, as Gelasius I had written, God wished the clergy to be ordered not by civil laws and worldly powers, but by pontiffs and priests.[29] Secular laws could be invoked only if they did not contradict ecclesiastical sanctions. Indeed, priests took precedence over kings in the promulgation of laws, for God first established His laws for kings and other believers through the agency of priests.[30]

Consequently, when they wrote of ecclesiastical law, the reformers thought chiefly of the canons of synods and councils and of papal

[26] Leicht, "Gregorio VII," 109.

[27] Cf. Alexander II, PL 146, 1403, 1406, and Peter Damian, Opusc. 8, PL 145, 191.

[28] Werminghoff, "Bruckstück," *NA* 27, 673: "*Quam* [regulam apostolicam] *utique in sui regni provinciis inventam nec Ludovicus mutare qualibet ratione debuit aut potuit sine auctoritate et consensu sanctae Romanae et apostolicae sedis, quia quamvis imperator et devotus tamen erat laicus sed nec episcoporum quisquam, quia non est illorum novam in ecclesias solo suo magisterio vel arbitrio regulam introducere praesertim illi contrariam quam beatus Gregorius testatur discretione praecipuam, sermone luculanter.*" Cf. Bonizo, *Lib. ad amic.*, III, MGH Ldl. 1, 579.

[29] *Lib. contr. invas. et symon.* I, 17, MGH Ldl. 2, 316f. Above, pp. 126, 140f.

[30] *Ibid.*, III, 12, 13. MGH Ldl. 2, 353f.

decretals, "the venerable councils of holy Fathers and the precepts of the Apostles, and of apostolic men."[31] Upon these documents they exercised their very keen powers of historical and textual criticism; from them, and especially from the canons of the synods they themselves held, they sought to justify their tightening of ecclesiastical discipline.[32] In that body of laws, if anywhere, lay restraints on papal discretion.

Perhaps the most influential and extreme summary of the Gregorians' view on law occurs in the letters of Gregory VII. Though far less refined a canonist than Peter Damian, Anselm of Lucca, or Deusdedit, Gregory possessed a sound knowledge of the canons, and his decretals were the chief instruments by which the reformers' legal program was enacted. Gregory wrote once that "the image of God is the form of justice,"[33] and he generally identified contempt for law, collapse of order, and schism from the true faith. Sacrilege and rapine enfeebled France because the laws were neglected and justice was utterly crushed.[34] Likewise, disorders in the Church occurred precisely because wicked men had striven to overturn the decrees of the Fathers and, with them, orthodox belief.[35] Gregory's letters indeed are characterized by insistence that violators of "Christian law" (*lex christiana*) or the "law of Christ" (*lex Christi*) be punished, that canonical order be preserved, and that priests and bishops obey God rather than the princes and potentates of this world, diligently honoring the law of their Creator and preferring to sacrifice their lives rather than justice.[36] Priests who infringed the law of God, the rules established by the holy Fathers through the inspiration of the Holy Ghost, denied the faith.[37]

The law on which the preservation of the faith depended was in part

[31] Peter Damian, *Liber Gomorrhianus*, c. 21, PL 145, 182.

[32] Blum, "Monitor," 473; Becker, *Studien*, 41; Fliche, "Collection," 349, 356f.

[33] Epp. Coll. 12, ed. Jaffé, *Bib. Greg.*, 533f; Santifaller, no. 106, 94f; Ladner, "Letters," 222.

[34] Reg. II, 5, MGH Epp. Sel. 2, 130.

[35] Reg. I, 12; IV, 7, MGH Epp. Sel. 2, 20, 305. Cf. Epp. Coll., no. 46, ed. Jaffé, *Bib. Greg.* 572: "*In omnibus enim terris licet etiam pauperculis mulierculis, suae patriae lege suaque voluntate virum accipere legitime; sanctae vero ecclesiae, quae est sponsa Dei et mater nostra, non licet secundum impiorum votum et detestabilem consuetudinem divina lege propriaque voluntate suo sponso legaliter in terris adherere.*"

[36] Reg. II, 31; II, 9; VIII, 21; III, 19; V, 11; II, 12, MGH Epp. Sel. 2, 166, 139, 547, 285, 364, 143f; Santifaller, no. 133, 139.

[37] Reg. II, 66; I, 23, MGH Epp. Sel. 2, 222, 39.

an unwritten moral law.[38] But, in its positive aspects, it was a law moderated by papal discretion. In his decrees, Gregory often maintained that he was not establishing new regulations, but merely renewing the rules of the Fathers.[39] His hierarchic policies showed the same character. He attempted, for example, to establish his direct ecclesiastical headship by sending legates, a practice which some Bohemians repudiated as an innovation, but which Gregory defended as merely the restoration of a practice which the negligence of his predecessors and other bishops had interrupted.[40] His office compelled him, he wrote, to keep vigilant watch over all churches to see that they rightly held the "documents of the faith and the holy rules of Scripture";[41] for to subvert the canons was to rend the unity of Christ's body.[42] Yet the Dictatus Papae asserted that only the pope might "establish new laws according to the need of the time," and that no chapter or book could be considered canonical without his approval.[43] And Gregory's letters reiterate that the Roman Church "has always been and will always be permitted to provide new decrees and remedies against newly arisen aberrations," that those new decrees were indisputably binding, and that Rome likewise had the power "to tolerate some things, even to conceal some things, following the temperance of discretion rather than the rigor of the canons."[44] He used this discretion most notably in making allowances for bishops who had unwittingly violated his own decree against lay investiture, due to its novelty,[45] though in a letter to Henry IV he wrote

[38] Cf. Reg. II, 37, MGH Epp. Sel. 2, 173: "Omnipotens Deus qui omnem legem suam in precepto adbreviavit caritatis det vobis se toto corde, tota anima tota virtute diligere. . . ."

[39] E.g., Reg. II, 68, IV, 6; V, 3, MGH Epp. Sel. 2, 225f, 303f, 353.

[40] Reg. I, 17, MGH Epp. Sel. 2, 27.

[41] Reg. II, 1, MGH Epp. Sel. 2, 124: "Suscepti nos officii cura compellit omnium ecclesiarum sollicitudinem gerere et, ut fidei documenta ac sacrae scripturae regulas recte teneant, vigilanti circumspectione perquirere ac docere."

[42] Reg. IV, 6, MGH Epp. Sel. 2, 304.

[43] DP 7, 17, Reg. II, 55 a., MGH Epp. Sel. 2, 203, 205.

[44] Reg. II, 67, MGH Epp. Sel. 2, 224: "huic sanctae Romanae ecclesiae semper licuit semperque licebit contra noviter increscentes excessus nova quoque decreta atque remedia procurare quae rationis et auctoritatis edita iudicio nulli hominum sit fas ut irrita refutare." Reg. V, 17, MGH Epp. Sel. 2, 378: "Quia consuetudo sanctae Romanae ecclesiae cui Deo auctore licet indigni deservimus, quedam tolerare quedam etiam dissimulare, discretionis temperantiam potius quam rigorem canonum sequentes. . . ." See Ullmann, Growth, 292ff.

[45] Reg. IV, 22; V, 18, MGH Epp. Sel. 2, 331, 381.

that he had in that decree resorted to the decrees and teaching of the Fathers and "established nothing new, nothing by our own invention." Rather, he declared, men must cast aside their error and follow "the first and only rule of ecclesiastical discipline and the narrow way of the saints."[46] A similar ambivalence appears in his concept of ecclesiastical privilege. Some allegations to the contrary,[47] he declared that privileges were granted according to circumstances of person, time, and place, as necessity or utility required, that they could subsequently be changed subject to the "authority of the holy Fathers,"[48] and that even privileges established by popes could be overturned, if it could be shown that the issuing pontiffs had been deceived into acting contrary to the establishments of the Fathers.[49]

For Gregory, and for the other reformers whose position he represented, ecclesiastical law was a constantly developing body of regulations, the components of which were established by bishops—singly, in their individual letters and treatises, or collectively, in their synodal decrees. The Roman Church held general supervision over the administration of law, and in their decretals bishops of Rome added to the body of law according to necessity. Their attitude toward antiquity as a legal sanction was ambivalent, but, on balance, they subordinated it to the general rule of papal discretion. Gregory VII wrote that the "law of Roman pontiffs" had prevailed in more lands than the law of Roman emperors.[50]

This characteristic of general applicability followed naturally from the argument, common among papal thinkers, that decrees of Roman bishops were normative among legal sources, and that the canonicity of a given text depended upon its presumed concordance with, or explicit approval by, papal decretals.[51]

Against doctrines which tended to curtail their powers, papal writers advanced with ever-greater refinement the doctrine that the Roman See was the epitome of the universal Church, and that the pope epitomized the Roman See. The reformers of the early twelfth century, no

---

[46] Reg. III, 10, MGH Epp. Sel. 2, 266: "*ad sanctorum patrum decreta doctrinamque recurrimus nichil novi, nichil adinventione nostra statuentes sed primam et unicam ecclesiasticae disciplinae regulam et tritam sanctorum viam relicto errore repetendam et sectandam esse censuimus.*"

[47] Reg. I, 24; VI, 34, MGH Epp. Sel. 2, 41, 447f.

[48] Reg. VI, 2, MGH Epp. Sel. 2, 393.

[49] Reg. VII, 24, MGH Epp. Sel. 2, 504.

[50] Reg. II, 75, MGH Epp. Sel. 2, 237f.

[51] Kuttner, "Liber canonicus," 393f.

less than their predecessors, resolutely argued that their work honored the ancient traditions and decrees of the Fathers[52] and the Apostles.[53] Still, the emphasis upon papal discretion which led the early Gregorians to an ambivalent view of tradition operated also among their successors.

Like earlier reformers, papal thinkers recalled that Christ said not "I am custom," but "I am truth."[54] More clearly than his immediate predecessors, Innocent II exposed the hierarchic implications of that distinction. Innocent wrote that no dishonesty or change of circumstance should upset or disturb what the holy Fathers instituted;[55] he professed to uphold the decrees of the sacred canons and the general custom of the Church.[56] Indeed, he said, the essential character of the priesthood itself was fidelity to the establishments of the Fathers: the priest ignorant of the law was no priest, for the priest's function was to know the law and to answer questions concerning the law.[57] Still, though he once inveighed against "new laws and customs,[58] he admitted on another occasion the "most recent establishments of councils" together with decrees of the Fathers and ancient conciliar decrees as authoritative.[59] For Innocent, the criterion between "custom" and "truth," the reconciling factor between ancient law and authentic change, was the hierarchic supremacy of Rome, particularly as expressed in adjudication. "According to the custom of the ancients," St. Peter and his successors established bishops, archbishops, and primates in appropriate sees to teach the divine law to the people.[60] The holy Fathers wished diverse ranks and orders to be in the Church so that, through subjection and reverence of lesser officers to greater, one unifying bond would prevail over diversity and the administration of each office would be rightly discharged.[61] In this order, Rome was the "head and hinge" (*caput et cardo*), the "mother" of the office held by all bishops. The Lord established St. Peter His vicar and the master of all the Church. Consequently, the Apostolic See could receive appeal from any part of the Church; and Innocent bitterly denounced attempts to curtail that power

---

[52] Paschal II, PL 163, 38, 91, 92, 100, 214, 225. Cf. PL 163, 442: *traditio Christi*, concerning the Eucharist. Calixtus II, PL 163, 1170, 1297, 1299; Anacletus II, PL 179, 706, 710.

[53] Paschal II, PL 163, 408, 428.      [54] Above, n. 20.

[55] Concerning privileges of churches and monasteries, see PL 179, 459.

[56] PL 179, 283, 495f.

[57] PL 179, 99, 264.

[58] PL 179, 469: "*novas leges sive consuetudines.*"

[59] PL 179, 192.      [60] PL 179, 134.

[61] PL 179, 134; cf. PL 179, 399.

279

in its broadest construction as presumption against the canons and blasphemy against the Holy Ghost.[62] Innocent indeed wrote that charity bound the orders in the Church together and produced the reverence of the lesser toward the greater officers.[63] But the effective manifestation of charity was obedience, especially to the privilege of St. Peter, juridically conceived; for that was the sum of the Church's law, the safeguard of ancient establishments, and the assurance of authentic change.

Tradition conveyed principally faith and practices; order was foremost in the Gregorians' minds. Tradition had required either stability or the constant historical elaboration of a deposit of doctrine. The Gregorians argued for expedience. As Gregory VII wrote, the primitive Church dissembled some things until the age of the Fathers, when they were set right, and the normal practice of the Roman Church was to relax canonical regulations or to conceal some things entirely, according to the need of the time.[64] Sudden change, or innovation, which the apologists and Fathers feared, was thus accommodated in the reformers' thought. Indeed, it became a normal instrument of hierarchic government. Tradition had been general to all believers. The Gregorians were ambivalent toward tradition when they did not simply ignore it, for they defined cohesion within the Church in terms of obedience to papal decrees. Tradition was, at best, a skeleton in their closet, a potential threat to their doctrine of full discretion.

$$+$$

The Gregorian view of Church law, the very antithesis of the idea of tradition, was part of a much broader concept of papal authority. For Victor II's statement that the papacy always had the power to uproot and to plant, and to adapt the order of the Church according to the changing times, applied to every aspect of ecclesiastical life.

Long after Victor's death, this position as interpreted and enacted by Gregory VII, incited the Great Controversy. There was little, conceptually, in the reformers' thought that had not been anticipated in statements of ninth-century popes. In the spirit, and sometimes in the

[62] By action of that sort, he wrote, Archbishop Henry of Sens had attempted to make himself the equal of St. Peter, or even to rise above him (PL 179, 264f); disobedience goaded bishops to become the equal of Jesus Christ and to ascend to the Apostolic See (PL 179, 226f).

[63] PL 179, 226f.                              [64] Above, pp. 64f, 277.

words, of Nicholas I, they argued that Rome was the custodian and the interpreter of true doctrine, and that popes conveyed the means of salvation to the rest of the world through the hierarchy. The cohesive element in the Church was obedience to Rome; the network of ecclesiastical offices was the channel of communication.

There was, however, an element in the reformers' thought which was only hinted at in the ninth century, a symptom of loftier aspirations than their predecessors had held.

For papal thinkers in the eleventh century, the Church was more than the Church as Cyprian and Augustine conceived it, strengthened by the refinements of Pseudo-Isidore.[65] The identification of the papacy with imperial qualities, particularly in the field of law, was symptomatic of the creation of an administrative body and of claims to universal juridical competence quite unknown in the ages of the apologists and Fathers.[66] The Gregorians' thought tended toward this conclusion by applying to the bishop of Rome imperial characteristics of administrative and juridical headship,[67] and by pressing to the extreme the irresponsibility implicit in the statement, "the Apostolic See is judged by no one."

From the ninth century onward, imperial attributes reinforced the liturgical acclamations of the Roman bishop as "supreme pontiff and universal pope," the ceremonial cry that St. Peter himself elected his successors,[68] the papal claims to a divine vicariate,[69] and other conventional assertions of spiritual supremacy. The forged Donation of Constantine shows that as early as the eighth, perhaps the early years of the ninth, century some thinkers ascribed to the Roman bishop insignia, privileges, and powers of imperial government.[70] Though apparently regarded with suspicion by some early reformers, the Donation itself may have inspired Gregory VII's claims to territorial dominance, and by the end of the eleventh century it stood in the papacy's normal canonistic repertory.[71] Even when the reformers accepted the Donation with

[65] Mirbt, *Publizistik*, 551.

[66] Mayer, "Kirchenbild," 284.

[67] Kempf, "Gewalt," *passim*; Ullmann, *Growth*, esp. 310ff; Ladner, "Concepts," 50, 52; Merzbacher, "Wandlungen," 277; Schmale, *Studien*, 247, n. 42.

[68] Opfermann, *Herrscherakklamationen*, 20 and *passim*; Kantorowicz, *Laudes*, 115.

[69] Maccarone, *Vicarius, passim*.

[70] See above, p. 155f.

[71] Laehr, *Schenkung*, 26, 29, 30f, 34, 38.

reserve, they followed its "imperializing" leads. For example, an elliptical sentence attributed to Gregory VII prescribed that only the pope might use the imperial insignia,[72] and it is clear that the early reformers normalized the use of two imperial symbols by the pope: the crown and the purple cape (*cappa rubea*).[73]

When reproved for the magnificence of his garments (presumably including these two insignia), Innocent II defended himself by saying that they were prescribed not by his own judgment, but "by the ancient constitution of the holy Fathers."[74] But, the use of the imperial symbols, the references to cardinals as "senators" and to legates as "proconsuls,"[75] and the conscious and increasingly refined development of papal bureaucracy betrayed an important new development in the concept of papal supremacy. References to the Roman bishop as "your majesty," known as early as the ninth century, suggested the tendency which led gradually to the assertion in the late twelfth century that "the pope is true emperor" (*papa ipse verus imperator*), and even in the time of Gregory VII to the assertion that the pope could depose emperors.[76]

This imperializing tendency among the reformers implied at least the inception of a concept of unitary world government in which all power of doctrinal teaching and physical coercion rested in the hands of the pope. The reformers, however, did not formulate this position clearly. They still understood Church unity primarily in terms of spiritual government. Imperial attributes ornamented an intellectual substructure composed of the ancient Petrine theory, as enhanced particularly by ninth-century authorities. For the reformers, the pope may well have been like an emperor in his power over Church order, but he was not "true emperor" over spiritual and temporal government.

[72] DP 8, Reg. II, 55 a, MGH Epp. Sel. 2, 204.

[73] Kantorowicz, *Laudes,* 137; Klewitz, "Krönung," 98ff, 106f, 116, 120; Schramm, "Austauch," 434, 442, 443.

[74] Arnulf of Séez, *Invectiva,* 4, MGH Ldl. 3, 96; cf. Schmale, *Studien,* 42.

[75] Sydow, "Untersuchungen," 33.

[76] Kantorowicz, *Laudes,* 90, 140; Schramm, "Austausch," 447f; DP 12. Reg. II, 55 a, MGH Epp. Sel. 2, 204. This assertion of headship was expressed ceremonially when temporal rulers did grooms' service for the pope, leading his horse, and, on one occasion, holding his stirrup as he dismounted (Holtzmann, "Kaiser," 3ff, 33). Four instances are recorded in the period under review: in 754, when Pippin did service for Stephen II; in 858, when Louis II met Nicholas I; in 1095, when King Conrad served Urban II; and, in 1131, when Lothaire III both led Innocent II's horse and assisted the Pope in dismounting.

The letters of Leo IX show this development at an early stage.[77-78] In large measure, Leo reiterated concepts which had long been conventional. He wrote that upon the integrity of Rome's privileges depended the stability, not of one Church, but of all Christendom;[79] and he judged the special responsibility of the pope to St. Peter, in whose imperishable apostolate all Roman bishops shared, to be the very essence of papal authority.[80] He acknowledged the apostolic character of men other than the Apostles themselves; for example, in allowing the local cult of St. Remigius to flourish in Rheims, he wrote that although Remigius was not an Apostle to other men, he was one to the French, for they were "the first fruits in the Lord of his apostolate."[81] Only St. Peter held a general apostolate for all believers, and consequently, only his successor held general care of all churches.

The fullest elaboration of Leo's thought occurs in his dealings with Constantinople. The Donation of Constantine, to which Leo never referred in western affairs,[82] provided admirable justification of Roman primacy against the pretensions of Michael Cerularius, patriarch of Constantinople, to parity with Rome and, particularly, to supremacy over the sees of Alexandria and Antioch.[83] Acting as the defender of

---

[77-78] He wrote to North African bishops rejoicing that they had sought the advice of Rome, the origin of their religion. After the Roman bishop, "the foremost archbishop and principal metropolitan of all Africa" was the bishop of Carthage, by whose authority bishops must be consecrated, and synods convoked within the province. Without the judgment of the Roman bishops, however, the African clergy could not celebrate a universal council or definitively condemn and depose bishops; for according to divine commission, "the greater and more difficult cases of all churches must be settled through the holy and principal See of St. Peter, by his successors" (PL 143, 728: "*omnium ecclesiarum maiores et difficiliores causae per sanctam et principalem beati Petri sedem a successoribus eius sunt diffiniendae*"). Rome, he wrote, had granted Carthage its precedence, on the pattern described by his venerable predecessors (Pseudo-) Clement, (Pseudo-) Anacletus, (Pseudo-) Anicetus, and others, paralleling hierarchic ranks with ranks in the pagan civil administration (PL 143, 729f). Leo's comments upon a dispute between the bishop of Forojulio and the patriarch of Grado, "primate and patriarch," likewise betray the Pseudo-Isidorian system of appellate recourse, requiring Grado's suffragans to air quarrels against their patriarch before their comprovincial bishops or to carry them to the papal presence (PL 143, 727).

[79] PL 143, 767, c. 36; cf. PL 143, 667.

[80] Cf. PL 143, 665, 693, 736ff; Ullmann, "Pontifex," 236f.

[81] PL 143, 617. See also the acknowledgement Leo seems to have given the "*sedes apostolica episcopalis*" of St. Martial, Limoges (Kantorowicz, *Laudes*, 138). Urban II also wrote that St. Martin "*apud Galliarum populos apostoli vicem optinere promeruit . . .*" (PL 151, 459). Cf. PL 151, 456, 458.

[82] Laehr, *Schenkung*, 24f.

[83] Cf. PL 143, 774.

Antiochene rights, Leo wrote to Peter of Antioch commending the profession of faith he had sent to Rome, recalling the common relation of the two Apostolic Sees to St. Peter, "the head and hinge of the Apostles," affirming the juridical primacy of Rome as declared by the "venerable councils," "human laws," and the Lord Himself, and urging Bishop Peter to stand fast against Constantinople.[84]

In his letters to Michael Cerularius, Leo stated his position more fully. At the end of time, Michael had arisen, a member of Antichrist;[85] by new presumption and incredible audacity, he had condemned the "apostolic and Latin church unheard and uncondemned," for commemorating the Lord's Passion with unleavened bread. In this, he strove, with human argumentation and conjecture, to confound the ancient faith. After almost one thousand twenty years, Michael had begun to teach the Roman Church how to keep Passiontide, as though the confession of St. Peter and the Apostle's continual presence had not enlightened the Roman Church.[86] The entire Church indeed was founded upon the faith of Peter, which had never failed and would never fail until the end. St. Peter and his successors had struggled against more than ninety heresies which had arisen in the East, or among the Greeks, for many of which bishops of Constantinople had been major advocates.[87] Leo recalled particularly the "reprehensible" (*nefanda*) Synod of Hiereia, which cast images of the Lord and of the saints into flames or submerged them in water, and tore paintings from the walls of basilicas. Aside from their heretical beliefs, many of the bishops of Constantinople had acceded uncanonically; some had been eunuchs; one had been a woman.[88] Furthermore, Michael's predecessors, like Michael himself, erred presumptuously in adopting the title "oecumenical patriarch."[89] Leo repeated a lengthy part of Gregory the Great's repudiation of the title, pointing out that Rome had not used it, even when Chalcedon offered it to Leo I. Even after Gregory's day, bishops of Constantinople continued to use the title, although it had not been granted to them, and although their use of it had been forbidden under anathema by the "holy and orthodox Fathers."[90]

In his condemnation of Latin practices and of Roman establishments, Michael presumed authority to judge what neither he nor any other mortal could judge. For St. Sylvester had decreed, with the approval of

---

[84] PL 143, 770.  [85] PL 143, 746, c. 4.  [86] PL 143, 747f, cc. 5, 6.
[87] PL 143, 748f, c. 8.  [88] PL 143, 760, c. 23.  [89] Cf. PL 143, 774.
[90] PL 143, 749f, c. 9.

Constantine and the Council of Nicaea, that the supreme see could be judged by no one. Moreover, on the fourth day after his baptism, Constantine established that all priests must be subject to the bishop of Rome in the same degree as all judges were subject to the king.[91] And he granted to the Roman bishops imperial power, dignity, insignia, and ministers forever,[92] adding earthly dominion to the heavenly dominion which the Apostolic See already held, and erecting "a royal priesthood of the holy Roman and Apostolic See"[93] over all believers and over the conversion of the nations in the four parts of the world.[94] Consequently, Rome begot the Latin Church in the West; that she was also the mother of the church in Constantinople was shown by the Byzantines when they sang liturgical acclamations to their emperors in Latin and recited Latin lections in their churches.[95] Indeed, Constantinople owed such eminence as it had to its "pious mother, the Roman Church," and to Constantine's munificence; for Rome out of love for Constantine had agreed that the city which he adorned with human honors should also enjoy ecclesiastical precedence, always preserving the ancient dignity of "the principal and apostolic sees," Antioch and Alexandria.[96]

Perhaps the clearest epitome of Leo's thought occurs in his famous comment upon Christ's commission to St. Peter, and His promise to pray for that Apostle's steadfastness in the faith. The faith of Peter, he wrote, was the faith of the Church. "No one denies this except the man who openly attacks these words of Truth. For as the whole door is ruled by the hinge, so is the work of the whole Church determined by Peter and his successors. And as the immovable hinge continually opens and closes the door, so Peter and his successors have free judgment of all the Church, since no one may abolish their place; for the supreme see is judged by no one. Thus its clergy are called cardinals, for they adhere quite closely to the hinge by which the rest is moved."[97] The growing importance of the Sacred College did not, for Leo, limit the powers of

[91] PL 143, 751, c. 10.          [92] PL 143, 752, c. 12.
[93] PL 143, 752f, 768, cc. 12, 13, 38.    [94] PL 143, 757, c. 17.
[95] PL 143, 761, c. 23.          [96] PL 143, 763, c. 28.

[97] PL 143, 765, c. 32: "*Quod nemo negat nisi qui evidenter haec ipsa verba Veritatis impugnat quia sicut cardine totum regitur ostium ita Petro et successoribus ejus totius ecclesiae disponitur emolumentum. Et sicut cardo immobilis permanens ducit et reducit ostium, sic Petrus et sui successores liberum de omni ecclesia habent judicium cum nemo debeat eorum dimovere statum, quia summa sedes a nemine judicatur. Unde clerici ejus cardinales dicuntur cardini utique illi quo cetera moventur vicinius adhaerentes.*" See Ullmann, "Humbert," 123; *Growth*, 321.

the pope. The cardinals were not the hinge, as the College wrote to Pope Eugenius in 1148; but they were near the hinge.[98]

Therefore, the imperial power which, Leo alleged, Constantine had granted to the Roman Church merely enhanced the powers which Rome had by virtue of St. Peter's continual presence. Leo's argument is that because of Christ's commission to St. Peter, the Roman bishop was supreme guardian of teaching and discipline. He was the authentic interpreter, and his doctrine was conveyed by the establishment of churches, like Constantinople, and by the obedience which bound bishops to him as judges were bound to their king. His means of enforcement was the free and incontrovertible judgment he held over the entire Church. Imperial attributes were but a useful ornament on this structure; they did not change the character or enlarge the jurisdictional competence of the Roman bishop.

The works of Peter Damian provide additional evidence of the identity the reformers drew between pope and papacy, and of the sweeping powers they ascribed to the pope by virtue of St. Peter's apostolate. To be sure, they too showed the effects of the imperializing tendency. The pope wielded powers beyond ecclesiastical authority. Peter related the papal consecration with the anointing of David as king;[99] he drew parallels between the cardinals, the "spiritual senators of the universal Church," and the ancient curia of the Romans;[100] and he wrote that Christ, having conferred upon the Roman bishop the keys of the universal Church, added monarchies as well, for, as delegated guardian of Henry IV, Pope Victor II held the powers of the entire Roman Empire.[101] But for Peter Damian, hierarchic order could be understood only in other, spiritual terms.

He wrote that St. Peter had obtained three sees: Antioch, where, having laid the foundation of faith, he ordained Ignatius as bishop; Alexandria, where his disciple St. Mark taught and suffered martyrdom; and, finally, Rome, where he presided for five years, adorning the City, together with St. Paul, with the triumphal victory of martyrdom.[102] In rank, Rome held the first "principate" (*principatus*), Alexandria the second, and Antioch the third.[103] Aquileia, he wrote, deserved to be

[98] See Tierney, *Foundations*, 70, n. 3; below, p. 312.
[99] Opusc. 20, PL 145, 455.
[100] Opusc. 31, c. 7, PL 145, 540: *"spiritales sunt universalis ecclesiae senatores."*
[101] Epp. I, 5, PL 144, 210.
[102] Epp. I, 20, PL 144, 238.
[103] Serm. 14-16, PL 144, 574, 582, 583.

an "apostolic see" because it possessed the body of St. Mark;[104] but, even though Peter himself recorded that the body of St. Matthew had been moved from Ethiopia to Salerno, and those of Sts. Luke and Andrew from "the regions of Bithynia" to Constantinople, he did not attribute to those two cities equivalent claims to apostolicity.[105] His negative comments upon Jerusalem revealed the legalistic principle behind his concept of patriarchal order. According to a common mode of thought, Jerusalem, rather than Rome, should take precedence over all churches, since the Lord died at Jerusalem. But the order of churches was "disposed according to the privilege of Peter, not according to the incomparable excellency of the Redeemer."[106] Consequently, according to the authority of the canons, Rome held first place, Alexandria the second, Antioch the third, Constantinople, the fourth, and Jerusalem the fifth.

Further, Peter identified the fate of all churches with that of Rome. To attempt to gain control of the Apostolic See by simony was nothing other than to strive to purchase control of all churches.[107] The pope shared the honor of his see. He was the vicar of Christ, who succeeded the supreme pastor in the apostolic dignity;[108] and, in addressing Hildebrand as pope-elect, Peter even wrote, "You are the Apostolic See; you are the Roman church."[109] The bishop of the Apostolic See was the "common father" of the entire world; he alone, in the term Gregory the Great feared, was the "universal bishop" (*universalis episcopus*) of all churches.[110] The judgment of Peter loosed and bound the entire world (*orbis universitas*); the sentence of Peter preceded the sentence of the Redeemer, for Peter did not bind what Christ bound, but Christ bound what Peter bound; and, in the words of Leo I, St. Peter alone of men shared in divine majesty and presided with the Lord.[111] Amidst all the

---

[104] Serm. 15, 16, PL 144, 582, 585. About 1053, Bishop Dominicus of Grado also claimed the patriarchal title on the assertion that his see had been founded by St. Mark (see Fuhrmann, "Patriarchate" [1954], 58).

[105] Serm. 15, PL 144, 582.

[106] Opusc. 35, c. 4, PL 145, 594.

[107] Epp. I, 21, PL 144, 250f. Cf. above, pp. 271, 274.

[108] Epp. I, 5, PL 144, 210; Opusc. 17, c. 4, PL 145, 386; Ullmann, "Pontifex," 256.

[109] Opusc. 20, c. 1, PL 145, 443: *"vos apostolica sedis, vos Romana estis ecclesia."*

[110] Opusc. 23, c. 1, PL 145, 474, on the general concern caused by the deaths of popes. See also, col. 480.

[111] Serm. 26, PL 144, 646.

changes in the Church, the primacy of St. Peter continued in the Roman See, epitomized, or even incarnated, in the pope. It was the safeguard of ecclesiastical truth and cohesion.

Under severer attack than previous reformer-popes on personal as well as on official grounds, Gregory VII composed particularly clear statements of this doctrine. The *Dictatus Papae* asserted that the Pope alone could use the imperial insignia, that his feet only were to be kissed by all princes, and that he might depose emperors.[112] What were the counterparts of such lofty, imperializing assertions in Gregory's thought about the Church? If the Lord commanded His Apostles to obey the scribes and Pharisees in reverence for the seat of Moses which they held, the apostolic and Gospel doctrine, as defined by the Roman See, also commanded the veneration of all the faithful.[113] The rock of the holy Roman Church was immobile,[114] and the gates of hell, "that is the tongues of heretics,"[115] would not prevail against it. Gregory strongly identified the qualities of the Roman See with the official character of the pope. The divine will had summoned him to the Apostolic See.[116] He governed jointly with Christ and St. Peter;[117] and, amidst the crushing burdens of the papacy, Christ sustained him.[118] On the day of his consecration, Gregory himself standing before the body of St. Peter, had been addressed with the words, "Whatever you bless will be blessed, and whatever you bind upon earth will also be bound in heaven."[119] St. Peter indeed spoke through the mouth of the pope,[120] who, by divine privilege and the right of inheritance, received the principate and power which Christ had granted to St. Peter, and which would abide in the Apostle's throne until the end of the world.[121] Through the merits of St. Peter,[122] papal judgments were divine judgments, and, even more, the pope, if canonically ordained, became "holy."[123] His own character thus transmuted by the sanctity of his office, the pope was able to claim for his own actions the obedience owed to the Apostolic See. His decrees

[112] DP 8, 9, 12. Above, nn. 72, 76.   [113] Reg. III, 10, MGH Epp. Sel. 2, 265f.
[114] Reg. I, 11, *ibid.*, 18.   [115] Reg. I, 64, *ibid.*, 93.
[116] Reg. I, 39, *ibid.*, 61.   [117] Reg. V, 21, *ibid.*, 384f.
[118] *Loc.cit.*
[119] Epp. Coll., no. 18, ed. Jaffé, *Bib. Greg.*, 544.
[120] Reg. II, 15; IV, 2, MGH Epp. Sel. 2, 148, 293.
[121] Reg. IX, 35, *ibid.*, 622f.
[122] Reg. II, 31, *ibid.*, 165; cf. Reg. IX, 35, *ibid.*, 626f.
[123] DP 23, Reg. II, 55 a; *ibid.*, 207; Ullmann, "Pontifex," 229, 240f, 243, 247f, 252; Becker, *Studien*, 54f.

and those of the Roman Church were identical.[124] Disobedience to them cast the offender outside the Church; it was the sin of paganism, or idolatry.[125]

Gregory showed how aptly Peter Damian had addressed him with the words, "You are the Roman Church."[126] By virtue of the identification between pope and see, Gregory claimed authority to interpose his judgment before that of any patriarch or primate,[127] following the pattern of hierarchic relations established by Pseudo-Isidore.[128] Moreover, he regarded bishops as his vicars, since other churches were subordinate to the Roman Church. The bishop of Rome, he said, had divided his care among individual bishops. He did not thereby deprive himself of his universal and supreme power, just as a king did not diminish his royal power by dividing his kingdom among dukes and counts. The Roman bishop consequently could order the affairs of any church, even if its bishop resisted.[129] The elliptical sentences of the *Dictatus Papae* amplify this thought: the pope held sole power to establish new churches by dividing wealthy bishoprics and uniting poor ones.[130] He alone could depose and reconcile bishops without synodal hearing.[131] He could depose absent persons in judicial process.[132] His legates, regardless of their rank, took precedence over all bishops in synods and they could issue the sentence of deposition against bishops.[133] His name only was to be recited in all churches.[134] He could translate bishops and ordain clergy in any church.[135] Greater cases in every church must be referred to Rome.[136]

Gregory pressed these claims through his legatine missions in the West.[137] He asserted them in his negotiations with eastern churches, which he judged had been led away from the orthodox faith by the Devil and divided among "diverse opinions"[138] which had "in the spirit

[124] E.g., Reg. V, 15, MGH Epp. Sel. 2, 375.

[125] Epp. Coll., no. 28, ed. Jaffé, *Bib. Greg.*, 554f; Reg. IV, 2, 23, 24, 14 a., MGH Epp. Sel. 2, 296, 336, 338, 486.

[126] See above, p. 287.

[127] Reg. I, 60, MGH Epp. Sel. 2, 87f.

[128] Reg. VI, 35, *ibid.*, 450ff.

[129] Roman Synod (1074), c. 23, PL 148, 783.

[130] DP 7, Reg. II, 55 a., MGH Epp. Sel. 2, 203.

[131] DP 3, 25, *ibid.*, 202, 207.   [132] DP 5, *ibid.*, 203.

[133] DP 4, *ibid.*, 203.   [134] DP 10, *ibid.*, 204.

[135] DP 13, 14, *ibid.*, 204f.   [136] DP 21, *ibid.*, 206.

[137] E.g., epp. coll. 21, ed. Jaffé, *Bib. Greg.*, 547.

[138] Reg. II, 31, 49, MGH Epp. Sel. 2, 167, 189. Cf. Reg. VIII, 1, *ibid.*, 511.

of presumption or by ignorance" acted without regard for Rome's jurid-ical supremacy,[139] and which he wished to redeem by a crusade under his personal leadership.[140] He declared them in his claim that all other patriarchates—those of Aquileia and Grado as well as Constantinople, the "daughter" of Rome—were subject to his direction.[141]

These were the attitudes of three exceptional men, Leo IX, Peter Damian, and Gregory VII, toward the central premise of the Gregorians: that the means of salvation was conveyed by the imperishable apostolate of St. Peter acting in the pope. His character transformed by his office, the bishop of Rome became the font of pure doctrine for all believers. Ascriptions of imperial power to the papacy corroborated the posi-tion of the pope as supreme interpreter and judge in the Church.

And yet, heightened assertions of papal pre-eminence merely sharp-ened doctrines which tended to limit papal discretion in Church law and order. Many thinkers, even among the reformers, objected to the piv-otal role that the Gregorians gave papal discretion. Proponents of these counterdoctrines argued that, far from fulfilling the establishments of the Apostles and the Fathers, the reformer-popes corrupted authen-tic Church order and enslaved the Church rather than freeing it. Among these thinkers the power to conserve counted for more than the power to change; tradition, for more than discretion. The Gregorians had ob-literated the primitive side of the Roman Janus: their antagonists meant to restore it.

If we look behind the veil of ideas into the real world, we see the great danger that awaited the imperialized papacy. From the practical point of view, the Gregorians' assertions were, at least at the begin-ning, hardly more than charades. The vastness of the patrimony of St. Peter and the campaigns of warrior popes—such as John VIII, John XII, Leo IX in the eleventh century, and Innocent II in the twelfth—belied the essential vulnerability of the papacy. Since the papacy had title over vast lands, it is easy to overestimate the power of the Roman bishops as civil rulers. In fact, their economic position varied greatly, sometimes within the space of a few years. However, from the ninth century on, deterioration was fairly constant. By the end of that century, the Lateran Church had collapsed, and in the mid-tenth century Liut-

---

[139] Reg. VI, 4, *ibid.*, 396f, concerning the case of St. Athanasius.

[140] Reg. I, 49, II, 31, *ibid.*: 75: 166.

[141] Reg. I, 18, 42: II, 39, 62; V, 5; VI, 5b (cc. 17, 18), 17a; *ibid.*, 29, 64f, 175f, 217, 353, 401, 428f.

prand observed that the roof above St. Peter's main altar leaked, and that the whole building threatened to fall. The poverty of their church was one condition which the eleventh-century reformers strove particularly to change. In 1045, the papal treasury was empty; and there is no evidence that the papacy had a system of accounting. That the reformers built or renovated few churches, and that Gregory VII apparently undertook no building activity at all, is a measure of the papacy's very grave economic difficulty. By the same token, the revival of construction, restoration, and ornamentation under Paschal II reflects the economic relief which the papacy derived from the Mathildine lands and from new techniques of administration learned in part from the Normans in south Italy. Under these circumstances, the papacy between the eighth and the late eleventh centuries was very susceptible to temporal influence and control, especially from groups within the city of Rome and from other Italian princes. The constant antagonism between the papacy and the people of Rome, and the intervention of the Roman nobility, of the Empire, and, less important, of the Normans in papal affairs blocked the efforts of Roman bishops to make good their supraterritorial claims. They all produced diversion and dissipation of the patrimony of St. Peter; they made the popes dependent upon other political authorities and thus committed them to political enterprises which they had not framed and which were often alien to the interests of their see. These circumstances deprived the papacy of sufficient resources to establish its universal administrative and juridical supremacy. Only in the early twelfth century did the papacy begin to move from under this incubus; Urban II for most of his pontificate was still dependent on the largesse of wealthy Roman matrons. In a divided and impoverished see, the advocates of tradition could bargain from strength.

CHAPTER 12

# Tradition: Watchword of Resistance

PETER DAMIAN had assured Gregory VII that, as pope, he was the Roman Church, the head of Christendom, and Gregory maintained that divergence from papal decrees was idolatry. Anti-Gregorians considered both statements open to dispute; for them, the unity of the Church could not be defined in terms of communion with one man, or of a monopoly of legislative power. In each of its manifestations, anti-Gregorian thought centered on one principle: that Gregory widely overstepped the limits of his office, and thus disrupted Church unity. The limits that they invoked were in fact those acknowledged by Gregory's defenders and successors: the rules of consensus, universality, and antiquity. In administrative terms, they argued that Gregory had abridged the rightful power of bishops, the instruments of consensus, and that he had impinged on powers of temporal government outside the Church's concern. In moral terms, they held that Gregory's personal wickedness invalidated his actions. Cardinal Humbert and Gregory had attacked temporal practices which they thought obstructed the means of salvation. But Gregory's actions aroused the ancient conviction that, while the Roman See might never err, the pope could pervert authentic doctrine and discipline. In Wido of Osnabrück's words, Gregory VII repudiated the command of God and "established his own tradition."[1] The Anti-Gregorians understood the antithesis of tradition and discretion; and they were in search of a doctrine of responsible government.

$+$

## A. THE IMPERIALISTS

Together with most of the great crises of his pontificate, Gregory VII inherited the animosity which earlier disputes generated. In the pontificate of Alexander II, the Milanese resisted Roman intervention, claiming that the Ambrosian church should not be subject to Roman laws, and that the Roman pontiff had no right to judge or to administer

[1] De Controv. Hild. et Hen., MGH Ldl. 1, 469.

affairs in their see.[2] Likewise, the Papal Election Decree of 1059 aroused toward Rome bitter hostility at the German court, since it seemed to deprive the German king of his customary powers in papal accessions. Bitterer still was the sense of injury in 1061, when even the powers acknowledged in 1059 were ignored and the royal court received formal notice neither of Nicholas II's death, nor of Alexander II's accession. Rome argued that the court had forfeited its rights under Nicholas's edict by repudiating the decree. The court had assembled a synod which condemned Nicholas and nullified his edict, and it refused to receive the legate whom Nicholas sent to proclaim the decree. It therefore deprived itself of the rights which Nicholas had preserved.[3] Moreover, the Donation of Constantine had conferred upon Rome principate over all churches, judgment over the kingdom of Italy, and other rights which disproved any argument that the German king could, on historical precedent, intervene in the elections of popes. But, the imperialists argued, law and convention could be changed, and this in fact occurred when Henry III became *patricius* of the Romans and received "the principate of always supervising the election of a pontiff." Nicholas II had confirmed this new privilege.[4] Furthermore, since the pope was "universal pontiff" (*universalis pontifex*), and since both the "Roman people" and the "Roman emperor" owed him obedience, the assent of the "Roman king" was necessary to complete the papal election; the king could not be expected to obey a man whom he had not elected.[5] Theory and dispute joined when the Synod of Basle (1061), meeting under Henry IV's summons and in the presence of Roman representatives, including Cardinal Hugh Candidus, elected Cadalus of Parma as Pope Honorius II. Under arbitration, the imperial court subsequently acknowledged Alexander II. Far from renouncing Cadalus, the German court allowed him to remain in possession of Parma, still claiming to be pope, a useful counterbalance in any further struggle with Alexander II.[6]

These points of opposition prepared directly for the conflict between Gregory and Henry, and they were reinforced by the widespread antag-

---

[2] Peter Damian, Opusc. 5, PL 145, 90. See Fliche, *Histoire*, 30. Alexander II's actions in Spanish affairs incited similar reactions (Tellenbach, "Bedeutung," 137f).

[3] Peter Damian, *Disceptio Synodalis*, MGH Ldl. 1, 87; cf. Deusdedit, below, p. 308. On Peter's treatise, see Zimmermann, "Papstabsetzungen," III, 98.

[4] *Ibid.*, 80: "*Heinricus* [III] *imperator factus est patricius Romanorum a quibus etiam accepit in electione semper ordinandi pontificis principatum.*"

[5] *Ibid.*, 78f.

[6] Zimmermann, "Papstabsetzungen," III, 92ff, 102.

onism with which Gregory's early reform decrees had been met. His release of laymen from obedience to simoniac or Nicolaite clergy, like his release of Henry's subjects from their oaths of fealty, aroused determined protests.[7] Sigebert of Gembloux objected that Gregory had dishonored the clergy with the result that laymen no longer obeyed Christian commands or respected the sacraments.[8] The bishops in the Synod of Worms (1076) condemned him for transferring the administration of ecclesiastical affairs from bishops to "popular madness," thus scattering the flame of discord through all the churches of Italy, Germany, Gaul, and Spain. The bishops objected that this was only one of many bad results of Gregory's subverting their authority by claiming immediate jurisdiction over all Christians.[9]

Gregory's particular decrees likewise elicited violent responses. Curiously, his original decree against lay investiture (1075), and the renewal of the edict in 1077 passed almost without comment in the controversial literature.[10] But the clergy throughout Europe vehemently decried his prohibitions of simony and Nicolaitism. Leo IX had witnessed violent protests against his prohibitions of the same abuses at synods in Rome (1049) and Mantua.[11] But Gregory's decrees against simony prompted resistance of that sort throughout Europe,[12] and even the charge of hypocrisy arose on the allegation that Gregory himself had acceded to the papacy through simony, and that he had ordained simoniacs.[13] A similar reaction met his decrees on clerical celibacy. In 1059, Peter Damian's attempt to enforce clerical celibacy in Milan led to a popular rising, and the Roman clergy under Stephen IX considered clerical continence "vain and frivolous."[14] When the Bishop of Brescia read

[7] Mirbt, *Publizistik*, 450ff.

[8] Apol., cc. 2, 8, MGH Ldl. 2, 439, 447; Chron. (a. 1074), MGH SS. 6, 362f.

[9] Ed. Erdmann, 66; cf. the letter of Liemar of Hamburg to Hezil of Hildesheim, in Sudendorf, *Registrum*, 1, no. 5, 9. Liemar complained that Gregory had, without due synodal deliberation, suspended him from office and summoned him to trial in Rome.

[10] Several decrees against lay investiture had been issued before the accession of Gregory VII, but they seem to have aroused little opposition (see Becker, *Studien*, 55, 138). Decrees were issued at Limoges (1031), Rheims (1049), Rome (1059), and Tours (1060). Gregory's first decree (1075) caused no comment, and its text has been lost.

[11] Fliche, *Réforme*, 1, 132, 151; Mirbt, *Publizistik*, 391f.

[12] Fliche, *Histoire*, 106.

[13] Fliche, *Histoire*, 244; Mirbt, *Publizistik*, 365f.

[14] Mirbt, *Publizistik*, 271f.

Nicholas II's prohibition of marriage among the clergy, his clergy beat him to the point of death.[15] Gregory's decrees met the same reception. For his defense of Gregory's prohibition, an Abbot was set upon in the Synod of Paris (1074), and the Archbishop of Rouen's clergy stoned him out of his church. The clergy of Cambrai was in open rebellion.[16] Similar conditions prevailed in some German churches.[17] And at least one thinker denounced Gregory's teaching as doctrinally erroneous.[18]

Resistance to the reform movement before Gregory's accession thus consolidated into general opposition when Gregory, as pope, pressed for general conformity to the reformers' goals. Particular churches, like the Milanese, the German court, bishops and lower clergy, all sensed the infringement of the rights they considered normal and legitimate, and their resistance was only stiffened by Gregory's insistence on liturgical uniformity according to Roman standards,[19] and on the collection of papal levies.[20]

In view of the general and bitter antagonism Gregory incurred even before his excommunication and deposition of Henry, it is remarkable that the treatises his adversaries wrote both before and after 1076 are generally moderate concerning principles of Church order and the coordination of ecclesiastical and temporal government. Only exceptional treatises insist on the programmatic subordination of the Church to the temporal power; and it would be fair to say that, on balance, the anti-Gregorian thinkers were arguing from their own viewpoints to the same position Gregory's followers took. A measure of their agreement is shown by the fact that Wibert absolved Henry IV of excommunication on the ground that he had been despoiled of his goods (i.e., the royal office) without having been duly summoned and convicted, but not on the ground that kings and emperors were immune to excommunication and deposition.[21] Toward Gregory himself they were merciless in their abuse; but they never ceased to profess reverence for the Roman See as the supreme head of all churches on earth. Indeed, the burden of their

---

[15] *Ibid.*, 272.

[16] Fliche, *Réforme* 1, 94; Bouquet, 14, 779f.

[17] Mirbt, *Publizistik*, 272f.

[18] Sigebert of Gembloux, Apol., cc. 3-8, MGH Ldl. 2, 439-448; Mirbt, *Publizistik*, 273, 393.

[19] Tellenbach, "Bedeutung," 133.

[20] Jordan, "Finanzgeschichte," 81; cf. Vehse, "Herrschaft," 157f.

[21] MGH Ldl. 1, 622.

thought was to distinguish between popes, who could err even in matters of faith, and the papacy, which Christ preserved from error, and to maintain that Gregory, having claimed powers not rightly his, had deposed himself.

It would be wrong, however, to imply that extremists were entirely absent from Henry's camp. The long poem by Benzo of Alba is testimony enough to the fact that what might now be called the "lunatic fringe" was indeed present there and vociferously active.[22] Learned in the works of classical antiquity, gifted in poetry, masterly in invective, Benzo cast aside all thought of equity or search for compromise. He considered neither the legitimacy of Rome's claim to ecclesiastical primacy, nor the intricate problem of right and abuse within the order of proprietary churches. His mind was entranced by delusions of the universal power which, he thought, came to Henry IV in succession from Caesar, and which preserved the right order of the world.[23] Gregory VII had attacked that vision; Benzo retaliated with blind invective. His assertions that the emperor rightly elected the pope and that he governed the clergy as the "vicar of the Creator"[24] are startling in their formulation; but, together with Benzo's allegation that the emperor ruled over all the kings of the earth,[25] they reveal the author's loose grasp both of the theoretical issues in the Controversy and of reality itself.

The earliest theoretical statements of the anti-Gregorian position occur in the letters of Henry IV and in the decrees of the Synods of Worms and Brixen. Henry's letters have sometimes been judged expressions of a doctrine of "regal pontificalism," or Caesaropapism.[26] But, as in dealing with Carolingian and Ottonian thought, it is necessary to weigh such terms carefully before applying them to Salian doctrines of kingship. A general sociological, or even anthropological, problem was involved. And, as one scholar has wisely observed: ". . . the idea that kings are magical or sacred goes back to primeval folklore. It was more a matter of popular sentiment than of developed political or constitutional theory. It hovered in the background of men's minds and was often contradicted by their more conscious views and practices. Besides, although the king might be a magical personage, this by no means exempted him from having to keep rules, by no means made him absolute. The vestal virgins were exceedingly sacred but, for that very reason,

---

[22] See Ullmann, *Growth*, 387ff.
[23] MGH SS. 11, 603, 611, 656.
[24] MGH SS. 11, 599, 634, 671.
[25] MGH SS. 11, 596, 602, 656.
[26] E.g., Morrison, *Lives*, 29ff.

had to remain exceedingly virginal. Just because he is something so primeval, a magic king is rigidly circumscribed by custom and tabu, and a *roi thaumaturge* is very apt to become a *roi fanéant*."[27]

The interpretation of Henry's actions as evidence of a doctrine of regal sacerdotalism places an unnecessarily extreme emphasis upon Henry's conventional assertions that God bestowed the royal power and preserved his kingdom from danger, that kings and priests must work in collaboration for the welfare of the Church, and indeed that Henry must take the initiative in securing the peace of the Church. The letters dealing with Henry's conflict with Gregory indeed state the familiar doctrine of institutional separation.[28] In 1076, Henry published four letters denouncing Gregory, in addition to the decree of the Synod of Worms. The Synod condemned Gregory for acceding to the papacy undeservedly through perjury, for polluting the Church with private scandals, and for denying bishops their rightful powers by inciting their flocks against them and superseding their juridical powers with his own. They declared that they had never promised obedience to him as pope, and they utterly repudiated his title.[29] Henry ratified this judgment with a letter to the Romans, two letters to "Hildebrand," and an encyclical to his bishops. In addressing the Roman clergy and people, Henry merely repeated the text of one of his denunciatory letters to Gregory and urged the recipients to rise up against Gregory, as an oppressor of the Church and a subverter of the Roman commonwealth and Henry's kingdom. He admonished them to spare Gregory's life, and, having forced him from his see, to elect another pope jointly with Henry and "all the bishops."[30] In a brief letter to Gregory, Henry complained that the Pope had treated his obedience with contempt, deprived him of the "hereditary dignity," the patriciate, which Rome owed him, and conspired to subvert his authority in Italy. He had abused bishops contrary to divine and human laws. Confirming the decree of Worms, Henry revoked every prerogative of the papacy from him and commanded him to descend from the See of Rome, whose patriciate Henry claimed by virtue of God's bestowal and the sworn assent of the Romans.[31] A

[27] Morris, "Politics," 299.

[28] Dr. Ullmann interprets this dualistic formulation as "withdrawal" from the *Rex-Sacerdos* position he ascribes to Henry III (*Growth*, 345). He argues that subsequently, at the Synod of Brixen, the *Rex-Sacerdos* position was revived (*ibid.*, 352).

[29] Ed. Erdmann, 68; Ullmann, *Growth*, 351.

[30] Ep. 10, ed. Erdmann, 12f.          [31] Ep. 11, *ibid.*, 14f.

second, more extensive letter addresses Gregory as "false monk," and combines the charges made by the Synod and by Henry in the previous letters. Here, and in the encyclical letter to his bishops, Henry came to grips with the problem of institutional coordination. In threatening to depose him, Gregory acted as though the pope granted kingship instead of God. Indeed, God granted the royal power to Henry; Jesus Christ called him to the kingship; and the "tradition of the holy Fathers" taught that he must not be deposed unless he deviated from the faith, for the judgment of kings belonged to God alone. Christ had not called Gregory to the priesthood. Gregory had rather risen to it by cunning, money, favor, and the sword. From the throne of peace, he destroyed peace and corrupted the true doctrine of St. Peter.[32] By arrogating both kingship and priesthood to himself he impaired the powers of both offices, and confused the pious ordination of God which required that they be distinct.[33]

The decree of the Synod of Brixen and Henry's two related letters to the Roman clergy and people rehearse these points. The Synod elaborately described Gregory's personal unworthiness for the papacy, alleging that he acceded by simony, by murdering his four immediate predecessors, by perjury, by plotting Henry's physical and spiritual death, by defending the traitorous Rudolf, and by scattering schism and discord at every level. He was, they declared, a heretic concerning the nature of the Eucharist, and a necromancer. Thus he must be canonically deposed.[34] In his own letters, Henry praised the Romans for their constancy toward him and declared his intention to receive the imperial crown in Rome, and to restore peace between the priesthood and the kingship.[35] In the later of the two letters, Henry wrote as though the decrees of Worms and Brixen were not definitive, for he summoned "Hildebrand" to an assembly where he could answer the charges against him, and where it could be decided whether he were to be retained in the Apostolic See or deposed. He professed that if Gregory could and should be pope, he would obey him. But he made his own position clear by writing that "Hildebrand" strove to destroy the ordination of God by conspiring against Henry, by wishing there to be only one sword, though God had said that two swords were sufficient.[36]

---

[32] Epp. 12, 13, *ibid.*, 15ff.   [33] Ep. 13, *ibid.*, 19.

[34] *Ibid.*, 70ff. On other imperialist correspondence in 1080, see Fliche, *Histoire*, 148f.

[35] Ep. 16, *ibid.*, 22f.   [36] Ep. 17, *ibid.*, 25.

Clearly, Henry's proposal of a further synod to try Gregory's case was mere diplomatic finesse; he concluded his letter with a reference to the office which Gregory "unjustly" held.[37] But throughout his comments in 1076 and again in 1081-1082 ran the thought that Gregory's ecclesiastical claims to omnicompetence wrongfully deprived bishops of their administrative powers, and that his arrogation of the authority to depose Henry destroyed God's ordination by uniting two offices which God wished to remain discrete.

Between 1090 and 1093, a long treatise was composed anonymously summarizing the imperialist position at that time. It received limited, if any, circulation in the Middle Ages, but the high quality of the work commands serious attention. The treatise, *De unitate ecclesiae conservanda*, reveals synthetic and analytic abilities of a very high order and a finely balanced judgment somewhat removed from the personal ambition and sense of injury which marked many other treatises of the period. The author prepared a judicious statement of principles, disclosed in a lengthy historical account of the conflict between empire and papacy from Gregory's accession onward. Alone among the anti-Gregorian writers, he stated at least the bare outlines of his ecclesiological position and related them to his particular objections against Gregory. The title of the treatise copies that of a work by St. Cyprian, and the author's concept of cohesion within the Church is in many ways similar to that of the African Father.

The unity of the Church, as commended by the Lord, depended upon the common charity of its members, and the author lamented that discord prevailed among most men, while there remained only among a few that concord through which the Church was unified, and in which it subsisted.[38] He considered the hierarchic structure of the Church essential to the proper conduct of ecclesiastical affairs. In particular, he strongly asserted Rome's juridical supremacy: according to the canons, all appeals in the Church must be deferred to the Apostolic See from which there could be no appeal,[39] and of which there could be no review.[40] Rome was the "mother of all churches." The author also fully understood the importance of the laws and customs by which the hierarchy must govern.[41] But the fulfillment of the law, he wrote, was char-

---

[37] Ep. 17, *ibid.*, 26.
[38] I, 1, MGH Ldl. 2, 184f. See the discussion in Ullmann, *Growth*, 404ff.
[39] I, 12, II, 25, *ibid.*, 200, 245.
[40] II, 39, *ibid.*, 268.
[41] II, 42, *ibid.*, 275.

ity,[42] and, in the last analysis, "necessity has no law."[43] Laws, customs, and even hierarchic order were mutable. Even the rights of the Apostolic See could be temporarily suspended by a pope's illicit conduct.[44] The author explicitly rejected the claims of headship epitomized in the *Dictatus Papae* by commenting that Gregory III had committed sacrilege when, contrary to the canons, he had performed ordinations in dioceses other than his own, thus depriving metropolitan churches of their rightful privileges.[45] Superior to the structure of offices and regulations was the rule of concord and charity as expressed in the consensus of all bishops. Many false Christians, he wrote, confessed that Jesus Christ came in the flesh, but they denied their confession by deeds which lacked charity.[46] The author paraphrased St. Cyprian when he wrote that the orthodox Church was composed of many churches, and that, although there were many bishops, there was only one episcopate, because of the Church's unity.[47] Only bishops could perform offices that unified the Church.[48] He appealed for ultimate sanction to "the assent of the whole Church" (*totius ecclesiae assensus*)[49] and observed, in some particular instances, very like Hincmar of Rheims, that the whole Church confirmed papal decrees by its consent.[50] The "catholic Church" was the universal Church, participating in the same sacraments;[51] but even sacraments performed by heretics or schismatics were valid, if they were offered according to correct liturgical order.[52]

Hildebrand had sown the disorder which afflicted the Church,[53] overthrowing the juridical order which the Roman See had held from its earliest days,[54] and, by trampling the privileges of other churches under foot, loosing the privileges of his primacy.[55] His partisans preached that the sacraments of heretics and schismatics were no more than offal,[56] and, on his counsel, Herman of Metz suspended in his dioceses for more than ten years all episcopal functions, "without which the Church of God cannot exist."[57] In contradicting the Gospel and spurning apostolic doc-

---

[42] *Loc.cit.*
[43] II, 6, *ibid.*, 217: Necessitas autem non habet legem.
[44] II, 23, *ibid.*, 241.     [45] II, 24, 40, *ibid.*, 241f, 269f.
[46] I, 15, *ibid.*, 207.     [47] II, 19, *ibid.*, 236.
[48] II, 30, *ibid.*, 257.     [49] II, 25, *ibid.*, 245.
[50] E.g., III, 23, 24, *ibid.*, 241, 244. The usage is frequent.
[51] II, 15, *ibid.*, 227.
[52] III, 2, *ibid.*, 283. Cf. III, 3, *ibid.*, 284.
[53] I, 1, *ibid.*, 185.     [54] I, 12, *ibid.*, 200.
[55] II, 23, 40, *ibid.*, 241, 269f.     [56] II, 17, *ibid.*, 233.
[57] II, 30, *ibid.*, 257. See also II, 17, *ibid.*, 233.

trine, Gregory ceased even to be a Christian,[58] and withdrew simultaneously from the episcopacy and the body of the Church.[59] His episcopal followers in Germany proved themselves unworthy men and irresponsible bishops by fleeing from their churches and forsaking their rightful obligations.[60] In his administration, Gregory had disregarded divine and human laws and begun to create a palatine court of bishops around them, "and from their face went out so cruel a sentence that they might call bad good and good, bad, preaching that they were blessed who, on Hildebrand's behalf, did robberies, seditions, and murders."[61] Gregory himself ultimately fled from his church.[62]

The author most emphatically asserted that the confusion Gregory precipitated created a state of necessity in which, for the safety of the Church, normal canonical procedure could not be observed. In these circumstances, Wibert was elected pope.[63] Against the objection that, as Archbishop of Ravenna, Wibert could not become pope because the canons forbade translation of bishops, the author argued that the canons allowed translation for reason of necessity or utility, and that, in consideration of utility, St. Peter himself had been translated from Antioch to Rome.[64] The Roman Church and Henry, as *patricius* of the Romans, had jointly elected Wibert to succeed the fugitive Hildebrand,[65] and the author vigorously argued that Urban II's accession had been sheer usurpation, the fruit of ambition and conspiracy among the Saxon bishops.[66]

The author maintained that Gregory's doctrinal error and wrongful administration centered in his decrees against Henry. The Pope professed to hold "the faith of the holy Fathers" (*fidem sanctorum patrum*) in honoring the command of St. Peter to be subject to all higher powers because of God.[67] But, in resisting Henry, Gregory contended against the ordination of God[68] and overthrew the usage and the discipline of the Church.[69] Through this especially, he divided himself from the body of the Church.[70]

The Apostle commanded that the royal power should be honored.

---

[58] II, 15, *ibid.*, 230.    [59] II, 15, *ibid.*, 228.    [60] II, 29, 30, *ibid.*, 253ff.
[61] II, 8, *ibid.*, 219: "*Inde divinis humanisque legibus posthabitis coepit apud eiusmodi episcopos esse palatium atque curia; et a facie eorum egressa est tam crudelis sententia ut dicant malum bonum et bonum malum, praedicantes beatos esse, qui pro parte Hildebrandi faciant praelia, seditiones, et homicidia.*"
[62] *Loc.cit.*    [63] II, 6, *ibid.*, 217.    [64] *Loc.cit.*
[65] II, 7, 21, *ibid.*, 217f, 238.    [66] II, 23, *ibid.*, 240.    [67] II, 3, *ibid.*, 215.
[68] II, 25, *ibid.*, 245.    [69] II, 15, *ibid.*, 226.    [70] II, 15, *ibid.*, 228.

Hildebrand dishonored it[71] by asserting that he held power over kings and over kingdoms, though the Apostles ruled the Church, not the kingdom.[72] Gregory alleged that precedents proved his right to depose Henry; but the author refuted them by careful historical examinations. Gregory had claimed that Pope Zacharias deposed the last of the Merovingians, and that through anointing Pope Stephen raised Pippin to be king of the Franks. The author answered that, though the popes did indeed participate in the events cited, they merely assented to what the Frankish princes had already established by common consent. It was not true that Zacharias had deposed Chilperic and absolved his subjects from their oaths of fealty toward him. Though St. Ambrose barred Theodosius the Great from communion, he intended to achieve no political effect; and bishops had not used excommunication against other emperors even if they were heretical.[73] Indeed, the letters of earlier popes repeatedly emphasized the duality of Church and Empire, and, rather than attesting the power of popes to depose emperors, they proved that popes left wicked rulers to the judgment of God.[74] Gregory paid no heed to Henry's hereditary accession to the kingship,[75] but, through his decrees and the military force he commanded, he divided both Church and commonwealth,[76] and scattered wars throughout the Roman Empire.[77] The example of Saul showed that kings must be honored, despite personal defects; for Saul ruled for many years after the Lord had rejected him.[78] According to the apostolic admonitions to obey kings, charges could not legitimately be entered against rulers, for even that was to struggle against the Lord and His anointed.[79]

The Roman Church's dealings with temporal rulers began with Constantine, who established that the Old Rome should have primacy of apostolic honor and the New, the principate of royal majesty. After the Byzantine emperors became heretics, or defenders of heretics, Rome sought other sons distinguished in nobility and virtue, and chose the peoples of Gaul and Germany to be their sons, and their kings to be emperors and *patricii* of the Roman Church.[80] Thereafter, until Hildebrand's day, popes had honored the duality of Church and Empire, and respected, as beyond their competence, the political processes, such

---

[71] I, 12, *ibid.*, 200.
[72] II, 1, *ibid.*, 212.
[73] I, 2, 3, 8, 16, *ibid.*, 185f, 194f, 208f.
[74] I, 3, *ibid.*, 187f.
[75] Cf. II, 15, *ibid.*, 227.
[76] *Loc.cit.* and *passim.*
[77] II, 2, *ibid.*, 212.
[78] II, 15, *ibid.*, 227.
[79] I, 12, II, 40, *ibid.*, 201, 268.
[80] I, 2, *ibid.*, 185.

as inheritance and war, by which the royal power was transferred.[81] Gregory's actions confused men who owed obedience to the Roman pontiff, because of his see's primacy, and fidelity to the king, because of their solemn oaths. And his release of Henry's subjects from their vows of fealty compounded disorder. The power to bind and to loose concerned only the bonds of sins,[82] and, through his abuse of that power, Gregory rent the unity of the Church.[83] Even after Henry went to Rome to gather the scattered flock of Christ, Gregory refused to receive him as king or even to see him, unless Henry surrendered to him the royal scepter as token of his power, honor, and kingdom; for, like the prince of Tyre, his heart was lifted up, and he said, "I am God, and I sit in the seat of God. There is no power but of God."[84]

The author nowhere explicitly discussed the formal depositions uttered against Gregory by the Synods of Worms or Brixen, or in Rome (1084). To his mind, Gregory's great wrongs had effectively stripped him of his primatial powers, and the urgent necessity to which he had given rise forced the suspension of normal canonical order and the election of Wibert. In very elegant fashion, he argued first, that Gregory's disregard for rightful privileges of other churches and his erroneous belief concerning the sacraments, together with the administrative disorders to which his maladministration led, proved him a faithless pastor, and, second, that, by usurping powers over the royal office, he fought against the disposition of God. On both counts, he set himself outside the orthodox Church by disrupting the charity which united all believers, by casting under foot the universal consensus of all bishops as expressed in the Church's authentic order and laws, and by claiming to dispense the royal power, which only God could grant and withdraw.

This position had radical consequences only when pressed to the extreme. Another author whose work went uncirculated in the Middle Ages showed by implication where the perils lay. That man was the Norman Anonymous, who flourished early in the twelfth century, probably in Rouen, and whose thought survives in thirty-one treatises of varying lengths and themes.[85] Despite obvious differences in purpose and tech-

---

[81] I, 2, 3, ibid., 185ff.  [82] I, 4, ibid., 188f.

[83] I, 5, ibid., 191. Cf. I, 2, 7, 10, ibid., 185f, 193, 198.

[84] II, 7, ibid., 217f; Ezech. 28:2; Rom. 13:1.

[85] On recent scholarly views, including the dispute over the author's identity, see the summary of Nineham, "Anonymous," 31ff; Pellens, "Tracts," 155; Texte: XV, XXXII. We await with interest Dr. Pellens' promised study of the Norman's ecclesiology.

303

nique, the German and the Norman shared views on hierarchic authority.

The Cyprianic emphases on charity as the cohesive element in the Church and on equality among bishops recur in these tracts.[86] The Gregorians claimed that the pope's judgments were unlimited and irreviewable, that, in the words of the Symmachian forgeries, "the supreme pontiff cannot be judged by anyone." The Norman Anonymous, however, held that the pope, as supreme pontiff, could indeed be judged by his successor. Even during his pontificate, he was liable to judgment, not in his official quality, but in his quality as a criminal—for example, as a murderer, an adulterer, or a fornicator.[87] This distinction between the pope as pontiff and as man had wide implications: for the author went on to say that, in any case, obedience was due to the bishop personally, rather than to the church over which he presided.[88]

As for the Roman See, the Norman was concerned to show that Roman primacy did not begin in the Church's earliest days. Christ did not decree it; the Apostles did not sanction it; the 72 Disciples, the Protomartyr Stephen and his companions had nothing to do with it. Indeed, the history of the early Church gave Jerusalem precedence over Rome on many points.[89] It might be true that the decrees of the holy Fathers established Rome as the "mother and mistress of all churches, and her bishop, the chief (*summus*) of all bishops."[90] But "necessity has no law."[91] When the Roman bishop acted as an apostle, he deserved the reverence the canons commanded. If he sought his own glory and did his own will rather than Christ's, there was no need to acknowledge him as an apostle.[92]

Latterly, the bishop of Rome had commanded many things that neither Christ nor the Apostles ordained, solely to indulge his own will and to display his power. As a result, episcopal authority was despised; episcopal power, diminished; the strength of justice, enfeebled; and the

[86] In the following remarks, I am especially indebted to the brilliant analysis by G. H. Williams in *Anonymous*. For the *Anonymous*'s comments on differences in legal procedure and liturgical observance, see J. 9, 11, ed. K. Pellens (Wiesbaden, 1966), 66, 82. On charity, *loc.cit.*, and J. 31, ed. Pellens, 180ff. For parity among bishops, see J. 2, 4, ed. Pellens, 14, 36ff, 38. See also Williams, *Anonymous*, 132ff.

[87] J. 1, ed. Pellens, 5ff.

[88] J. 29, ed. Pellens, 227. But cf. J. 12, ed. Pellens, 90.

[89] J. 4, 12, ed. Pellens, 40f, 84ff.

[90] J. 4, ed. Pellens, 40f.

[91] J. 6, ed. Pellens, 49.

[92] J. 28, ed. Pellens, 214; Williams, *Anonymous*, 137f.

severity of ecclesiastical discipline, broken.[93] There was no need to observe, or even to hear, commands such as these, which ran counter to the ordination of God, the doctrine of the Apostles, and the teaching of earlier saints. The Roman pontiff was not ordained to resist God's ordinance himself and to make others withstand it, to act against the Apostles' doctrine, to overturn the statutes of his own predecessors, and to sow schism and desolation. As evidence of right thinking in St. Peter's chair, the author quoted a series of excerpts from papal decretals on the need to uphold ancient order. The tradition side of the Roman Janus was for him more authoritative than the discretion side. Siricius, Zosimus, Nicholas I, and others were made to speak for tradition and against the powers of discretion they built and exercised.[94]

Recent popes attacked the very basis of right order. They excommunicated bishops, men whom God had anointed and sanctified with His holy oil, and to whom he had given the power to bind and to loose.[95] They imposed new orders of precedence[96] and, contrary to established practice, they compelled bishops to go to Rome at great danger to themselves and to their churches.[97] Thus it was clear that two Roman churches existed, one Christ's, the other Satan's.[98] Popes had departed from the rule of antiquity; they need no longer be obeyed.

This much the German and the Norman had in common. Danger appeared when the Norman took up the theme that rulers could not be resisted and developed it into a thorough-going doctrine of temporal supremacy. He protested against the popes' excommunications of bishops. Yet even graver, to his mind, was their attempt "to remove the royal power from the principate and rule of all churches."[99] His extravagant parallels between royal coronations and episcopal consecrations claiming that the king's unction was "the greater and holier" are well known.[100] The king was the counterpart of Christ; bishops represented the Apostles.[101] The king was priestly, if not a priest; he was "*presul princeps et summus*"; and, in installing bishops, he used the power of God.[102]

---

[93] J. 28, ed. Pellens, 215.

[94] J. 28, ed. Pellens, 215, 219f.

[95] J. 28, ed. Pellens, 221.

[96] J. 4, ed. Pellens, 39.

[97] J. 4, 28, ed. Pellens, 40, 215.

[98] J. 30, ed. Pellens, 230; Williams, *Anonymous*, 139.

[99] J. 28, ed. Pellens, 222.

[100] J. 24 a, ed. Pellens, 141.

[101] J. 24 a, ed. Pellens, 161.

[102] J. 24 a, ed. Pellens, 135. The Norman used the word "*traditio*" occasionally, but not frequently enough to show that the word had any special meaning

In these curious tracts, then, there does appear a concept of regal pontificalism. But, far from being a representative spokesman, the Norman Anonymous had struck out on his own. He took the royalist argument that kings must be obeyed as a religious duty and that lay investiture was right, and he developed it into an eccentric doctrine quite contrary to the dualistic thought stated, for example, in *De unitate ecclesiae conservanda.* Yet standard dualistic thought did contain the potential for his development.

It would be wrong to call this Erastianism, but it is hard to find a term that describes it more exactly. Could kings set aside ancient rules and observances of the Church? What if rulers were heretics or Muslim? Could a council be "universal" if some kings withheld their clergy from it and forbade them to assent to its decrees? If so, would its canons apply to unrepresented and unassenting clergy? The author gave no answers to these questions, nor to other critical issues raised by his views. His thought is incompletely expressed, and perhaps only partially reasoned out.

He certainly seems not to have realized the disintegrative implications of his doctrine for the transmission and interpretation of doctrine. His defense of particularistic forms of discipline and liturgy in the Church and his attack on the centralizing work of the Gregorians were of a piece with his concept of kings as in some sense priests and heads of the priesthoods in their lands. He obviously understood that the church in each kingdom must convey the Church's common religious experience in its own idiom, and under the guidance of its temporal ruler. In his view, charity was strong enough to override the anarchy that must have ensued, and to bind all believers in one body of Christ.

### B. DISSIDENT REFORMERS

On the defensive, the imperialists sought to retrench in their old positions. By contrast, the reformers who contested the Gregorians' concept of papal discretion were on the attack; they meant to gain new ground. In fact, they agreed entirely with the Gregorian goals for reform, and

---

for him. In contesting the Roman bishop's censure against the bishop of Rouen for disobedience, the Norman invoked *"traditio apostolica"* (J. 4, ed. Pellens, 36). Clerical celibacy *"traditio igitur hominis est, non Dei, non apostolorum institutio"* (J. 14, ed. Pellens, 95f. See also p. 205, for a similar reference to *"apostolica traditio"*). His other references to *"traditio"* and *"traditiones"* are in quotations from St. Paul's letters.

some of them sided with the Gregorians against the Empire. At issue was how to rule the new ground once it had been gained. On this point there were many fundamental differences, even between the popes and their partisans; and, for reformers who opposed papal omnicompetence as well as for imperialists, the démodé concept of tradition was charged with meaning.

Though they understood the question of ecclesiastical cohesion in ways similar to that of Gregory VII, their emphases differed greatly. For example, Manegold of Lautenbach considered Gregory the true pope, not only because he had acceded canonically, but also because the general consensus of the whole Church acknowledged him. Gebehard saw, as a body of authority beside papal decrees, the laws which the Church had held from the beginning, which the Fathers had established to last forever, and which had been transmitted by a succession of authentic teachers until Gebehard's own "monstrous times." The two authors agreed entirely with Gregory that lay investiture and the Synod of Brixen jeopardized the cohesion of the Church.[1] But, in their strictly ecclesiological thought, they did not ascribe to Rome the complete legislative flexibility which Gregory claimed. Consensus, antiquity, and universality, the ancient tests of authentic tradition, were also categories of authority, independent of papal government—though in the present case they confirmed the rightfulness of Gregory's cause. These authors were therefore closer in principle, though not in sentiment, to Gregory's enemies than to the Pope himself, and the positions they represented led to conflict among the Gregorians in the time of Paschal II.

Concerning administrative order, Manegold had appealed to consensus, and Gebehard to Church law as transmitted by a long succession of authentic teachers, as normative authorities independent of papal decrees. Other cautious thinkers set general limits to papal discretion explicitly in legislation. Bonizo of Sutri, for example, wrote that the Roman pontiff could not utterly destroy the canons, although he could temper them according to necessity. He equated destruction of the canons with infringing papal decrees and violating decrees of the first

[1] Gebehard to Herman of Metz, cc. 5, 13. MGH Ldl. 1, 265f, 268, 270f; Manegold, Contra Wolfelmum, c. 23; *ibid.*, 306f; Ad Gebehardum, c. 50; *ibid.*, 399.

four oecumenical councils "which men must venerate as the Gospels."[2] Other writers suggest the same view.[3]

Cardinal Deusdedit added a still more explicit limit. Arguing that the Papal Election Decree of 1059 wrongly ascribed powers of electoral review to the German king, Deusdedit concluded that the decree itself was invalid, for three reasons: first, because the German bishops, in repudiating Nicholas II had invalidated his decree; second, because the Germans had themselves violated the decree by intruding Cadalus of Parma and Wibert of Ravenna into the Apostolic See, and because they had so far corrupted the text of the decree that no readings were indisputable; and, finally, because Nicholas, as one patriarch, could not violate or change the canons on episcopal election established by authority of the five patriarchs and of more than 1,250 Fathers. Deusdedit maintained that he intended no disrespect to Nicholas, who, as a man, was liable to reproof. Boniface II retracted and burned his nomination of Vigilius as his successor when the Roman clergy judged it contrary to the canons, Deusdedit was sure that Nicholas would have done the same thing, if he had seen collected the patristic sentences opposing his decree.[4]

Tradition in its historically correct sense appears explicitly in some writings. The letters of Sigebert of Gembloux, Ivo of Chartres, and Godfrey of Vendôme are most instructive examples of this usage.

Sigebert composed a dignified protest when Paschal condemned the people of Liège and Cambrai for supporting Henry IV. Sigebert denounced the Pope's approval of the assaults Count Robert of Flanders had launched against the two churches in support of his decree, and the interdict which Paschal had imposed upon Liège for opposing the measure against Cambrai. His letter begins with a lament that the Church had become Babylon, a city of confusion, through diversity of tongues and opinions among believers. The Church ought to be united by "fraternal unanimity" (*per fraternam unanimitatem*),[5] but Roman commands had disrupted canonical authority by destroying churches, oppressing paupers and widows, promoting vast depredations, and slay-

---

[2] *Lib. ad amic.*, IX, MGH Ldl. 1, 615. Cf. Wido of Ferrara, *De schismate Hildebrandi*, II, MGH Ldl. 1, 552: "*et Romanae ecclesiae salva fide novum aliquid condere semper licuit et licebit.*"

[3] E.g., Urban II, PL 151, 495; Bernald, Apol., cc. 7, 8, MGH Ldl. 2, 67.

[4] *Lib. contr. invas. et symon.* I, 11-13, MGH Ldl. 2, 309ff; Mirbt, *Publizistik*, 555.

[5] C. I., MGH Ldl. 2, 451.

ing alike good and evil.[6] Paschal's measures were "new traditions" (*novae traditiones*)[7] contrary to the "law of God" (*legem Dei*),[8] and to the "ancient Fathers" (*antiquos patres*),[9] whom the people of Cambrai and Liège followed. Paschal spoke with the same "Roman ambition" which led many of his predecessors to deposition or abdication as "pseudo-popes."[10] His enlistment of Robert's military force confused the distinction Christ made between the material and the spiritual swords[11] and continued the work of "Pope Hildebrand," the author of this new schism, who first raised the priestly lance against the diadem of kingship.[12] As for the interdict against the people of Liège, Sigebert argued that God absolved those whom the Roman pontiff unjustly excommunicated.[13] There was no precedent for Paschal's actions, he argued, in all the "ancient expositors." Only Hildebrand had tampered with the sacred canons; Paschal opposed "new authority" to the established order of the Church.[14]

Ivo of Chartres similarly appealed to tradition when he wrote to Hugh of Lyons, a papal legate, defending Daimbert of Sens's refusal to make a formal submission to Hugh as the price for his consecration. Ivo charged that Hugh sought to change, as he wished, what antiquity sanctioned, custom (*consuetudo*) preserved, and the hallowed authority of the venerable Fathers confirmed. He quoted the assertion of Pope Zosimus that the decrees of the Fathers commanded that reverence be shown the antiquity which abided with him; he added words from the papal accession oath, as in the *Liber Diurnus*, to the effect that the pope would intrude no diminution, change, or innovation into the tradition preserved and handed down by his predecessors, but would, on the contrary, observe and venerate all things canonically transmitted. Ivo professed utter amazement that Hugh claimed to renew ancient traditions and customs by what were in fact private laws and new traditions, and he admonished him to return to what antiquity truly established and custom preserved.[15] In another letter, Ivo wrote similarly to Hugh's successor Ioserannus denying that Ioserannus had the power to summon bishops from the province of Sens to his synod. Writing in

---

[6] C. 4., *ibid.*, 454.   [7] Cc. 5, 6, *ibid.*, 456, 458f.   [8] C. 5, *ibid.*, 456.
[9] C. 7, *ibid.*, 459.   [10] C. 8, *ibid.*, 459f.
[11] C. 2, *ibid.*, 452f. Cf. Paschal II to Robert, PL 163, 108.
[12] C. 8, *ibid.*, 460: "*Hildebrandus papa qui auctor est huius novelli scismatis et primus levavit sacerdotalem lanceam contra diadema regni primo indiscrete Heinrico faventes excommunicavit.*"
[13] C. 11, *ibid.*, 462f.   [14] C. 13, *ibid.*, 464.   [15] MGH Ldl. 2, 642ff.

the name of his comprovincials, Ivo professed that they could not obey the summons without transgressing the ancient limits which the Fathers had set. Neither the venerable authority of the Fathers nor antiquity gave Ioscerannus the right to summon bishops outside his province to a synod, unless the Apostolic See commanded it or a special appeal were entered before him concerning provinces other than his. The summons was therefore an "unheard of novelty" and an attempt to alter the ancient rights of churches.[16]

Finally, Godfrey of Vendôme, a member of the Sacred College, condemned on grounds of tradition Paschal II's decree approving lay investiture. Some men claim, he wrote (ca. 1116), that the Roman Church can do whatever it pleases, and that by some dispensation it can even do other than the Scriptures command. But the Roman Church could surely not do what Peter could not do, and, as Paul showed by resisting Peter to his face, Peter could not dissolve the law of the divine Scriptures. Rome, therefore, must use the power to bind and loose not according to its own will, but "according to the tradition of Christ."[17]

Argument from tradition was a convenient defense for men who, like Sigebert and Ivo, opposed the growing centralization of papal government, or, like Godfrey, resisted a pope's abrupt deviation from the policies generally approved by the Sacred College and other clergy of the Roman See. It intrinsically sustained conservative thought against the doctrine of papal centralization and irresponsibility.

Concerning administrative order, there was as critical a division in the reformers' ranks as there was over legislation. The reformers themselves acknowledged or introduced flaws in the Gregorians' monarchic structure; for they rejected absolute identification of pope and papacy.

In any case, there were several checks upon the Gregorians' lofty doctrine of unlimited power. Contemporary thought attributed divine vicariate not only to popes, but to bishops, priests, and kings.[18] For all his powers, the bishop of Rome was forbidden to nominate his suc-

---

[16] *Ibid.*, 649f, 652.

[17] Ep ad Bernarium, *ibid.*, 688: "*secundum Christi traditionem*," repeated in Godfrey's letter to Petrus Leonis, *ibid.*, 696. As he wrote earlier (1111) to Paschal II, the Church lived by faith, chastity, and freedom; lay investiture weakened all three. According to the "traditions of the holy Fathers," lay investiture was a heresy, incompatible with the ancient rules and the continuing vigor of the Church (ep. ad Paschalem, *ibid.*, 682).

[18] Maccaroni, *Vicarius*, 75, 77, 99f.

cessor, a disability not imposed upon his imperial counterpart.[19] The memories of heretical or apostate popes—Marcellinus, Liberius and Felix, Anastasius II and Honorius I—lingered to detract from assertions of doctrinal infallibility.[20] Practical circumstances sometimes forced the Gregorian reformers to modify their claims and to temporize in their most urgent measures.[21] For, as St. Anselm of Canterbury wrote to Paschal II: "It is often necessary for the sake of compromise to withdraw from apostolic and canonical establishments, especially in a kingdom where almost everything is so corrupt and perverse that hardly anything can be done according to ecclesiastical establishments."[22] There were at the same time formal doctrines which entirely repudiated the concept of unlimited papal authority and argued that there were regular, institutional checks upon the power of the bishop of Rome.[23]

The newest of these doctrines came from among the reformers themselves in the College of Cardinals.[24] The full development of this ecclesiology came in the fourteenth century,[25] but its basic elements were present in Gregory VII's last years. In 1058 the cardinals showed their power by repudiating Benedict X as pope;[26] in 1059 the Papal Election Decree made the cardinal bishops principal electors of Roman bishops. Peter Damian referred to the cardinals as men "by whose counsel and

[19] Harnack, "*Christus praesens*," 441, n. 3. But cf. the nomination of Boniface II by Felix IV (530) and of Vigilius by Boniface II (ca. 531). Boniface's clergy forced him to withdraw his cession as uncanonical (Caspar, *Geschichte* 2, 193ff).

[20] Döllinger, *Papst-Fabeln*, 57ff, 126ff, 146ff, 162, 166f; Mirbt, *Publizisttk*, 566ff.

[21] Tellenbach, *Church*, 122ff.

[22] PL 163, 93, no. 74: "*Saepe necesse est aliquid de apostolicis et canonicis statutis pro compensationibus relaxare, maxime in regno in quo fere omnia sic corrupta et perversa sunt ut vix ibi aliquid omnino* [iuxta] *statuta ecclesiastica fieri possit.*"

[23] Even Peter Damian seems occasionally to have modified the Petrine doctrine with a doctrine of apostolic collegiality by saying that what Christ granted to St. Peter, he also conferred upon the other Apostles in common (Serm. 41, PL 144, 723), by affirming that "there was one superiority of judicial power among them [and] the same dignity of order, nor was the authority of power in binding or loosing considered of different sorts" (Serm. 42, PL 144, 726: Una scilicet inter eos excellentia iudiciariae potestatis eadem dignitas ordinis nec diversa in ligando sive solvendo virtutis habetur auctoritas), and by his frequent reference to the "Apostolic Senate" as exercising collective powers, particularly in the Last Judgment. Serm. 16; Serm. 41; Serm. 49; Serm. 57; Serm. 63, PL 144, 584, 722, 726, 777, 827, 864.

[24] Fliche, *Réforme*, 3, 249; Ullmann, *Growth*, 319ff.

[25] Merzbacher, "Wandlungen," 346f.

[26] On the general background, see Krause, *Papstwahldekret.*

311

judgment the state and discipline of the whole catholic church ought to be governed,"[27] and as "the spiritual senators of the universal Church."[28] After 1059 their powers greatly increased.[29] The first major breach between pope and cardinals occurred in 1084, when more than half the College deserted Gregory VII and joined the anti-pope, Clement III.[30] The complaint of the dissidents that Gregory had acted arbitrarily without due consultation with the cardinals, and their assertion that the powers of St. Peter resided not in the pope alone, but in the entire Roman See, made their position clear.[31] The cardinals were the true representatives of the Roman See; their privileges were proof against any pope; indeed, they argued that the pope represented the Roman See only so long as the cardinals supported him, and that he and the whole Church were subject to their judgment.[32] Learning from Gregory's rejection, Urban II and his followers gave the cardinals additional authority in the Roman See.[33] In time, the doctrine of papal government accommodated the claims of the cardinals so far as to allow them, like the pope, to be liturgically acclaimed as the elect of St. Peter,[34] and to share the imperialized symbols of the papacy itself. Despite this accommodation, there remained the doctrine with which the College reproved Eugenius III in 1148: that Eugenius had been raised from private status to the office of universal pope by the "sacred senate of Cardinals," on which, as on hinges, the axis of the universal Church moved; that his office obliged him to consult the Roman curia for the good of all men; and that, following the pattern of synodal deliberation before all patriarchs, particularly those of Alexandria and Antioch, nothing could be permanently decided without the authority of the cardinals.[35]

The reform program itself raised another critical issue, which jeopar-

[27] Epp. I, 20, PL 144, 239.

[28] Opusc. 31, c. 7, PL 145, 540. Cf. epp. I, 20, II, 1, PL 144, 239, 258.

[29] Kuttner, "Cardinalis," 173ff; Sydow, "Untersuchungen," 33ff.

[30] Klewitz, "Entstehung," 137, 167, 175; Krause, *Papstwahldekret*, 55f; Sydow, "Untersuchungen," 23, 36, 38, 51. The situation became still more critical after Gregory's death (Klewitz, "Entstehung," 137, 141f).

[31] Fliche, *Réforme*, 3, 250ff; Lulvès, "Machtbestrebungen," 456; Sydow, "Untersuchungen," 36.

[32] Mirbt, *Publizistik*, 561.

[33] Fliche, *Histoire*, 208f; Sydow, "Untersuchungen," 64; Gossman, *Urban II*, 148.

[34] Kantorowicz, *Laudes*, 127.

[35] Otto of Freising, *Gesta Frederici*, I, 60, MGH SS. in us. sch., 3rd ed., 85f.

dized the very premises of the Roman doctrine: namely, the question of whether personal unsuitability impaired official powers. The reformers posed this question most often concerning unworthy priests or bishops. But it also touched the papacy itself, which even the reformers agreed had been corrupted by simony.

Cardinal Humbert expressed the extreme view that the sacraments performed by a simoniac or uncelibate priest were invalid. A heretic, he wrote, was not a man who simply understood something contrary to true faith, but one who obstinately and unreasonably defended his own understanding.[36] Simoniacs were such men, far worse than the Arians or Eutychians.[37] The sale of control over Church property was the sale of episcopal or priestly powers over the Church,[38] and thus marked the end of the Church's liberty, and of the freedom to follow the dictates of the Holy Spirit as expressed in canonical elections and in the teaching of bishops appointed by the Spirit's free operation.[39]

Humbert insisted that simoniacs did nothing less than sell to the Devil the world for which God gave His only begotten Son, that they became bondsmen of the Devil, the equals of Judas, or worse, "the clergy of the Devil and the Synagogue of Satan, since they refuse to be the clergy and Church of God,"[40] "For just as the mystery of eternal justice and equity, which is Christ, operated then among our ancient Fathers and operates now among catholics, so the mystery of injustice and inequity, which is Antichrist, operates among heretics as though among the sons of disobedience."[41] The Holy Ghost was not enticed or bound by money to obey the will and voices of simoniacs; their sacrilegious offices and execrable consecrations utterly lacked the fullness of the Spirit's powers.[42] If he were a true believer, a layman could under necessity "baptize in remission of sins through the Holy Spirit"; but a

---

[36] Adv. sim., praef. MGH Ldl. 1, 101f. On Humbert's ecclesiology, see the interpretation in Ullmann, *Growth*, 265ff.

[37] Adv. sim. II, 36, MGH Ldl. 1, 185.

[38] Adv. sim., III, 1, MGH Ldl. 1, 198f.

[39] Adv. sim., praef., MGH Ldl. 1, 102. Cf. Tellenbach, *Church*, 16f.

[40] Adv. sim. II, 18, 20, 32, MGH Ldl. 1, 161f, 164, 181. Cf. Adv. sim. II, 46, *ibid.*, 194.

[41] Adv. sim. I, 40, *ibid.*, 189: "*Nam sicut in antiquis patribus nostris tunc operabatur et nunc in catholicis operatur mysterium sempiternae iustitiae et aequitatis quae est Christus; sic et in hereticis tanquam in filiis diffidentiae operatur mysterium iniustitiae et iniquitatis quae est antichristus.*"

[42] Adv. sim. I, 3, *ibid.*, 106.

313

simoniac could not, even if he were called a bishop,[43] and even if he seemed to lead a righteous life.[44]

Peter Damian, however, argued that sacraments were valid, regardless of the priest's personal qualities. With full regard for the high dignity of the priesthood, Peter compared priests with the angels who proclaimed Christ's birth.[45] But in condemning a world where there was "nothing but gluttony, avarice, and lust,"[46] he also condemned with great forthrightness priests, bishops, and even monks who disdained the true simplicity and humility of their professions in favor of carnal desires, luxury, and worldly honors.[47] Still, he maintained that canonical authority prohibited the rebaptism of persons baptized by heretics, lest the name of God, as invoked by the heretical priest, should seem to be invalidated or invoked in vain.[48] God disdained to receive the sacrifices of the impious[49] and showed this by sending fire from heaven to cremate Nadab and Abihu as they stood at the altar.[50] But as for the recipients of the sacraments, Christ, not the priest, worked in the sacred mysteries, and their recipients took them to salvation or damnation, according to their own merits. "That which is given is on all accounts good, although the recipient may be criminous."[51] Such was particularly the case with simoniacs, who became heretical by wrongful dealings, but were orthodox in faith.[52] For, as he observed regarding Caiaphas, unworthy men sometimes received the gift of prophecy; light was sometimes set in the hands of the blind, not so that he could see, but so that he could minister to others.[53]

---

[43] Adv. sim. I, 2, *ibid.*, 105.

[44] Adv. sim. I, 17, *ibid.*, 130.

[45] Epp. VIII, 1, PL 144, 462; cf. Opusc. 25, c. 2, PL 145, 494: *"Nobilem ergo necesse est esse ecclesiae sacerdotem, ut qui minister est Domini erubescat se servum esse peccati."*

[46] Epp. I, 15, PL 144, 231: *"Totus itaque mundus hoc tempore nihil est aliud nisi gula, avaritia, atque libido."*

[47] Epp. I, 15; VII, 7, PL 144, 227, 446. Opusc. 12, cc. 1, 15; Opusc. 13, c. 1; Opusc. 17, praef., c. 3; Opusc. 22, praef., c. 2; PL 145, 251f, 268, 291, 379, 385, 463, 467. Cf. Peter's own requests for endowments, e.g., Epp. VIII, 5, VII, 14, 15; PL 144, 453, 455, 470.

[48] Opusc. 31, c. 3, PL 145, 527f.

[49] *Liber gomorrihanus*, c. 20, PL 145, 181.

[50] Opusc. 18, c. 4, PL 145, 405.

[51] *Liber gratissimus*, c. 6, MGH Ldl. 1, 24: *"Id tamen quod datur omnino bonum est, licet reus sit ille qui accipit."* See also c. 12, *ibid.*, 34.

[52] *Liber Gratissimus*, c. 5, *ibid.*, 23; Opusc. 30, c. 2, PL 145, 526. Cf. Fliche, *Réforme*, 1, 192, 207f, 215.

[53] *Liber gratissimus*, c. 10, MGH Ldl. 1, 30f.

In their decretals, the reformer popes expressed still a third view: that, by the very act of simony or by cohabitation with women, priests and bishops suspended themselves from their offices. Alexander II, for example, declared that men guilty of these offenses must not celebrate divine offices; that, if they persisted in their priestly functions, the people must not hear them;[54] and, finally, that a bishop who knowingly consecrated a simoniac as bishop incurred the sentence of deposition together with the man he had consecrated.[55] The letters of Gregory VII likewise suggest the position that simoniac and Nicolaite clergy, together with bishops who refused to punish them, ceased at the moment of their wrongful act to exercise their priestly functions legitimately. Special trials must be held to judge individual cases, but according to existing canons, deprivation was incurred instantaneously with the crime. By their disobedience to the decrees of the Apostolic See concerning simony and clerical celibacy, bishops lost claims to obedience from the laity. They became, not bishops, but enemies of Christ.[56] Gregory forbade laymen to receive their offices[57] and, in some cases, he urged them to rise up and expel culpable prelates.[58]

This position ignored the question of the validity of sacraments performed by unworthy priests at the same time as it denied simoniacs and Nicolaites any legitimate title to priesthood or episcopate. On the issue of sacramental validity, therefore, it differed both from the thought of Humbert and from that of Peter Damian. But, in the matter of legitimacy, it corresponded with Humbert's argument by holding that wrongful actions of specific kinds nullified title to ecclesiastical office. Like Humbert's view, it argued that official legitimacy was lost when individual men violated approved norms of faith or discipline. Either view, followed to its logical conclusion, jeopardized the Roman claim to unfailing orthodoxy.

Only Peter Damian's argument that the sacraments of heretics were valid, and his silence concerning official legitimacy presented no fundamental challenge to the Roman doctrine. Indeed, Peter included in his *Liber gratissimus* some enlightening comments upon Pope Liberius,

---

[54] PL 146, 1383. Cf. PL 146, 1389.

[55] PL 146, 1289, c. 2.

[56] Reg. IV, 11, MGH Epp. Sel. 2, 310f; Epp. Coll., nos. 9, 10; ed. Jaffé, *Bib. Greg.*, 530, 532.

[57] Epp. Coll., nos. 3, 4, 5, ed. Jaffé, *Bib. Greg.*, 523f, 525f.

[58] Epp. Coll., nos. 40, 41, ed. Jaffé, *Bib. Greg.*, 567, 569. Cf. Pflugk-Hartung, 1, no. 47, 46. See Becker, *Studien*, 83f.

who was a "heretic and an inciter of sedition" (*hereticus et sediciosus*), subscribed to the Arian heresy, and remained an apostate for six years, and upon Pope Vigilius, a "wicked and impious man" (*sceleratus et impius*), who sacrilegiously strove to obtain the Apostolic See before the death of Boniface II, and by treachery to secure the deposition of Silverius and his own accession to the papacy. The ordination and statutes even of these "infamous pontiffs" (*flagitiosi pontifices*) had been acknowledged; for "the Holy Spirit is given through him who manifestly does not have [the Spirit]."[59] Recalling that St. Paul withstood St. Peter to his face,[60] Peter Damian reproved Victor II, whose negligence in executing the law had driven Christ from the papal courts.[61] He blamed Clement II for failing to spread ecclesiastical reform abroad.[62] He censured Alexander II, who had purloined a book from him, indulged too much in frivolities, and perpetrated legal abuse.[63] Like St. Peter, popes were rightly open to censure by the people,[64] and Peter Damian also recalled that the Prince of the Apostles, being fond of balsam, cursed a pope who had sold a balsam-producing property which the Roman Church owned in the region of Babylon.[65] Peter Damian knew that heresy, misdemeanor, and irresponsibility had all deflected individual popes from true belief or practice. Such defects did not impair their official powers.[66] No matter how reprehensible their lives, kings and bishops were still called "gods" and "christs" because of their respective offices.[67] If a pope were duly called to the papacy by the cardinal bishops, elected by the lower clergy, and approved by the people "not at the ends of the earth, but within the walls of the Romans and in the bosom of the Apostolic See itself," his establishments and his sacramental functions were valid, however profound his personal iniquities.[68] Otherwise,

[59] *Liber gratissimus*, c. 16, MGH Ldl. 1, 38f: "*Spiritus enim sanctus per eum datur a quo procul dubio non habetur.*"
[60] Opusc. 46, cc. 5, 6, PL 145, 708ff; epp. 1, 12, PL 144, 217.
[61] Epp. I, 5, PL 144, 210.
[62] Epp. I, 3, PL 144, 207f.
[63] Epp. I, 12; II, 6; Vita Ss. Rodulphi et Dominici, prolog. PL 144, 214ff, 270, 1009; Blum, "Monitor," 463ff, 472f.
[64] Epp. I, 12, PL 144, 215ff.
[65] Epp. I, 20, PL 144, 243.
[66] Ullmann, "Pontifex," 238.
[67] *Liber gratissimus*, c. 10, MGH Ldl. 1, 31.
[68] Epp. I, 20, PL 144, 238f, 243; Discept. synodal., MGH Ldl. 1, 91: "*Quis ergo istorum iusto videbitur examine preferendus, utrum is, quem elegit unus vir perpetuae maledictionis anathemate condemnatus an ille potius quem cardi-*

he might wear the mitre and the purple cape as empty symbols of his own perversity.[69]

Even though they held in general the doctrine that personal unsuitability impaired official powers, other writers concurred in the special case of the Apostolic See with Peter Damian's thought that the sins of individual popes did not vitiate their sacramental and legal acts. Leo IX, one of whose first acts as pope, at the Roman Synod of 1049, was to deny priestly functions to Nicolaites and simoniacs, covered the sins of his predecessors as well as his own shortcomings when he wrote that he was the same as Peter in office, but unlike him in merit.[70]

Not all thinkers were convinced by this distinction, and much of the Investiture Controversy turned on the questions of whether an unworthy pope actually conveyed the means of salvation, and whether the Gregorians might have exceeded the papacy's rightful powers in their adaptations of law and order.

---

*nales episcopi unanimiter vocaverunt, quem clerus elegit, quem populus expetivit, non in extremitate terrarum, sed intra moenia Romanorum et in ipsius sedis apostolicae gremio?"*

[69] Epp. I, 20, PL 144, 242.

[70] PL 143, 766, c. 35: *"Qua de re, fratres utinam non ad iudicium nostrum dicamus, profecto sumus qualis Petrus et non sumus qualis Petrus, quia idem sumus officio et non idem merito."*

CHAPTER 13

# Conflict Among the Reformers

THE reformers were divided into two camps. There were some for whom Rome's ecclesiological Janus was dead. They understood that unlimited papal discretion, incarnate in the bishop of Rome, moderated the Church's law and order according to the changing times. For the others, the Janus complex survived. They distinguished between pope and papacy, and considered other standards—all subsumed under the name "tradition"—superior to papal decrees. These two schools agreed on many fundamental points, but the crises of the age focused on the Chair of St. Peter; the profound disagreement between the schools could not be suppressed. Three conflicts in particular brought voices of dissent into the open: the Investiture Conflict itself, and two other controversies to which it gave rise, the Privilegium Dispute and the contested papal election of 1130.

## A. THE ISSUE OF A HERETICAL POPE: THE SCHISM OF 1084

Thus far, we have considered the anti-Gregorian position as stated by imperialist writers. Between 1084 and the end of the eleventh century, another body of anti-Gregorians produced several short treatises stating a radically new doctrine of Church government, in which the principal question was neither the relation of the spiritual to the temporal power, nor the relative powers of pope and bishop, but the proper mode of government in the Roman Church itself.[1] The authors of these treatises were the schismatic cardinals who repudiated Gregory in 1084.[2]

The defense of Henry IV which the cardinals offered was only incidental to their principal argument. It was little more than a gesture of diplomatic courtesy to the ruler with whom they had made common cause against Gregory, but from whose ideological position their own greatly differed. They were not so much pro-Henry as anti-Gregory. The bishops at Worms and Brixen, and the author of *De unitate ec-*

---

[1] Fliche, *Réforme* 3, 249.
[2] See Klewitz, "Entstehung," 137, 167, 175; Krause, *Papstwahldekret*, 55f.

*clesiae conservanda* vehemently protested against the centralization of ecclesiastical order which Gregory strove to achieve. The schismatic cardinals insisted that the program of centralization be continued and even extended; their objection was not that Gregory had suppressed the canonical privileges of other bishops, but that he had excluded the lesser cardinal clergy from full participation in governing the monarchic order he wished to erect.

From the beginning of his pontificate, Gregory encountered bitter opposition in Rome.[3] In 1083, Henry found the Romans prepared and even eager to repudiate Gregory.[4] It was in a sense natural that this animosity found foothold among the cardinal clergy, especially among the cardinal priests and deacons, who, despite their majority in the Sacred College, did not participate fully in the affairs of the Roman See.[5] Cardinal Beno stated their points of contention in two letters written in 1084 and 1089. In the earlier letter, Beno wrote that Gregory had excommunicated Henry without synodal hearing, in utter disregard of the canons. No cardinal subscribed his decree, and when Gregory rose from his seat to declare the sentence, God's displeasure splintered the beams of the chair. This was a sign, Beno wrote, that the tenant of the chair would, by his dangerous and presumptuous excommunication, scatter terrible schisms against the Church of Christ and the See of Peter, and cruelly overthrow the seat of Christ by trampling underfoot the laws of the Church. He rent the unity of the Church and created two churches.[6] Gregory had also plotted Henry's assassination,[7] and thus given one more example of his unbridled bloodlust.[8] The blood of the Church cried out against him; the Church most justly withdrew from his

[3] Cf. *Liber Pontificalis, Vita Gregorii VII*, ed. Duchesne, 2, 282; Gregory VII, Epp. coll. no. 18, ed. Jaffé, *Bib. Greg.*, 544; Lerner, "Hugo," 49, 55f.

[4] Sigebert of Gembloux, Chron. (a. 1083), Ekkehard Chron. (a. 1083), MGH SS. 6, 364, 205.

[5] On the complaints of the cardinals, see Fliche, *Réforme* 3, 250ff; Lulvès, "Machtbestrebungen," 456; Mirbt, *Publizistik*, 561. Profiting from the unhappy example of his predecessor, Urban II strove to reconcile the estranged clergy and to strengthen his ties with loyal cardinals by acknowledging that the cardinals had special powers during vacancies of the Roman See and, under normal circumstances, very considerable consultative powers in Church administration (Fliche, *Réforme* 3, 208f; Sydow, "Untersuchungen," 38; Becker, *Urban* II). The schismatic cardinals fully accepted Gregory's program of reform, and his rejection of sacraments performed by simoniacs or Nicolaites (Mirbt, *Publizistik*, 385f).

[6] Ep. I, c. 3, MGH Ldl. 2, 370.

[7] Ep. I, c. 5, *ibid.*, 371.

[8] Cf. ep. I, c. 8, *ibid.*, 372f.

communion, as, in the persons of Roman clergy, it had withdrawn from the "apostates" Anastasius II and Liberius, the latter of whom Gregory followed in heresy by celebrating a feast day in his honor.[9] Gregory had been elected by laymen, contrary to the canons; the cardinals did not subscribe to his election. Under threat of anathema, they had commanded that no one should be elected pope before the third day after the dead pope had been buried. Alexander II's body was hardly cold before Gregory was elected, and after he acceded, he remembered the cardinals' affront by removing them from the counsel of the Holy See, even though the canons required that three cardinal priests and two deacons always be with the pope as witnesses.[10] He violently distorted the Scriptures to serve falsehood, thus falling into idolatry.[11] And, at Eastertide, 1080, he revealed his sinful divinations and simultaneously deposed himself by prophesying that by the next feast of St. Peter Henry would either be dead or so utterly deposed that he could muster no more than six soldiers, and by adding that, if this did not come to pass, the bishops, cardinals, and all who heard him should no longer consider him pope, but drag him from the altar. God, however, preserved the emperor, and thus, by his own words, Hildebrand stood condemned.[12]

In his second letter, Beno repeated with considerable elaboration his point that the cardinals had rightly abandoned Gregory as heretical. The cardinals were the "venerable Fathers of the Roman Church,"[13] and they had preserved their church from error throughout history. They had withdrawn from Liberius and Anastasius II;[14] they had risen up against the necromancy, conspiracy, and gross immorality of popes;[15] they had initiated reform by electing Leo IX.[16] Again, when Hildebrand and Urban II lapsed into the heresy of Liberius, presuming to set aside the decrees of Chalcedon concerning baptism by heretics, the "Fathers of the Roman Church" had withdrawn from their communion and cursed their heresies and their abuse of the power to bind and loose.[17] Beno described in considerably more detail than in his earlier letter the circumstances which blemished Gregory's election: that he had made com-

---

[9] Ep. I, cc. 1, 9, *ibid.*, 369, 373. See Klewitz, "Krönung," 123.

[10] Ep. I, c. 2; Ep. II, 12, c. 2, *ibid.*, 370, 380.

[11] Ep. I, c. 2, *ibid.*

[12] Ep. I, c. 7, *ibid.*, 371. The same prophecy is mentioned by Bonizo of Sutri in *Liber ad Amicum*, c. 9, MGH Ldl. 1, 616f.

[13] Ep. II, *ibid.*, 373: "*venerandis aeclesiae Romanae patribus.*"

[14] Ep. II, c. 2, *ibid.*, 375f.          [15] Ep. II, cc. 4-8, *ibid.*, 376ff.

[16] Ep. II, cc. 8, I, *ibid.*, 378f.          [17] Ep. II, c. 2, *ibid.*, 375f.

mon cause with the Jews, that he had plotted the murders of six popes in the space of thirteen years and the forcible ejection of Benedict X,[18] that he had perjured himself by forswearing the papacy and later grasping it uncanonically by military force, and that the cardinals declined to subscribe to his election.[19] Perversity, duplicity, and satanic divinations marked his pontificate,[20] and yet the common people called him "holy." But thirteen "wiser and more religious cardinals" (*cardinales sapientiores et religiosiores*) together with many other clergy from the Lateran, perceived his heresy. They knew that, by his own words, he had deposed himself. They judged his apostasy intolerable, and withdrew from his communion.[21]

Between 1076 (?) and 1089, the schismatic cardinals issued a series of three tractates. The special interest of these essays lies, first, in their comments upon the proper relation of the Church to temporal government, and, second, in the limits they prescribed for papal authority. In terms very like those used in *De unitate ecclesiae conservanda*, the cardinals judged that Gregory abused his powers in excommunicating Henry, and that he grossly exceeded them in absolving Henry's subjects of their oaths.[22] By textual analysis, the cardinals showed that Gregory had created precedents for his actions by taking out of context and distorting the sense of a decree of Gregory the Great, by drawing false inferences from St. Ambrose's excluding Theodosius from communion, and by other dishonest representations. Gregory the Great had, in any case, spoken of a "provincial king," not of an emperor; Ambrose had not presumed to make any declaration concerning the Empire or tribute, and, in dealing with the Arian Valentinian, he had imposed no sanctions at all. Jesus commanded, concerning pagan rulers, that what was Caesar's should be rendered to Caesar, and, even in the days of Arian emperors, the Roman church had never denied that "Caesar's right" (*ius Caesaris*) should be satisfied. Gregory was right in arguing by precedent that Ambrose excommunciated Theodosius, but wrong in his further deductions.[23] And, in his violation of the greater precedents of Christ and St. Peter, who rendered tribute and honor to Caesar, he became a member of Antichrist, or even Antichrist himself.[24]

The power to bind and to loose must be exercised "according to

---

[18] Ep. II, c. 9, *ibid.*, 379f.
[20] Ep. II, cc. 1, 3, 7, *ibid.*, 373, 376, 378.
[22] Mirbt, *Publizistik*, 217f, 229.
[24] Ep. III, c. 4, *ibid.*, 383.

[19] Ep. II, cc. 11, 12, *ibid.*, 380.
[21] Ep. II, c. 2, *ibid.*, 374f.
[23] Ep. III, c. 9, *ibid.*, 391f.

the rules of the Church" (*ex regulis ecclesiae*), and Gregory had fallen into heresy and idolatry by distorting the precepts of the law to suit himself.[25] The cardinals argued against the Gregorian position that, once duly elected and consecrated, the pope was "holy." They referred to the examples of Anastasius II and Liberius who had been canonically elected, but whom God and the Church subsequently condemned for their errors.[26] Hildebrand had violated the Nicene canons, by admitting as Henry's accusers persons whom those canons barred, by allowing the accusation to be entered in Henry's absence, and by excommunicating the King though he had not confessed his wrong voluntarily nor had he been legally convicted. Gregory was thus "dubious in the faith and almost an infidel" especially as he revived the erroneous decree of Anastasius II concerning baptism performed by heretics, for which the Roman Church had condemned, and divine wrath killed, Anastasius.[27] Hildebrand had claimed to be the Apostolic See,[28] but day after day revealed his iniquity in claiming to judge secular things as well as spiritual, in renewing Anastasius's decree,[29] and in utterly disregarding the canons. Since he had fallen irrevocably into error, the "Fathers of the Roman Church" rightly abandoned him.[30]

Aside from these programmatic statements by Beno and his colleagues, the schismatic cardinals produced several other letters in 1098, largely restating their earlier position. Of these, the most instructive are two letters by the Cardinal Hugh, one to Cardinal Hugh Candidus, and another to the Countess Mathilda. Hugh rehearsed the apostasies of Liberius and Anastasius, and observed that the cardinals could in such cases condemn popes, since the privilege of Peter belonged to the whole Roman See, not just to the pope alone.[31] Indeed, public declarations of the supreme pontiff were invalid without the subscription of the cardinals.[32] Cardinal Hugh also commented on the special circumstances in the case of Pope Marcellinus, observing that the synod which heard Marcellinus's case declined to judge him before he had condemned himself and subscribed to his own condemnation, "since the first see will not be judged by anyone," and especially since three cardi-

[25] Ep. III, c. 11, *ibid.*, 394.　　[26] Ep. III, c. 15, *ibid.*, 400.

[27] Ep. III, cc. 10, 13, *ibid.*, 393, 398f.　　[28] Ep. III, c. 12, *ibid.*, 396.

[29] *Loc.cit.*: "*A patribus sanctae sedis derelictum, sedem apostolicam esse reputasti cum iam non solum spiritualia, sed etiam secularia a te non possent iudicari.*"

[30] Ep. III, cc. 10, 12, *ibid.*, 393f, 396.

[31] Epp. IV, X, *ibid.*, 404f, 418f.

[32] Ep. X, *ibid.*, 418.

nal priests and two deacons, Marcellinus's official companions, were implicated in his fall.[33] Canonical election by no means made a pope "holy"; for Marcellinus, Liberius, and Anastasius had all been canonically elected and later deposed for their errors.[34] He vigorously repudiated Urban II as an inventor of new heresies and a reviver of ancient error,[35] who, with irrevocable hardness of heart, had shaken the foundations of the faith and opposed new laws to divine laws, and turned the privilege of apostolic power into abuse.[36] The Roman Church had synodically condemned Urban's errors and, by the judgment of the Holy Ghost, withdrawn from his communion.[37]

+

The reconstitution of papal government by the reformers culminated three centuries' search for a basis of ecclesiastical cohesion in patterns of hierarchic order. This was particularly true in the erection of the Sacred College as a coordinate of the Roman bishops in administrative affairs. But the conflict between Gregory VII and the schismatic cardinals showed that, even among thinkers who agreed that the chief cohesive element in the Church was the administrative powers of the Roman See, points of dispute arose concerning the order of that supreme government. The questions of the relationship between ecclesiastical and temporal offices did not greatly concern the schismatic cardinals. They were content to affirm the conventional concept of duality. Their primary concern was with the structure of government within the Roman Church, and, distinguishing between pope and papacy, they advanced their doctrine that the special powers of St. Peter belonged to the Roman See, and particularly to the cardinals, and that popes were responsible for their actions to the Sacred College.

Gregory's actions and his enemies' responses left open one supreme question: Could the successor of St. Peter in office cease to be the successor of the Apostle in faith? The Saxons reproached Gregory with the charge that, in his vacillation between Henry and Rudolf, the throne of Peter had lost the constancy of Peter. The royalists considered him heretical in denying the validity of sacraments performed by heretical priests, in forbidding Nicolaitism, and in his teaching on the Eucharist. They judged that he had overturned the canonical order in the Church

---

[33] *Loc.cit.*      [34] Ep. X, *ibid.*, 420.      [35] Ep. VIII, *ibid.*, 411.
[36] Ep. VIII, c. 3; Ep. X, *ibid.*, 410f, 417f, 420f.
[37] Ep. XI, *ibid.*, 420f.

and interrupted the performance of sacraments, the sign and seal of the Church's unity. The schismatic cardinals withdrew from him because of his alleged heresy, gross immorality, and schismatic actions concerning Church order. To his enemies, Gregory was a simoniac, schismatic, heretic, necromancer, murderer. Finally, there was the charge that his accession had been uncanonical, and that his actions were consequently invalid, and his assertions, sheer pretense. The dispute had posed the great problem of whether a pope might, by wrongful teaching, suspend his powers or even lose them. Was there a criterion of law and justice apart from, and higher than, the discretion of a pope? To ask this question was to strike at the very basis of the Gregorian equivalence between pope and papacy, the view that only Rome, through the pope, could communicate the means of salvation. The controversy had laid the authenticity of papal action and of the papal title itself open to debate. In the forty years after the death of Urban II, these issues were the crux of the dispute.

### B. AUTHENTICITY OF PAPAL ACTS: THE PRIVILEGIUM DISPUTE

Directly or by implication, the great schisms of the late eleventh century uniformly raised the issue of papal responsibility and the proper limits of papal power. From the accession of Paschal II until the end of the Gregorian reform movement, the Investiture Controversy as a whole tended to center upon the premise which the schismatic cardinals shared with "national" churches: that even in the hierarchic grouping the pope's powers were limited by a standard of authority higher than papal discretion. All thinkers could accept the limit which Paschal II described when he wrote that the power to bind and loose passed from St. Peter to all "who preside justly in his see and strive to dispose the Church of God by canonical order."[1] But there were vast differences in judgment as to whether the successors of St. Peter might not themselves decide what was just and within canonical order; whether there were offices capable of certifying a pope's actions as licit or not, and of correcting his wrongful acts; and whether illicit government deprived a Roman bishop of his official powers. Above all, there was the limit

---

[1] PL 163, 39, 40f: "*Quam potestatis suae successionem ipse beato Clementi et per eum omnibus transfudit qui eius sedi iuste praesidere et ecclesiam Dei canonica studuerint ordinatione disponere.*" On changes in the papal reform program in the early twelfth century, see Cantor, *Church*, 309ff.

of secular power to which John of Salisbury alluded when he wrote that
Henry II of England boasted of having gained the same powers which
Henry I had held, "being, in his land, king, apostolic legate, patriarch,
emperor, and everything he wished."[2] These questions of cohesion within the hierarchic grouping had arisen even in the early days of Gregorian
reform; they recurred throughout the Investiture Controversy and received pragmatic answers as the Controversy closed.[3]

+

From the beginning of his pontificate, Paschal[4] strongly upheld the
decrees of Gregory VII and Urban II against lay investiture. He "renewed" the decrees of the Fathers against it, "the root of simoniac
madness."[5] Before the Settlement of Bec, he wrote a series of letters to
Henry I of England strongly rejecting Henry's request that he confirm
that practice which Paschal denounced as the result of tyrannical usurpation by kings.[6] Paschal assured the King that to reject lay investiture
was not to detract from royal powers or prerogative, but merely to
uphold the divine right of Him who said, "I am the door."[7] At the same
time, he vigorously encouraged Anselm of Canterbury in opposing Henry's defense of practices "alien to the Church and forbidden by the holy
canons."[8] He likewise prosecuted the struggle against Henry IV with
great vigor: the Emperor was "the head of heretics," who set up an
idol of Simon Magus in the Holy Place and whom the Apostles and
their vicars had expelled from the Church.[9] As in his English correspondence, Paschal affirmed that he wished to honor the rights which
kings properly held and not to diminish them in any way. "But what
does the episcopal staff or the sacerdotal ring have to do with a warrior?
Let [kings] have their eminence in the Church by being the Church's
defenders and enjoying the support of the Church. Let kings have what
belongs to kings; let bishops have what belongs to bishops. Let them

---

[2] Ep. 239, PL 199, 271: *"qui in terra sua erat rex, legatus apostolicus, patri-
archa, imperator et omnia quae volebat."*

[3] Fliche, *Histoire*, 339ff.

[4] For a comparison of Paschal's policies with those of Gregory VII, see Becker,
*Studien*, 28.

[5] PL 163, 91.                [6] PL 163, 70f, 94.                [7] PL 163, 119f.

[8] PL 163, 106, 91f, 154. Cf. Paschal's letters to French clergy on the buying
and selling of Church offices (PL 163, 100, 436).

[9] PL 163, 108.

325

thus keep peace between them and be venerated together in the one body of Christ."[10]

After the death of Henry IV, Paschal renewed the decree against lay investiture in the synod of Guastalla; then, on the invitation of Henry V, he agreed to go to Germany. Uncertain of his reception there, Paschal went instead to Chalons, where he held an inconclusive conference with Henry V's envoys, and thence to Troyes, where he held a synod in which he repeated the prohibition.[11] It was then agreed that Henry V would attend a general council which Paschal proposed to convene in Rome the next year to judge the whole issue. This plan came to nothing, but negotiations between Paschal and Henry continued. In 1110, Henry set out for Italy.

Two years earlier, Anselm of Canterbury had been scandalized by reports that in his negotiations Paschal inclined to countenance lay investiture by the German king.[12] The results of the negotiations in 1111-1112 more than justified these apprehensions. Before Henry arrived in Rome, Paschal sent representatives to him promising to perform the imperial coronation and to surrender all regalia—cities, duchies, counties, the rights to collect tolls and strike coins, supervision of markets, and the like—which kings had granted to the Church, if Henry, in return, would assure the Church's liberty by renouncing lay investiture. Henry agreed, on condition that this undertaking be ratified by the assent of the whole Church and of his princes.[13] Formal promises were exchanged to this effect.[14] Henry then advanced to Rome. The two surviving accounts of what followed there do not agree. An encyclical letter composed later to vindicate Henry's actions alleges that at the gates of St. Peter's Henry professed his benevolent intentions toward the Church and asked Paschal to discharge his promise. When the Pope proclaimed his undertaking, all bishops, abbots, and sons of the Church resisted him to his face, denouncing the decree as manifest heresy.[15] The subsequent portion of the encyclical is lost. Another ac-

---

[10] PL 163, 175: "*Quid enim ad militem baculus episcopalis, quid annulus sacerdotalis? Habeant in ecclesia primatum suum, ut sint ecclesiae defensores, et ecclesiae subsidiis perfruantur. Habeant reges quod regum est; quod sacerdotum est, habeant sacerdotes. Sic pacem invicem teneant, et se invicem in uno Christi corpore venerentur.*"

[11] See PL 163, 215.

[12] PL 163, 246.

[13] Ekkehard, Chron. (a. 1111), MGH SS. 6, 244.

[14] MGH Const. 1, nos. 83-88, 137ff.

[15] MGH Const. 1, no. 100, 151.

count, composed by an eyewitness among Paschal's followers, reports that Pope and King entered St. Peter's, that Paschal asked Henry to execute his promise, and that Henry withdrew for consultation with his bishops and princes. A stalemate ensued when the German bishops denied that the agreement could be enacted, and Paschal insisted that the evils of lay investiture and simony had come about through the wrongful involvement of bishops in temporal affairs.[16] After protracted discussions, Henry placed Paschal and his entourage under custody and, when the Romans attacked the German forces the next day, Henry withdrew with the captives to a camp outside the city. Casting aside the previous agreement, Henry pressed Paschal to acknowledge the right of lay investiture. At the same time, the King specified that investiture by laymen in no way concerned churches or spiritual powers of bishops, but only the regalia. On this understanding and under great duress, Paschal acceded to Henry's demands, protesting that in order to guarantee the freedom of the Church, he was forced to permit a settlement to which he would never have consented in order to save his own life.[17]

By the privilege then issued, Paschal declared that bishops and abbots must be elected freely without simony or violence, and with the king's assent. Investiture by the king with ring and staff must follow; episcopal consecration could not be performed without prior investiture, even if a man had been elected by clergy and people. This arrangement was just, Paschal declared, because his predecessors (Hadrian I and Leo III) had granted the right of investiture to Henry's predecessors, and because the security of the kingdom depended upon the cession of regalia to bishops and abbots. He cursed violators of his decree with the anathema and with a threat of deposition, and invoked divine mercy upon those who obeyed it.[18]

This reversal of the policy for which Gregory VII, Urban II, and Paschal himself had bitterly fought, this acceptance of the practice which represented for the reformers the complex of abuses they sought to eradicate, brought the severest opprobrium upon Paschal. Paschal himself condemned the privilege almost immediately after his release from Henry's camp.[19] The controversy which Paschal's Privilegium

---

[16] MGH Const. 1, no. 99, 148f.

[17] *Ibid.*, 149.

[18] MGH Const. 1, no. 96, 144f.

[19] See also his letter to the Spanish clergy (1115), PL 163, 385.

aroused among the reformers showed that, obscured but not suppressed by the doctrine of papal omnicompetence, was the doctrine that popes could err, and that there was an authority higher than the papal discretion by which the validity of papal decrees must be gauged. We have seen that Godfrey of Vendôme called that authority "tradition." Other thinkers described it in legal or institutional terms,[20] invoking principles related to those of later canonists, who argued that consent by the community of the faithful was necessary validation of papal decrees.

Paschal himself rejected the decree on the ground that it departed from the judgment of earlier popes. Subsequently, in negotiations with Henry I of England, he offered a settlement "contrary to the authority of the Apostolic See" in the hope that Henry would be persuaded thereby to render satisfaction to the Roman Church.[21] He may well have acted in the same hope early in 1111, but the defiant and bitter reproaches he encountered both from distant bishops and from those around him forced him to withdraw the Privilegium so as to spare the Church even graver confusion.[22] In a letter to the cardinals written soon after his release, Paschal protested that their censure of him exceeded their canonical powers; it had proceeded, he wrote, from envy rather than from charity. He promised to correct what he had done to end the devastation of the city and the surrounding province, and he admonished the cardinals thenceforth to act "for the Church, in the Church."[23] In another letter, written to Guido of Vienne, he explicitly nullified the Privilegium, and cursed it with eternal damnation. He forbade, condemned, established, and confirmed what the "Canons of the Apostles, the Antiochene, and the universal councils" and his predecessors, especially Gregory VII and Urban II, had forbidden, condemned, established or confirmed, and he promised to observe their sanctions.[24]

Such admonitions and professions were insufficient. Paschal's action had precipitated a dispute among the reformers which a recent study has described as a breach "between the two wings of the reform movement, sacerdotalists and ascetics," of which the latter approved Paschal's cession.[25] Accordingly, the Lateran Synod of 1112 convened, and after hearing Paschal profess his adherence to the decrees of Gregory VII

[20] Luca, "L'Accetazione," 193ff.
[21] PL 163, 377: "*quamvis contra auctoritatem sedis apostolicae satisfecimus sperantes et vos deinceps sedi apostolicae in suae dignitatis iustitia satisfacturos.*"
[22] PL 163, 291.   [23] PL 163, 290f.   [24] PL 163, 292.
[25] White, "Gregorian Ideals," 328, 333f; White, "Pontius," 200.

and Urban II, "by judgment of the Holy Spirit," condemned and nullified the Privilegium.[26] On his own authority and with the support of Louis VI, Guido of Vienne held a synod in his see which declared lay investiture heretical, excommunicated Henry V (an action not taken at the Lateran Synod), and exhorted Paschal to confirm these actions on pain of losing the obedience of the Synod's members.[27] Paschal confirmed the Vienne decrees and, at another Lateran Synod in 1116, he repeated the sentences of 1112.

Intimidation by the cardinals, reminiscent of Gregory VII's pontificate, Paschal's condemnation of the Privilegium, the separate condemnation by the Lateran Synod in 1112, and the action and threat of the Synod of Vienne all expressed institutional modes of recourse against papal judgments. The intellectual warrants for some of these actions were stated in six principal works, composed in 1111-1112, before the Privilegium had been synodically condemned.

Two of these works issued from the Sacred College. The earlier of them was the letter of Godfrey of Vendôme to Paschal, which invoked tradition as authoritative. Godfrey distinguished sharply between the See of St. Peter, which had never erred in the faith, and the man holding the see, who might by wrongful acts deprive himself of participation in the beatitude of Sts. Peter and Paul, and who might also, "like another Peter," penitently correct his error. Paschal needed such repentance for, by the Privilegium, he had become no pastor, but a ravening wolf among the flocks, "a prophet corrupted by Satan." The Psalmist spoke of him, saying, "The words of his mouth are iniquity and guile,"[28] and Godfrey refused to follow Paschal or to close his eyes to the Pope's "impiety."[29] In 1111-1112, some cardinals issued a defense of Paschal which, though more moderate in tone than Godfrey's letter, has much in common with it.[30] The treatise was composed in answer to "some foolish and schismatic men, or rather heretics," who maintained that Paschal could no longer be considered pope because he had first granted the right of investiture to Henry, and then excommunicated the King.[31] The cardinals contended that kings who did evil or were

---

[26] Mansi 21, 51; MGH Const. 1, no. 399, 570ff. See Fliche, *Histoire*, 370; McKeon, "Council," 3ff and esp. 10f which shows that Paschal's reversal was due in large part to the political enterprise of Louis VI, who feared the potential alliance of Empire and Papacy represented by the Privilegium.

[27] Mansi 21, 75f.    [28] Ps. 36, 3.    [29] MGH Ldl. 2, 680-83.

[30] On the power of the cardinals at this time, Sydow, "Untersuchungen," 64.

[31] Defensio Paschalis Papae, MGH Ldl. 2, 659f.

"unprofitable" (*inutiles*) must be excommunicated, urged to repent,[32] that Henry deserved excommunication because of the fraud and coercion with which he had extorted the Privilegium, that, at any rate, lay investiture was forbidden by the Scriptures and the Fathers, and that it manifestly transgressed the boundary between temporal and spiritual government.[33] The cardinals contended that Paschal made the disputed cession under great duress,[34] and that it was in any case invalid, since it ran counter to the canons, to the decrees of the Fathers, and to the universal councils.[35] But Paschal had given joy to the sons of the Church by repenting of his wrongful act and condemning the Privilegium, as Pope Marcellinus, having sacrificed under persecution to false gods, repented and won the crown of martyrdom.[36]

The four remaining works likewise emphasize Paschal's departure from the canons. Hildebert of Le Mans lamented that the "seat of sanctity" (*cathedra sanctitatis*) had been laid waste, that unclean canons had polluted the Church, and that the "crude barbarity of the Germans" had slain and enslaved ministers of the divine law. At the same time, he rejoiced that Paschal had been worthy to imitate the sufferings of the Apostles,[37] and he strongly rejected the proposal that a synod sit to judge whether Paschal's act should stand or be voided, or whether the Pope himself should remain in his see or be sent into exile. "The universal bishop," he wrote, "has the power to review the laws and rights of all men."[38] Hildebert seems to have contemplated the sort of self-correction for which Bruno of Segni explicitly called in his letter to Paschal. Bruno declared that, though he loved Paschal, he loved Jesus more, and that consequently he had to denounce the Privilegium. Paschal had broken his own earlier decree, which accorded with the canons and the establishments of the Fathers from the age of the Apostles until his own day: the faith had been violated; the Church had lost its freedom; the priesthood had been despoiled. Bruno condemned as heretics men who ran counter to the faith and teaching of the orthodox Church. He admonished Paschal to condemn once more what he had earlier condemned as heretical, and to restore to the Church the freedom of which his Privilegium had deprived it.[39]

---

[32] *Ibid.*, 665.  [33] *Ibid.*, 660, 663f.  [34] *Ibid.*, 660f.
[35] *Ibid.*, 661.  [36] *Ibid.*, 664f.

[37] Lamentatio pro captione papae Paschalis, *ibid.*, 668.

[38] Dispensatio Papae pro captione sua, *ibid.*, 672: "*Universalis episcopus omnium habet leges et iura rescindere.*"

[39] Ep. ad Paschalem, *ibid.*, 564; see also Bruno's letter to Peter of Porto (*ibid.*,

By far the longest and most thoroughly considered treatise of protest was Placidus of Nonantula's *Liber de honore ecclesiae*. Placidus saw that one of the most critical issues in the debate was whether the bishop of Rome had complete discretion in establishing new laws. In his view, the pope could establish new laws only to regulate circumstances on which the Fathers, the Apostles, and the Evangelists had said nothing. If the Lord, or the Apostles, or the Fathers had defined an issue, the pope could only uphold—even at the cost of death—the previous definition. If he strove to overturn what the Apostles and prophets had taught, his judgment was not a juridical sentence, but an error.[40] Paschal's Privilegium was contrary to the grace of the Holy Spirit and to the holy canons. If what Paschal granted were actually conceded to kings, the whole Church would be subjected to them and secular princes would allow simoniacs and other canonically disqualified men to receive the sacrament of holy orders. After the example of St. Peter, Paschal must therefore correct his action,[41] and remedy what he had done contrary to the authority of the Old and the New Testaments.[42] In another vein, Placidus discussed the contention that Hadrian I had granted the right of investiture to Charlemagne and his successors. Though he strongly doubted the authenticity of that cession, Placidus was not prepared to denounce it frankly as false. To his mind, lay investiture had not been a heresy in the Church's early days because it had been performed simply, and because it had led to no contention. The adamant defenders of the practice only made it heretical in the time of Gregory VII and Urban II.[43] Therefore, Hadrian did not sanction a heretical practice, even if the cession attributed to him were genuine. Placidus, moreover, found it incredible that Hadrian should have intended to approve anything other than a symbolic act expressing the prince's duty to defend the Church.[44] Either Hadrian had acted in answer to conditions which no longer existed, or he had made the grant through human weakness and error, since Hadrian himself forbade temporal intervention in episcopal elections on another occasion.[45] In

---

563) and his Libellus de Simoniacis (*ibid.*, 546f), both composed about 1111; White, "Pontius," 201. On Paschal's efforts to retaliate by having Bruno removed as abbot of Monte Cassino and expelled from Segni, see McKeon, "Council," 5.

[40] C. 70, *ibid.*, 597. On this treatise, see Ullmann, *Growth*, 409f.

[41] C. 118, *ibid.*, 625f.

[42] C. 119, *ibid.*, 626. See McKeon, "Council," 5f.

[43] C. 82, *ibid.*, 604.          [44] C. 67, *ibid.*, 596.

[45] Cc. 69, 70, 102, 103, 117, *ibid.*, 596f, 618f, 623.

any case, Paschal's concession opposed the commands of God and had to be corrected.[46]

If an emperor were not orthodox, the Church had to resist him on all counts, and, if he imposed upon the Roman See a man of his own choice, the man could not be considered a true bishop.[47] But Placidus acknowledged that orthodox kings and emperors rightly had the power to confirm episcopal elections,[48] that the Church owed tribute and services to them,[49] and even that, under special circumstances, a king might invest a bishop with a fief using the normal form of investiture, but not bestowing the ring and staff.[50] Though he excerpted and quoted the Donation of Constantine,[51] he did not deduce from it any doctrine of papal supremacy over temporal rulers. His argument was simply that, though lay investiture need not be wrongful, it had by Gregory VII's day become detrimental to Church order. The "supreme and universal pontiffs, Gregory VII, Urban II, and Paschal II," saw the evils it engendered and forbade it.[52] The Privilegium therefore contradicted Paschal's own declarations and those of his spiritual Fathers; it violated the circumstances under which the Roman bishop could establish new laws.

Paschal himself, the men who repudiated the Privilegium synodically, and the authors of these critical treatises were all concerned to define the conditions which validated papal decrees. They all agreed that the Scriptures, the decrees of earlier popes, establishments of the Fathers, and canons of oecumenical councils composed a legal standard against which the validity of papal sentences had to be judged. They likewise agreed that if a papal decree flagrantly departed from the standard, it had to be corrected by papal authority.[53] Paschal satisfied this demand with his repeated condemnations of the Privilegium, but the problem of correcting a pope obdurate in his error clearly occurred to the cardinals who reproved Paschal and to the members of the Synod of Vienne who threatened to withdraw their obedience from him. If there were a canon of legal validity higher than papal decrees, there must also be executive authority higher than that of the bishop of Rome. In the eleventh century, the Synods of Worms and Brixen, and

[46] C. 117, *ibid.*, 623.      [47] C. 99, *ibid.*, 618.
[48] Cc. 37, 93, *ibid.*, 585, 615.      [49] C. 118, *ibid.*, 624ff.
[50] C. 86, *ibid.*, 612. See also, cc. 56, 82, 153, *ibid.*, 591, 604f, 635.
[51] Cc. 58, 91, *ibid.*, 593, 613f.
[52] C. 118, *ibid.*, 624.      [53] Cf. Kern, *Kingship*, 183f.

the schismatic cardinals explicitly declared that. The controversy over the Privilegium revived in practice the latent principle, and elaborated both the doctrine of magisterial authority which it expressed, and the doctrine of assent which it foretold.

### C. AUTHENTICITY OF THE PAPAL TITLE: THE CONTESTED ELECTION OF 1130

Unfortunately, no treatises concerning the Privilegium dispute survive from the period after 1112, although the issues which the controversy raised remained acute throughout the rest of Paschal's pontificate. The dispute posed the question of the authority of papal acts; the thought concerning papal responsibility formulated then was the intellectual framework for a second great controversy, the contested papal election of 1130, in which the essential question concerned the authenticity of the papal title itself. The decisive element, again, was the assent of the faithful.

$$+$$

When he deserted Gregory VII, Cardinal Hugh Candidus sought support from Robert Guiscard, arguing that Gregory was not "pontiff according to the decrees of the holy Fathers," and promising that he and his followers would give Robert the imperial crown if he expelled Gregory from the Church by force. To this, Robert answered that it was outrageous to think that a pope could be deposed, "who was enthroned by election of the clergy and the approval of the Roman people, when the pontifical chair was vacant, and consecrated at the altar of St. Peter by cardinal bishops."[1] Robert's response epitomized the elements of valid papal election upon which the reformers insisted from 1059 onward. It omitted the approval of the German king; for, as we have seen, the reformers themselves considered that inessential. But it retained as constitutive acts canonical election and consecration by the cardinal bishops at St. Peter's altar.

These criteria were insufficient to decide the election dispute of 1130, for each party rightly met them.[2] The election expressed abiding differ-

---

[1] Bonizo of Sutri, *Liber ad amicum*, c. 7, MGH Ldl. 1, 604: "*Nefas enim est credere per tuas inimicias vel alicuius posse papam deponi, qui electione cleri et laude populi Romani, cum kathedra pontificalis vacaret, intronizatus, ad altare sancti Petri ab episcopis cardinalibus consecratus est.*"

[2] See the description of the preliminaries to the election and of the election itself, in Schmale, *Studien*, 146ff.

ences within the Sacred College which have been traced to the pontificate of Paschal II, and it is generally considered a schism between cardinals who advanced a "curialist" program of Church government and those who represented the doctrine of papal monarchy.[3] According to one interpretation, some cardinals continued the "curialist" thought which the schismatic cardinals expressed in its most extreme form in the age of Gregory VII, and which largely effected Paschal II's withdrawal of the Privilegium.[4] Their opponents held the position according to which Gregory himself seems to have acted: namely that supreme administrative powers in the Apostolic See belonged to the successor of St. Peter, not to the Curia. These latter thinkers were, moreover, influenced by the ascetic ideals being preached in their own day by such monastic reformers as Hugh of Grenoble, Norbert of Magdeburg, and Bernard of Clairvaux.[5] The antagonism within the Sacred College reflected stages of development in two "Gregorian" concepts of Church government. It was not a conflict between a "new" concept and an "old" one;[6] nor did it wholly reflect a difference between age groups, even though many of the curialists had entered the College before the pontificate of Honorius II;[7] Cardinal Peter Pierleone (Anacletus II) and Cardinal Gregory Paperesche (Innocent II) were of the same generation.[8]

The antagonism became strong in the time of Calixtus II; it showed itself in the divided election of 1124, in which Honorius II, one of the anti-curialists, ultimately won general acceptance as pope. Hostility remained acute throughout Honorius's pontificate; curialists were seldom nominated as legates or entrusted with other major duties,[9] and there was constant danger that the parties would fall into open contention. The equipoise of power was all the more threatening since the Frangipani supported Honorius's party, and the Pierleoni were patrons of the curialists. To avert a catastrophic schism, the parties agreed, before 1130, that a commission of eight cardinals should be constituted after Honorius's death to choose his successor, and that, if they failed to agree, the choice would pass to another commission of cardinals.[10]

---

[3] Schmale, *Studien*, 58.    [4] Cf. White, "Gregorian Ideal," 334.

[5] White, "Pontius," 206. On Innocent II's encouragement of canons regular and of the Premonstratensians, see Schmale, *Studien*, 272ff.

[6] Cf. Schmale, *Studien*, 58.

[7] Klewitz, "Ende," 372ff, and below, pp. 344ff.

[8] Schmale, *Studien*, 58f.

[9] Klewitz, "Reformpapsttum," 405; Schmale, *Studien*, 89; White, "Pontius," 211.

[10] Henry of Lucca to Norbert of Magdeburg, PL 179, 40ff.

This plan was never executed. An effort by the Pierleoni to gain the papacy by a premature election was foiled when Honorius's party exhibited the moribund Pope to the Roman people. Immediately upon Honorius's death, his party prevented news of the event from becoming public until, hastily burying the dead Pope to conform with canonical requirements, they proceeded to elect Cardinal Gregory as Honorius's successor.[11] With conspiratorial haste, they exhumed Honorius's body and marched with it to the Lateran, joined by about ten other cardinals and some laymen. After burying Honorius a second time, they enthroned Innocent and invested him with the papal insignia. Within a few hours, the Pierleoni had mustered their forces. The majority of the cardinals, a large company of the Roman people, almost all the Roman nobility, and the municipal officials gathered in the church of St. Mark, and, according to canonical order, elected Peter Pierleone as pope. A few days later, Innocent II fled from the Lateran to a Frangipane fortress and Anacletus broke through the doors of St. Peter's, received consecration by the bishop of Porto, seized the Lateran, where he was enthroned, and finally confiscated the treasures of several churches, stripping even statues of their precious metal casings. By armed force and liberal bribes, Anacletus won control of the City; he won even the Frangipani to his side, and Innocent fled to Pisa, Genoa, and, finally, to France.

Despite conspiracy and violence on each side, both claimants had been elected by the clergy and people of Rome; each had been consecrated by cardinal bishops at one of St. Peter's altars; both had been enthroned in the Lateran. These canonical elements were insufficient to recommend one claimant over the other; and the establishment of legitimate title became a matter of diplomacy rather than of canonistic evidence.

Anacletus remained in possession of the city, and, by granting Roger II of Sicily the royal title, he gained the support of Norman Italy. His other efforts to win recognition failed, including his offer of the imperial crown to Lothair III of Germany, as ratified by a letter from the Roman people to that King and by Anacletus's excommunication of Lothair's enemy, the Anti-King, Conrad of Hohenstaufen.

Under the advocacy of St. Bernard of Clairvaux, Innocent won almost immediate recognition in France, Germany, Spain, England, and

[11] *Ibid.*, 40f.

part of northern Italy. Innocent, like Anacletus, confirmed Lothair's title and excommunicated Conrad.[12]

For Innocent, that gesture was fruitful. In 1133, he returned to Rome under Lothair's protection, crowned Lothair as emperor and invested him with the Mathildine lands. Anacletus, however, remained in possession of St. Peter's, the Castello Sant' Angelo, and other parts of Rome, and Innocent fled once again when Roger II arrived with his troops. Lothair's second Italian expedition in 1137 restored some lands in southern Italy to Innocent's control, and, after Anacletus's death in 1138, the people of Rome acknowledged Innocent as pope. Anacletus's cardinals, after electing a successor to him, were also persuaded to submit to Innocent; and in 1139, the First Lateran Council ended the dispute by annulling Anacletus's official acts and excommunicating Roger II.

For our purposes, it is important to know the ecclesiological defense advanced by each claimant and the Church institutions employed to settle the controversy. Anacletus emphasized his election by cardinals, clergy, and people, with complete unanimity, the honor and joy with which the Romans conducted him to his enthronement in St. Peter's seat.[13] He emphasized particularly the participation and the perfect harmony of all officers in the ecclesiastical and urban administration of Rome; his consecration by Peter of Porto before the altar of St. Peter; his investiture with the phrygium "after the fashion of our predecessors"; and the fact that he was performing all normal episcopal functions in his see.[14] Beyond these proofs, he adduced his acceptance as true pope by Roger II, and by the archbishops and abbots of Apulia and Calabria, and by the whole oriental Church—Jerusalem, Antioch, and Constantinople—with which he claimed to have close relations.[15] The "heresiarch Gregory"[16] stood in pathetic contrast, elected as he had been "by a very few men,"[17] none of whom had any rightful part in the election of the Roman pontiff,[18] "false brethren"[19] and "false bishops,"[20] who had presumed with bloody hands to make him their idol, surreptitiously, under cover of darkness.[21] Though "Gregory" had attempted

---

[12] PL 179, 53.   [13] PL 179, 690f.

[14] PL 179, 696f, 699f, 702f, 704, 706f, 708f, 710, 712, 713f.

[15] PL 179, 718.   [16] PL 179, 723.

[17] PL 179, 699: a paucissimis.

[18] PL 179, 697f.   [19] PL 179, 696.   [20] PL 179, 697.

[21] PL 179, 702, 703. Anacletus frequently used variants of this metaphor. See also cols. 697, 700, 702, 703, 709.

to subvert Anacletus's authority by encouraging perjury, he had been compelled to flee by night to Pisa, where he lived "most wretchedly," while, by God's grace, Anacletus remained with his "brethren and sons, cardinal bishops, priests, and deacons, the entire clergy of the City, and the people," whole and prosperous, celebrating Church festivals in the Lateran palace peacefully and honorably, according to the ancient custom of his predecessors.[22]

Except for possession of the Roman See, the same elements appear in the arguments of Innocent and his supporters. His cardinals wrote to Lothair III announcing that they had elected him "as supreme pontiff," and enthroned him "in the supreme seat" amidst an "infinite throng of the Faithful"; and that they had then, according to established practice, bestowed upon him the pontifical insignia of Honorius II, Calixtus II, Paschal II, and their predecessors. They declared that all eastern and western churches venerated Innocent as "universal Father and vicar of St. Peter, orthodoxly chosen by orthodox men, and orthodoxly consecrated."[23] Vulgrinus of Bourges declared: "The orthodox bishops and orthodox cardinals who suffer persecution with the Lord Pope Innocent for justice's sake are the Roman Church";[24] and he argued that this was proven by the unity between Innocent and "innumerable" patriarchs, primates, metropolitans, and bishops, the kings of England, Germany, Spain, and Jerusalem, and the dukes and princes of almost all the world. "This," he wrote, "is the catholic and universal Church, which shines in the East and is seen even in the West."[25] Walter of Ravenna similarly assured Norbert of Magdeburg, Lothair's chancellor, that Innocent had acceded canonically by the election of the orthodox cardinals, and that the whole Church of Italy accepted him as "universal Father, pope, and *apostolicus*."[26]

In his own letters, Innocent emphasized that he had the unanimous support of the "catholic" cardinals,[27] that he had received letters of

[22] PL 179, 723 (A.D. 1134).

[23] PL 179, 37f.

[24] PL 179, 44f: "*Catholici episcopi et catholici cardinales qui cum domino papa Innocentio persecutionem patiuntur propter iustitiam hi sunt Romana ecclesia. . . .*" Cf. Innocent's cardinals to Lothair III, PL 179, 37f: "*Posthac Palladium in quo dominus noster papa Innocentius cum catholica ecclesia residebat, aggreditur* [Anacletus]."

[25] PL 179, 46.

[26] PL 179, 39. Cf. Henry of Lucca to Norbert of Magdeburg, PL 179, 42, on the support Innocent had in Tuscany, Lombardy, and "ultramontane regions."

[27] PL 179, 53, 55, 55f.

submission from the Patriarch of Jerusalem and the Bishop of Bethlehem,[28] and, soon after, from the Patriarch of Antioch,[29] and that the kings of France, England, and Germany had acknowledged him.[30] His flight from Rome was not a sign of divine displeasure, as Anacletus understood, but an act of God's mercy, delivering him from the "assembly of evil-doers"; and Innocent interpreted his brief return to the City in 1133 as a token of God's continual blessing.[31]

Innocent and his partisans flatly asserted that Anacletus's election was invalid, performed as it was after Innocent's canonical accession,[32] and accompanied by bloodshed and spoliation of the churches.[33] Anacletus had "dishonorably" put on the *cappa rubea* and seized counterfeit copies of the pontifical insignia, taken St. Peter's with siege machinery, broken into the Lateran with smoke, fire, and bloodshed, and plundered the treasury of St. Peter's which Roman pontiffs and emperors had enriched with gold lamps, images, crosses, gems, precious vases, liturgical vestments, and other costly offerings. Eastern and western churches alike repudiated him.[34] He was a schismatic, apostate and heretic.[35]

In these apologies and recriminations, one vindicating element stood out beside the canonical aspects of papal elections: namely acknowledgment of claims, the consent of the faithful. Both Innocent and Anacletus were ultimately forced to contend that their elections were valid because they had followed canonical procedure, and that this validity was proven by the acknowledgment of orthodox Romans, of eastern prelates, and of the kings and princes. These assertions were in some instances exaggerated and premature; for, while Innocent did win general recognition in northern Europe, even there, and much more in Italy, Anacletus retained strong support until his death.[36]

Still, the appeal to universal consensus was fundamental to both

---

[28] PL 179, 119 (A.D. 1132).  [29] See Schmale, *Studien*, 248f.
[30] PL 179, 76 (A.D. 1131).  [31] PL 179, 178.
[32] See Arnulf of Séez, *Invectiva*, c. 5, MGH Ldl. 3, 100.
[33] PL 179, 39, 41f, 55f.  [34] PL 179, 37f.
[35] PL 179, 39, 126.

[36] Bernhardi, *Lothar III*, 347. A defender of Gregory VII had argued similarly that Gregory had been acknowledged as true pope by the entire world for more than ten years. By wrongful intrusion of the secular power, Wibert, whom Gregory had excommunicated, usurped the Apostolic See, consecrated, not by the cardinal bishops to whom alone belonged the privilege of consecrating popes, but by bishops who had been excommunicated for three years (Anon., *Liber canon. contra Heinr.*, c. 46, MGH Ldl. 1, 515).

claimants, and it found institutional expression in a series of synods, culminating in the Lateran Council of 1139. Before Anacletus's death, formal synods were held at Étampes (1130), Rheims (1131), Piacenza (1132), Würzburg (1133),[37] and Pisa (1135) to judge the case; they all decided in favor of Innocent, who presided in person at Rheims, Piacenza, and Pisa. In addition, Roger II arranged a conference between the two parties at Salerno in 1137-1138 to guide his politically wavering decision, but Anacletus's death ended his temporizing. Anacletus and his followers had earlier proposed that a general council be summoned to settle the dispute.[38] And, when Lothair III entered Italy in 1133, Anacletus petitioned him to hold an imperial synod to hear and judge the rival claims. Lothair was persuaded only with difficulty to abandon the project in view of the existing sentences in Innocent's favor.

The principles which dictated the judgments of these synods were not, on balance, canonical. St. Bernard set the standard of judgment at the Synod of Étampes, where he insisted that the principal issue was the personal worthiness of the two claimants. Bernard's vigorous misrepresentation of Anacletus's actions, together with the virulent hostility Anacletus had earlier aroused as papal legate in France and England, won the Synod to Innocent's camp.[39] Innocent's reputation among the regular clergy for personal purity and devoutness seems also to have won him prevalent support in Germany.[40] And yet, Lothair's indecision concerning the proposal of an imperial synod in 1133, the Synod of Pisa, and the conference at Salerno all showed that the synods which had

---

[37] Bernhardi, *Lothar III*, 339ff.

[38] Bernard of Clairvaux, ep. 12, PL 182, 276ff, esp. c. 12, col. 279. See c. 11, col. 279: Universae quippe ecclesiae negotium est, non unius causa personae. Similarly, in 1160, a Synod of Pavia was convened to judge the claims of Victor IV and Alexander III.

[39] Schmale, *Studien*, 226; White, "Gregorian Ideal," 336f, 338f. Cf. Suger, *Vita Ludovici VI*, 32, in ed. H. Waquet (Paris, 1929), 256ff: "*Quo rex ut erat piissimus ecclesie defensor, cito compunctus concilium archiepiscoporum episcoporum, abbatum et religiosorum virorum Stampis convocat et eorum consilio magis de persona quam de electione investigans—fit enim sepe ut Romanorum tumultuanciam quibuscumque molestiis ecclesie electio minus ordinarie fieri valeat—ei assensum electioni consilio virorum prebet et deinceps manutenere promittit.*" Cf. Arnulf of Séez, *Invectiva*, c. 5, MGH Ldl. 3, 100f. On contemporary descriptions of Innocent's character, see Schmale, *Studien*, 195.

[40] Schmale, *Studien*, 238f, 242. See also Arnulf of Séez, *Invectiva*, c. 4, MGH Ldl. 3, 97: "*Verum oportet nunc ex meritis non ex gratia iudicare nec gratiosum tantum sed et dignum constituere sacerdotem.*" Cf. ibid., c. 5, ibid., 101.

approved Innocent's title as authentic did not have general or definitive authority. As Anacletus and his followers suggested, only a general council could terminate the dispute, and, after Anacletus's death had rendered the issues moot, Innocent summoned the Second Lateran Council to clear his title.

The formal impact of this protracted controversy upon later writings was slight. Some mediaeval commentators on the early twelfth century ignored it altogether and mentioned only Innocent's election;[41] and no document from it entered Gratian's *Decretum*, which was being compiled in Bologna while the dispute raged.[42]

Still, the election of 1130 was critically important both as an expression of tensions within the government of the Roman Church and as an indicator of currents in ecclesiology. The dispute concerning Paschal II's Privilegium had raised the issue of each pope's personal responsibility for his official actions. For many thinkers, it had shattered the identity between the Roman Church and the pope which existed in the minds of Peter Damian and Gregory VII; it established that papal discretion in the establishment of new laws was limited by the earlier laws of the Church and that violation of previous regulations must be corrected. The disputed election of 1130 raised the equally fundamental issue of personal worthiness as a qualification for the papacy and of what office could rightly judge the suitability of claimants to the See of St. Peter. The powers of the papacy itself were insufficient to determine disputes concerning the authenticity of a papal claimant's title, once normal requirements for canonical election had been met. In the dispute concerning the Privilegium, the dissident cardinals and Guido of Vienne had acted to judge the authority of papal acts by synodal deliberation. In the dispute following the election of 1130, all parties appealed to synodal judgment as expressing the universal consensus which both Innocent and Anacletus invoked to authenticate their claims. The ancient rule of consensus was being transformed into the political doctrine of assent.

The election of 1130 was the first in a long series of papal elections in which the Sacred College split and elected factional claimants to the papacy. The arguments advanced by the two parties before Anacle-

[41] Bernhardi, *Lothar III*, 347, n. 22.

[42] The only decretals by Innocent II in the Decretum concern the purgation of clergy (P. II, C. II, qu. V, c. 17) and vows to be taken by persons assisting at synods (P. II, C. XXXV, qu. VI, c. 7).

tus's death lacked the fullness and the sophistication of arguments advanced later in comparable schisms. But in lines of argumentation, in concepts of authority, and in ultimate appeal to universal consensus, they expressed principles which received fullest expression in the Great Schism and in the Conciliar Epoch.

## CHAPTER 14

# Results of the Controversy

FROM the time of Constantine on, Roman thinkers had conflicted with thinkers in Gaul over matters of Church order. Since Christianity's earliest days, believers had wrestled with the question of what was owed to Caesar, and what to God. The Investiture Controversy stood apart from all earlier conflicts. Advantageous alliances with some of the emergent civil groupings—especially with the Norman principalities in Italy—enabled Gregory VII and his successors to hang on. They were not overwhelmed, as earlier popes had been, by the sheer political and military predominance of their enemies. Their survival meant, furthermore, that the Dispute was protracted. It was a struggle over principle, rather than over such political disobedience as had prompted other Roman revolts against German domination; and, because it lasted half a century, it inspired vigorous and repeated sifting of basic ideas. The winnowing was not fine; but the questions at issue were fundamental to Church order.

The controversy began with the problem of moral reform of the clergy, progressed to a conflict about the relation between the papacy and kings, and finally issued in a series of crises concerning the nature of the papacy itself.

Its results in terms of concrete issues are relatively easy to state. The moral reform of the clergy, the original goal of the Gregorian movement, was accomplished in principle, though it fell far short of realization, especially as regards the lower clergy.[1]

As for the temporal power in Germany, Gregory VII discovered that it was not easy to correct illicit change intruded into the Church by the secular power. A stubbornly offensive king could be excommunicated; Gregory held that he could also be deposed. The execution of such decrees was, however, beyond the power of the Roman See. Even among the reformers themselves arose the damaging thought that, if a wicked king renounced obedience to a pope, the pontiff had no further

---

[1] Becker, *Studien*, 169.

authority over him.[2] This seems also to have been the guiding principle for Peter Damian and, after him, Cardinal Deusdedit, when they argued that the German court had voided the Papal Election Decree of 1059 by repudiating both the decree and Nicholas II.[3]

The dispute between papacy and Empire ended in the Concordat of Worms, perhaps little more than the seal on a diplomatic impasse, or "a Pyrrhic triumph for the Papacy when the king was left in possession of the field."[4] Henry V indeed retained the substance of his control over the German church, though he had to sacrifice the symbolic act of investing bishops-elect with ring and staff. By the Concordat, the papacy for a time renounced the prospect of achieving in reality the universal and immediate headship of all churches that it claimed in theory. As compensation, Calixtus II secured imperial assurance of free elections to abbacies and episcopacies, and important curtailment of imperial powers in Burgundian and Italian elections.

The uncanonical intrusion of secular power into episcopal and abbatial accessions was repulsed; though the powers of kings over their bishops remained secure and were perhaps even strengthened,[5] the principle of free election had become generally accepted.

This settlement reasserted the conventional doctrine that kingship and episcopacy had discrete legal competences.[6] The tortuous route by which it was concluded also had new consequences of the greatest importance, particularly as regards the concept of papal powers. The doctrine of Gregory VII that popes could depose kings yielded under fiercest opposition to more moderate positions which reaffirmed the principle of institutional separation by acknowledging that, though the pope might excommunicate kings, he could not depose them. Indeed, the doubt was growing in some quarters that he could even confer the imperial title. When they wrote to Lothair III on Anacletus's behalf, the Roman people declared that the power to bestow the imperial title was theirs, not the pope's. The course of institutional separation was set toward the lapse of imperial coronations in the thirteenth century,[7] the secular

---

[2] Above, p. 400.    [3] Above, pp. 293, 308. Below, p. 400.

[4] Brooke, "Lay Investiture," 30. On Leo IX's reform synods, see Fliche, *Réforme* 1, 151.

[5] Becker, *Studien,* 169f. Cf. Hoffmann, "Schwerter," 95, 113f.

[6] Cf. Tellenbach, *Church,* 124f, 157f; Hoffmann, "Cluny," 169.

[7] Even in the twelfth century, Conrad III was not crowned as emperor by a pope (1137-1152). Philip of Swabia (1197-1208) was never crowned, and the imperial coronation of Frederick II (1220) was the last until that of Henry VII (1312), by cardinals.

343

coronation of Louis IV by a Roman nobleman in St. Peter's (1328), and the imperial bull *Licet Iuris* (1338) which denied the pope all power in the elevation of emperors. The king did not convey the Church's message of salvation; but the pope could not rearrange the order of temporal government which God had established.

By contrast, when we turn to sum up the results of the Investiture Conflict for the broader issue of ecclesiastical cohesion, the elements to be counted in seem hazy and imprecise. Doctrines of discretion and tradition clashed in one catastrophe after another over a period of fifty years. What came of it? We can, of course, say exactly how the schism in the Sacred College under Gregory VII turned out, trace the course of the Privilegium dispute, and make score-cards for different stages in the conflict between Innocent II and Anacletus II. But even in these historically precise cases, there were no easy answers to the great questions at issue. Contemporaries must have seen the same jagged and shifting intellectual landscape: the Gregorian schism ended only years after Gregory was buried in Salerno; the Privilegium haunted Paschal for nearly a decade; the contest between Innocent and Anacletus dragged on until Anacletus died, eight years after the election. It was an age brave, or desperate, enough to pose questions that were beyond its power to answer.

In the conflict, even the venerable concept of tradition, one of the pillars of debate, took on a new meaning. All parties agreed that the troubles of their day occurred because illicit change had affected the Church. The Gregorians argued that the temporal power had intruded such a change by usurping control of spiritual functions through simony and lay investiture; and the anti-Gregorians, including the schismatic cardinals, maintained that Gregory had perpetrated wrongful innovation by deposing Henry, and according to some authors, by uncanonically excommunicating him.

A new tendency ran through these conventional objections. The tracts of the schismatic cardinals illustrate it most incisively, for, in stating their position, the most unprecedented and originative thought of the eleventh century, the cardinals defended rights which were scarcely half a century old. Their claims that cardinals had even in Christian antiquity exercised the powers they themselves claimed shows all the more sharply the common impulse of thinkers to justify their actions by invoking ancient practice. Gregory VII, in appealing to precedent, Henry IV, in resorting to "the tradition of

344

the holy Fathers," and the authors of Gregorian and imperialist treatises all similarly alleged that they were continuing modes of conduct which had been normal from the earliest days of Christianity. For Gregory, his followers, and the different schools of anti-Gregorians, historical fact and consistency of argumentation were secondary to the defense of existing commitments. Antiquity, patristic consensus, universal assent or testimony—the ancient canons of authenticity—were all invoked to support the most antagonistic views. Thinkers judged that whatever was right must by definition be "ancient," even if it were an utterly new device. The implications of this tendency for the concept of tradition were great.

Certainly, the transvaluation of tradition had gone very far, even though among some writers the older concept survived. Wenric of Trier, for example, set great value upon the Scriptures and the writings of the Fathers as a supreme rule of faith and life. They enjoined righteousness of every sort, particularly in submission to kings. And understanding of them, he wrote, was that "sweet gentleness which was poured out from the very breast of Christ the Lord into His Apostles, and which the humility of apostolic men devoutly received from the Apostles, carefully guarded, and faithfully fulfilled."[8] Most thinkers would have found this view of doctrinal communication acceptable; some writers explicitly invoked the rule of tradition as a vague, but effective rallying-cry of opposition. And yet, even these writers thought first of laws and offices as channels conveying true doctrine to believers.

The apologists and Fathers invoked earlier practices and judgments as testimonies to a primordial truth which they in their own times had to reaffirm. By contrast, thinkers in the late eleventh century referred to them as precedents for particular juridical or administrative actions, or for a pattern of institutional relationships. The past served not so much to prove eternal, abstract verity, as to warrant modes of official conduct. It was not so much the continuous existence of the good itself as a guide for achieving a greater good.

Eleventh-century thinkers of all parties found the cohesive element in the Church less in spiritual factors than in administrative order. Henry IV saw it in the divine establishment of kingship and episcopacy in two distinct orders. The author of *De unitate ecclesiae conservanda*

---

[8] MGH Ldl. 1, 290f: "*Haec est illa, quae ab ipso Christi Domini pectore in eius apostolos transfusa est, dulcedinis suavitas, quam ab apostolis apostolicorum virorum humilitas devote suscepit, sollicite custodivit, fideliter inplevit.*"

345

judged it to be charity reinforced by law and the general assent of the Church. The schismatic cardinals declared that it rested in the laws, to which popes were subject, and in the collective powers of the Fathers of the Roman Church. Gregory VII and his followers found it in law and in unlimited papal discretion which transcended law. For them, of all thinkers, the transvaluation of tradition was most complete; the essence of their reform program contradicted a continuum of sacred knowledge; tradition had given way to a thorough doctrine of discretionary authority.

The Gregorians all but suppressed what we have called the "Janus complex" in papal thought. They understood that the idea of tradition—even when perceived as Nicholas I had understood it, as a bulwark of papal discretion—inevitably undermined the structure it was meant to support. Their contempt for antiquity struck at the base of the idea of tradition; the concept that truth was conveyed by a long succession of authentic teachers was also cancelled out by the Gregorians' argument that corruption had intervened between the remote past and the present day. Now and then, they remembered to use the language of tradition for polemical reasons. But they used it to describe the fact of discretion.

Though tradition still carried weight among some thinkers, its transvaluation and especially the Gregorians' doctrine of administrative omnicompetence shifted the grounds of debate.

The points of conflict were submitted to new forms of inquiry, to new modes of reasoning, which transformed them gradually into abstract, constitutional principles of the most general importance, the premises of representative government.

Even in Gregory VII's day, the unsystematized thought which he expressed was being slowly superseded by legalistic reasoning. A sign of this change was the production of canonistic anthologies: between 1083 and 1099, all the major compilations of the Gregorian era were made.[9] Petrus Crassus heralded the revival of Roman law; Cardinal Deusdedit and Ivo, the growth of canonistic method and knowledge; Anselm of Canterbury, new forms of rationalization. In the age of Calixtus II and Innocent II, Irnerius, Gratian, and Abelard continued the fusing of Ro-

---

[9] The collections of Anselm of Lucca (c. 1083), Cardinal Atto (c. 1084), and Cardinal Deusdedit (1083-1087), Bonizo of Sutri's *Liber de vita christiana* (c. 1089-1095), and, by canonists outside the papal court, the anonymous Collectio Britannica (c. 1090), Ivo of Chartres' Decretum (c. 1094), and the Panormia (c. 1094, perhaps by Ivo).

man law, canonistic science, and scholastic reasoning. Beyond them lay the supreme achievements of mediaeval canonistic jurisprudence.

The Investiture Controversy was in a sense a "world-revolution";[10] for it projected onto the conscience of all Europe questions of authority which had occurred in local disputes countless times before. Debate could not be cut off and the issues could not be prematurely smothered, as they had been before. But the Controversy itself only posed the questions, provided some conceptual leads toward feasible solutions, and arrayed pope, council, and king for later tests of strength and theory. It translated the authorities of antiquity, universality, and consensus into new terms, relevant to contemporary institutions. The complete answers were found slowly in the course of the next century with the new tools of legal knowledge and philosophy.

When the Controversy ended, the greater issues of hierarchic administration had not achieved resolution. Without abstract, constitutional definitions, the combatants were awash in a stormy sea of relationships whose dimensions and complex interconnections they could not measure. Maxims of juristic theology and subtle understanding of special points were inadequate for full comprehension of the issues and thus for a thorough treatment of them. Eleventh and early twelfth-century thinkers generally had no better tools for the work. They saw the issues as essentially pragmatic matters of administration, rather than aspects of a broad system of right government. Lay investiture, excommunication of kings, or depositions of popes were right or wrong in concrete instances, but there was as yet no rationalization of them in abstract theories of equality or justice, no acknowledged successor to the primitive idea of tradition as a control on authentic teaching that had its origin, force, and ultimate purpose outside the Church's law and order.

Still, the scope of dispute required systematization. Necessity demanded its invention; constitutional theory must supersede pragmatic administrative thought. The Investiture Controversy and its echo in the contested election of 1130 showed that the first step toward a genuinely rational ecclesiological theory must be the most difficult: a definition of papal powers. It was clear, however, that that step would lead men in very different directions. The outset of their divergencies was perhaps the most important result of the Controversy; it was a turning point in the history of political thought.

The whole controversy raised the issue of how the Church could

[10] Cantor, *Church*, 6f.

deal with the temporal world in the social context of mediaeval Europe. The schism of 1084 brought home the problems of heresy in St. Peter's chair and of the relative powers of pope and cardinals. The Privilegium dispute and the contested election of 1130 cast new and powerful light on the assent of the faithful as a legitimizing force in the Church. These were profound issues indeed. It is small wonder that the age on which they broke could frame only partial, *ad hoc*, answers. But great honor belongs to the men who framed them, for their work was the seed from which came the bountiful harvest of late mediaeval jurisprudence.

Ecclesiology and constitutional thought owed much to the Investiture Controversy; but, among the different concepts of Church order and just government to which the Dispute gave rise, there was essentially no common ground. As doctrines of limited and irresponsible power in ecclesiastical and temporal government, they expressed anew ancient problems of political relationships in terms which were to divide men throughout the Middle Ages. As the greatest Carolingian thinker wrote, "every man shall abound in his own sense until that Light comes which turns the false light of the philosophers into shadows and changes into light the shadows of them that rightly understand."[11]

[11] John Scottus Erigena, *De Divisione Naturae*, V, 39, PL 122, 1022: "*Unusquisque in suo sensu abundet donec veniat illa lux quae de luce falso philosophantium facit tenebras et tenebras recte cognoscentium convertit in lucem.*"

## CHAPTER 15

# Summary: From Law to Jurisprudence

FROM the age of the Apostles until our day, the character and goals of the Church have been subjects of almost continuous debate. Beyond the relatively few metaphysical doctrines which early won general acceptance, important problems of faith and discipline have arisen ever since St. Paul withstood St. Peter at Antioch (Galatians 2:11). Out of these problems have come the reforms, schisms, and heresies which mark the history of the Church as a history of dissent and estrangement.

The principal issue has been the nature of authority in the Church. Because the Church's purpose was to save men by preaching a specific doctrine, the same that Christ taught the Apostles, questions naturally arose about the preservation of the original, saving doctrine as the Apostolic Age became increasingly remote, and as divergencies in practices and belief developed.

It was universally agreed that Christ had preached the necessary doctrine of salvation in its fullness, and that any addition to or subtraction from it would corrupt its purpose and destroy its effect. Dispute turned on the precise means of preservation.

In this essay, we have taken the idea of tradition as a window on some great conflicts of the early Christian era. From the struggle with the pagan Empire to the Investiture Dispute, the same fundamental questions arose. Medieval thinkers framed these issues in theological terms. We have examined their arguments. Perhaps, in summary, it may be useful to offer another perspective on the forces we have repeatedly observed.

Let us examine the ancient concept of the Church as a society, and cast the question of Church unity as a matter of social cohesion. The cohesive element of any society is consensus, especially in the tacit agreement of its members concerning channels of legitimate authority. Such consensus establishes not only governmental orders, but, more widely, norms of conduct on every level of existence. It is a check on man's dealings with his fellows individually or by corporative action.

349

In different societies, and at different times in the history of each society, it sanctions highly diverse standards of right order. But, under any conditions, the character and history of a society are determined by the objects of assent and the means of its communication.

From the aspect of sociology, what part does tradition have in maintaining the cohesion of the Church as a "society"?

A logical distinction should be drawn between tradition, as communication, and the matter conveyed. The content of tradition is, of course, the *raison d'être* of tradition itself. It is sometimes called the "common religious experience" in which all members of the group participate, and without which the group would not exist. The group can preserve its cohesion only as long as it continues to participate in its peculiar experience, no matter how distant in time the believers may be from the historical occurrence which they consider the initiation of their faith. For the Church, the common religious experience is the Incarnation.

The channels of participation in the experience must remain open, the transmission of the experience must be constant. Still, pressures within the group and outside it endanger authentic transmission. Among believers, the unrelenting tension between conservatism and change, and the need to adapt received institutions and practices to unfamiliar circumstances create a dialectic of interpretation which is seldom resolved. The unifying effect of the common experience is further counteracted by centrifugal attractions from outside the institutional structure of the group.

Especially among proselytizing religions, the exclusivism of the group conflicts with and complements the group's efforts to assimilate an ever-increasing number of converts. Exclusivism requires a constant effort to resolve the tension between conservatism and change, and thus to establish the basis and safeguards of religious cohesion. Assimilation, on the other hand, requires the proselytizers to come to terms with the alien society which they wish to convert. This was the fundamental crisis which the Church encountered after the conversion of Constantine, when great numbers of nominal converts followed their Emperor's example.

The assimilation of converts produces simultaneous assimilation of the religious group by society. For, to communicate its common experience to aliens, the religious group adopts as its own modes of expression—in iconography, forms of argumentation, cult practices, and the like—originally foreign to it, but meaningful to those it wishes to convert. The disputes in the early Church between men who believed that pagan learning, specially rhetoric, might be useful to Christians, and those who held that the same mouths could not sing the praises of God and Jupiter, reveals this pressure.

In seeking to communicate its common experience and thus to affirm its identity, the religious group normally adopts the techniques of doctrine, cult, and organization. These are the channels of tradition. They are usual in the history of any religion, and they may follow parallel or even virtually identical courses of evolution among widely-separated groups adhering to the same religion. Different problems of social accommodation, however, may produce variations in doctrine, cult, or order; and these may lead to schisms, or secessions, and consequent regroupings. For religious attitudes are determined not only by the common religious experience of the believers, which is constant, but also by the variable of tradition, which purports to teach what the common experience was, and what it meant. Tradition is particularly subject to the effects of assimilation.

Especially in a preliterate society, but also in any society which is not fully literate, tradition assumes paramount authority in determining the norms of cohesion within the group. Efforts are made to insure the accurate transmission and understanding of the common experience. Mnemonic devices may be introduced; schools of specialists may be instituted to train authorities in authentic teaching and observance; proprietary rights or privileges may be attached to the accurate transmission of the cohesive element. In the Church, this corresponded to the development of religious symbolism, the distinction of clergy from laity, and the definition of ranks within the clergy.

Even within a numerically small religious group, the modes of transmission imperceptibly change and, thus, the understanding of the common experience changes. Despite safeguards, failure of memory on the part of the guardians of tradition may occur; and changes may likewise occur through instruction designed not so much to transmit the focal teaching as to explain critical terms or practices the meanings of which are obscure. The exegesis becomes, in practice, more important than the text. This was the case in the Arian, Monophysite, and Monothelite conflicts, which centered upon thoroughly unscriptural terms, terms devised by exegetes to clarify their arguments.

When the believers are widely dispersed among several ethnic groups, diversity inevitably enters the understanding of the common religious experience. Different mnemonic devices are chosen; the specialists are differently selected, taught, and supervised; and explanatory teachings vary according to the understanding of the men who frame them and the relevance of the obscure point to the value system of a given society. The original religious experience might thus be common to all adherents of the religion, together with an emphasis on the normative role of tradition and some important modes of conveying that experience in doctrine, cult, or order. Social values and conditions quite extraneous to the immediate concerns of the religious group may, however, produce widely diverse understandings of the content and proper communication of the common experience. This was the source of conflict in the Iconoclast Dispute.

+

On all these points, we have seen that the Church never existed as a unitary society, and that there was correspondingly never a unitary tradition drawing all believers together. Tradition indeed united the faithful and separated them from those outside the Church. But, in communication, its essential function, tradition responded with the greatest sensitivity to circumstances of time and place. It worked cohesively within individual social groupings, but divisively on the multisocial level.

Sociologically construed, this was the way tradition actually worked as an acknowledged authority in the Church. We have seen that the world of men conditioned the world of ideas, that the social variability of tradition critically affected the way mediaeval men thought about it.

What were the means of salvation, and how were they conveyed? These common problems engaged both the early Fathers, who struggled to describe the mystery of the Incarnation in theological terms, and thinkers in eleventh and twelfth-century Europe who, like Cardinal Humbert, considered Christ "the mystery of eternal justice and equity."[1] Often they used the same words. From the age of Constantine on, the essential tensions in Christian thought—the issues of Church-State relations and of patterns of authority within the Church—also remained constant. But the modes of reasoning out these problems and the attempted resolutions varied.

[1] See above, p. 313.

The earliest writers invoked tradition's continuum as a paramount authority, but, at the same time, they acknowledged that powers of spontaneous action inherent in some offices could also direct men to true belief and right order. In the highly improvised thought of the Apostolic Fathers and the Apologists, there was room enough for both these views of authority, which we have subsumed under the general headings "Jewish" and "Gentile." Indeed, the two strands of thought, closely interwoven, became part of the Church's standard intellectual hardware, as the persistent Janusism of Roman thinkers showed. The primitive concept was never entirely lost. But, by and large, the emphasis of western thought moved away from tradition, the idea of anciently transmitted authority, and toward a concept of administrative power which Richard Hooker much later described. "All things," he wrote, "cannot be of ancient continuance." New problems arise; unprecedented challenges demand new responses. "The Church being a body which dieth not, hath always power, as occasion requireth, no less to ordain that which never was than to ratify what hath been before."[2]

By what authority could the unanticipated problem be resolved? In what terms could the solution be cast? Because men understood authority and, more explicitly, tradition in the Church differently, they answered these questions differently. Schism was the normal result. The doctrinal interpretation and the ritual act became more relevant than the incomprehensible mystery they were designed to express.

Apologetic and patristic thinkers understood that the irreducible function of tradition was to guard the interest of the Church by unifying it, and by separating its members from outsiders. But distance in time and in space, and variations in language, class distinctions, and social, hierarchic, and civil groupings fundamentally affected the interpretation of the sacred body of knowledge which tradition was thought to convey. Tradition was subject to adaptation by new values, aspirations, and social myths; for its very nature was to reflect, explain, and enable the adaptation of the community of believers to its environment.[3] We have let the impact of politics represent the kind of decisive influence that all these social factors had.

It may be a truism to observe that even exceptionally gifted persons cannot go beyond the limits of their cultures. But this simple premise is essential to an understanding of all the variations which the concept

---

[2] *Of the Laws of Ecclesiastical Polity*, V, 8.
[3] Vansina, *Tradition*, 78, 106; Wach, *Sociology*, 35.

of tradition experienced before the eighth century, and its subsequent transvaluation among western thinkers. As long as the Church was interstitial in society, it was natural that tradition should be regarded as an unwritten but necessary guide to understanding the Christian mysteries, charismatically preserved among the true believers. The Judaic heritage of the Church provided the idea; the disarray which persecution visited upon Church order assured it. Within the cadre of late Roman and Byzantine society, law superseded charisma as a means of communication and a safeguard of cohesion when the clergy became fully integrated into society as a privileged class having powers of administration over property, over its own hierarchic structure, and, in religious matters, over the laity. Finally, in the West, law grew into jurisprudence. The unifying and authoritative functions formerly ascribed to tradition were gradually assumed by laws and legal systems, and even the word tradition lost general currency. That this occurred was principally due to the social and political integration of the clergy into Germanic society. By office and often by birth, prelates belonged to the higher nobility; they held vast political powers as well as social pre-eminence; they were full members of the military, landed aristocracy of proto-feudal and feudal society. Under these conditions, it was inevitable, given the canonical privileges of clergy, that a general system of appellate jurisdiction should emerge among the Germanic peoples, independent of secular courts, and that an orderly body of regulations should likewise gain currency to rule that judiciary system. The concept of tradition, which had become all things to all men, yielded to more distinct authorities. The word survived; the concept was transvaluated.

This tendency toward jurisprudence in the early twelfth century was one important continuation of the concept of tradition, a fact that the Waldensians saw when they said "that the tradition of the Church is the tradition of Pharisees."[3a] The development we have described issued from the irresoluble tension between conservatism and change, and the broader tension, of which that was part, between estrangement from the world and the desire to convert the world. Even among contemporaries, there was no uniform approach to these problems: while Gratian undertook a dialectical study in jurisprudence, Bernard of Clairvaux denounced the legalism of the papal curia, and Hugh of St. Victor composed the earliest treatise expressly on ecclesiology, a work

[3a] Leff, *Heresy* 2, 460.

profoundly mystical in its concept though scholastic in its method.[4] Moreover, reverence for the authority of the old expressed itself in the conflict between "Ancients" and "Moderns" in the late twelfth century,[5] in scattered references to "statutes of the elders" or "traditions of the Fathers," and in the concept of custom which St. Thomas Aquinas epitomized in his statement that "custom has the force of law, abolishes law, and is the interpreter of law."[6] But tradition as a definable concept had little place in the works of mystics, for whom it ran counter to the immediate and instantaneous communion between the believer and his God. Further, conservatism had never accounted for the whole character of tradition; veneration of antiquity, or at least of the old familiar ways, is present in any civilization, and at any time. For three centuries, social pressures had led western thinkers toward formulation in the later twelfth century of the concept that the Church's common religious experience was conveyed through a corporation, or an interlocking complex of corporations, regulated by a systematized body of legal principles.[7] And the concept of tradition chiefly survived, not as an intellectual entity, but in the categories of authority to which it had given rise among different schools—for example, in the decretists' theories limiting papal authority,[8] and in the growth of the conciliar doctrine.[9]

Though always challenged by doctrines of irresponsible power within the Church, the principle of accountability was perhaps the most important vestige of the idea of tradition as a control on true teaching.

Casting an eye toward disputes in the late Middle Ages, it would be easy to fall into the thicket of exaggeration, and to say that the idea of tradition lay at the heart of those titanic struggles of popes, cardinals, and councils over official limits. But by its very nature, exag-

---

[4] Seeburg, *Studien*, 59; Merzbacher, "Recht," 190ff; "Wandlungen," 283f. On other protests against growing legalism, see Mayer, "Kirchenbild," 282f, 286f; Jordan, "Entstehung," 123f, 149.

[5] Chenu, *La théologie*, 386ff.

[6] *Summa Theologiae*, P. 2, qu. 97, art. 2. See also Gratian's *Decretum*, D. 1, i. 5.

[7] Ladner, "Aspects," 407ff. Cf. Tierney, "Theory," 437f; Tellenbach, *Church*, 16.

[8] Tierney, *Foundations*, 42f, 46; cf. *ibid.*, 24f, 87, 91, 93. On the importance of tradition in the theology of the canonists, see Tierney's excellently balanced essay, " 'Scriptura.' "

[9] Tierney, *Foundations, passim*; Merzbacher, "Wandlungen," 318, 321, 325, 327. For a general characterization of later mediaeval ecclesiology, see Merzbacher, "Wandlungen," *passim*; Mayer, "Kirchenbild," 290.

geration must have a kernel of truth. A common problem did indeed unite men who invoked tradition in the early Middle Ages and men who advocated the refined constitutional checks and balances of the thirteenth and fourteenth century canonists. From the beginning, the whole structure of theology and order had been meant to express the Church's common religious experience and to communicate the means of salvation. Neither they, nor official functions as their expressions, were the indispensable essence of the Church; they were all tools. The cause and purpose of the Church lay outside the structure of doctrine and law, however elaborate, however systematized. Indeed, it could even conflict with the system of order. This was clear when men reopened the ancient issue of whether the apostolate died with the Apostles—as the Synod of Sens (1140) accused Abelard of doing—by arguing that the power of binding and loosing had not passed to the Apostles' successors. The Incarnation was of a nature utterly different from the channels that led believers to participate in it.

We have examined tradition both as a conveyance of the common experience and as a check on the communication of that experience. In its way, the dialectical structure of Gratian's *Decretum* set corresponding controls in systematized standards of action derived from rational principles, and the decretists were not slow in working out its implications.

On a more general, but closely related level, some canonistic thinkers from the twelfth century on took up other issues raised by the primitive idea of tradition. Here, the language of mediaeval theology blends with that of modern sociology. They increasingly defined the Church as a community of believers; by the early fourteenth century, they declared that that community held the plenitude of power in the Church, and exercised it through general councils. At the same time, advocates of papal supremacy, the intellectual heirs of the Gregorians, refined their own position. The pope, they argued, was supreme: all authority in the Church flowed from him to all bishops, to the cardinals, and even to general councils, which had no power either to restrict or to augment his authority. Against this view, men who saw the community of the faithful as the supreme reservoir of power defended their thought on two points: first, that popes were elected by the cardinals acting as representatives of the whole community, or explicitly of the general council; and second, that, when popes fell into heresy, they could be deposed by the judgment of the universal Church, expressed in a council. A doctrine of an accountable, representative pope emerged. In time, advocates of

356

the conciliar view elaborated this position: they argued that, without falling into heresy, the universal Church could act without the pope's advice or consent and even against him when he was delinquent by virtue of flagrant wrongdoing, schism, and other urgent matters. Indeed, during a vacancy of the Roman See, the council or its vicars could exercise the papal powers. One hears more than an echo of Sts. Irenaeus and Cyprian.

The old tests of authentic tradition, consensus, and universality reappeared in this argument. Even advocates of papal supremacy acknowledged them when they conceded that, though the pope normally held unlimited authority over the Church, he was subject to the Church and to the council as its representative in matters of faith. They sometimes mitigated this thought with the argument that the bishop of Rome, falling into heresy, instantly lost his office, that consequently no pope could be heretical, and that in such a case it only remained for a universal council, as the surviving representative of the Church, to declare the see vacant. The cogency of universal witness was generally admitted; and beyond these canonistic arguments lay critical doctrines of popular sovereignty in the Church, as expressed for example by Nicholas of Cusa, and the more radical ideas of a "lay Church" as set forth by Marsiglio of Padua and William of Ockham.

The Great Schism and its antecedents reinforced this view. "It could never be admitted that the 'seamless robe' had been rent apart, and if the hierarchical organization which should have manifested the intrinsic unity of the Church had become riven by inveterate schism, it was natural that well-intentioned churchmen should turn with new enthusiasm to the ancient doctrine of a unity inherent in the whole *congregatio fidelium*, a mystical unity that could never be compromised by the dissensions of popes and prelates."[10] The language and the thought of the age we have reviewed appeared again in the appeals of Wycliff and Hus to the generality of the Church, though they at times shared the Waldensian view that "tradition" described the "Pharisaism" of the papacy.

What we have in fact traced under the name "tradition" is the idea that the cohesive element of the Church, as a community, lay outside any system of laws and offices, and that the legitimacy of legal and administrative orders depended on their consonance with that external element. We have also seen that general consensus of the community was constantly taken to be the chief touchstone of authenticity. The de-

[10] Tierney, *Foundations*, 222.

velopment toward abstract principles of justice and doctrines of popular sovereignty, as represented by the late mediaeval conciliarists, suggests that these basic premises may have had wider implications in political thought.

Indeed, it is reasonable to assume that intensification of issues of authority within the Church had natural ramifications in questions of secular power, the nucleus of "national" Churches. The view of the imperialists and of the schismatic cardinals in the late eleventh century that a pope's heresy freed the faithful of obedience to him, the thought of Peter Damian and Cardinal Deusdedit that a papal decree was binding only upon those who accepted it, and the position expressed in the electoral crisis of 1130 that the authenticity of the papal title depended upon universal acceptance by believers had counterparts in secular political thought.[11] The technical importance of the coronation oath as a condition of accession, Manegold of Lautenbach's more abstract contractual doctrine, and the thought of Gregory VII and the rebellious Saxons that personal unworthiness impaired or negated a king's official powers, showed that some thinkers were qualifying the concept of secular authority along corresponding lines. The incumbent, pope or king, was not the incarnation of powers, but the servant of abstract principles of justice.[12] Certainly from the ninth century onward, the principle emerged in ecclesiological and in political thought that governmental authority derived from the consent of the articulate governed, and that a ruler's assumption of office and the validity of his acts depended upon approval, or at least acceptance, by his more powerful subjects.

Certainly it would be excessive to see these tendencies in political thought, and especially the drive toward a contract theory of government, as aspects of thought about tradition as an authority in the Church. Their relation to our theme is more analogous than direct. The same may be true of the currents in late mediaeval canonistic thought which we have mentioned, but to a lesser degree, since the issues and even the language of debate were linearly related on many levels to the conflicts we have described.

It would be wrong to claim too much for the idea of tradition; it would likewise be wrong to underestimate the impact of an idea that

[11] Cf. the theory of some twelfth-century Byzantine canonists that Rome lost its primacy to Constantinople when, in their view, the pope became a heretic (Dvornik, *Apostolicity*, 289). Above, p. 343. Below, p. 400.

[12] Cf. Fliche, *Réforme* 3, 323.

purported to define both the authentic doctrine of salvation, the warrant of the Church's very existence, and the means by which that doctrine was conveyed and preserved from corruption. From the standpoint of one important current in constitutional thought, ecclesiology, we can say this: In each religious grouping according to its own idiom, the concept of tradition conditioned men to seek ultimate standards of authority outside laws and offices, and to see rulers of the Church as servants of abstract principles. With the growth of Church order in the West, this fundamental element brought men at least to the threshold of doctrines of responsible, representative government. Disputes over the idea of tradition raised the basic questions of Church order and set the terms of authenticity which were commonly acknowledged, and by which later generations framed their answers.

Whatever its ramifications, the idea of tradition itself has remained one of the great open questions in European history. It has always flourished among some thinkers, especially among those who wish to limit administrative powers without a revolutionary change of system.

Is Christianity mainly a way of life, as men thought who appealed to the generality of the faithful, or a system of order, as advocates of formalism held? Despite the transference of its effective functions to administrative and juridical apparatus, tradition has remained a rallying cry of all parties in the great theological controversies of the western Church. It was so for St. Thomas Aquinas and for thinkers during the Reformation of the sixteenth century; it is so in our own day. The debate in the first Vatican Council concerning papal infallibility epitomized the timeless impasse and the disinterest in underlying social diversity which different views of tradition have met since the age of the apologists; for, opposed by bishops who pleaded that the tradition of the Church contradicted the doctrine of infallibility, Pope Pius IX declared simply, "*La tradizione son' io.*" Ideas cannot be abstracted from the world of men. In the renewed theological consideration of tradition in the twentieth century, and in the great movements toward community of hope among Christians, that confrontation is an exhortation to charity, and an admonition.

> Thy sacred Academie above
> Of Doctors, whose pains have unclasp'd and taught
> Both bookes of life to us . . .
> . . . pray for us there

359

That what they have misdone or mis-said, wee to that may
    not adhere;
Their zeale may be our sinne. Lord, let us runne
Meane waies and call them stars, but not the Sunne.

        John Donne, *Divine Poems*, xiii, "The Doctors."

# Appendices

# Second Thoughts on the Attitudes of Popes Nicholas I and John VIII Toward Temporal Government

In *The Two Kingdoms*, I described Nicholas I and John VIII as thorough-going papal monists, who understood Church order and temporal government as parts of a unitary system under the command of the papacy. I have since then come to a very different conclusion. To elucidate my comments in the preceding text, it seems advisable to add here a summary of these second—and, I believe, more correct—thoughts.

The bishops who wrote that Nicholas counted himself an Apostle among the Apostles also protested that "he made himself the emperor of the whole world,"[1] and a later chronicler wrote that "he commanded kings and tyrants, and presided over them with authority, as though he were the lord of the world."[2] In responding to enquiries of the Bulgarians, he compiled books of secular law for their consultation.[3] He admonished Frankish bishops to reproach their sinful kings,[4] reminding Adventius of Metz that rulers who governed wickedly were not kings to be obeyed, but tyrants to be resisted.[5] These facts suggest that Nicholas adopted an assertive attitude of ecclesiastical superiority over temporal government.

Instead, he held the conventional view that the Church and the civil power were institutionally discrete, and his concept of tradition led him further to consider temporal intervention in Church affairs a positive threat to authentic faith and discipline. Concerned to maintain the distinction between secular powers and priestly orders,[6] Nicholas thought

---

[1] PL 121, 379.

[2] Regino, Chronicon (a. 868); MGH SS. I, 579. Cf. Ullmann, *Growth*, 200, concerning Nicholas: "The point to bear in mind is that Christ's distribution of the functions, sacerdotal and regal, is now suggested to be vicariously in papal hands." Cf. also *ibid.*, 201: "The mother-function of the Roman Church is, by virtue of the approximation of the pope's vicariate of St. Peter to a vicariate of Christ, greatly, though logically, extended to those who even refused to acknowledge the primacy of the 'mother church.' Nevertheless, the mother-function of the Roman Church is paralleled by the father-function of the pope himself."

[3] MGH Epp. VI, k. a. 4, no. 99, cc. 13, 19: 575, 578.

[4] *Ibid.*, nos. 47, 53: 327, 340f.

[5] *Ibid.*, no. 31, 299. Cf. no. 24, 288.

[6] *Ibid.*, no. 39, 313f.

that a complete functional distinction excluded clergy from temporal affairs and laymen from spiritual matters.[7] His objection to Photius's accession was that, though Sardica forbade the election of bishops from the laity,[8] Photius had been elevated from the daily concerns of public administration to usurp what belonged to bishops,[9] that he had become a doctor before he had been taught, a master before he had been a disciple, an illuminator before he had received light.[10] Lacking spiritual authority, laymen could not bind and loose pontiffs,[11] nor could they judge priests.[12] Divine law sometimes forbade what human law allowed;[13] and despite many points of agreement between the two bodies of law,[14] the Church remained subject exclusively to Gospel, apostolic, and canonical decrees.[15]

In the Photian controversy, Nicholas argued explicitly that, by not respecting the institutional integrity of the Church, Michael III had violated tradition. Descending from the imperial throne, he wrote, Michael had ascended the pontifical seat and assumed the episcopal ministry.[16] Bishops had been neglected, and canonical order cast aside when laymen were employed in ecclesiastical government and given the power to remove bishops at will, replacing them with men of their own choosing.[17] Acting without the consent of the Roman pontiff,[18] Michael and his pseudo-synod had committed the "execrable apostasy" of falsifying Nicholas's letters concerning Photius;[19] they had undone "ecclesiastical traditions,"[20] "those traditions which we received of old from our Fathers,"[21] "the traditions of the Roman See."[22]

Violations of ecclesiastical order such as these and the general threat they represented had no effective remedy. Nicholas wrote that Christian kings should willingly serve "their mother, the Church, of whom they have been spiritually born";[23] that they governed "the people of God";[24] and that, among ancient kings, many were truly called kings,

[7] *Ibid.*, no. 104, 613. Cf. no. 99, c. 95, 597.
[8] *Ibid.*, no. 82, 434f.   [9] *Ibid.*, no. 86, 448.   [10] *Ibid.*, no. 82, 434f.
[11] *Ibid.*, no. 88, 486.   [12] *Ibid.*, no. 99, c. 70, 592.   [13] *Ibid.*, no. 57, 357.
[14] E.g., *ibid.*, nos. 88, 165: 461, 463, 686f.
[15] *Ibid.*, no. 57, 357.   [16] *Ibid.*, no. 88, 469f.   [17] *Ibid.*, no. 91, 531.
[18] *Ibid.*, no. 90, 492.
[19] *Ibid.*, nos. 91, 98: 516, 554f, 562.
[20] *Ibid.*, no. 88, 483.   [21] *Ibid.*, no. 100, 604.
[22] *Ibid.*, no. 100, 605. Cf. no. 90, 508.
[23] *Ibid.*, no. 99, c. 18, 578.
[24] *Ibid.*, no. 7, 274. Cf. no. 22, 287.

since they were worthy of the company of saints.[25] But Nicholas saw no institutional means of impairing the official powers of rulers who prejudiced the interests of the Church, and who proved themselves tyrants instead of true kings. He wrote urging Michael not to appear an ungrateful son toward his mother (the Church), from whom he and his fathers received the Empire, and to struggle against the enemies of the Church with religion rather than with material force.[26] Nicholas claimed the Emperor as his "dearest son," and urged him to choose whether he wished to be numbered among the persecutors of the Church, such as Nero and Diocletian, or among those "who exalted the Church of God, and especially the Roman Church," such as Constantine the Great and Theodosius the Great.[27] When Michael persisted in the policy Nicholas condemned, the Pope "strongly grieved" that he had chosen to follow in the footsteps of wicked princes, neglecting the decrees of the Apostolic See.[28] Angered by the contemptuous, "indeed blasphemous" attitude of Michael's envoy,[29] Nicholas resorted to an irrelevant flourish, forbidding Michael to call himself "Emperor of the Romans" on the ground that, not knowing the language of the Romans, he disparaged it as "barbaric and Scythic."[30] In institutional terms, Nicholas summarized his position by paraphrasing the dualistic thought set forth by Gelasius I in his *De Anathematis Vinculo*.[31]

Nicholas observed the functional distinction explicit in this passage even in dealing with Louis II, whom Pope Sergius II had crowned as king (844) and Leo IV as emperor. Louis had received his kingdom, Nicholas wrote, by hereditary right, which the authority of the Apostolic See confirmed with the imperial diadem.[32] When the king of the Bulgars sent his weapons to Nicholas as tokens of his victory "in the name of Christ," Louis commanded that the arms and other gifts which the King had presented to St. Peter be sent him. Nicholas sent some things, and made an excuse about others,[33] a sign of acquiescence to the temporal headship of his "spiritual and dearest son."[34] Similarly,

---

[25] *Ibid.*, no. 99, c. 42, 583.     [26] *Ibid.*, no. 90, 508f.     [27] *Ibid.*, no. 88, 484.

[28] *Ibid.*, no. 90, 504.     [29] *Ibid.*, no. 91, 529.

[30] *Ibid.*, no. 88, 459. Louis II commented upon the same attitude in his famous letter to Basil I (MGH Epp. VII, k. a. 5, 390).

[31] MGH Epp. VI, k. a. 4, no. 88, 485f. See above, pp. 101f.

[32] *Ibid.*, no. 34, 305.

[33] Annal. Bertin. (a. 866). MGH SS. in us. schol., 86.

[34] *Liber pontificalis*, Vita Nicolai I, 7, ed. Duchesne 2, 152. Cf. MGH Epp. VI, k. a. 4, no. 33, 303.

Nicholas neglected to press claims of institutional superiority in the case of Lothair II. Appealed to both by Lothair and by Theutberga, the King's rejected wife, Nicholas first left adjudication of the case to the Synod of Metz (863); he instructed his legate to declare his sentence only if the Synod should not meet, or if Lothair failed to appear before the Synod.[35] The judgment of the Synod, which ran counter to Nicholas's opinion, and Lothair's subsequent profligacy, kept the case open; Nicholas wondered whether Lothair were truly to be called king,[36] and, at length, excommunicated him.[37] Nicholas wrote that he had hesitated to excommunicate Lothair, fearing bloodshed and war;[38] and, though he urged Charles the Bald and Louis the German to seek Lothair's "correction," he never appealed to them as executors of his decree or identified excommunication with deposition.[39] In other matters, Lothair defied Nicholas's attempt to curtail his power in filling episcopal sees,[40] Louis the German withheld for two years revenue which Nicholas claimed as due St. Peter,[41] and Louis the German and Charles the Bald forced the Pope to cancel a scheduled synod of Rome by denying their clergy permission to attend. In each case, Nicholas was outraged. He was especially angry that Louis and Charles, in prejudice to his summons, should have required the constant presence of their bishops in military defense against pirates, a violation of the episcopacy's spiritual functions.[42] But in none of these instances did Nicholas adopt any measure stronger than emphatic protest. The functional division which Gelasius described allowed no institutional means of reconciling disputes between the Church and the civil power; Nicholas's thought did not supply that deficiency.

Against wicked kings, Nicholas sometimes urged resistance, but the weapons he prescribed for bishops were admonition and reproof. His excommunication of Lothair II was a unique act, despite the grave provocation which other rulers offered, and Nicholas seems to have attributed no political implications to it.

[35] MGH Epp. VI, k. a. 4, no. 11, 276f.
[36] *Ibid.*, nos. 18, 35: 284, 306.
[37] *Ibid.*, nos. 15, 26, 32 (c. 4), 44, 47: 232, 291, 301, 318f, 326.
[38] *Ibid.*, no. 38, 311.
[39] *Ibid.*, nos. 2, 38, 44: 268, 311, 318f.
[40] *Ibid.*, nos. 13, 14, 15, 23: 279, 281, 288.
[41] *Ibid.*, no. 51, 338.
[42] *Ibid.*, nos. 38, 39: 309f, 313.

Discretion and compromise for political purposes characterized John's ecclesiastical policies, and this in turn led him to resolve the further question of relations with temporal powers in terms of reciprocal engagements.

John's diplomacy in the East, particularly with Byzantium and Bulgaria, suggests his methods and his goals. The case of Photius involved, directly or indirectly, John's aspirations to gain ecclesiastical hegemony, not only in Bulgaria, but also in other eastern provinces, such as Dalmatia[43] and Moravia,[44] where Byzantine influence was ascendant. He was also eager to obtain military assistance from Byzantium. But in the very years when his diplomacy brought Byzantine forces to his assistance during their reconquest of southern Italy,[45] John began separate negotiations to undermine Byzantine influence over Michael, king of the Bulgars. Repeating the claim that the Bulgarian province had anciently belonged to Rome, John warned the King in strong terms against the heresy and guile of the Greeks. Michael had first chosen to follow St. Peter, but latterly he seemed won to the consistently false and crafty arguments of Byzantium. John warned him with the example of the Goths, whom the Byzantines had infected with heresy, and urged him to return to St. Peter, who first recognized and confessed the Son of God, who received the Lord's flocks to rule, and who was promised the keys of the heavenly kingdom.[46] John repeatedly emphasized Rome's headship of all churches. All nations came to Rome, he wrote, as to one mother and one head;[47] all kings and princes had received the word of truth from her;[48] in Rome alone was to be found the faith which Sts. Peter and Paul had preached.[49] Earlier, John had protested that he sought from Michael neither glory nor honor nor emolument nor yet temporal power, but only supervision of dioceses in the King's lands.[50] He offered Basil I recognition of Photius in exchange for military assistance and the concession of Bulgaria; he offered Michael the favor of the Heavenly Keybearer in return for ecclesiastical obedience. But, at the end of his pontificate, John found these negotiations fruitless; excommunicating Photius for failing to withdraw from Bulgaria, he likewise threatened Michael with excommunication for fail-

---

[43] MGH Epp. VII, k. a. 5, no. 196, 157.
[44] *Ibid.*, no. 255, 222.
[45] Cf. *ibid.*, nos. 47, 72, 217, 245, 263: 45, 67, 194, 214, 233.
[46] *Ibid.*, no. 66, 59f. Cf. no. 182, 146.     [47] *Ibid.*, no. 198, 159.
[48] *Ibid.*, no. 192, 154.     [49] *Ibid.*, no. 67, 61.
[50] *Ibid.*, no. 66, 59.

ing to acknowledge Roman ecclesiastical headship as he had promised Nicholas I.[51]

In negotiating with western rulers, John also sought to establish formal relationships of mutual advantage. Far from contesting the political order of "national" churches, he accepted and even approved the decisive powers of temporal government in episcopal elections,[52] and the obligations of fealty which bound bishops to kings.[53] Benedict III had written that "by a special prerogative" (*speciali tamen praerogativa*) Roman bishops cared for the churches of Gaul next after those of Rome and Italy,[54] and John continued that emphasis. His letters to Frankish rulers especially suggest a revival of the terms concluded between the papacy and the early Carolingians to be friends of the ally's friends and enemies of his foes.[55] To the Franks, John offered spiritual sanctions and, in special cases, the imperial crown. From them, he required defense of Rome and of the Petrine patrimony.[56]

The terms of alliance became particularly clear in the negotiations with Charles the Bald before and after Charles's imperial coronation. Soon after his accession, John had written angrily to Charles, threatening to inflict upon him the punishment which Hadrian II had threatened.[57] But in 876, "John, the supreme pontiff and universal pope," received Charles as his "spiritual son," secured his election as king of Italy, and crowned him emperor.[58] Soon after the death of Louis II, John wrote to Charles recalling that his imperial accession had been hoped for even in the time of Nicholas I, to serve "the honor and exaltation of the holy Roman Church and the security of the Christian people."[59] In a later sermon, John described more fully the functions

[51] *Ibid.*, nos. 182, 192, 308: 146, 154, 267.

[52] E.g., *ibid.*, nos. 248, 252, 4: 217, 220, 316f.

[53] E.g., *ibid.*, no. 5, 318.

[54] PL 115, 693f.

[55] Wallach, "Amicus." Cf. MGH Epp. VII, k. a. 5, no. 44, 43: "*ita ut ipsius amicos et inimicos nostros amicos et inimicos existere teneamus.*"

[56] Cf. his dealings with Charles the Bald in 876-877, *ibid.*, nos. 24, 31, 33, 36: 22, 29, 33, 35f. See Engreen, "John," 325ff.

[57] *Ibid.*, no. 6, 277, ii. John apparently referred to Hadrian's threat of excommunication in the case of Hincmar of Laon.

[58] MGH Cap. 2, no. 200, 99. The evidence presented in this section seems to warrant modification of the view that John was a *Papstkaiser*, who "never let the initiative slip from his hands." See Ullmann, *Growth*, 164ff.

[59] MGH Epp. VII, k. a. 5, no. 59, 311. Cf. *ibid.*, no. 7, 321, where he alleged that both Nicholas I and Hadrian II had elected Charles because he had brought the church of Gaul to a new flowering. See Ullmann, *Growth*, 161ff.

Charles was expected to discharge. Charles, he said, had been elected by divine providence from before the creation of the world to follow the Great Charles, who had exalted all churches, and had especially "reformed the Roman church into its ancient state and order,"[60] conferring upon it many honors and emoluments, restoring cities to its government and adding not a few cities from his own realm to its control. Charlemagne had purified religion with sacred learning, and encouraged both divine and human knowledge to the eradication of error. To continue this work, God had established Charles the "savior of the world"; the Roman Senate, clergy, and people elected him as emperor. By anointing him, John conferred upon Charles through grace the kingly character which Christ possessed through nature.[61] The comments on Charlemagne's munificence toward the Roman church were perhaps more to the point than the conventional references to divine election; for Charles had taken the "royal vows" (*vota regia*) at the tomb of St. Peter, before he received the imperial dignity through the imposition of John's hands.[62]

The exact terms of Charles's oath are unknown, as indeed are those of the vows of Pippin and Charlemagne on which it was probably patterned. That it established obligations of reciprocal assistance can, however, be judged from John's subsequent letters. He repeatedly appealed to Charles for military defense, especially against Saracen attacks, urging Charles to come quickly to assist the Roman Church, his "mother," from whom he had received both government and faith [63] For his part, John used the full strength of spiritual sanctions to defend Charles from his enemies. At the Synod of Ravenna (877), which met to confirm Charles's coronation, the Pope had anathematized anyone who should attempt to overthrow Charles,[64] an obvious allusion to Louis the German, who had invaded Charles's lands in 876 when Charles was in Italy for his imperial coronation. In his letters to the bishops and nobility of Gaul, John admonished them to honor their vows of loyalty to Charles,[65] and contrasted Charles, whose vows befitted "the most Christian defender of Christ's Church," with Louis, whose invasion raised

---

[60] Bouquet 7, 694f.
[61] *Loc.cit.*
[62] PL 126, 658, no. 13.
[63] MGH Epp. VII, k. a. 5, no. 22, 20. Cf. *ibid.*, no. 32, 31.
[64] Bouquet 7, 697, no. 50.
[65] MGH Epp. 7, k. a. 5, no. 5, 318.

doubts as to whether he should rightly be called a king.[66] He urged Louis's bishops to dissuade him from his aggression and forbade his counts to support it.[67] For Charles, he wrote, had become emperor, not by human cession, but by divine, through John's ministry,[68] and their undertaking against him was in fact against God.[69]

After Charles's death, John again sought a protector. Louis' son, Carloman, invaded Italy and demanded the imperial crown. He was aided by Lambert of Spoleto, who attacked Rome and kept John under guard. On Lambert's withdrawal, John set sail for Gaul, "seeking peace and aid" where his predecessors had sought it.[70] He wished to take council with the West Frankish rulers "concerning joint deliverance of the Holy Roman Church and the state of the commonwealth."[71] He seems at one time to have had in mind a sort of collective defense afforded by the heirs of Charles the Bald and those of Louis the German.[72] At another, he held the promise of the Roman Empire before Louis III of West Francia.[73] At the Synod of Troyes, he secured the anathematization of Lambert of Spoleto and his other enemies, and he took the occasion particularly to exhort Louis the Stammerer to defend the Roman Church from which, through his ancestors, he received pure doctrine and imperial distinction.[74] But he found no sure hope of support; and he returned to Rome complaining that his search had failed and that he had experienced the fulfillment of the verse, "Since iniquity has abounded, the love of many waxes cold."[75]

John had, in the meantime, entered negotiations with Boso of Vienne, whom he had adopted as his "spiritual son."[76] When Carloman of Bavaria, who also controlled northern Italy, was rumored to be so ill as to have become incapable "of retaining the kingdom," John proposed a synod to consider electing his successor, possibly Boso. He forbade the archbishop of Milan to accept anyone as king without his consent, on the grounds that the man whom John was to consecrate as emperor

---

[66] *Ibid.*, no. 6, 318f.

[67] *Ibid.*, nos. 7, 8: 321f, 323.

[68] *Ibid.*, no. 7, 321.    [69] *Ibid.*, no. 8, 325.    [70] *Ibid.*, no. 109, 101.

[71] *Ibid.*, no. 88, 84: "*de communi salvatione sanctae Romanae ecclesiae et reipublicae statu.*" Cf. no. 64, 57: "*de statu reipublicae totiusque Christiani populi salvatione.*"

[72] *Ibid.*, no. 109, 101.

[73] *Ibid.*, no. 205, 165.

[74] *Ibid.*, no. 87, 82. Cf. *ibid.*, nos. 115, 150, 105f, 126.

[75] *Ibid.*, no. 116, 106; Matt. 24:12.

[76] *Ibid.*, no. 110, 102.

should have John as his first elector.[77] John wished to consider the matter in synod,[78] but Carloman's partial recovery[79] and the diplomacy of Carloman and his brothers ultimately brought John to abandon Boso as an imperial candidate and to accept Charles the Fat as emperor.

Charles the Fat's failure to answer John's summons to conference during the Pope's journey into Gaul had signified to John that Charles did not wish to fulfill the vows which his father and grandfather had made to the Roman Church. John had reproved him for his "disobedience."[80] But in 879, John addressed him as a "beloved and spiritual son," and urged him to delay no longer in going to the defense of the Roman Church.[81] Under extraordinary pressures from "pagans and wicked Christians," John conferred on Charles the unusual honor of meeting him at Ravenna as he advanced to Rome for his coronation (880).[82] But neither extraordinary honors nor John's constant pleas for assistance brought the defense he wished.[83] In his last letters, John repeated the complaint that Charles had not given the Roman Church the protection to which the imperial office obliged him.[84]

It is difficult in John's negotiations with temporal rulers to discover the workings of any programmatic ideological principles. Some authors have considered as expressions of a sweeping concept of papal supremacy over temporal government John's exalted view of Rome as "the head of the world," his wish to consider synodically the question of Carloman of Bavaria's successor, his view of the sacramental office he performed in imperial coronations, and his fervent admonitions to Frankish emperors that their first duty was to defend Rome.[85]

But circumstances suggest another plausible, and more moderate interpretation. The terms concerning Roman supremacy were conventional, and in themselves, they implied nothing beyond predominance within the ecclesiastical hierarchy. John's proposal to consider Carloman's successor presupposed that Carloman was already incapable of government; the Pope did not specifically refer to deposition, and it is at least possible that he proposed to seek a man who would tech-

---

[77] *Ibid.*, no. 163, 133.
[78] *Loc.cit.*
[79] Cf. *ibid.*, nos. 179, 186, 193, 241: 143f, 148, 155, 212.
[80] *Ibid.*, no. 110, 102.   [81] *Ibid.*, no. 180, 144.   [82] *Ibid.*, no. 224, 199.
[83] E.g., *ibid.*, nos. 251, 309: 219, 268.
[84] *Ibid.*, no. 304, 263.
[85] E.g., Ullmann, *Growth*, 222ff; Morrison, *Kingdoms*, 264ff.

371

nically be co-regent with Carloman until the latter's death, assuming then sole powers of government. That would have been a variation on the normal Carolingian practice of acknowledging sons as co-regents with their fathers. In any case, John proposed to act, not arbitrarily, but with the counsel of others, particularly of the archbishop of Milan; and, when Carloman seemed likely to recover, the Pope abandoned the project altogether. While writing in lofty terms of his powers to conse-crate emperors, John was always careful to affirm that particular em-perors came to the purple by divine election, which his own actions in some sense confirmed. His earnest petitions for imperial defense were inspired by the reciprocal understanding which he wished the corona-tion to establish, on his side by the act of consecration, and, on the part of the emperors, by the "royal vows."

These particular points, therefore, are insufficient to establish that John acted according to a systematic doctrine of papal supremacy over temporal power. Considered in their historical context and in con-junction with John's Byzantine negotiations, they suggest diplomacy rather than ecclesiology. Instead of the implementation of ideological principles, they indicate the effort of the Pope, as head of an inde-pendent, but beleaguered principality, to gain military defense in ex-change for the unique spiritual sanctions he claimed to command.

# Saxon Germany and the Myth of the Sacerdotal King

A HIGHLY RESPECTED SCHOOL of historical opinion has recently sprung up, holding that the Saxon kings of Germany were in some sense "sacerdotal," and that they considered themselves and were considered at least quasi-papal. This is a matter of great importance for anyone who studies the concepts of Church authority in the tenth century. It is central to the question of how sacred knowledge was thought to be transmitted; for it suggests that the Saxons modified or discarded entirely the Fathers' view that only priests, and especially bishops, were bearers of tradition.

I do not belong to the *Rex-Sacerdos* school of interpretation, which, in my view, distorts our perspective by overemphasizing the evidence of liturgy and the language of controversy at the expense of plain history.[1] Since this attitude colors my treatment of the tenth century, and especially my discussion of the Investiture Conflict, I think it only honest to say why I dissent from a fashionable and cogent school.

It has rightly been said that the imperial coronation of Otto I (962) drew a chronological caesura through the middle of the tenth century.[2] Afterwards the relations between Germany and Italy, and between the papacy and northern Europe, changed radically and permanently. But what concept of empire guided those new relations? Ecclesiastical cohesion was understood in legal and administrative terms. Where did imperial authority fit into that pattern, and what part did it play in communicating the means of salvation?

Perhaps because of scant documentation, scholarly opinions vary extremely on these points. One learned author has described the Ottonian concept of empire as reaching its fullest development in Otto III, who, in his interpretation, acted jointly with Pope Gregory V "as an ideational universal *Rex-Sacerdos*."[3] "Otto III," he wrote, "was emperor and 'pope.' "[4] This interpretation rests on the identification of the Ot-

---

[1] For similar reservations concerning the supposed "sacral kingship" of the ancient Teutons, see the very convincing essay by Baetke, *Yngvi*.

[2] Zimmermann, "Papstabsetzungen" II, 75f.

[3] Ullmann, *Growth*, 240, n. 6. See p. 237, n. 1: "Governmentally, of course, Otto I was Rex-Sacerdos (in the sense in which we use the term, see supra p. 156). . . ."

[4] Ullmann, *Growth*, 240.

tonian Empire with the Roman Empire, and on the further premise that the *imperium christianum* and the *imperium Romanum* were identical.[5] It strengthens these identifications by pointing out that mediaeval thinkers understood that the Germanic Empire, like the Roman, was an amalgam of several kingdoms.[6] And it extends them to include the so-called *Rex-Sacerdos* idea by pointing to the concept of sacral kingship which flourished among the Germanic peoples.[7] This latter concept received expression in coronation rituals as described, for example, in a letter supposedly sent from Bishop John XII of Ravenna to Berengar (ca. 905): "For the empire differs little from priesthood, and, no doubt, the prince of empire is sometimes called priest, since clearly priests and kings are sanctified from one horn of oil."[8] Empire was "sacred";[9] the emperor was "holy."[10]

There are, however, distinct limits to this interpretation. The identification of the Ottonian Empire with the Roman is not entirely secure. The words *Renovatio imperii Romanorum* do appear on a seal of Otto III; Hrothsvitha and, in one letter, Gerbert call the Ottonian realm *imperium Romanum*.[11] Still, in a letter written in the name of

[5] *Loc.cit.* and pp. 234, 236. Dr. Ullmann argues (p. 89) that Romanus= Christianus in Carolingian and post-Carolingian thought. As support, he points out: "In other prayers the amalgamation of 'Christianitas' and 'Romanitas' went so far that the original term 'Romanus' was exchanged for 'Christianus.' Thus, for example, in the Gelasian sacramentary the reference to the 'Romani' was altered in the Frankish sacramentaries to 'Christiani.' " I may venture to suggest, in view of the particularistic ecclesiology and the overt dislike of Rome which Franks and Germans sometimes expressed (below, pp. 375f.), that this substitution may be explained in terms of aversion, rather than those of identity. For the thought among some tenth-century writers that "*Romani* gab es nur in Rom . . . ," see Beumann, *Widukind, passim*, and esp. p. 264f. On Charlemagne's "Entrömisierung von Karls Kaisertum," see Ohnsorge, *Abendland*," 122, 125.

[6] In addition to Dr. Ullmann's comments, see Löwe, "Kaisertum," 534f; Johnson, *Activities*, 32, 112, 197; Schieffer, "Kanzlei," 27, 36, 145f, 148.

[7] On the cults of Sigismund and Guntram, see Folz, "Frage," esp. 317. On the Ottos, see Beumann, "Legitimierung," 44f.

[8] Loewenfeld, "Briefe," 531: "*Nam imperium a sacerdotio parum distat, et aliquando imperii principem sacerdotem vocari non est dubium quia ex uno cornu olei sacerdotes et reges sanctificari manifestum est.*" See also, a letter to Ardingus of Brescia, *ibid.*, 534: "*Legitur in quibusdam, regem sacerdotem appellari et parum distare imperium a sacerdotio.*" See also Ullmann, *Growth*, 154f.

[9] Loewenfeld, "Briefe," 531.

[10] Liutprand, *De Gestis Ottonis*, cc. 8, 18, MGH in us. schol., 3rd ed., 164, 173.

[11] Erdmann, "Reich," 421ff, 424ff. On Adso of Montier-en-Der, see *ibid.*, 426. The passage, written shortly before Otto I's imperial coronation (949-954), refers to the Roman Empire as enfeebled, and adds: ". . . *quidem vero doctores*

Hugh Capet to the Byzantine emperors, Gerbert himself acknowledged that the Roman Empire had ended. In his diatribe against Arnulf of Rheims, the Bishop of Orleans said the same thing.[12] Otto III's cousin, Bruno of Querfurt, lamented that the Emperor had spent his strength trying to renew the dead beauty of an aged Rome,[13] and in the minds of other thinkers the Roman Empire was a thing of the past.[14]

The identification of the Roman and the Ottonian Empires was not, therefore, generally taken for granted, even in the Ottonian chancery. Neither was universality or regal sacerdotalism an inevitable attribute of Ottonian government, least of all in dealings with Rome itself.

If the emperor was the vicar of Christ, Rome was surely his crown of thorns. Divided by language from the Romans,[15] the Saxons were caught in strong cross currents of mutual animosity between their own

---

nostri dicunt, quod unus ex regibus Francorum Romanum imperium ex integro tenebit." It is unclear whether Adso refers to Otto I, who was crowned "rex Francorum" in Aachen (936), or to the "reges Francorum" in France (citations, n. 51). See also Beumann, "Kaisertum," 539. As for Otto III's seal, Beumann's conclusions concerning Widukind are certainly relevant—Widukind, 265: "Widukind müsste auch dies verleugnet haben, wenn sein imperator Romanorum universal gemeint wäre. Dass er ihn Romanorum und nicht Romanus nennt, kann daher geradezu als Beweis dafür gelten, dass er ihn nur partikular im Sinne der Herrschaft über die Römer seiner Zeit, als eine gesteigerte Patriziuswürde verstanden wissen wollte."

[12] Löwe, "Kaisertum," 544f; Erdmann, "Reich," 432; Ullmann, Growth, 234. "And, so it was held, this Roman Empire could never perish." See above, pp. 261f ; Erdmann, "Reich," 430.

[13] Vitae quinque fratrum Poloniae, c 7, MGH SS. 15, pt. 2, 722. Bruno seems to exaggerate when he writes of Otto's positive aversion to Germany, especially in view of the Emperor's reverence for Charlemagne, which led to his burial at Aachen.

[14] Hammer, "Concept," 53, the Versus Romae, attributed to various periods between the seventh and the tenth century. Löwe, "Kaisertum," 537, the Vita Radbodi both failed to identify the Ottonian Empire with the Roman, and predicted that Otto I's empire would not last long. Cf. the letter of William of St. Benigne to Pope John XIX (written 1025-1032)—PL 141, 1157: "Quoniam licet potestas Romani imperii, quae olim in orbe terrarum monarches viguit, nunc per diversa terrarum loca innumeris regatur sceptris, ligandi solvendique in caelo et in terra potestas incumbit magisterio Petri."

[15] E.g., Liutprand, De Gestis Ottonis, c. 11, MGH in us. schol., 3rd ed., 167: "His auditis imperator [Otto I at the trial of John XII] quia Romani eius loquelam propriam, hoc est Saxonicam, intellegere nequibant, Liudprando Cremonensi episcopo precepit, ut Latino sermone haec Romanis omnibus quae secuntur exprimeret."

people and the Romans.[16] They were never able to break the power of the great Roman families—the descendants of Theophylact among the Crescentii and the counts of Tusculum—[17] and thus they were never masters of the papacy, which was constantly a pawn moved by the Roman nobility and people against the emperors, the invaders from the north.

From Otto I's imperial coronation until the death of Otto III there was an unbroken series of plots and armed risings against the Germans and the popes they installed.[18] This constant unrest is epitomized in John XVI's alleged offer of the *decus Romani imperii* to the Byzantines,[19] and in the known conspiracy of John XII with the Magyars and the Byzantines against Otto I, immediately after his imperial coronation.[20] It is difficult to see that harmony of purpose and identity of interest which one scholar saw when he argued: "The universality of the Church is reflected in the ideational universality of Roman emperorship. The emperor's universality is a reflection, not indeed in degree, but in kind of that universality which is epitomized in the Roman Church which confers the dignity of emperorship through the medium of the pope."[21] The Romans and the men they elected as popes had no idea of such a thing. For them, Ottonian headship in Rome was universal neither in an "ideational" nor in a political sense, and the whole history of the Ottos' dealings with Rome can be summarized by one author's description of Otto I's retreat from Italy in 972: "When he returned, nothing

[16] Aside from numerous revolts against the Ottos, see Benedict of St. Andrea's lament after Otto I's imperial coronation that the "king of the Saxons" had captured Rome and reduced her strength to nothing (Chron., c. 39, MGH SS. 3, 719). Cf. the Roman's earlier attitude toward the Burgundians—Liutprand, Antapodosis III, 45, MGH in us. schol., 2nd ed., 74. On the hostility of the Germans, see Beumann, "Legitimierung," 20f; Liutprand, Legatio, c. 12, MGH in us. schol., 3rd ed., 183: "*Dicamus, hoc solo, id est Romanorum nomine quicquid ignobilitatis, quicquid timiditatis, quicquid avaritiae, quicquid luxuriae, quicquid mendacii, immo quicquid vitiorum est, comprehendentes.*" See Hauck, *Kirchengeschichte* 3, 229. On this animosity in the eleventh century, see Löwe, "Kaisertum," 539, 541; Zimmermann, "Papstabsetzungen," III, 77f.

[17] On Alberic II and the fortunes of his family early in the century, see Zimmermann, "Papstabsetzungen," II, 242.

[18] Erdmann, "Reich," 440; Santifaller, *Geschichte*, 29; Zimmermann, "Papstabsetzungen," II, 243, 251ff, 268-279, 284f, 278f; Hauck, *Kirchengeschichte* 3, 223ff.

[19] Arnulf of Milan, *Gesta episc. Mediol.*, c. 11, MGH SS. 8, 9f; Löwe, "Kaisertum," 541; Zimmermann, "Papstabsetzungen," II, 274.

[20] Zimmermann, "Papstabsetzungen," II, 247.

[21] Ullmann, *Growth*, 235.

that he had begun was finished. Stable conditions were far from being created in Rome; the Greeks and Arabs were far from being driven out of Italy; least of all was the relationship with the Papacy clarified. Political predominance had not developed into supremacy."[22]

"Ideational" and "universal" qualities did not determine Ottonian dealings with Rome. Neither do they appear in relations between the German kings and other rulers in northern Europe. To be sure, the imperial title and the special responsibilities it entailed in defense of the Roman Church might have given the emperor an honorific precedence over other rulers. But Europe, outside of Germany and Burgundy, generally failed to acknowledge even that, much less any political supremacy. Even in Italy, the Saxons' imperial title was contested when it was not frankly ignored.[23] Tenth-century kings in France, Mercia,[24] Bulgaria,[25] and perhaps in Spain[26] likewise used the imperial title. Excluding the Byzantines, Charlemagne and his successors had no monopoly on the title in the ninth century.[27] Their adoption of the title may in fact have been inspired by Anglo-Saxon usage, and similar influence may have worked in Otto I's mind, for his first wife was an Anglo-Saxon princess.[28] Even among the Franks in the late ninth century, at least one author considered the title "king" merely an ancient *nomen imperii*.[29] There seems, in other words, to have been a general tendency

[22] Hauck, *Kirchengeschichte* 3, 239: "*Als er zurückkehrte, war nichts von dem, was er begonnen hatte, vollendet; so wenig in Rom gesicherte Zustände geschaffen waren, so wenig waren Griechen und Araber aus Italien vertrieben; am wenigsten war das Verhältnis zum Papsttum geklärt: die politische Übermacht war nicht zur Herrschaft fortgebildet worden.*"

[23] Löwe, "Grenzen," 357f, 373; Löwe, "Kaisertum," 562.

[24] Keller, "Kaisertum," 353f, 355; Stengel, "Kaisertitel," 3ff. Hugh Capet was "Augustus" (Gerbert, ep. 179, in ed. Havet, 160).

[25] Löwe, "Kaisertum," 551.

[26] Löwe, "Grenzen," *passim*.

[27] E.g., Louis the German was called emperor (Stengel, "Kaisertitel," 33). On Anglo-Saxon king-emperors in the ninth century, see Löwe, "Grenzen," 370. The Carolingians' imperial title was also ignored in England and Italy (Löwe, "Grenzen," 353ff). On Paulus Albarus's view concerning the kingdoms of the Franks and the Greeks, see Löwe, "Grenzen," 351f.

[28] Stengel, "Kaisertitel," 28f; Loyn, "Style," 111-15.

[29] Monk of St. Gall, *Gesta Caroli*, I, 5, MGH SS. 2, 733: "*Et dixit rex, quod nomen imperii veteribus in usu fuit: 'Bene!'*" See Beumann, "Nomen," *passim*. Löwe, "Kaisertum," 556: "*Die Theorie vom König als Kaiser in seinem Reich kann also nicht einfach als Reaktion auf Barbarossa und Heinrich VI. verstanden werden. Ihre Wurzeln reichen weit zurück in frühere Jahrhunderte; nur die präzise wissenschaftliche Formulierung und die verschäfften politischen Gegensätze sind für das 12. Jahrhundert in Anspruch zu nehmen.*"

to identify a king as an emperor, especially when he ruled a number of kingdoms.[30] And, if they were Christians, kings naturally understood that an *imperium christianum* existed in their own lands as well as in the realm of men who had been crowned at Rome.[31]

On another level, there is no evidence that the Ottos claimed hegemony over other rulers by virtue of their special *imperium*. Their actual policy of alliance is shown particularly well in the missionary work that they encouraged. At the beginning of the tenth century, all the lands to the north, east, and southeast lay open for Christianization.[32] Military conquest, colonization, and ecclesiastical organization went together; like Charlemagne, the Ottos had "the missionary follow the flag."[33] The establishment of episcopal sees and the nomination of bishops were instruments of political control. Despite every effort to make Hamburg-Bremen the center of missionary work in the north, the Scandinavian kings allowed Anglo-Saxon missionaries to compete with German for converts, and utterly declined political subjection to the German kings.[34]

Perhaps the Ottos' most enduring success occurred in the East, but even there the Saxon rulers were forced to yield political headship in order to retain some measure of influence.

Even in Poland and the Slavic provinces, acquisitions were impermanent. After 962, Otto I saw them begin to slip away. By the death of Otto III, they had all but vanished; there was no question at all of universal supremacy.[35] Miesko I removed himself from German suzerainty by surrendering his lands to the Pope and receiving them back in fief (990). His son, Boleslas Chrobry, having demonstrated Poland's independence by force of arms, secured a temporary peace with Otto III at the price of total ecclesiastical freedom from German control. Gnesen was erected as an archiepiscopal see, and the new bishoprics of Breslau, Kolberg, and Krakau were subordinated to it.[36] Re-

[30] Stengel, "Kaisertum," 11.

[31] Löwe, "Kaisertum," 562.

[32] Johnson, *Activities*, 166.

[33] Johnson, *Activities*, 171; Sullivan, "Missionary," 722f; Kirchberg, *Kaiseridee*, 47.

[34] Johnson, *Activities*, 169. On the same tension in the eleventh century, see Kirchberg, *Kaiseridee*, 99ff, 107f.

[35] Beumann, "Kaisertum," 531f: "*Von einer Universalherrschaft über das christliche Abendland, wie die Karl d. Gr. noch hatte ausüben können, konnte ohne hin keine Rede mehr sein.*"

[36] Cf. Johnson, *Activities*, 180. This independence received complete symbolic

peated revolts from the death of Otto II onward also shook German rule over northern and Slavic lands. In the north, bishops were expelled from Oldenburg, Havelburg, and Brandenburg; sees among the Slavs were all but extinguished.[37]

By the year 1001, the Ottos had lost Rome, Bohemia, Poland, and the Slavic and Danish lands. Otto II's expeditions against the Byzantines and Saracens in Italy were as disastrous as his military undertakings in France and Germany. Otto III had no time to recover the losses. The Saxons' imperial title was not universally acknowledged, nor, in fact, did the Ottos themselves ever claim in negotiations with other rulers that "ideational" universality which had been ascribed to them. Their relations with Rome and with the missionary fields to the north and east likewise gave reason to doubt that they thought of their office in terms of the *Rex-Sacerdos* idea. They certainly sought political control of bishoprics and, indeed, of Rome itself. But sacerdotalism seems not to have colored those efforts. Otto I scrupulously sought papal establishment of new sees in 947-948, 962, and again in 967;[38] Merseburg was extinguished by Gregory V, not by Otto II. With Boleslas Chrobry, Otto III secured the erection of the Polish sees by Sylvester II and, with Stephan of Hungary, that of Gran (Esztergom). Later, Merseburg was likewise restored and Bamberg erected by papal action. A distinction must be drawn between the very great political influence which these rulers patently had and used to arrange Church order advantageously, and the rightful, even constitutional, functions of a ruler who, as both king and priest, holds the power to convey the means of salvation. The latter, the Saxon rulers never claimed or exercised.

In this regard, much attention has been given the title which Otto III assumed in the year 1000, after his pilgrimage to Gnesen: *servus Jesu Christi*, a title assumed by St. Paul. In the next year, Otto adopted a second title: *servus apostolorum*.[39]

Did Otto arrogate an apostolic character? Perhaps he did, in the sense of a putative decree of John XIX which declared that anyone could be called an apostle whom divine revelation sent to preach and who freed

---

expression in 1024, when Boleslas was crowned king of Poland. In 1003, Henry II was forced to make common cause with the heathen Liutizi against Boleslas (Kirchberg, *Kaiseridee*, 72f).

[37] Johnson, *Activities*, 174ff; Hauck, *Kirchengeschichte* 3, 242-53.

[38] See esp. Keller, "Kaisertum," 362ff.

[39] Ullmann, *Growth*, 239f; Kirchberg, *Kaiseridee*, 59.

his people from the devil.[40] But to the emperor who had watched the missionary sees of his grandfather overturned and had just participated in freeing the Polish church from his allegiance, the title can only have been an "ideational" compensation for real loss, an expression of piety and dedication, but not an assumption of sacerdotal character.

To return to the question: What concept of Empire did guide the Saxons? What coordinates of political thought directed their ecclesiastical actions? It is perfectly agreed that there was no common understanding of the powers the Empire held in its relation to Rome and to the papacy, in ecclesiastical administration, or even in matters of temporal government. There was no imperial constitution and thus there could be no imperial constitutional theory.[41] One scholar has argued cogently that "it is impossible to speak of the operation of a specific 'imperial' idea in this period."[42]

The thought has been advanced most convincingly that the concept of Empire was in constant flux, both at the Ottonian court and among contemporary historical writers. Widukind, Hrothsvitha, and Liutprand each conceived the Empire in diverse ways and, in some instances, differently at different times.[43] We have already observed that Gerbert at one time wrote that the Roman Empire had ended, and at another, that Otto III governed it.[44]

The character of the imperial office was certainly not settled in the days of Otto I, or perhaps even in his own mind.[45] Otto himself seems to have come by stages to the concept of imperial dignity which achieved fullest expression in the Roman coronation in 962, but which popular speech had given him at least in 955, on the Lechfeld.[46] There is reason

[40] PL 141, 1150; Dvornik, *Apostolicity*, does not discuss this document (JL 4092 [3114]).

[41] For schematic discussions of major views on the subject, see Beumann, "Romkaiser," 157f; Löwe, "Kaisertum," 558f; Stengel, "Kaiser," 157.

[42] Mommsen, *Studien*, 66: "*Es ist für diese Periode nicht möglich von Auswirkungen einer spezifisch 'imperialen' Idee zu sprechen.*" Mommsen continues to say that such an idea did emerge in the twelfth century. See also Löwe, "Grenzen," 345.

[43] Keller, "Kaisertum," 385f.          [44] See above, pp. 374f.

[45] Keller, "Kaisertum," 387.

[46] Mommsen, *Studien*, 57f; Keller, "Kaisertum," 328, 344f; Stengel, "Kaiser," 263ff. Widukind calls Otto "emperor" in his narrative from the battle of the Lechfeld onward, though he never mentioned Otto's imperial coronation (Stengel, "Kaiser," 270; "Kaisertitel," 30f). Beumann, "Kaisertum," 545, rightly points out, however, that Widukind neglected other critical things, such as Otto's preoccupation with missionary work in the East.

to argue that for Otto I and his immediate successors, their empire was not a universal, Roman realm, but a particularistic "non-Roman," or "Rome-free," kingdom.[47]

Post-Ottonian thinkers may suggest a solution to the problem by arguing that the empire was not at all Roman. It had passed, they held, from the Romans to the Greeks, from them to the Franks, and, finally, from the Franks to the Germans.[48] Like the king-emperors in France, England, and Spain, the Ottonians seem to have rested their imperial power on government of a specific people, or of a number of peoples.[49] In the terms of one author, the emperor was "Roman," but the imperial people, the bearers and the conferrants of the imperial title, were Frankish.[50] When he was crowned as king in 936, Otto the Great heard the Archbishop of Cologne say: "Receive this sword, with which you may cast out all enemies of Christ, barbarians and wicked Christians, by the divine authority given to you, with all the power of the whole empire of the Franks, to establish the peace of all Christians."[51] In 966, Otto's chancery for a time used the title *imperator augustus Romanorum ac Francorum.*[52] Despite his desire to revive the "Empire

[47] Beumann, "Romkaiser," 174f, and esp. Beumann, *Widukind von Korvei,* 258ff; Mommsen, *Studien,* 174f; Brundage, "Widukind," 15ff; Keller, "Kaisertum," 361: "*Ein solcher universaler Anspruch war der karolingischen Kaiseridee noch durchaus fremd; auch Otto d. Gr. hat ihn nicht aufgenommen.*"

[48] The thought is implied even in Ottonian times by Widukind, and, soon after him, by Notker III of St. Gall, who argued that the Roman Empire had ended. It reached full expression in Otto of Freising (Goez, *Translatio,* 91ff, 109, 116, 206).

[49] Stengel, "Kaiser," 261f.

[50] Beumann, "Romkaiser," *passim,* esp. p. 179f, concerning Charlemagne. P. Classen takes a different view of Charlemagne's concept by tracing the words "*Romanum gubernans imperium*" in one of his titles to Byzantine usage, by way of Ravenna. In Classen's view, the title was precisely a challenge to the Byzantines' assertions of universal government. "Romanum gubernans imperium," esp. 120f.

[51] Widukind, Res gestae Saxonicae, II, 1, MGH SS. in us schol., 5th ed., 66: "*Accipe hunc gladium, quo eicias omnes Christi adversarios barbaros et malos christianos, auctoritate divina tibi tradita omni potestate totius imperii Francorum ad firmissimam pacem omnium Christianorum.*" Kirchberg, *Kaiseridee,* 24. Otto's choice of Aachen as a coronation city and the emphasis on his succession to the *imperium Francorum* was certainly part of his effort to establish firm control over Lorraine, which his father had acquired little more than a decade earlier. See Beumann, "Kaisertum," 538; Schulte, *Aachen,* 10. On the election of Louis the Child, cf. PL 134, 33: "*Et quia reges Francorum semper ex uno genere procedabant. . . .*"

[52] Erdmann, "Reich," 417; Keller, "Kaisertum," 375.

of the Romans," Otto III continued this thought in his profound veneration for Charlemagne, in his plan to establish his residence in Aachen,
and in his desire to be buried near the first Emperor of the Franks.[53]
Under Henry II, the position continued in modified form in the inscrip-
tion around the royal seal: *Renovatio regni Francorum*.[54]

For the Saxons, then, the Empire was basically not Roman, but the
*imperium* (or *regnum*) *Francorum*. What they considered the rightful
place of imperial power in the Church can be judged by their dealings
with the German episcopate.

The terms "State-Church" and "Church System," or a felicitous German amalgam, *Reichskirchensystem*, are often used to describe the directive powers which the Saxon rulers exercised in Church affairs. It is
very plausible to argue that these terms are inexact and, specifically,
that the Ottonians neither thought in terms of institutional structure nor
created a system of government, temporal or ecclesiastical.[55] The point
can readily be granted that the Saxons governed the church as opportunity allowed, rather than as system required—such is always the
nature of politics. This is an important point. But it is still true that, as
occasion offered, they sought and exercised predominance in the German church, and that they may well have wished to extend the same
control over the papacy; Otto III counted the pope among the *opti-
mates* of his realm.[56]

One of the great achievements of Otto I was his incorporation of the
Bavarian episcopate into his own sphere of influence, despite strong regional separatism. The work was a critical part of Bavaria's political
subordination to the German king.[57] The distinction between royal
lands and church lands was gradually obliterated and, by the procedure of investiture, the kings came to control enfeoffment of bishops
with the lands of their churches, and, to some degree, the enfeoffments
by bishops of their own tenants. Church synods met at royal summons

[53] Folz, *Souvenir*, passim.

[54] Kirchberg, *Kaiseridee*, 71. The kings of France continued to be called "*reges
Francorum*." E.g., PL 132, 1072; PL 133, 1015; PL 141, 1145; Gerbert, ep. 111,
in ed. Havet, 101.

[55] See Nitschke, "Einstimmigkeit," 57.

[56] Ullmann, *Growth*, 241ff; Hauck, *Kirchengeschichte* 3, 259. For a general
survey of the Saxons' ecclesiastical activities, see Santifaller, *Geschichte*, 34f.
Santifaller's schematic outline of the *Reichskirchensystem* of the Ottonians and
Salians is in *Geschichte*, 21ff.

[57] Beumann, "Kaisertum," 542.

and often in the presence of the kings.[58] Most important, canonical election of bishops, though observed in form, was most frequently nullified by royal nomination.[59]

The bishops at Gerbert's election wrote of France, but their words apply equally to Germany. They confessed that they had elected Arnulf to the see of Rheims, "impelled by the clamor of the multitude, since Scripture says, 'The voice of the people is the voice of God,' " and since the canons required the desire of clergy and people to be taken in episcopal elections. "But the voice of the people shouting 'Crucify, crucify' was surely not the voice of God. Not every voice of the people, therefore, is the voice of God." With the favor and approval of both their princes, "Lord Hugh, Augustus, and the most excellent King Robert," the bishops of the province of Rheims, "with the assent of those who are God's in the clergy and people," they declared the election of Gerbert. It was convenient for them to forget that Arnulf had also been elected with Hugh's approval.[60]

The scene had many counterparts in Germany. Yet it is important to remember that, although in fact kings nominated men to episcopal sees, they insisted that the form of election be observed. The force of the canons might be nullified in practice, but it could not be utterly abolished. Election by the king was one part of episcopal accession; it must be confirmed through election by the people and, in both acts, the corroborating election of God must be apparent.[61] However arbitrary it may have been, royal intervention in ecclesiastical affairs was not understood as the arbitrary act of a *Rex-Sacerdos*, consecrated by holy oil as a sort of superior bishop. Unanointed kings and on occasion even dukes exercised the same powers.[62] It seems to have been warranted by the belief that God indeed acted through kings who were in unity with him; this unity was shown by God's favor to the king in worldly matters, prosperity in peace and victory in war. When God forsook a king, these outward signs fell away. Thus, the strong king's voice in episcopal elections was indeed the voice of God, and the concurrence of the people with his nomination was pious acceptance of God's will.[63]

---

[58] Santifaller, *Geschichte*, 24f.
[59] On Italy, see Johnson, *Activities*, 146f.
[60] Gerbert, ep. 179, in ed. Havet, 159f.
[61] These are Nitschke's distinctions in "Einstimmigkeit," 29, 33.
[62] Nitschke, "Einstimmigkeit," 36.
[63] Nitschke, "Einstimmigkeit," 39f, 54, 56.

A concept of sacral kingship thus certainly characterized Ottonian dealings with the German church. Independent in origins from Christian liturgy, the concept was greatly strengthened by ritual coronation and unction. But in the words of a great student of the age: "There can be as little question of a real Royal Priesthood in the age of German kings and emperors as in the Carolingian period; the king or emperor is and remains a layman, and lay and clerical orders are sharply distinguished by Church law. If the king had belonged to the clerical order by virtue of the ecclesiastical consecration he received, and if his place had been above bishops in the hierarchy, the prohibition of lay investiture would not have affected him and the Investiture Controversy could not have happened."[64]

The intervention of the Saxons in Church matters came, not from political thought, but from political necessity, not from emperors who imagined themselves as popes, but from rulers who saw the episcopal order as a possible counterpoise to a troublesome and increasingly powerful temporal nobility. It is a very obvious and commonly acknowledged truth that the Saxons saw and used the conventional interdependence of Church and king, and the uninheritable character of the episcopacy and of episcopal lands, to create the order of bishops as a non-hereditary princely class allied with the king against the entrenched interests of the hereditary nobility. Toward this end, Otto I fostered new sees in missionary lands, and, closer to home, secured the election of his uncle Robert to Trier, his brother Bruno to Cologne, and his illegitimate son William to Mainz. He and his successors tended the other German sees with equal care.

However, this care was in the way of alliance, not of pure domination. The rich endowments and the positions of government which the Ottos granted bishops did indeed create a large and enormously powerful class. Like their secular counterparts, the bishops were becoming territorial princes. "The bishops, it must never be forgotten, were as feudally ambitious, as particularistically minded, as the most inde-

---

[64] Santifaller, *Geschichte*, 24: ". . . *von einem eigentlichen Königpriestertum kann aber ebensowenig wie in der Karolingerzeit so auch in der deutschen Königs- und Kaiserzeit die Rede sein; der König bzw. der Kaiser ist und bleibt Laie, und Laien- und Klerikerstand sind kirchenrechtlich scharf geschieden. Hätte der König auf Grund der empfangenen kirchlichen Weihen dem Klerikerstande angehört und wäre sein Platz der Hierarchie über den Bischöfen gewesen, dann hätte ihn das Verbot der Laieninvestitur nicht treffen und daher hätte es auch nicht zu einem Investiturstreit kommen können.*"

pendent-spirited noble. Their loyalty could be as fickle and as transient as that of any secular, if they felt their independence of action circumscribed, or their own interests, no matter what they were, violated by the king. Their aims were to a large extent identical with those of the feudal nobility, i.e., the accumulation of wealth and power to support as independent an existence as possible.[65] It was, in a sense, every man for himself. Despite obligations to their kings, the Ottonian bishops' interest were in the first instance local. They wished to build up the power of their individual sees against the temporal aristocracy and, if necessary, against the king.[66]

In some degree, the interests of the bishops and those of the king coincided: they could make common cause against external enemies, like the Magyars, or a hostile pope, or, on occasion, against hereditary nobles.[67] But their collaboration could not be taken for granted. Their power gave them independence and peculiar interests; their backgrounds—until the time of Henry II, bishops were chosen from the families of the hereditary aristocracy—[68] gave them concepts of class and privilege often at variance with royal policy. Finally, their own positions were in some cases insecure. In Lorraine, several Ottonian bishops were withstood or expelled by their people.[69] In other sees the contest between bishop and local nobles reduced the support which the bishop could give his king.

Despite the temptations of power and the pressure of danger, some bishops were unswervingly loyal to their kings. Bruno of Cologne, Notger of Liège, Leo of Vercelli, and Bernward of Hildesheim conformed to the Ottonian ideal of cooperation between mitre and crown. But other bishops defected from the royal camp under pressure or honest conviction and defied their kings in temporal and ecclesiastical matters. Lotharingian rebels against Otto the Great were supported by their bishops in 938-940 and 953-954, and in 939, as well, by Rothad of Strassburg and Frederick of Mainz, and in 953 by Harold of Salzburg and Frederick.[70] Abraham of Freising and Henry of Augsburg sup-

---

[65] Johnson, *Activities*, 97.
[66] Köhler, *Bild*, 46ff, 65f.
[67] Köhler, *Bild*, 135.
[68] Johnson, *Activities*, 74f.
[69] Johnson, *Activities*, 114ff. See the reproach that Gerbert addressed to the people of Verdun after they had expelled Adalbero: "*Ideo pastorem non recognoscis, quia regem tuum* [Otto III] *regno privare moliris. Non est tui juris creare novos reges ac principes, id est sub insolita transire juga*" (ep. 79, in ed. Havet, 72f).
[70] Johnson, *Activities*, 29, 31, 106; Hauck, *Kirchengeschichte* 3, 33ff.

ported Henry of Bavaria in his revolts against Otto II. Towards the end of Otto III's reign, the Saxon bishops connived with rebels.[71]

As for major ecclesiastical policies, the Ottos ran afoul of episcopal opposition or insubordination twice. The earlier occasion concerned Otto I's plans to establish ecclesiastical order in the eastern provinces. He originally intended to withdraw Halberstadt from its allegiance to Mainz, to translate the see to Magdeburg, and to erect it as an archiepiscopal see. After the death of Frederick of Mainz, who had opposed or failed to support Otto in every rebellion of his reign, Otto secured the accession of his son, William, to the see. The new bishop, however, declined to reduce the power of Mainz, and resisted his father so fiercely as to break off communications with the court for a time. A compromise was found: Magdeburg would be erected as an archbishopric, and a new see would be established at Merseburg, partly with lands taken from the diocese of Halberstadt. Halberstadt itself would remain a suffragan see of Mainz. Even though this proposal was approved by king, pope, and papal synod, and provisions were taken to guard the interests of Halberstadt in the future, the settlement was unswervingly resisted by the bishop of Halberstadt, and it could not be executed until he died. Even then, the bishops of Halberstadt cherished bitter resentment against their kings and the bishops of Magdeburg and Merseburg for the reduction of their diocese.[72]

The issue in the second dispute was control of the convent of Gandersheim. It arose in the last years of Otto III as a jurisdictional dispute between Mainz and Hildesheim. A Roman synod in 1001 awarded the judgment to Hildesheim. The sentence was approved by both Sylvester II and Otto III, and a legate was commissioned to promulgate the decree at a synod of Saxon bishops to be held at Pöhlde. At Pöhlde, Willigis of Mainz secured the presidency of the synod, attempted to prevent the decree's being read and, that failing, admitted an unruly mob to dissolve the synod. Though he was suspended from his office and summoned to Rome with his supporters to defend his action, Willigis remained in possession of his office and did not go to Rome. Synods and imperial hearings were held. Gandersheim was again awarded to Hildesheim; Henry II forced Willigis to renounce his

---

[71] Johnson, *Activities*, 36ff. On the part of bishops in the struggle attending Henry II's accession, see *ibid.*, 389.

[72] Johnson, *Activities*, 40ff; Keller, "Kaisertum," 362ff, 369f.

claims. But when Aribo succeeded to Mainz, he revived the dispute and protracted it—contrary to the clear wishes of his kings—until 1030.[73]

The episcopal resistance in these two cases, and the bitter opposition with which the bishops of Mainz, Würzburg, and Eichstätt later met Henry II's proposal to establish the see of Bamberg,[74] show how far the Saxon kings were from being the complete masters of the German church. Nomination of bishops, summoning of synods, and, in some degree, the management of Church lands were royal prerogatives. But the bishops had become territorial princes in their own right, largely through the grants of lands and privileges with which the Ottos sought their favor. They did not see their king as their ecclesiastical head, and the concept of sacral kingship fortified by liturgical sacring and crowning was not sufficient to prevent them from resisting their rulers in the synod and on the battlefield. There was more than ceremonial meaning in Bishop Meingöz of Eichstädt's refusal to stand when Henry II entered: "I am known to be the elder," he said, "and the heathen and Holy Writ alike command that the elder be honored."[75]

The Ottonians, therefore, seem to have acted in ecclesiastical affairs not according to principles of political thought, but according to political advantage. The concept of the *Rex-Sacerdos*, an emperor who was also in some sense head of the ecclesiastical order, appears neither in their writings nor in their actions, and the glory of Roman emperorship seems to have been for them merely an exalted expression of the power they already held in the *imperium Francorum*. Otto III was *imperator Romanorum*; his uncle, Hugh Capet, was *augustus*; *rex* was an ancient *nomen imperii*. For the Saxon kings, their empire was not a universal realm; nor was their imperial power in any sense sacerdotal. They did not attempt, as "popes," to convey or to interpret the Church's doctrine and sacraments. Even within the limits of practical politics, they saw their authority decay, their missions overturned, their "colonial" churches absorbed into the fabrics of independent, eastern duchies, their own bishops a source of opposition. The tension which Hincmar of Rheims had found irresoluble between the liberty of the Church and royal power was resolved in tenth-century Germany by the emergence of bishops as territorial princes.

---

[73] Johnson, *Activities*, 48ff; Hauck, *Kirchengeschichte* 3, 417ff.

[74] Johnson, *Activities*, 46f.

[75] Anon. Haser., c. 24, MGH SS. 7, 260: *"Ego inquiens senior sum cognatus, et seniorem honorare tam gentiles quam sacrae iubent litterae."* On this passage, Johnson, *Activities*, 245.

This fragmentation of authority was not, however, complete. Raoul Glaber rightly observed the change toward stability about the year 1000 when he later wrote: ". . . it was as though the very world, shaking itself, cast off the old and put on a white robe of churches."[76] The very strong reigns of Henry II and Conrad II consolidated royal authority in Germany and confirmed the predominance of the king in ecclesiastical matters. These gains reached their apogee in the Synod of Sutri.[77] But the developments of the Ottonian period could not be utterly overcome. They left to the next century a mixed heritage: the independence of German clergy toward Rome which the structure of a "national" church ensured, the hereditary role of the German king as emperor of the Romans in papal affairs, and, finally, the power of German bishops, as territorial princes, to check the ecclesiastical and temporal efforts of their kings. The political cohesion of the "national" church and the metaphysical cohesion of the Church universal, once represented by the concept of tradition, were uneasily combined. In these elements lay the seeds of ecclesiological and political thought which flowered in the Investiture Controversy, that great conflict in which the structure of the Ottonian church collapsed.[78] The bitterness of Arnulf of Orleans and Gerbert toward the See of St. Peter, implicit also in the action of Willigis toward the papal legate, found new and sharper expression in the disastrous struggles of the eleventh century. Raoul Glaber was right. The barbarian invasions had ended in the tenth century; prosperity and social stability returned. But the "white robe of churches" was to be rent. It was in its way a great harbinger of false hope, such as Alcuin had seen two centuries earlier when he wrote to comfort the Abbot of Lindisfarne, after the Northmen had sacked his monastery: "Be not cast down in mind by this misfortune. God chastises every son whom He receives; and so perhaps He has chastised you the more because He has loved you the more. Jerusalem, God's beloved city, perished in the Chaldean flame with the temple of God. Girt about with a crown of the Holy Apostles and of innumerable martyrs, Rome was torn asunder by the devastation of pagans; but she soon revived through the compassion of God. Almost all Europe

---

[76] Hist. III, iv, 13, in ed. M. Prou (Paris, 1886), 62: "*Erat enim instar ac si mundus ipse, excutiendo semet, rejecta vetustate, passim candidam ecclesiarum vestem indueret.*" Cf., *ibid.*, III, vi, 19, 68.

[77] T. Schieffer, "Heinrich II. und Konrad II," 384-437; Ullmann, *Growth*, 246ff.

[78] Santifaller, *Geschichte*, 35.

was emptied by the swords and fires of the Goths and Huns. But now, by God's mercy, Europe shines, adorned with churches as the sky is with stars, and in them the offices of the Christian religion flourish and increase."[79]

[79] MGH Epp. 4, k. a. 2, no. 20, 57.

APPENDIX C

# The Gregorian Reformers' View
# of Temporal Government

IN GENERAL, the attitude of the early reformer popes concerning secular government was conventional: they held that the proper offices of king and bishop were discrete but interdependent, in that kings could supply clergy needed offices of defense and emolument, and bishops could lead princes to eternal life.[1]

Cardinal Humbert, however, had sharper things to say. In his view, temporal rulers had impeded the Church's communication of the means of salvation, when they had not utterly prevented it. Kings and emperors had fostered simony and lay investiture, with the destruction of order, the dissipation of Church property, and the interruption of the valid sacraments they entailed. After its appearance in Simon Magus, simony vanished until the accession of Christian princes. Then, with the rich endowments which emperors conferred upon churches, the ancient bane returned.[2] Fostered by the practice of lay investiture from the time of the Ottos onward,[3] it had grown so virulent that no canons or synods of the holy Fathers, or edicts of religious princes could resist it. Lay investiture was a peculiarly western practice; for, despite manifold errors, the Church of Constantinople was free of it.[4] In vowing at their consecrations to preserve existing privilege, western emperors were forced to vow to perpetuate the violation of their predecessors' edicts in favor of the Church; the empire was no longer Christian, but pagan,

---

[1] Such was the tenor of Leo IX's remarks to Constantine Monomachus (PL 143, 778), and to Edward the Confessor (PL 143, 674). Cf. col. 1002, Bonizo of Sutri, *Lib. ad amic.*, V, MGH Ldl. 1. 589. Alexander II wrote in the same vein to William the Conqueror, urging him to patronize the practice of religion, to defend ecclesiastical persons from harm, and to protect widows, orphans, and the oppressed (PL 146, 1365; cf. col. 1413). And again, he admonished Wratislav of Bohemia that, as king, he must give account in the Last Judgment for the churches and monasteries, and for the chaste and religious service of God in his lands (PL 146, 1367. See also Alexander's letter to Gervasius of Rheims, *ibid.*, col. 1300).

[2] Adv. sim. II, 35, MGH Ldl. 1, 183; cf. Ullmann, *Growth*, 265ff. On the general problem of lay investiture, see Russell, *Dissent*, 132ff.

[3] See above, pp. 383f.

[4] Adv. sim. III, 7, 8, MGH Ldl. 1, 206f.

or worse than pagan, since it apostatized from God.[5] Henry II, to be sure, attempted to uproot the sacrilegious practice, unlike the flagrant simoniac Henry of France, whom God allowed to rule as punishment for the sins of the people so that he would drag them utterly into the Devil's lot. But Henry II's work ended with his premature death.[6]

On every hand, laymen violated their proper duties—to defend churches, paupers, orphans, and widows—and cast aside the limits of their own juridical order to usurp the powers in episcopal elections which the canons ascribed to primates, metropolitans, clergy, and people.[7]

Humbert argued that episcopacy and kingship were distinct, and that the episcopal dignity, a heavenly office, was more excellent than the royal, an earthly dignity.[8] By this, he intended to imply no institutional superiority of the priesthood over the kingship. The burden of his argument was rather that ecclesiastical and secular affairs were discrete. The latter must be decided by laymen; the former by clergy, according to the rules established by popes, by the words of holy Fathers, and by orthodox princes.[9] "The Church has her own laws and her own judges," he wrote, "to censure or correct the wrongs of her officers and ministers, with the advice of religious and wise men." Only in the failure of those appointed judges could laymen rise to defend the Church.[10]

Peter Damian likewise argued that the clerical and the lay orders were separate, and protested against their wrongful interpenetration. And yet, though Peter strongly opposed the practice of lay investiture,[11] he considered secular intervention in Church affairs on balance a great good which enabled the Church to communicate the message of salvation.

---

[5] Adv. sim. II, 36, *ibid.*, 184f.    [6] Adv. sim. III, 8, *ibid.*, 206.

[7] Adv. sim. III, 5, *ibid.*, 204.    [8] Adv. sim. III, 21, *ibid.*, 225f.

[9] Adv. sim. III, 9, *ibid.*, 208. Dr. Ullmann's interpretation is the reverse (*Growth*, 265ff).

[10] Adv. sim. III, 11, *ibid.*, 212: "*Habet enim ecclesia suas leges suos judices, quibus cum consilio religiosorum et sapientum aut corripiantur aut corrigantur culpae praepositorum et ministrorum eius.*" See Ullmann, "Humbert," 111.

[11] Epp. I, 13, PL 144, 219f, 221, 223; Blum, "Monitor," 474f. Among the works of Peter Damian, there is a very famous sermon (no. 69) which numbers unction of kings among the Church's sacraments. Since even very eminent scholars (e.g., Hoffmann, "Schwerter," 79) still discuss it as genuine, I think it may be useful to repeat that since the eighteenth century the sermon has been acknowledged as a forgery by Damian specialists. See K. Reindel, "Studien," I, 27f; Morrison, *Lives*, 16 n. 50.

Certainly, he distinguished between the "tribunal of the judge" and the "cathedra of the bishop," assigning to each its proper and discrete juridical, administrative, and moral functions.[12] But he urgently admonished great and powerful laymen to advance the reform of the Church, breaking with "unjust canons" (*iniustos canones*), overturning the false idols, and restoring the priesthood to its rightful purity.[13] He lavishly praised the memory of Henry III, who had destroyed simony, by whose decree the Roman Church was governed, and without whose authority no one could be elected bishop of the Apostolic See.[14] He fervently admonished Henry IV to follow his father's example so that, through him, the fallen Church might rise again, the Church's confounded discipline might reflower, and Henry might take a place in history with Nerva, who pacified the Church, Constantine, who confirmed it, and Theodosius, who exalted it.[15]

The variations between the comments of Peter Damian and Humbert largely reflect differences in emphasis and in immediate polemical goals rather than in principle. Neither thinker went much further than Leo IX or Alexander II toward defining in institutional terms the relationship between the Church and the civil power, or even between the Roman Church and the German emperors, whom Humbert blamed for the prevalence of simony and Peter praised for their efforts to reform clerical morals. The reformers could well agree that the interpenetration of temporal and ecclesiastical powers violated the proper limits of each, but they left unestablished the nice balance of legitimate interests, the precise definition of juridical competence, and the basis for compromise of disputes between the Church and temporal rulers which any complete analysis of the problem would have required. For them, as for ecclesiastical thinkers since the age of the apologists, ecclesiastical and temporal institutions might benefit one another, but they were ultimately discrete, each governed by its own offices and laws.

Within what limits could secular rulers participate in the Church's work? Did their intervention in Church administration, according to ancient practice, obstruct transmission of the doctrine of salvation in word and in sacrament? The issue of simony, with its attendant prob-

[12] E.g., Opusc. 57, c. 2, PL 145, 821; Epp. VII, 3, PL 144, 440.

[13] E.g., epp. VII, 18; VIII, 1, PL 144, 458, 461; Opusc. 18, diss. 3, PL 145, 416. See Mirbt, *Publizistik*, 453.

[14] *Liber gratissimus*, c. 38, MGH Ldl. 1, 71.

[15] Epp. VII, 3, PL 144, 438, 441.

lem of lay investiture, proved the dualistic view insufficient to serve the reform program; for that position conceded the Church, and especially the Roman See, no power to correct abuses by forcing kings and other temporal lords to surrender the rights over churches which centuries of usage had given them. This deficiency endangered the progress of reform in the pontificate of Gregory VII; his bold solution precipitated the Investiture Conflict.

The complex history of the conflict, Gregory's acceptance of temporizing as a diplomatic technique, his lack of a genuinely systematic and consistent concept of relations between temporal and ecclesiastical offices, and, finally, the need to accommodate in negotiations the election of Rudolf which the Saxons unexpectedly executed without direct consultation with Gregory, all militate against deducing any categorical position from Gregory's letters. On another level, much of that apparent inconsistency in his conduct against which the Saxons vehemently protested derived from his unfailing anticipation that Henry might repent and again govern as a Christian king.[16] Above all, there is the possibility that Gregory himself did not fully control the administration of the Roman See itself. There is indeed a great *caveat* against seeing Gregory as the complete master of the Roman Church and the cunning practitioner of *Realpolitik*. In a letter to his legate, Hugh of Lyon, Gregory explained an apparent contradiction in papal policy. "Your Prudence knows," he wrote, "that many things are issued as though they were from us, both in writing and orally, without our knowledge."[17] Gregory was sole master neither in Germany nor in his own house, and his ambiguous policy toward Henry came about largely from circumstances beyond his control.

Aside from the ambivalence, on the one hand, of declaring Henry excommunicate and deposed, and, on the other, of continuing to call him "king" and to negotiate with him and his party, there was an even greater inconsistency: namely, that Gregory obviously exercised the power to declare Henry deposed, but, at the same time, steadfastly maintained that he could not nominate a new king.

From the early patristic age onward, it had been a commonplace among ecclesiastical thinkers that no one could withdraw an office

---

[16] See Tierney, *Crisis,* 55f.

[17] Reg. IX, 32, MGH Epp. Sel. 2, 618: "*Noverit itaque prudentia tua, quia multa tanquam a nobis deferuntur et scripta et dicta nobis nescientibus.*" On this passage, see Murray, "Gregory VII," 175.

which he could not bestow. Thus, a deacon could not depose a bishop, nor could a layman defrock a priest. Gregory's actions suggest a departure from this principle. And yet, any assessment of their constitutional implications should take into account several possible qualifications. It is important to know, for example, whether Gregory considered his decrees against Henry constitutive or declaratory, and in what degree (that is, whether he judged that they established a new state of affairs or acknowledged an existing one), and whether he intended his measures to be definitive. Next, the decrees should be defined as issuing from normal judicial review (i.e. from established appellate procedure) or from extraordinary appellate jurisdiction. In other words, it should be considered whether Gregory saw the powers exercised against Henry as generally valid or as limited to the special circumstances of one case.

Some scholars have maintained that, to Gregory's mind, Henry's personal unworthiness stripped him of office, and the papal decrees merely declared his self-deposition, just as, by the act of simony, men deprived themselves of their spiritual powers only to have that fact recognized later by synodal deposition.[18] But the terms of the decrees against Henry are distinctly originative. They do not profess to confirm or declare a pre-existing state of affairs. Rather, they initiate some critical effects: the deposition of Henry and, in 1080, the confirmation of Rudolf's succession in Germany. The question as to whether these effects were intended to be definitive is, however, far less easy to answer. Gregory's persistent hope for Henry's repentance and his acknowledgment of Henry as king before and after each decree of deposition indicates very strongly that he did not consider either decree final. He nowhere stated, as he did in the cases of bishops whom he irreversibly deposed, that Henry had been cast down "without hope of recovery." Indeed, he recorded after the first decree against Henry that he had warned Henry of irretrievable deposition, but the decrees themselves lack the technical phrase "*sine spe recuperationis.*"[19] Gregory seems to have thought that the deposition of an unjust king could definitely be accomplished only by divine judgment, as expressed, for example, in battle. His appeals to St. Peter in the first decree and to Sts. Peter and Paul in the second, seek ratification of his sentence by heavenly action. He asked, in the second decree, that Henry should win no victories, and that Sts. Peter and Paul should cast him down quickly so

[18] Voosen, *Papauté*, 281, 283; Kern, *Gottesgnadentum*, 200.
[19] Morrison, "Canossa," 141f.

as to show their powers to grant and to withdraw secular offices. Gregory himself disclaimed the first of these powers, and he never arrogated the second in absolute terms.[20]

In considering the place of the decrees in specific legal procedures, it is important to observe that the processes against Henry were from the first extraordinary, and that, in the second period of the conflict, both Henry and Rudolf appealed to Gregory for judgment and agreed to abide by his arbitration. Even in the period before the first decree, Henry sent Gregory assurances of good will and professions of repentance and obedience,[21] which he had confirmed by oath to papal legates in 1074.[22] Gregory had entered into negotiations with the Saxons, and, at least in 1073, he proposed to send legates to hear their case.[23] Although he wrote to congratulate Henry IV on his victory over the Saxons in 1075,[24] Gregory's expression of regret at the consequent loss of Christian blood and his earlier encouragement of Rudolf to press ecclesiastical reforms despite opposition from the king's court,[25] suggest that he wished to keep a foot in each camp. The dispute between Henry and the Saxons was thus potentially under arbitration by Gregory or his legates, as Gregory had thought it to be in 1073. Henry momentarily destroyed that prospect. Gregory considered Henry excommunicate by association with the men whom Alexander II had explicitly condemned; and when Henry deliberately violated Gregory's decree against lay investiture and carried his opposition to the ultimate by securing Gregory's deposition by the Synod of Worms, Gregory had no alternative to retaliation in kind. Gregory's fresh resolve to arbitrate the civil conflict in Germany, the reconciliation at Canossa, and the election of Rudolf as king determined the course of the process until Rudolf's death. Both sides appealed to Gregory as judge. Gregory temporized, acknowledging both Henry and Rudolf as kings, until, by obviously premeditated affronts to the Pope, Henry again provoked a retaliatory sentence of excommunication and deposition. Before a de-

[20] Morrison, "Canossa," 142f. I agree entirely with Ladner, "Concepts," 51, n. 10, that, for Gregory, "kingdoms are worldly institutions both in origin and character." Opposed to this view are the interesting interpretations in Hoffmann, "Schwerter," 87; Ullmann, *Principles*, 79; and Kempf, "Problem," 112.

[21] Epp. 5, 7, ed. Erdmann, 8f, 10f.

[22] Epp. Coll., no. 14, ed. Jaffé, *Bib. Greg.*, 537.

[23] Reg. I, 39, MGH Epp. Sel. 2, 62.

[24] Reg. III, 7, *ibid.*, 256.

[25] Reg. II, 45, *ibid.*, 182.

cision had been handed down, he defied the arbitration to which he had appealed. He consequently defaulted his case.

The deduction of clearly defined, constitutional premises from this series of juridical and diplomatic improvisations is hazardous. Obviously, Gregory believed that he could rightly excommunicate and depose kings. This is shown most clearly by his actions against Henry, by his assertions of the qualitative superiority of spiritual over temporal government, by his appeals to his own understanding of Gregory the Great's statements concerning papal authority over temporal officers and of Pope Zacharias's favor toward Pippin, and, perhaps, by the unqualified statement of the Dictatus Papae (1075) that the pope could depose emperors, although Henry was not emperor until 1084. The apparent inconsistencies in his dealings with Henry and the special circumstances in which the decrees of deposition and excommunication were issued suggest that Gregory himself had no fully developed concept of general conditions under which popes could depose temporal rulers, or even of the practical effect which a pope's deposition of a king could be expected to have.

Gregory's distinction between the forces of Antichrist and those of Christ achieved practical importance in his allegation that, through pride, Henry had joined the members of the Devil, and that those who followed him were likewise "enemies of God." Gregory absolved "Christians" of their oaths of fealty to Henry and forbade them to serve him as king. But, by their disobedience, they, like Henry, ceased to be true Christians, fell into idolatry, and joined forces with the Prince of Darkness. Over the unrighteous, Gregory had no powers; he explained his inability to enforce the decree of deposition in terms of duality of good and evil, and he looked for definitive confirmation of his judgment by supernatural action.

Before Gregory's position that popes might depose kings could be systematically expressed, administrative procedures had to be devised which assured the ejection of deposed kings from office, and regulated the accession of their successors, all under the effective supervision of the Apostolic See. Gregory made tentative efforts toward creating this pattern of relationships when he specified in 1081 that the king whom the Germans should elect had to promise fidelity and obedience to the Roman See.[26] The analogy is clear between the proposed oath and

[26] Reg. IX, 3, *ibid.*, 575f.

the oaths of homage Gregory actually received from temporal princes. Like them, it was a specific legal measure, binding only upon the man who swore it, and he was to take it after the election of the nobles had established him as king. The proposal in effect brought Gregory no closer to resolving the tension in his thought that he could withdraw an office which he could not bestow.

It has been eloquently argued that the pontificate of Gregory VII marked a radical change in the Church's concept of its place in the world; mistrust and withdrawal gave way to a new attitude demanding militant conversion of the world, in which society was conceived as unitary, and all social and political orders were in some way subordinate to ecclesiastical direction.[27] But this, in general, is an oversimplification. Withdrawal from the world received great encouragement in the eleventh century from new foundations, such as the Carthusians, the Camaldolensians, the Congregation of Vallombrosa, and, in the early twelfth century, from Cîteaux. The success of these foundations reflected the same sense of estrangement from the world which inspired heresies and popular religious movements to require apostolic poverty and mortification of the flesh, and which gave rise to communities following the *vita apostolica*.

Particularly concerning Gregory VII's thought, this interpretation discounts the thorough ambivalence of that Pope's measures.

By excommunicating and deposing Henry, Gregory manifestly did overstep the juridical division between temporal and spiritual, the separation of competences between the Church and the world, which thinkers from the age of the Apologists onward largely took for granted. But his distinction between temporal and ecclesiastical law, between institutional functions proper to laymen and those of clergy, the limits which he himself acknowledged on his powers over the royal office, and his concept of the world as divided between the righteous and the enemies of God suggest that he did not entirely cast aside the old distinctions and adopt a completely unitary concept of world order, subordinated to direction by the Apostolic See. In these reservations, he continued the thought of earlier men.[28] But in his insistence that obedience to the Apostolic See was the cohesive element in the Church, and

---

[27] Tellenbach, *Church*, 165. See also R. Bennett's introduction, p. xif. Cf. Ullmann, *Growth*, 269f. There is an apparent contradiction between Tellenbach's interpretation on the point of conversion and his view that the world was already considered a Christian community (p. 2 and *passim*).

[28] E.g., Gelasius I; above, pp. 102ff.

in his unsystematized contention that rulers who defied Roman jurisdiction ceased to be Christians or even rightful kings, and that the bishop of Rome might decree their depositions, he anticipated indistinctly the later thought of canonistic jurisprudence.

+

Gregory's thought was abstract, incomplete, and extemporaneous. In 1076, his dispute with Henry led him to take an extreme position from which circumstances never allowed him to escape, a position in a personal struggle which deflected attention from the initial object of the reform: namely, the moral reform of the clergy, and the reversal of the interpenetration of secular and ecclesiastical offices as expressed in lay investiture and simony. From 1076 onward, Gregory never ceased to insist that these were his goals. But the ferocious hostility between him and Henry and the need to vindicate his actions both before his enemies and before those of his followers who, like Gebehard, held that he might have dealt too harshly with the King, brought him to the ambivalent position we have described. His expressions were dictated in part by immediate diplomatic necessities, and in part by his own anticipation of Henry's repentance. The scope of his ideological improvisation was limited, first, by his insistence that Henry must be reconciled with Rome before normal relations between them as king and pope could be resumed, and, second, by the exclusive power of the German nobles to confer the royal office, exercised, as in Rudolf's election, independently of papal supervision.

Gregory's thought on ecclesiastical cohesion centered on three major articles: that those in communion with the Roman See constituted the true Church; that the sign and condition of communion was obedience to papal commands; and that heretics, apostates, and pagans, being outside the Church, were beyond Roman jurisdiction. Gregory's partisans, on balance, accepted these points. But, free of the diplomatic pressures which weighed upon him, they differed from the Pope in one significant aspect: they argued for the separation of temporal from ecclesiastical powers rather than for the submission of secular government, even in special circumstances, to ecclesiastical direction. Gregory's defenders were prepared to acknowledge that popes held sweeping powers over Church order—that, for example, the legislative competence of bishops of Rome was superior even to that of oecumenical councils,[29] and that other bishops stood in the same relation to the pope as judges to their king.[30] But they stopped short of extending that broad authority over temporal government.

The treatises of Gebehard, Manegold, and Bonizo show that even Gregory's devoted supporters failed to accept, perhaps to grasp, the full institutional significance of the Pope's conduct toward Henry. Gregory seems never to have composed a categorical pattern of institutional hierarchy, subordinating the royal power to the papal. There is reason to doubt that he himself clearly understood the broad legal implications of what he did and wrote. Gebehard, Manegold, and Bonizo concurred in his lofty assertions of papal supremacy within the Church, and they defended his actions against Henry, chiefly by arguing that the pope could dissolve oaths wrongfully taken or tending to destructive effects. But, in their defenses remained the institutional distinction between Church and State which Gregory had breached, which had marked Christian thought from the age of the apologists, and which, in the next centuries, the great lawyer popes obscured.

Like Gregory's contemporary partisans, Roman thinkers in the fifteen years after Gregory's death both confirmed his concept of Roman supremacy within the hierarchy and stopped short of extending that supremacy over temporal government. In Gregory's last years, and especially in the pontificate of Urban II, the practical limits which checked Gregory's actions gradually declined in importance for them. The dominance of German kings over the papacy, exercised in varying degrees since the time of Charlemagne, ended, and Urban II set the course of later alliances by seeking his major support in France. A recent study[31] has pointed out that, in his reorganization of legatine missions and establishment of primatial sees in France, according to Pseudo-Isidorian concepts, Urban actually departed from Gregory's precedents and achieved in some degree the goal of ecclesiastical centralization which had largely eluded Gregory.

These diplomatic and hierarchic developments freed Urban from the pressures which had put Gregory into a diplomatic strait jacket. Urban renewed the sentence of excommunication against Henry; on the elec-

[29] Cf. Mirbt, *Publizistik*, 563; Gebehard, *Ad Hermannum*, c. 20, MGH Ldl. 1, 271f.

[30] Mirbt, *Publizistik*, 560f.

[31] Becker, *Studien*, 80f. It is hoped that this development will be taken up in the second volume of Dr. Becker's *Urban II*.

tion of Italian nobles, he crowned Henry's son Conrad king of Italy (1093). He condemned Henry as the "subverter of Christian peace, the sacrilegious seller of churches, the destroyer of the Roman Empire, the author and defender of heretics."[32] Henry had tyrannically cast down from the pontifical throne the supreme pontiff to whom, through St. Peter, the Lord gave the unique privilege of opening and closing the gates of heaven, and he had set up a golden statue in the holy places and forced all whom he could to worship it. Urban excommunicated him and confirmed Conrad's usurpation of his title in Italy; but he refrained from issuing a decree of deposition. The question of the German crown remained open; the way to compromise was open.

Cardinal Deusdedit's treatise, *Libellus contra invasores et simoniacos* (ca. 1097), is a cohesive statement of the position which Urban's actions and scattered remarks seem to reflect. Writing more than a decade after Gregory's death, Deusdedit did not discuss in detail that Pope's conflict with Henry. Indeed, his comments were brief and somewhat equivocal. Henry, he wrote, had repented of his wrongdoing, but Wibert plunged him again into simony. He violated the oath taken at Canossa. When Gregory threatened him first with excommunication and, if he did not submit, with deposition, Henry was forced to give satisfaction by taking another oath. He violated that vow also, as though kings were not obliged to comply with any judgment of the Apostolic See. And, Deusdedit concluded, he was surely free of that obligation if he did not belong to the flock of St. Peter.[33] Deusdedit therefore considered Gregory's actions against Henry mere threats, rather than constitutional measures, and he judged that they could be effective only if Henry were obedient to the Roman See.

The Cardinal stated in his prologue the conceptual premise of this opinion and of his broader comments on the relation between ecclesiastical and temporal powers. The kingship, he wrote, was a great office, having control over the material sword, just as the priesthood held the sword of the Divine Word. The office of priests was one thing; that of kings, another. The king must provide for the peace of the kingdom and assist the priest by forcing to obedience those whom the priest could not correct by verbal admonition. Each office required the other; neither

[32] PL 151, 396: "*christianae pacis eversor et ecclesiarum sacrilegus venditor, Romani imperii destructor, haereticorum auctor et defensor.*"
[33] II, 11, MGH Ldl. 2, 328f. See above, pp. 343, 358.

could presume to discharge the other's functions, "lest what was built by one should be destroyed by the other."[34]

The theme of Deusdedit's treatise is that this interdependence and equipoise had been upset when secular princes usurped the power to elect bishops, a power which properly belonged to clergy and people. Even if kings and laymen lived holy lives, they were bound to obey priests, no matter how personally unmeritorious the priests were; for out of honor to the priestly seat of Moses, the Lord commanded His Apostles to obey their priests, who were to crucify Him.[35] This obedience was to extend particularly to ecclesiastical persons and property, over which laymen had no rightful authority, and most of all to episcopal elections.[36] The Apostolic Canons proved that from the time of the Apostles onward, the "holy custom" (*sancta consuetudo*), the "apostolic tradition" (*traditio apostolica*),[37] of the Church had required free election by clergy and people. Pious emperors had confirmed the apostolic order by law.[38] Intrusion of bishops by the temporal power was a "damnable custom" (*dampnabilis consuetudo*) to which antiquity gave no authority: if kings were adulterers, he argued by analogy, they did not oblige their successors to be adulterers.[39] To be sure, some Greek emperors imposed bishops on vacant sees without regard for canonical process, and for a time they exercised powers of review over the election of Roman bishops; but other emperors abandoned these precedents, understanding that they were contrary to God's ordination.[40] The wrongful intrusion of secular power had aroused unworthy conduct among men who aspired to the episcopate; they busied themselves with secular activities, spending vast sums of money, serving in temporal courts for decades, patiently bearing heat, rain, cold, and all other discomforts, incessantly hoping for the deaths of their bishops so that they could finally receive the episcopal office from the prince.[41] But even when this occurred, their simoniac dealings branded them as heretics, cast them outside the Church, and thus deprived them of all priestly powers.[42] Temporal laws, canonistic authorities, and the Scriptures all forbade this temporal intrusion, as did indeed the precedents of pagans who

[34] Prol., *ibid.*, 300.
[35] III, 8, *ibid.*, 348.
[36] IV, 1, 5, *ibid.*, 355, 357.
[37] See above, p. 273 n. 18.
[38] I, 2, MGH Ldl. 2, 301f.
[39] I, 14, *ibid.*, 313.
[40] I, 4, 9, *ibid.*, 303, 307f.
[41] I, 15, *ibid.*, 314.
[42] II, 4, 10; IV, 10, *ibid.*, 322, 327f, 363.

greatly honored priests serving gods of wood and stone.[43] In Deusdedit's mind, royal disposition of episcopal offices therefore violated both the specific "apostolic tradition" of the Church and the normal order of human affairs, as represented by the honor pagans gave their priests. On the other hand, the Cardinal was very far from asserting papal dominance over the royal office.

Deusdedit's terse and closely reasoned treatise, the letters of Urban II, and the Gregorian treatises we have mentioned all espoused Gregory's cause without adopting or even approving the extreme measures Gregory had used. The personal and diplomatic pressures which diverted Gregory from his main purpose and forced him into his fiercely controversial position were not relevant or perhaps even understandable to his contemporary defenders. The ambivalence of his thought enabled them to resume the conventional thought concerning the relationship between the Church and the civil power without openly modifying or rejecting his position. The dispute between Henry and the Roman Church continued until the Emperor's death. But the later Gregorians' new reliance upon France, Henry's distraction by civil war in Germany, and the development of canonistic thought freed the reformers from the troubles which had deflected Gregory from the original purposes of the reform movement. They could resume the primary tasks of the reform movement: the centralization of Church order and the moral reform of the clergy. They had resumed the position of the early reformer popes concerning temporal government: worldly government could assist or hinder the communication of the means of salvation. Lay investiture was an evil practice which impeded it; but temporal power was ultimately irrelevant to that communication. As Manegold wrote, "lacking a king, a man can also discharge the whole cult of Christianity with no diminution, as the inhabitants of many lands do, having no king, and yet preserving Christianity with supreme devotion through the priestly ministry."[44] In an utterly different historical context, the reformers' indifference, or even hostility, to temporal government repeated the thought of the early apologists. A millennium earlier Hermas had spoken for them all when he distinguished between the earthly city, dominated by Satan, and the heavenly city, to which the Christian belonged. The

[43] III, 3, *ibid.*, 343f.

[44] C. 48, MGH Ldl. 1, 394: "*quia sine rege omnem christianitatis cultum absque diminutione etiam potest inplere, sicut multarum terrarum incole fatiunt, qui non habent regem et tamen per sacerdotale ministerium summa devotione servant christianitatem.*"

Christian, Hermas declared, was foreign to the earthly city, and its prince could rightly expel the servant of God, if he refused to obey that city's law: "You may leave his city, and go to your own city, and, without loss, joyfully follow your own law."[45]

$+$

Toward the end of Deusdedit's life, the conflict reached a turning point. The early reformers and the initial participants in the Investiture Conflict died about that time, or earlier; the Countess Mathilda strengthened the hand of the reformers in 1102 by renewing the cession of lands she had originally made to the papacy in 1077; the reformers themselves healed the schism in their ranks which followed the death of Gregory VII,[46] and regained possession of the city of Rome for the first time since Gregory's flight in 1084. In diplomatic relations, the reformers initiated the contact with France which ultimately superseded the interdependence of Empire and Papacy with the French dominance of the papacy in the late Middle Ages.

These changes were material to the final settlement of the Dispute, as was the principle of duality which Deusdedit and other Gregorians reaffirmed. The precise form of reconciliation, however, was difficult to achieve. The pontificate of Paschal II, indeed, saw the tension between the centralizing papacy and kings spread along an ever-widening front. Paschal's letters concerning communion with Constantinople and Baldwin of Jerusalem's seizure of lands over which Antioch claimed hierarchic control dealt with eastern manifestations of the same royal particularism which Paschal encountered in western princes. In confirming to Roger II the legateship Urban II granted to Roger I and his successors (1117), Paschal carefully specified that Roger would have to yield precedence to *legati a latere* and accomplish by his "secular power" what "ecclesiastical humility" commanded but could not achieve. Roger did not have the power to pronounce ecclesiastical judgments or to summon synods, and Paschal exhorted Roger not to deny the Roman Church the power the Lord granted it, not to oppress churches, but to assist them, and not to judge bishops, but to revere them as vicars of God.[47] When Henry I forbade communication between the English

[45] Similitudines I, 6, in ed. K. Lake, *Apostolic Fathers* (London, 1913) 2, 140. On this passage, see Frend, *Martyrdom*, 195.
[46] Becker, *Studien*, 80.
[47] PL 163, 425f.

bishops and Rome, and neglected to collect Peter's pence, Paschal likewise had occasion to admonish the King not to deny St. Peter his due reverence (1115, 1116). He complained that, unless Henry commanded their admittance, Roman envoys and letters were barred from England, and that the appeal of cases from England to Rome was forbidden.[48] Under those circumstances, he could not confirm English bishops in their office, having no evidence that their manner of life or their learning qualified them for the episcopate. Consequently, he could not discharge the Lord's commands to St. Peter, "Feed my sheep; feed my lambs," and "Confirm thy brethren." Without Paschal's knowledge, Henry had even presumed to decide disputes concerning bishops.[49] He had thus doubly detracted from the honor of the Roman Church by arrogating its functions for himself, and by thwarting Rome's custom, transmitted from the Apostles themselves, of sending representatives into every province to consider the more weighty cases.[50] "How, therefore," Paschal asked, "can we feed lambs or sheep whom we have neither known nor seen?"[51]

Similarly when he sent the pallium to the archbishop of Spalato and required the archbishop to render a vow of fidelity to the papal representative, the king of Hungary and his magnates protested vehemently. They argued that Christ forbade all oath-taking, and that neither the Apostles nor any councils had established the practice. Paschal maintained that the "custom of the Apostolic See and of the entire Church" forbade metropolitans to consecrate bishops or celebrate synods before receiving the pallium; that, without such testimony of faith and character as the oath he had requested, the pallium could not be bestowed; that the Council of Chalcedon had in fact approved the procedure; and, finally, that, in any case, councils met and their decrees received legal force by the authority of the Roman church, on which authority conciliar decrees were never binding.[52] Then Paschal turned to the essential issue. He asked the archbishop: "Does it seem to you a Gospel judgment that the King and magnates have decided that you abstain from the above condition of the oath? Does the honor of our primacy seem supreme? Has that sentence of the Lord fallen to

---

[48] PL 163, 376f.      [49] PL 163, 379.      [50] PL 163, 379, 408.
[51] PL 163, 378.

[52] PL 163, 429: *"Aiunt in conciliis statutum non inveniri quasi Romanae ecclesiae legem concilia ulla praefixerint, cum omnia concilia per ecclesiae Romanae auctoritatem et facta sint et robur acceperint et in eorum statutis Romana patenter auctoritas excipiatur."*

404

ruin in your mind: 'The disciple is not above the master'? Was it said to the Prince of Hungary: 'And when thou art converted, confirm thy brethren'? . . . They can despise the Apostolic See. They can trample us under foot. They can not overturn or withdraw the privilege given by God when it was said to Peter, 'Thou art Peter, and upon this rock I shall build my Church,' and 'To you I shall give the keys of the kingdom of Heaven.' "[53]

In the early twelfth century, however, as in the eleventh, the classic expression of the struggle between the "national" church and the papacy was the Investiture Controversy. The reform had arisen among thinkers who judged that clerical immorality impaired the Church's transmission of the message of salvation through preaching and through the sacraments. At a later stage, the reformers came to understand that the great power which temporal princes exercised in accessions to Church offices at every level was partially responsible for the corruption of the clergy, since it encouraged simony and allowed the accession of canonically disqualified men, and, most of all, since these abuses excluded the action of the Holy Ghost in lawful election. Men thus acceded to bishoprics having the name of bishop, but not the spiritual powers which only the free operation of the Holy Ghost conferred; they were unable by inspired teaching or by valid sacraments to impart the great mysteries of the faith. This same view prevailed among twelfth-century reformers. But by 1119 a mediating influence was at work at the papal court, and Godfrey of Vendôme showed its effects in a letter he addressed to Calixtus II in that year. For a layman to invest a bishop with ring and staff was indeed a heresy, he wrote;[54] and it was clearly episcopal consecration, not any secular act, which bestowed his essential powers upon a bishop. Yet, kings and emperors governed men "by divine right" (*ex iure divino*). By the same right, they must be honored as the anointed of the Lord. The Church was in fact

---

[53] *Loc.cit.*: "*Itaque quod censuerint rex et magnates a supradicta sacramenti conditione te quiescere, videturne vobis iudicium evangelicum? Videturne primatus nostri honor praecipuus? Nunquid animo cecidit illa sententia Domini: Non est discipulus supra magistrum? Nunquid Hungarico principi dictum est: Et tu conversus confirma fratres tuos? Nunquid haec nos commodi nostri profectione requirimus; et non unitatis catholicae statuimus firmamentum? Possunt apostolicam sedem contemnere; possunt adversum nos calcaneum elevare. Datum a Deo privilegium evertere vel auferre non possunt quo Petro dictum est: 'Tu es Petrus et super hanc petram aedificabo ecclesiam meam,' et 'Tibi dabo claves regni coelorum.'* "

[54] MGH Ldl. 2, 690f.

obliged to them for the possessions that they and their predecessors granted it.[55] After a bishop's canonical election and consecration, he could without offense receive "through royal investiture" (*per investituram regalem*) the possessions of his church by some sign unobjectionable to the king, to the pontiff, or to the catholic faith. Thus peace could be restored to the Church.[56]

As this position gained favor among papal thinkers, the German bishops and princes more resolutely determined to end the controversy, and in 1121 they solemnly declared at Würzburg that they would undertake to impose an equitable settlement both upon Henry and upon the Church.[57]

On assurances from Calixtus that he wished to deprive Henry of no right proper to the royal office,[58] a conference was held at Worms in September, 1122. A compromise was reached. Henry renounced investiture with ring and staff and granted all churches in the Empire the right of canonical election and free consecration. He promised restitution of the "possessions and regalia of St. Peter" which Rome had lost during the Controversy, similar restitution to other injured persons in the Dispute, peace to Calixtus and his party, and assistance to the Roman Church. For his part, Calixtus granted Henry the right to be present at any election to a bishopric or abbacy in Germany, providing that the elections were held without simony or violence. In disputed elections, he might, jointly with the metropolitan and comprovincial bishops, give his assent to the "sounder part." Bishops-elect and abbots-elect must receive the regalia from Henry by investiture "*per sceptrum*," and they must discharge the legal obligations they thus incurred. Outside Germany, bishops or abbots, except those directly subject to the bishop of Rome, were to receive investiture with the regalia "*per sceptrum*" within six months of their consecrations, and to honor their consequent obligations.[59]

This settlement accepted lay investiture as normal procedure, though it barred the ring and staff as symbols of investiture. It confirmed the decisive power of the king in German episcopal and abbatial accessions by establishing his presence in elections as normal, and by requiring in-

[55] *Ibid.*, 691.
[56] *Ibid.*, 692.
[57] Ekkehard, Chron. (a. 1121), MGH SS. 6, 257; MGH Const. 1, no. 106, 158.
[58] PL 163, 1232.
[59] MGH Const. 1, no. 107, 159f. Calixtus's undertaking is no. 108, 161.

vestiture with regalia to precede consecration. The king therefore retained power to represent his own views in the election itself and, if confronted with a candidate he considered unacceptable, to reopen the electoral process by refusing investiture. On the other hand, the guarantee of free and canonical elections technically prevented wholly arbitrary royal action; and investiture after consecration in imperial territories outside Germany greatly limited royal influence over episcopal accessions in Burgundy and Italy. For its part, the papacy had re-established the clear distinction between the administrative competence of the Church and that of temporal government which lay investiture with ring and staff blurred, and confirmed the power in elections to some sees which royal claims had challenged.

The Concordat of Worms did not end lay investiture, and after 1122 some authors, like Honorius Augustodunensis,[60] continued to discuss lay investiture as an aspect of the broader question of relations between the Church and secular rulers. Honorius could write of the duality of spiritual and temporal offices, and the superiority of the spiritual,[61] dilating upon the subjection of kings to popes,[62] and upon the control of laws which priests had from the time of the Old Dispensation onwards, which Christ granted St. Peter.[63] He could distinguish between the royal unction and the episcopal anointing to show that the royal ceremony did not change the lay character of kings.[64] He could read into the Donation of Constantine a cession to the pope of power to review imperial elections,[65] and attribute to bishops power to establish kings, leaving to laymen only the right of assent.[66] Later popes could likewise declare the superiority of their office over the kingship, as Innocent II declared in words like those of Gregory VII, that the Roman church held principate both over earthly and over heavenly things.[67] But the long, bitter controversy which the Concordat of Worms ended showed that such doctrines fell far short of reality. By the settlement of Bec, the Concordat of Worms, and other diplomatic engagements between the papacy and temporal rulers in the first third of the twelfth century, the papal reformers were forced to compromise their programmatic centralization of Church order to suit the political structure of "national"

---

[60] Summa gloria, c. 28, MGH Ldl. 3, 76.

[61] *Ibid.*, prol., cc. 1, 2, *ibid.*, 63ff.

[62] *Ibid.*, c. 8, *ibid.*, 68. Cf. c. 14, *ibid.*, 70.

[63] *Ibid.*, c. 15, *ibid.*, 71.  [64] *Ibid.*, c. 9, *ibid.*, 69.

[65] *Ibid.*, c. 17, *ibid.*, 71.  [66] *Ibid.*, cc. 18, 21, 22, *ibid.*, 72f.

[67] PL 179, 483.

churches. They had fought the conflict between the demands of metaphysical and political cohesion to an impasse. Their program was compromised, not thwarted; and indeed their successes were considerable enough to encourage the continual growth of the doctrine of papal monarchy. But the royal power remained a distinct limit upon the degree to which that doctrine could be realized, a barrier of nonsacerdotal authority monitoring the lines of association between pope and bishops.

# Bibliography

Aland, K. "Die religiöse Haltung Kaiser Konstantins," *Studia Patristica*, 1 (1957), 549-600.

———. "Petrus in Rom," *HZ*, 183 (1957), 497-516.

Alexander, P. J. "Church Councils and Patristic Authority. The Iconoclastic Councils of Hiereia (754) and St. Sophia (815)." *Harvard Studies in Classical Philology*, 63 (1958), 493-505.

———. "The Iconoclastic Council of St. Sophia (815) and its Definition (*Horos*)," *DOP*, 7 (1953), 35-66.

———. *The Patriarch Nicephorus of Constantinople. Ecclesiastical Policy and Image Worship in the Byzantine Empire*. Oxford, 1958.

———. "The Strength of Empire and Capital as Seen Through Byzantine Eyes," *Speculum*, 37 (1962), 339-57.

Alföldi, A., trans. H. Mattingly. *A Conflict of Ideas in the Late Roman Empire. The Clash Between the Senate and Valentinian I*. Oxford, 1952.

———. *The Conversion of Constantine and Pagan Rome*. Oxford, 1948.

Amann, E. "L'Affaire Nestorius vue de Rome," *RevSR*, 23 (1949), 5-37, 207-44; 24 (1950), 28-52, 235-65.

Anastos, M. V. "The Ethical Theory of Images Formulated by the Iconoclasts in 754 and 815," *DOP*, 8 (1954), 151-60.

Andrieu, M. "La carrière ecclésiastique des papes et les documents liturgiques du moyen-âge," *RevSR*, 21 (1947), 90-120.

Arnold, W. R. "The Relation of Primitive Christianity to Jewish Thought and Teaching," *HTR*, 23 (1930), 161-79.

Arquillière, H. X. *L'Augustinisme politique*. 2nd ed.; Paris, 1955.

Ashworth, H. "The Influence of the Lombard Invasions on the Gregorian Sacramentary." *Bulletin of the John Rylands Library*, 36 (1953-1954), 305-27.

Autenrieth, J. "Der bisher unbekannte Schluss des Briefes Gregors VII. an Mathilde von Tuscien von 16. Februar 1074 (Reg. I, 47)," *DA*, 13 (1957), 534-38.

Auvray, P. "Saint Jérôme et saint Augustin. La controverse au sujet de l'incident d'Antioche," *RSR*, 29 (1939), 594-610.

Baar, P. A. van den. *Die kirchliche Lehre der Translatio Imperii Romani bis zur Mitte des 13. Jahrhunderts.* (Analecta Gregoriana, 78.) Rome, 1956.

Bach, E. "Imperium Romanum: Étude sur l'idéologie politique du XII<sup>e</sup> siècle." *Classica et Mediaevalia,* 7 (1945), 138-45.

Baetke, W. *Yngvi und die Ynglinger: Eine quellenkritische Untersuchung über das nordische "Sakralkönigtum."* Berlin, 1964. (SB. d. Sächsischen Akademie der Wiss. zu Leipzig.)

Bakhuizen van den Brink, J. N. "Traditio im theologischen Sinne," *VigC,* 13 (1959), 65-86.

――――. "Tradition and Authority in the Early Church," *Studia Patristica,* 7 (1966), 3-22.

Bardy, G. "La culture grecque dans l'occident chrétien au IV<sup>e</sup> siècle," *RSR,* 29 (1939), 5-58.

――――. "La culture latine dans l'orient chrétien au IV<sup>e</sup> siècle." *Irénikon,* 14 (1937), 313-38.

――――. "Grecs et Latins dans les premières controverses pélagiennes," *Bulletin de littérature ecclésiastique,* 49 (1948), 3-20.

――――. "La latinisation de l'église d'occident." *Irénikon,* 14 (1937), 3-20, 113-30.

――――. "L'occident et les documents de la controverse arienne," *RevSR,* 20 (1940), 28-63.

――――. "Le patriotisme égyptien dans la tradition patristique," *RHE,* 45 (1950), 5-24.

――――. *La question des langues dans l'église ancienne,* Vol. 1. Paris, 1948.

――――. "Les répercussions des controverses théologiques des V<sup>e</sup> et VI<sup>e</sup> siècles dans les églises de Gaule." *Revue d'histoire de l'Eglise de France,* 24 (1938), 23-46.

――――. "La rivalité d'Alexandrie et de Constantinople au V<sup>e</sup> siècle." *France Franciscaine,* 19 (1936), 5-19.

――――. "Saint Jérôme et ses maîtres hébreux," *RevB,* 46 (1934), 145-64.

――――. "Le sens de l'unité dans l'église et les controverses du V<sup>e</sup> siècle." *L'Année théologique,* 9 (1948), 156-74.

Barion, H. *Das fränkisch-deutsche Synodalrecht des Frühmittelalters.* (Kanonistische Studien und Texte. Bd. 5-6.) Bonn, 1931.

Batiffol, P. *Cathedra Petri. Études d'histoire ancienne de l'Église.* (Unam Sanctam, 4.) Paris, 1938.

————. "L'empereur Justinien et le siège apostolique," *RSR*, 16 (1926), 193-264.

————. "Papa, sedes apostolica, apostolatus." *Rivista di Archeologia Cristiana della Pontificia Commissione di Archeologia Sacra*, 2 (1925), 99-116.

————. " 'Princeps apostolorum.' Esquisse de l'histoire de cette expression." *Actes du premier congrès national des historiens français, 1927* (Paris, 1928), 27.

Bauerreiss, R. "Servus servorum dei als Titel frühmittelalterlicher baiuvarischer Äbte." *Studien und Mitteilungen zur Geschichte des Benediktinerordens und seiner Zweige*, 66 (1955), 58-60.

Baynes, N. H. "Alexandria and Constantinople. A Study in Ecclesiastical Diplomacy." *Journal of Egyptian Archaeology*, 12 (1926), 145-56. Reprinted in *Byzantine Studies and Other Essays* (London, 1955), 97-115.

————. "Eusebius and the Christian Empire." Mélanges Bidez, II. *Annuaire de l'Institut de Philologie et d'Histoire Orientales*, 2 (1934), 13-18.

————. "The Icons Before Iconoclasm," *HTR*, 44 (1951), 93-106.

Beck, H.G.J. *The Pastoral Care of Souls in Southeast France During the Sixth Century*. (Analecta Gregoriana, 51.) Rome, 1950.

Becker, A. *Papst Urban II., I. Herkunft und kirchliche Laufbahn. Der Papst und die lateinische Christenheit*. (MGH Schriften, 19, 1.) Stuttgart, 1964.

————. *Studien zum Investiturproblem in Frankreich. Papsttum, Königtum und Episkopat im Zeitalter der gregorianischen Kirchenreform* (1049-1119). (Schriften der Universität des Saarlandes.) Saarbrücken, 1955.

Below, G. v. *Die Entstehung des ausschliesslichen Wahlrechts der Domkapitel mit besonderer Rücksicht auf Deutschland*. (HistStud, 11.) Leipzig, 1883.

Berges, W. "Gregor VII. und das deutsche Designationsrecht." *Studi Gregoriani*, 2 (1947), 189-209.

Bernhardi, W. *Lothar von Supplinburg*. Leipzig, 1879.

Beskow, P., trans. E. J. Sharpe. *Rex Gloriae. The Kingship of Christ in the Early Church*. Stockholm, 1962.

Beumann, H. "Das Kaisertum Ottos d. Gr. Ein Rückblick nach Tausend Jahren," *HZ*, 195 (1962), 529-73.

411

Beumann, H. "Nomen Imperatoris. Studien zur Kaiseridee Karls d. Gr."
*HZ*, 185 (1958), 515-49.

————. "Romkaiser und fränkisches Reichsvolk." *Festschrift Edmund E. Stengel* (Münster-Cologne, 1952), 157-80.

————. "Die sakrale Legitimierung des Herrschers im Denken der ottonischen Zeit," *ZfRG*, g. A., 66 (1948), 1-45.

————. *Widukind von Korvei. Untersuchungen zur Geschichtsschreibung und Ideengeschichte des 10. Jahrhunderts.* Weimar, 1950.

Bévenot, M. " 'Primatus Petro Datur.' St. Cyprian on the Papacy," *JTS*, 5 (1954), 19-35.

Bezzola, G. A. *Das Ottonische Kaisertum in der französischen Geschichtsschreibung des 10. und beginnenden 11. Jahrhunderts.* Graz-Cologne, 1956. (Veröffentlichungen des Instituts für Oesterreichische Geschichtsforschung, Bd. 18.)

Bierbach, K. *Kurie und nationale Staaten im früheren Mittelalter (bis 1245).* Dresden, 1938.

Bietenhard, H. "Kirche und Synagoge in den ersten Jahrhunderten," *TZ*, 4 (1948), 174-92.

Bischoff, B. "The Study of Foreign Languages in the Middle Ages," *Speculum*, 36 (1961), 209-24.

Bloch, H. "Monte Cassino, Byzantium, and the West in the Earlier Middle Ages," *DOP*, 3 (1946), 163-224.

————. "The Pagan Revival in the West at the End of the Fourth Century," in ed. A. Momigliano, *Conflict*, 193-218.

————. "The Schism of Anacletus II and the Glanfeuil Forgeries of Peter the Deacon of Monte Cassino." *Traditio*, 8 (1952), 159-264.

Bloch, M. *Les rois thaumaturges.* Strasbourg-Paris, 1924.

Bloch, R. "Écriture et tradition dans le Judaïsme." *Cahiers Sioniens* (1954), 9-34.

Blum, O. J. "The Monitor of the Popes: St. Peter Damian." *Studi Gregoriani*, 2 (1947), 459-76.

————. *St. Peter Damian: His Teaching on the Spiritual Life.* (Catholic University Studies in Mediaeval History, N. S. 10.) Washington, 1947.

Blumenkranz, B. "Augustin et les juifs. Augustin et le judaïsme." *Recherches Augustiniennes* (suppl. to *Revue des Études Augustiniennes*), 1 (1958), 225-41.

————. "Les auteurs chrétiens latins du moyen-âge sur les juifs et le judaïsme." *Revue des études juives*, 9 (1948), 3-67; 10 (1951-1952), 5-61.

————. *Les auteurs chrétiens latins du moyen-âge sur les juifs et le judaïsme*. Paris, 1963.

————. "Die Juden als Zeugen der Kirche," *TZ*, 5 (1949), 396-98.

————. *Die Judenpredigt Augustins: Ein Beitrag zur Geschichte der jüdisch-christlichen Beziehungen in den ersten Jahrhunderten*. (Basler Beiträge zur Geschichtswissenschaft, Bd. 25.) Basel, 1946.

————. "Die jüdischen Beweisgründe im Religionsgespräch mit den Christen in den christlich-lateinischen Sonderschriften des 5. bis 11. Jahrhunderts," *TZ*, 4 (1948), 119-47.

————. "Vie et survie de la polémique antijuive." *Studia Patristica*, 1 (1957), 460-76.

Bolton, W. F. "The Supra-historical Sense in the Dialogues of Gregory I." *Aevum. Rassegna di Scienze storiche, linguistiche, filologiche*, 33 (1959), 206-13.

Bonhomme, P. "La littérature polémique autour de la querelle des investitures. Le plaidoyer en faveur d'Henri IV de Pierre Crassus," *RevSR*, 31 (1957), 217-48, 343-63.

Borino, G. B. "L'investitura laica dal decreto di Nicolò II al decreto di Gregorio VII." *Studi Gregoriani*, 5 (1956), 345-59.

Bouman, C. A. *Sacring and Crowning. The Development of the Latin Ritual for the Anointing of Kings and the Coronation of an Emperor Before the Eleventh Century*. Groningen, 1957.

Bouyer, L. "The Fathers of the Church on Tradition and Scripture," *Eastern Churches Quarterly*, 7 (1947), 1-16.

Braak, M. T. *Kaiser Otto III: Ideal und Praxis im frühen Mittelalter*. Amsterdam, 1928.

Brackmann, A. "Gregor VII. und die kirchliche Reformbewegung in Deutschland. Eine Zusammenfassung früherer Forschungen." *Studi Gregoriani*, 2 (1947), 7-30.

Bréhier, L. "L'investiture des patriarches de Constantinople au moyen-âge." *Miscellanea G. Mercati*, 3, *Studi e Testi*, 123 (1946), 368-72.

————. *La querelle des images (VIIIᵉ-IXᵉ siècles)*. Paris, 1904.

Brooke, Z. N. "Lay Investiture and its Relation to the Conflict of Empire and Papacy." *Proceedings of the British Academy*, 25 (1939), 217-47.

Brühl, C. "Hinkmariana," *DA* 20 (1964), 48-77.

Brundage, J. A. "Widukind of Corvey and the 'Non-Roman' Imperial Idea." *Mediaeval Studies*, 22 (1960), 15-26.

413

Brunhès, G., "L'idée de tradition dans les trois premiers siècles." *Revue Apologétique*, 2 (1906-1907), 54-61, 114-23.

Brutzkus, J. "Trade with Eastern Europe, 800-1200." *Economic History Review*, 11-13 (1941-1943), 31-41.

Bruyne, D. de. "La correspondance échangé entre Augustin et Jérôme," *ZNTW*, 31 (1932), 233-48.

Cam, H. M. "The Adolescent Nations." *MH*, 9 (1955), 7-9.

Campenhausen, H. v. *Ambrosius von Mailand als Kirchenpolitiker.* (Arbeiten zur Kirchengeschichte, 12.) Berlin, 1929.

———. "Der urchristliche Apostelbegriff." *Studia Theologica*, 1 (1948), 96-130.

Cantor, N. F. *Church, Kingship and Lay Investiture in England, 1089-1135.* Princeton, 1958.

Carlyle, R. W. and A. J. *A History of Mediaeval Political Theory in the West.* 6 vols., 4th impression; London, 1950.

Caspar, E. "Das Papsttum unter fränkischer Herrschaft," *ZfKG*, 54 (1935), 132-264.

———. *Geschichte des Papsttums.* 2 vols. Tübingen, 1930, 1933.

———. "Die Lateransynode von 649," *ZfKG*, 51 (1932), 75-137.

———. "Papst Gregor II. und der Bilderstreit." *ZfKG*, 52 (1933), 29-89.

———. "Primatus Petri," *ZfRG*, k. A. 16 (1927), 253-331. Published separately, Berlin, 1926.

Cavallera, F. "La doctrine sur le prince chrétien dans les lettres pontificales du V^me siècle." *Bulletin de la littérature ecclésiastique*, 38 (1937), 67-78, 119-35, 167-79.

Chadwick, H. "The Exile and Death of Flavian of Constantinople: A Prologue to the Council of Chalcedon," *JTS*, 6 (1955), 17-34.

Chany, W. A. "Paganism to Christianity in Anglo-Saxon England," *HTR*, 53 (1960), 197-217.

Charanis, P. *Church and State in the Later Roman Empire. The Religious Policy of Anastasius the First, 491-518.* Madison, Wisc., 1939.

———. "Ethnic Changes in the Byzantine Empire in the Seventh Century," *DOP*, 13 (1959), 23-44.

Charlesworth, M. P. "The Fear of the Orient in the Roman Empire." *Cambridge Historical Journal*, 2 (1926), 1-16.

Chenu, M. D. *La théologie au XII^e siècle.* Paris, 1957.

Chydenius, J. *Medieval Institutions and the Old Testament.* (Societas

414

Scientiarum Fennica, Commentationes Humanarum Litterarum, XXXVII.2.) Helsinki, 1965.

Classen, P. "Romanum gubernans imperium. Zur Vorgeschichte der Kaisertitulatur Karls des Grossen," *DA*, 9 (1951-1952), 103-21.

Congar, Y.M.J. *La tradition et la vie de l'église.* Paris, 1963.

————. *La tradition et les traditions. Essai historique.* Paris, 1960.

————. "Traditions apostoliques non écrites et suffisance de l'écriture." *Istina*, 6 (1959), 279-306.

Conybeare, F. C. "Newly Discovered Letters of Dionysius of Alexandria to the Popes Stephen and Xystus," *EHR*, 25 (1910), 111-14.

Courtois, C. "Grégoire VII et l'Afrique du Nord." *Revue historique*, 195 (1945), 97-122, 193-226.

Cranz, F. E. "Kingdom and Polity in Eusebius of Caesarea," *HTR*, 45 (1952), 47-66.

Cullmann, O. *La tradition. Problème exégétique, historique et théologique.* (Cahiers théologique, 33.) Neuchâtel, 1953.

Daniélou, J. "The Conception of History in the Christian Tradition," *JR*, 30 (1950), 171-79.

————. "Écriture et Tradition," *RSR*, 51 (1963), 550-57.

David, M. *La souveraineté et les limites juridiques du pouvoir monarchique du IX^e au XV^e siècle.* Paris, 1954.

Delaruelle, E. "La connaissance du grec en occident du V^e au IX^e siècle." *Mélanges de la Société Toulousaine d'Etudes Classiques*, 1 (1946), 207-26.

————. "L'Église romaine et ses relations avec l'église franque jusqu'en 800." *Settimane di Studio del Centro Italiano di Studi sull'alto Medioevo*, 7. Vol. I (Spoleto, 1960), 143-84.

————. "La pietà popolare nel secolo XI." *Relazioni del X. Congresso Internazionale di Scienze Storiche*, 1955. Vol. 3, 307-32.

Demougeot, E. "À propos des interventions du pape Innocent I^er dans la politique séculiere." *Revue historique*, 212 (1954), 23-38.

Deneffe, A. *Der Traditionsbegriff. Studie zur Theologie.* (Münster Beiträge zur Theologie, 18.) Münster, 1931.

————. "Tradition und Dogma bei Leo dem Grossen." *Scholastik*, 9 (1934), 543-54.

Dereine, C. "L'élaboration du Statut Canonique des chanoines réguliers spécialement sous Urbain II," *RHE*, 46 (1951), 534-65.

Dereine, C. "La prétendue règle de Grégoire VII pour chanoines réguliers," *RevB*, 71 (1961), 108-18.

——. "Vie commune, règle de Saint Augustin et chanoines réguliers au XIᵉ siècle," *RHE*, 41 (1946), 365-406.

Devisse, J. *Hincmar et le loi*. Dakar, 1962.

DeWailly, I. M. "Notes sur l'histoire de l'adjectif apostolique." *Mélanges de science religieuse*, 5 (1948), 141-52.

Dix, G., ed. *The Treatise on the Apostolic Tradition of St. Hippolytus of Rome, Bishop and Martyr*. London, 1937.

Dölger, F. *Byzanz und die europäische Staatenwelt*. Ettal, 1953.

——. "Nihil innovetur nisi quod traditum est. Ein Grundsatz der Kulttradition in der römischen Kirche." *Antike und Christentum*, 1 (1929), 79-80.

——. "Rom in der Gedankenwelt der Byzantiner," *ZfKG*, 56 (1937), 1-42.

Döllinger, I. v. *Die Papst-Fabeln des Mittelalters*. Stuttgart, 1890.

Dörries, H. *Das Selbstzeugnis Kaiser Konstantins* (Abh. d. Ak. der Wiss. in Göttingen, phil.-hist. Kl. 3. Folge, nr. 34.) Göttingen, 1954.

Downey, G. "Coptic Culture in the Byzantine World. Nationalism and Religious Independence." *Greek, Roman, and Byzantine Studies*, 1 (1958), 119-35.

Dressler, F. *Petrus Damiani. Leben und Werk*. (Studia Anselmiana, 34.) Rome, 1954.

Duchesne, L., trans. M. L. McClure. *Christian Worship: Its Origin and Evolution*. 5th ed.; London, 1923.

——. *L'Église an VIᵉ siècle*. Paris, 1925.

Duke, J. A. *The Columban Church*. 2nd ed.; Edinburgh, 1957.

Dümmler, E. "Brief des Erzbischofs Walter von Ravenna an den Erzbischof Konrad von Salzburg." *Forsch DG*, 8 (1868), 164-65.

——. "Über den Dialog de statu sanctae ecclesiae," *SB der kgl. preuss. Akad. der Wiss. zu Berlin*, 1. Halbband (1901), 362-86.

Dvornik, F. "Emperors, Popes, and General Councils," *DOP*, 6 (1951), 1-23.

——. *The Idea of Apostolicity in Byzantium and the Legend of the Apostle Andrew*. (*DOS*, 4.) Harvard, 1958.

——. *National Churches and the Church Universal*. Westminster, 1944.

——. "The Patriarch Photius and Iconoclasm," *DOP*, 7 (1953), 67-97.

————. *Le Schisme de Photius. Histoire et Légende.* (Unam Sanctam, 19.) Paris, 1950.

————. *Les Slaves, Byzance et Rome au IX<sup>e</sup> siècle.* Paris, 1926.

Ehrhardt, A. *The Apostolic Succession in the First Two Centuries of the Church.* London, 1953.

Eichmann, E. "Die Adoption des deutschen Königs durch den Papst," *ZfRG*, g. A., 37 (1916), 291-312.

————. *Die Kaiserkrönung im Abendland.* 2 vols. Würzburg, 1942.

————. *Weihe und Krönung des Papstes im Mittelalter.* Munich, 1951.

Ellspermann, G. L. *The Attitude of the Early Christian Latin Writers Toward Pagan Literature and Learning.* (Catholic University Patristic Studies, 82.) Washington, 1949.

Elze, R., ed. *Die Ordines für die Weihe und Krönung des Kaisers und der Kaiserin.* (MGH, Fontes Iuris Germanici Antiqui, 9.) Hanover, 1960.

————. "Die päpstliche Kapelle im 12. und 13. Jahrhundert," *ZfRG*, k. A. 36 (1950), 145-204.

————. "Das 'sacrum palatium Lateranense' im 10. und 11. Jahrhundert." *Studi Gregoriani*, 4 (1952), 27-54.

Engelmann, O. *Die päpstlichen Legaten in Deutschland bis zur Mitte des 11. Jahrhunderts.* Diss. Marburg, 1913.

Engreen, F. E., "Pope John the Eighth and the Arabs." *Speculum*, 20 (1945), 318-30.

Ensslin, W. "Das Gottesgnadentum des autokratischen Kaisertums der frühbyzantinischen Zeit." *Studi bizantini e neoellenici*, 5 (1939), 154-66.

————. "Justinian I. und die Patriarchate Rom und Konstantinopel." *Symbolae Osloenses*, 35 (1959), 113-27.

Erdmann, C. "Die Aufrufe Gerberts und Sergius' IV. für das Heilige Land," *QFIAB*, 23 (1931-1932), 1-21.

————. "Gesta Romanae Ecclesiae contra Hildebrandum," *ZfRG*, k. A. 26 (1937), 433-36.

————. "Mauritius Burdinus (Gregor VIII.)," *QFIAB*, 19 (1927), 205-61.

————. "Das ottonische Reich als Imperium Romanum," *DA*, 5 (1941), 412-41.

Ewig, E. "Zum christlichen Königsgedanken im Frühmittelalter," *Vorträge und Forschungen*, 3 (1954), 7-73.

Eynde, D. van den. *Les normes de l'enseignement chrétien dans la littérature patristique des trois premiers siècles*. Paris, 1933.

Fauser, A. *Die Publizisten des Investiturstreites. Persönlichkeiten und Ideen*. Diss. Würzburg, 1935.

Fedele, P. "Le famiglie di Anacleto II e di Gelasio II." *Archivio della Reale Società Romana di Storia Patria*, 27 (1904), 399-440.

Feine, H. E. "Kirchenreform und Niederkirchenwesen. Rechtsgeschichtliche Beiträge zur Reformfrage vornehmlich im Bistum Lucca im 11. Jahrhundert." *Studi Gregoriani*, 2 (1947), 505-24.

———. "Die Periodisierung der kirchlichen Rechtsgeschichte," *ZfRG*, k. A. 36 (1950), 1-14.

———. "Vom Fortleben des römischen Rechts in der Kirche," *ZfRG*, k. A. 42 (1956), 1-24.

Felbinger, A. "Die Primatialprivilegien für Italien von Gregor VII. bis Innocenz III. (Pisa, Grado und Salerno)," *ZfRG*, k. A. 37 (1951), 95-163.

Fichtenau, H. *Das karolingische Imperium. Soziale und Geistige Problematik eines Grossreiches*. Zurich, 1949.

Fichtner, J. A. "Scripture and Tradition in the *Commonitorium*." *American Ecclesiastical Review*, 149 (1963), 145-61.

Fischer, J. *Oriens—Occidens—Europa. Begriff und Gedanke "Europa" in der späten Antike und im frühen Mittelalter*. Wiesbaden, 1957.

Flemming, J. *Akten der Ephesinischen Synode vom Jahre 449 syrisch mit Georg Hoffmanns deutscher Übersetzung und seinen Anmerkungen*. (Abh. der kgl. Gesell. der Wiss. zu Göttingen, philol.-hist. Kl., N. F. 15, nr. 1.) Berlin, 1917.

Flesseman-Van Leer, E. *Tradition and Scripture in the Early Church*. Assen, 1954.

Fliche, A. *Histoire de l'Église*. Vol. 8: *La réforme grégorienne et la réconquête chrétienne*. Paris, 1940.

———. *La Réforme grégorienne*. 3 vols. Louvain, 1924, 1925, 1937.

———. "La valeur historique de la collection canonique d'Anselme de Lucques." *Miscellanea historica in Honorem Alberti de Meyer*. Vol. 1 (Louvain-Brussels, 1946), 348-57.

Fohrer, G. "Tradition und Interpretation im Alten Testament," *ZATW*, 73 (1961), 1-29.

Folz, R. *L'idée d'empire en occident du V^e au XVI^e siècle*. Paris, 1953.

418

————. *Le Souvenir et la légende de Charlemagne dans l'empire germanique médiéval.* Paris, 1950.

————. "Zur Frage der heiligen Könige: Heiligkeit und Nachleben in der Geschichte des burgundischen Königtums," *DA,* 14 (1958), 317-44.

Freeman, A. "Further Studies in the *Libri Carolini.*" *Speculum,* 40 (1965), 203-89.

Frend, W.H.C. *Martyrdom and Persecution in the Early Church: A Study of a Conflict from the Maccabees to Donatus.* Oxford, 1965.

Friedberg, E. *Lehrbuch des katholischen und evangelischen Kirchenrechts.* 2nd ed.; Leipzig, 1884.

Fuhrmann, H. "Konstantinische Schenkung und Silvesterlegende in neuer Sicht," *DA,* 15 (1959), 523-40.

————. "Pseudoisidor und die Abbreviatio Ansegisi et Benedicti Levitae," *ZfKG,* 69 (1958), 309-11.

————. "Studien zur Geschichte mittelalterlicher Patriarchate," *ZfRG,* k. A. 39 (1953), 112-76; 40 (1954), 1-84; 41 (1955), 95-183.

Gaffrey, B. *Hugo der Weisse und die Opposition im Kardinalskollegium gegen Papst Gregor VII.* Diss. Greifswald, 1914.

Ganshof, F. L. "L'église et le pouvoir royal dans la monarchie franque sous Pépin III et Charlemagne." *Settimane di Studio del Centro Italiano di Studi sull'alto Medioevo,* VII. Vol. 1 (Spoleto, 1960), 95-141.

————. "Note sur l'élection des évêques dans l'empire romain au IVme et pendant la premières moitié du Vme siècle." *Mélanges F. de Visscher,* 3. *Revue internationale des droites de l'Antiquité,* 4 (1950), 467-98.

Ganzer, K. *Die Entwicklung des auswärtigen Kardinalats im hohen Mittelalter.* (Bibliothek des deutschen hist. Inst. in Rom, 26.) Tübingen, 1963.

Gaudemet, J. "Droit romain et droit canonique en Occident aux IVe et Ve siècles." *Actes du Congrès de droit canonique, 1947.* (Paris, 1950), 254-67.

————. *L'Église dans l'empire romain (IVe-Ve siècles).* Paris, 1958.

————. *La formation du droit séculier et du droit de l'Église aux IVe et Ve siècles.* (Publ. Inst. de Droit rom. de l'Univ. de Paris, 15.) Paris, 1957.

————. "Survivances romaines dans le droit de la monarchie franque du V^ème au X^ème siècle." *Tijdschrift voor Rechtsgeschiedenis*, 23 (1955), 149-206.

Gay, J. *L'Italie méridionale et l'empire byzantin depuis l'avènement de Basile Ier jusqu'à la prise de Bari par les normands (867-1071).* (Bibliothèque des écoles françaises d'Athènes et de Rome, fasc. 90.) Paris, 1904.

Geanakoplos, D. J. *Byzantine East and Latin West: Two Worlds of Christendom in Middle Ages and Renaissance.* New York, 1966.

————. "Church and State in the Byzantine Empire: A Reconsideration of the Problem of Caesaropapism," *CH*, 34 (1965), 381-403.

Gelzer, H. *Ausgewählte kleine Schriften.* Leipzig, 1907.

————. *Byzantinische Kulturgeschichte.* Tübingen, 1909.

————. "Der Streit über den Titel des ökumenischen Patriarchen." *Jahrbücher für protestantische Theologie*, 13 (1887), 549-84.

Geraets, T. F. "Apostolica Ecclesiae Traditio. Over de apostolische Traditie bij Irenaeus van Lyon." *Bijdragen. Tijdschrift voor Filosofie en Theologie*, 18 (1957), 1-18.

Gerhardsson, B., trans. E. J. Sharpe. *Memory and Manuscript. Oral Tradition and Written Transmission in Rabbinic Judaism and Early Christianity.* Uppsala, 1961.

————. *Tradition and Transmission in Early Christianity.* Lund-Copenhagen, 1964.

Gericke, W. "Das Constitutum Constantini und die Silvesterlegende," *ZfRG*, k. A. 44 (1958), 343-50.

————. "Das Glaubensbekenntnis der 'Konstantinischen Schenkung,' " *ZfRG*, k. A. 47 (1961), 1-76.

————. "Konstantinische Schenkung und Silvesterlegende in neuer Sicht," *ZfRG*, k. A. 47 (1961), 293-304.

————. "Wann entstand die Konstantinische Schenkung?" *ZfRG*, k. A. 43 (1957), 1-88.

Gérold, T. *Les Pères de l'Église et la musique.* (Publ. de la Fac. de théol. prot. de l'Univ. de Strasbourg, 25.) Paris, 1931.

Ghellinck, J. de. "Diffusion, utilisation et transmission des écrits patristiques." *Gregorianum*, 14 (1933), 356-400.

————. *Le mouvement théologique du XIIᵉ siècle.* 2nd ed.; Paris, Brussels, 1948.

————. "Patristique et argument de tradition au bas moyen-âge." *Aus der Geisteswelt des Mittelalters, Festgabe M. Grabmann.* Vol. 1

(Münster, 1935), 403-26. *Beiträge zur Geschichte der Philosophie und Theologie des Mittelalters.* Supplementband III. 1. Halbband.

Gigli, G. *L'ortodossia, l'arianesimo e la politica di Costanzo II* (337-361). Rome, 1949.

Gilchrist, J. T. "Canon Law Aspects of the Eleventh Century Gregorian Reform Programme," *JEH*, 13 (1962), 21-38.

————. "Humbert of Silva-Candida and the Political Concept of *Ecclesia* in the Eleventh Century Reform Movement." *Journal of Religious History*, 2 (1962-1963), 13-28.

Ginzberg, L. *Die Haggada bei den Kirchenvätern*, I. Amsterdam, 1899.

Gmelin, U. "Auctoritas. Römischer princeps und päpstlicher Primat." *Forschungen zur Kirchen- und Geistesgeschichte*, 11 (1937), 1-154.

————. "Die Entstehung der Idee des Papsttums," *DA*, 2 (1938), 509-31.

Goez, W. *Translatio Imperii. Ein Beitrag zur Geschichte des Geschichtsdenkens und der politischen Theorien im Mittelalter und in der frühen Neuzeit.* Tübingen, 1958.

Goffart, W. "Byzantine Policy in the West under Tiberius II and Maurice. The Pretenders Hermenegild and Gundovald (579-585)." *Traditio*, 13 (1957), 73-118.

Gossman, F. J. *Pope Urban II and Canon Law.* (Catholic University of America Canon Law Studies, no. 403.) Washington, 1960.

Grabar, A. *L'iconoclasme byzantin. Dossier archéologique.* Paris, 1957.

Grabmann, M. "Die Eröterung der Frage, ob die Kirche besser durch einen guten Juristen oder durch einen Theologen regiert werde, bei Gottfried von Fontaines (+ nach 1306) und Augustinus Triumphus von Ancona (+ 1328)." *Festschrift E. Eichmann* (Paderborn, 1940), 1-19.

Grabowski, S. J. *The Church: An Introduction to the Theology of St. Augustine.* London, 1952. St. Louis, 1957.

Grant, R. M. "The Appeal to the Early Fathers," *JTS*, 11 (1960), 13-24.

————. *The Formation of the New Testament.* London, 1965.

————. "Hermeneutics and Tradition in Ignatius of Antioch. A Methodological Investigation." *Archivio di Filosofia*, 1/2 (1963), 181-201.

————. "Historical Criticism in the Ancient Church," *JR*, 25 (1945), 183-96.

————. "Scripture and Tradition in St. Ignatius of Antioch." *Catholic Biblical Quarterly*, 25 (1963), 322-35.

Greenslade, S. L. "The Illyrian Churches and the Vicariate of Thessalonica, 378-395," *JTS*, 46 (1945), 17-30.

———. *Schism in the Early Church*. London, 1953.

Grégoire, H. "Patriarche oecuménique = 'évêque supérieur.' " *Byzantion*, 8 (1933), 570-71.

Grillmeier, A. trans., J. S. Bowden. *Christ in the Christian Tradition. From the Apostolic Age to Chalcedon (451)*. London-New York, 1965.

———, and H. Bacht, eds. *Das Konzil von Chalkedon*. 3 vols. Würzburg, 1951-1954.

Grumel, V. "Chronologie des patriarches iconoclastes du IX$^e$ siècle," *EO*, 34 (1935), 162-66, 506.

———. "Jerusalem entre Rome et Byzance," *EO*, 38 (1939), 104-17.

———. "La politique religieuse du patriarche saint Méthode," *EO*, 34 (1935), 385-401.

———. "Les préliminaires du schisme de Michel Cérulaire ou la question romaine avant 1054." *Revue des études byzantines*, 10 (1953), 5-23.

———. "Le problème de la date pascale aux III$^e$ et IV$^e$ siècles. L'origine du Conflit: Le nouveau cadre du comput pascal juif." *Revue des études byzantines*, 18 (1960), 161-78.

Grundmann, H. "Oportet et haereses esse. Das Problem der Ketzerei im Spiegel der mittelalterlichen Bibelexegese." *Archiv für Kulturgeschichte*, 45 (1963), 129-64.

Guinan, A. "The Christian Concept of Kingship as Manifested in the Liturgy of the Western Church. A Fragment in Suggestion," *HTR*, 49 (1956), 219-69.


Haendler, G. *Epochen karolingischer Theologie: Eine Untersuchung über die karolingischen Gutachten zum byzantinischen Bilderstreit*. (Theologische Arbeiten, 10.) Berlin, 1958.

Hagel, K. F. *Kirche und Kaisertum in Lehre und Leben des Athanasius*. Diss. Tübingen. Borna-Leipzig, 1933.

Hagendahl, H. *Latin Fathers and the Classics*. (Studia Graeca et Latina Gothob., VI.) Stockholm, 1958.

Hahn, V. "Schrift, Tradition und Primat bei Irenaeus." *Trierer Theologische Zeitschrift*, 70 (1961), 233-43, 292-302.

Haller, J. "Die Formen der deutsch-römischen Kaiserkrönung," *QFIAB*, 33 (1944), 49-100.

————. *Das Papsttum: Idee und Wirklichkeit.* 2 vols. Berlin-Stuttgart, 1934-1939.

Halphen, L. *Charlemagne et l'empire carolingien.* Paris, 1949.

Hammer, W. "The Concept of the New or Second Rome in the Middle Ages." *Speculum*, 19 (1944), 50-62.

Hampe, K. *Deutsche Kaisergeschichte in der Zeit der Salier und Staufer.* 10th ed. by F. Baethgen. Heidelberg, 1949.

Hanson, R.P.C. *Origen's Doctrine of Tradition.* London, 1954.

————. *Tradition in the Early Church.* London, 1962.

Hardy, E. R. *Christian Egypt: Church and People. Christianity and Nationalism in the Patriarchate of Alexandria.* Oxford, 1952.

————. "The Patriarchate of Alexandria: A Study in National Christianity," *CH*, 15 (1946), 81-100.

Harnack, A. v. "Christus Praesens—Vicarius Christi. Eine kirchengeschichtliche Skizze." SB der preuss. Akad. der Wiss. (Berlin), phil.-hist. Kl. (1927), 415-46.

————. "Ecclesia Petri propinqua. Zur Geschichte der Anfänge des Primats des römischen Bischofs," SB der preuss. Akad. der Wiss. (Berlin), phil.-hist. Kl. (1927), 139-52.

————. "Der erste deutsche Papst (Bonifatius II., 530/32) und die beiden letzten Dekrete des römischen Senats," SB der preuss. Akad. der Wiss. (Berlin), phil.-hist. Kl. (1924), 24-42.

Hauck, A. *Kirchengeschichte Deutschlands.* 5 vols. 3rd-4th ed.; Leipzig, 1922-1929.

Hefele, K. J. v. and H. LeClercq, *Histoire des Conciles*, 11 vols. Paris, 1907-1952.

Heiler, F. *Altkirchliche Autonomie und päpstlicher Zentralismus.* Munich, 1941.

Hergenröther, J. "Das griechische Kirchenrecht bis zum Ende des neunten Jahrhunderts." *Archiv für katholisches Kirchenrecht*, 23 (1870), 185-227.

Hermann, E. "Chalkedon und die Ausgestaltung des konstantinopolitanischen Primats," in A. Grillmeier and H. Bacht eds., *Konzil*, vol. 1 (Würzburg, 1953), 459-90.

Hess, H. *The Canons of the Council of Sardica. A.D. 343. A Landmark in the Early Development of Canon Law.* Oxford, 1958.

Heussi, K. *Die römische Petrustradition in kritischer Sicht.* Tübingen, 1955.

Hirsch, E. "Die Auffassung der simonistischen und schismatischen Weihen im elften Jahrhundert, besonders bei Kardinal Deusdedit." *Archiv für katholisches Kirchenrecht*, 87 (1907), 25-70.

Hirsch, H. *Das Recht der Königserhebung durch Kaiser und Papst in hohen Mittelalter*. Darmstadt, 1962.

Hoffmann, H. "Die beiden Schwerter im hohen Mittelalter," *DA*, 20 (1964), 78-114.

————. "Ivo von Chartres und die Lösung des Investiturproblems," *DA*, 15 (1959), 393-440.

————. "Politik und Kultur im ottonischen Reichskirchensystem. Zur Interpretation der Vita Brunois des Ruotger." *Rheinische Vierteljahrsblätter*, 22 (1957), 31-55.

————. "Von Cluny zum Investiturstreit." *Archiv für Kulturgeschichte*, 45 (1963), 165-209.

Hoffmann, K. "Der 'Dictatus Papae' Gregors VII. als Index einer Kanonessammlung?" *Studi Gregoriani*, 1 (1947), 531-37.

Hofmann, G. "Papst Gregor VII. und der christliche Osten." *Studi Gregoriani*, 1 (1947), 169-81.

Holstein, H. "Traditio et Scriptura in Patristica Occidentali inde a Sancto Augustino," in Pontificia Acad. Mariana Int., *Scriptura*, 205-23.

————. *La tradition dans l'Église*. Paris, 1960.

Holtzmann, R. *Der Kaiser als Marschall des Papstes*. (Schriften der Strassburger Wissenschaftlichen Gesellschaft in Heidelberg, NF, 8. Hft.) Berlin-Leipzig, 1928.

————. "Der Weltherrschaftsgedanke des mittelalterlichen Kaisertums und die Souveränität der europäischen Staaten," *HZ*, 159 (1938-1939), 251-64.

————. *Der Weltherrschaftsgedanke des mittelalterliche Kaisertums und die Souveränität der europäischen Staaten*. Tübingen, 1953.

Holtzmann, W. "Imperium und Nationen." *Relazioni del X. Congresso Internazionale di Scienze Storiche*, 1955. Vol. III, 271-303.

————. "Studien zur Orientpolitik des Reformpapsttums und zur Entstehung des ersten Kreuzzuges," *HistVjs*, 22 (1924-1925), 167-99.

Honigmann, E. "Juvenal of Jerusalem," *DOP*, 5 (1950), 209-79.

————. "The Patriarchate of Antioch: A Revision of Le Quien and the Notitia Antiochena." *Traditio*, 5 (1947), 135-61.

Hove, A. van. "Een inleiding tot de bronnen van het Kerkelijk Recht op het einde der XIe eeuw." *Miscellanea Historica in Honorem Alberti de Meyer*. Vol. 1 (Louvain-Brussels, 1946), 358-72.

Huhn, J. "Bewertung und Gebrauch der Heiligen Schrift durch den Kirchenvater Ambrosius," *HJb*, 77 (1958), 387-96.

Hürten, H. "Gregor der Grosse und der mittelalterliche Episkopat," *ZfKG*, 73 (1962), 16-41.

Jacqueline, B. "À propos des *Dictatus papae*: Les *Auctoritates apostolice sedis* d'Avranches." *Revue historique de droit français et étranger*, 34 (1956), 569-74.

――――. "Bernard et le schisme d'Anaclet II." Commission d'histoire de l'Ordre de Cîteaux, III. *Bernard de Clairvaux* (Paris, 1953), 349-54.

Janin, R. "L'empereur dans l'église byzantine." *Nouvelle Revue Théologique*, 77 (1955), 49-60.

――――. *La géographie ecclésiastique de l'empire byzantine*, I. Paris, 1953.

――――. "Rôle des commissaires impériaux byzantins dans les conciles." *Revue des études byzantines*, 18 (1960), 97-108.

Jarry, J. "Hérésies et factions à Constantinople du Ve au VIIe siècle." *Syria, Revue d'Art oriental et d'archéologie*, 37 (1960), 348-71.

Johnson, E. N. *Secular Activities of the German Episcopate: 919-1024.* (University of Nebraska Studies, 30/31.) Lincoln, 1930-1931.

Jones, A.H.M. *Constantine and the Conversion of Europe.* London, 1948.

――――. *The Later Roman Empire, 184-602.* 3 vols. and map folder. Oxford (Blackwell) and Norman, Okla., 1964.

――――. "The Social Background of the Struggle Between Paganism and Christianity," in Momigliano, ed., *Conflict*, 17-37.

――――. "Were Ancient Heresies National or Social Movements in Disguise?" *JTS*, 10 (1959), 280-98.

Jonkers, E. J. "Application of Roman Law by Councils in the Sixth Century." *Tijdschrift voor Rechtsgeschiedenis*, 20 (1952), 340-43.

――――. "Pope Gelasius and Civil Law." *Tijdschrift voor Rechtsgeschiedenis*, 20 (1952), 335-39.

Jordan, K. "Das Eindringen des Lehnswesens in das Rechtsleben der römischen Kurie," *AUF*, 12 (1931-1932), 13-110.

――――. "Die Entstehung der römischen Kurie," *ZfRG*, k. A. 28 (1939), 97-152.

――――. "Zur päpstlichen Finanzgeschichte im 11. und 12. Jahrhundert," *QFIAB*, 25 (1933-1934), 61-104.

425

Jordan, K. "Der Kaisergedanke in Ravenna zur Zeit Henrichs IV. Ein Beitrag zur Vorgeschichte der staufischen Reichsidee," *DA*, 2 (1938), 85-128.

———. "Die päpstliche Verwaltung im Zeitalter Gregors VII." *Studi Gregoriani*, 1 (1947), 111-35.

———. "Die Stellung Wiberts von Ravenna in der Publizistik des Investiturstreites," MIÖG, 62 (1964), 155-64.

Jouassard, G. "Réflexions sur la position de saint Augustin relativement aux Septante dans sa discussion avec saint Jérôme." *Revue des Études Augustiniennes*, 2 (1956), 93-99.

Jugie, M. "L'ecclésiologie des Nestoriens," *EO*, 34 (1935), 5-25.

———. "Interventions de Saint Léon le Grand dans les affaires intérieures des églises orientales." *Miscellanea Pio Paschini, I. Lateranum*, 14 (1948), 77-94.

———. "Photius et la primauté de Saint Pierre et du pape." *Bassarione*, 35 (1919), 120-30; 36 (1920), 16-76.

———. "La primauté romaine d'après les premiers théologiens monophysites (V$^e$-VI$^e$ siècles)," *EO*, 33 (1934), 181-89.


Kaegi, W. E., Jr. "The Byzantine Armies and Iconoclasm." *Byzantinoslavica*, 27 (1966), 48-70.

Kampers, F. "Rex et Sacerdos," *HJb*, 45 (1925), 495-515.

———. "Roma Aeterna und Sancta Dei Ecclesia Rei Publicae Romanorum," *HJb*, 44 (1924), 240-49.

Kantorowicz, E. H. "Deus per Naturam, Deus per Gratiam. A Note on Mediaeval Political Theology," *HTR*, 45 (1952), 253-77.

———. *The King's Two Bodies. A Study in Mediaeval Political Theology*. Princeton, 1957.

———. *Laudes Regiae. A Study in Liturgical Acclamations and Mediaeval Ruler Worship*. Berkeley, 1946.

Kehr, P. F. *Die Belehnungen der süditalienischen Normannenfürsten durch die Päpste* (1059-1192). Abh. der preuss. Akad. der Wiss. zu Berlin, phil.-hist. Kl., 1934, no. 1.

———. "Zur Geschichte Wiberts von Ravenna (Clemens III)," I. SB der preuss. Akad. der wiss. (Berlin), 1921, 355-68.

Keller, H. "Das Kaisertum Ottos des Grossen im Verständnis seiner Zeit," DA, 20 (1964), 325-388.

Kemp, E. W. "Bishops and Presbyters at Alexandria," *JEH*, 6 (1955), 125-42.

426

Kempf, F. "Das mittelalterliche Kaisertum." *Vorträge und Forschungen*, 3 (1954), 225-42.

―――. "Die päpstliche Gewalt in der mittelalterlichen Welt. Eine Auseinandersetzung mit Walter Ullmann." *Saggi Storici Intorno al Papato* (Miscellanea Historiae Pontificiae, 21) Rome, 1959: 117-69.

―――. "Das Problem der Christianitas im 12. und 13. Jahrhundert," *HJb*, 79 (1960), 104-23.

―――. "Untersuchungen über das Einwirken der Theologie auf die Staatslehre des Mittelalters: Bericht über ein neues Buch." *Römische Quartalschrift*, 54 (1959), 203-33.

―――. "Zur politischen Lehre der früh- und hochmittelalterlichen Kirche," *ZfRG*, k. A. 47 (1961), 305-19.

Kern, F. *Gottesgnadentum und Widerstandsrecht im frühen Mittelalter.* 2nd ed. by R. Buchner; Münster, 1954.

―――, trans. S. B. Chrimes. *Kingship and Law in the Middle Ages.* Oxford, 1939.

Kirchberg, J. *Kaiseridee und Mission unter den Sachsenkaisern und den ersten Saliern von Otto I. bis Heinrich III.* (HistStud, 259). Berlin, 1934.

Kitzinger, E. "The Cult of Images in the Age Before Iconoclasm," *DOP*, 8 (1954), 83-150.

Klauser, T. "Der Übergang der römischen Kirche von der griechischen zur lateinischen Liturgiesprache." *Miscellanea G. Mercati*, I. *Studi e Testi*, 121 (1946), 467-82.

Klewitz, H. W. "Das Ende des Reformpapsttums," *DA*, 3 (1939), 371-412.

―――. "Die Entstehung des Kardinalkollegiums," *ZfRG*, k. A. 25 (1936), 115-221.

―――. "Kanzleischule und Hofkapelle," *DA*, 4 (1940-1941), 224-28.

―――. "Die Krönung des Papstes," *ZfRG*, k. A. 30 (1941), 97-130.

―――. "Montecassino in Rom," *QFIAB*, 28 (1937-1938), 36-47.

―――. "Papsttum und Kaiserkrönung: Ein Beitrag zur Frage nach dem Alter des Ordo Cencius II," *DA*, 4 (1940-1941), 412-43.

―――. "Studien über die Wiederherstellung der römischen Kirche in Süditalien durch das Reformpapsttum," *QFIAB*, 25 (1933-1934), 105-57.

―――. "Zur Geschichte der Bistumsorganisation Campaniens und Apuliens im 10. und 11. Jahrhundert," *QFIAB*, 24 (1932-1933), 1-61.

Klinkenberg, H. M. "Papsttum und Reichskirche bei Leo d. Gr.," Z*fRG*, k. A. 38 (1952), 37-112.

――――. "Der römische Primat im 10. Jahrhundert," Z*fRG*, k. A. 41 (1955), 1-57.

Koch, H. *Cathedra Petri. Neue Untersuchungen über die Anfänge der Primatslehre.* Beiheft 11, *ZNTW.* Giessen, 1930.

Kohler, K. *The Origins of the Synagogue and the Church.* New York, 1929.

Köhler, O. *Das Bild des geistlichen Fürsten in den Viten des 10. 11. und 12. Jahrhunderts.* (AbhMNG, Hft 77.) Berlin, 1935.

Kölmel, W. *Rom und der Kirchenstaat im 10. und 11. Jahrhundert bis in die Anfänge der Reform. Politik, Verwaltung: Rom und Italien.* (AbhMNG, Hft 78.) Berlin, 1935.

Königer, A. M. "Prima sedes a nemine iudicatur." *Beiträge zur Geschichte des christlichen Altertums und der byzantinischen Literatur. Festgabe A. Ehrhard* (Bonn-Leipzig, 1922), 273-300.

Kraft, H. "Kaiser Konstantin und das Bischofsamt." *Saeculum*, 8 (1957), 32-42.

Krämer, F. "Über die Anfänge und Beweggründe der Papstnamenänderungen in Mittelalter," *Römische Quartalschrift*, 51 (1956), 148-88.

Krause, H. G. *Das Papstwahldekret von 1059 und seine Rolle im Investiturstreit.* (*Studi Gregoriani*, 7.) Rome, 1960.

Krauss, S. "The Jews in the Works of the Church Fathers." *Jewish Quarterly Review*, 5 (1892-1893), 122-57; 6 (1893-1894), 82-99, 225-61.

Krautheimer, R. "The Carolingian Revival of Early Christian Architecture." *Art Bulletin*, 24 (1942), 1-38.

Kuttner, S. "Cardinalis: The History of a Canonical Concept." *Traditio*, 3 (1945), 129-214.

――――. "Liber canonicus. A Note on 'Dictatus Papae,' c. 17." *Studi Gregoriani*, 2 (1947), 387-401.

Laarhoven, J. van. " 'Christianitas' et Réforme grégorienne." *Studi Gregoriani*, 6 (1959-1961, published 1962), 1-98. Published separately as *Recherches sur le concept 'Christianitas' pendant la réforme ecclésiastique de Grégoire VII jusqu'à Bernard.* Rome, 1959.

Labriolle, P. de. "Papa." *Bulletin du Cange, Archivium Latinitatis Medii Aevi*, 4 (1928), 65-75.

————. *La réaction païenne. Étude sur la polémique anti-chrétienne du Iᵉʳ au VIᵉ siècle.* Paris, 1934.

Lacey, T. A., ed. and introd. *Appellatio Flaviani.* (Publ. of the Church Historical Society, 70.) London, 1903.

Ladner, G. B. "Aspects of Mediaeval Thought in Church and State." *Review of Politics,* 9 (1947), 403-22.

————. "Der Bilderstreit und die Kunstlehren der byzantinischen und abendländischen Theologie," *ZfKG,* ser. III, 1 (1931), 1ff.

————. "The Concept of the Image in the Greek Fathers and the Byzantine Iconoclastic Controversy," *DOP,* 7 (1953), 3-33.

————. "The Concepts of 'Ecclesia' and 'Christianitas' and their Relation to the Idea of Papal 'Plenitudo Potestatis' from Gregory VII to Boniface VIII." *Sazerdozio e Regno de Gregorio VII a Bonifacio VIII. Miscellanea Historiae Pontificiae,* 18 (1954), 49-77.

————. *The Idea of Reform. Its Impact on Christian Thought and Action in the Age of the Fathers.* Harvard. 1959.

————. "Die mittelalterliche Reform-idee und ihr Verhältnis zur Idee der Renaissance," *MIÖG,* 60 (1952), 31-59.

————. "Origin and Significance of the Byzantine Iconoclastic Controversy." *Mediaeval Studies,* 2 (1940), 127-49.

————. *Theologie und Politik vor dem Investiturstreit.* Vienna, 1936.

————. "Two Gregorian Letters on the Sources and Nature of Gregory VII's Reform Ideology," *Studi Gregoriani,* 5 (1956), 221-42.

Laehr, G. *Die konstantinische Schenkung in der abendländischen Literatur des Mittelalters bis zur Mitte des 14. Jahrhunderts.* (*HistStud.* 166.) Berlin, 1926.

Laistner, M.L.W. "The Christian Attitude to Pagan Literature." *History,* 20 (1935-1936), 49-54.

————. *Christianity and Pagan Culture in the Later Roman Empire.* Cornell, 1951.

————. "Pagan Schools and Christian Teachers." *Liber Floridus. Festschrift P. Lehmann.* (Erzabtei St. Ottilien, 1950.), 47-61.

Lauras, A. "Saint Léon le Grand et la tradition," *RSR,* 48 (1960), 166-84.

Laurent, V. "Le titre de patriarche oecuménique et la signature patriarchale." *Revue des études byzantines,* 6 (1948), 5-26.

————. "Le titre de patriarche oecuménique et Michel Cérulaire." *Miscellanea G. Mercati,* 3. *Studi e Testi,* 123 (1946), 373-96.

Laurin, J. R. *Orientations maîtresses des apologistes chrétiens de 270 à 361.* (Analecta Gregoriana, 61.) Rome, 1954.

Lebon, J. "La christologie de Timothée Aelure, archevêque monophysite d'Alexandrie, d'après les sources syriaques inédites," *RHE*, 9 (1908), 677-702.

Le Bras, G. "Les problèmes des institutions de la chrétienté médiévale," *Rapports du XI^e Congrès international des sciences historiques (21-28. Août, 1960).* Vol. 3 (Stockholm, 1960), 121-39.

————. "Sociologie de l'église dans le haut moyen-âge." *Settimane di Studio del Centro Italiano di Studi sull'alto Medioevo,* 7. Vol. 2 (Spoleto, 1960), 595-611.

Leclercq, J. "Simoniaca Heresis." *Studi Gregoriani,* 1 (1947), 523-30.

————. "Un témoignage sur l'influence de Grégoire VII dans la réforme canoniale." *Studi Gregoriani,* 6 (1959-1961, published 1962), 173-227.

Leff, G. *Heresy in the Later Middle Ages: The Relation of Heterodoxy to Dissent, c. 1250 - c. 1450.* 2 vols. Manchester and New York, 1967.

Lehmgrübner, H. *Benzo von Alba. Ein Verfechter der kaiserlichen Staatsidee unter Henrich IV.* Berlin, 1887.

Leib, B. *Rome, Kiev et Byzance à la fin du XI^e siècle. Rapports religieux des Latins et des Gréco-Russes sous le pontificat d'Urbain II (1088-1099).* Paris, 1924.

Leicht, P. A. "Il Pontefice S. Gregorio VII ed il Diritto Romano." *Studi Gregoriani,* 1 (1947), 93-110.

Leipoldt, J. *Der soziale Gedanke in der altchristlichen Kirche.* Leipzig, 1952.

Lerner, F. *Kardinal Hugo Candidus.* (*HZ*, Beiheft 22.) Munich-Berlin, 1931.

Levison, W. "Konstantinische Schenkung und Silvester-Legende." *Miscellanea F. Ehrle,* 2. *Studi e Testi,* 38. (Rome, 1924), 159-247.

Liebermann, F. "Lanfranc and the Antipope," *EHR*, 16 (1901), 328-32.

Lintzel, P. *Die Kaiserpolitik Ottos des Grossen.* Munich, 1943.

Lopez, R. S. "À propos d'une virgule. Le facteur économique dans la politique africaine des papes." *Revue historique,* 198 (1947), 178-88.

————. "Le problème des relations anglo-byzantines du septième au dixième siècle." *Byzantion,* 18 (1946-1948), 139-62.

————. "The Role of Trade in the Economic Readjustment of Byzantium in the Seventh Century," *DOP*, 13 (1959), 67-85.

————. "Some Tenth Century Towns," *MH*, 9 (1955), 4-6.

————. "Still Another Renaissance?" *AHR*, 57 (1951-1952), 1-21.

Lot-Borodine, M. "La doctrine de la déification dans l'église grecque jusqu'au XI<sup>e</sup> siècle." *Revue de l'histoire des Religions*, 105/6 (1932), 5-43, 525-74; 107/8 (1933), 8-55.

Löwe, H. "Kaisertum und Abendland in ottonischer und frühsalischer Zeit," *HZ*, 196 (1963), 529-62.

————. "Von den Grenzen des Kaisergedankens in der Karolingerzeit," *DA*, 14 (1958), 345-74.

Löwenfeld, S. "Acht Briefe aus der Zeit König Berengars," *NA*, 9 (1884), 513-40.

Loyn, H. R. "The Imperial Style of the Tenth Century Anglo-Saxon Kings." *History*, 40 (1955), 111-15.

Lubac, H. de. *Corpus Mysticum. L'eucharistie et l'Église au moyen-âge.* 2nd ed.; Paris, 1949.

————. *Exégèse médiévale. Les quatre sens de l'Ecriture.* Vol. 1, Paris, 1959.

Luca, L. de "L'Accettazione popolare della Legge Canonica nel Pensiero di Graziano e dei suoi Interpreti." *Studia Gratiana*, 3 (1955), 194-276.

Lulvès, J. "Die Machtbestrebungen des Kardinalkollegiums gegenüber dem Papsttum," *MIÖG*, 35 (1914), 455-83.


Maassen, F. *Geschichte der Quellen und der Literatur des canonischen Rechts im Abendlande bis zum Ausgange des Mittelalters*, vol. I, Graz, 1870.

Maccarrone, M. " 'Cathedra Petri' und die Idee der Entwicklung des päpstlichen Primats vom 2. bis. 4. Jahrhundert." *Saeculum*, 13 (1962), 278-92.

————. "La dottrina del Primato papale dal IV all' VIII secolo nelle Relazioni con le Chiese occidentali." *Settimane di Studio del Centro Italiano di Studi sull'alto Medioevo*, 7. Vol. 2 (Spoleto, 1960), 633-742.

————. *Vicarius Christi: Storia del Titolo Papale.* (*Lateranum*, 18.) Rome, 1952.

Macdonald, J. "Who Instituted the Papal Vicariate of Thessalonika?" *Studia Patristica*, 4 (1961), 478-82.

McIlwain, C. H. *The Growth of Political Thought in the West from the Greeks to the End of the Middle Ages.* London, 1932.

McKeon, P. R. "The Lateran Council of 1112, the Heresy of Lay Investiture and the Excommunication of Henry V," *MH*, 17 (1966), 3-12.

Madoz, G. *El Concepto de la Tradición en San Vicente de Lerins.* (Analecta Gregoriana, 5.) Rome, 1933.

Manoir, H. du. "L'argumentation patristique dans la controverse nestorienne," *RSR*, 25 (1935), 441-61, 531-59.

Marot, D. H. "La collégialité et le vocabulaire épiscopal du V$^e$ au VII$^e$ siècle." *Irénikon*, 36 (1963), 41-60; 37 (1964), 198-226.

Marot, H. "Les conciles romains des IV$^e$ et V$^e$ siècles et le développement de la primauté." 1054-1954, *L'Église et les églises,* vol. I (Chevtogne, 1954. Collection Irénikon.), 209-40.

Martin, E. J. *A History of the Iconoclastic Controversy.* London, 1930.

Maurer, M. *Papst Calixt II.* I. Theil. Diss. Munich, 1886.

Mayer, A. L. "Das Kirchenbild des späten Mittelalters und seine Beziehungen zur Liturgiegeschichte." *Vom christlichen Mysterium. Gesammelte Arbeiten zum Gedächtnis von Odo Casel, O.S.B.* (Düsseldorf, 1951), 274-302.

Merzbacher, F. "Recht und Gewaltenlehre bei Hugo von St. Victor." *ZfRG*, k. A. 44 (1958), 181-208.

――――. "Wandlungen des Kirchenbegriffs im Spätmittelalter. Grundzüge der Ekklesiologie des ausgehenden 13., des 14. und 15. Jahrhunderts," *ZfRG*, k. A. 39 (1953), 274-361.

Meyer, O. "Reims und Rom unter Gregor VII," *ZfRG*, k. A. 28 (1939), 418-52.

Miccoli, G. "Ecclesiae primitivae forma." *Studi medievali,* ser. terz., 1, fasc. 2 (1960), 470-98.

Michel, A. "Die Kaisermacht in der Ostkirche (843-1204)." *Ostkirchliche Studien,* 2 (1953), 1-35, 89-109; 3 (1954), 1-28.

――――. "Humbert und Hildebrand bei Nikolaus II. (1059-1061)," *HJb,* 72 (1953), 133-61.

――――. *Humbert und Kerullarios.* 2 vols. Paderborn, 1924-1930.

――――. *Papstwahl und Königsrecht oder das Papstwahl-Konkordat von 1059.* Munich, 1946.

Mikoletzky, H. L. "Der 'fromme' Kaiser Heinrich IV," *MIÖG,* 68 (1960), 250-65.

Mirbt, K. *Die Publizistik im Zeitalter Gregors VII.* Leipzig, 1894.

Mohr, W. *Die karolingische Reichsidee.* Münster, 1962.

Mohrmann, C. "Linguistic Problems in the Early Christian Church," *VigC,* 11 (1957), 11-36.

Molland, E. "Le développement de l'idée de succession apostolique." *Revue d'histoire et de philosophie religieuses*, 34 (1954), 1-29.

———. "Irenaeus of Lugdunum and the Apostolic Succession," *JEH*, 1 (1950), 12-28.

Momigliano, A. "Christianity and the Decline of the Roman Empire," in Momigliano, ed., *Conflict*, 1-16.

———, ed. *The Conflict between Paganism and Christianity in the Fourth Century*. Oxford, 1963.

Mommsen, T. E. *Studien zum Ideengehalt der deutschen Aussenpolitik im Zeitalter der Ottonen und Salier*. Diss. Berlin, 1930.

Monks, G. R. "The Church of Alexandria and the City's Economic Life in the Sixth Century." *Speculum*, 28 (1953), 349-62.

Morgenthaler, R. "Roma—Sedes Satanae. Röm. 13, 1 ff. im Lichte von Luk. 4, 5-8." *TZ*, 12 (1956), 289-304.

Morris, C. "Shakespeare's Politics." *The Historical Journal*, 8 (1965), 293-308.

———. *Western Political Thought*, vol. I: *Plato to Augustine*. London, 1967.

Morrison, K. F. "Canossa: A Revision." *Traditio*, 18 (1962), 121-48.

———. "Introduction." in T. E. Mommsen and K. F. Morrison, *Imperial Lives and Letters of the Eleventh Century* (Columbia, 1962), 3-51.

———. *Rome and the City of God: An Essay on the Constitutional Relationships of Empire and Church in the Fourth Century*. (Transactions of the American Philosophical Society, N.S., 54, pt. 1.) Philadelphia, 1964.

———. *The Two Kingdoms: Ecclesiology in Carolingian Political Thought*. Princeton, 1964.

Moynihan, J. M. *Papal Immunity and Liability in the Writings of Medieval Canonists*. Rome, 1961.

Muckle, J. T. "Greek Works Translated Directly into Latin Before 1350." *Mediaeval Studies*, 4 (1942), 33-42; 5 (1943), 102-14.

Mühlbacher, E. *Die streitige Papstwahl des Jahres 1130*. Innsbruck, 1876.

Müller, L. "Die Bedeutung der Tradition in der orthodoxen Theologie und Kirche." *Kirche und Kosmos: Orthodoxes und Evangelisches Christentum*. Studienheft, 2 (Witten, 1950), 77-97.

Murnier, C. *Les sources patristiques du droit de l'église du VIII<sup>e</sup> au XII<sup>e</sup> siècle*. Muhlhausen, 1957.

433

Murphy, F. X. *Peter Speaks Through Leo. The Council of Chalcedon. A.D. 451.* Washington, 1952.

Murray, A. "Pope Gregory VII and his Letters." *Traditio*, 22 (1966), 147-202.

Nineham, R. "The So-called Anonymous of York," *JEH*, 14 (1963), 31-45.

Nitschke, A. "Die Einstimmigkeit der Wahlen im Reiche Ottos des Grossen," *MIÖG*, 70 (1962), 29-59.

――――. "Die Wirksamkeit Gottes in der Welt Gregors VII. Eine Untersuchung über die religiösen Äusserungen und politischen Handlungen des Papstes." *Studi Gregoriani*, 5 (1956), 115-219.

Nock, A. D. *Conversion. The Old and the New in Religion from Alexander the Great to Augustine of Hippo.* Oxford, 1933.

Norden, W. *Das Papsttum und Byzanz. Die Trennung der beiden Mächte und das Problem ihrer Wiedervereinigung bis zum Untergange des byzantinischen Reichs (1453).* Berlin, 1903.

Norwood, F. A. "Attitude of the Ante-Nicene Fathers Toward Greek Artistic Achievement." *Journal of the History of Ideas*, 8 (1947), 431-48.

――――. "The Political Pretensions of Pope Nicholas I." *CH*, 15 (1946), 271-85.

Nyman, J. R. "The Synod at Antioch (324-325) and the Council of Nicaea." *Studia Patristica*, 4 (1961), 483-89.

Obermann, H. A. *The Harvest of Medieval Theology.* Harvard, 1963.

Oesterley, W.O.E. *The Jewish Background of the Christian Liturgy.* Oxford, 1925.

Opfermann, B. *Die liturgischen Herrscherakklamationen im Sacrum Imperium des Mittelalters.* Weimar, 1953.

Ortiz de Urbina, I. "Traditio et Scriptura apud Primaevos Patres Orientales," in Pontificia Acad. Mariana Int., *Scriptura*, 185-203.

Ostrogorsky, G. "The Byzantine Empire in the World of the Seventh Century," *DOP*, 13 (1959), 2-21.

――――. trans. J. Hussey. *History of the Byzantine State.* Oxford, 1956.

――――. *Studien zur Geschichte des byzantinischen Bilderstreites.* (Historische Untersuchungen, Hft 5.) Breslau, 1929.

Outler, A. C. "Augustine and the Transvaluation of the Classical Tradition." *Classical Journal*, 54 (1958-1959), 213-20.

――――. *The Christian Tradition and the Unity We Seek.* Oxford, 1957.

Pacaut, M. *La Théocratie: L'Église et le pouvoir au moyen-âge.* Paris, 1957.

Pargoire, J. *L'Eglise byzantine de 527 à 847.* 2nd ed., Paris, 1905.

Parker, T. M. "The Medieval Origins of the Idea of the Church as a 'Societas Perfecta.' " *Miscellanea historiae ecclesiasticae, Bibliothèque de la RHE,* fasc. 28 (1960), 23-31.

Peitz, W., ed. H. Förster, *Dionysius-Exiguus Studien.* (Arbeiten zur Kirchengeschichte, 33.) Berlin, 1960.

Pellens, K. "The Tracts of the Norman Anonymous: CCCC 415." *Transactions of the Cambridge Bibliographical Society,* 4 (1965), 155-65.

———. *Die Texte des Normannischen Anonymus.* Wiesbaden, 1966.

Pilcher, A. *Geschichte der kirchlichen Trennung.* 2 vols. Munich, 1864, 1865.

Plöchl, W. M. *Geschichte des Kirchenrechts, I: Das Recht des ersten christlichen Jahrtausends.* Vienna, 1953.

Pollard, T. E. "The Exegesis of Scripture and the Arian Controversy." *Bulletin of the John Rylands Library,* 41 (1958-1959), 414-29.

Pontificia Academia Mariana Internationalis, *De Scriptura et Traditione.* Rome, 1963.

Post, G. "*Ratio publicae utilitatis, ratio status* und 'Staatsräson.' (1100-1300)." *Die Welt als Geschichte,* 21 (1961), 8-28, 71-99.

———. *Studies in Mediaeval Legal Thought. Public Law and the State, 1100-1322.* Princeton, 1964.

Quasten, J. "Tertullian and 'Traditio.' " *Traditio,* 2 (1944), 481-84.

Rady, L. *Les papes Pascal et Gélase dans la querelle des investitures.* Brussels, 1908.

Rees, S. "Leontius of Byzantium and his Defence of the Council of Chalcedon," *HTR,* 24 (1931), 111-19.

Reindel, K. "Studien zur Überlieferung der Werke des Petrus Damiani," *DA,* 15 (1959), 23-102; 16 (1960), 73-154; 18 (1962), 317-417.

Reynders, D. B. "Paradosis. Le progrès de l'idée de tradition jusqu'à Saint Irenée." *Recherches de théologie ancienne et médiévale,* 5 1933), 155-91.

Richardson, R. D. "Eastern and Western Liturgies. The Primitive Basis of their Later Differences," *HTR,* 42 (1949), 125-48.

Riddle, D. W. "The So-called Jewish Christians." *Anglican Theological Review,* 12 (1929-1930), 15-33.

Rieker, K. "Die Entstehung und Geschichtliche Bedeutung des Kirchenbegriffs." *Festgabe für Rudolph Sohm* (Munich-Leipzig, 1914.), 1-22.

Russell, J. B. *Dissent and Reform in the Early Middle Ages.* Berkeley-Los Angeles, 1965.

Ryan, J. J. *Saint Peter Damiani and His Canonical Sources.* Toronto, 1956.

Ryan, John. "The Early Irish Church and the See of Peter." *Settimane di Studio del Centro Italiano di Studi sull'alto Medioevo*, 7. Vol. 2 (Spoleto, 1960), 549-74.

Sägmüller, L. "Die Idee von der Kirche als Imperium Romanum im kanonischen Recht." *Theologische Quartalschrift*, 80 (1898), 50-80.

Salaverri, J. "La Idea de Tradición en la Historia Ecclesiástica de Eusebio Cesariense." *Gregorianum*, 13 (1932), 211-40.

Salaville, S. "Saint Augustin et l'Orient." *Angelicum*, 8 (1931), 1-23.

Santifaller, L. *Zur Geschichte des ottonisch-salischen Reichskirchensystems.* SB der Oesterreichischen Akademie der Wissenschaften, phil.-hist. Kl. 229, Bd. 1, Abh. Vienna, 1954.

Schade, H. "Die Libri Carolini und ihre Stellung zum Bild," *ZkTh*, 79 (1957), 69-78.

Schelkle, K. H. "Staat und Kirche in der patristischen Auslegung von Rm. 13, 1-7," *ZNTW*, 44 (1953-1954), 223-36.

Schieffer, T. "Cluny et la querelle des Investitures." *Revue historique*, 225 (1961), 47-72.

———. "Heinrich II. und Konrad II. Die Umprägung des Geschichtsbildes durch die Kirchenreform des 11. Jahrhunderts," *DA*, 8 (1951), 384-437.

———. "Die lothringische Kanzlei um 900," *DA*, 14 (1958), 16-148.

Schmale, F. J. "Die Bemühungen Innocenz' II. um seine Anerkennung in Deutschland," *ZKG*, 65 (1953-1954), 240-69.

———. "Papsttum und Kurie zwischen Gregor VII. und Innocenz II," *HZ*, 193 (1961), 265-85.

———. *Studien zum Schisma des Jahres 1130.* (Forschungen zur kirchlichen Rechtsgeschichte und zum Kirchenrecht, 3.) Cologne, 1961.

Schmeidler, B. "Heinrichs IV. Absetzung 1105/6, kirchenrechtlich und quellenkritisch untersucht," *ZfRG*, k. A. 12 (1922), 168-221.

Schmid, P. *Der Begriff der kanonischen Wahl in den Anfängen des Investiturestreits.* Stuttgart, 1926.

Schmidt, K. D. "Papa Petrus ipse," *ZKG*, 54 (1935), 267-75.

Schneemelcher, W. "Athanasius von Alexandrien als Theologe und als Kirchenpolitiker," *ZNTW*, 43 (1950-1951), 242-56.

Schnitzer, J. *Die Gesta Romanae Ecclesiae des Kardinals Beno und andere Streitschriften der schismatischen Kardinäle wider Gregor VII.* Bamberg, 1892.

Schramm, P. E. *Herrschaftszeichen und Staatssymbolik.* 3 vols. (MGH Schriften, 13.) Stuttgart, 1954-1956.

———. *Kaiser, Rom und Renovatio*, 2nd ed.; Darmstadt, 1957.

———. "Die Ordines der mittelalterlichen Kaiserkrönung," *AUF*, 11 (1929-1930), 285-390.

———. "Sacerdotium und Regnum im Austausch ihrer Vorrechte. Eine Skizze der Entwicklung zur Beleuchtung des 'Dictatus Papae' Gregors VII." *Studi Gregoriani*, 2 (1947), 403-57.

———. "Der 'Salische Kaiserordo' und Benzo von Alba. Ein neues Zeugnis des Graphia-Kreises," *DA*, 1 (1937), 389-407.

———. "Das Versprechen Pippins und Karls des Grossen für die römische Kirche," *ZfRG*, k. A. 27 (1938), 180-217.

———. "Das Zeitalter Gregors VII. Ein Bericht." *Göttingische Gelehrte Anzeigen*, 207 (1953), 62-140.

Schrörs, J. H. *Hinkmar, Erzbischof von Reims. Sein Leben und seine Schriften.* Freiburg i. D., 1884.

Schulte, A. *Die Kaiser- und Königskrönungen zu Aachen: 813-1531.* Bonn-Leipzig, 1924.

Schwartz, E. *Der Prozess des Eutyches.* SB der Bayerischen Akad. der Wiss., phil.-hist. Abt. 1939, Hft. 5.

———. "Zweisprachigkeit in den Konzilsakten." *Philologus*, 88 (1933), 245-253.

Seaver, J. E. *Persecution of the Jews in the Roman Empire (300-438).* Lawrence, Kans., 1952. University of Kansas Humanistic Studies, No. 30.

Seckel, E. "Studien zu Benedictus Levita," *NA*, 26 (1901), 37-72; 29 (1904), 275-331; 31 (1906), 59-139; 34 (1909), 319-81; 35 (1910), 105-91; 39 (1914), 327-431; 40 (1915), 15-130; 41 (1916), 157-263. Continued by J. Juncker in *ZfRG*, k. A., 23 (1934), 269-377.

Seeberg, R. *Der Begriff der christlichen Kirche*, I. Teil. *Studien zur Geschichte des Begriffes der Kirche*. Erlangen, 1885.

Sellers, R. V. *The Council of Chalcedon: A Historical and Doctrinal Survey*. London, 1953.

————. *Two Ancient Christologies*. London, 1940.

Semmler, J. "Reichsidee und kirchliche Gesetzbegung," *ZKG*, 71 (1960), 37-65.

Serraz, L. "Les lettres du pape Hadrien I$^{er}$ lues au II$^e$ concile de Nicée," *EO*, 25 (1926), 407-20.

Seston, W. "Constantine as a 'Bishop.'" *Journal of Roman Studies*, 37 (1947), 127-31.

Setton, K. M. *Christian Attitude Towards the Emperor in the Fourth Century*. Columbia, 1941.

Sharkey, N. *St. Gregory the Great's Concept of Papal Power*. (Catholic University Studies in Sacred Theology, 2nd ser., 35.) Washington, 1950.

Simard, G. "La querelle de deux saints, saint Jérôme et saint Augustin." *Revue de l'Université d'Ottawa*, 12 (1942), 15-38.

Simon, M. "La polémique anti-juive de S. Jean Chrysostome et le mouvement judaïsant d'Antioche." *Mélanges Cumont. Annuaire de l'Institut de Philologie et histoire orientales*, 4 (1936), 403-21.

————. "Les saints d'Israël dans la dévotion de l'église ancienne." *Revue d'histoire et de philosophie religieuses*, 34 (1954), 98-127.

————. *Verus Israël. Étude sur les relations entre chrétiens et juifs dans l'Empire romain (135-425)*. (Bibl. des écoles françaises d'Athènes et de Rome, 166.) Paris, 1948.

Smalley, B. *The Study of the Bible in the Middle Ages*. New York, 1952.

Smith, M. "A Comparison of Early Christian and Early Rabbinic Tradition." *Journal of Biblical Literature*, 82 (1963), 169-76.

Smulders, P. "Le mot et le concept de 'tradition' chez les pères grecs," *RSR*, 40 (1951-1952), 41-62.

Spörl, J. "Das Alte und das Neue im Mittelalter. Studien zum Problem des mittelalterlichen Fortschrittsbewusstseins," *HJB*, 50 (1930), 297-341, 498-524.

Steinacker, H. "Die römische Kirche und die griechischen Sprachkenntnisse des Frühmittelalters," *MIÖG*, 62 (1954), 28-66. This article is a revision of an essay published in the *Festschrift für Theodor Gomperz*. Vienna, 1902.

Stengel, E. E. "Den Kaiser macht das Heer. Studien zur Geschichte eines politischen Gedankens." *Historische Aufsätze Karl Zeumer zum sechsigsten Geburtstag als Festgabe dargebracht* (Weimar, 1910), 247-310.

————. "Kaisertitel und Suveränitätsidee. Studien zur Vorgeschichte des modernen Staatsbegriffs," *DA*, 3 (1939), 1-56.

Stickler, A. M. "Concerning the Political Theories of the Medieval Canonists." *Traditio*, 7 (1949-1951), 450-63.

Stockmeier, P. " 'Imperium' bei Leo dem Grossen." *Studia Patristica*, 3 (1961), 413-20.

————. *Leos I. des Grossen Beurteilung der kaiserlichen Religionspolitik.* (Münchner Theologische Studien, Hist. Abt., Bd. 14.) Munich, 1959.

Straub, J. "Kaiser Konstantin als ἐπίσκοπος τῶν ἐκτός." *Studia Patristica*, 1 (1957), 678-95.

Sullivan, R. E. "The Carolingian Missionary and the Pagan." *Speculum*, 28 (1953), 705-40.

————. "The Papacy and Missionary Activity in the Early Middle Ages." *Mediaeval Studies*, 17 (1955), 46-106.

Sydow, J. "Untersuchungen zur kurialen Verwaltungsgeschichte im Zeitalter des Reformpapsttums," *DA*, 11 (1954-1955), 18-73.

Telfer, W. "The Author's Purpose in the *Vita Constantini.*" *Studia Patristica*, I (1957), 157-67.

————. "Constantine's Holy Land Plan." *Studia Patristica*, 1 (1957), 696-700.

————. "Episcopal Successions in Egypt," *JEH*, 3 (1952), 1-13.

————. "The Fourth-Century Greek Fathers as Exegetes," *HTR*, 50 (1957), 91-105.

————. "Meletius of Lycopolis and Episcopal Succession in Egypt," *HTR*, 48 (1955), 227-37.

Tellenbach, G. "Die Bedeutung des Reformpapsttums für die Einigung des Abendlandes." *Studi Gregoriani*, 2 (1947), 125-49.

————. trans. R. F. Bennett. *Church, State and Christian Society at the Time of the Investiture Contest.* Oxford, 1940.

————. ed. *Neue Forschungen über Cluny und die Cluniacenser.* Freiburg, 1959.

————. "Zwischen Worms and Canossa (1076/77)," *HZ*, 162 (1940), 316-25.

Thery, G. "Rôle des Byzantins dans l'activité littéraire de l'abbaye de

Saint-Denis au IXᵉ siècle," in *Comptes rendus de l'Académie des Inscriptions et Belles-Lettres* (1934), 276-277.

Thompson, E. A. "Christianity and the Northern Barbarians." In Momigliano, ed., *Conflict*, 56-78.

Tierney, B. "A Conciliar Theory of the Thirteenth Century," *CathHR*, 36 (1951), 415-40.

———. "The Continuity of Papal Political Theory in the Thirteenth Century. Some Methodological Considerations." *Mediaeval Studies*, 27 (1965), 227-45.

———. *The Crisis of Church and State*. Englewood Cliffs, N.J., 1964.

———. *Foundations of the Conciliar Theory*. Cambridge, 1955.

———. "Pope and Council. Some New Decretist Texts." *Mediaeval Studies*, 19 (1957), 197-218.

———. " 'Sola Scriptura' and the Canonists," *Studia Gratiana*, 11 (1967), 345-66.

Townsend, W. T. "Councils Held Under Pope Symmachus," *CH*, 6 (1937), 233-59.

———. "The So-Called Symmachian Forgeries," JR, 13 (1933), 165-74.

Treitinger, O. *Die oströmische Kaiser- und Reichsidee nach ihrer Gestaltung im höfischen Zeremoniell*. Diss. Munich, 1938.

Tuilier, A. "Le sens de l'adjectif οἰκουμενικός dans la tradition patristique et dans la tradition byzantine." *Studia Patristica*, 7 (1966), 413-26.

Ullmann, W. "Cardinal Humbert and the Ecclesia Romana." *Studi Gregoriani*, 4 (1952), 111-27.

———. "The Development of the Medieval Idea of Sovereignty," *EHR*, 64 (1949), 1-33.

———. *The Growth of Papal Government in the Middle Ages. A Study in the Ideological Relation of Clerical to Lay Power*. 2nd ed.; London, 1962.

———. "Leo I and the Theme of Papal Primacy," *JTS*, 11 (1960), 25-51.

———. *Medieval Papalism. The Political Theories of the Medieval Canonists*. London, 1949.

———. "On the Use of the Term 'Romani' in the Sources of the Earlier Middle Ages." *Studia Patristica*, 2 (1957), 153-63.

———. *Principles of Government and Politics in the Middle Ages*. New York, 1961.

————. "Romanus pontifex indubitanter efficitur sanctus: Dictatus Papae 23 in Retrospect and Prospect." *Studi Gregoriani*, 6 (1959-1961, published 1962), 229-64.

————. "The Significance of the *Epistola Clementis* in the Pseudo-Clementines," *JTS*, 11 (1960), 295-317.

————. "Some Remarks on the Significance of the *Epistola Clementis* in the Pseudo-Clementines." *Studia Patristica*, 4 (1961), 336-40.

Vailhé, S. "Le titre de patriarche oecuménique avant saint Grégoire le Grand," *EO*, 11 (1908), 65-69.

Vansina, J., trans. H. M. Wright. *Oral Tradition: A Study in Historical Methodology*. Chicago, 1965.

Vasiliev, A. A. *Justin the First. An Introduction to the Epoch of Justinian the Great.* (DOS 1.) Harvard, 1950.

Vehse, O. "Die päpstliche Herrschaft in der Sabina bis zur Mitte des 12. Jahrhunderts," *QFIAB*, 21 (1929-1930), 120-75.

Visser, W.J.A. *Die Entwicklung des Christusbildes in Literatur und Kunst in der frühchristlichen und frühbyzantinischen Zeit.* Diss. Utrecht. Bonn, 1934.

Voigt, K. "Papst Leo der Grosse und die 'Unfehlbarkeit' des oströmischen Kaisers," *ZKG*, 47 (1928), 11-17.

Voosen, E. *Papauté et pouvoir civil à l'époque de Gregoire VII.* Gembloux, 1927.

Vries, W. de. *Der Kirchenbegriff der von Rom getrennten Syrer.* (Oriental. christ. Analecta, 143.) Rome, 1955.


Wach, J. *Sociology of Religion*. Chicago, 1944.

Wallach, L. *Alcuin and Charlemagne.* Cornell, 1959.

————. "Amicus amicis, inimicus inimicis," *ZKG*, 52 (1933), 614-15.

————. "Education and Culture in the Tenth Century," *MH*, 9 (1955), 18-22.

————. "The Greek and Latin Versions of II. Nicaea and the Synodica of Hadrian I (JE 2448)." *Traditio*, 22 (1966), 103-25.

————. "Libri Carolini and Patristics, Latin and Greek: Prolegomena to a Critical Edition," in L. Wallach, ed., *The Classical Tradition: Literary and Historical Studies in Honor of Harry Caplan* (Cornell, 1966), 451-98.

————. "The Roman Synod of December 800 and the Alleged Trial of Leo III," *HTR*, 49 (1956), 123-42.

————. "The Unknown Author of the *Libri Carolini*; Patristic Exegesis,

Mozarabic Antiphons and the Vetus Latina." *Didascaliae, Studies in Honor of Anselm M. Albareda* (New York, 1961), 469-515.

Wallace-Hadrill, J. M. "Rome and the Early English Church. Some Questions of Transmission." *Settimane di Studio del Centro Italiano di Studi sull'alto Medioevo,* 7 Vol. 2 (Spoleto, 1960), 519-48.

Watt, John A. *The Theory of Papal Monarchy in the Thirteenth Century: The Contribution of the Canonists.* New York, 1965.

Weigl, E. *Christologie vom Tode des Athanasius bis zum Ausbruch des nestorianischen Streites (373-429).* (Münchner Stud. zur hist. Theologie, 4.) Munich, 1925.

Welsersheimb, L. "Das Kirchenbild der griechischen Väterkommentare zum Hohen Lied," *ZkTh,* 70 (1948), 393-449.

Weltin, E. G. "Quid Athenae Hierosolymis?" *Classical Journal,* 51 (1956), 153-61.

White, H. V. "Pontius of Cluny, the *Curia Romana* and the End of Gregorianism in Rome," *CH,* 27 (1958), 195-219.

————. "The Gregorian Ideal and Saint Bernard of Clairvaux." *Journal of the History of Ideas,* 21 (1960), 321-48.

Wilde, R. *The Treatment of the Jews in the Greek Christian Writers of the First Three Centuries.* (Catholic University Patristic Studies, 81.) Washington, 1949.

Wilks, M. J. "The *Apostolicus* and the Bishop of Rome," *JTS,* 13 (1962), 290-317; 14 (1963), 311-54.

————. "*Papa est nomen iurisdictionis*: Augustinus Triumphus and the Papal Vicariate of Christ," *JTS,* 8 (1957), 71-91, 256-71.

————. *The Problem of Sovereignty in the Later Middle Ages.* Cambridge, 1963.

Williams, G. H. "Christology and Church-State Relations in the Fourth Century," *CH,* 20 (1951), no. 3, 3-33; no. 4, 3-25.

————. *The Norman Anonymous of 1100 A.D. Toward the Identification and Evaluation of the So-Called Anonymous of York.* (Harvard Theological Studies, 18.) Cambridge, Mass., 1951.

Winkler, M. *Der Traditionsbegriff des Urchristentums bis Tertullian.* Munich, 1897.

Winston, R. *Charlemagne. From the Hammer to the Cross.* London, 1956.

Wolfson, H. A. "Philosophical Implications of Arianism and Apollinarianism," *DOP,* 12 (1958), 3-28.

442

————. *The Philosophy of the Church Fathers.* Vol. I, *Faith, Trinity, Incarnation.* Harvard, 1956.

Woodward, E. L. *Christianity and Nationalism in the Later Roman Empire.* London, 1916.

Zeiller, J. "La conception de l'Église aux quatre premiers siècles," *RHE*, 29 (1933), 571-85, 827-48.

Zema, D. B. "Economic Reorganization of the Roman See During the Gregorian Reform." *Studi Gregoriani,* 1 (1947), 137-68.

————. "The Houses of Tuscany and of Pierleone [*sic*] in the Crisis of Rome in the Eleventh Century." *Traditio,* 2 (1944), 155-75.

————. "Reform Legislation in the Eleventh Century and its Economic Impact," *CathHR,* 27 (1941), 16-38.

Ziegler, A. K. "Pope Gelasius I and his Teaching on the Relation of Church and State," *CathHR,* 27 (1942), 412-37.

Zilliacus, H. *Zum Kampf der Weltsprachen im oströmischen Reich.* Diss. Helsingfors, 1935.

Zimmermann, H. "Papstabsetzungen des Mittelalters." *MIÖG,* 69 (1961), 1-84, 241-91; 70 (1962), 60-110.

Zoepffel, R. *Die Papstwahlen vom 11. bis zum 14. Jahrhundert.* Göttingen, 1871.

Zwölfer, T. *Sankt Peter, Apostelfürst und Himmelspförtner: Seine Verehrung bei den Angelsachsen und Franken.* Stuttgart, 1929.

# Index

449